D0388350

A Glossary of English Food Terms

When you're in England, you speak English. American English, that is, of course. Like a major credit card, it's accepted everywhere. But you may come across a few unfamiliar terms, particularly when the subject is food. The following "translations" can help (see the reverse side for general terms):

British English	American English	British English	American English
Afters	Dessert	Jacket potato	Baked potato served with various toppings
Aubergine	Eggplant	Jelly	jello
Bangers	Sausages	Joint	Meat roasted on the bone
Bap	Soft sandwich bun	Kipper	Smoked fish
Biscuit	Cracker or cookie	Liquor	Green, salty, parsley-based gravy
Black or white	Refers to coffee; white is coffee with cream	Mange tout	Snow peas
Broad bean	Lima bean	Marrow	Squash
Bubble and Squeak	Mashed potatoes mixed with cabbage or meat and then fried	Mash	Mashed potatoes
Chicory	Endive	Mince	Ground meat, usually beef
Chips	French fries	Ploughman's lunch	Pub grub consisting of crusty bread with cheese or pâté
Cornish pasties	Pastry filled with meat, onion, and vegetables	Pudding	Dessert
Cottage pie	Ground meat and mashed potatoes baked in a pie	Rasher	Slice of bacon
Courgettes	Zucchini	Rocket	Arugula
Crisps	Potato chips	Salt beef	Corned beef
Crumpet	Holier version of an "English muffin"	Scotch egg	Hard-boiled egg fried in a jacket of ground sausage and bread crumbs
French beans	Green beans	Shepherd's pie	Baked pie of meat and vegetables covered with gravy and mashed potatoes
Fry-up	Big English breakfast of eggs, sausage/bacon, baked beans, tomatoes, and more	Spotted dick	Sponge cake with fruit and raisins steamed and served with custard sauce
Gateau	Cake	Steak and kidney pie	Pastry-topped pie of steak, kidneys, and mushrooms in gravy
Haricots vert	Green beans	Sticky toffee pudding	Spotted dick (see preceding entry) without the fruit and served with warm butterscotch sauce

England For Dummies, 3rd Edition

(continued)

British English	American English	British English	American English
Sultana	Raisin	Trifle	Sponge cake soaked in sherry, layered with raspberry preserves, covered with custard sauce, and capped with whipped cream
Sweet	Dessert	Welsh rarebit	Melted cheddar cheese and mustard or Worcestershire sauce served on toast
Treacle	Molasses	Whitebait	Small, whole, deep-fried fish

Minding Your Teas and Queues

British English differs a bit from the English spoken in the New World. You may encounter the following "foreign" words and phrases, which are listed below with their American-English translations (see the reverse side for food terms):

British English	American English	British English	American English
Bonnet	Hood of a car	Mac (mackintosh)	Raincoat
Boot	Trunk of a car	Mate	Male friend
Brilliant	All-purpose, enthusiastic superlative	Nappy	Diaper
Brolly	Umbrella	Peckish	Hungry
Cheers	Goodbye (or said when raising a glass in a toast)	Petrol	Gasoline
Cinema	Movie ("theatre" is only live theater)	Queue	To line up (The Brits are excellent queuers.)
Coach	A long-distance bus	Quid	One pound sterling (£)
Concessions	Special discounts for students, seniors, and the disabled	Return ticket	Round-trip ticket
Cooker	Stove (sometimes called an Aga, a brand name)	Ring	Call on the phone ("Ring me in the morning.")
First floor	Second floor (and so on)	Rubber	Eraser
Flat	Apartment	Serviette	Napkin
Fortnight	Two weeks	Single ticket	One-way ticket
Ground floor	First floor	Subway	Underpass
Jumper	Sweater	Ta	Thanks
Knackered	Tired	Teatime	Period between 3:30 and 6 p.m.
Knickers	Underwear ("Don't get your knickers in a twist.")	Tights	Pantyhose
Lift	Elevator	Torch	Flashlight
Loo	Toilet/restroom ("I need to use the loo.")	Underground/Tube	Subway
Lorry	Truck		

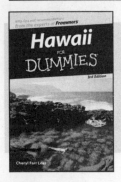
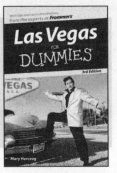

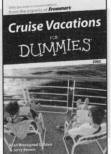

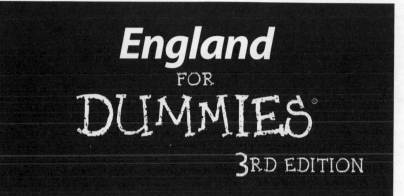

England

FOR

DUMMIES

3RD EDITION

by Donald Olson

WILEY

Wiley Publishing, Inc.

England For Dummies,® 3rd Edition

Published by
Wiley Publishing, Inc.
111 River St.
Hoboken, NJ 07030-5774
www.wiley.com

WILEY

About the Author

Donald Olson is a novelist, playwright, and travel writer. His newest novel, *Confessions of a Pregnant Princess*, was published in 2005 under the pen name Swan Adamson. An earlier Swan Adamson novel, *My Three Husbands*, has been translated into French and published in several European countries. Donald Olson's novel *The Confessions of Aubrey Beardsley*, was published in the United Kingdom by Bantam Press, and his play, *Beardsley*, was produced in London. His travel stories have appeared in the *New York Times, Travel + Leisure, Sunset, National Geographic* books, and many other publications. *England For Dummies*, 1st Edition won a 2002 Lowell Thomas Travel Writing Award for best guidebook. His other guidebooks *London For Dummies*, *Best Day Trips from London, Irreverent London, Germany For Dummies,* and *Frommer's Vancouver & Victoria* are all published by Wiley Publishing, Inc. London is one of Donald's favorite cities, and England is one of his favorite countries.

Dedication

This book is dedicated to all those Londoners who showed the world in July 2005 that they are stronger than any terrorists.

Author's Acknowledgments

I would like to thank BritRail for helpful assistance while I was researching this new edition of *England For Dummies*. Thanks also go to Gary Larson and Stephen Brewer.

Publisher's Acknowledgments

We're proud of this book; please send us your comments through our Dummies online registration form located at www.dummies.com/register/.

Some of the people who helped bring this book to market include the following:

Editorial

Editors: Naomi Black, Christine Ryan, Project Editors; M. Faunette Johnston, Production Editor; and Jennifer Moore, Development Editor

Copy Editor: Laura Miller

Cartographer: Andrew Murphy

Senior Photo Editor: Richard Fox

Cover Photos: *Front cover:* © Steve Bidler/eStock Photo; Dorset: Shaftesbury: family walking on Gold Hill, thatched cottages beyond

Back cover: © Nick Bodle/ Alamy Images; Cumbria: Derwent Water scenic

Cartoons: Rich Tennant (www.the5thwave.com)

Composition Services

Project Coordinator: Jennifer Theriot

Layout and Graphics: Carl Byers, Lauren Goddard, Denny Hager, Joyce Haughey, Barbara Moore, Heather Ryan, Julie Trippetti

Proofreaders: Laura Albert, Leeann Harney, TECHBOOKS Production Services

Indexer: TECHBOOKS Production Services

Publishing and Editorial for Consumer Dummies

Diane Graves Steele, Vice President and Publisher, Consumer Dummies

Joyce Pepple, Acquisitions Director, Consumer Dummies

Kristin A. Cocks, Product Development Director, Consumer Dummies

Michael Spring, Vice President and Publisher, Travel

Kelly Regan, Editorial Director, Travel

Publishing for Technology Dummies

Andy Cummings, Vice President and Publisher, Dummies Technology/General User

Composition Services

Gerry Fahey, Vice President of Production Services

Debbie Stailey, Director of Composition Services

Contents at a Glance

Introduction *1*

Part 1: Introducing England *7*

Chapter 1: Discovering the Best of England 9
Chapter 2: Digging Deeper into England 15
Chapter 3: Deciding When and Where to Go 24
Chapter 4: Following an Itinerary: Five Great Options 41

Part 11: Planning Your Trip to England *55*

Chapter 5: Managing Your Money 57
Chapter 6: Getting to England.. 69
Chapter 7: Getting Around England 77
Chapter 8: Booking Your Accommodations 87
Chapter 9: Catering to Special Needs or Interests 95
Chapter 10: Taking Care of the Remaining Details 103

Part 111: London and Environs *113*

Chapter 11: Settling Into London 115
Chapter 12: Exploring London 158
Chapter 13: Day-tripping from London 201

Part 1V: The Southeast *221*

Chapter 14: Kent and Sussex 223
Chapter 15: Kent's Best Castles, Stately Homes,
and Gardens 247

Part V: The West Country *259*

Chapter 16: Hampshire and Wiltshire:
Old Wessex and New Sarum 261
Chapter 17: Devon: Moors, Tors, and Sandy Shores 274
Chapter 18: Cornwall: Saints, Salts, Sea, and Sun.................. 292

Part V1: England's Heartland *309*

Chapter 19: Stratford-upon-Avon and Warwick Castle 311
Chapter 20: Bath and the Best of the Cotswolds 325

Part V11: Way Up North *349*

Chapter 21: Yorkshire 351
Chapter 22: The Lake District 377

Part V111: The Part of Tens *399*

Chapter 23: Ten Writers and the Places They Lived 401
Chapter 24: Ten Great English Gardens.................................. 405

Chapter 25: Ten (Or So) Great English Churches 409
Chapter 26: Ten Important Royals — Past and Present 413
Appendix: Quick Concierge 422
Index 433

Maps at a Glance

The Regions in Brief 25
London's Neighborhoods 122
London's Top Hotels 132
London's Top Restaurants...144
London's Top Attractions 160
British Museum..163
St. Paul's Cathedral..171
Tower of London..173
Westminster Abbey 175
West End Shopping...186
London's Clubs, Pubs, and Bars 194
Day Trips from London 202
Cambridge 203
Oxford 215
The Southeast 224
Canterbury 227
Rye 231
Brighton 239
Kent's Castles, Stately Homes, and Gardens..............................248
Hampshire and Wiltshire...262
Winchester 264
Salisbury 269
Devon 275
Exeter 276
Dartmoor National Park...282
Cornwall...293
England's Heartland 312
Stratford-upon-Avon...314
Bath 327
Yorkshire 352
York 353
York Minster 363
The Lake District 378
Keswick 393

Table of Contents

Introduction *1*

    About This Book...1
    Conventions Used in This Book 2
    Foolish Assumptions 3
    How This Book Is Organized................................3
        Part I: Introducing England............................4
        Part II: Planning Your Trip to England.......................4
        Part III: London and Environs........................4
        Part IV: The Southeast...................................4
        Part V: The West Country 4
        Part VI: England's Heartland 5
        Part VII: Way Up North 5
        Part VIII: The Part of Tens............................5
    Icons Used in This Book.......................................6
    Where to Go from Here...6

Part 1: Introducing England *7*

    Chapter 1: Discovering the Best of England 9

        The Best of Legendary London 9
        The Best Cities, Towns, and Villages 10
        The Best Castles, Palaces, and Stately Homes 11
        The Best Cathedrals and Churches 11
        The Best Historic Places 12
        The Best Gardens...13
        The Best Romantic Landscapes 13
        The Best Shopping..14

    Chapter 2: Digging Deeper into England 15

        The Main Events: A Brief History of England 15
        Building Blocks: An Overview of English Architecture 18
        Dining English Style from Traditional to Modern 20
        Visiting the Local Pub..20
        Background Check: Finding England
        in Books and Movies..21
            Books...22
            Movies 23

    Chapter 3: Deciding When and Where to Go 24

        Going Everywhere You Want to Be 24
            Looking at London: from Buckingham Palace
            to the British Museum..................................24

Exploring Southeast England: Canterbury,
castles, and historic towns 26
Sightseeing at Stonehenge and in
the West Country: Hampshire,
Wiltshire, Devon, and Cornwall............................27
Discovering England's heartland: Stratford-
upon-Avon, the Cotswolds, and Bath 28
Heading north: Yorkshire and the Lake District 28
Scheduling Your Time..29
Revealing the Secrets of the Seasons 30
Traveling during high and low seasons 30
Watching those unpredictable skies 31
Blooming in spring..32
Shining (and raining) in summer 32
Glowing in autumn..33
Welcoming in winter..34
Perusing a Calendar of Events......................................35
January...35
February...35
March 36
April..36
May 36
June...37
July..38
August 38
September...39
October 39
November 39
December..40

**Chapter 4: Following an Itinerary:
Five Great Options...41**

Seeing England's Highlights in One Week 42
Touring the Best of England in Two Weeks.......................45
Discovering England with Kids..47
Strolling through England's Greenery:
An Itinerary for Garden Lovers 49
Visiting England's Past: An Itinerary for History Buffs 51

Part II: Planning Your Trip to England................55

Chapter 5: Managing Your Money 57

Planning Your Budget 57
Lodging...57
Transportation 58
Dining 59

Sightseeing..59
Shopping and nightlife 60
Cutting Costs — But Not the Fun....................62
Handling Money 63
Using ATMs and carrying cash....................64
Charging ahead with credit cards.................64
Toting traveler's checks............................65
Dealing with a lost or stolen wallet 66
Taking Taxes into Account..........................67
Tipping Like You Mean It.............................68

Chapter 6: Getting to England.....................69
Finding Out Who Flies Where.......................69
Getting the Best Deal on Your Airfare 70
Working with Consolidators 71
Booking your flight online 71
Arriving by Other Means.............................72
Taking the train 72
Riding a ferry or hovercraft........................73
Joining an Escorted Tour 73
Choosing a Package Tour............................75
Locating package tours..............................75
Checking out airline and hotel packages.......76

Chapter 7: Getting Around England.............77
Weighing the Options: Train or Car? 77
Riding the Rails...77
Buying your train ticket 78
Negotiating the rail system.........................78
Getting to know London's train stations 79
Saving with BritRail passes.........................80
Hopping a Coach: Bus Travel 81
Driving on the Left, Passing on the Right: Car Travel 81
Renting a car in London — or not 82
Renting a car in England 83
Hitting the road: Motorways, dual carriageways,
and roundabouts..................................84
Following the rules of the road 85
Coping with emergencies on the road 85
Filling up the tank 86

Chapter 8: Booking Your Accommodations.................87
Finding the Right Place for You.....................88
Understanding the pros and cons of B&Bs 88
Exploring hotel choices 89
Finding the Best Room at the Best Rate.........92

Surfing the Web for Hotel Deals 93
Reserving the Best Room...94

Chapter 9: Catering to Special Needs or Interests.....95

Traveling with the Brood: Advice for Families...................95
Locating family-friendly accommodations
and restaurants 96
Hiring a baby-sitter in England.....................................97
Making Age Work for You: Tips for Seniors 97
Accessing England: Information for
Travelers with Disabilities 98
Considering the benefits of escorted tours...........100
Dealing with access issues 100
Following the Rainbow: Resources for
Gay and Lesbian Travelers...101

Chapter 10: Taking Care of the Remaining Details...103

Getting a Passport..103
Applying for a U.S. passport......................................103
Applying for other passports 104
Entering England with your passport 105
Dealing with a (gulp) lost passport 105
Playing It Safe with Travel and Medical Insurance.........105
Staying Healthy When You Travel.....................................106
Staying Connected by Cellphone 107
Accessing the Internet Away From Home 109
Keeping Up with Airline Security 111

Part III: London and Environs 113

Chapter 11: Settling into London...................................115

Getting There...115
Flying to London 115
Taking the train 119
Orienting Yourself in London 119
Introducing the Neighborhoods..120
The City of London 120
West End 121
West London...124
The South Bank 126
Finding Information After You Arrive 126
Getting Around London..127
By Underground (subway) 127
By bus...129
By taxi...130
On foot..130

Staying in Style 131
    The top hotels 134
    Runner-up accommodations 141
Dining Out 143
    Neighborhoods for ethnic eats 143
    Strategies for budget dining 143
    The top restaurants..................................146
Treating Yourself to a Tea 155
    Casual tearooms and patisseries............155
    Elegant spots for high tea.......................156

Chapter 12: Exploring London 158

Discovering the Top Attractions....................158
Finding More Cool Things to See and Do 175
Seeing London by Guided Tour 181
    Bus tours 181
    Boat tours 182
    An amphibious tour...................................183
    Walking tours...183
Following an Itinerary.......................................184
Shopping in London...184
    When to shop and how to find deals.......184
    Where to shop and what to buy..............185
Living It Up After Dark......................................190
    Finding out what's happening 190
    Getting tickets 190
    Raising the curtain on performing arts
      and music...190
    Checking out the club and bar scenes ...192
Fast Facts: London 197

Chapter 13: Day-tripping from London 201

Cambridge: Medieval Colleges on the River Cam 201
    Getting to Cambridge 201
    Finding information and taking a tour 204
    Getting around Cambridge 204
    Exploring the best of Cambridge 204
    Finding more to see and do in Cambridge...........207
    Dining in Cambridge.................................208
Greenwich: The Center of Time and Space.....209
    Getting to Greenwich................................209
    Finding information and taking a tour 209
    Exploring Greenwich 210
    Dining in Greenwich 211
Hampton Court Palace: Henry VIII's Riverside Estate....211
    Getting to Hampton Court 211
    Exploring Hampton Court..........................212

Royal Botanic Gardens (Kew Gardens):
Royal Pleasure Grounds 212
Getting to Kew Gardens 213
Exploring Kew Gardens 213
Oxford: Town and Gown...213
Getting to Oxford 214
Finding information and taking a tour 214
Exploring the best of Oxford 214
Finding more to see and do in Oxford....................216
Dining in Oxford..217
Blenheim Palace: Ancestral Home of the Churchills 218
Getting to Blenheim Palace 218
Exploring Blenheim Palace..218
Windsor Castle: Official Royal Residence 219
Getting to Windsor Castle..220
Exploring Windsor Castle 220

Part IV: The Southeast 221

Chapter 14: Kent and Sussex 223
Canterbury: Tales from the Great Cathedral 224
Getting to Canterbury 225
Finding information and taking a tour 225
Staying in or near Canterbury...................................225
Dining in or near Canterbury 226
Exploring Canterbury...228
Rye: Smugglers, Mermaids, and Writers 229
Getting to Rye..230
Finding information 230
Taking a tour of Rye...231
Staying in Rye..232
Dining in Rye 233
Exploring Rye 234
Battle: 1066 and All That 236
Getting to Battle..236
Finding information 236
Dining in Battle...237
Exploring the Battle of Hastings Abbey
and Battlefield 238
Brighton: Fun Beside the Seaside 238
Getting to Brighton...239
Finding information 240
Getting around Brighton 240
Staying in or near Brighton..240
Dining in Brighton...242

Exploring Brighton..243
Shopping in Brighton......................................245
Stepping out in Brighton, night or day.................245

Chapter 15: Kent's Best Castles, Stately Homes, and Gardens..................................247

Knole: A Room for Every Day of the Year 248
Getting to Knole..249
Exploring Knole...249
Hever Castle: Anne Boleyn Slept Here.................250
Getting to Hever Castle 250
Exploring Hever Castle....................................251
Chartwell: The Private Life of a
Famous Prime Minister...................................252
Getting to Chartwell 252
Exploring Chartwell House...............................252
Leeds Castle: Castle of Queens, Queen of Castles 253
Getting to Leeds Castle 253
Exploring Leeds Castle....................................253
Sissinghurst Castle Garden: Romance
amongst the Roses 254
Getting to Sissinghurst Castle Garden 255
Exploring Sissinghurst Castle Garden.................255
Dover Castle: Towers and Tunnels 256
Getting to Dover Castle...................................256
Exploring Dover Castle....................................256

Part V: The West Country *259*

Chapter 16: Hampshire and Wiltshire: Old Wessex and New Sarum....................................261

Winchester: King Alfred Meets Jane Austen..................263
Getting to Winchester 263
Finding information and taking
a tour of Winchester....................................263
Staying in Winchester.....................................264
Finding lunch or a spot of tea 264
Exploring Winchester and
the surrounding area...................................265
Salisbury: High-Spire Act.................................268
Getting to Salisbury..268
Finding information on Salisbury 268
Staying in or near Salisbury 269
Dining in Salisbury...270
Exploring Salisbury and the surrounding area 271

Stonehenge: Visiting the Standing Stones........................272
Getting to Stonehenge.................................272
Exploring Stonehenge 273

Chapter 17: Devon: Moors, Tors, and Sandy Shores **274**

Exeter: Sea Captains and Silversmiths 275
Getting to Exeter......................................276
Finding information and taking a tour 277
Staying in Exeter......................................277
Dining in Exeter.......................................278
Exploring Exeter.......................................279
Shopping for Exeter silver 280
Dartmoor National Park: Back to Nature 281
Getting to the park....................................281
Finding information 281
Taking a tour of the park..............................283
Staying in Dartmoor National Park......................283
Dining in Dartmoor National Park 284
Exploring in and around Dartmoor
National Park......................................285
Torquay: Relaxing on the English Riviera 286
Getting to Torquay.....................................287
Getting around and touring Torquay 287
Finding information 287
Staying and dining in Torquay 287
Exploring Torquay 288
Plymouth: Where the Pilgrims Set Sail 289
Getting to Plymouth 289
Taking a cruise in Plymouth 289
Finding information 289
Locating a spot for lunch or tea.......................290
Exploring Plymouth.....................................290

Chapter 18: Cornwall: Saints, Salts, Sea, and Sun...**292**

Penzance: As in "The Pirates of . . ." 294
Getting to Penzance....................................294
Finding information and taking a tour
of Penzance.......................................295
Staying in Penzance 295
Dining in Penzance 296
Exploring in and around Penzance......................298
The Penwith Peninsula: A Driving Tour
from Penzance to Land's End 300
Stop #1: Newlyn.......................................300
Stop #2: Mousehole 301

Stop #3: The Minack Theatre 301
Stop #4: Land's End 302
St. Ives: Artists' Haven by the Sea.............................302
Getting to St. Ives..302
Finding information about St. Ives..........................303
Staying in St. Ives 303
Dining in St. Ives...304
Exploring St. Ives 304
Finding more to see near St. Ives 305
Fowey and the Saint's Way: River Town
and Holy Track 306
Cotehele, Eden Project, and Lanhydrock:
Three Great Cornish Gardens 307
Cotehele..307
Eden Project 308
Lanhydrock...308

Part VI: England's Heartland 309

Chapter 19: Stratford-upon-Avon and Warwick Castle 311

Stratford-upon-Avon: In the Bard's Footsteps 311
Getting to Stratford-upon-Avon...............................312
Finding information about
Stratford-upon-Avon 313
Getting around and touring
Stratford-upon-Avon 313
Staying in Stratford-upon-Avon 313
Dining in Stratford-upon-Avon................................315
Exploring the best of Stratford-upon-Avon...........317
Finding more to see and do in
Stratford-upon-Avon 320
Seeing a play in Stratford-upon-Avon 321
Shopping in Stratford-upon-Avon 321
Warwick Castle: Warlords and Ladies 321
Getting to Warwick 322
Dining at Warwick Castle 322
Exploring Warwick Castle 322
Finding more to see and do in Warwick................324

Chapter 20: Bath and the Best of the Cotswolds 325

Bath: Hot Mineral Springs and
Cool Georgian Splendor...326
Getting to Bath 326
Finding information and taking a tour of Bath......328
Exchanging money and locating ATMs 328

Staying in and around Bath 329
Dining in Bath...330
Exploring Bath..332
Cheltenham: A Little Bath 334
Getting to Cheltenham 335
Traveling among the local villages 335
Finding information and taking a tour
of Cheltenham 335
Staying in Cheltenham 335
Dining in Cheltenham..336
Exploring Cheltenham..337
Shopping in Cheltenham..338
Bourton-on-the-Water: Bridges on the Windrush 338
Getting to Bourton-on-the-Water 338
Stopping for a spot of tea in
Bourton-on-the-Water......................................339
Exploring Bourton-on-the-Water..........................339
Upper Slaughter and Lower Slaughter:
Quiet and Atmospheric 340
Broadway: Village Shopping 340
Getting to Broadway..340
Finding information about Broadway 341
Staying in Broadway 341
Stopping for a spot of tea in Broadway................341
Exploring Broadway and vicinity..........................341
Chipping Campden: Picture Perfect 342
Getting to Chipping Campden...............................342
Staying and dining in Chipping Campden.............342
Exploring Chipping Campden 344
Cirencester: Market Town with a Roman Past 344
Getting to Cirencester...344
Finding information about Cirencester..................344
Staying in Cirencester 344
Dining in Cirencester...345
Exploring Cirencester..346
Shopping in Cirencester..347

Part VII: Way Up North *349*

Chapter 21: Yorkshire...**351**

York: Ancient Walls and Snickelways 352
Getting to York 353
Renting a car or calling a taxi...............................354
Finding information about York.............................354
Exchanging money and locating ATMs 354

Taking a tour in York 355
Staying in York.......................................356
Dining in York 357
Exploring York.......................................359
Shopping in York....................................364
Stepping out at night in York...................364
Day-tripping from York: Castle Howard
    and Eden Camp 365
Scarborough: Cliffs and Arcades.....................366
Getting to Scarborough...........................367
Getting around Scarborough.....................367
Finding information and taking a tour of
    Scarborough 367
Staying in Scarborough 367
Dining in Scarborough.............................369
Exploring Scarborough 369
Seeing the performing arts In Scarborough 372
Yorkshire's Two National Parks: Moors and Dales 372
North York Moors National Park 372
Yorkshire Dales National Park...................374
Haworth: On the Trail of the Brontës 375
Getting to Haworth 375
Finding Information and taking a tour
    of Haworth 375
Dining in Haworth 376
Exploring Haworth.................................376

Chapter 22: The Lake District 377

The Lake District: Natural Beauty
    and Literary Treasures 379
Getting to the Lake District 379
Getting around the Lake District...............380
Taking a tour of the Lake District 380
Lake Windermere: The Largest Lake in England.............381
Finding information and exchanging money
    near Lake Windermere 381
Touring by boat or foot...........................381
Staying near Lake Windermere 382
Dining near Lake Windermere...................383
Exploring around Lake Windermere.............385
Grasmere: Wordsworth Territory 387
Finding information about Grasmere...........387
Touring on foot......................................387
Staying in and around Grasmere...............388
Dining in Grasmere 389
Exploring in and around Grasmere.............390

Keswick: Lakeland Central 392
    Getting to Keswick..392
    Finding information and exchanging money
        at Keswick 392
    Staying in or near Keswick 392
    Dining in Keswick...394
    Exploring in and around Keswick 395
    Shopping in Keswick 397
    Discovering Keswick's performing arts 397

Part VIII: The Part of Tens...................................*399*

Chapter 23: Ten Writers and the Places They Lived 401

    Jane Austen...401
    Charlotte, Emily, and Anne Brontë.....................402
    Charles Dickens..402
    Henry James (and E. F. Benson)..........................403
    Beatrix Potter 403
    Vita Sackville-West 403
    William Shakespeare...404
    William Wordsworth 404

Chapter 24: Ten Great English Gardens 405

    Castle Howard 405
    Chelsea Physic Garden 406
    Eden Project..406
    Hever Castle..406
    Hidcote Manor..407
    Kew Gardens 407
    Lanhydrock..407
    Sissinghurst Castle Garden 407
    Stourhead 408
    Warwick Castle 408

Chapter 25: Ten (Or So) Great English Churches.......409

    Canterbury Cathedral: Pilgrim Central 409
    Exeter Cathedral: A Medieval Sculpture Gallery............410
    King's College Chapel: Unparalleled Lightness 410
    St. Martin-in-the-Fields: West End Landmark...................410
    St. Paul's Cathedral: Wren's Crowning Achievement......411
    Salisbury Cathedral: High in the Sky 411
    Westminster Abbey: England's Crowning Glory 411
    Winchester Cathedral: Saxon Power Base.........412
    York Minster: England's Largest Gothic Church 412

**Chapter 26: Ten Important Royals —
Past and Present** **413**

Queen Boudicca (A.D. 30?–60):
Braveheart of the Britons 413
Alfred the Great (849–899): A Warrior and a Scholar 414
William the Conqueror (1028–1087): Winner Takes All ...415
Henry II (1133–1189): Family Plots 416
Henry VIII (1491–1547): Take My Wife — Please! 416
Elizabeth I (1533–1603): Heart and Stomach of a King ...417
George III (1738–1820): "My Lords and Peacocks . . ." 418
George IV (1762–1830): A Dandy King for the Regency ...419
Queen Victoria (1819–1901): Mother of Monarchs 420
Queen Elizabeth II (1926–): Monarchy Amid Media 421

Appendix: Quick Concierge *422*

Toll-Free Numbers and Web Sites 427
Major airlines serving England 427
Major car-rental agencies operating in England ...428
Major hotel chains in England 428
Where to Get More Information 429
Locating tourist offices 429
Surfing the Net 430

Index *433*

Introduction

● ●

So you're going to England. Great! But what parts of England do you want to visit? The country stretches from the English Channel in the south to the Scottish border in the north, and from Wales and the Irish Sea in the west to the North Sea in the east. England isn't a huge country — you can drive its length in a day — but sightseeing possibilities pack the interior.

I have a hunch that London is on your itinerary, but what other cities, regions, or specific attractions do you want to see? The walled city of York? Stratford-upon-Avon, the birthplace of William Shakespeare? Are you interested in nightclubbing at a seaside resort, like Brighton, or strolling through an elegant 18th-century spa town, like Bath? Are there specific landscapes you want to see, such as the Yorkshire moors or the cliffs of Cornwall? What castles, cathedrals, and stately homes do you want to visit? And how about other historic sites? Do you want to visit Roman ruins, spend all day in the Tower of London, or walk around the field where the Normans and the Saxons fought the Battle of Hastings in 1066? England promises so much to see, do, and enjoy that you may find planning a trip here a real challenge.

But don't worry, lucky traveler — in this book, I help you assemble your perfect itinerary from England's sightseeing riches. With a bit of planning and some useful information under your belt, you may find taking that trip to England easy.

About This Book

This book serves as a selective guide to England. By definition, England is the southern part of Great Britain, excluding Wales. Wales and Scotland, although part of the United Kingdom of Great Britain and Northern Ireland, don't appear in this book.

My goal throughout this book is to give you a good selection of the country's highlights, which means I exclude places that other, more exhaustive guidebooks routinely include. Birmingham, Manchester, and Bristol are important cities, but from the perspective of a first-time visitor to England, they don't have much to offer. England has so much worth seeing that you don't need to waste your time with the second-rate, the overrated, or the boring.

Use this book as a reference guide. You can, of course, start at the first page and read all the way through to the end. Or, if you've already been to England and know the basics of international travel, you can easily flip to the specific part you need or hone in on one specific chapter.

Please be advised that travel information can change at any time — this is especially true of prices. I suggest that you write or call ahead for confirmation when making your travel plans. The author, editors, and publisher can't be held responsible for readers' experiences while traveling. Your safety is important, however, so I encourage you to stay alert and be aware of your surroundings. Keep a close eye on cameras, purses, and wallets, all favorite targets of thieves and pickpockets.

Conventions Used in This Book

I recently tried to extract some information from a guidebook and felt that I needed training in hieroglyphics to interpret all the different symbols. I'm happy to report that user-friendly *England For Dummies* isn't like that. I keep the symbols and abbreviations to a minimum.

I do use the following credit card abbreviations to indicate which cards hotels, restaurants, and attractions accept

AE: (American Express)

DC: (Diners Club)

MC: (MasterCard)

V: (Visa)

All local, U.K. telephone numbers in this book begin with a zero, followed by a city or area code. A slash divides the zero and city or area code from the local number. For information about calling U.K. numbers from either within or outside the United Kingdom, see the Appendix.

I divide the hotels into two categories: my personal favorites and those that don't quite make my preferred list but still get my hearty seal of approval. Don't be shy about considering these runner-up accommodations if you can't get a room at one of my favorites or if your preferences differ from mine — the amenities that the runners-up offer and the services they provide make all these accommodations good choices to consider as you determine where to rest your head at night.

I also include some general pricing information to help you as you decide where to unpack your bags or dine on the local cuisine. In addition to giving you exact prices, I use a system of dollar signs ($) to show a range of costs for hotels or restaurants. The dollar signs for hotels correspond to *rack rates* (nondiscounted, standard rates) and reflect a hotel's low to high rates for a double room. For restaurants, the dollar signs denote the *average* cost of dinner for one person, including appetizer, main course, dessert, one nonalcoholic drink, tax, and tip (usually 10 percent, unless the bill already includes a service charge). The scale for hotels goes up to five $ signs; the priciest restaurants get four $ signs. Check out the following table to decipher the dollar signs:

Cost	Hotel	Restaurant
$	$175 and under	$25 and under
$$	$176–$275	$26–$40
$$$	$276–$375	$41–$60
$$$$	$376–$475	$61 and up
$$$$$	$476 and up	

I always give prices in this book first in British pounds sterling (£), followed by U.S. dollars ($) rounded off to the nearest dollar over $10 and to the nearest nickel under $10. Although the exchange rate fluctuates daily, this book uses £1 – $1.85.

For those hotels, restaurants, and attractions that I plot on a map, the listing information gives you a page reference to the map. If a hotel, restaurant, or attraction falls outside the city limits or in an out-of-the-way area, this book may not include it on a map.

Foolish Assumptions

As I wrote this book, I made some assumptions about you, dear reader, and your needs as a traveler. Here's what I assumed about you:

- ✔ You may be an experienced traveler who hasn't had much time to explore England and wants expert advice on how to maximize your time and enjoy a hassle-free trip.

- ✔ You may be an inexperienced traveler looking for guidance when determining whether to take a trip to England and how to plan for it.

- ✔ You're not looking for a book that provides all the information available about England or that lists every hotel, restaurant, or attraction. Instead, you're looking for a book that focuses on the places that can give you the best or most original experience in England.

If you fit any of these criteria, *England For Dummies,* 3rd Edition, gives you the information that you're looking for!

How This Book Is Organized

I break this book down into eight parts. The first two parts deal with trip planning and organization. They provide information, advice, and suggestions that can help you map out a wonderful vacation. I devote the other parts of the book to London and specific regions of the country. For each region, I list the best towns and cities to visit, with hotel and restaurant choices, and the top attractions, including castles, stately homes, and gardens.

Part I: Introducing England

This first part introduces England and gives you some excellent reasons for going there. This section gives you an overview of the best England has to offer and helps you get the big picture. These chapters provide background information on the history, architecture, and dining scene in England; recommend books and movies to enhance your trip; help you to decide when to visit and what to see; and provide sample one- and two-week itineraries.

Part II: Planning Your Trip to England

This part helps take some of the wrinkles out of the trip-planning stage. I give you sound advice on planning a realistic budget and talk about your options for airlines and airfares, how package tours can save you big bucks, and what kinds of guided tours you can join. This part helps you to decide what form of transportation (train, bus, or rental car) to use to get around the country, and it explains what kind of accommodations you can expect for your money. I provide tips for England-bound travelers with special needs and interests: families, seniors, travelers with disabilities, and gay and lesbian travelers. I also deal with some pretrip loose ends, from passports to medical insurance.

Part III: London and Environs

All you need to know about England's greatest city makes up this part. You find detailed information on London's airports and thumbnail descriptions of the city's diverse neighborhoods. Also, I help you get around like a Londoner on the Underground, on the bus, or in a taxi. You can find a list of London's best hotels and an appetizing survey of London's best restaurants. I cover the top attractions in and around this exciting city, plus shopping and nightlife. Making side trips from London is easy, and I provide details on several possible destinations: Greenwich, Hampton Court Palace, Kew Gardens, Windsor Castle, Oxford, Blenheim Palace, and Cambridge.

Part IV: The Southeast

In this part, I outline the highlights of Kent and Sussex, counties close to London that border the English Channel. I also recommend overnight destinations, such as Canterbury, with its ancient cathedral; the swinging seaside resort of Brighton; and the cobblestoned town of Rye. I devote a chapter to Kent's greatest castles, stately homes, and gardens — including Knole, Hever Castle, Sissinghurst Castle Gardens, Dover Castle, and Leeds Castle.

Part V: The West Country

This part explores the West Country counties of Hampshire, Wiltshire, Devon, and Cornwall. Winchester is Hampshire's most historic city. Neighboring Wiltshire is the home of Salisbury, with its towering cathedral, and that great prehistoric monument Stonehenge. In Devon, you find the unique moorland landscape of Dartmoor National Park; Torquay, a laid-back seaside resort; and Plymouth, where the Pilgrims set sail for the New World. Vacationers often flock to mysterious Cornwall, which includes Land's End in England's southwesternmost corner, with its colorful seaside towns, such as Penzance and St. Ives.

Part VI: England's Heartland

I devote this part to central England. You may know Stratford-upon-Avon in Warwickshire as the home of William Shakespeare, and nearby Warwick Castle is one of the country's most popular attractions. Such an amazing collection of 18th-century buildings fills beautiful Bath that UNESCO (United Nations Educational, Scientific, and Cultural Organization) designated the city a World Heritage Site. The Cotswolds region, with its picture-perfect villages built of honey-colored stone, is one of England's premier touring destinations. Cheltenham and Cirencester make good bases for exploring the Cotswolds.

Part VII: Way Up North

Yorkshire and the Lake District are highly scenic areas close to England's northern border with Scotland. York is one of the most beautiful and historic cities in the North; Scarborough is a Yorkshire resort town on the North Sea; and amazing Castle Howard lies between them. North York Moors National Park and the Yorkshire Dales National Park protect Yorkshire's distinctive landscape of heather-covered moors, gentle dales, and rugged coastline. The Lake District, in Cumbria, is a spectacularly beautiful region of mountains and lakes, all within Lake District National Park. You can stay on Lake Windermere, England's largest lake, or in nearby Grasmere or Keswick.

Part VIII: The Part of Tens

The Part of Tens allows me to focus a little more attention on the extra-special places and sights I want you to know about. My "tens" include ten famous writers and how you can visit where they lived and worked, ten great English gardens, ten magnificent churches and cathedrals, and ten famous royals and the events that characterized their reign.

You can also find two other elements in this book. Near the back, I include an A-to-Z appendix — your Quick Concierge — containing plenty of handy information, such as how the telephone system works and what numbers to call in an emergency. You also find a list of toll-free telephone numbers and Web sites for airlines, car-rental agencies, and hotel chains serving England, plus Web sites where you can find additional information on specific cities or areas. Finally, I include a tear-out Cheat Sheet that can help you with unfamiliar British words.

Icons Used in This Book

In this book's margins, you can find six different icons: little pictures that clue you in on some important trip-planning matters and a few things that are just for fun.

 This icon points out my report on the most newsworthy scandals — I mean stories — about people and places. I throw in these tidbits about English personalities and places just for the fun of it.

 I'm not cheap, but I love to save money, and I suspect you do, too. Keep an eye out for the Bargain Alert icon as you seek out money-saving tips and/or great deals.

 Best of the Best highlights the best the destination has to offer in all categories: hotels, restaurants, attractions, activities, shopping, and nightlife.

 Watch for the Heads Up icon to identify annoying or potentially dangerous situations such as tourist traps, unsafe neighborhoods, budgetary ripoffs, and other things to beware.

 Look to the Kid Friendly icon for attractions, hotels, restaurants, and activities that welcome children or people traveling with kids.

 Find out useful advice on things to do and ways to schedule your time when you see the Tip icon.

Where to Go from Here

To England, of course! How you use this book is up to you. You can start from the beginning and read straight through, or you can start anywhere in between and extract information as you want or need it. Throughout the book, I hope you think of me as your guide or companion on this journey to England. However you use the book, I want you to have a great time.

Part I
Introducing England

The 5th Wave   By Rich Tennant

"This afternoon I want everyone to go online and research Native American culture, history of the old West, and discount airfares to England for the two weeks I'll be on vacation."

In this part . . .

This part helps to get you going. If you've never been to England, you need advice and information to start planning your trip. And if you've been to England before, you may want to refresh your knowledge and look for some new places to visit.

Chapter 1 gives you a brief overview that fills you in on the best England has to offer, from the edge-of-your-seat excitement of London to the sleepy splendor of ancient villages. I give you a round-up of the greatest gardens, the coolest castles, the stateliest of stately homes, the most historically charismatic towns and cities, the most beautiful churches and cathedrals, and the most romantic landscapes.

Chapter 2 digs deeper into the culture and history of England in a way that can only add to your enjoyment of what you see and experience once you're there. I give you a brief outline of the main events in English history, right up to the latest royal scandals. I cover the dining and drinking scene, from haute restaurants to historic pubs where you can enjoy a pint of ale with the locals. I outline England's main architectural trends. And, finally, I recommend some books and movies that you may want to check out.

Chapter 3 offers more specific information to help you plan when and where you want to go. I present a general overview of the main areas I cover in the book and include a calendar of events and a description of the seasons.

In Chapter 4, I suggest two possible itineraries: one for visitors who have one week in England, the second for visitors with two weeks. I also include itineraries for families, gardening enthusiasts, and history buffs. Even if you don't use them, the itineraries may give you some ideas for your own trip and how to budget your time.

Chapter 1

Discovering the Best of England

In This Chapter

▶ Discovering London and England's most fascinating towns and villages

▶ Exploring England's unrivaled collection of castles, palaces, cathedrals, and churches

▶ Experiencing the great historic landmarks of England

▶ Enjoying glorious gardens and the English countryside

▶ Going shopping in London and beyond

*E*ngland claims a special place in the hearts and minds of many people. English speakers (and readers) in the United States, Canada, Australia, and New Zealand often feel a kinship with the land of their mother tongue. England shares many cultural ties and hundreds of place names with those countries. So for some people, a trip to England is like going home. The country's great age, and the sheer weight of its history, can induce a sense of awe and wonder. England is a land of ancient cities, royal palaces, massive cathedrals, and legendary sites. You can see the layers of its long history everywhere you look. And travelers can enjoy the country in so many different ways. Mighty castles, stately homes, glorious gardens, and picturesque villages enhance the country-side's natural beauty. The cooking is unique, and so is the English pub.

This chapter gives you as an at-a-glance reference to the absolute best — the best of the best — that England has to offer. In the categories that I outline, you can find some of the things that make traveling in England so much fun and so endlessly fascinating. I discuss each of these places in detail later in this book; you can find them in their indicated chapters, marked with a Best of the Best icon.

The Best of Legendary London

London is one of the world's great cities, and I give it plenty of coverage in this book because almost every visitor to England heads here first. London is exciting, historic, cultured, cutting-edge, and romantic. See Chapters 11 and 12 for more on all of these highlights:

✔ London is where you can visit truly world-class museums. **The British Museum,** the **National Gallery,** the **Tate Modern,** the **Tate Britain,** the **Victoria & Albert Museum,** and the **Natural History Museum** — to name the best known — display a mind-boggling array of artwork and unique treasures.

✔ The **Tower of London, Westminster Abbey,** and **Buckingham Palace** are just three of the famous historic places you can visit. **Hyde Park, Kensington Gardens, Green Park,** and **St. James's Park** form a vast network of green space shared by Londoners and visitors to the capital of the United Kingdom.

✔ London's **dining scene** is phenomenal, and the **entertainment choices** — theater, music, dance, opera, film — are almost limitless. The **shopping opportunities** are endless, too.

The Best Cities, Towns, and Villages

England isn't that large, so you can base yourself in London and take day trips to many historic cities and towns in other parts of the country. Or you can make them part of an itinerary that showcases the country's best cities:

✔ One of the most elegant of English cities is the former spa town of **Bath,** with its amazing Georgian *crescents* (row houses built in a long curving line) and 18th-century architecture. See Chapter 20.

✔ **Oxford** and **Cambridge** are famous university towns where centuries-old colleges cluster around quadrangles. See Chapter 13.

✔ For some laid-back fun beside the seaside, you can visit **Brighton,** on the south coast, or head up north to **Scarborough,** on the North Sea in Yorkshire. **Cornwall** has several picturesque towns, many of them former fishing villages with colorful histories of smuggling and pirates: **Penzance** is the largest, but you also find **St. Ives,** an artists' colony with a beautiful beach; **Mousehole;** and **Fowey.** See Chapters 14, 21, and 18 respectively.

✔ **Rye,** in Sussex, is one of the best-preserved and most attractive towns in England, full of Elizabethan homes and buildings. See Chapter 14.

✔ **York,** two hours north of London by train, is still surrounded by its medieval walls; has narrow, medieval lanes; and is home to York Minster, one of the largest churches in the world. See Chapter 21.

✔ The scenic **Cotswolds** region is dotted with charming, honey-colored stone villages — **Broadway, Bourton-on-the-Water, Chipping Campden,** and **Cirencester** — that all grew rich on wool during the Middle Ages. See Chapter 20.

✔ In the **Lake District,** a scenically splendid area in northwest England, you find picturesque villages, such as **Grasmere,** and lakeside towns, such as **Keswick,** in stunning countryside. See Chapter 22.

The Best Castles, Palaces, and Stately Homes

Step into one of England's castles, palaces, or stately homes, and all you can do is marvel at the way people used to live. *Some* people, I should say, because these enormous estates belonged to an elite minority with royal connections or private fortunes. Usually set amid spectacular grounds, these places are treasure troves of history and art, packed with rare paintings and beautiful furniture.

✔ In London, you can visit **Buckingham Palace,** the queen's official residence, and **Kensington Palace,** once the home of Princess Diana. Henry VIII's **Hampton Court Palace** is a short train ride from London, as is 900-year-old **Windsor Castle,** another official residence of Queen Elizabeth II. See Chapter 12 for more on Buckingham and Kensington palaces; see Chapter 13 for more on Hampton Court Palace and Windsor Castle.

✔ **Knole,** which has 365 rooms (some with their original 17th-century furnishings), and moated **Hever Castle,** birthplace of Anne Boleyn, are just two of the many castles and stately homes you can visit in Kent. See Chapter 15.

✔ One of the most dramatically sited castles in England is **St. Michael's Mount,** on its own rocky island in Mount's Bay, Penzance. **Castle Drogo,** in nearby Dartmoor National Park, is the last private castle to be built in England (it was completed in 1930). See Chapters 18 and 17, respectively.

✔ **Blenheim Palace,** near Oxford, was the palatial childhood home of Winston Churchill, who later moved to **Chartwell,** a house in Kent that is filled with Churchill memorabilia. See Chapters 13 and 15, respectively.

✔ Farther north, just a few miles from Stratford-upon-Avon, is mighty **Warwick Castle,** surrounded by thick stone walls and towers. The wax artisans at Madame Tussauds have "peopled" the castle with its former owners and some of their famous guests. See Chapter 19.

✔ **Castle Howard,** in Yorkshire, is one of the most beautiful stately homes in England, an enormous domed wonder set amidst landscaped grounds with classically inspired buildings. See Chapter 21.

The Best Cathedrals and Churches

England's mighty cathedrals, still in use 800 years and more after they were built, dominate the heart of England's cities. Their stupendous size never fails to impress, and some of their architectural details are stunning. I include several of my favorite cathedrals and churches in this book:

- ✔ English monarchs have been crowned in London's **Westminster Abbey** since the time of William the Conqueror. **St. Paul's Cathedral** is the masterpiece of Sir Christopher Wren, who rebuilt London after the Great Fire of 1666. See Chapter 12.

- ✔ Chaucer's pilgrims in *The Canterbury Tales* were headed toward **Canterbury Cathedral,** and tourists still flock there in droves. See Chapter 14.

- ✔ The west front of **Exeter Cathedral** is remarkable for its rows of sculptured saints and kings, the largest surviving array of 14th-century sculpture in England. See Chapter 17.

- ✔ Massive **York Minster,** the largest Gothic building in northern Europe, contains more medieval stained glass than any other cathedral in England. See Chapter 21.

The Best Historic Places

England markets its history big time, and with good reason: Its history stretches back some 2,000 years, to a time when Latin-speaking Roman soldiers built forts, roads, and temples from Kent to Northumberland. But England was inhabited for thousands of years before the Romans arrived. No soap opera can beat the stories associated with England's most famous historic sites. The great historical landmarks of England stir the imagination because they've witnessed so much — from glorious triumphs to bloody tragedies.

- ✔ When you visit the **Tower of London,** you can walk on a piece of ground where the great dramas and terrors of a turbulent kingdom were played out, where Elizabeth I was held captive while still a princess, and where Sir Thomas More and Anne Boleyn were beheaded. See Chapter 12.

- ✔ In southern England, at a place called **Battle,** you can walk around the battlefield where in 1066 William of Normandy defeated Harold, the Saxon king of England. The battle changed the course of English history. See Chapter 14.

- ✔ Long-vanished peoples erected mysterious monuments that still fill the country. The most famous is **Stonehenge,** a massive stone circle on the plains of Wiltshire. In **Cornwall,** you can visit other tantalizing prehistoric sites, including **Chysauster,** the remains of an Iron Age village. In northern England, up in the Lake District, **Castlerigg Stone Circle,** near Keswick, is another enigmatic reminder of early human presence in England. See Chapters 16, 18, and 22, respectively.

The Best Gardens

In England, gardening has been raised to an art form. Chalk it up to a temperate climate (especially in the southeast and southwest) that can support all kinds of rare and exotic plant species, including azaleas and rhododendrons. I include several great English gardens in this book because gardens are a growing (pardon the pun) interest for visitors from around the globe. The gardens usually surround a stately home or castle that you can also visit.

- Perhaps the most famous garden in England is at **Sissinghurst Castle,** in Kent. The plantings there, and at equally beautiful **Hidcote Manor,** in Gloucestershire, form living "rooms" of shape, color, scent, and texture. See Chapters 15 and 20.

- **Stourhead,** in Wiltshire, was laid out in 1741 and is one of the oldest landscape gardens in England. See Chapter 16.

- In **Cornwall, Cotehele,** and **Lanhydrock** are estates known for their superb riverside gardens. Cornwall is also the site of England's newest garden, a massive world-environment learning center called the **Eden Project.** See Chapter 18.

- You can find immaculately landscaped grounds, where every shrub and blade of grass is clipped to perfection, at **Hever Castle,** in Kent; **Warwick Castle,** near Stratford-upon-Avon; and **Castle Howard,** up north in Yorkshire. See Chapters 15, 19, and 21, respectively.

- Closer to London, you find historic gardens at **Hampton Court Palace** and the Royal Botanic Gardens at **Kew.** See Chapter 13.

The Best Romantic Landscapes

England has been settled for thousands of years, and truly wild places are rare in this densely populated country where 46,382,000 people inhabit 50,357 square miles of land. Yet travelers always comment on the countryside's beauty, a domesticated blend of farms, enclosed fields, and small villages that seem to snooze under a blanket of history. The way humans have interacted with the environment for thousands of years — leaving behind grand monuments, such as Stonehenge, humble country churches, thatched cottages, and hedgerows — contributes to the enduring charm of the English countryside. Many visitors respond to the sense of human continuity evoked by the following landscapes:

- If you explore **Cornwall,** you encounter rocky coastal headlands, windswept moors, and Celtic crosses left by Irish missionaries 14 centuries ago. See Chapter 18.

- Touring the **Cotswolds,** you see picturesque villages of honey-colored stone that date back to the Middle Ages interspersed with lightly forested valleys and high open fields where sheep graze as they've done for a thousand years. See Chapter 20.

✔ Luckily, the country's wildest and most unique landscapes are protected as national parks, limiting commercial development and opening the countryside to walkers, thus preserving the regions' essential character. Places like **Dartmoor National Park** in Devon, **North York Moors** and **Yorkshire Dales** national parks in Yorkshire, and **Lake District National Park** in semi-remote Cumbria are all great places for you to experience the most romantic landscapes of England. See Chapters 17, 21, and 22, respectively.

The Best Shopping

London is one of the world's greatest shopping cities, and my credit cards aren't doing all the talking. From mighty Harrods to the superchic boutiques of Bond Street, from the 200-year-old shops on Jermyn Street to the wonderland of bookstores on Charing Cross Road, London offers a seemingly endless array of goods and goodies. Custom-made shirts, hand-tooled leather shoes, high-quality woolens — in London, you can still find such things. You can hunt for an old engraving, paw through bric-a-brac at an outdoor market stall, or wander through the London silver vaults in your quest for a Georgian soup ladle. See Chapter 12.

Nowhere else in the country can match London's abundance of shopping opportunities. Outside the capital, however, small shops and one-of-a-kind places draw the shopper's eye:

✔ Antiquarian bookstores abound in **Cambridge** and **Oxford.** See Chapter 13.

✔ **Exeter** is a good place to look for silver. See Chapter 17.

✔ The **Cotswolds** has more antique stores than anywhere else in England. See Chapter 20.

✔ Many areas of the country feature locally made handicrafts. Look for pottery in **Devon, Cornwall,** and the Lake District. See Chapters 17, 18, and 22, respectively.

You may also stumble across some treasure at a rural car-boot (trunk) sale or jumble sale. At these informal sales in school or church buildings or in parking lots, you can buy secondhand odds and ends. And of course, every major historic attraction in England — from Sissinghurst Castle Garden in Kent to Castle Howard in Yorkshire — has a gift shop.

Chapter 2

Digging Deeper into England

In This Chapter

▶ Running through the main events in England's history

▶ Building your architecture appreciation

▶ Diving into English food and beer

▶ Discovering books and movies about England

This chapter helps you find out more about England and deepens your experience of the country. I distill the essence of England's complicated and tumultuous past so you can get a clear, quick sense of the major eras. Then I highlight the main architectural trends, whet your appetite with a primer on English food and drink, and recommend some excellent books and movies about England.

The Main Events: A Brief History of England

England's history is an inexhaustible subject. Huge tomes have been written on individual monarchs, colorful personalities, architectural styles, and historical eras. But in this section, I'm going to be as brief as a bikini and give you a history of England that covers only the bare essentials:

✔ **Prehistory:** Beginning about 5,000 years ago, a Neolithic civilization was cutting and hauling megaton slabs of stone over dozens of miles and erecting them in elaborate geometric configurations. Stonehenge is the most famous example of their work. (See Chapter 16 for details on Stonehenge.)

✔ **The Romans arrive:** When the Romans conquered England in A.D. 43, they suppressed or subdued the local Celtic tribes. The legendary Queen Boudicca (or Boadicea) was a Celtic warrior queen who fought back the invading Romans. You can see a statue of her on Westminster Bridge in London. The Romans brought their building and engineering skills to England, and you can see the remains of Roman walls, roads, forts, temples, villas, and baths throughout the country — most notably in Bath. (See Chapter 20 for more on Bath.)

✔ **Northern invaders:** With the Roman Empire's breakup in A.D. 410, Jutes, Angles, and Saxons from northern Europe invaded England and formed small kingdoms. For the next 600 years or so, the Anglo-Saxon kingdoms fought off Viking raiders. In the north, Eboracum, a Roman settlement, became Jorvik, a Viking city, and eventually York (See Chapter 21 for more on York.)

✔ **William the Conqueror:** The next major transitional period in England started in 1066, when William of Normandy fought and killed Harold, the Anglo-Saxon king of England, at the Battle of Hastings (the site of today's town of Battle, which you can read about in Chapter 14). William and his French nobles took over the land and built castles — Windsor Castle (see Chapter 13) and the Tower of London (see Chapter 12) are two examples — and cathedrals that still stand today. Every monarch up to the present day claims descent from William the Conqueror.

✔ **Magna Carta:** King John, a Plantagenet, signed the Magna Carta in 1215, granting more rights to the nobles. What about the common man and woman? As serfs and vassals in a closed, hierarchical, class-ridden society, their lot wasn't an easy one. Geoffrey Chaucer (1342–1400) was the first writer to give us some recognizable portraits of folks who lived during the medieval period, in *The Canterbury Tales*. (For more on Canterbury, see Chapter 14.)

✔ **Hundred Years' War:** At home and abroad, war and bloodshed tore England apart for more than 300 years. The Hundred Years' War between France and England began in 1337. During this same period, in the War of the Roses, the Houses of York and Lancaster fought for the right of succession to the English crown.

✔ **Tudor and Elizabethan England:** Henry VIII, the Tudor king famous for taking six wives, brought about the next great shift in what had been Catholic England. In 1534, he dissolved all the monasteries and became head of the Church of England. His daughter, Elizabeth I, ruled during a period of relative peace, power, and prosperity. The Elizabethan period was England's Golden Age, the time when Shakespeare's plays were being performed at the Globe Theatre in London.

✔ **Civil war:** In 1603, James VI of Scotland became King James I of England, uniting the crowns of England and Scotland. But conflicts between monarchs and nobles were endless. Charles I, seeking absolute power, dissolved Parliament in 1629. He was beheaded in 1649 after Oliver Cromwell led a bitter civil war between Royalists and Parliamentarians. Cromwell's armies destroyed churches and royalist strongholds throughout the country. Cromwell was elevated to Lord Protectorate of the Realm, but by 1660 a new king, Charles II, was on the throne. This time, however, his powers were limited.

✔ **Fire and plague:** London, which had been growing steadily, was devastated by two back-to-back catastrophes: the Great Plague of 1665 and the Great Fire of 1666.

✔ **The Victorian Empire:** England reached its zenith of power and prestige during the reign of Victoria (1837–1901), who ruled over an empire so vast that "the sun never set" on it. The Industrial Revolution spawned another major change during this period, moving England away from its agrarian past and into a mechanized future. Charles Dickens and other social reformers exposed the wretched working conditions in Victorian England, where children as young as 6 had to labor in mines and factories. The late Victorian age was the time of Sherlock Holmes, a fictional detective created by Arthur Conan Doyle, and Jack the Ripper, a real-life serial killer who terrorized London's West End.

✔ **England in the World Wars:** England suffered terrible losses during World War I (1914–1918) but emerged victorious. During World War II, from the fall of France in 1940 until the United States entered the war in 1941, England stood alone against Hitler. Winston Churchill was the country's prime minister during the war years. With strictly rationed food, mandatory blackouts, and terrible bombing raids that destroyed cities and killed tens of thousands of civilians, life in wartime England had a profound effect on its citizens. Shortages continued for many years afterward.

✔ **The welfare state:** Another major societal shift occurred in 1945 when the Labour Party began to dismantle the empire and introduced the welfare state. Under the National Health System, every citizen in the United Kingdom can receive free health care (the quality of that care is another story). It wasn't until Margaret Thatcher and the Tory Party came into power during the 1980s that England began privatizing formerly state-run agencies, such as the railroad (with what some say are disastrous results).

✔ **Queen Elizabeth II:** Queen Elizabeth II ascended the throne in 1952. The fairy-tale wedding of her son Prince Charles to Lady Diana Spencer was the last high point for the House of Windsor. Charles and Diana's subsequent divorce seemed to unleash a floodgate of royal scandals, with the result that the popularity of the British monarchy is at an all-time low. In 2002, the queen celebrated her 50th anniversary on the throne. But the queen is no longer the richest woman in England: J. K. Rowling, the author of the Harry Potter books, now holds that title.

✔ **New Labour:** In 2001, Tony Blair was elected to a second term as prime minister, and New Labour, with its centrist approach, was firmly in control of the government. However, in the 2005 elections, the party lost one-third of its seats as voters expressed their discontent with Blair's continuing support of the war in Iraq.

✔ **Terrorist bombings:** In July 2005, a day after exultant Londoners learned that their city would host the 2012 Olympics, terrorists detonated bombs in the London Underground and on a double-decker bus, killing 54 people and wounding hundreds more. Londoners stood together and carried on, showing the world that they would not be cowed by acts of violence.

Building Blocks: An Overview of English Architecture

You can determine the period in which a building was constructed (or reconstructed) by its architectural and decorative details. In a country like England, where the age of buildings can span a thousand-year period (a few Anglo-Saxon churches are even older than that), many different styles evolved. The architectural periods are often named for the monarch or royal family reigning at the time. You can enhance your enjoyment of England's abundance of historic buildings if you know a few key features of the different styles. The following list is a brief primer in English architectural history, from Norman to Victorian times:

ANGLO FILES
ENGLAND

Recent royal events

In 2005, Prince Charles, the heir to the British throne, finally married his longtime mistress, Camilla Parker-Bowles, in a ceremony that his mother, Queen Elizabeth, did not attend. The wedding was something of a highlight — if you can call it that — in a royal year full of royal embarrassments. For one thing, it became apparent that the British public did not want Camilla to be their eventual queen. She will, though, unless the governments of England and 15 Commonwealth nations change the law. In the meantime, you can call the pre-queen Her Royal Highness the Duchess of Cornwall. Earlier in the year, a picture of Prince Harry, youngest son of Charles and his first wife, Princess Diana, wearing a WWII German desert uniform with a Nazi swastika on his armband shocked the British public. It seems the party-boy prince didn't realize wearing such an outfit to a costume party might offend some. Harry was forced to apologize — just about the time a former art teacher charged that she actually painted the paintings Harry submitted for his art exams at Eton. Not a minute too soon, Harry was packed off to Sandhurst Military Academy for the usual pseudomilitary training of a royal. Then news erupted that Prince Andrew and Prince Edward, younger sons of Queen Elizabeth, were in essence receiving royal housing benefits that made them look like welfare cheats. Andrew (Fergie's ex), whose wealth is estimated at £13 million ($24 million), pays no annual rent for a 30-room lodge in Windsor Great Park. Edward, with a fortune estimated at £9 million ($17 million), pays £10,000 ($18,500) a year for a 57-room house set on 87 acres in Bagshot Park. No wonder the queen was so eager to claim that the monarchy — which costs every citizen of the United Kingdom about 59p ($1.10) per year — provides the British taxpayers real value for money. It must have warmed the heart of every hardworking commoner.

- **Norman** (1066–1189): Round arches, barrel vaults, and highly decorated archways characterize this period's Romanesque style.

- **Early English Gothic** (1189–1272): The squat, bulky buildings of the Norman period gave way to the taller, lighter buildings constructed in this style.

- **Decorated Gothic** (1272–1377): Buildings in this style have large windows, *tracery* (ornamental work with branching lines), and heavily decorated gables and arches.

- **Perpendicular Gothic** (1377–1483): Large *buttresses* (exterior side supports) allowed churches to have larger windows than ever before. Tracery was more elaborate than in previous Gothic buildings; the four-centered arch appeared; and architects perfected *fan vaulting* (a decorative form of vaulting in which the structural ribs spread upward and outward along the ceiling like the rays of a fan).

- **Tudor** (1485–1553): During this period, buildings evolved from Gothic to Renaissance styles. Large houses and palaces were built with a new material: brick. England has many half-timbered Tudor and Elizabethan domestic and commercial buildings. This method of construction used brick and plaster between visible wooden timbers.

- **Elizabethan** (1553–1603): The Renaissance brought a revival of classical features, such as columns, *cornices* (prominent rooflines with brackets and other details), and *pediments* (a decorative triangular feature over doorways and windows). The many large houses and palaces of this period were built in an E or H shape and contained long galleries, grand staircases, and carved chimneys.

- **Jacobean** (1603–1625): In England, Inigo Jones adopted the symmetrical, classically inspired Palladian style that arrived from Italy, but he used it in a freer and more fanciful way. Buildings in this style incorporate elements from ancient Greek and Roman architecture. Columns and pilasters, round-arch arcades, and flat roofs with openwork parapets became common.

- **Stuart** (1625–1688): Elegant classical features, such as columns, cornices, and pediments, are typical of this period, in which Sir Christopher Wren was the preeminent architect.

- **Queen Anne** (1689–1714): Buildings from the English baroque period mix heavy ornamentation with classical simplicity.

- **Georgian and Regency** (1714–1830): During these periods, elegant terraced houses were built; many examples survive in Brighton and Bath. Form and proportion were important elements; interior decoration inspired by Chinese motifs became fashionable.

- **Victorian** (1830–1901): A whole range of antique styles emerged — everything from Gothic and Greek Revival to pseudo-Egyptian and Elizabethan. Hundreds of English churches were renovated during the Victorian era.

Dining English Style from Traditional to Modern

Once upon a time, you could always count on getting lousy meals in England. English "home cooking" — all too often dull, insular, and uninspired — was the joke of Europe. That began to change in the 1980s, with the influx of new cooking trends that favored foods from France and Italy. Since then, London has become a major food capital, and the rest of the country has raised its food consciousness considerably. London is certainly the easiest place to find restaurants serving inventive Modern British cuisine, but you also encounter the new cooking style in smaller towns and even in some pubs. And don't forget that spicy Indian cooking is England's second "national" cuisine. You find thousands of Indian and other ethnic restaurants throughout the country.

But traditionalists have nothing to worry about. You can still get your hands on all those wonderful Old English faves — eggs, kippers, beans, and fried tomatoes for breakfast; bubble and squeak; roast beef and Yorkshire pudding; meat pies; fish and chips; cottage pie; sticky toffee pudding; and trifle. (See the Cheat Sheet at the front of this book for a glossary of English food terms.) When traditional, nonfancy English dishes are done well, they're supersatisfying and delicious. If you travel around the country, look for local and regional specialties, such as sausage, lamb, cheese, and desserts.

While you're in England, you can also look forward to the world of afternoon tea. In the West Country, you get a cream tea, which consists of tea; homemade scones; strawberry jam; and thick, rich, clotted cream from Devon or Cornwall. (You put the cream on your scones, not in your tea, and then top it all with the jam.) Elsewhere, you may find whipped cream in place of the clotted cream. You can have teas as simple or as fancy as you want.

Visiting the Local Pub

The pub (short for *public house*) is an English institution. England is awash with historic pubs, where you can sit all evening with a pint of ale, bitter, stout, or cider and soak up the local color. No matter how tiny the village or town, you always find at least one pub. In London and larger towns, you can do a *pub crawl*, walking (upright) from pub to pub and sampling the diverse brews on tap. Although you can get a hard drink at both bars and pubs, when you're in a pub, you're better off confining yourself to beer.

Parliament has instituted the strict hours that most pubs adhere to: Monday through Saturday from 11 a.m. to 11 p.m. and Sunday from noon to 10:30 p.m. Americans, take note: You won't be asked or expected to pay a cover charge in an English pub, and you *never* tip the bartender;

A beer primer: Are you bitter or stout?

Most of the pubs in London and throughout the United Kingdom are "tied" to a particular brewery and sell only that brewery's beers (you see the name of the brewery on the sign outside). Independent pubs can sell more brands than a tied pub. Either way, you still have to choose from what may seem like a bewildering variety. The colorful names of individual brews don't provide much help — you can only wonder what Pigswill, Dogs Bollocks, Hobgoblin, Old Thumper, Pommies Revenge, or Boondoggle taste like. Depending on all sorts of factors — the water, the hops, the fermentation technique, and so on — the brewery crafts the taste of any beer, whether on draught or in a bottle. You can get a few U.S. and international brands, but imports are more expensive than the homegrown products.

When ordering beer in a pub, specify the type, the brand, and the amount (pint or half-pint) you want. Feel free to ask the bartender to recommend something based on your taste preferences. Just remember that pubs serve most English beer at room temperature. The following brief descriptions of beer may come in handy in a pub:

✔ **Ale:** Not as strong as bitter, ale has a slightly sweeter taste. You can order light or pale ale in a bottle; export ale is a stronger variety.

✔ **Bitter:** What most locals drink. It's a clear, yellowish, traditional beer with a strong flavor of hops. *Real ale* is a bitter that's still fermenting *(alive)* when it arrives from the brewery; the pub pumps and serves it immediately.

✔ **Lager:** When chilled, lager is probably the closest you can come to an American-style beer. You can get lager in bottles or on draught.

✔ **Shandy:** Equal parts bitter and lemonade (sometimes limeade or ginger beer), it's for those who like a sweet beverage that only sort of tastes like beer.

✔ **Stout:** A dark, rich, creamy version of ale. Guinness is the most popular brand. A *black and tan* is half lager and half stout.

the best you can do is offer to buy him or her a drink, an acceptable practice in England. Ten minutes before closing, a bell rings, signaling that the time has come to order your last round.

Background Check: Finding England in Books and Movies

It's always fun to whet your appetite for a place by reading about it or watching a movie filmed on location. When it comes to reading about England or seeing it on the screen, you have almost endless possibilities. Here are a few suggestions.

Books

Has any country produced as many great and enduring writers as England? It's impossible in a brief survey to even scratch the surface. In Chapter 23, "Ten Writers and the Places They Lived," I provide a quick rundown of the works and workplaces associated with **Jane Austen; Charlotte, Emily,** and **Anne Brontë; Charles Dickens; Henry James** and **E.F. Benson; Beatrix Potter; Vita Sackville-West; William Shakespeare;** and **William Wordsworth.** The wonderful thing about England — at least, if you love literature — is that you can visit the homes of many great poets and novelists, and see with your own eyes the towns, cities, and landscapes that inspired them.

Here are some additional suggestions for English novels:

- If you're going to visit Dorset or Devon, you may want to read a novel or two by **Thomas Hardy,** who set his works in the fictional county of Wessex. Hardy's best-known works are *Tess of the D'Urbervilles, Jude the Obscure,* and *The Mayor of Casterbridge.*

- **Daphne du Maurier**'s famous romantic novel *Rebecca* is set in a great house on the coast of Cornwall.

- The fascinating historical novels of **Edward Rutherfurd** follow the fates of families and fortunes in specific places or regions of England over thousands of years: *Sarum* is about Salisbury; *London* is about London; *The Forest* is about life in the New Forest.

- The Cazalet Chronicles, four novels by **Elizabeth Jane Howard,** take place in London and on the south coast of England between the two world wars.

- **Alan Hollinghurst**'s Booker Prize-winner, *The Line of Beauty,* etches a portrait of London during the Thatcher years.

- **Zadie Smith**'s brilliantly hilarious *White Teeth* is the story of two immigrant families in North London.

- **Ian McEwan**'s best-selling *Saturday* evokes the life of an upper-middle-class family in London today.

- **Kate Fox**'s entertaining pop-psych book *Watching the English* deals humorously with the "hidden rules" of English behavior as it relates to social class and "Englishness."

Thousands of tomes have been written about the history of England. One recent and noteworthy offering is **Simon Schama**'s three-volume *History of Britain,* which accompanied a program of the same name on the BBC History Channel. For popular biographies of historical figures, try **Antonia Fraser**'s *The Wives of Henry VIII* and *Cromwell.* You can find many good biographies of Elizabeth I, including **Alison Weir**'s *The Life of Elizabeth I.*

Movies

The Brits are great filmmakers and beat Hollywood cold when it comes to honesty in acting, re-creation of period detail, and human-scale cinematic storytelling. If you've ever watched British television, you know how completely different it is from American TV. The characters actually look like human beings and inhabit recognizable worlds.

When it comes to British film, you have to pick the genre that interests you. Over the past 30 years or so, television imports from the BBC have appeared on *Masterpiece Theatre, Mystery!,* and cable channels in the United States, and they've won legions of fans. Many of these popular series, from *Upstairs, Downstairs* and *The Forsythe Saga* to *Absolutely Fabulous* and *Queer as Folk,* are available on DVD. *Masterpiece Theatre* has also shown outstanding historical dramas such as *Elizabeth R,* with Glenda Jackson playing Queen Elizabeth I, and *The Six Wives of Henry VIII.* In addition, you can find filmed-for-television BBC versions of all the Shakespeare plays. Your library may have some of these versions on DVD or video.

If you're looking for sweeping historic epics filmed for the big screen, check out **Anne of the Thousand Days** (with Genevieve Bujold and Richard Burton), **Mary Queen of Scots** (with Vanessa Redgrave), *A Man for All Seasons* (with Paul Scofield), **Lady Jane** (with Helena Bonham Carter), and **Becket** (with Richard Burton and Peter O'Toole). The recent **Ladies in Lavender** with Maggie Smith and Judi Dench was filmed in Cornwall. Judi Dench played Queen Victoria in the delightful **Mrs. Brown,** and Cate Blanchett was a memorable Elizabeth I in **Elizabeth.** Other period costume films that I recommend include *Women in Love; A Room with a View; Howard's End;* and the film/TV versions of Jane Austen's *Pride and Prejudice, Sense and Sensibility,* and *Persuasion.* Charlotte Brontë's *Jane Eyre* has been adapted several times, starting with the Laurence Olivier/Merle Oberon Hollywood version of 1939. And don't forget that the Harry Potter movies are filmed in England.

For a look at contemporary England, some of the following movies may appeal to you: *Calendar Girls, The Full Monty, Billy Elliott,* and *Closer.*

Chapter 3

Deciding When and Where to Go

In This Chapter

▶ Exploring England's main points of interest

▶ Making the most of your time in England

▶ Getting a grip on the seasons

▶ Checking out the country's calendar of events

So when and where do you want to go in England? In a country full of options, I help you narrow your focus. This chapter tells you the highlights of each region, and gives you a rundown on the seasons and the country's main events so that you can determine the best destinations and time of year for your visit.

Going Everywhere You Want to Be

England For Dummies, 3rd Edition, is a selective book, geared to savvy travelers who want to know more about England's leading sights. I don't cover every city, county, and region — I focus on only the country's essential highlights. I want this book to introduce you to the best cities, castles, cathedrals, gardens, and countryside that England has to offer. (Wales and Scotland, although part of the United Kingdom, aren't included in this book.) To help figure out which regions to visit during your trip, check out the following thumbnail sketches. For locations, see "The Regions in Brief" map on p. 25.

Looking at London: from Buckingham Palace to the British Museum

The Romans founded **London,** the capital of the United Kingdom, 2,000 years ago. Today, London is the largest, fastest, and most important city in England. Over the centuries, this seat of power has accrued an unrivaled collection of treasures, from historic cathedrals and royal palaces to matchless museums and parks. London's top sights include the **British Museum, Buckingham Palace,** the **Tower of London, Westminster**

The Regions in Brief

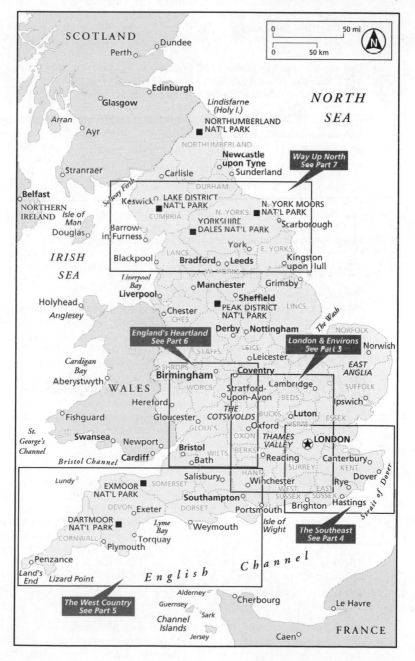

Abbey, the **Houses of Parliament, St. Paul's Cathedral,** the **National Gallery,** the **National Portrait Gallery,** the **Tate Modern,** the **Victoria & Albert Museum,** the **Natural History Museum, Kensington Palace,** and **Kensington Gardens.** (See Chapters 11 and 12 for details on all these attractions.)

London can easily consume all your time, but you can make many easy day trips from the city. In less than an hour, you can reach **Hampton Court Palace, Windsor Palace, Kew Gardens, Greenwich** (site of the Prime Meridian, the line from which the world measures longitude), and the ancient college towns of **Cambridge** and **Oxford.** Close to Oxford, you can find another excellent destination, **Blenheim Palace,** one of the greatest country estates in England. All these day trips are covered in Chapter 13.

London offers all the delights of a great international city. It has more than its share of revered monuments and historic sites, but it's not a city that dozes in the past. London is both traditional and trendsetting. It's a crowded, fast-paced, multiethnic metropolis. If you love art, culture, and people watching, you'll love London.

Exploring Southeast England: Canterbury, castles, and historic towns

East and **Southeast England** include the counties of Kent and Sussex (see Chapter 14), with their abundance of fascinating castles, famous gardens, and picturesque towns. **Canterbury,** in Kent, is one of the most beautiful and historic cathedral towns in England. Tourists (formerly called *pilgrims*) have been visiting Canterbury's magnificent cathedral since before Chaucer wrote *The Canterbury Tales* more than 600 years ago.

Many people want to visit the Kentish coastal town of **Dover** to see the famous white cliffs. To be honest with you, you probably don't want to make Dover a special destination. **Dover Castle,** with its 1,000 years of history (the castle was in use right through World War II), is well worth visiting, but the town of Dover contains little else of interest.

Rye, on the other hand, is a Sussex town whose charms are irresistible. More historic buildings (the earliest dates to 1250) line the cobblestone streets and time-warped lanes than in any other town in England. With its fine restaurants and cozy inns, Rye makes a good base for further exploration of this area along the Channel coast. If the date 1066 means anything to you, you may want to visit nearby **Battle,** where William the Conqueror defeated King Harold at the Battle of Hastings and thus gained control of England. Walk around the famous battlefield and explore the ruins of the abbey William erected to commemorate his victory. You can't get much closer to English history than that!

Brighton is a popular resort town on the south coast, within commuting distance to London (the town makes for an easy day trip). Brighton has been a seaside destination since the early 19th century, when the prince regent built the remarkable **Royal Pavilion,** now the town's major tourist attraction. With its long beach, amusement pier, promenades, and late-night club scene, Brighton remains a favorite weekend getaway spot.

In addition to the preceding towns, I devote a chapter to the castles, stately homes, and magnificent gardens of **Kent** (see Chapter 15), which are all special places that you can visit as day trips from London or as part of a car tour. The American Astor family purchased, restored, and lived in **Hever Castle,** the childhood home of Anne Boleyn, second wife of Henry VIII. **Knole,** with 365 rooms and many of its original Elizabethan furnishings, is the largest and one of the most splendid country homes in England. Knole was the birthplace of Vita Sackville-West, who later created, with her husband, Harold Nicholson, the world-famous gardens at **Sissinghurst,** now a place of pilgrimage for garden lovers from around the world. Kings and queens who spent time at **Leeds Castle,** built more than 900 years ago, added to the moated castle over the centuries.

Sightseeing at Stonehenge and in the West Country: Hampshire, Wiltshire, Devon, and Cornwall

Part V of this book, which focuses on the **West Country,** fills you in on the feast of sightseeing possibilities in the adjoining counties of Hampshire and Wiltshire (see Chapter 16), Devon (see Chapter 17), and Cornwall (see Chapter 18). **Winchester,** in Hampshire, is a graceful town with an amazing history (in Anglo-Saxon days, it was more important than London) and a wonderful cathedral. Jane Austen, who penned the "Eng Lit" hits *Pride and Prejudice* and *Sense and Sensibility,* is buried in Winchester Cathedral; you can also visit her modest home in nearby **Chawton.** Bare, brooding Salisbury Plain in Wiltshire, west of Hampshire, is the setting for **Stonehenge,** the stone circle that's one of the world's most famous ancient monuments. A few miles from this Neolithic wonder is **Salisbury.** The soaring spires of its Gothic cathedral dominate this busy country town.

Thrusting out into the Atlantic, Devon and Cornwall occupy the south-westernmost corner of England. The cathedral town of **Exeter** is a good starting place for a tour of these two counties surrounded by the sea. **Dartmoor National Park** lies a few miles west of Exeter. If you want to explore this open, treeless moorland with its gray stone fences and tunnel-like lanes winding beneath tall hedgerows, the area around **Chagford** is a good place to stay. Devon's southern coastline boasts sandy beaches and comfortable, old-fashioned resort towns, such as **Torquay,** clustered in a mild-weather zone called the English Riviera. Many people want to visit **Plymouth** because in 1620, the Pilgrims set sail from Plymouth for the New World, but after you see the Mayflower Steps (the departure point for the Pilgrims), not much else can spark your interest.

Thousands of years ago, Cornwall was a Celtic land known for its tin mines. Ancient mysteries still cling to Cornwall's rocky coastline in the form of stone circles. You find some of these *cromlechs,* as they're called, in the vicinity of **St. Ives,** a beautiful Cornish seaside town that became famous as an artists' colony. South of St. Ives, overlooking the island castle of **St. Michael's Mount** on Mount's Bay, is the bustling market town of **Penzance.** A five-hour train ride from London, Penzance is the last station before windy **Land's End,** where you can walk along the headlands that face the Atlantic. You can best explore the Land's End Peninsula, with its tiny, stone-built fishing villages, such as **Mousehole** (pronounced *Muz*-zle) and the lovely town of **Fowey** (pronounced *Foy*) farther along the coastline to the east, by car.

Discovering England's heartland: Stratford-upon-Avon, the Cotswolds, and Bath

William Shakespeare, whose plays still enchant, grip, amuse, and move audiences 400 years after his death, was born in **Stratford-upon-Avon** (see Chapter 19), a small Warwickshire village. This town, located in central England, only one and a half hours northwest of London by train, is one of England's top tourist destinations. If you're a Shakespeare fan, you can easily spend a day visiting the various shrines. Consider staying overnight if you want to see a play performed by the Royal Shakespeare Company. From Stratford, local train service runs to Warwick, whose top attraction is mighty **Warwick Castle** (see Chapter 19). Behind its thick stone ramparts, this imposing hilltop fortress features beautiful Victorian-era living rooms (with wax figures by the artisans at Madame Tussauds), a creepy dungeon, and beautifully landscaped grounds.

The **Cotswolds** (see Chapter 20) is a mostly rural area of bare rolling hills, river valleys, and woodlands south of Stratford-upon-Avon and west of Oxford. The region is known for its small, beautiful villages built of honey-colored stone during the prosperous years of the medieval wool trade. Although they have inevitably lost some of their soul to the flourishing tourist trade that now supports them, you may still want to pay Cotswold villages, such as **Broadway, Chipping Campden, Bourton-on-the-Water,** and **Cirencester,** a visit. Tour the villages by car because public transportation to the small villages is spotty. In these villages, you can shop for hours (the Cotswolds has more antiques shops than anywhere else in England) and then relax in an old-fashioned tea shop for an afternoon cream tea. **Hidcote Manor,** one of the greatest of English gardens, is a must for flower lovers visiting this region of England. You may want to make **Cheltenham,** a lively county town laid out as a spa in the early 19th century, your headquarters in the Cotswolds. You can also visit beautiful **Bath,** the queen of spa towns and a picture of Regency elegance. Located at the southern edge of the Cotswolds, Bath, with its superb Georgian terraces and renowned **Roman Baths Museum,** deserves at least a full day.

Heading north: Yorkshire and the Lake District

Northern England has a different character (and a different accent) from softer, greener southern England. The North is where you find the walled city of **York** (see Chapter 21), with its Viking heritage, medieval buildings, and glorious cathedral — the largest Gothic cathedral in Europe. Crammed with museums, restaurants, and plenty to do day and night, York is an excellent headquarters for exploring England's northern climes. With a car, you can make the easy drive to **North York Moors National Park** and **Yorkshire Dales National Park,** two areas of haunting beauty where the heather-covered moors and winding river valleys draw walkers and nature lovers. Emily Brontë's novel *Wuthering Heights* or Charlotte Brontë's equally beloved *Jane Eyre* may have formed your images of bleak, windswept Yorkshire moors. The Brontë homestead in the village of **Haworth** is a place of literary pilgrimage year-round. East of York, in a vast, landscaped park, sits the greatest country house in Yorkshire: **Castle Howard.** The television series *Brideshead Revisited* used this castle for filming, and visitors can get in year-round. **Scarborough,** on the Yorkshire coast, is a fun-loving seaside resort with a wide, curving beach and plenty of gaudy seaside arcades. You can easily get from Scarborough to **Whitby,** a small, attractive fishing village.

Cumbria, the northern county west of Yorkshire, offers some of the most beautiful and unusual countryside in England. Here, you find high, bare hills (or small, bare mountains, if you prefer), numerous lakes, and villages nestled in the unspoiled countryside that characterizes the **Lake District** (see Chapter 22), a national park area. **Bowness,** one of the region's resort centers, sits on 16km-long (10-mile) **Lake Windemere,** the largest lake in England. Literature lovers associate the Lake District with the poet William Wordsworth, whose homes in **Grasmere** and **Rydal** you can visit, and with Beatrix Potter, the author and illustrator of children's classics such as *The Tale of Peter Rabbit.* Potter's home in **Near Sawrey,** on the north side of Lake Windemere, is open to the public. **Hawkshead,** a short distance away, is a charming village constructed of the distinctive gray Lakeland stone. **Keswick,** a few miles north, is a large, important county town on the shores of Derwentwater. Like the rest of the Lake District, Derwentwater buzzes with visitors from Easter to October.

Scheduling Your Time

If you're flying into England, you have your choice of two major cities: **London** and **Manchester.** Four airports serve London; the majority of international flights arrive at Heathrow or Gatwick. From either airport, you can easily reach London and every other part of England by train. (Both airports also have car-rental facilities.) Here are some travel times from London to other parts of England:

- ✔ From London, you can reach the northern city of **York** by fast train in about two hours. Driving takes twice as long.

- ✔ The trip from London to **Penzance** in southwesterly Cornwall takes about seven hours by fast train, closer to nine hours if you drive.

> ✔ By train, you can get to Oxenholme, in England's northwesterly **Lake District,** from London in about five hours; driving takes at least eight hours.
>
> ✔ You can make places like **Bath, Canterbury, Oxford, Winchester,** and **Stratford-upon-Avon** an easy day trip from London, none of them more than two hours away by fast train.

If you want to explore the Lake District, Yorkshire, or the Cotswolds — areas in northern and northwestern England — you may want to avoid the congestion of London's airports and fly into Manchester (only a few airlines offer this option from the U.S., however). The Manchester airport connects to the country's rail network, so you can hop on a train at the airport and be on your way to any place in England.

 On average, each of England's top attractions takes about two hours to visit, after you're actually there and inside. Some, such as the Tower of London or Warwick Castle, take more time, but others, such as Westminster Abbey, take less. A local museum outside London may take as little as 15 to 30 minutes to visit. But other variables enter in: whether you're taking a guided tour (usually about 60–90 minutes, no matter where) and if crowds make lines move slowly. Another variable is the difficulty of allotting a certain amount of time to a great institution, such as the British Museum, which is loaded with so many treasures you can easily spend a full day or more there, or to a great English garden that beguiles you into dawdling.

Revealing the Secrets of the Seasons

How do you decide what time of year to travel to England? This section presents the pros and cons of each season so you can choose the best time for your visit.

Traveling during high and low seasons

 Roughly speaking, the high season for travel in England lasts from Easter to the end of September. The country gets the most crowded and the prices go sky-high during the peak summer months of June, July, and August. October to Easter make up the low season, when tourism dwindles, prices drop, and attractions shorten their open hours.

During your trip, you probably want to visit London, a destination on almost every English itinerary. London is popular year-round. In fact, London is one of the world's most popular tourist destinations.

 In the winter months, generally from October through March, castles, museums, and tourist offices outside London have shorter hours and may close certain days of the week. Hours and open days increase during the crowded months of June, July, and August. During the summer tourist season in popular cities like Cambridge or York, you can choose among three daily walking tours rather than the one that's offered in the winter. If you're a garden lover, time your visit to fall between Easter and September — peak tourist months, but also peak garden months. You can visit most castles and palaces year-round, but in summer, when lines are longest, you may find yourself waiting to get in and feeling rushed after you do. Long-distance train and bus schedules don't change much between winter and summer. However, local public transportation options in outlying regions, such as the Lake District or the Cotswolds, are curtailed during the less touristy months.

Watching those unpredictable skies

England's weather is what you might call "changeable." Except in the most general terms, you can have real problems predicting just what the weather will be like in any given season. Remember that England is part of an island, and the surrounding seas, as well as its northerly location, determine its weather patterns. In general, however, London and the south of England remain fairly mild year-round, rarely dipping below freezing or rising above 80° F (27° C) (at least for extended periods). Table 3-1 gives you an idea of London's temperature and rainfall variations. But don't rely on these figures too much: In 2001, London and the rest of England (and Europe) experienced the coldest and wettest winter and spring since written records originated in the 18th century. And then, in August 2003, 2004, and 2005, the mercury soared to the mid-90s for several days and even reached 100° F.

Table 3-1   London's Average Temperatures and Rainfall

	Jan	Feb	Mar	Apr	May	June	July	Aug	Sep	Oct	Nov	Dec
Temp (°F/°C)	40/4	40/4	44/7	49/9	55/13	61/16	64/18	64/18	59/15	52/11	46/8	42/6
Rainfall (in.)	2.1	1.6	1.5	1.5	1.8	1.8	2.2	2.3	1.9	2.2	2.5	1.9

Wherever you end up in England, you may find the weather drizzly, brisk and windy, still and muggy, dry and hot, clammy, or even glorious. Some days, you get a combination. But whatever the weather, whatever the season, England is well worth seeing.

Spring comes earliest to Cornwall and Devon in the southwest, where camellias, azaleas, and rhododendrons start to bloom in March. Northern counties, such as Yorkshire and Cumbria, take longer to warm up. Anyone who's spent a winter's day trying to enjoy a walk on the windswept moors of Yorkshire can tell you to postpone a walking tour there until spring is well advanced or summer has arrived. The Lake District in Cumbria tends to be rainy year-round, so expect sudden squalls even in summer.

Weather patterns

According to 18th-century writer Dr. Samuel Johnson (1709–1784), "When two Englishmen meet, their first talk is of the weather." Things haven't changed much since then. The unpredictability of the English climate has led to another sound British maxim: There is no such thing as bad weather; there is only inappropriate clothing. For an Englishman (and woman), appropriate foul-weather gear includes a *mac* (short for mackintosh, a raincoat), a *brolly* (umbrella), and *Wellingtons* (rubber boots).

Blooming in spring

England is at its greenest, freshest, blooming best in April and May. Highlights of the season include the following:

- ✔ The great English parks and gardens, such as Sissinghurst in Kent or Hidcote Manor in Gloucestershire, are at their peak of lushness. Bright yellow fields of *rape* (a European plant in the mustard family) brighten the countryside. Daffodils blooming along the lovely River Cam in Cambridge and throughout the Lake District form an unforgettable image of an English spring.

- ✔ In London, the Chelsea Flower Show is the quintessential spring event.

- ✔ Airfares are lower than in summer.

- ✔ The sky stays light well into the evening.

But keep in mind these springtime pitfalls:

- ✔ During the half-term school holidays in late February and for three weeks around Easter, visitors pour into London. As a result, the major attractions have longer lines (*queues* in Britspeak), and hotel rooms may be harder to find. During Easter week, towns and major attractions outside London get crowded as well.

- ✔ The weather is even more unpredictable than usual.

- ✔ Public transportation throughout England is reduced during holiday periods.

- ✔ Many museums, stores, and restaurants close on Good Friday, Easter, and Easter Monday.

Shining (and raining) in summer

Notoriously chilly England becomes irresistible under the sun. Unfortunately, many tourists flock to England to enjoy the fine weather, which can often turn into rain in July and August. The crowds descend to enjoy the following:

✔ Everyone moves outdoors to take advantage of the fine weather with alfresco theaters, concerts, and festivals. Tables sit outside cafes, pubs, and restaurants all over the country.

✔ Roses and colorful plants bloom in the great English gardens and in front of small cottages.

✔ Summer evenings are deliciously long and often cool, even if the day has been hot.

✔ The evening stays light past 10.

But keep in mind:

✔ July and August have the highest amount of rainfall for the year in London and the midsection of England, so skies can stay gray and cloudy.

✔ Occasional summer heat waves can drive the mercury into the 80s and even 90s, making July and August hot and muggy. Many businesses and budget-class hotels in London don't have air-conditioning.

✔ Most overseas visitors converge on London and the rest of England from July to September. Lines for major attractions can be interminably long.

✔ Hotels are more difficult to come by, especially on weekends, and high-season rates apply.

✔ Vacationers pack the beach resorts along the southern coast and up into Yorkshire.

✔ Roads in the beautiful Lake District, which receives millions of visitors annually, are clogged in July and August.

Glowing in autumn

Autumn's golden glow casts a lovely spell over England. This is my favorite time of year here, and I can think of only one disadvantage to counteract the many advantages:

✔ In Kent, apples and pears ripen in the orchards, and roadside stands sell fresh produce. Country farms harvest hay. Falling leaves skitter down ancient streets and through town squares, and the heather and *bracken* (a type of fern) on the moors and hillsides turn russet and gold. A crispness is in the air, and the setting sun gives old stone buildings and church spires a mellow patina.

✔ After mid-September, you have fewer tourists to contend with, so everything feels less crowded, and you may encounter more natives than visitors.

✔ With the drop in tourism, hotel rates and airfares may go down as well.

✔ London's cultural calendar springs to life in the fall.

✔ Although you may experience rain at this time of year, you're just as likely to encounter what Americans call "Indian summer."

But autumn has one drawback: Like every season in England, autumn can bring rain.

Welcoming in winter

The English love being cozy, and English winters provide the perfect time for coziness. Although most overseas visitors to London arrive in July and August, the highest number of visitors from *within* the United Kingdom come to England between January and March. What do they know that you should know? Consider the points that make winter wonderful:

✔ The season has a cozy feeling. Country inns welcome guests with crackling fires in ancient stone fireplaces. Game appears on restaurant menus. A sprinkling of snow gives a sparkling new charm to parks, cathedrals, gardens, and old towns.

✔ London and the rest of England become a bargain in winter. Businesses consider the country's off season to run November 1 to December 12 and December 25 to March 14. Winter off-season rates for airfares and hotels can sometimes be astonishingly low — airline package deals don't get any cheaper (see Chapter 6). At these times, hotel prices in London and throughout England can drop by as much as 20 percent.

✔ Although the winter winds may blow, nothing in London stops — in fact, everything gets busier. The arts — theater, opera, concerts, and gallery shows — stay in full swing.

✔ London and many other cities and towns throughout England develop a lovely buzz during the Christmas season: The stores decorate; lights glow; carolers sing; entertainers perform special holiday pantomimes; and in London, the giant Norwegian spruce goes up in Trafalgar Square. On Christmas Day, the boys' choir of King's College Chapel in Cambridge performs the Festival of Nine Lessons and Carols, a traditional Christmas service with music that broadcasts throughout the world.

Naturally, winter has its downside:

✔ Although the yuletide holidays are always jolly, they also add up to another peak London tourist season from mid-December to Christmas. You know what that means: bigger crowds and higher prices.

✔ The entire country virtually shuts down on December 25 and 26 and January 1. Stores, museums, and other attractions close, and public transportation is severely curtailed. On December 26

(Boxing Day, so called because in Victorian times, service workers, such as postmen, received gift boxes on this day), you can have a hard time finding any open restaurants.

✔ Wintertime England may be gray and wet for weeks on end; in midwinter, the skies get dark by about 3:30 p.m. The English usually keep their thermostats set rather low (about 10° F lower than most Americans). Rather than turn up the heat, the English don their *woollies* (long underwear). You should do the same — or prepare for a chronic case of goose pimples.

Perusing a Calendar of Events

England hums with festivals and special events of all kinds, some harking back to centuries past. If London is going to take up all or part of your trip, write or call **VisitBritain**, the country's official tourist agency (see the Appendix at the back of this book for the address and phone number), and request a copy of its monthly *London Planner*, which lists major events, including theater and the performing arts. Do this at least a month before your departure date. The VisitBritain Web site (www.visitbritain.com) is another good resource for checking Englandwide events and dates before you go.

For recorded information on weekly London events while in London, call VisitBritain's 24-hour **London Line** at ☎ 0870/1-LONDON; calls cost 60p ($1.10) per minute. You can't call the London line from outside the United Kingdom. To find out what's going on while you're traveling throughout the rest of England, stop in at the tourist information centers. (I list street addresses, phone numbers, and Web addresses of these centers throughout this guide and in the Appendix.) You may just happen upon some unique local event.

January

In January, the **London New Year's Day Parade** features marching bands, floats, and the Lord Mayor of Westminster traipsing in a procession from Parliament Square to Berkeley Square. Call ☎ 020/8566-8586 for more details. January 1 (noon to 3 p.m.).

Late January/early February brings in the **Chinese New Year,** marked by colorful street celebrations on and around Gerrard Street in Soho, London's Chinatown. Date varies.

February

In mid-February, the **Jorvik Viking Festival** in York features a combat event and parade to celebrate this Yorkshire city's thousand-year Viking heritage. For more information, call ☎ 01904/621-756 or check the Web at www.vikingjorvik.com. Dates vary.

March

Bath hosts its highly regarded **Literature Festival,** with new and established writers giving readings and leading seminars. For more information, contact the Bath Festivals Box Office (☎ **01225/463-362**) or check out the city's Web site at www.visitbath.co.uk. Early March.

St. Patrick's Day is a big to-do in London, which has the third-largest Irish population after Dublin and New York. No parades are held, but you see plenty of general merriment. March 17.

The **BADA Antiques & Art Fair** (formerly known as the Chelsea Antiques Fair) draws antiques lovers to Duke of York Square in London's Chelsea for six days. For more information, call ☎ **020/7589-6108.** Mid-March.

At the **Oxford and Cambridge Boat Race** between Putney Bridge and Mortlake Bridge, rowers from the two famous universities compete for the Beefeater Cup. A good viewing spot is the Hammersmith Mall. Last Saturday in March or first Saturday in April (check local press or www.theboatrace.org for an exact date).

April

The **London Marathon** was first held in 1981 and has become one of the most popular sporting events in the city. Some 30,000 men and women, from champion athletes to first-timers, take part. The race begins in Greenwich; winds its way past the Tower of London and along the Thames; and finishes in The Mall in front of Buckingham Palace, one of the best viewing spots. For more information, call ☎ **020/7902-0199** or visit www.london-marathon.co.uk. Mid-April.

May

The **Brighton International Festival** brightens up venues all over the resort town of Brighton on the Sussex coast with a wide array of drama, literature, visual art, dance, and concert programs ranging from classical to hard rock. Call ☎ **01273/292-950** for more information or check www.visitbrighton.com. Most of May.

The **Football Association FA Cup Final** usually takes place at Wembley Stadium. Remember that *football* in the United Kingdom is soccer, and tickets are difficult to get hold of, given the sport's popularity. Contact the box office at Wembley Stadium Ltd., Wembley HA9 0DW; ☎ **020/8795-9000;** www.wembleystadium.com. Mid-May.

Bath's 18th-century buildings provide wonderful settings for performances during the **International Music Festival.** For more information, contact the Bath Festivals Box Office at ☎ **01225/463-362** or check out the city's Web site at www.visitbath.co.uk. Mid-May.

One of London's most famous spring events, the **Chelsea Flower Show,** held on the grounds of the Chelsea Royal Hospital, draws tens of thousands of visitors from around the world. Ordering tickets in advance is a good idea; in the States, you can order them from Keith Prowse at ☎ **800/669-7469.** For more information, call the Royal Horticultural Society at ☎ **020/7834-4333** or check out the Web site, www.rhs.org.uk. Third week in May.

June

The Derby, pronounced "darby" and now called the Vodafone Derby, is one of the highlights of the racing season at Epsom Racecourse in Surrey. Posh fashions, corporate suits, and champagne abound. Call ☎ **01372/470047** for more information or visit www.epsomderby.co.uk. Early June.

April 21 is Queen Elizabeth II's birthday, but her official birthday parade, **Trooping the Colour,** takes place on a Saturday in June. The Horse Guards celebrate "Ma'am's" birthday in Whitehall with an equestrian display full of pomp and ceremony. For free tickets, send a self-addressed envelope and International Reply Coupon (or U.K. stamps) from January 1 to February 28 to Brigade Major Horseguards, Whitehall, London SW1A 5BJ (☎ **020/7414-2279**). Mid-June.

The most prestigious horse-racing event in England is **Royal Ascot,** held at the Ascot Racecourse (near Windsor in Berkshire, about 48km/30 miles from London) in the presence of the royal family. For information, call ☎ **01344/876-876** or visit the Web site at www.ascot.co.uk. You can order tickets online for this event. Note: In 2005, Royal Ascot was held in York while the Ascot racecourse was being refurbished; this location switch happens again in 2006. Mid- to late June.

The world's top tennis players whack their rackets at the **Wimbledon Lawn Tennis Championships,** held at Wimbledon Stadium. Getting a ticket to this prestigious event is complicated. August 1 to December 31, you can apply to enter the public lottery for the next year's tickets by sending a self-addressed envelope and International Reply Coupon to All England Lawn Tennis Club, P.O. Box 98, Church Rd, Wimbledon, London SW19 5AE. For more information, call ☎ **020/8944-1066** or 020/8946-2244 (recorded information) or visit www.wimbledon.com. Late June to early July.

The **City of London Festival** presents a series of classical concerts, poetry readings, and theater in historic churches and buildings, including St. Paul's Cathedral and the Tower of London. For more information, call ☎ **020/7377-0540** or visit www.colf.org. Late June to mid-July.

Living artists from all over the world present more than 1,000 works of art at the juried **Royal Academy Summer Exhibition.** For more information, call the Royal Academy at ☎ **020/7300-8000** or visit www.royal academy.org.uk. Early June to mid-August.

Kenwood, a lovely estate at the top of Hampstead Heath, is the bucolic setting for the **Kenwood Lakeside Concerts,** a summer season of Saturday-night open-air concerts. For more information, call ☎ 020/8233-7435. Mid-June to early September.

July

Pride in the Park, the U.K.'s largest gay and lesbian event, begins with a march and parade from Hyde Park to Parliament Square, followed by live music, dancing, and fun. For more information, visit www.prideinthe park.com. First Saturday in July.

Cheltenham hosts the **International Festival of Music,** which brings in soloists and ensembles from around the world. For more information, call ☎ 01242/227-979 or check out the festival Web site, www.cheltenhamfestivals.co.uk. Early July.

The **Henley Royal Regatta,** one of England's premier sporting and social events, is a championship rowing event with a long tradition. The regatta takes place on the Thames just downstream from Henley, an Oxfordshire town 56km (35 miles) west of London. For more information, call ☎ 01491/572-153 or visit the regatta Web site at www.hrr.co.uk. First week in July.

The **Hampton Court Flower Show,** held on the palace grounds in East Molesey, Surrey (part of Greater London), shows off one of the loveliest gardens in England. For more information, call Hampton Court Palace at ☎ 0870/752-7777 or visit the palace Web site at www.hrp.org.uk. Second week in July.

In July, you can attend the much-loved **BBC Henry Wood Promenade Concerts.** Known as "The Proms," this series of classical and popular concerts takes place at London's Royal Albert Hall. To book by credit card, call the box office at ☎ 020/7589-8212 or visit www.bbc.co.uk/proms. Mid-July to mid-September.

August

Buckingham Palace opens to the public August through September. For details and to charge tickets, call ☎ 020/7766-7300. For more information on visiting the palace, see Chapter 12 or the palace Web site, www.royal.gov.uk. August 1 to October 1 (dates vary by a day or two every year).

The **Houses of Parliament** open for guided tours in late summer. You can reserve tickets by phone at ☎ 0870/906-3773 or order tickets online at www.firstcalltickets.com. July 26 until the end of August.

During London's **Notting Hill Carnival,** steel bands, dancing, and Caribbean fun take over the streets of Notting Hill (Portobello Road, Ladbroke Grove, and All Saints Road). This enormous street fair is one of Europe's largest. For more information, call ☎ **020/8964-0544.** Bank Holiday weekend in August (last Mon in Aug).

September

The **Thames Festival** celebrates the mighty river with giant illuminated floats. For more information, call ☎ **020/7928-8998.** Mid-September.

October

Rural towns and villages all over the country hold **harvest festivals.** Contact the tourist office in the region you want to visit for details. (Check out the relevant regional chapter in this book for tourist-office phone numbers.) Weekends throughout the month.

Cheltenham hosts the **Cheltenham Festival of Literature,** showcasing the talents of internationally known writers. For more information, call ☎ **01242/227-979** or www.cheltenhamfestivals.co.uk. Early to mid-October.

The **Chelsea Crafts Fair** is the largest such fair in Europe, with scores of artisans selling handmade crafts of every description. For details, contact the Crafts Council at ☎ **020/7806-2512** or www.craftscouncil.org.uk. Last two weeks of October.

November

Although based at the National Film Theatre on the South Bank, the **London Film Festival** (www.bfi.org.uk) presents screenings all over town. Call ☎ **020/7815-1433** in November for recorded daily updates on what's showing and where. Throughout November.

The Lord Mayor of London goes on the grand **Lord Mayor's Procession** through The City from Guildhall to the Royal Courts of Justice in his gilded coach; festivities include a carnival in Paternoster Square and fireworks on the Thames. For more information, call ☎ **020/7606-3030.** Early November.

For the **State Opening of Parliament,** Queen Elizabeth II, in all her finery, sets out from Buckingham Palace in her royal coach and heads to Westminster, where she reads out the government's program for the coming year. (This event is nationally televised.) For more information, call ☎ **020/7971-0026** or visit www.parliament.uk. First week in November.

On **Guy Fawkes Night,** throughout England, bonfires and fireworks commemorate Guy Fawkes's failure to blow up King James I and Parliament in 1605. For the locations of celebrations in London, check *Time Out* magazine, available at newsstands around the city. (For a brief history of Guy Fawkes, see Chapter 14.) November 5.

December

Christmas lights go on in London's Oxford Street, Regent Street, Covent Garden, and Bond Street. Mid-November to early December.

The **lighting ceremony** of the huge Norwegian spruce Christmas tree in London's Trafalgar Square officially announces the holiday season. Check with the Britain Visitor Centre or Tourist Information Centre for the time. First Thursday in December.

Many revelers focus their New Year's Eve celebrations on Trafalgar Square. December 31.

Chapter 4

Following an Itinerary: Five Great Options

In This Chapter
▶ Seeing England's top attractions in one or two weeks
▶ Visiting England with kids
▶ Hitting the highlights for garden lovers and history buffs

*E*very visitor to England faces the same questions: How can you see as much as possible in a limited amount of time? How can you sort out what's really worth seeing and fit those attractions into a realistic itinerary? This chapter provides the answers. If you budget your time wisely and choose your sights carefully, you can enjoy a satisfying and manageable trip from beginning to end.

The secret to any "successful" trip is to be well organized yet flexible. If you travel by train in England, for example, you need to be aware of train schedules. Always call the train information number that I provide (see Chapter 7) and get exact departure times. But don't pack your schedule so tightly that a late train ruins your day. Even with limited time, you can see more if you organize your days efficiently and use common sense. Don't assume, for instance, that every museum or sight is open every day, all day. Take a moment to look at the details for each attraction that you can find throughout the rest of this book.

This chapter offers five itineraries for people with limited time or special interests. The daily itineraries are commonsense, limited-time suggestions only. Maybe you prefer to spend all day in the British Museum rather than the couple of hours that I suggest. Maybe shopping and cafe-hopping in York appeals to you more than visiting York Minster. Or you really just want to get outdoors and go walking in the Lake District. Whatever your preference, go for it! You can enjoy England in countless ways, depending on your own individual interests. See Chapters 1 and 2 for some preliminary information on the best that England has to offer.

Seeing England's Highlights in One Week

Spend at least three days of a weeklong trip to England in **London.** You may, in fact, want to stay in London for the entire week, making easy day trips from the city and returning to your hotel at night (that's the premise I use in this itinerary). This saves you the wear and tear of lugging your baggage around. Plus you can often get special rates for a weeklong stay.

To maximize your sightseeing time, try to book flights that arrive in the morning and depart in the evening.

To avoid wasting time in lines (*queues* in Britspeak), try to hit the top London sights early in the day, preferably right when they open or late in the afternoon. I mean in particular Buckingham Palace (when it's open to the public during Aug and Sept), the Tower of London, Westminster Abbey, and Madame Tussauds wax museum. Westminster Abbey, to cite just one example, can receive more than 15,000 visitors a day!

For information on all the London attractions mentioned in this itinerary, see Chapter 12 unless noted otherwise.

Spend part of **Day One** settling into your London hotel, getting your bearings, and fighting jet lag. Don't make it a big day, but make walking part of your itinerary. Walking gets you into the swing of London and helps your body adjust to the new time. Start your trip with a visit to majestic **Westminster Abbey,** visiting the Royal Tombs and Poets' Corner. Afterward, because they're right next door, stroll around **Big Ben** and the **Houses of Parliament.** Unless you queue up to hear a debate or come in August when Parliament offers guided tours, you can't get inside, but you get a great riverside view from Westminster Bridge. On the opposite side of the Thames sits the **British Airways London Eye,** a 450-foot-high observation wheel. Reserve in advance for the trip up and over London; otherwise, you may spend at least a half-hour waiting in line for a ticket and another hour before your scheduled ride. You're not far from the **Tate Modern,** so if you're in the mood to look at modern art, walk along the Thames to London's newest museum (open until 6 p.m. Mon–Thurs, until 10 p.m. Fri and Sat). If you'd rather look at 18th- and 19th-century masterpieces of British painting, head over to **Tate Britain** in Pimlico instead. Have dinner in the Covent Garden area or on the Thames (see the listing for R.S. *Hispaniola,* passenger boat turned quaint restaurant, in Chapter 11).

Greet **Day Two** with a walk through **Green Park.** You're on your way to **Buckingham Palace** to witness the pageantry of the **Changing of the Guard** (check beforehand to make certain it's taking place that day). For details on touring Buckingham Palace's **State Rooms** during August and September, see Chapter 12. Reserving tickets so you know your specific entry time is a good idea; otherwise, you may have to wait in line for an hour or more to get in. If you don't tour the palace itself, visit the **Royal**

Mews (the stables that surround the palace) or the newly renovated **Queen's Gallery.** From Buckingham Palace, you can stroll down The Mall, through **St. James's Park,** passing **Clarence House,** the home of the Queen Mother until 2002 and now the official London residence of the Prince of Wales, and **St. James's Palace.**

Next, stop at **Trafalgar Square,** London's grandest and certainly most famous plaza. You can have lunch or tea at the National Gallery's restaurant or in the restaurant in the crypt of St. Martin-in-the-Fields church on the square's east side. Spend your afternoon viewing the **National Gallery's** treasures. Renting one of the self-guided audio tours helps you to hone in on the collection's most important paintings. You can instead spend your afternoon in the **National Portrait Gallery,** next door to the National Gallery. The fascinating portrait gallery offers a concise but comprehensive display of famous Brits, from the Tudors to the Spice Girls. If you haven't already reserved a seat for a West End show, you may want to stop by the half-price-ticket booth in nearby **Leicester Square** to see what's available. Have dinner in **Soho** before the show (see Chapter 11 for my restaurant recommendations).

On **Day Three,** arrive as early as you can at the **Tower of London,** and immediately hook up with one of the one-hour tours led by the Beefeaters, the tower guides in the distinctive red coats. Later, you can explore the precincts on your own, making certain that you allot enough time to see the Crown Jewels. From the Tower, head over to nearby **St. Paul's Cathedral,** which you can see in about a half-hour if you're not on a tour. The **British Museum,** your next stop, has enough to keep you occupied for several days; if you want to see only the highlights, allow yourself a minimum of two hours. Later in the afternoon, explore **Piccadilly Circus,** the teeming epicenter of London's West End. Regent Street, Piccadilly, and Jermyn Street offer great shopping.

On **Day Four,** hop on a train from Waterloo Station, and make the half-hour trip to **Hampton Court Palace.** Or, for a much longer but far more scenic alternative, take a boat. Boats usually depart Westminster Pier at 10 a.m. from April to September for the four-hour journey to the palace; you can also take the train there and the boat back. Give yourself a minimum of three unhurried hours at Hampton Court. Touring the various staterooms and apartments with an audio guide can give you a good historical perspective. The gardens can easily take up an hour. Have lunch or tea on the premises, and be back in London in plenty of time for dinner and a show. (For information on Hampton Court Palace, see Chapter 13.)

On **Day Five,** take an early train from King's Cross Station, and head up north to Yorkshire, where you can spend the day in the walled city of **York.** The train trip takes two hours, making York a relatively easy day trip from London. Or you may want to stay overnight. For an overview of York, considered northern England's most beautiful city, hook up with a guided walking or bus tour — several options exist. Give yourself at least an hour to visit spectacular **York Minster,** the largest Gothic church in northern Europe. The stained glass is marvelous, and a fascinating museum lies beneath the church, where excavations have revealed Roman-era buildings. Two other attractions in York are definitely worth seeing: The **National Railway Museum** has royal train cars used by Queen Victoria and Queen Elizabeth II, and the **Jorvik Viking Centre** lets you time-travel back to York in the Viking era. Set aside some time for wandering down York's winding medieval lanes. You may also want to walk along the circuit of amazingly preserved medieval walls. (For details on visiting York, see Chapter 21.)

For **Day Six,** take your pick: **Cambridge** (trains from King's Cross) or **Oxford** (trains from Paddington Station) are both easy-to-reach destinations for day trips from London. If you spent the night in York, you can take the train to either destination from there. Oxford and Cambridge are fascinating university towns with medieval colleges built around quadrangles. (See Chapter 13 for more details on both cities.)

If you opt for Oxford, sign up for the two-hour walking tour that leaves at 11 a.m. and 1 p.m. from the Oxford Information Centre. This tour is the best way to gain an overall perspective on the town and get into some of the major colleges, which you may not otherwise get access to. Later, you can spend an hour in the **Ashmolean Museum,** famed for its antiquities, coins, and porcelain and painting collections.

You can also take a two-hour walking tour in Cambridge, or you may prefer the open-top bus tour. You have to see **King's College Chapel,** one of the most beautiful churches in England, in Cambridge; hearing the famous boys' choir sing *Evensong* (an evening church service in which part of the liturgy is sung) is an unforgettable experience. Set aside an hour to tour the **Fitzwilliam Museum;** its fine and varied collection includes Egyptian, Greek, and Roman antiquities, and some modern British paintings. **"The Backs"** — so named because some of the colleges back onto the River Cam — is a beautiful place for strolling. If you feel adventurous, you can rent a *punt* (small boat) and pole yourself down the Cam; you can also pay to have someone do the punting for you.

Day Seven is your last day in London. Ideally, you booked your return flight for the evening, so you can have at least a few morning hours for more sightseeing, shopping, or both. Checkout time is probably no later than noon, so ask the hotel front desk if the hotel can store your luggage. Alternatively, if you plan to take a fast airport train from Victoria (Gatwick) or Paddington (Heathrow) station, you can check in with your luggage early in the day (airline counters are in the train stations) and ask that your luggage go on to the airport; you can then take a later train. (See Chapter 11 for detailed information on getting to and from London airports.) If you haven't made it to **Harrods** department store yet, do that first, or check out the other shopping options in Knightsbridge. Instead of shopping, you may want to squeeze in one last museum. Several major South Kensington museums aren't far from Harrods, including the

Natural History Museum, with its famous dinosaur exhibits, and the Victoria & Albert Museum, renowned for its superlative art and design collections. Instead of visiting a museum, you can visit Kensington Palace in Kensington Gardens, but allow yourself at least two hours if you do so. Following your morning activities, grab a quick lunch or snack and then make your way to the airport to catch your plane.

Touring the Best of England in Two Weeks

Lucky you — with two weeks, you can explore so much of the country!

For the first week, follow the itinerary in the previous section, "Seeing England's Highlights in One Week." But because you don't have a plane to catch, Day Seven for you begins at the National Portrait Gallery, if you haven't visited it yet. From the portrait gallery, you can easily walk to Covent Garden Market, where you find scores of interesting shops. Covent Garden Piazza, a perfect spot for lunch, is a lively hub filled with restaurants. Alternatively, spend your seventh morning in one of the famous South Kensington museums, such as the Natural History Museum or the Victoria & Albert Museum. From there, you can easily stroll to Kensington Gardens and visit Kensington Palace, the former home of Princess Diana. In the evening, go for a traditional English dinner at Rules, London's oldest restaurant, or Simpson's-in-the-Strand. Other options for the evening include a play or concert, or maybe a stop in a couple of good pubs. (See Chapter 11 for information on restaurants and Chapter 12 for attractions and nightlife.)

On Day Eight, hop a train from Paddington Station to Exeter, in Devon. In Exeter, you can rent a car and drive into nearby Dartmoor National Park and other parts of the West Country. (Renting a car in Exeter makes more sense than renting one in London.) Chagford is a good place to stay overnight. Before you leave Exeter, though, give yourself an hour to explore beautiful Exeter Cathedral. If you don't want to rent a car, you can explore the town on foot and continue by train to Penzance or St. Ives in Cornwall. (See Chapter 17 for information on Exeter and Chagford.)

Devote Day Nine to Cornwall, the southwestern tip of England. From Exeter or Chagford, make the fairly short drive to Penzance, where you need at least two hours to visit the fabulous island castle of St. Michael's Mount. If you have a car, you can easily drive from Penzance to Land's End, stopping at the picturesque fishing village of Mousehole on the way. Don't waste your time with the theme-park attractions at Land's End; go for the stupendous views westward out over the Atlantic and then head on to St. Ives. If you're without a car, skip Land's End, and take the train from Penzance to St. Ives, an artists' colony that's become a seaside resort town. Loaded with charm, good restaurants, and hotels, St. Ives makes a good place to stay overnight. The town's big draw is Tate St. Ives, a museum that exhibits artists who live and work in Cornwall. More interesting is the Barbara Hepworth Museum and sculpture garden, located in and around the great sculptor's former studio. On a beautiful summer evening, when the sun lingers late in the sky, you may want to drive (if you have a car) to **Chysauster,** a prehistoric site near St. Ives. (I describe Cornwall, including Penzance, Land's End, and St. Ives, in Chapter 18.)

From St. Ives or Penzance, you can reach **Bath** on **Day Ten** in about four hours by car or train (depending on connections); you may want to spend the night there. Bath is a wonderfully walkable city, filled with outstanding examples of Regency-era architecture, including the **Royal Crescent** and the **Pump Room,** a charming place to have your afternoon tea. Set aside at least two hours for the wonderful **Roman Baths Museum.** (Check out Chapter 20 for Bath's many attractions.)

You need a car for **Day 11**'s tour of the nearby **Cotswolds.** (If you've been traveling by train until now, you can rent a car in Bath.) You can visit several lovely villages, all built of mellow, honey-colored Cotswold stone. **Broadway** and **Bourton-on-the-Water** no longer depend on the wool trade, as they did in the Middle Ages, but now depend on visitors who come to stroll, shop, and have cream teas. Near Broadway, you can find **Hidcote Manor,** one of England's great gardens. If you're a garden lover, don't miss it; plan on spending at least two hours here. Overnight in **Cheltenham,** a small but lively spa town, or **Cirencester,** a beautiful Cotswolds market town with a noteworthy church and the **Corinium Museum,** full of Roman mosaics and artifacts from the area. Both towns are full of good restaurants and hotels. (See Chapter 20 for information on the Cotswolds.)

From Cheltenham or Cirencester, on **Day 12,** drive (or take the train) northeast to **Stratford-upon-Avon,** a good place to spend the night. The trip takes about two hours. In Stratford, you want to spend at least three hours visiting the **Shakespeare sites.** If you're a theater lover, see a production at one of the **Royal Shakespeare Festival** theaters. You want to reserve tickets in advance if you can; if you don't, head directly for the box office before doing anything else. In the afternoon, you may want to drive or take the local train from Stratford to nearby **Warwick Castle.** The castle, nearly 1,000 years old, is one of England's premier tourist attractions and can easily keep you occupied for several hours. (For details on Stratford-upon-Avon and Warwick Castle, see Chapter 19.)

From Stratford, on **Day 13,** drive south to **Stonehenge,** a few miles outside Salisbury. If you don't have a car, take the train to **Salisbury,** and hop on a local bus to Stonehenge. This great stone circle, believed to be about 5,000 years old, is the most famous prehistoric site in England. Afterward, take a couple of hours to wander through Salisbury, with its magnificent Gothic **cathedral.** You can spend the night in Salisbury, or you may want to head back to London. (See Chapter 16 for details on Salisbury and Stonehenge.)

On **Day 14,** return your rental car, and get to the airport. You may be able to return your car in Salisbury, even if you rented it in Exeter. If you can, I recommend returning your car in Salisbury and taking a train (a one-and-a-half-hour trip) back to London. Otherwise, see whether you can drop the car directly at Heathrow or Gatwick, the most likely departure points for your flight. From Salisbury, just to be on the safe side, give yourself at least three hours to drive back to London.

Discovering England with Kids

So you want to spend five days in England and bring along your kids? No problem. Perhaps this trip will be your kids' introduction to the country or their first experience of any foreign country. You may know what *you* want to see, but where do you take *them?* I have a few suggestions to keep both you and your kids excited and entertained.

Much, of course, depends on your children's ages and their interests. Activities that toddlers and preteens find enthralling probably bore teens out of their minds.

 Try to get their interest up before you buckle your seat belts for the transatlantic flight. A visit to your local library can give you some real treasures in this regard: children's books set in England (the *Harry Potter* series), children's travel books with maps, and even travel videos that the whole family can watch. For more tips on traveling with kids, see Chapter 9.

For this itinerary, I assume that you want to spend at least three of your five days entirely in London. Who wouldn't want to spend several days in the capital city, jam-packed with sights that kids of all ages can enjoy? Plus staying in London and making day trips mean that you don't have the additional hassle of a car. You can get everywhere on public transportation.

For information on all the London attractions in this itinerary, see Chapter 12 unless noted otherwise.

Don't schedule too much on **Day One.** Exercise helps ward off jet lag. After sitting in a plane for several hours, take smaller children to one of London's great parks so they can run and let off steam. Depending on where your hotel is located, your destination may be Hyde Park, Kensington Gardens, Green Park, St. James's Park, or Regent's Park. During your stay, you may want to visit them all. If you're traveling with a teen, you can introduce yourselves to the city with a stroll through London's four royal parks, following the **Princess Diana Commemorative Walk** (see Chapter 11).

More focused sightseeing begins on **Day Two.** Consider a guided bus tour that helps orient everyone and gives you at least a glimpse of all the major sights. Several outfits provide tours on double-decker buses — always a treat for kids — and Frog Tours uses amphibious vehicles to show you the main sights on land and from the Thames. More expensive guided tours may include the **Changing of the Guard** at **Buckingham Palace,** a bit of pageantry that both children and adults find exciting. After the tour, make the **British Airways London Eye** your first stop. This giant, high-tech observation wheel revolves on the South Bank, beside the Thames, across from the Houses of Parliament. Reserve your ticket beforehand to avoid waiting in a long line. All ages enjoy the half-hour "flight." Afterward, cross Westminster Bridge, and stroll over to view the **Houses of Parliament** and **Big Ben** (hopefully the clock strikes the hour while you're in the vicinity). And because it's close at hand, use this opportunity to visit **Westminster Abbey.** Younger children may not get much out of the place, but you will. Later in the afternoon, take a ferry ride down the Thames to the **Tower of London;** you can catch the ferry at Westminster Pier near the Houses of Parliament. After you get inside the Tower, hook up with one of the Beefeater tours; the red-coated custodians of the Tower have plenty of dramatic tales to tell. If you're with a child age 10 to 17, you may want to have dinner at the **Hard Rock Cafe** in Mayfair (see Chapter 11).

Begin **Day Three** at the **Natural History Museum** in South Kensington, where the dinosaur exhibit, complete with life-size animatronic raptors and a T-Rex, captures the imaginations of both young and old(er). If your child's a budding Einstein, the **Science Museum,** with its many hands-on, interactive exhibits, may be a better choice. Afterward, if you have small children in tow, stroll over to **Kensington Gardens** for a look at the famous statue of Peter Pan. The **Princess Diana Memorial Playground** in the northwest corner of Kensington Gardens enchants little ones. You can have lunch in the **Orangery** of adjacent Kensington Palace or make your way to **Café-in-the-Crypt** in St. Martin-in-the-Fields church in Trafalgar Square. If you're with a teen, you may want to spend the morning or afternoon in **Madame Tussauds wax museum** or the **London Dungeon** on the South Bank; some of the gorier exhibits are unsuitable for young children. In the evening, older kids and teens may also enjoy one of the West End's razzmatazz musicals.

Make **Day Four** a day trip to **Brighton,** on the Sussex coast. The quick trip takes less than an hour. There, you can visit the **Royal Pavilion** and take the kids over to **Palace Pier,** a spot filled with games and souvenir stands. If the weather's warm, rent a deck chair and sit on the beach. Brighton is a fun place just to stroll around, with plenty to keep you and the family entertained. (For details on Brighton, see Chapter 14.)

On **Day Five,** head out to **Hampton Court Palace,** another quick train ride of less than an hour. (You can also take a boat, but the trip takes about four hours.) Hampton Court offers you much to explore, so give yourself at least four hours. Small children may not get much out of the visit, but they will probably find the staff members who wear period costumes intriguing. You can eat on the premises. Save the best part for last: The famous maze in the gardens brings out the kid in everyone. (For information on Hampton Court, see Chapter 13.) Following your visit to Hampton Court Palace, you can depart from London on a flight that leaves later in the evening; however, that may require too much rushing for most families. A better plan may be to fly out the next morning.

Strolling through England's Greenery: An Itinerary for Garden Lovers

England is a paradise for gardeners. In London and throughout the country, you find superb gardens created in a variety of styles. You can reach many of England's great gardens by train and taxi, but a car definitely comes in handy if you're intent on seeing several gardens in different parts of the country. Serious garden lovers may want to consider a guided garden tour. (See Chapter 6 for information on the garden tour offered by Maupintour.)

 If you want to tour English gardens at their best, you need to travel between May and August. Although a great garden is interesting at any time of year, spring to late summer are the peak blooming seasons, when English gardens are at their best, showing off with a blazing dazzle of color.

The gardens in England are often part of a stately home, which you may also want to visit. Touring a house and its gardens usually takes a minimum of three hours. If you're a gardener, you may want to make these excursions the focal point of your day and plan other activities accordingly.

If you have one week in England and want to spend part of your time in London, what gardens can you see? Well, you have many beautiful options.

Spend **Day One** strolling around London's magnificent royal parks (St. James's Park, Green Park, Hyde Park, and Kensington Gardens). Former hunting grounds, they've been landscaped over the centuries to accommodate millions of visitors each year. Visit the lovely formal gardens around Kensington Palace in **Kensington Gardens.** If you plan to spend part of May in London, you may want to attend the famous **Chelsea Flower Show,** which kicks off the gardening season. Reserve tickets in advance for this yearly event. (See Chapter 12 for information on the gardens and Chapter 3 for details on the flower show.)

On **Day Two,** take a half-day to visit the **Royal Botanic Gardens** at Kew, which include wonderful Victorian-era glass conservatories. You can reach Kew by Underground or by boat. Charming Kew Palace and an 18th-century Chinese pagoda are part of this once-royal pleasure garden. (See Chapter 13 for details on visiting Kew.)

Devote **Day Three** to the gardens at **Hampton Court Palace,** Henry VIII's extravagant showplace beside the Thames. In addition to viewing formal plantings in the geometric Tudor style, you can visit the ancient greenhouse, see a 300-year-old grapevine, and wind your way through the famous maze. You may want to time your visit to coincide with the **Hampton Court Flower Show** in July. (See Chapter 3 for details on the flower show and Chapter 13 for information on Hampton Court Palace.)

Reserve **Day Four** for your visit to **Sissinghurst Castle Gardens** in Kent. Sissinghurst is a major highlight of any garden tour of England. From London, you can get there by train. Laid out and planted by Vita Sackville-West and Harold Nicholson in the 1930s, Sissinghurst is one of the greatest and most romantic gardens in the world. Now a National Trust property, the gardens are so popular that they use a timed-entry system at peak periods during the spring and summer. You can find a restaurant and tea shop on the premises. (See Chapter 15 for information on Sissinghurst.)

If you have a car and get an early start, you can combine a visit to Sissinghurst with a visit to **Hever Castle,** Anne Boleyn's childhood home. Remarkable Italianate gardens, designed for William Waldorf Astor in 1903, surround the moated castle. (See Chapter 15 for details on Hever Castle.)

If you don't have a car, you can travel to Hever Castle by train and taxi on **Day Five.** If you visit both Sissinghurst and Hever Castles on Day Four, use Day Five to visit those royal parks you may have missed on Day One.

Among the hundreds of gardens in England, two more unforgettable ones await garden lovers. In order to see them as part of your weeklong trip, however, you need to rent a car.

Spend part of **Day Six** at **Stourhead,** located a few miles west of Salisbury, in Wiltshire. Laid out in 1741, Stourhead is one of the oldest landscape gardens in England. A lake, a bridge, and classically inspired buildings serve as focal points in a graceful landscape. (See Chapter 16 for details on Stourhead.)

You may want to spend the night in Salisbury, or continue north to Bath or one of the Cotswolds towns that I describe in Chapter 20.

Day Seven belongs to **Hidcote Manor** in the Cotswolds. The plantings at this remarkable garden in Gloucestershire form living "rooms" of shape, color, scent, and texture. The gardens at Hidcote, begun in 1907, have influenced gardeners from around the world. Strolling through this magnificent creation, patiently fashioned from inhospitable terrain, is a perfect way to end your weeklong garden tour of England. (For information on Hidcote Manor, see Chapter 20.)

Visiting England's Past: An Itinerary for History Buffs

Many travelers thrill at the experience of standing in a place where history was made. England, as you probably know, is loaded with these hallowed spots. In this ancient realm, you can see places that span roughly 5,000 years of human history. My suggested itinerary covers only a fraction of the sites you can visit. Using London as a base for several day trips, this itinerary is geared for an eight-day stay in England. With this itinerary, you don't need a car.

On **Day One,** you arrive in London, a city that's hardly lacking in historic monuments. Start off with a trip to the granddaddy of them all, the 900-year-old **Tower of London.** Join one of the guided tours led by the Beefeaters, and wander around afterward on your own. Tower Green is the spot where political prisoners, such as Anne Boleyn and Sir Thomas More, were beheaded during the reign of Henry VIII. You have to see the Crown Jewels, housed in a high-security armory.

From the Tower, travel by boat (you find a ferry pier right outside) to Westminster Pier, the stop for the **Houses of Parliament** and your next destination, **Westminster Abbey.** This ancient Gothic edifice, where almost every British monarch since William the Conqueror has been crowned, resonates with history. In the chapels, you find the tombs of Queen Elizabeth I; her half-sister, Mary Tudor ("Bloody Mary"); and her onetime rival, Mary Queen of Scots. Great English statesmen, war heroes, and writers are commemorated throughout. Have dinner at **Rules,** London's oldest restaurant, to cap off your history-filled day. (For details on the sights in this paragraph, see Chapter 12; for the restaurant Rules, see Chapter 11.)

On **Day Two,** head over to **Buckingham Palace,** ideally on a day when the historic pomp and pageantry of the **Changing of the Guard** is taking place (daily from April 1 through early June, on alternate days the rest of the year). The palace itself, Queen Elizabeth's official London residence, is open to the public in August and September. If you can't get into the palace, stop in at the **Royal Mews,** where you can see the amazing gilded coach in which the queen rides to open Parliament. After your royal tours, make your way to the **Imperial War Rooms** in Westminster. The fascinating underground bunker was the World War II headquarters for Prime Minister Winston Churchill and his War Cabinet. The bunker has been preserved exactly as it was during England's "darkest hour" in the 1940s. Your last major stop of the day is **St. Paul's Cathedral,** site of the famous fairy-tale wedding of Prince Charles and Princess Diana in 1981. (See Chapter 12 for information on all these London attractions.)

Day Three, if you're up for it, can be your day to compare and contrast a royal palace and a royal castle. Start the day early at **Kensington Palace,** used by monarchs from William and Mary to Queen Victoria, who was born there. An audio guide fills you in on the history. On display in the historical dress collection are gowns worn by Queen Victoria, Queen Elizabeth, and Princess Diana. (For details on Kensington Palace, see Chapter 12.) Afterward, travel to **Windsor Castle,** less than an hour by train from London. Another one of the queen's official residences, the historic castle set in its Great Park is open to visitors most of the year. The sumptuous interior was redone in the 19th century. (You can find information on Windsor Castle in Chapter 13.)

Treat yourself to a full-day trip to **York,** one of England's most historic cities, on **Day Four.** Get an early start, because the train takes two hours to get there. You can find a wealth of historic attractions in York. Start your explorations at awe-inspiring **York Minster,** the largest Gothic structure in northern Europe. Its enormous windows shimmer with medieval stained glass. Then head over to **Jorvik Viking Centre** for a ride back to York of a thousand years ago, when the city was a Viking settlement called Jorvik. York is wonderfully walkable, although its ancient lanes can be confusing. Stroll through the **Shambles,** a medieval street where butchers had their shops, and make a full or partial circuit of the medieval city walls. You can have dinner in York, on the train ride back, or in London. (See Chapter 21 for details on York and its attractions.)

Make another day trip on **Day Five,** this time to **Winchester,** the ancient Anglo-Saxon capital of Wessex under King Alfred. By train from London, the trip takes about one and a half hours. Winchester is a small, delightful town and a pleasure to explore. Begin at mighty **Winchester Cathedral,** which houses the remains of some of the Anglo-Saxon kings of England. You also can see the grave of Jane Austen, the brilliant author of *Pride and Prejudice* and other early-19th-century classics. Making a circuit of the town, passing Winchester College (founded in 1382) and following the River Itchen, is easy. The famous King Arthur's Round Table hangs in **Castle Hall,** the largest medieval hall in England after Westminster. Sir Walter Raleigh heard his death sentence in Castle Hall in 1603. In the small **City Museum,** you can see Roman mosaics from the period when Winchester was a Roman settlement. You can be back in London in time for dinner at **Ye Olde Cheshire Cheese,** the onetime hangout of Dr. Johnson and Charles Dickens. (See Chapter 16 for information on Winchester; see Chapter 11 for the restaurant Ye Olde Cheshire Cheese.)

Day Six is another day trip, this time to **Canterbury,** about one and a half hours east of London, in Kent. In terms of England's religious history, you can call only a few places more important. More than 700 years ago, pilgrims began flocking to the shrine of St. Thomas à Becket, who had been murdered by King Henry II's henchmen in **Canterbury Cathedral.** Becket's shrine was destroyed during the reign of Henry VIII, but the site is marked near the high altar. The poet Geoffrey Chaucer wrote about a group of those Old English–speaking pilgrims in *The Canterbury Tales,* and you may want to step into the **Canterbury Tales,** an entertaining museum and exhibition on nearby St. Margaret's Street, to renew your acquaintance with or discover more about them.

For a glimpse of how the locals lived 2,000 years ago, when Canterbury was a Roman settlement called Cantuaria, spend some time in the small but informative **Canterbury Roman Museum.** Then make your way to the ruins of **St. Augustine's Abbey,** a Christian site that predates the cathedral by about 600 years. You can take an audio-guided tour of this UNESCO World Heritage site, one of the oldest Anglo-Saxon monastic sites in the country. Nearby is another ancient treasure: **St. Martin's Church,** perhaps the oldest church in England. It was already in existence when St. Augustine arrived to convert the natives in A.D. 597. (You can find more information on Canterbury and its sights in Chapter 14.)

On **Day Seven,** go prehistoric and visit **Stonehenge,** possibly the world's most famous ancient monument. Ride a bus from Salisbury, about one and a half hours west of London. The ancient stone circle retains its mystery even in the face of thousands of daily tourists. Was the circle used as an astronomical laboratory, as one popular theory holds? Even the date is uncertain — it's estimated to be at least 5,000 years old. In Salisbury, before heading back to London, visit beautiful **Salisbury Cathedral,** a masterpiece of English Gothic architecture. Its spire is the tallest in England. (Details on Stonehenge and Salisbury are in Chapter 16.)

On **Day Eight,** go into **Battle** — Battle, Sussex, that is. In this small town just north of Hastings, you find one of the most historically hallowed spots on English soil: the battlefield where, in 1066, William of Normandy fought King Harold for the throne of England. William won and became known as William the Conqueror. His defeat of Harold spelled the end of Anglo-Saxon rule and marked the beginning of a new French culture imposed upon the country. At the 1066 Battle of Hastings Abbey and Battlefield, you can walk on the battlefield. A clever audio guide that tells the story from three different perspectives enhances your experience. William the Conqueror built the Battle Abbey, now in ruins, on the spot where Harold was slain and English history moved into a new phase. The town of Battle, about 90 minutes south of London by train, has several good restaurants for lunch or tea. (See Chapter 14 for information on Battle.)

Part II
Planning Your Trip to England

"And how shall I book your flight to London - First Class, Coach, or Medieval?"

In this part . . .

This part helps you with the practical details of planning your trip to England.

In Chapter 5, I get into the nitty-gritty of money. You have to deal with British money every day of your trip, so this chapter tells you all about pounds and pence. Any traveler who's trying to come up with a workable budget needs to have a general idea of what things currently cost. I also include useful information on changing your home currency into pounds and pence, and provide plenty of practical info on using ATMs and credit cards while in England.

In Chapter 6, I go over the transportation options for getting you to England. I discuss the various types of escorted and package tours and give you the rundown on what airlines fly to England, where to find special deals, and how to book your flight online.

After you're in England, you may want to get out of London and travel around the rest of the country. In Chapter 7, I tell you about traveling by train, bus, and car.

Booking your accommodations ahead of time is wise, and Chapter 8 tells you how to do so. I explain hotel rack rates and give you some pointers to help you find the best room for the best rate. I list the various hotel options available to you, from world-famous luxury hotels in London and spectacular country-house hotels to simple B&Bs.

In Chapter 9, I offer some specific information and tips for visitors with special needs or interests: You can find advice and resources for families traveling with children, senior travelers, travelers with disabilities, and gay and lesbian travelers.

Chapter 10 deals with last-minute details. I discuss getting a passport, buying travel and medical insurance, and staying healthy on your trip.

Chapter 5

Managing Your Money

In This Chapter

▶ Planning a realistic budget for your trip
▶ Changing your money into pounds and pence
▶ Using ATMs, traveler's checks, and credit cards
▶ Paying and recouping British sales tax
▶ Knowing when — and how — to tip

*O*kay, you want to go to England. You're excited and eager to pack, but can you really afford it? At this point, a financial reality check is in order. You may have heard that London is an expensive city, but just how expensive? And what about destinations outside London? What does it cost to stay overnight in romantic Cornwall, for example, and how much do you have to pay for train fare from London? This chapter helps you answer all these questions and assemble a budget.

Planning Your Budget

Planning a budget for your trip to England isn't as difficult as you may think. To come up with a workable figure, you need to break your trip down into its various components: airfare, transportation while in England, hotels, meals, entertainment, and so on. In the following sections, you can find vital clues on how to create a realistic budget that works for you.

Lodging

The cost of accommodations takes the biggest bite from your budget. And you have to pay more for accommodations in London than anywhere else in England. If you book your rooms in advance, especially for the London part of your trip, you can know this expense before you leave on vacation.

Chapter 8 discusses what kind of lodgings you can expect for your money and how to get the best rate. After you get a firm handle on prices and locations, check out Chapter 11 for my recommendations of top-notch London B&Bs (bed-and-breakfasts) and hotels in all price ranges and locations. You can also find good hotels and B&Bs in the regional chapters of the book.

In London, rates vary considerably from B&B to B&B and from hotel to hotel, so I can't give you a very reliable average. For the recommendations in this book, however, the rates for a double room generally fall between £83 and £100 ($154–$185) for an inexpensive property, between £100 and £150 ($185–$278) for a moderately priced one, and between £150 and £200 ($278–$370) for an expensive one. After that, you hit the stratosphere of £200-plus ($370-plus) for a luxury B&B or hotel. Keep in mind that all B&Bs and many midrange London hotels include at least a continental breakfast as part of the room rate, so you can save a few pounds with a "free" meal each day.

In other parts of England, the rates for accommodations are more uniform and much lower, generally £30 to £35 ($56–$65) per person, per night. Overall, you pay less for everything after you leave London. However, you still can find plenty of opportunities to drop a king's ransom for a room, especially in some of those truly elegant country-house hotels.

Check for special deals when you're outside of London. Many country-house hotels offer bed, breakfast, and a full dinner at bargain prices. Throughout England, properties offer special price breaks for stays of two nights or a full weekend (Fri and Sat night).

Transportation

You can get to London from anywhere in the world by plane, train, or boat. Transportation costs vary widely, of course, depending on your point of departure, time of year, and method of travel. You can look over all your transportation options in Chapter 6, where I also give you tips on landing a good airline deal to England. After you arrive in London, yon can take a number of steps to stretch your budget.

I have some good news that can save you a bundle: You may not need to rent a car in England because you can tour London using public transportation and reach many destinations outside of the city by train.

Within London, you can take advantage of the fast, convenient, and easy-to-use subway system, the Underground (called the "Tube"). Special reduced-price transportation passes, **Visitor Travelcards** (see Chapter 11), make getting around the city relatively inexpensive (approximately £4.90/$9 per day for a one-day pass).

Trains can take you to many of England's castles and other destinations. If you plan to do much traveling in the countryside, consider getting a **BritRail pass** (see Chapter 7 for details). You have to buy these passes, which offer substantial savings over individual fares, before you arrive in England. In England's smaller towns and cities, you can walk almost everywhere because the city centers are so compact. Or you can hop on a bus, as the locals do. Sometimes you may need to take a taxi, which can get expensive, depending on the distance from the rail stations to your destinations in the towns.

 In some areas, a car makes exploration of the countryside much easier. However, renting a car can be a very expensive proposition. You may find a great rate, but gasoline (*petrol* in Britspeak) costs more than twice what it does in the States. See Chapter 7 for more details on renting a car in England.

Dining

The food in England used to be the butt (or shank) of many a joke, but in recent years, London has emerged as one of the great food capitals of the world. You find superb restaurants in the rest of the country, too. Of course, eating at the top restaurants, no matter where you are, can cost you. However, in London and in every town and village throughout England, you can find countless pubs and restaurants where you can dine cheaply and well — and where you can enjoy your meal along with the locals. In addition, many of the best restaurants in London and elsewhere offer special fixed-price meals at real bargains.

Again, everything costs more in London. If you eat lunch and dinner at the moderately priced London restaurants recommended in Chapter 11, you can expect to pay £25 to £40 ($46–$74) per person per day for meals, not including wine (assuming that your hotel rate includes breakfast). Outside of London, unless you splurge on really high-class restaurants, food costs about £20 to £35 ($37–$65) per person per day. In the countryside, many hotels offer full board — that is, bed, breakfast, and dinner. In most cases, full board adds up to considerable savings.

If you have breakfast at a cafe rather than your hotel and are content with coffee and a roll, expect to pay about £4 to £6 ($7.40–$11) in or out of London. Depending on the restaurant, an old-fashioned English breakfast with eggs, bacon or sausage, toast, and tea or coffee can run anywhere from £7 to £12 ($13–$22) in London, about one-third that outside London — but remember, your hotel cost nearly always includes breakfast. Likewise, a simple afternoon tea at a cafe in London sets you back about £5 to £8 ($9.25–$15), but a lavish high tea with sandwiches, scones, clotted cream, and cakes at one of the great London hotels may cost you £25 ($46) or more. Elsewhere, expect to pay about £6 ($11) for a scrumptious cream tea (with scones, jam, and Cornish or Devon clotted cream).

Sightseeing

Your budget for admission fees depends on what you want to see, of course. But don't cut costs with your sightseeing. After all, you came all this way to see the sights, right? Sure, an adult ticket to the Tower of London is £15 ($28), but do you really want to miss seeing this historic landmark and the extraordinary Crown Jewels housed there? Keep in mind that if you're a senior or a student, you can often get a reduced-price admission. Plus many attractions offer reduced family rates for two adults and two children.

You can get into all the top national museums — the British Museum, National Gallery, National Portrait Gallery, Tate Britain, Tate Modern, Victoria & Albert Museum, Natural History Museum, and Science Museum — for free. And it costs nothing to stroll through London's great parks or to view Buckingham Palace (okay, from the outside) and see the Changing of the Guard.

As a general rule, expect to pay about £13 to £17 ($24–$31) for admission to famous castles and palaces, such as Castle Howard in Yorkshire and Warwick Castle near Stratford-upon-Avon. Some of the great English cathedrals, such as Salisbury and York, charge admission fees of £5 to £7 ($9.25–$13) to help pay the enormous cost of upkeep. You rarely pay more than £7 ($13) for museums and local attractions outside of London.

Unless they're students with valid identification, those 16 and over usually have to pay the adult admission charge at attractions.

If your plans call for visiting castles, such as Windsor or Warwick; palaces, such as Hampton Court or Blenheim; historic properties, such as Shakespeare's Birthplace in Stratford-upon-Avon; and gardens, such as Sissinghurst in Kent, you can save money by purchasing a **Great British Heritage Pass.** The passes are good for 4 days ($50), 7 days ($75), 15 days ($95), and one month ($130). These passes include almost all major historic properties in England, and you get 50 percent off the admission price at the Tower of London. You can order one by phone at ☎ **888/BRITRAIL** in North America, from a travel agent in Australia or New Zealand, or online at www.britrail.com. In London, you can buy the Heritage Pass at the Britain Visitor Centre, 1 Regent St., SW1. For more information, check VisitBritain's Web site, www.visitbritain.com/heritagepass.

Shopping and nightlife

Shopping and entertainment are the most flexible parts of your budget. You don't have to buy anything at all, and you can hit the sack right after dinner instead of seeing a play or dancing at a club. You know what you want. Flip through the London shopping options and the London entertainment and nightlife venues in Chapter 12. If anything strikes you as something you can't do without, budget accordingly. Keep in mind that a pint in a pub sets you back about £3.50 ($6.50), and a London West End theater ticket can range from £25 to £75 ($46–$139). You may want to budget for a theater ticket at Stratford-upon-Avon, too; seats cost between £8 and £42 ($15–$78). Coastal resort towns, like Brighton, are big with club-goers, so you may want to check out the scene while you're there; club cover charges rarely cost more than £5 ($9.25), but drinks are always expensive, about £4 to £6 ($7.40–$11) for nonpremium alcohol.

Table 5-1 and Table 5-2 give you an idea of what things typically cost in London and the rest of England, so you can avoid some sticker shock.

Table 5-1   What Things Cost in London

Item	Cost
Transportation from airport to Central London	
From Heathrow by Underground	£3.80 ($7.05)
From Gatwick by train	£12 ($22)
One-way Underground fare within Central London	£2 ($3.70)
Double room at the Cadogan Hotel	£244–£340 ($451–$629)
Double room at Hazlitt's 1718	£202–£254 ($374–$470)
Double room with breakfast at Aster House	£145–£195 ($268–$361)
Double room at Astons Apartments	£90–£125 ($167–$231)
Double room with breakfast at Luna Simone Hotel	£60–£80 ($111–$148)
Lunch for one at Oxo Tower Brasserie	£25 ($46)
Set-price dinner for one at Rules, excluding wine	£20 ($37)
Dinner for one at Wagamama Noodle Bar	£14 ($26)
Pizza at Gourmet Pizza Company	£6.50 ($12)
Afternoon tea for one at the Lanesborough	£26 ($48)
Coffee and cake at Pâtisserie Valerie	£6 ($11)
Pint of beer at a pub	£3.50 ($6.50)
Admission to the Tower of London (adult/child)	£15/£9.70 ($28/$18)
Admission to Madame Tussauds (adult/child)	£18/£17 ($33/$31)
Theater ticket	£5–£50 ($9.25–$93)
Theater program	£3 ($5.55)

Table 5-2	What Things Cost Outside of London
Item	*Cost*
Round-trip train ticket London–Cambridge	£17 ($31)
Round-trip train ticket London–Bath	£35 ($65)
Admission to Roman Baths Museum, Bath	£9.50 ($18)
Combined ticket price for all Shakespeare sights in Stratford	£13 ($24)
Lunch for one at Hathaway Tea Rooms, Stratford	£6.50 ($12)
Theater ticket, Stratford-upon-Avon	£5.50–£45 ($10–$83)
Admission to Warwick Castle	£10 ($19)
Double room with private bath and breakfast, Hamlet House B&B, Stratford	£42–£52 ($78–$96)
Admission to Stonehenge	£5.50 ($10)
Room and breakfast for two, Mt. Prospect Hotel, Penzance	£115 ($213)
Admission to St. Michael's Mount Castle, Cornwall	£5.50 ($10)
Combined admission to Tate St. Ives art museum and Barbara Hepworth Museum and Sculpture Garden	£8.50 ($16)
Cornish cream tea	£6 ($11)
Room, dinner, and breakfast for two, White Moss House, Lake District	£158 ($292)
Tank of unleaded gas, economy car	£50 ($93)

Cutting Costs — But Not the Fun

Throughout this book, Bargain Alert icons highlight money-saving tips and great deals. Check out these additional cost-cutting strategies:

- ✔ **Go in the off season.** If you can travel at nonpeak times (Oct to mid-Dec or Jan–Mar), hotel prices can be as much as 20 percent less than during peak months.

- ✔ **Travel midweek.** If you can travel on a Tuesday, Wednesday, or Thursday, you may find cheaper flights to London. When you ask about airfares, find out whether you can get a cheaper rate by flying on a different day.

- ✔ **Try a package tour.** For popular destinations like London, you can make just one call to a travel agent or packager to book airfare, hotel, ground transportation, and even some sightseeing. You pay much less than if you try to put the trip together yourself (see Chapter 6 for package-fare deals).

✔ **Reserve a hotel room with a kitchen** (in England, they call them *self-catering units*), and do at least some of your own cooking. You may not feel like you're on vacation if you do your own cooking and wash your own dishes, but you can save money by not eating in restaurants two or three times a day. Parents traveling with children often find this strategy useful.

✔ **Always ask for discount rates.** Membership in AAA, frequent-flier programs, trade unions, AARP, or other groups may qualify you for discounts on plane tickets and hotel rooms that you book before you go. When you're in England, seniors and students with ID usually get a lower admission rate to attractions.

✔ **Try expensive restaurants at lunch rather than dinner.** At most top London restaurants, lunches cost you a lot less than dinners, and the menu often includes many of the dinnertime specialties. Also, wherever you travel in England, look for fixed-price menus.

✔ **Travel off peak, standard class.** A train ticket always costs more if you travel at peak commuter times (before 9:30 a.m.). A first-class train ticket generally costs about one-third more than a standard class.

✔ **Walk.** London is large, but you can still walk just about anywhere. And every historic English town or city is compact. A good pair of walking shoes can save you money on taxis and other local transportation. As a bonus, you get to know the city and its inhabitants more intimately, and you can explore at a slower pace.

Handling Money

Britain's unit of currency is the pound sterling (£). Every pound is divided into 100 pence (p). Coins come in denominations of 1p, 2p, 5p, 10p, 20p, 50p, £1, and £2. Notes are available in £5, £10, £20, and £50 denominations. As with any unfamiliar currency, British pounds and pence take a bit of getting used to. The coins have different sizes, shapes, and weights according to value. Each banknote denomination has its own color and bears a likeness of the queen. The Bank of England draws all the currency.

The *exchange rate,* which fluctuates daily, is the rate you get when you use your own currency to buy pounds sterling. In general, **£1 = $1.85** (see Table 5-3). I use this approximate exchange rate for prices in this book. (If the U.S. price is less than $10, I round it off to the nearest nickel; if more than $10, to the nearest dollar.)

Table 5-3	Simple Currency Conversions			
U.S.	*U.K.*		*U.S.*	*U.K.*
$1	55p		$1.85	£1
$5	£2.70		$3.70	£2
$10	£5.40		$9.25	£5
$20	£11		$19	£10
$50	£27		$37	£20
$100	£54		$92	£50

When you're about to leave on your trip, check with your bank or look in the newspaper to find out the current exchange rate. You can also check currency conversions online at www.xe.com.

Using ATMs and carrying cash

The easiest and best way to get cash away from home is from an ATM (automated teller machine), sometimes called a *cashpoint* in England. You can find 24-hour ATMs all over London: outside banks, in large supermarkets, and in some Underground (Tube) stations. In other English cities and towns, look for ATMS in local banks on the town's main street (often called High Street).

The **Cirrus** (☎ 800-424-7787; www.mastercard.com) and **PLUS** (☎ 800-843-7587; www.visa.com) networks span the globe; look at the back of your bank card to see which network you're on and then call or check online for ATM locations at your destination. Be sure you know your personal identification number (PIN) and find out your daily withdrawal limit before you depart. Also keep in mind that many banks impose a fee every time your card is used at a different bank's ATM, and that fee can be higher for international transactions (up to $5 or more) than for domestic ones (where they're rarely more than $1.50). On top of this fee, the bank from which you withdraw cash may charge its own fee. For international withdrawal fees, ask your bank.

Charging ahead with credit cards

Credit cards are a safe way to carry money: They also provide a convenient record of all your expenses. Credit card purchases are translated from pounds to dollars at a favorable exchange rate. Keep in mind that when you use your credit card abroad, most banks assess a 2 percent fee above the 1 percent fee that Visa, MasterCard, and American Express charge for currency conversion on credit charges. But you may still want to go with credit cards when you factor in things like exorbitant ATM fees and higher traveler's check exchange rates (and service fees).

In smaller towns and villages outside London, you may have trouble paying for B&Bs and restaurants with credit cards. Many B&Bs with one to three guest rooms operate on a cash-only basis, as do some tearooms.

You can use credit cards to withdraw cash advances at banks or ATMs if you know your PIN. If you've forgotten yours or didn't even know you had one, call the number on the back of your credit card, and ask the bank to send it to you. If your bank debit card works with one of the international credit card systems (such as Cirrus), you can use it in England. Using debit cards in England has one major difference, however: You can't get extra cash back.

Some credit card companies recommend that you notify them of any impending trip abroad so that they don't become suspicious when you use the card a number of times in a foreign destination, which may lead them to block your charges. Even if you don't call your credit card company in advance, you can always call the card's toll-free emergency number if a charge is refused — a good reason to carry the phone number with you. Basically, just remember to carry more than one card with you on your trip; a card may not work for any number of reasons, so having a backup is the smart way to go.

Toting traveler's checks

These days, traveler's checks are less necessary because most cities have 24-hour ATMs that allow you to withdraw small amounts of cash as needed. However, keep in mind that you will likely be charged an ATM withdrawal fee if the bank is not your own, so if you're withdrawing money every day, you might be better off with traveler's checks — provided that you don't mind showing identification every time you want to cash one.

Your traveler's checks will be issued in your local currency. After you arrive in England, you need to convert them to pounds and pence. (See the box "Changing your currency in England," which follows.)

You can get traveler's checks at almost any bank. **American Express** offers denominations of $20, $50, $100, $500, and (for cardholders only) $1,000. You pay a service charge ranging from 1 percent to 4 percent. You can also get American Express traveler's checks over the phone by calling ☎ 800-221-7282; Amex gold and platinum cardholders who use this number don't have to pay the 1 percent fee.

Visa offers traveler's checks at Citibank locations nationwide, as well as at several other banks. The service charge ranges between 1.5 percent and 2 percent; checks come in denominations of $20, $50, $100, $500, and $1,000. Call ☎ 800-732-1322 for information. AAA members can get Visa checks without a fee at most AAA offices or by calling ☎ 866-339-3378. **MasterCard** also offers traveler's checks. Call ☎ 800-223-9920 for a location near you.

Changing your currency in England

Changing money is a simple and straightforward operation. Just remember that every time you exchange money, you need to show your passport. By using a currency-exchange service, called a *bureau de change,* you can easily change cash or traveler's checks. These services are available at major London airports, any branch of major banks (throughout the country), all major rail and Underground stations in Central London, post offices countrywide, many Tourist Information Centres, and American Express or Thomas Cook offices. *Bureaux de change* in airports and rail stations are generally open daily between 8 a.m. and 9 p.m.

Almost every major bank in Central London and in cities throughout England has a foreign-currency window where you can exchange traveler's checks or cash. Weekday hours for banks are generally 9:30 a.m. to 3:30 p.m. The big bank names in England currently include Barclays Bank (☎ 020/7441-3200), Midland Bank (☎ 020/7599-3232), and NatWest (☎ 020/7395-5500). These companies have branches throughout England.

Steer clear of *bureaux de change* that offer good exchange rates but charge a heavy commission (up to 8 percent). You find them in major tourist sections. (Some are open 24 hours.) Some hotels also cash traveler's checks, but they have a much higher commission than a bank or *bureau de change.* Before exchanging your money, always check the exchange rate, the commission rate, and additional fees.

If you choose to carry traveler's checks, be sure to keep a record of their serial numbers separate from your checks in the event that they are stolen or lost. You get a refund faster if you know the numbers.

Dealing with a lost or stolen wallet

Contact all of your credit card companies the minute you discover that your wallet has been lost or stolen, and file a report at the nearest police precinct. Your credit card company or insurer may require a police report number or record of the loss. Most credit card companies have an emergency toll-free number to call if your card is lost or stolen; they may be able to wire you a cash advance immediately or deliver an emergency credit card in a day or two. Call the following U.K. number that applies to you:

- ✔ **American Express:** ☎ **01273/696933** or 800-221-7282 in the U.S. (for cardholders and traveler's check holders)

- ✔ **MasterCard:** ☎ **01702/362988** or 800-307-7309 in the U.S.

- ✔ **Visa:** ☎ **01604/230230** or 800-847-2911 in the U.S.

For other credit cards, call the toll-free number directory at ☎ **800/555-1212** in the U.S.

Identity theft or fraud are potential complications of losing your wallet, especially if you've lost your driver's license along with your cash and credit cards. Notify the major credit-reporting bureaus immediately; placing a fraud alert on your records may protect you against liability for criminal activity. The three major U.S. credit-reporting agencies are **Equifax** (☎ 800-766-0008; www.equifax.com), **Experian** (☎ 888-397-3742; www.experian.com), and **TransUnion** (☎ 800-680-7289; www.transunion.com). Finally, if you lose all forms of photo ID, call your airline and explain the situation; it may allow you to board the plane if you have a copy of your passport or birth certificate and a copy of the police report you filed.

Taking Taxes into Account

Allow me to introduce you to Britain's version of sales tax — the *value-added tax (VAT)*. Brace yourself. The tax amounts to 17.5 percent. The VAT is part of the reason prices (particularly in London) are so high. The tax is added to the total price of consumer goods (the price on the tag already includes the tax) and to hotel and restaurant bills. The VAT isn't a hidden expense, but not all quoted room rates, especially in the luxury tier, include the tax. Make sure to ask whether your quoted room rate includes the VAT. (In the hotel listings in this book, I tell you if the rate doesn't include the VAT.)

Getting your VAT back

If you're not a resident of the European Union, you can get your VAT refunded on purchases made in England (but not the VAT paid at hotels and restaurants). Every store requires a minimum purchase of at least £50 ($93) to qualify for a VAT refund. The exact amount varies from store to store. To get the refund, you must get a **VAT refund form** from the retailer, and the retailer must complete the form at the time of purchase. Don't leave the store without a completed refund form. Present the form — along with the goods — at the VAT Refunds counter in the airport. After you get the paperwork stamped, you have two choices:

✔ You can mail in the papers and receive your refund in a British check (no!) or a credit-card refund (yes!).

✔ You can go directly to the Cash VAT Refund desk at the airport and get your refund in cash.

VAT doesn't apply to goods shipped out of the country, no matter how much you spend. You can avoid VAT and the hassle of lugging large packages back with you by having stores ship your purchases for you; many happily do so. However, shipping charges can double the cost of your purchase, and you may have to pay duties when the goods arrive. Rather than use this costly strategy, consider paying for excess baggage (rates vary with the airline).

On top of the VAT, a few restaurants add a service charge of 12.5 to 15 percent to your bill. If they include a service charge, the menu must state this policy ("A 15% service charge has been added to your bill"). This charge amounts to mandatory tipping, so if your credit card receipt comes back with a space for you to add a tip, put a line through it.

Tipping Like You Mean It

As a general rule, except for tips in restaurants (12.5–15 percent) and to cab drivers (10 percent), you don't have to tip a lot in London. An exception is if you stay in an expensive hotel with porters who carry your bags (£1/$1.85 per bag) and doormen who hail you a cab (£1/$1.85 per successful hail). In fancier country-house hotels, like Gidleigh Park, where the service is extremely attentive, tipping is left to the discretion of the guests. In such cases, you may want to leave a minimum of £20 ($37) per guest for the staff. In a pub, *never* tip the bartender — if you want to acknowledge the service, offer to buy him or her a drink.

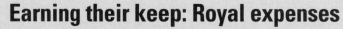

Earning their keep: Royal expenses

In 2005, in an attempt to prove how cheap royalty is, Buckingham Palace said the queen costs U.K. taxpayers the equivalent of 60p ($1.10) per person per year. That amount adds up to the yearly total of £37 million ($68 million), which the queen receives in public money to carry out her duties and maintain her palaces. But that figure doesn't include the unknown but rising cost of security or the ceremonial duties of the armed services. Does the House of Windsor earn its keep? According to published reports, members of the royal family carried out 2,900 official engagements in 2004. Garden parties cost some £514,000 ($950,900); food and kitchens ran £432,000 ($799,200); and wines and beverages cost £6,000 ($11,100). Travel costs included £2.2 million ($4.1 million) on helicopters, £812,000 ($1.5 million) on civilian air travel, £534,000 ($987,900) with the Royal Air Force, and £782,000 ($1.4 million) on the Royal Train.

Chapter 6

Getting to England

• •

In This Chapter

▶ Traveling to England by plane, train, or ferry
▶ Finding the best airfare
▶ Looking into escorted tours and package deals

• •

Now that you've decided to visit England, you need to find a way to get there. In this chapter, I discuss getting you to England. What are your options for direct, nonstop flights? How can you save money on your flight (and your hotel)? What are the pros and cons of taking an escorted tour?

Finding Out Who Flies Where

Most regularly scheduled international flights from the United States, Canada, Australia, and New Zealand arrive at London's Heathrow and Gatwick airports. Flights from the Continent land at Heathrow, Gatwick, Stansted, or London City. Charter flights from the Continent usually fly into Luton, the smallest of London's five airports. Manchester, in northern England, has an international airport, but I don't recommend flying into it unless you plan to skip London entirely. Here's a brief description of each of the London airports, who flies to them, and how to travel from them to Central London (see the Appendix for the contact information for these airlines):

✔ **Heathrow:** The main international airport, 24km (15 miles) west of Central London. It's served by **Air Canada** (flights from Calgary, Montreal, Ottawa, Toronto, Vancouver, and St. John's), **Air New Zealand** (flights from Australia and New Zealand), **American** (flights from Boston, Chicago, Los Angeles, New York, and Miami), **British Airways** (U.S. flights from Boston, Chicago, Detroit, Los Angeles, Miami, Newark, New York JFK, Philadelphia, San Francisco, Seattle, and Washington Dulles; Australian flights from Brisbane, Melbourne, Perth, and Sydney; New Zealand flights from Auckland), **Continental** (flights from Los Angeles, New York JFK, Newark, San Francisco, and Washington Dulles), **Icelandair** (flights from Baltimore, Boston, Minneapolis/St. Paul, and New York JFK), **Qantas** (Australian flights from Melbourne, Perth, and Sydney; New Zealand flights from

Auckland); **United** (flights from Boston, Chicago, Los Angeles, Newark, New York JFK, San Francisco, and Washington Dulles), and **Virgin Atlantic** (flights from Chicago, Newark, New York JFK, San Francisco, and Washington Dulles).

For information on getting into London from Heathrow, check out Chapter 11.

✔ **Gatwick:** A smaller airport than Heathrow, about 40km (25 miles) south of London. It's served by **American** (flights from Boston, Dallas/Ft. Worth, and Raleigh/Durham), **British Airways** (flights from Atlanta, Baltimore, Charlotte, Dallas/Ft. Worth, Denver, Houston, New York JFK, Miami, Orlando, Phoenix, and Tampa), **Continental** (flights from Boston, Cleveland, Houston, Miami, Newark, and Orlando), **Delta** (flights from Atlanta and Cincinnati), **Northwest** (flights from Detroit and Minneapolis/St. Paul), **Qantas** (flights from Sydney, Australia), and **Virgin Atlantic** (flights from Boston, Las Vegas, Miami, Newark, Orlando, and San Francisco).

For information on getting into London from Gatwick, see Chapter 11.

✔ **Stansted:** Eighty kilometers (50 miles) northeast of London, this airport handles national and European flights. The Stansted Sky Train to Liverpool Street Station takes 45 minutes and costs £13 ($24).

✔ **London City:** Only 10km (6 miles) east of Central London, this airport services European destinations. A bus charges £5 ($9.25) per person to take passengers on the 25-minute trip from the airport to Liverpool Street Station.

✔ **Luton:** Forty-five kilometers (28 miles) northwest of London, this airport services mostly charter flights. Travel by train from the airport to King's Cross Station for £9.50 ($18); the trip takes about an hour.

✔ **Manchester Airport,** in Yorkshire, is served by **Air Canada** (flights from Toronto), **American** (flights from San Francisco and New York JFK), **British Airways** (flights from Boston and New York JFK), **British Midland** (flights from Washington, D.C.; Chicago; and Toronto), **Continental** (flights from Newark), **Delta** (flights from Atlanta), **SAS** (flights from Toronto), **United** (flights from Washington, D.C., and Chicago), **US Airways** (flights from Orlando), and **Virgin Atlantic** (flights from Orlando).

Getting the Best Deal on Your Airfare

Competition among the major U.S. airlines is unlike that of any other industry. Every airline offers virtually the same product (basically, a coach seat is a coach seat is a . . .), yet prices can vary by hundreds of dollars.

Business travelers who need the flexibility to buy their tickets at the last minute and change their itineraries at a moment's notice — and who want to get home before the weekend — pay the premium rate, known as the *full fare*. But if you can book your ticket far in advance, stay over Saturday night, and are willing to travel midweek (Tues, Wed, or Thurs), you can qualify for the least expensive price — usually a fraction of the full fare. On most flights, even the shortest hops within the United States, the full fare runs close to $1,000 or more, but a 7- or 14-day advance-purchase ticket may cost you less than half that amount. Obviously, planning ahead pays.

The airlines also periodically hold sales, in which they lower the prices on their most popular routes. These fares have advance-purchase requirements and date-of-travel restrictions, but you can't beat the prices. As you plan your vacation, keep your eyes open for these sales, which tend to take place in seasons of low travel volume — in England, that's basically October through March. You almost never see a sale around the peak summer vacation months of July and August or around Thanksgiving or Christmas, when many people fly regardless of the fare they have to pay.

Working with Consolidators

Consolidators, also known as bucket shops, are great sources for international tickets (although they usually can't beat the Internet on fares within North America). Start by looking in Sunday newspaper travel sections; U.S. travelers should focus on the *New York Times, Los Angeles Times,* and *Miami Herald.*

Bucket-shop tickets are usually nonrefundable or rigged with stiff cancellation penalties, often as high as 50 to 75 percent of the ticket price. And some put you on charter airlines with questionable safety records.

Several reliable consolidators are worldwide and available on the Web, and most of them offer flights to London. **STA Travel** (☎ 800/781-4040; www.statravel.com), the world's leader in student travel, offers good fares for travelers of all ages. **ELTExpress** (☎ 800/TRAV-800; www.flights.com) started in Europe and has excellent fares worldwide. Flights.com also has "local" Web sites in 12 countries. **Air Tickets Direct** (☎ 800/778-3447; www.airticketsdirect.com) is based in Montreal and leverages the currently weak Canadian dollar for low fares.

Booking your flight online

The "big three" online travel agencies — **Expedia** (www.expedia.com), **Travelocity** (www.travelocity.com), and **Orbitz** (www.orbitz.com) — sell most of the air tickets bought on the Internet. (Canadian travelers can try www.expedia.ca and www.travelocity.ca; U.K. residents can go for expedia.co.uk and opodo.co.uk.) Each has different business deals with the airlines and may offer different fares on the same flights, so you may want to shop around. Expedia and Travelocity send you an

e-mail notification when a cheap fare becomes available to your favorite destination. Of the smaller travel-agency Web sites, **SideStep** (www.sidestep.com) receives good reviews from users. It's a browser add-on that purports to "search 140 sites at once," but in reality, it beats competitors' fares only as often as other sites do.

You can find great **last-minute deals** through free weekly e-mail services provided directly by the airlines. Most of these deals are announced on Tuesday or Wednesday and must be purchased online. Most deals work only for travel that weekend, but you can book some (such as Southwest's) weeks or months in advance. Sign up for weekly e-mail alerts at airline Web sites or check megasites that compile comprehensive lists of last-minute specials, such as **Smarter Living** (smarterliving.com). For last-minute trips, www.site59.com in the U.S. and www.last minute.com in Europe often have better deals than the major-label sites.

If you're willing to give up some control over your flight details, use an opaque fare service, like **Priceline** (www.priceline.com) or **Hotwire** (www.hotwire.com). Both offer rock-bottom prices in exchange for travel on a "mystery airline" at a mysterious time of day, often with a mysterious change of planes en route. The mystery airlines are all major, well-known carriers — and you don't really have to worry about being sent from Philadelphia to London via Tampa. But you have a pretty good chance of getting a 6 a.m. or 11 p.m. flight. Hotwire tells you flight prices before you buy; Priceline usually has better deals than Hotwire, but you have to play its "name our price" game. Note: In 2004, Priceline added nonopaque service to its roster. You now have the option to pick exact flights, times, and airlines from a list of offers — or opt to bid on opaque fares as before.

Arriving by Other Means

If you're traveling to London from another destination in Europe, flying isn't the only way to get there. Train and car ferries and high-speed hovercrafts cross the English Channel throughout the year from ports in France, Holland, and Belgium. And the Eurostar high-speed train zips beneath the channel through the Chunnel, a tunnel beneath the English Channel.

Taking the train

London has several train stations, and the one you arrive at depends on your point of departure from the Continent. The three-hour Eurostar service connecting Paris and Brussels to London via the Chunnel arrives at **Waterloo International Station.** Trains from Amsterdam arrive at **Liverpool Street Station.** Other London train stations include **Victoria, Paddington, King's Cross,** and **Euston Station.**

You can't use a Eurail pass on trains in England and the rest of the United Kingdom, so if you plan to travel within England or the rest of the United Kingdom, check out the various **BritRail passes** available (see Chapter 7 for more information).

 The high-speed **Eurostar** train runs from London to Paris or Brussels. Several types of Eurostar fares are available. Senior fares (for passengers over 60) and youth fares (for passengers under 26) can cut the price of a first-class fare by 20 percent or more. The same reductions apply for passengers traveling with validated Eurail and BritRail passes. To check out current and special promotional fares for Eurostar, visit Rail Europe's Web site at www.raileurope.com.

Riding a ferry or hovercraft

Crossing time for the car, train, or passenger ferries that regularly criss-cross the English Channel can take anywhere from 90 minutes to 5 hours, depending on the point of departure. Various *hovercrafts* (high-speed ferries with propellers that lift them off the surface of the water) skim over the water in as little as half an hour. Frequent train service to London is available from all the channel ports. The following lists the major ferry and hovercraft companies:

- **Hoverspeed UK** (☎ **08705/240-241** in the U.K.; www.hoverspeed.co.uk): Operates hovercrafts that zip across the channel between Calais and Dover in 35 minutes; the SuperseaCats (jet-propelled catamarans) run between Newhaven and Dieppe in 55 minutes.

- **P&O European Ferries** (☎ **870/242-4999** in the U.K. or 561-563-2856 in the U.S.; www.poportsmith.com): Offers daily ferry/car crossings between Cherbourg and Portsmouth (crossing time is five hours), and Le Havre and Portsmouth (5½ hours).

- **P&O Stena Line** (☎ **08705/980333** in the U.K.; www.poferries.com): Operates ferries between Calais and Dover (crossing time is 75 minutes).

- **Sea France** (☎ **01304/212-696** in the U.K.; www.seafrance.co.uk): Runs ferries between Dover and Calais (crossing time is 90 minutes).

Joining an Escorted Tour

You may be one of the many people who love escorted tours. The tour company takes care of all the details and tells you what to expect at each leg of your journey. You know your costs upfront, and in the case of the tame ones, you don't get many surprises. Escorted tours can take you to the maximum number of sights in the minimum amount of time with the least amount of hassle.

If you decide to go with an escorted tour, I strongly recommend purchasing travel insurance, especially if the tour operator asks to you pay upfront. But don't buy insurance from the tour operator! If the tour operator doesn't fulfill its obligation to provide you with the vacation you paid for, it probably doesn't fulfill its insurance obligations, either. Get travel insurance through an independent agency. (I tell you more about the ins and outs of travel insurance in Chapter 10.)

When choosing an escorted tour, along with finding out whether you have to put down a deposit and when final payment is due, ask a few simple questions before you buy:

- ✔ **What is the cancellation policy?** Can they cancel the trip if they don't get enough people? How late can you cancel if you are unable to go? Do you get a refund if you cancel? If they cancel?

- ✔ **How jam-packed is the schedule?** Does the tour schedule try to fit 25 hours into a 24-hour day, or does it give you ample time to relax by the pool or shop? If getting up at 7 a.m. every day and not returning to your hotel until 6 or 7 p.m. sounds like a grind, certain escorted tours may not be for you.

- ✔ **How large is the group?** The smaller the group, the less time you spend waiting for people to get on and off the bus. Tour operators may dodge this question because they may not know the exact size of the group until everybody makes reservations. But the operator should be able to give you a rough estimate.

- ✔ **Does the tour have a minimum group size?** Some tours have a minimum group size and may cancel the tour if they don't book enough people. If a quota exists, find out what it is and how close they are to reaching it. Again, tour operators may dance around these questions, but the information may help you select a tour that you know will actually happen.

- ✔ **What exactly does the tour include?** Don't assume anything. You may have to pay to get yourself to and from the airport. A box lunch may be included in an excursion, but drinks may be extra. Beer may be included, but not wine. How much flexibility do you have? Can you opt out of certain activities, or does the bus leave once a day, with no exceptions? Are all your meals planned in advance? Can you choose your entree at dinner, or does everybody get the same chicken cutlet?

Here are a few companies that offer escorted tours to London and the rest of England (with prices per person, based on double occupancy):

- ✔ **Globus and Cosmos** (www.globusandcosmos.com): Well-known budget tour companies working in partnership. Current offerings include an eight-day tour of the scenic and historic highlights in southern England starting at $1,676, airfare included.

- ✔ **Maupintour** (www.maupintour.com): A nine-day garden tour includes the Chelsea Flower Show; the great gardens at Sissinghurst, Stourhead, and Blenheim Palace; plus excursions to Bath, Oxford, and London. Prices start at $3,479, airfare not included. Other tours go to Yorkshire and the Lake District, and the West Country.

- ✔ **Trafalgar Tours** (www.trafalgartours.com): Provides more upscale choices; prices for the 15-day "Best of Britain" tour start at $2,099, airfare not included.

Choosing a Package Tour

For lots of destinations, package tours can be a smart way to go. In many cases, a package tour that includes airfare, hotel, and transportation to and from the airport costs less than the hotel alone on a tour you book yourself. That's because tour operators buy packages in bulk, so they can resell them to the public for less.

Package tours vary greatly in what they provide. Some offer a better class of hotels than others; others provide the same hotels for lower prices. Some book flights on scheduled airlines; others sell charters. In some packages, you may have a limited choice of accommodations and travel days. Some packages let you choose between escorted vacations and independent vacations; others let you add on just a few excursions or escorted day trips (also at discounted prices) without booking an entirely escorted tour.

To find package tours, check out the travel section of your local Sunday newspaper or the ads in the back of national travel magazines, such as *Travel & Leisure, National Geographic Traveler,* and *Condé Nast Traveler.* **Liberty Travel** (call ☎ 888-271-1584 to find the store nearest you; www.libertytravel.com) is one of the biggest packagers in the northeastern U.S. and usually boasts a full-page ad in Sunday papers.

Another good source of package deals is the airlines themselves. Most major airlines offer air/land packages. Several big **online travel agencies** — Expedia, Travelocity, Orbitz, Site59, and Lastminute.com — also do a brisk business in packages.

Locating package tours

Information about package tours is available from a variety of sources. A few companies that offer packages to England are

- ✔ **British Travel International** (☎ 800-327-6097; www.britishtravel.com): A good source for discount packages.

- ✔ **Liberty Travel** (☎ 888-271-1584; www.libertytravel.com): One of the biggest packagers in the northeastern United States, offers reasonably priced packages.

✔ **Trailfinders** (www.trailfinders.com): A good source for discount packages for Australian visitors, it has several offices in Australia: Sydney (☎ 02/9247-7666), Melbourne (☎ 03/9600-3022), Cairns (☎ 07/4041-1199), Brisbane (☎ 07/3229-0887), and Perth (☎ 08/9226-1222).

Checking out airline and hotel packages

Airlines are good sources for package tours, especially to London, because they package their flights together with accommodations. The following airlines offer packages to England:

✔ **American Airlines Vacations** (☎ 800-321-2121; www.aavacations.com)

✔ **British Airways Holidays** (☎ 800-AIRWAYS; www.britishairways.com/holiday)

✔ **Continental Airlines Vacations** (☎ 800-525-0280; www.continental.com)

✔ **Northwest Airlines World Vacations** (☎ 800-800-1504; www.nwaworldvacations.com)

✔ **United Airlines Vacations** (☎ 800-328-6877; www.unitedvacations.com)

✔ **Virgin Atlantic Vacations** (☎ 888-YESVIRGIN; www.virgin.com/vacations)

Chapter 7

Getting Around England

In This Chapter

▶ Deciding on the best way to travel
▶ Traveling through England by train
▶ Seeing the country by bus
▶ Exploring the countryside by car

I strongly recommend that you explore at least a portion of England that has nothing to do with London. Out of the city and in the countryside or an ancient village, the quiet magic of this country comes over you like a spell. The gently unfolding and sometimes dramatic landscapes vary from region to region, and so do the cities and towns. Great and unforgettable sights await you at every turn, and so do small, local surprises. This chapter helps you decide whether train travel, bus travel, or auto-motion is for you.

Weighing the Options: Train or Car?

Because of England's small size and easy access to train and road networks, the country is a joy to explore. Many cities and sites are workable as day trips from London. You can reach Bath, Brighton, and Canterbury from London in 90 minutes or less by train and in about two hours by car or bus. The trip to Stratford-upon-Avon or to Salisbury (the closest large town to Stonehenge) takes about two hours by train and about three hours by car. If London is your home base, and you get an early start, you can explore any one of these places, have lunch, and be back in London in time for dinner.

Riding the Rails

In England, people still take trains to travel around the country. I recommend traveling by train over all other forms of transportation — especially if you're a first-time visitor to England. Traveling by train is fun, safe, and convenient. In smaller cities, the train stations are never more than a few minutes' walk or a simple bus ride from the town center. If you want to explore the countryside, you can easily take a train to a new city and then rent a car.

The sleek, high-speed **Intercity trains** that run between London and heavily traveled main-line routes are the most dependable and comfortable trains you can take. You can ride these fast trains to York, Stratford-upon-Avon, Bath and Cheltenham (both good bases for exploring the Cotswolds), Oxenholme (closest station to the Lake District), Exeter (in Devon), and Penzance (in Cornwall). For shorter trips, such as to Brighton and Cambridge, you can take a **commuter train.** In some cases, you may need to transfer to a **local train** to reach your destination.

The local trains connect larger towns to smaller ones and are very basic. Unlike all other trains, local trains don't have toilets or food service. Smoking isn't permitted on local trains, and it's confined to strictly designated areas on commuter and Intercity trains. The local stations are small; sometimes (particularly on Sun) no one is available to help with information or ticket sales. You can always find train schedules posted in the local stations, and if no window service is available, you can buy your ticket on the train.

For the most current train schedules and fares, call **National Rail Enquiries** at ☎ **08457/484950** in the United Kingdom. You can also find timetable information online at www.nationalrail.com, but always call National Rail Enquiries to verify schedules.

Buying your train ticket

You can purchase your train ticket with cash or credit card at a ticket window or ticket machine in the train station. If the windows are closed, you have to buy your ticket on the train with cash. If you have a BritRail pass (see "Saving with BritRail passes," later in this chapter), you don't have to bother with buying tickets; just board the train.

In England, you call a one-way train ticket a *single.* A round-trip ticket is a *return.* If you go on a day trip, ask for a *day return.*

When you buy your ticket, you have to choose between first and standard (second) class. First-class tickets cost about one-third more than standard class. The first-class cars have roomier seats, but you can travel quite comfortably in standard class. If you want a first-class ticket, you have to request one — otherwise, the agent will sell you a standard-class ticket.

First-class service on some Intercity train routes includes free meals; complimentary coffee, tea, beverages, and snacks served at your seat; and a free newspaper. Standard-class passengers can buy sandwiches and drinks in a cafe car. On some lines, an employee comes through with a food-and-beverage trolley.

Negotiating the rail system

The British rail system is currently emerging from a crisis. It had seriously deteriorated since being privatized in the 1980s and is in the midst of a multibillion-pound, five-year restoration plan scheduled to end in 2008. Service has already improved, at least on the main routes, but you may still encounter canceled trains, departure tracks changed without notice, and railway employees who don't always have the correct information to help you on your journey.

For all these reasons, I urge you to keep your wits about you when traveling by train in England. Keep the following in mind:

✔ Always call **National Rail Enquiries** (☎ 08457/484950) the night before your train trip to verify departure times and departure stations.

✔ Whenever possible, **choose a direct train** over one that requires a change along the way. In some cases, trains going to the same destination (such as Canterbury or Dover) depart from different London stations. Ask National Rail Enquiries or information agents at the station for the quickest and most direct routes to a destination.

✔ Tracks can change without an announcement, so always **verify with a railway employee** before you board that the train is going to your destination.

✔ On some lines, **Sunday is one of the worst days to travel** because fewer trains run, and they tend to be slow. Track work often takes place on Sunday, sometimes causing long delays or requiring that you complete part of the journey by bus.

Getting to know London's train stations

One of the busiest transportation hubs in the world, London has 11 major stations, so you need to get to the right station in order to catch your train. (Throughout this book, I tell you which London station serves the destination that I describe.) The Underground (subway) serves all London's train stations. In every station, a large overhead display, usually near the platforms, lists the departing trains and platforms.

If you travel around England or the rest of the United Kingdom from London, you'll depart from one of the following stations:

✔ **Charing Cross Station:** Trains from here travel southeast to Canterbury, Hastings, Dover, and English Channel ports that connect with ferry service to the Continent.

✔ **Euston Station:** Trains from this station head north to the Lake District and up to Scotland.

✔ **King's Cross Station:** Trains from here travel to destinations in the east of England, including Cambridge and York.

✔ **Liverpool Street Station:** Trains from this station head to English Channel ports, with continuing service to the Netherlands, northern Germany, and Scandinavia.

✔ **Paddington Station:** Trains from Paddington travel southwest to Bath, Plymouth, and Penzance in Cornwall, stopping at cities along the way.

✔ **St. Pancras Station:** Currently being renovated, this station will eventually provide expanded Eurostar service to Paris and Brussels from the Midlands.

✔ **Victoria Station:** Head here for trains traveling to the south and southeast of England, including Canterbury, Brighton, and Gatwick Airport.

✔ **Waterloo International:** Primarily for trains going to the south of England, you need to head to Waterloo International, which connects to Waterloo Station, to catch Eurostar trains to and from Paris and Brussels.

Saving with BritRail passes

If you plan to travel around England by train, consider purchasing a **BritRail pass** before you arrive. BritRail passes are really convenient because you don't have to stand in line to buy train tickets; if a train is in the station, you can just hop on. In peak summer travel months, you may want to reserve your seat, which you can do for a small fee.

BritRail passes are sold only outside the United Kingdom; therefore, you must purchase them *before* you arrive in England. You can order the passes through a travel agent or by contacting **RailEurope** (☎ **877-257-2887** in the U.S. or 800-361-RAIL in Canada; www.raileurope.com). The various kinds of BritRail passes are

✔ **BritRail London Plus Pass:** This pass covers a large area around London and gets you to Cambridge, Oxford, Canterbury, Dover, Winchester, Salisbury, and as far west as Exeter in Devon. With this pass, the cost for first-class travel for any two days in an eight-day period is $91 for adults; children ages 5 to 15 travel free with a parent; standard class is $69 for adults. Four- and seven-day London Plus Passes are also available. The first-class, round-trip full fare between London and Exeter costs you about $334, so with this pass you save money the farther you travel from London (within the allowed area). If you take day trips only to Hampton Court Palace and Windsor, for example, you're better off paying the regular train fares.

✔ **BritRail Flexipass:** This pass allows you to travel any 4, 8, or 15 days within a two-month time period. A four-day, first-class Flexipass costs $395 for adults, $336 for seniors over 60; children ages 5 to 15 travel free with a parent. In standard class, the four-day pass costs $265 for adults; children ages 5 to 15 travel free with a parent (there's no standard-class senior rate). The Flexipass allows you to visit Wales and Scotland.

✔ **BritRail England Consecutive Pass:** Good if you're going to be on the go, this pass lets you visit all of England over a specific number of consecutive days (but you don't get to go to Wales or Scotland). An eight-day, first-class pass costs $249 for adults, free for children ages 5 to 15 traveling with a parent. An eight-day standard-class pass costs $365 for adults, free for children ages 5 to 15 traveling with a parent.

✔ **BritRail Family Pass:** This pass makes traveling with kids cheaper and easier. Buy any adult or senior pass, and you get one free youth pass (ages 5–15) of the same type and duration; additional children pay 50 percent of adult fares. Children under 5 travel free at all times.

Hopping a Coach: Bus Travel

A long distance touring bus in England is a *coach*. (You take buses for local transportation.) The main long-distance coach company is National Express. Its routes cover the entire country, and its comfortable coaches have reclining seats and a toilet; they often have food-and-beverage service. Tickets usually cost half of what the train does, and they're even cheaper if you buy a return ticket. The one drawback, at least for the busy traveler without much extra time, is that coaches take at least one or two hours longer than the train.

If you travel around England by coach from London, you'll depart from **Victoria Coach Station,** Buckingham Palace Road (☎ **020/7730-3466;** Tube: Victoria), located just two blocks from Victoria Station. Coach stations in cities outside of London are always close to the city center, often next to the train station. For information on travel by coach and the various money-saving passes available, contact **National Express** (☎ **08705/808080**); you can view schedules and fares online at www. nationalexpress.com.

Driving on the Left, Passing on the Right: Car Travel

I always suggest that people travel through England by train rather than car. You usually spend much of a long-distance car trip on motorways without much scenery, so what's the point? But having a car does open up whole regions of the English countryside for exploration. In areas, such as the Cotswolds, where trains don't serve villages and local bus service is sporadic or infrequent, having a car is almost a necessity. Additionally, parts of Cornwall and the Lake District aren't accessible by train or bus.

Cough up the congestion charge

Traffic in central London was such a snarl that in February 2003, a new congestion charge went into effect. Drivers must now pay £8 ($15) to enter central London from 7 a.m. to 6:30 p.m. Monday through Friday. You can make this payment online (www.cclondon.com), at retail outlets, or by phone (☎ **0845/900-1234**). There are no tollbooths, but high-tech cameras read the plate numbers of all cars entering the charge zone and match them to a database; if you haven't paid by 10 p.m., you get fined. The Inner Ring Road forms the boundary for the congestion charge.

Americans renting a car in England need a valid U.S. driver's license that they've had for at least one year. The same holds true for Canadians, Australians, and New Zealanders. In most cases, depending on the agency, you must be at least 23 years old (21 in some instances, 25 in others) and no older than 70. (Some companies have raised this age to 75.)

Renting a car in London — or not

Having a car in London is far more of a hassle than a help for the following reasons:

- ✔ Finding your way through the city in heavy traffic while driving on the *left-hand side* of the road can turn even the best American driver into a gibbering nutcase.

- ✔ Maneuvering through London's congested and complicated maze of streets can be an endurance test even for Londoners.

- ✔ Parking is difficult to find and expensive. (Street meters cost a minimum of £1/$1.85 for 20 minutes.)

- ✔ Just entering central London by car on weekdays sets you back £8 ($15); for details, see the box "Cough up the congestion charge" that follows.

- ✔ Paying for gas (*petrol* in Britspeak) costs almost £3.50 ($6.50) a gallon.

- ✔ Riding public transportation — especially the Underground — gets you everywhere you want to go at a fraction of the cost.

Do yourself a favor: Forget about renting a car in London. If you want to be with Londoners on their own turf (or in their own tunnels), the Tube (Underground) is a great way to do it. Even if you plan excursions outside London, the trains are a better option than a car. If you need a car to explore the countryside, you can rent one in a hub city or town after you arrive by train.

Renting a car in England

Although the car-rental market in Britain is highly competitive, renting a car in England costs more than in the United States — unless, that is, you can find a special promotional offer from an airline or a car-rental agency. When I last rented a car in England, in 2005, without benefit of any special offers, the total cost was more than £135 ($250) for a four-day rental of a compact car with manual transmission. That price included unlimited mileage and all the insurance but not gas *(petrol),* which added another £54 ($100). Car-rental rates vary even more than airline fares. The price depends on a host of factors, including car size, the length of time that you keep it, where and when you pick the car up and drop it off, and how far you drive it.

Asking a few key questions can save you hundreds of dollars when renting a car. Keep the following factors in mind:

- ✔ You can often get a lower car-rental rate if you reserve seven days in advance by using a toll-free reservations number. (See the Appendix for a list of international car-rental firms that rent cars in England.)

- ✔ Find out whether the quoted price includes the 17.5 percent value-added tax (VAT). (See Chapter 5 for more on this tax.)

- ✔ If you plan to do much driving, a rental package with unlimited mileage is your best option.

- ✔ Weekend rates may be lower than weekday rates.

- ✔ If you keep the car for five or more days, a weekly rate may be cheaper than the daily rate.

- ✔ The rate may be cheaper if you pick up the car at a central town office rather than at an airport.

- ✔ Don't forget to mention membership in AAA, AARP, frequent-flier programs, and trade unions. These affiliations usually entitle you to discounts ranging from 5 to 30 percent. Check with your travel agent about any and all of these rates.

- ✔ Most car rentals are worth at least 800km (500 miles) on your frequent-flier account.

- ✔ Some airlines offer package deals that include car rental. (See Chapter 6 for more on package tours.)

In addition to the standard rental prices, other optional charges apply to most car rentals. Many credit card companies cover the *collision-damage waiver* (CDW), which requires you to pay for damage to the car in a collision. Check with your credit-card company before you go so you can avoid paying this hefty fee (as much as $15 per day).

The royal fast lane

In 2001, Princess Anne, the 50-year-old daughter of Queen Elizabeth, was found guilty of driving her Bentley at 93 mph in a 70-mph zone on a two-lane road in rural Gloucestershire. The princess had a unique defense: She claimed that she thought the police cars flashing their lights behind her were offering an escort, so she didn't slow down. A local magistrate fined her several hundred pounds.

The car-rental companies also offer *additional liability insurance* (if you harm others in an accident), *personal accident insurance* (if you harm yourself or your passengers), and *personal effects insurance* (if your luggage is stolen from your car). If you have insurance on your car at home, you're probably covered for most of these unlikelihoods. If your own insurance doesn't cover you for rentals, or if you don't have auto insurance, consider the additional coverage.

 As with other aspects of planning your trip, using the Internet can make comparison-shopping for a car rental much easier. The major booking Web sites — **Travelocity** (www.travelocity.com), **Expedia** (www.expedia.com), and **Yahoo! Travel** (http://travel.yahoo.com), for example — have search engines that can dig up discounted car-rental rates. Just enter the car size you want, the pickup and return dates, and the city where you want to rent, and the server returns a price. You can even make the reservation through these sites.

Hitting the road: Motorways, dual carriageways, and roundabouts

What some countries call a freeway, the Brits call a *motorway*. England has a good motorway network. Don't stop on a motorway (indicated as *M* plus a number on maps) unless you have an emergency. You don't have to pay a toll to drive on British motorways if you're going to any of the places described in this book.

The English call a two-way road a *single carriageway* and a four-lane divided highway (two lanes in each direction) a *dual carriageway*. Country roads, some of them paved-over tracks dating back centuries, are full of twists and turns, and often barely wide enough for two cars to pass. One element of British roads that invariably throws non-native drivers is the *roundabout* — a traffic junction where several roads meet at one traffic circle. At a roundabout, the cars already circulating in the roundabout always have the right of way, as do cars entering the roundabout from entrances to one's right.

On certain sections of the motorway, where speeding is especially dangerous, speed cameras have been installed. The cameras take a photograph of any car exceeding the speed limit so that the police can trace the culprit. You can see a camera symbol on entering these areas. Surveillance cameras have also been installed at some traffic lights to catch anyone who doesn't stop for the red.

Following the rules of the road

You need to know some general facts if you plan to drive in England:

✔ All distances and speed limits are shown in miles and miles per hour (mph). If you need to translate from the metric system, a kilometer is 0.62 of a mile, and a mile is 1.62 kilometers. Speed limits are usually

- 30mph (49kph) in towns

- 40mph (65kph) on some town roads where posted

- 60mph (97kph) on most single-carriageway (two-way) roads

- 70mph (113kph) on dual carriageways and motorways

✔ Road signs are usually the standard international signs. Buy a booklet (available at many shops and in airports) called *Highway Code* for about £1 ($1.85) before you set out. The information in this book is essential for driving in England.

✔ On major motorways, lanes closest to the outside edge of the road are intended for general driving, while the lanes closest to the median are intended for overtaking (passing) slower moving vehicles.

✔ The law requires you to wear a seat belt. If you have children, make sure that you ask the car-rental agency about seat belts or car seats before you rent.

✔ At roundabouts, traffic coming from the right has the right of way.

✔ You can pass other vehicles only on the right.

✔ Parking in the center of most big towns is difficult and expensive. Make sure that you read all posted restrictions or park in a lot.

✔ You *must* stop for pedestrians in crosswalks marked by striped lines (called *zebra crossings*) on the road. Pedestrians have the right of way.

Coping with emergencies on the road

 All motorways have emergency telephones stationed a kilometer apart. Markers at every tenth of a kilometer point to the nearest phone. The phone operator can get emergency or automotive services for you if you need them. Motorway service stations are usually about 40km (25 miles) apart and occasionally as far as 80km (50 miles) apart.

Filling up the tank

Petrol (gasoline) stations are self-service. Use the green filler pipe for unleaded petrol, the red filler pipe for leaded petrol, and the black filler pipe for diesel fuel.

Petrol is often cheapest at supermarkets. (Yes, they may have pumps outside.) But going to a motorway service station is more convenient. You buy petrol by the liter (3.78 liters = 1 gallon). Expect to pay about 90p ($1.65) per liter (approximately $6.30 per gallon) for unleaded petrol.

Chapter 8

Booking Your Accommodations

In This Chapter

▶ Checking out the options
▶ Getting the best rates
▶ Surfing for cyber-deals
▶ Upgrading your room

*C*hant this as your mantra: "I will not arrive in London without a hotel reservation. I will not arrive in . . . " Reserving a room is especially important if you plan to be in London from mid-April to early October (high season). If you arrive in London with a hotel reservation, you don't have to waste your precious time trying to find a place to stay.

Booking ahead isn't quite as important in the rest of England, but I recommend that you do it — particularly if you're going to spend a Friday or Saturday night in a major tourist spot like Stratford-upon-Avon or in a resort town like Brighton. Hotels in popular tourist areas, such as the Cotswolds, Cornwall, and the Lake District, also fill up fast in June, July, and August. Off season, and especially in the middle of winter, you don't have a problem booking a room on the spot, wherever you are. In a small village, finding a room may be as simple as spotting a "room-to-let" sign in the front window of a house.

 You find tourist information centers in all the larger towns and the national parks, and they can always help you find a room. In most cases, tourist information centers charge 10 percent of the first night's hotel rate, but you get that back at the hotel, so the service ends up costing nothing.

Finding the Right Place for You

Accommodations in England are available in varying price ranges and degrees of luxury. Places to stay generally fit into one of two categories: hotels and bed-and-breakfast inns (B&Bs).

The situation in London — one of Europe's most visited cities — differs from the rest of England. The selection of hotels is far greater than you'll find elsewhere in England, and they cost considerably more money. But London does offer good budget hotels and plenty of B&Bs that won't render you unconscious when you see the bill. If you have a few more dollars (*pounds,* that is) to throw around, you can choose among unique boutique hotels, large chain hotels, and several ultraluxurious places. Other options include self-catering hotels (where the rooms come equipped with small kitchens) or fully equipped *flats* (apartments).

Outside London, prices generally drop by half for small B&Bs and by about one-third or more for hotels. The distinction between B&B and hotel is less obvious outside of the capital because most places, even large hotels, include breakfast with the room, which isn't the case at most high-end hotels in London. In small towns and rural villages, you can also experience a "real" B&B — a home where a family resides and rents out one or two bedrooms. You can also find marvelous country-house hotels, where you get impeccable service and astronomical prices. Away from the big city, many hotels also offer dinner to guests for a special half-board rate.

Brits, and Europeans in general, aren't as committed to smoke-free environments as Americans. But this attitude is changing. More and more hotels and B&Bs in England reserve special rooms or an entire floor for nonsmokers. In the hotel descriptions in this book, I always note completely smoke-free hotels.

Understanding the pros and cons of B&Bs

Bed-and-breakfast inns (B&Bs) in England are different from what you may have experienced elsewhere. Most are former — usually old — homes, and the comfort and services vary widely. (Some are current homes where you stay with the family.) The plumbing can be unpredictable, as can the water temperature. Space is often scarce. But they do offer a slice of domestic life that you can't get in a larger, more anonymous hotel.

Because B&Bs are often private homes and not hotels, typical amenities can also vary widely, especially in the bathroom facilities. Nearly all B&B rooms contain washbasins, but you may have to share a bathroom down the hall. Most B&Bs usually keep their facilities scrupulously clean, but many travelers prefer private bathrooms. Keep in mind, however, that *en-suite* (in-the-room) bathrooms are generally so small that you feel as if you haven't left the airplane, and squeezing into the super tiny showers can be a trial.

The decor in many of the lowest-priced B&Bs is fairly unimpressive. Coming back to a small room with mismatched furniture, avocado walls, and a tiny bathroom down the hall with no hot water may be an inconvenience you're willing to suffer for saving money, but I don't recommend any such places in this book. You do have to pay more for the more popular and well-appointed B&Bs, but their comforts and conveniences make them worth the price.

What about the breakfast part of the B&B? Well, gone are the days when the staff of every B&B cooked you up a *full English breakfast* (also known as a *fry-up*) of eggs, sausages, bacon, fried tomatoes, and beans. Many still do — especially outside London — but others put out a *continental buffet,* which consists of cereals, fruits, and breads. The B&B descriptions in this book say "rate includes English breakfast" or "rate includes continental breakfast," so you know what to expect.

Licensed B&Bs, like hotels, are inspected regularly, and the quality of B&Bs has improved greatly over the years. I recommend them for people who don't require many extras, although the most successful B&Bs continually upgrade their services or offer some enticing amenities. For example, many B&Bs now provide cable TV and direct-dial phones in the rooms.

 If you're physically disabled or infirm in any way, B&Bs may not be the choice for you. B&Bs usually don't have elevators, so you may have to carry your luggage up steep, narrow stairs. Be sure to check how accessible the B&B is before making reservations.

Exploring hotel choices

England boasts a wide choice of hotels. Some inexpensive ones provide breakfast with a room rental; others charge an additional fee for the most important meal of the day. At a four- or five-star hotel, you pay a hefty price to eat breakfast on the premises. The guest rooms at a self-catering hotel (see the section "Self-catering options," later in this chapter, for more on these rooms) come equipped with small kitchens so that you can make breakfast in your room.

In the following sections I describe the kinds of services and amenities you can expect based on the type of accommodation you choose. But you can get a pretty good sense of the level of pampering you'll receive based on price alone. Table 8-1 tells you what to expect from your holiday digs based on the amount of cash you dish out.

Table 8-1		Key to Hotel Dollar Signs
Dollar Sign(s)	**Price Range**	**What to Expect**
$	Less than £95 ($176)	You are more likely to find these relatively simple accommodations in B&Bs than in hotels. Rooms will likely be small, and you don't necessarily get in-room amenities, such as telephone and televisions. You may have to share a bathroom. In a B&B, you do get breakfast.
$$	£96–£149 ($178–$276)	A bit classier, these midrange accommodations offer you more room, more extras (such as irons, hair dryers, or a microwave), and a more convenient location than the preceding category. You probably get breakfast.
$$$	£150–£203 ($278–$376)	Higher-class still, these accommodations begin to look more upscale, and service begins to factor in. Many chain hotels fall in this category. You get a roomier private bathroom, cable TV, and other in-room amenities, and you can probably find a café or restaurant on the premises. You may or may not get breakfast.
$$$$	£204–£257 ($377–$475)	Hotels in this category generally meet high international standards, and you find them in upscale neighborhoods. Porter and room service are available. Think fine furnishings, larger bathrooms with designer toiletries, high-quality bedding, chocolates on your pillow, a classy restaurant, and maybe even expansive or romantic views. A fine breakfast will be available, but you probably have to pay for it.
$$$$$	£257 ($475) and up	These top-rated accommodations generally come with luxury amenities, such as valet parking, 24-hour room service, a gourmet restaurant, on-site spa and health club, large bathrooms, high-end furnishings and high-quality sheets, DVD/CD players, and turn-down service — you get a great experience, and you pay through the nose for it. The great London hotels and the exclusive country-house hotels generally fall into this category, and they may include a gourmet dinner and breakfast.

Boutique and deluxe hotels

London offers a few *boutique hotels,* such as the 41 (see Chapter 11), that are midrange in size but not price; sumptuously furnished, they offer state-of-the-art amenities and full service.

Older deluxe hotels, full of charm and character, offer a distinctly English style. Older London hotels, such as The Gore or Hazlitt's 1718, have been around for a century or more (see Chapter 11). Outside London, you can routinely find hotels (such as The Mermaid Inn, in Rye; see Chapter 14) that served as coaching inns 400 years ago. Perhaps the most atmospheric hotels in England, they're full of twisting stairways and oak-beamed bedrooms (the bathrooms are always modern, however).

Chain properties

Maybe you *always* stay at one of the chain hotels — a Hyatt, a Sheraton, a Best Western, or a Marriott. These newer places are basically the same no matter where they are: They rely on their brand name and a no-surprise approach to win customers. London is chock-full of chain hotels, if that's what you fancy. Outside the capital, you also find chain hotels in most medium-size towns and in tourist-heavy areas (such as the Lake District), but you may not recognize the names. Keep your eyes open for Thistle, one reliable British chain. Its hotels aren't always new; some are in historic properties. Most chain hotels cater to large groups, and you may feel rather anonymous in them. On the other hand, these hotels usually come well equipped for people with disabilities and families with children. For a list of chain hotels in England, see the Appendix.

Landmark and country-house hotels

At the top of the hotel spectrum, in both price and prestige, are the landmark hotels and country-house hotels. In London, the Dorchester, Claridge's, the Park Lane Sheraton Hotel, and the Savoy (see Chapter 11 for all) rank among the world's best hotels. You can expect glamorous public salons (and glamorous fellow guests), a generously proportioned and well-decorated room with a large private bath, an on-site health club or access to one nearby, and top-of-the-line service.

Country-house hotels are a world onto themselves. Former private estates set within landscaped gardens, they typify a world of privilege and tradition, and work hard to make their guests feel pampered and comfortable. You can always expect fine gourmet cooking and a full range of amenities, including room service and an on-site health club. You can find two outstanding country-house hotels in Gidleigh Park in Devon (see Chapter 17) and Middlethorpe Hall in Yorkshire (see Chapter 21).

Self-catering options

In London, you can also consider staying at a *self-catering hotel,* where you do the cooking in your own hotel room. (Astons Apartments in London, which you can read about in Chapter 11, is the only self-catering hotel that I list in this book.) For short stays and for one or two people, self-catering hotels don't always beat the competition's price. But for families and people who can't afford or don't want to eat every meal out, self-catering hotels can really save your budget. Outside of London, you find few self-catering hotels; instead, you find self-catering *flats* (apartments) or holiday homes that you can rent for a week or more.

Finding the Best Room at the Best Rate

 The rate you pay for a room depends on many factors, the most important being the way you make your reservation. The strategies in this section can help you get the best rate available.

The *rack rate* is the maximum rate a hotel charges for a room. It's the rate you get if you walk in off the street and ask for a room for the night. You sometimes see these rates printed on the fire/emergency exit diagrams posted on the back of your room's door, and these are the rates I've listed in this book. Hotels are happy to charge you the rack rate, but you can almost always do better. Perhaps the best way to avoid paying the rack rate is surprisingly simple: Just ask for a cheaper or discounted rate. You may be pleasantly surprised.

A travel agent may be able to negotiate a better price with certain hotels than you can get by yourself. (That's because the hotel often gives the agent a discount in exchange for steering his or her business toward that hotel.)

 You may get a lower rate by reserving a room through the hotel's toll-free number rather than calling the hotel directly. On the other hand, the central reservations number may not know about discount rates at specific locations. Your best bet is to call both the local number and the toll-free number, and see which one gives you a better deal.

Room rates (even rack rates) change with the season, as occupancy rates rise and fall. But even within a given season, room prices are subject to change without notice, so the rates quoted in this book may be different from the actual rate you receive when you make your reservation. Be sure to mention membership in AAA, AARP, frequent-flier programs, any other corporate rewards programs you belong to when you call to book. Budget hotels and small B&Bs rarely offer these organization discounts, but you never know unless you ask.

 You may be able to save 20 percent or more by traveling off season, which is mid-October to mid-December and January to March.

The best hotel and B&B rates are probably available through package tours that include airfare and hotel (see Chapter 6 for more on package tours). With these packages, which are sometimes astonishingly cheap, you have to choose a hotel that's part of the package. Packages offered by airlines tend to include larger chain hotels. So what? The money you save may amount to hundreds of dollars.

Surfing the Web for Hotel Deals

You generally shop online for hotels in one of two ways: by booking through the hotel's own Web site or through an independent booking agency (or a fare-service agency, like Priceline). These Internet hotel agencies have multiplied in mind-boggling numbers of late, competing for the business of millions of consumers surfing for accommodations around the world. This competitiveness can be a boon to consumers who have the patience and time to shop and compare the online sites for good deals — but shop you must, for prices can vary considerably from site to site. And keep in mind that hotels at the top of a site's listing may be there for no other reason than that they paid money to get the placement.

Of the "big three" sites, Expedia (www.expedia.com) offers a long list of special deals and "virtual tours" or photos of available rooms so you can see what you're paying for (a feature that helps counter the claims that hotels often hold back the best rooms from bargain booking Web sites). Travelocity (www.travelocity.com) posts unvarnished customer reviews and ranks its properties according to the AAA rating system. Also reliable are Hotels.com and Quikbook.com. An excellent free program, TravelAxe (www.travelaxe.net), can help you search multiple hotel sites at once, even ones you may never have heard of — and conveniently lists the total price of the room, including the taxes and service charges. Another booking site, Travelweb (www.travelweb.com), is partly owned by the hotels it represents (including the Hilton, Hyatt, and Starwood chains) and therefore plugs directly into the hotels' reservations systems — unlike independent online agencies, which have to fax or e-mail reservation requests to the hotel, a good portion of which get misplaced in the shuffle. More than once, travelers have arrived at the hotel only to be told that they have no reservation. To be fair, many of the major sites are undergoing improvements in service and ease of use, and Expedia will soon be able to plug directly into the reservations systems of many hotel chains — none of which can be bad news for you. In the meantime, it's a good idea to get a confirmation number and make a printout of any online booking transaction.

In the opaque Web site category, Priceline (www.priceline.com) and Hotwire (www.hotwire.com) get even better prices for hotels than for airfares; with both sites, you get to pick the neighborhood and quality level of your hotel before offering up your money. Priceline's hotel product even covers Europe and Asia, though it's much better at getting five-star lodging for three-star prices than at finding anything at the bottom of the scale. On the down side, many hotels stick Priceline guests in their least desirable rooms. Be sure to go to the BiddingforTravel Web site (www.biddingfortravel.com) before bidding on a hotel room on Priceline; BiddingforTravel gives you a fairly up-to-date list of hotels that Priceline uses in major cities. For both Priceline and Hotwire, you pay upfront, and the fee is nonrefundable. Note: Some hotels don't provide loyalty program credits or points or other frequent-stay amenities when you book a room through opaque online services.

Some good England-specific Web sites that you can use to track down and make online reservations at hotels in England are

- **LondonRooms.com** (www.londonrooms.com): An excellent search engine that can set you up in a B&B or hotel anywhere in London. One click on an area lets you view the available choices; another click gives you information on an individual property.

- **British Hotel Reservation Centre** (www.bhrc.co.uk): Lists current and seasonal specials at selected London and U.K. hotels.

- **Independent Traveler** (www.gowithit.co.uk): Lists hundreds of self-catering accommodations in London. These are private flats, not hotels, and are available for a one-week minimum period; they can be a fantastic bargain.

- **London Bed & Breakfast** (☎ 800/872-2632 in the U.S. or 020/7351-3445 in the U.K.; www.londonbandb.com): Provides inexpensive accommodations in select private homes.

- **Londontown.com** (www.londontown.com): Hotel Web site that has a long list of London properties among which you can choose. Some properties on the list offer special low rates if you book through the site.

- **SeniorSearch U.K.** (www.ageofreason.com): A site for seniors looking for special hotels and other forms of accommodation, including home and apartment exchanges.

- **Uptown Reservations** (www.uptownres.co.uk): Provides listings for dozens of B&Bs in private homes in London.

Reserving the Best Room

After you make your reservation, asking one or two more pointed questions can go a long way toward making sure you get the best room in the house. Always ask for a corner room. These rooms are usually larger, quieter, and have more windows and light than standard rooms, and they don't always cost more. Also ask if the hotel is renovating; if it is, request a room away from the renovation work. Ask, too, about the location of the restaurants, bars, and discos in the hotel — all sources of annoying noise. And if you aren't happy with your room when you arrive, talk to the front desk. If they have another room, they should be happy to accommodate you, within reason.

If you need a room where you can smoke, request one when you reserve. If you can't bear the lingering smell of smoke, tell everyone who handles your reservation that you need a smoke-free room. Hotels in England usually have nonsmoking rooms; some establishments are entirely smoke free.

Chapter 9

Catering to Special Needs or Interests

In This Chapter

▶ Bringing the family
▶ Discovering discounts and special tours for seniors
▶ Locating wheelchair-accessible attractions
▶ Finding lesbian and gay communities and special events

*M*any of today's travelers have special interests or needs. Parents may want to take their children along on trips. Seniors may like to take advantage of discounts or tours designed especially for them. People with disabilities need to ensure that their itineraries offer wheelchair access. And gays and lesbians may want to know about welcoming places and events. In response to these needs, this chapter offers you advice and resources.

Traveling with the Brood: Advice for Families

If you have enough trouble getting your kids out of the house in the morning, dragging them thousands of miles away may seem like an insurmountable challenge. But you may find family travel immensely rewarding, giving you new ways of seeing the world through smaller pairs of eyes.

Familyhostel (☎ 800-733-9753; www.learn.unh.edu/familyhostel) takes the whole family, including kids ages 8 to 15, on moderately priced domestic and international learning vacations. A team of academics guides lectures, fields trips, and sightseeing.

You can find good family-oriented vacation advice on the Internet from sites like the **Family Travel Forum** (www.familytravelforum.com), a comprehensive site that offers customized trip planning; **Family Travel Network** (www.familytravelnetwork.com), an award-winning site that offers travel features, deals, and tips; **Traveling Internationally with Your Kids** (www.travelwithyourkids.com), another site that offers customized trip planning; and **Family Travel Files** (www.thefamily travelfiles.com), which offers an online magazine and a directory of off-the-beaten-path tours and tour operators for families.

 Admission prices for attractions in London and throughout England are reduced for children 5 to 15 years old. Children under 5 almost always enter free. If you're traveling with one or two children ages 5 to 15, always check to see whether the attraction offers a money-saving family ticket, which considerably reduces the admission price for a group of two adults and two children.

Locating family-friendly accommodations and restaurants

Most hotels can happily accommodate your family if you reserve your rooms in advance and let the staff know that you're traveling with kids. The establishment may bring in an extra cot or let you share a larger room; these types of arrangements are common. Smaller bed-and-breakfasts (B&Bs) may present problems, such as cramped rooms and shared toilet facilities, and some places don't accept children at all. Ask questions before you reserve.

London and many of England's midsize cities have plenty of American-style fast-food places, including Burger King, McDonald's, Pizza Hut, and KFC. You don't find these chains in smaller villages and towns, however. If you need a family-friendly spot, consult the pages of this book. I point out plenty of places where you can take the kids.

 Expensive, high-toned restaurants in England aren't particularly welcoming to young children. The menus aren't geared to the tastes of American youngsters; the prices are high; and the staff can be less than accommodating.

 To keep costs down, rent a hotel room with a kitchen (in England, these rooms are called *self-catering units*), and prepare your own meals. Another option, when the weather cooperates, is to take the family on a picnic. London's **Kensington Gardens** (see Chapter 12) and the parks of **Windsor** and **Warwick castles** (check out Chapters 13 and 19, respectively) are great outdoor destinations. When in London, you can also take advantage of pretheater fixed-price menus (usually served 5:30–7 p.m.), which usually give you a good deal.

Younger teens traveling in London probably want to check out the **Hard Rock Cafe** (check out Chapter 11) or the scene at the **Trocadero** in **Piccadilly Circus** (see Chapter 11 for information on this neighborhood), which offers theme restaurants, such as **Planet Hollywood** and the **Rainforest Cafe.** For adventurous teens and younger children, London may be a good place to introduce them to Chinese or Indian cuisine.

Letting your younger children read *Peter Pan* or *Peter Pan in Kensington Gardens* and telling them about his statue there can generate excitement about the trip. Slightly older children may enjoy the *Harry Potter* series, which takes place in real and fictional settings in London and around the country. (If your kids have already read the series, they know that Harry shops in Diagon Alley in London before he goes off to school at Hogwarts.) Older children may enjoy the thought of traveling around London in the Underground (called the Tube) or taking a boat trip down the Thames. With the information in this book and some online investigating, you can also incite your kids' curiosity about historic sites, such as the **Tower of London** (see Chapter 12), **Stonehenge** (see Chapter 16), and **Warwick Castle** (see Chapter 19).

Hiring a baby-sitter in England

Maybe you really need a relaxing evening at the opera and a romantic late dinner. But you can't take Junior along on this special evening. What are your options? Ask your hotel staff if they can recommend a local baby-sitting service. Most of the hotels marked with a Kid Friendly icon in this book can help arrange baby-sitting. London also has several respected and trustworthy baby-sitting agencies that provide registered nurses and carefully screened mothers, as well as trained nannies, to watch children. One old and trustworthy baby-sitting service is **Universal Aunts** (☎ 020/7386-5900; www.universalaunts.co.uk), which charges £6.50 ($12) per daytime hour, £5 ($9.25) after 6 p.m. (four-hour minimum), plus a £3.50 ($6.50) agency fee.

Making Age Work for You: Tips for Seniors

England doesn't present any problems for you if you're a senior who gets around easily. If this is not the case for you, be aware when planning your trip that some hotels don't have elevators — particularly less expensive B&Bs. The steep staircases in some places are a test for *anyone* with luggage. When you reserve a hotel, ask whether you have access to an elevator (or *lift,* as Brits call it).

Being a senior may entitle you to some terrific travel bargains, such as lower prices for BritRail passes and reduced admission at theaters, museums, and other attractions. Always ask, even if the attraction doesn't have the reduction posted. Carrying ID with proof of age can pay off in all these situations. *Note:* You may find that some discounts, such as public transportation reductions in London, are available only to U.K. residents.

Members of **AARP** (formerly known as the American Association of Retired Persons), 601 E St. NW, Washington, DC 20049 (☎ **888-687-2277** or 202-434-2277; www.aarp.org), get discounts on hotels, airfares (including discounts of 12 to 25 percent on Virgin Atlantic flights to London from eight U.S. cities), and car rentals. AARP offers members a wide range of benefits, including *AARP: The Magazine* and a monthly newsletter. Anyone over 50 can join.

Many reliable agencies and organizations target the 50-plus market. **Elderhostel** (11 Ave. de Lafayette, Boston, MA 02110; ☎ **877/426-8056;** www.elderhostel.org) offers people 55 and over a variety of university-based education programs in London and throughout England. These courses are value-packed, hassle-free ways to travel. Travel packages include airfare, accommodations, meals, tuition, tips, and insurance. And you'll be glad to know that no grades are given. Tours focus on London's legal, music, and art scenes; the gardens of the Cotswolds, Kent, or the Lake District; literary sights in Wessex and Yorkshire; or a number of other topics and locations. **Grand Circle Travel** (347 Congress St., Boston, MA 02210; ☎ **800/597-3644;** www.gct.com) is another agency that escorts tours for mature travelers. Call for a copy of its publication *101 Tips for the Mature Traveler* or order a copy online.

Recommended publications offering travel resources and discounts for seniors include: the quarterly magazine *Travel 50 & Beyond* (www.travel50andbeyond.com); *Travel Unlimited: Uncommon Adventures for the Mature Traveler* (Avalon); *101 Tips for Mature Travelers,* available from Grand Circle Travel (☎ **800-221-2610** or 617-350-7500; www.gct.com); *The 50+ Traveler's Guidebook* (St. Martin's Press); and *Unbelievably Good Deals and Great Adventures That You Absolutely Can't Get Unless You're Over 50* (McGraw-Hill), by Joann Rattner Heilman.

Accessing England: Information for Travelers with Disabilities

Most disabilities shouldn't stop anyone from traveling. There are more options and resources out there than ever before. Most hotels and restaurants happily accommodate people with disabilities. London's top sights and many of the attractions in other towns and regions are wheelchair accessible. (Call first to make arrangements and get directions to special entrances and elevators.) Theaters and performing-arts venues are usually wheelchair accessible as well (again, call first).

Persons with disabilities often can get special discounts at sightseeing and entertainment venues in Britain. They call these discounts *concessions* (often shortened to *concs*).

Before departing on your trip, contact **VisitBritain** (see the Appendix for addresses and phone numbers) and request a copy of its *Disabled Traveler Fact Sheet,* which contains some helpful general information. *Access in London* ($15.95) is the best and most comprehensive London guide for people with disabilities and anyone with a mobility problem. The book provides full access information for all the major sites, hotels, and modes of transportation. You can order it at www.amazon.com.

The United Kingdom has several information resources for travelers with disabilities. The best of these resources include the following:

- **Artsline** (☎ 020/7388-2227; www.artsline.org.uk) provides advice on the accessibility of London arts and entertainment events. The **Society of London Theatres** (32 Rose St., London WC2E 9ET; www.officiallondontheatre.co.uk) also offers a free guide called *Access Guide to London's West End Theatres.*

- **Holiday Care Service** (Sunley House, 4 Bedford Park, Croyden, Surrey CR0 2AP; ☎ **0845/124-997** in the U.K. 020/8760-0072 outside the U.K.; www.holidaycare.org.uk) offers information and advice on suitable accommodations, transportation, and other facilities in England.

- **The National Trust** (☎ 020/7447-6742; www.nationaltrust. org.uk) is a British organization that owns and operates hundreds of historic properties (castles, gardens, and more) throughout England. The free booklet *Information for Visitors with Disabilities* provides details on accessibility at each site. Contact The National Trust Disability Office, 36 Queen Anne's Gate, London SW1H 9AS, to obtain a copy. Although not all National Trust sites are accessible, the organization provides powered four-wheeled vehicles free of charge at more than 50 properties; you can drive yourself or have a companion or volunteer drive for you.

- **RADAR** (Royal Association for Disability and Rehabilitation; 12 City Forum, 250 City Rd., London EC1 8AF; ☎ 020/7250-3222; www. radar.org.uk) publishes information for travelers with disabilities in Britain.

- **Tripscope, The Courtyard** (Evelyn Road, London W4 5JI; ☎ 08457/ 585-641 or 0117/939-7782; www.tripscope.org.uk) provides travel and transport information and advice, including airport facilities.

U.S.-based organizations that offer assistance to disabled travelers include **MossRehab** (www.mossresourcenet.org), which provides a library of accessible-travel resources online; **SATH (Society for Accessible Travel and Hospitality)** (☎ 212-447-7284; www.sath.org; annual membership fees: $45 adults, $30 seniors and students), which offers a wealth of travel resources for all types of disabilities and informed recommendations on destinations, access guides, travel agents, tour operators, vehicle rentals, and companion services; and the **American Foundation for the Blind** (AFB) (☎ 800-232-5463; www.afb.org), a referral resource for the blind or visually impaired that includes that includes information on traveling with Seeing Eye dogs.

For more information specifically targeted to travelers with disabilities, the community Web site **iCan** (www.icanonline.net/channels/travel/index.cfm) has destination guides and several regular columns on accessible travel. Also check out the quarterly magazine *Emerging*

Horizons ($15 per year, $20 outside the U.S.; www.emerginghorizons. com); **Twin Peaks Press** (☎ 360-694-2462), offering travel-related books for travelers with special needs; and Open World Magazine, published by SATH (subscription: $13 per year, $21 outside the U.S.).

Considering the benefits of escorted tours

Many travel agencies offer customized tours and itineraries for travelers with disabilities. **Accessible Journeys** (☎ 800/846-4537; www.disabilitytravel.com) offers tours of Britain and London in minibuses or motorcoaches. **The Guided Tour** (☎ 800/783-5841; e-mail: gtour400@aol.com) has one- and two-week guided tours for individuals, with one staff member for every three travelers. **Undiscovered Britain** (☎ 215/969-0542; www.undiscoveredbritain.com) provides specialty travel and tours for individuals, small groups, or families traveling with a wheelchair user.

Dealing with access issues

The United Kingdom doesn't yet have a law like the Americans with Disabilities Act. More and more businesses are becoming accessible, however, and access in general is easier than ever before.

Not all hotels and restaurants in Britain provide wheelchair ramps. Most of the less expensive B&Bs and older hotels don't have elevators, or they have elevators that are too small for a wheelchair. Ask about this issue when you reserve your room or table.

England's better-known museums and attractions are accessible, but in some cases, you have to use a different entrance. Call the attraction to find out about special entrances, ramps, elevator locations, and general directions.

Trains throughout the United Kingdom now have wide doors, grab rails, and provisions for wheelchairs. To get more information or to obtain a copy of the leaflet *Rail Travel for Disabled Passengers,* contact The Project Manager (Disability), British Rail, Euston House, Eversholt Street, London NW1 1DZ (☎ 020/7922-6984). You can also check out the Web site www.nationalrail.co.uk, which has a section on travel for people with disabilities and contact details for the various train operating companies.

Travelers with disabilities may want to keep the following in mind when traveling in London:

✔ Although London's streets and sidewalks are in good repair, you don't find as many modern curb cuts as in younger cities. (In other historic towns, such as Rye, you have to deal with cobblestones.)

✔ Not all the city's Underground ("Tube" or subway) stations have elevators and ramps.

✔ Most public buses aren't wheelchair accessible.

✔ You can fit a wheelchair in London's black cabs.

✔ Victoria Coach Station in Central London has Braille maps.

The following organizations provide access information and services for travelers with disabilities in London:

✔ **Transport for London** (☎ 020/7222-1234; www.tfl.co.uk) publishes a free brochure called *Tube Access*, available in Underground stations, and has information that you can download on its Web site. The organization also provides information on the wheelchair-accessible minibus service (called Stationlink) between all the major BritRail stations.

✔ **Wheelchair Travel** (1 Johnston Green, Guildford, Surrey GU2 6XS; ☎ 1483/233-640; fax: 01483/237-772; www.wheelchair-travel.co.uk) is an independent transport service for the traveler with disabilities arriving in London. The organization offers self-drive cars and minibuses (although I strongly discourage anyone, with a disability or not, from driving in London) and can provide wheelchairs. You can get a driver who acts as a guide if you ask.

Following the Rainbow: Resources for Gay and Lesbian Travelers

London has always been a popular destination for gays and lesbians, even in the days (up to 1967) when homosexuality was a criminal offense in Britain. Today, with a more tolerant government at the helm — and gay marriage an imminent possibility — gay pride is prominent. The government has actually *spent money* to promote gay tourism. Click the Gay Britain link on the VisitBritain Web site at www.visitbritain.com for information on gay venues and events throughout England.

In London, you can find gay theaters, gay shops, more than 100 gay pubs, famous gay discos, and gay community groups of all sorts. The gay-friendly resort town of Brighton is also known for its pub and club scene. Elsewhere in the country, at least in the larger cities, you can usually find a gay pub or two and clubs with at least one night a week for gays.

Old Compton Street in Soho is the heart of London's Gay Village. The area has dozens of gay pubs, restaurants, and upscale bars and cafes. The **Earl's Court area,** long a gay bastion, has a large gay population, gay pubs, and many gay-friendly restaurants.

Lesbigay events in London include the **London Lesbian and Gay Film Festival** in March, the **Pride Parade** and celebrations in June, and the big outdoor bash known as **Summer Rites** in August. You can obtain information and exact dates from **London's Lesbian and Gay Switchboard** (☎ **020/7837-7324;** www.llgs.org.uk).

Brighton (which you can read more about in Chapter 14) is one of the gayest seaside resort towns in Europe. From London, you can get there on the train in under an hour.

As you plan your trip, you may want to check out the following Web sites; all are specifically geared to gay and lesbian travelers to England:

- ✔ www.pinkpassport.com
- ✔ www.gayguide.co.uk
- ✔ www.gaybritain.co.uk
- ✔ www.timeout.com, the online edition of *Time Out* magazine, with a gay and lesbian section

Several gay magazines and publications, useful for their listings and news coverage, are available in London's gay pubs, clubs, bars, and cafes. The most popular are *Pink Paper* (www.pinkpaper.com) and *QX* (*Queer Xtra;* www.qxmagazine.com). *Gay Times* (www.gaytimes.co.uk), which covers all England, is a high-quality monthly news-oriented mag available at most news agents. *Gay and Lesbian Yellow Pages* (www.glyp.com) is good for its citywide listings, *Time Out* (www.timeout.com) appears at news agents on Wednesdays.

Gay's the Word (66 Marchmont St., WC1; ☎ **020/7278-7654;** www.gays theword.co.uk; Tube: Russell Square) is London's only all-around gay and lesbian bookstore. The store stocks a wonderful selection of new and used books and current periodicals.

Chapter 10

Taking Care of the Remaining Details

In This Chapter

▶ Obtaining a passport
▶ Insuring your trip in a number of ways
▶ Taking care of your health
▶ Communicating via cellphone and e-mail
▶ Breezing through airline security

*B*efore you depart for England to visit the British Museum in London or Shakespeare's birthplace in Stratford-upon-Avon, you need to take care of some final details. Do you have an up-to-date passport? Have you taken steps to meet your health needs while you're on your trip? Are you wondering how to use a cellphone or access e-mail while in England? This chapter gives you the information you need.

Getting a Passport

A valid passport is the only legal form of identification accepted around the world. You can't cross most international borders without it. Getting a passport is easy, but the process takes some time. For an up-to-date, country-by-country listing of passport requirements around the world, go to the Foreign Entry Requirement Web page of the U.S. State Department at http://travel.state.gov/foreignentryreqs.html.

Applying for a U.S. passport

If you're applying for a first-time passport, follow these steps:

1. Complete a **passport application** in person at a U.S. passport office; a federal, state, or probate court; or a major post office.

   To find your regional passport office, either check the **U.S. State Department** Web site, http://travel.state.gov/passport, or call the **National Passport Information Center** (☎ 877-487-2778) for automated information.

2. Present a **certified birth certificate** as proof of citizenship.

   You may also want to bring along your driver's license, state or military ID, or social security card.

3. Submit **two identical passport-size photos,** measuring 2x2 inches.

   You often find businesses that take these photos near a passport office. Note: You can't use a strip from a photo-vending machine because the pictures aren't identical.

4. Pay a **fee.**

   For people 16 and over, a passport is valid for 10 years and costs $85. For those travelers 15 and under, a passport is valid for 5 years and costs $70.

Allow plenty of time before your trip to apply for a passport; processing normally takes three weeks but can take longer during busy periods (especially spring).

If you have a passport in your current name that was issued within the past 15 years (and you were over age 16 when it was issued), you can renew the passport by mail for $55. Whether you're applying in person or by mail, you can download passport applications from the U.S. State Department Web site at http://travel.state.gov/passport_services.html. For general information, call the **National Passport Agency** (☎ 202-647-0518). To find your regional passport office, either check the U.S. State Department Web site or call the **National Passport Information Center's** toll-free number (☎ 877-487-2778) for automated information.

Applying for other passports

The following list offers information for citizens of Australia, Canada, and New Zealand:

- ✔ **Australians** can visit a local post office or passport office, call the **Australia Passport Information Service** (☎ 131-232 toll-free from Australia), or log on to www.passports.gov.au for details on how and where to apply.

- ✔ **Canadians** can pick up applications at passport offices throughout Canada, post offices, or from the central **Passport Office, Department of Foreign Affairs and International Trade,** Ottawa, ON K1A 0G3 (☎ 800-567-6868; www.ppt.gc.ca). Applications must be accompanied by two identical passport-size photographs and proof of Canadian citizenship. Processing takes five to ten days if you apply in person or about three weeks by mail.

- ✔ **New Zealanders** can pick up a passport application at any New Zealand Passports Office or download it from its Web site. Contact the **Passports Office** at ☎ 0800-225-050 in New Zealand or 04-74-8100, or log on to www.passports.govt.nz.

Entering England with your passport

If you're a citizen of the United States, Canada, Australia, or New Zealand, you must have a passport with at least two months remaining until its expiration to enter the United Kingdom. You need to show your passport at the customs and immigration area when you arrive at a U.K. airport. After your passport is stamped, you can remain in the United Kingdom as a tourist for up to three months. You don't need a visa if you're going to stay in England or the rest of the United Kingdom for less than three months.

Keep your passport with you at all times or at least keep it in a safe place. You need to show it only when you're converting traveler's checks or foreign currency at a bank or currency exchange. If you're not going to need your passport for currency exchanges, ask whether the hotel has a safe where you can keep it locked up.

Dealing with a (gulp) lost passport

Don't worry; you won't be sent to the Tower of London if you lose your passport in England, but you need to take steps to replace it *immediately*. First, notify the police. Then go to your consulate or high commission office (you can find them all in London). Bring all available forms of identification, and the staff can get started on generating your new passport. For the addresses of consulates and high commissions, see the Appendix. Always call first to verify open hours.

Playing It Safe with Travel and Medical Insurance

Three kinds of travel insurance are available: trip-cancelation insurance, medical insurance, and lost luggage insurance. The cost of travel insurance varies widely, depending on the cost and length of your trip, your age and health, and the type of trip you're taking, but expect to pay between 5 and 8 percent of the vacation itself. Here is my advice on all three:

- ✔ **Trip-cancellation insurance:** Helps you get your money back if you have to back out of a trip, if you have to go home early, or if your travel supplier goes bankrupt. Allowed reasons for cancellation can range from sickness to natural disasters to the U.S. State Department's declaring your destination unsafe for travel. (Insurers usually don't cover vague fears, though, as many travelers discovered who tried to cancel their trips in October 2001 because they were wary of flying.)

  Travel Guard International publishes **Travel Guard Alerts,** a list of companies it considers high risk (www.travelinsured.com). Protect yourself further by paying for the insurance with a credit card — by law, consumers can get their money back on goods and services that they don't receive if they report the loss within 60 days after the charge appears on their credit card statement.

✔ **Medical insurance:** For travel overseas, most health plans (including Medicare and Medicaid) don't provide coverage, and the ones that do often require you to pay for services upfront and reimburse you only after you return home. Even if your plan does cover overseas treatment, most out-of-country hospitals, including those in England, make you pay your bills upfront and send you a refund only after you've returned home and filed the necessary paperwork with your insurance company. As a safety net, you may want to buy travel medical insurance. If you want to get yourself additional medical insurance, try **MEDEX Assistance** (☎ **410/453-6300**; www. medexassist.com) or **Travel Assistance International** (☎ **800/ 821-2828**; www.travelassistance.com; for general information on services, call the company's Worldwide Assistance Services, Inc., at ☎ **800-777-8710**).

✔ **Lost luggage insurance:** Most travelers don't need this insurance. On domestic flights, checked baggage is covered up to $2,500 per ticketed passenger. On international flights (including U.S. portions of international trips), baggage coverage is limited to approximately $9.05 per pound, up to approximately $635 per checked bag. If you plan to check items more valuable than the standard liability, see if your homeowner's policy covers your valuables, get baggage insurance as part of your comprehensive travel-insurance package, or buy Travel Guard's BagTrak product. Don't buy insurance at the airport, as it's usually overpriced. Be sure to take any valuables or irreplaceable items with you in your carry-on luggage, as many valuables (including books, money and electronics) aren't covered by airline policies.

If the airline loses your luggage, immediately file a lost-luggage claim at the airport, detailing the luggage contents. For most airlines, you must report delayed, damaged, or lost baggage within four hours of arrival. The airlines are required to deliver luggage, once found, directly to your house or destination free of charge.

For more information, contact one of the following recommended insurers: **Access America** (☎ 866/807-3982; www.accessamerica. com), **Travel Guard International** (☎ 800/826-4919; www.travel guard.com), **Travel Insured International** (☎ 800/243-3174; www. travelinsured.com), and **Travelex Insurance Services** (☎ 888/ 457-4602; www.travelex-insurance.com).

Staying Healthy When You Travel

Getting sick can ruin your vacation, so I strongly advise against it (of course, last time I checked, the bugs don't listen to me any more than they probably listen to you).

Avoiding "economy-class syndrome"

Deep vein thrombosis or, as it's known in the world of flying, "economy-class syndrome," is a blood clot that develops in a deep vein. You can develop this potentially deadly condition by sitting in cramped conditions — such as an airplane cabin — for too long. During a flight (especially a long-haul flight), get up, walk around, and stretch your legs every 60 to 90 minutes to keep your blood flowing. Other preventive measures include frequently flexing your legs while sitting, drinking a lot of water, and avoiding alcohol and sleeping pills. If you have a history of deep vein thrombosis, heart disease, or another condition that puts you at high risk, some experts recommend wearing compression stockings or taking anticoagulants when you fly; always ask your physician about the best course for you. Symptoms of deep vein thrombosis include leg pain or swelling, or even shortness of breath.

For domestic trips, most reliable health-care plans provide coverage if you get sick away from home. For travel abroad, you may have to pay all medical costs upfront and be reimbursed later. For information on purchasing additional medical insurance for your trip, see the preceding section.

Talk to your doctor before leaving on a trip if you have a serious and/or chronic illness. For conditions such as epilepsy, diabetes, or heart problems, wear a **MedicAlert identification tag** (☎ **888/633-4298;** www.medicalert.org), which immediately alerts doctors to your condition and gives them access to your records through Medic Alert's 24-hour hotline. Contact the **International Association for Medical Assistance to Travelers (IAMAT)** (☎ **716/754-4883,** or 416/652-0137 in Canada; www.iamat.org) for tips on travel and health concerns in the countries you plan to visit.

Staying Connected by Cellphone

For some (and I'm one of them), a vacation means a vacation from the telephone and e-mail. But other travelers want or need to stay connected to home, family, or office wherever they go. You can stay connected in England, and quite easily. But there are few things you need to know about using a cellphone or laptop while there.

GSM (Global System for Mobiles), the three letters that define much of the world's **wireless capabilities,** describe a big, seamless network that makes for easy cross-border cellphone use throughout Europe and dozens of other countries worldwide. In the U.S., T-Mobile, AT&T Wireless, and Cingular use this quasiuniversal system; in Canada, Microcell and some Rogers customers are GSM; and all Europeans and most Australians use GSM.

If your cellphone is on a GSM system, and you have a world-capable multiband phone, such as many Sony Ericsson, Motorola, or Samsung models, you can make and receive calls across civilized areas on much of the globe, from Andorra to Uganda. Just call your wireless operator, and ask it to activate "international roaming" on your account. Unfortunately, per-minute charges can be high — usually $1 to $1.50 in England and Western Europe.

So you may want to buy an "unlocked" world phone from the get-go. Many cellphone operators sell "locked" phones that restrict you from using any other removable computer-memory phone-chip card (called a *SIM card*) other than the ones that they supply. Having an unlocked phone lets you install a cheap, prepaid SIM card (which you can find at a local retailer) in your destination country. (Show your phone to the salesperson; not all phones work on all networks.) You get a local phone number — and much, much lower calling rates. Getting an already locked phone unlocked can be a complicated process, but you can do it if you really want; just call your cellular operator, and say that you plan to go abroad for several months and want to use the phone with a local provider.

You may decide that **renting** a phone makes the most sense. Although you can rent a phone from any number of overseas sites, including kiosks at airports and at car-rental agencies, I suggest renting the phone before you leave home. That way, you can give loved ones and business associates your new number, make sure the phone works, and take the phone wherever you go — especially helpful for overseas trips through several countries, where local phone-rental agencies often bill in local currency and may not let you take the phone to another country.

Phone rental isn't cheap. It usually costs $40 to $50 per week, plus air-time fees of at least a dollar a minute. If you're traveling to England, though, local rental companies often offer free incoming calls within their home country, which can save you big bucks. The bottom line: Shop around.

Rent-a-Phone (☎ 800/400-7221 in the U.S. or 0800/317-540 in the U.K.) is an international cellphone rental company with offices in the U.S. and U.K.; per-minute charges from England are generally about $1.99 per minute to the U.S. and Europe, and you can have the phones delivered to your door in the U.S. before you leave. In Terminals 1 and 2 at Heathrow Airport, you can buy a range of mobile phones and services, including SIM cards, at **Primus** (☎ 020/8607-5960).

Two good wireless rental companies are **InTouch USA** (☎ 800/872-7626; www.intouchglobal.com) and **RoadPost** (☎ 888/290-1606 or 905/272-5665; www.roadpost.com). Give them your itinerary, and they can tell you what wireless products you need. InTouch can also, for free, advise you on whether your existing phone can work overseas; simply call ☎ 703/222-7161 between 9 a.m. and 4 p.m. EST, or go to http://intouchglobal.com/travel.htm.

Accessing the Internet Away From Home

Travelers can use any number of ways to check their e-mail and access the Internet on the road. Of course, using your own laptop — or even a PDA (personal digital assistant) or electronic organizer with a modem — gives you the most flexibility. But even if you don't have a computer, you can still access your e-mail and even your office computer from cybercafes.

Nowadays, you may have a hard time finding a city in England that *doesn't* have a few cybercafes, though you probably won't find any cyber-cafes in smaller towns and villages. Although there's no definitive directory for cybercafes — these are independent businesses, after all — you can start looking at www.cybercaptive.com and www.cybercafe.com.

Aside from formal cybercafes, most **youth hostels** nowadays have at least one computer you can use to get to the Internet. And most **public libraries** across the world offer Internet access free or for a small charge. If you want to save money, avoid **hotel business centers** unless you can use the service for free.

Most major airports now have **Internet kiosks** scattered throughout their gates. These kiosks, which you also see in shopping malls, hotel lobbies, and tourist information offices around the world, give you basic Web access for a per-minute fee that's usually higher than cybercafe prices. The kiosks' clunkiness and high prices mean you want to avoid them whenever possible.

To retrieve your e-mail, ask your **Internet Service Provider (ISP)** if it has a Web-based interface tied to your existing e-mail account. If your ISP doesn't have such an interface, you can use the free **mail2web** service (www.mail2web.com) to view and reply to your home e-mail. For more flexibility, you may want to open a free, Web-based e-mail account with **Yahoo! Mail** (http://mail.yahoo.com). (Microsoft's Hotmail is another popular option, but Hotmail has severe spam problems.) Your home ISP may be able to forward your e-mail to the Web-based account automatically.

If you need to access files on your office computer, look into a service called **GoToMyPC** (www.gotomypc.com). The service provides a Web-based interface for you to access and manipulate a distant PC from any-where — even a cybercafe — as long as your "target" PC is running and has an always-on connection to the Internet (such as with Road Runner cable). The service offers top-quality security, but if you're worried about hackers, use your own laptop rather than a cybercafe computer to access the GoToMyPC system.

Surfing at Internet cafes in London

The handy www.netcafeguide.com has a pretty good London listing, including the **easyInternetcafé** chain. You can find 18 of these giant Internet cafes in the capital — but *cafe* is really a misnomer because the hundreds of screens in the largest locations make them look like telemarketing sweatshops, and you don't hear any conversation, just the clicking of keyboards. The charging system is radical because surfers buy credit, not minutes. The minimum spend is £2 ($3.70), and the amount of time you get for those couple of pounds is in inverse proportion to how busy the branch is. The cafe adjusts the rate every five minutes and posts the new rate on video screens, a bit like a stock exchange. Your ticket has a user ID, which notes the current rate when you first log on. That becomes your rate. You never pay more during your visit, but if things quiet down, your credit can buy you more time — a pound can buy you up to six hours, or so they claim. easyInternetcafés hours vary, so check www.easyeverything.com for hours as well as new branches to add to this list: 358 Oxford St., W1 (Tube: Bond Street); 9–16 Tottenham Court Rd., W1 (Tube: Tottenham Court Road); 160–166 Kensington High St. (Tube: Kensington High Street); 456–459 Strand, WC2 (Tube: Charing Cross); and 9–13 Wilton Rd., SW1 (Tube: Victoria). As befitting a large chain, the telephone number for all locations is ☎ 020/7241-9000.

If you bring your own computer with you, the buzzword in Internet access to familiarize yourself with is **wi-fi** (wireless fidelity), and more and more hotels, cafes, and retailers are signing on as wireless "hotspots" from which you can get a high-speed connection without cable wires, networking hardware, or a phone line. You can get a wi-fi connection in one of several ways. Many laptops sold in the last year have built-in wi-fi capability (an 802.11b wireless Ethernet connection). Mac owners have their own networking technology, Apple AirPort. If you have an older computer, you can plug an 802.11b/**wi-fi card** (which costs around $50) into your laptop. You sign up for wireless access service like you do cellphone service, through a plan offered by one of several commercial companies that have made wireless service available in airports, hotel lobbies, and coffee shops, primarily in the U.S. (followed by the U.K. and Japan). **T-Mobile Hotspot** (www.t-mobile.com/hotspot) serves up wireless connections at Starbucks coffee shops throughout England. **Boingo** (www.boingo.com) and **Wayport** (www.wayport.com) have set up networks in airports and high-class hotel lobbies. iPass providers also give you access to a few hundred wireless hotel lobby setups. Best of all, you don't need to be staying at the Four Seasons to use the hotel's network; just set yourself up on a nice couch in the lobby. The companies' pricing policies can be byzantine, with a variety of monthly, per-connection, and per-minute plans, but in general you pay around $30 a month for limited access — and as more and more companies jump on the wireless bandwagon, prices are likely to get even more competitive.

There are also places that provide **free wireless networks** in cities around the world. To locate these free hotspots, go to www.personal telco.net/index.cgi/WirelessCommunities.

If wi-fi is not available at your destination, most business-class hotels throughout England and the rest of the U.K. offer dataports for laptop modems, and many offer free high-speed Internet access via an Ethernet network cable. You can bring your own cables, but most hotels rent them for around $10. **Call your hotel in advance** to see what your options are.

In addition, major ISPs have **local access numbers** around the world, letting you go online by simply placing a local call. Check your ISP's Web site, or call its toll-free number to ask how you can use your current account away from home and how much it can cost. If you're traveling outside the reach of your ISP, the **iPass** network has dial-up numbers in most of the world's countries. You have to sign up with an iPass provider, which then tells you how to set up your computer for your destination(s). For a list of iPass providers, go to www.ipass.com. One solid provider is **i2roam** (☎ **866/811-6209** or 920/235-0475; www.i2roam.com).

Wherever you go, bring a **connection kit** of the right power and phone adapters, a spare phone cord, and a spare Ethernet network cable — or find out whether your hotel supplies them to guests.

North American current runs 110V, 60 cycles; the standard voltage throughout Britain is 240V AC, 50 cycles. You need a current converter or transformer to bring the voltage down and the cycles up. Two pronged North American plugs don't fit into the three-pronged square British wall sockets, so you also need a three-pronged square adapter and converter if you use North American laptops or appliances while in England. You can find plug adapters and converters at most travel, luggage, electronics, and hardware stores. Some plug adapters are also current converters. Most contemporary laptop computers automatically sense the current and adapt accordingly.

Keeping Up with Airline Security

With the federalization of airport security, security procedures at U.S. airports are more stable and consistent than ever. Generally, you'll be fine if you arrive at the airport **one hour** before a domestic flight and **two hours** before an international flight; if you show up late, tell an airline employee, and she can probably whisk you to the front of the line.

Bring a **current, government-issued photo ID,** such as a driver's license or passport. Keep your ID at the ready to show at check-in, the security checkpoint, and sometimes even the gate. (Children under 18 don't need government-issued photo IDs for domestic flights, but they do for international flights.)

In 2003, the Transportation Security Administration (TSA) phased out **gate check-in** at all U.S. airports. And **e-tickets** have made paper tickets nearly obsolete. Passengers with e-tickets can beat the ticket-counter lines by using airport **electronic kiosks** or even **online check-in** from your home computer. Online check-in involves logging on to your airline's Web site, accessing your reservation, and printing out your boarding pass — and the airline may even offer you bonus miles to do so! If you're using a kiosk at the airport, bring the credit card you used to book the ticket or your frequent-flier card. Print out your boarding pass from the kiosk, and simply proceed to the security checkpoint with your pass and a photo ID. If you're checking bags or looking to snag an exit-row seat, you can do so using most airline kiosks. Even the smaller airlines are employing the kiosk system, but always call your airline to make sure these alternatives. **Curbside check-in** is also a good way to avoid lines, although a few airlines still ban curbside check-in; call before you go.

Security checkpoint lines are getting shorter than they were during 2001 and 2002, but some doozies remain. If you have trouble standing for long periods of time, tell an airline employee; the airline will provides you with a wheelchair. Speed up security by **not wearing metal objects,** such as big belt buckles. If you have metallic body parts, a note from your doctor can prevent a long chat with the security screeners. Keep in mind that only **ticketed passengers** are allowed past security, except for folks escorting disabled passengers or children.

Federalization has stabilized **what you can carry on** and what you can't. The general rule is that sharp things are out, nail clippers are okay, and food and beverages must be passed through the X-ray machine — but that security screeners can't make you drink from your coffee cup. Bring food in your carry-on rather than checking it, as explosive-detection machines used on checked luggage have been known to mistake food (especially chocolate, for some reason) for bombs. Travelers in the U.S. are allowed one carry-on bag, plus a "personal item" such as a purse, briefcase, or laptop bag. Carry-on hoarders can stuff all sorts of things into a laptop bag; as long as it has a laptop in it, it's still considered a personal item. The TSA has issued a list of restricted items; check its Web site (www.tsa.gov/public/index.jsp) for details.

Airport screeners may decide that they need to search your checked luggage by hand. You can now purchase luggage locks that allow screeners to open and relock a checked bag if they need to hand-search it. Look for Travel Sentry–certified locks at luggage or travel shops and at Brookstone stores (you can buy them online at www.brookstone.com). These locks, approved by the TSA, can be opened by luggage inspectors with a special code or key. For more information on the locks, visit www.travelsentry.org. If you use something other than TSA-approved locks, your lock will be cut off your suitcase if a TSA agent needs to hand-search your luggage.

Part III
London and Environs

The 5th Wave   By Rich Tennant

In this part . . .

For many travelers, a trip to England begins and ends in London. That's why I devote an entire part of this guide to the United Kingdom's capital. Chances are you'll fly into one of London's airports and use the city as your major transportation and cultural hub. London is one of the world's major tourist magnets. After you start exploring, you understand just why so many people love this city.

In Chapter 11, I help you settle into this exciting metropolis. I explain how to get into the city from the airport, and then I describe Central London's neighborhoods and tell you about the transportation options available. Next, I list my recommended hotels and give advice for finding a room if you arrive without a reservation. And finally, I give you a list of restaurants in all price ranges that feature different kinds of cuisine.

Chapter 12 helps you explore London in your own way and at your own pace. I describe the top attractions — those places you absolutely don't want to miss — and a host of other intriguing sights that may interest you. I explain options for touring by bus, boat, or foot. Next, I delve into London's truly mind-boggling shopping scene and its array of theater and nightlife possibilities.

Chapter 13 introduces you to several great side trips from London — places you can easily visit in a day, returning in time for dinner and a show. You'll find all you need for enjoyable day trips to Cambridge, Oxford, Hampton Court Palace, Blenheim Palace, the Royal Botanic Gardens at Kew (Kew Gardens), and Windsor Castle.

Chapter 11

Settling into London

In This Chapter

▶ Arriving in London
▶ Getting from the airport into the city
▶ Orienting yourself to the neighborhoods
▶ Traveling by Underground, bus, and taxi
▶ Choosing your hotel
▶ Picking a good restaurant
▶ Enjoying a scrumptious tea

As the oft-quoted Dr. Samuel Johnson observed more than 200 years ago, "When a man is tired of London, he is tired of life." Year-round, millions from all corners of the globe visit the U.K. capital. London is famed for its venerable monuments, splendid museums, royal palaces, magnificent parks, literary associations, exciting nightlife, and super shopping. For many visitors, a trip to England begins and ends in London.

This city may be old and full of quaint corners and age-old traditions, but London isn't a stodgy place. Trend-setting London is to the United Kingdom what New York City is to the United States: the spot where everything happens first (or ultimately ends up). This ancient metropolis is now as high-tech as a hyperlink, with mobile phones, cybercafes, and e-communications part of everyday life. In this city, you can see the traditional and the cutting edge on the same street corner. An enormous city with more than 7 million inhabitants, London harbors a diversity of sights, sounds, and experiences that make it as fascinating today as it was for Dr. Johnson.

Getting There

As the capital and largest city in the United Kingdom, London doesn't lack transportation options. The city acts as a huge international hub, which makes travel to London from overseas and the Continent easy.

Flying to London

London has five airports, but chances are you'll fly into Heathrow or Gatwick, which handle the bulk of London's international flights. The airports manage tens of thousands of visitors per day and are geared to moving people efficiently from point A to point B.

Arriving at Heathrow

About 24km (15 miles) west of Central London, **Heathrow** (☎ 0870/ 000-0123;** www.baa.co.uk) is the largest of London's airports, with four passenger terminals serving flights from around the globe. The corridors are surrealistically long, but moving walkways make your trek easier. And everything is signposted, so you won't get lost.

Your first stop after deplaning is **Passport Control and Customs,** which involves a fairly routine procedure. On the plane, you receive a landing card to fill out. You must provide your name, your address, your passport number, and the address where you're staying in the United Kingdom. Present this completed form and your passport to the passport official. After the official stamps your passport, you pick up your luggage. From there, you wend your way out through the Customs Hall.

After clearing Customs, you enter the terminal's main concourse. All sorts of services are available, including ATMs, hotel-booking agencies, theater-booking services, banks, and *bureaux de change* (currency exchange) windows, where you can swap your dollars or traveler's checks for pounds and pence. (See Chapter 5 for information about changing money.) If you want to pick up a free map and general info, go to the London Tourist Board's **Tourist Information Centre** in the Underground station for Terminals 1, 2, and 3 (open daily 8 a.m.–6 p.m.).

You have several options for getting into the city from Heathrow. You can travel by train, bus, or shuttle:

✔ **The London Underground** (☎ 020/722-1234): This subway system, called the Underground or the Tube, provides the cheapest mode of public transportation to Central London destinations. All terminals at Heathrow link up with the Tube system. Follow the Underground signs to the ticket booth. The **Piccadilly Line** gets you into Central London in about 45 minutes for a fare of £3.80 ($7.05). Underground trains run from all four Heathrow terminals every five to nine minutes Monday to Saturday 5:30 a.m. to 11:30 p.m. and Sunday 6 a.m. to 11 p.m. *Note:* Because of construction on a new Terminal 5, you can't get Underground service from Terminal 4 until late 2006. Buses take passengers from Terminal 4 to nearby Hatton Cross Tube station.

The one potential hassle with the Underground is that the trains don't have luggage racks. You have to stash your bags as best you can — behind your legs, on your lap, or to one side of the center doors where the cars have more space. To reach your hotel on the Underground, you may have to change trains or take a taxi from the Underground station closest to your destination.

Be sure to keep your luggage with you at all times; security has been stepped up since the Underground bombings of July 2005, and any bags or packages that you leave unattended, even for a couple of minutes, may be confiscated.

If the Underground is closed when you arrive, the **N97 night bus** connects Heathrow with Central London. Buses (located in front of the terminals) run every 30 minutes Monday to Saturday from midnight to 5 a.m. and Sunday from 11 p.m. to 5:30 a.m. The trip takes about an hour; the one-way fare costs is £1.20 ($2.20).

✔ **National** Express buses (☎ **0870/575747;** www.gobycoach.com): These buses may be a better alternative to the Underground if you're loaded down with heavy luggage because there's more room to store your bags. Two buses — the Express bus and the A2 Airbus — provide service from the airport to Central London. The Express bus goes from Heathrow to Victoria Station, making stops at Cromwell Road, Knightsbridge, and Hyde Park Corner. The A2 Airbus goes to King's Cross Station, stopping at Bayswater, Marble Arch, Euston, and Russell Square. Travel time for both is about 75 minutes, and the fare is £8 ($15), payable on the bus. Up to three buses an hour depart daily between 4 a.m. and 11:23 p.m. from the front of Heathrow's terminals.

✔ **The Heathrow Express train** (☎ **0845/600-1515;** www.heathrow express.co.uk): The fastest way into London, this train runs from all four Heathrow terminals to Paddington Station in just 15 minutes. The trains have air-conditioning, ergonomically designed seating, and plenty of luggage space. The standard-class fare is £14 ($26) one-way. You can buy tickets at the airport or, for a small extra charge, on the train. Service runs every 15 minutes Monday to Saturday 5:07 a.m. to 11:32 p.m. and Sunday 5:03 a.m. to midnight. All the major airlines have check-in counters right at Paddington, so when you return from London to the airport, you can conveniently check your luggage before boarding the train; when you arrive at Heathrow, you can go directly to your departure gate without further check-in.

✔ **Taxis:** You may find taking a taxi from Heathrow into Central London cost effective if you're traveling in a group of two or three people. You can order a taxi at the Taxi Information booths in Terminal 3 (☎ **020/8745-4655**) or Terminal 4 (☎ **020/8745-7302**). Expect to pay about £45 ($83), plus a 10 percent tip, for a trip of about 45 minutes. Taxis are available 24 hours a day.

Arriving at Gatwick

Gatwick (☎ **0870/0002-468;** www.baa.co.uk), located about 45km (28 miles) south of Central London, is considerably smaller than Heathrow. International flights arrive at the South terminal. Gatwick provides the same services Heathrow does, except that the London Tourist Board doesn't have an office there.

The highway system from Gatwick into London is far less efficient than from Heathrow, so buses, minivans, or cabs can end up taking two to three hours if traffic is in a snarl.

You find fewer transportation options for getting into Central London:

✔ **Gatwick Express train** (☎ 0845/850-1530; www.gatwickexpress. co.uk): Right in the South terminal, this is your best bet for getting into central London. The handy train serves airport passengers only and offers plenty of room for luggage and a flight check-in option at Victoria Station (convenient when you're returning to the airport from London). The train whizzes you from the airport to Victoria Station in half an hour for £12 ($22). Trains run daily every 15 minutes from 5:20 a.m. to midnight and hourly (1:30, 2:35, 3:35, and 4:35 a.m.) throughout the night. *Note:* Officials have been talking about cutting back on this service, so you may not have access to as many trains in 2006.

✔ **South Eastern train** (☎ 0845/748-49-50): A local train, the South Eastern runs to Victoria Station in half an hour and costs £8.20 ($15). Older than the Gatwick Express, these trains are regular passenger trains. Four trains run an hour during the day; they run every half-hour from midnight to 5 a.m.

✔ **Hotelink** (☎ 01293/552-251; www.hotelink.co.uk): A minibus service that charges £20 ($37) to take you directly to your hotel. Minibuses are available at the terminal on the half-hour in the summer or on the hour in winter.

✔ **Checker Cars:** Taxis provide 24-hour service between Gatwick and Central London. You find cars outside the terminals, or you can order a taxi from the South terminal (☎ 01293/502-808) or the North terminal (☎ 01293/569-790). Fares cost £65 ($120), plus tip, for the 90-minute journey.

Arriving at another London airport

If you fly from North America, you'll arrive at Heathrow or Gatwick. European travelers have three other airport options in London:

✔ About 53km (33 miles) northeast of Central London, **Stansted** (☎ 08700/000-303) is a single-terminal airport used for national and European flights. The **Stansted Express** (☎ 0845/600-1245; www.stanstedexpress.com) to Liverpool Street Station takes 45 minutes and costs £14.50 ($27). Trains run every half-hour daily 6 a.m. to 11:59 p.m. A taxi fare into the city averages about £60 ($111) plus tip.

✔ **London City Airport** (☎ 0207/646-000): A mere 9.5km (6 miles) from the city center, this airport services European destinations only. A **blue shuttle bus** (☎ 020/7646-0088) takes passengers from the airport to Liverpool Street Station in 25 minutes for £6 ($11).

The buses run every ten minutes daily 6 a.m. to 9:30 p.m. A taxi to the vicinity of Marble Arch costs about £25 ($46), plus tip.

✔ **Luton** (☎ **01582/405-100**): This small independent airport 53km (33 miles) northwest of the city services European charter flights. The **Greenline 757 Bus** (☎ **0870/608-7261**) runs from the airport to the Victoria Coach Station on Buckingham Palace Road daily every hour from 5:30 a.m. to midnight; the trip takes about 75 minutes and costs £8 ($15). The 24-hour **Railair Coach Link** also runs to Luton Station (5km/3 miles away), where it connects with the Thameslink City Flyer train to King's Cross Station in Central London. The fare is £10 ($19); trip time is one hour. Taxis into the city cost about £50 ($93), plus tip.

Taking the train

If you travel to London by train from the Continent, you'll probably get off the train near the English Channel and take a ferry or hovercraft (a high-speed ferry) across the water (see Chapter 6 for more information on crossing the Channel). You disembark at one of the United Kingdom's Channel ports. The ports closest to London are Dover, Ramsgate, and Folkestone to the east, and Southhampton, Portsmouth, and Newhaven to the south. From whichever port you end up at, you take another train into London. Trains connecting with ferries on the U.K. side of the Channel generally go to Liverpool Street Station, Victoria Station, or Waterloo International. Also, the Eurostar Chunnel trains arrive from Paris and Brussels at Waterloo. (The *Chunnel* is the tunnel beneath the English Channel.) On the superconvenient Eurostar, you don't have to make any train–boat–train transfers along the way.

London's train stations are bustling beehives of activity. In them, you find restaurants, bookstores, news agents, *bureaux de change,* and many of the services you find at an airport. A **tourist information center** is located in **Waterloo International Terminal Arrivals Hall** (☎ **020/ 7234-5800;** open daily 8:30 a.m.–10:30 p.m.).

London's train stations link to the Underground system. Just look for the Underground symbol (a circle with a horizontal line through it). Waterloo links to the Northern and Bakerloo lines; Victoria connects with the District, Circle, and Victoria lines; Liverpool Street links to the Circle, East London, Metropolitan, and Central lines. (See "Getting Around London," later in this chapter, for more information about the Underground.) Taxi ranks wait outside all the train stations.

Orienting Yourself in London

From its beginnings as a Roman garrison town called Londinium nearly 2,000 years ago, London has grown steadily and in a somewhat pell-mell fashion, swallowing up what were once small villages. Today, Greater London encompasses a whopping 1,611 sq. km (622 square miles), an area larger than some of England's national parks. The main tourist portion of London covers only a fraction of that (65 sq. km/25 sq. miles at the most).

 London's size, along with its confusing and sometimes oddly named streets and its seemingly endless plethora of neighborhoods, confounds many visitors — and Londoners as well. To help you find your way around, I strongly suggest that you buy a copy of *London A to Z* (*z* is pronounced "zed"). You can pick up this indexed street map at the airport, at just about any bookstore, or from any news agent.

Introducing the Neighborhoods

London grew up along the north and south banks of the **River Thames,** which snakes through the city in a long, loose *S* curve. This great tidal river has played a major role in London's growth and prosperity through the ages. London's major tourist sights, hotels, and restaurants are on the river's **north bank,** while many of the city's famous performing arts venues sit on the **south bank.**

Central London, on the north bank of the Thames, is considered the city center. Londoners think of this district as roughly the area covered by the Circle Line Underground route, with Paddington Station anchoring the northwest corner, Earl's Court at the southwest corner, Tower Hill at the southeast corner, and Liverpool Street Station at the northeast corner. Central London is divided into three areas: **The City of London,** the **West End,** and **West London.**

All London street addresses include a designation, such as SW1 or EC3. These codes represent **postal districts,** like ZIP codes in the United States. When you actually hit the streets, the postal district designations don't matter as much as the nearest Tube stop.

For the locations of the districts in the following sections, see the "London's Neighborhoods" map on p. 122.

The City of London

The City of London is a self-governing entity extending south from Chiswell Street to the Thames. The area is bounded to the west by Chancery Lane and to the east by the Tower of London, its most important historic monument. Fleet Street, the former heart of newspaper publishing, cuts through the center of the district to Ludgate Circus, where it becomes Ludgate and leads to St. Paul's Cathedral. Built on top of the original 1 square mile the Romans called Londinium is an area called The City. Today, this area is the Wall Street of England, home to the Bank of England, the Royal Exchange, and the Stock Exchange. The major Tube stops are Blackfriars, Tower Hill, St. Paul's, Liverpool Street Station (the main rail terminus in this area), Bank, Barbican, and Moorgate.

West End

The West End (that is, west of The City) may be loosely called "downtown" London. For most people, the West End is synonymous with the theater, entertainment, and shopping areas around Piccadilly Circus and Leicester Square. But the West End actually includes a host of neighborhoods:

- ✔ **Holborn:** Abutting the City of London to the west, you find the old borough of Holborn, the legal heart of London. Barristers, solicitors, and law clerks scurry to and fro among the Inns of Court, Lincoln's Inn Fields, Royal Courts of Justice, and Old Bailey. This in-between district is bounded roughly by Theobald's Road to the north; Farringdon Road to the east; the Thames to the south; and Kingsway, Aldwych, and Lancaster Place to the west. The major Tube stops are Holborn, Temple, and Blackfriars.

- ✔ **The Strand and Covent Garden:** The northern section of The Strand, the area west of Holborn, is Covent Garden, with Shaftesbury Avenue as its northern boundary. The Strand, a major street running from Trafalgar Square to Fleet Street, is the principal thoroughfare along the southern edge, with Charing Cross Road to the west and Kingsway, Aldwych, and Lancaster Place to the east. The major Tube stops are Covent Garden, Leicester Square, and Charing Cross.

- ✔ **Bloomsbury:** Just north of Covent Garden, New Oxford Street and Bloomsbury Way mark the beginnings of the Bloomsbury district. Home of the British Museum and several colleges and universities, this intellectual pocket of Central London is bounded to the east by Woburn Place and Southampton Row, to the north by Euston Road, and to the west by Tottenham Court Road. The major Tube stops are Euston Square, Russell Square, Goodge Street, and Tottenham Court Road.

- ✔ **Soho:** The Soho neighborhood occupies the warren of densely packed streets north of Shaftesbury Avenue, west of Charing Cross Road, east of Regent Street, and south of Oxford Street. This lively area is full of restaurants and nightclubs. London's Gay Village centers on Old Compton Street. The major Tube stops are Leicester Square, Covent Garden, and Tottenham Court Road.

- ✔ **Piccadilly Circus, Leicester Square, and Charing Cross:** Think of this area, just west of The Strand, as downtown London or Theatreland. Piccadilly Circus, the area's major traffic hub and best-known tourist destination, feeds into Regent Street and Piccadilly. Leicester Square and Shaftesbury Avenue, a few minutes' walk to the east, house most of the West End theaters. From Leicester Square, Charing Cross Road runs south to Trafalgar Square, the National Gallery, and Charing Cross Station. The Tube stops are Piccadilly Circus, Leicester Square, and Charing Cross.

- ✔ **Mayfair:** Elegant and exclusive Mayfair nestles comfortably between Regent Street on the west, Oxford Street on the north, Piccadilly on the south, and Hyde Park on the west. This area is the land of luxury

London's Neighborhoods

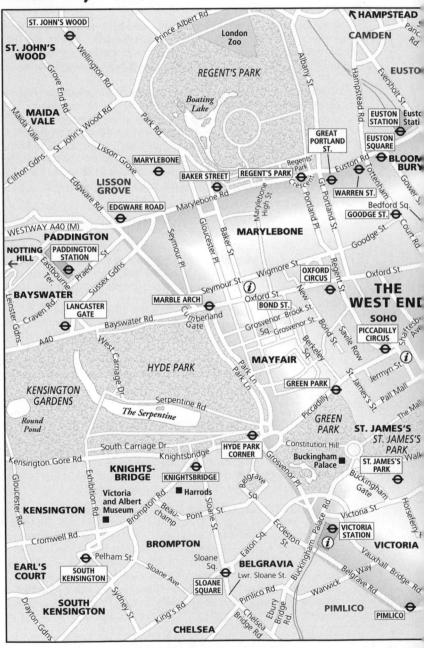

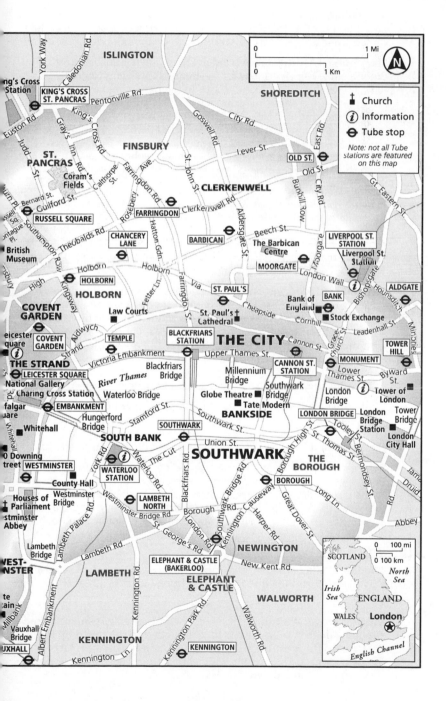

hotels and luxurious shopping. The major Tube stops are Piccadilly Circus, Bond Street, Marble Arch, and Hyde Park Corner.

✔ **Marylebone:** The neighborhood north of Mayfair and west of Bloomsbury, Marylebone (*Mar*-lee-bone) abuts giant Regent's Park. Marylebone Road runs south of the park. Great Portland Street marks the eastern boundary and Edgware Road the western. You may call this area "Medical London" because it has several hospitals and the famous Harley Street Clinic. But perhaps the most famous street is Baker Street, home of the fictional Sherlock Holmes. You can find Madame Tussauds wax museum on Marylebone Road. The major Tube stops are Baker Street, Marylebone, and Regent's Park.

✔ **St. James's:** Considered "Royal London," St. James's is a posh green haven beginning at Piccadilly and stretching southwest to include Green Park and St. James's Park, with Buckingham Palace between them and St. James's Palace across from St. James's Park. Pall Mall runs roughly east–west into the area and meets the north–south St. James's Street. Regent Street marks the eastern boundary. The Tube stops are St. James's Park and Green Park.

✔ **Westminster:** East and south of St. James's, Westminster draws visitors to Westminster Abbey and the Houses of Parliament, the seat of British government. Westminster extends from Northumberland Avenue just south of Charing Cross to Vauxhall Bridge Road, with the Thames to the east and St. James's Park to the west. Victoria Station, on the southwest perimeter, is a kind of axis for Westminster, Belgravia, and Pimlico (see the next two listings). The Tube stops are Westminster, St. James's Park, and Victoria.

✔ **Pimlico:** The pie-shaped wedge of London extending west from Vauxhall Bridge Road to Buckingham Palace Road is Pimlico. Crowning it to the north is Victoria Station, and here you also find the Tate Britain gallery. The Tube stops are Pimlico and Victoria.

✔ **Belgravia:** A posh quarter long favored by aristocrats, Belgravia begins west of Victoria Station and Green Park, and extends south to the river and west to Sloane Street; Hyde Park bounds the area to the north. Many foreign embassies are located in Belgravia. The Tube stops are Victoria, Hyde Park Corner, and Sloane Square.

West London

West London — still considered part of Central London — has several distinctive neighborhoods filled with hotels, restaurants, great shopping, and major tourist attractions:

✔ **Knightsbridge:** West of Belgravia is the fashionable residential and shopping district of Knightsbridge, bounded to the north by Hyde Park and to the west by Brompton Road, where you find Harrods, the neighborhood's chief shopping attraction. The Tube stops are Knightsbridge and Sloane Square.

✓ **Chelsea:** Below Knightsbridge and west of Belgravia, Chelsea begins at Sloane Square and runs south to the Thameside Cheyne Walk and Chelsea Embankment. King's Road, a bustling shopping artery, acts as its northern boundary and Chelsea Bridge Road as its eastern border. To the west, Chelsea extends as far as Earl's Court Road, Redcliffe Gardens, and Edith Grove. The Tube stop is Sloane Square.

✓ **South Kensington:** Kensington Gardens and Hyde Park form the green northern boundary of South Kensington. Frequently referred to as Museumland, South Ken hops with hotels, restaurants, and tourists flocking to the Natural History Museum, Science Museum, and Victoria & Albert Museum. The district is bounded to the west by Palace Gate and Gloucester Road, to the east by Fulham Road, and to the south by busy Brompton Road. The Tube stops are Gloucester Road and South Kensington.

✓ **Kensington:** The residential neighborhood of Kensington fills the gap between Kensington Gardens and Holland Park, with Notting Hill Gate and Bayswater Road marking its northern boundary. Kensington Church Street runs north–south between Notting Hill Gate and Kensington High Street. Kensington Palace, formerly the home of Princess Diana, sits on the western side of Kensington Gardens. The Tube stop is High Street Kensington.

✓ **Earl's Court:** Beginning south of West Cromwell Road and extending down to Lillie Road and Brompton Road is the down-to-earth Earl's Court neighborhood. Its western boundary is North End Road, and its eastern boundary is Earl's Court Road. You won't find any major tourist attractions in Earl's Court, which has long been a haven for budget travelers (particularly Australians — hence its nickname, "Kangaroo Court") and for gays and lesbians. The area is gradually being spruced up, but many streets still look a bit frayed. The Tube stop is Earl's Court.

✓ **Notting Hill:** Beginning north of Holland Park, Kensington Gardens, and Hyde Park (Holland Park Avenue and Bayswater Road run along the northern perimeter of the parks), you find Notting Hill and the rising subneighborhood of Notting Hill Gate. The area is bounded by Clarendon Road to the west, Queensway to the east, and Wesbourne Grove to the north. The most famous street, Portobello Road, runs north–south through the center. The super-hip neighborhood was a backdrop for the 1999 movie *Notting Hill,* starring Julia Roberts and Hugh Grant. The Tube stops are Notting Hill Gate, Bayswater, and Queensway.

✓ **Bayswater and Paddington:** Picking up where Notting Hill ends, Bayswater runs east to meet Marylebone at Edgware Road. The roaring A40 (Westway) highway acts as its northern boundary. Paddington Station sits in the northwestern corner of Bayswater. This area is fairly commercial and not particularly attractive. Here, you find no major tourist attractions and plenty of budget B&Bs. The Tube stops are Paddington, Lancaster Gate, Marble Arch, and Edgware Road.

The royal Dotty

Thanks to a dog named Dotty, Princess Anne, otherwise known as the Princess Royal, became the first member of the modern royal family to have a criminal record. On April 1, 2003, Anne and her husband were walking their three English bull terriers in the park around Windsor Castle (see Chapter 13). Dotty, one of the dogs, bolted away, knocked over two boys on bicycles, and bit them. In court, Anne pleaded guilty to charges of losing control of her dog and had to pay a £500 ($925) fine, £250 ($463) to the boys, and £148 ($274) in court costs. Dotty escaped destruction but had to undergo retraining and to be leashed and muzzled in public.

The South Bank

You probably don't want to stay on the South Bank, but you may go to the South Bank Centre for a play or a concert at one of its internationally known arts and performance venues, all clustered beside the river within easy walking distance of Waterloo Station. Closer to Westminster Bridge, you can find the city's newest high-rise attraction: the British Airways London Eye observation wheel. For a scenic route to the South Bank, take the Tube to Embankment, on the north bank, and walk across the Thames on the newly glitzed-up Hungerford pedestrian bridge. The Jubilee Walkway, a breezy riverside path, extends east from the South Bank Centre to the new Tate Modern art gallery, the Globe Theatre, the new London City Hall, and Tower Bridge. The new pedestrian-only Millennium Bridge spans the Thames from the Tate Modern to St. Paul's Cathedral. The Tube stops are Waterloo, London Bridge, and Southwark.

Finding Information After You Arrive

The **Britain & London Visitor Centre,** 1 Regent St., Piccadilly Circus, SW1 (Tube: Piccadilly Circus), provides tourist information to walk-in visitors; phone assistance isn't available. The office is open Monday from 9:30 a.m. to 6:30 p.m., Tuesday to Friday from 9 a.m. to 6:30 p.m., and Saturday and Sunday from 10 a.m. to 4 p.m. You can find hotel- and theater-booking agencies; a currency exchange; and plenty of free brochures on river trips, walking tours, and day trips from London.

You can find **Tourist Information Centres** in the following locations (please note that ☎ **020/7234-5800** is the information number for all Tourist Information Centres):

✔ **City of London,** St. Paul's Churchyard (St. Paul's Cathedral): Open Easter through September daily from 9:30 a.m. to 5 p.m., October through March Monday through Friday from 9:30 a.m. to 5 p.m., and Saturday from 9:30 a.m. to 12:30 p.m.

> ✔ **Waterloo International Terminal Arrivals Hall:** Open daily from
> 8:30 a.m. to 10:30 p.m.

For current listings and reviews of everything that's going on in London,
buy a copy of *Time Out.* This publication hits the newsstands on
Wednesday and costs about £2.50 ($4.65).

Getting Around London

You can choose among many ways to get around London. If you travel for
any distance, the fastest mode of transportation in this enormous city is
the Underground or Tube (the subway system). Many of the slower but
more scenic buses are double-deckers. Most convenient (unless you're
stuck in a traffic jam) is to go by taxi. But walking is the most fun of all.
When you're on foot, you see more and can explore some of the leafy
squares and cobbled lanes that contribute to London's enduring charm.

For general London travel information, call ☎ **020/7222-1234** or visit
the Transport for London Web site, www.tfl.gov.uk. You can get free
bus and Underground maps, and buy Travelcards and bus passes, at any
major Underground station or at the London Travel Information Centres
in the stations at King's Cross; Liverpool Street; Oxford Circus; Piccadilly
Circus; St. James's Park; Victoria; and Heathrow Terminals 1, 2, and 3.

By Underground (subway)

London has the oldest and most comprehensive subway system in the
world. The Tube is fast and convenient, and just about everyone but the
royals uses it. Everywhere you choose to go in London, you can find a
nearby Tube stop, clearly marked by a red circle with a horizontal line
through it. For an Underground map, see the inside back cover of this
book.

Using the Underground

Thirteen Underground lines crisscross the city and intersect at various
stations where you can change from one train to another. On Underground
maps, every line is color-coded (Bakerloo is brown, Piccadilly is dark blue,
and so on), which makes planning your route easy. All you need to know is
the name of your stop and the direction you're heading. After you figure
out which line you need to take, look on the map for the name of the last
stop in the direction you need to go. The name of the last stop on the line
appears on the front of the train and sometimes on electronic signboards
that display the name of the arriving train. (The one exception to this is
the Circle Line, which doesn't list a last stop because it runs in a loop
around Central London.) Inside all but the oldest trains are electronic
signs, recorded voices, or both that announce the name of each approaching stop.

Most of the Underground system operates with automated entry and
exit gates. You feed your ticket into the slot; the ticket disappears and

pops up again like a piece of toast; the gate bangs open; and you remove your ticket and pass through. At the other end, you do the same to get out, but the machine keeps the ticket (unless you have a multiuse Travelcard ticket, which the machine returns to you). Some stations outside of Central London are staffed by ticket collectors.

You may have to transfer from one Underground line to another to get to your destination. All Underground maps clearly show where various lines converge. Signs in the stations direct you from one line to another. To get from one line to another, you go through tunnels (which the Brits call *subways*), and you may have to go up or down a level or two.

Underground service stops around midnight (a little earlier on less-used lines). Keep this in mind when you're out painting the town red. If you miss the last train, you have to take a taxi or one of the night buses.

Buying tickets

You can purchase Underground tickets at the ticket window or from one of the automated machines in most stations. Machines can change £5, £10, and £20 notes. Fares to every station are clearly posted in all stations.

For fare purposes, the city is divided into zones. **Zone 1** covers all Central London. **Zone 6** extends as far as Heathrow to the west and Upminster to the east. Make sure your ticket covers all the zones you're traveling through (no problem if you're staying in Central London), or you may have to pay a £10 ($19) penalty fare.

A **single-fare one-way ticket** within one zone costs £2 ($3.70) for an adult and 60p ($1.10) for a child from 5 to 15 years of age. You don't have to pay more than this to reach any sight in Central London (provided you're also staying in Central London). Tickets are valid for use on the day of issue only.

If you plan to travel by Underground, you can save time and money by buying a book of ten tickets, called a *carnet*. **Carnet tickets** are valid in Zone 1 only. Each ticket is good for a single ride on any day. The price is £17 ($31) for an adult and £5 ($9.25) for a child. With a Travelcard (see the following section), you can save even more.

Saving with Travelcards

To make the most of London's public transportation system, consider buying a **Travelcard,** which allows unlimited travel by Underground *and* bus. You can purchase these cards in the following increments:

- ✔ **Day Travelcard:** For Zones 1 and 2 (everything in Central London), this card costs £4.70 ($8.70) for an adult and £2 ($3.70) for a child; the card is valid after 9:30 a.m. weekdays and all day Saturday and Sunday.

- ✔ **3-Day Travelcard:** For Zones 1 and 2, this card costs £15 ($28) for an adult and £7.50 ($14) for a child.

✔ **7-Day Travelcard:** For Zone 1 (all Central London), this card costs £19 ($35) for an adult and £7.50 ($14) for a child.

✔ **Family Travelcard:** This card is good for families or groups of one or two adults traveling with one to four children; to use it, you must travel together as a group. The Family Travelcard is valid after 9:30 a.m. Monday to Friday and all day Saturday and Sunday. Rates for one day of travel in Zones 1 and 2 are £3.10 ($5.75) per adult and 80p ($1.50) per child.

Another great way to save money on London transportation is the **Visitor Travelcard,** which you can buy in the United States and Canada before leaving home (you can't get it in London). You can choose between two kinds of Visitor Travelcards, the All Zone and the Central Zone (good for Zone 1 only); both allow unlimited travel on the Tube and bus, and you can get them in three-, four-, or seven-day increments. Prices for the Central Zone card are $24 for adults and $10 for children for three days, $29 for adults and $11 for children for four days, and $36 for adults and $13 for children for seven days. You can buy Visitor Travelcards by contacting a travel agent, calling **RailEurope** at ☎ 877/257-2887 from the United States or ☎ 800/361-RAIL from Canada, or going online to www.raileurope.com.

By bus

Distinctive red double-decker buses are very much a part of London's snarled traffic scene, but not all London buses are double-deckers, and some aren't red. Bus travel does have one drawback, especially for first-timers: You need to know the streets of London so you can get off at the correct stop. Get a free bus map at one of the Travel Information Centres (see the section "Finding Information After You Arrive," earlier in this chapter), or you may overshoot your destination. On the plus side, riding the bus is cheaper than taking the Tube; you don't have to contend with escalators, elevators, or tunnels; and you get to see the sights as you travel.

A concrete post with a red or white sign on top reading "London Transport Bus Service" clearly marks each bus stop. Another sign shows the routes of the buses that stop there. If the sign on top of the post is red, the stop is a *request stop,* meaning that you have to hail the approaching bus as you would a taxi (don't whistle; just put up your hand). If the sign is white, the bus stops automatically. Be sure to check the destination sign in front of the bus to make sure that the bus travels the entire route. Have some coins with you, because the drivers don't change banknotes.

Unlike the Underground, the bus network isn't divided into fare zones. The bus fare for a journey of any length costs £1.20 ($2.20) for adults, 40p (75¢) for children. Children 16 and under ride free if they have a **Child Photocard;** you must supply your own passport-size photo of your child to obtain this free ID card, which is available at a Tube station or one of the Travel Information Centres.

A **one-day bus pass** is a good thing to have if you plan to do much travel-ing by bus. You can use the pass all day, but it isn't valid on N-prefixed night buses (which you can read about in the following paragraph). You can purchase this one-day pass and bus passes good for longer periods at most Underground stations, selected news agents, and Travel Information Centres. A one-day bus pass for all Central London costs £3 ($5.55) for an adult and £1 ($1.85) for a child age 5 to 15. A **seven-day bus pass** for Central London costs £11 ($20) for an adult and £4 ($7.40) for a child 5 to 15. *Note:* Children must have a **Child Photocard** ID in order to buy and use any of these passes; you can get the card for free at major Tube stations and Travel Information Centres, but you need to have a passport-size photograph of your child.

At the witching hour of midnight, buses become **night buses** (N), and their routes change. Nearly all night buses pass through Trafalgar Square, Central London's late-night magnet for insomniacs.

By taxi

You can safely and comfortably get around the city by taking a taxi. Riding in the old-fashioned, roomy black taxis is a pleasure. Today, there are also many smaller and newer-model taxis. London cabs of any size or color don't come cheap. The fare starts at £1.40 ($2.60) for one person, with 40p (75¢) for each additional passenger. Then you have to deal with the surcharges: 10p (20¢) per item of luggage; 60p ($1.10) weeknights 8 p.m. to midnight; 90p ($1.65) from midnight until 7 a.m.; 60p ($1.10) Saturday and Sunday until 8 p.m. and 90p ($1.65) after 8 p.m. The meter leaps 20p (35¢) every 111 yards or 90 seconds. Tip your cabbie 10 to 15 percent of the total fare.

You can hail a cab on the street. If a cab is available, the yellow or white FOR HIRE sign on the roof is lit. You can order a **radio cab** by calling ☎ 02072/720-272 or 02072/535-000. Be aware that if you call for a cab, the meter starts ticking when the taxi receives notification from the dis-patcher, not when the taxi actually picks you up.

You don't have to worry about whether the cabdriver knows where he's going in London. When it comes to finding a street address, London cab-bies are among the most knowledgeable in the world. Their rigorous train-ing, which includes an exhaustive street test called "The Knowledge," gives them an encyclopedic grasp of the terrain.

On foot

Sure, you can hop from one place to the next by using the Tube, a bus, or a cab. But if you really want to get acquainted with the charming hodgepodge and monumental grandeur of London, bring along a good pair of walking shoes, and explore on foot. Everywhere you turn, you see enticing side streets, countrylike lanes, little *mews dwellings* (former sta-bles converted into homes), and picturesque garden squares. London's great parks are as safe to walk in as its streets. (In fact, crime is less prevalent in London than in many other major cities, and all the neighborhoods included in this book are safe.)

If you want to follow a detailed stroll or two around the city, perhaps of Dickens's London or of Westminster and Whitehall, check out the 11 tours in *Frommer's Memorable Walks in London,* by Richard Jones (Wiley Publishing, Inc.).

An 11km (7-mile) walk commemorating the life of Princess Diana passes through four of London's royal parks: St. James's Park, Green Park, Hyde Park, and Kensington Gardens. Along the way, 90 plaques point out sites associated with Diana, including Kensington Palace (her home for 15 years), Buckingham Palace, St. James's Palace (where she shared an office with Prince Charles), and Spencer House (her family's mansion, now a museum).

When you walk in London (or anywhere in England), remember

- ✔ **Traffic moves on the opposite side of the street from what you're accustomed to if you're from the U.S. or Canada.** This tip sounds simple enough on paper, but in practice, you need to keep reminding yourself to look in the "wrong" direction when crossing a street. Throughout London, you see LOOK RIGHT or LOOK LEFT painted on street crossings.

- ✔ **Striped lines (called *zebra crossings*) on the road mark pedestrian crossings.** Flashing lights near the curb indicate that drivers *must* stop and yield the right of way when a pedestrian steps out into the zebra to cross the street.

Staying in Style

As you probably expect, London's hotels are the most expensive in England. Accommodations come in all shapes, sizes, and prices (see Chapter 8 for more information on booking your accommodations). Nothing is going to be as inexpensive as that roadside motel on the freeway back home, but you do find a few good budget hotels and plenty of B&Bs that won't cost you an arm and a leg. Sliding up the scale, you come to unique boutique hotels, older traditional hotels, large chain hotels, and several ultraluxurious places known the world over. Basically, though, you find only two categories of accommodations in London: hotels and bed-and-breakfast inns.

You really don't want to arrive in London without a hotel reservation, especially if you visit from mid-April to early October (high season). If you do arrive without a reservation, you can book rooms through the agencies listed in Chapter 8.

London's Top Hotels

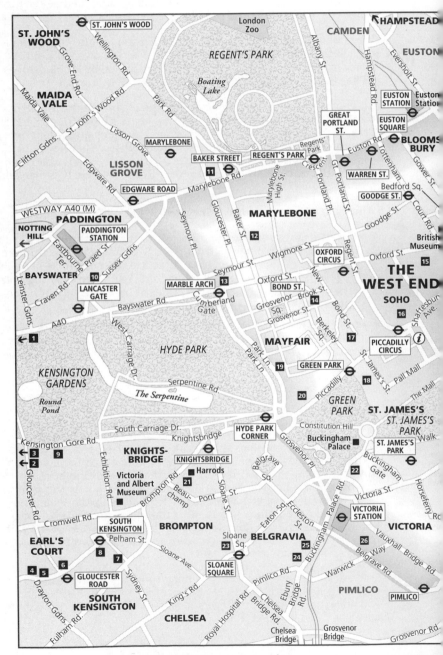

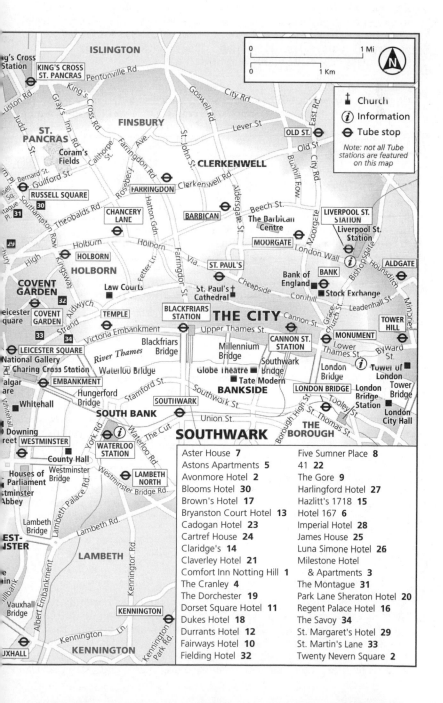

Aster House **7**
Astons Apartments **5**
Avonmore Hotel **2**
Blooms Hotel **30**
Brown's Hotel **17**
Bryanston Court Hotel **13**
Cadogan Hotel **23**
Cartref House **24**
Claridge's **14**
Claverley Hotel **21**
Comfort Inn Notting Hill **1**
The Cranley **4**
The Dorchester **19**
Dorset Square Hotel **11**
Dukes Hotel **18**
Durrants Hotel **12**
Fairways Hotel **10**
Fielding Hotel **32**

Five Sumner Place **8**
41 **22**
The Gore **9**
Harlingford Hotel **27**
Hazlitt's 1718 **15**
Hotel 167 **6**
Imperial Hotel **28**
James House **25**
Luna Simone Hotel **26**
Milestone Hotel
 & Apartments **3**
The Montague **31**
Park Lane Sheraton Hotel **20**
Regent Palace Hotel **16**
The Savoy **34**
St. Margaret's Hotel **29**
St. Martin's Lane **33**
Twenty Nevern Square **2**

If you stay in London over a weekend, ask if your hotel has a special weekend rate. Larger hotels that cater to business travelers often drastically reduce their rates and throw in a few extra perks for Friday-to-Sunday-night stays. Special weekend rates generally aren't available at smaller, less expensive hotels and B&Bs.

For a key to the dollar-sign ratings that I use in the hotel listings, see Chapter 8. For general information on U.K. accommodations and for definitions of such terms as *value-added tax* (VAT), *self-catering rooms,* and *English breakfast,* check out Chapter 8. For the locations of all the hotels that I discuss in this chapter, see the "London's Top Hotels" map on p. 132.

The top hotels

London has an enormous range of hotels in all price categories and in all parts of town. I list a fair range of accommodations; if you want more options or have particular needs that my picks don't meet, the **Britain & London Visitor Centre,** 1 Regent St. (walk-in or online service only; www.visitlondon.com), can help you find what you need.

Note: Remember that this book lists the *rack rates,* the highest published rates for a room with no discounts. You can often find a lower rate by checking the hotel's Web site for special promotional and weekend rates.

Aster House
$$–$$$ **South Kensington**

At the end of a street of early Victorian townhouses, this 12-unit, non-smoking B&B is a charmer. Each guest room is individually decorated in English country-house style, and many rooms have four-poster, half-canopied beds and silk wallpaper. The bathrooms come with power showers. Every room has a dataport for plugging in a laptop computer. The breakfasts, served in the glassed-in garden conservatory, are more health-conscious than you'd expect from an English B&B.

See map p. 132. 3 Sumner Place (near Onslow Square), London SW7 3EE. ☎ *020/ 7581-5888. Fax: 020/7584-4925.* www.AsterHouse.com. *Tube: South Kensington (then a five-minute walk west on Old Brompton Road and south on Sumner Place). Rack rates: £145–£195 ($268–$361) double; special winter rates posted on Web site. Rates include buffet continental breakfast. MC, V.*

Astons Apartments
$–$$ **South Kensington**

Astons offers value-packed accommodations in three carefully restored Victorian red-brick townhouses. Each studio has a compact kitchenette (great for families on a budget); a small bathroom; and bright, functional furnishings. (Because you can cook on your in-room stove, the English call these accommodations "self-catering" units.) The more expensive designer studios feature larger bathrooms, more living space, and extra pizzazz in the decor. If you like the idea of having your own cozy London apartment (with daily maid service), you can't do better. Free cribs, baby baths, and baby-bottle sterilization equipment are available.

See map p. 132. 39 Rosary Gardens (off Hereford Square), London SW7 4NQ. ☎ *800/525-2810 in the U.S. or 020/7590-6000. Fax: 020/7590-6060.* www.astons-apartments.com. *Tube: Gloucester Road (then a five-minute walk south on Gloucester Road and west on Hereford Square; Rosary Gardens is 1 block farther west). Rack rates: £90–£125 ($167–$231) double. Rates don't include 17.5% VAT. AE, MC, V.*

Avonmore Hotel
$–$$ **Kensington**

In 2000, the British Automobile Association awarded this small hotel four diamonds (out of a possible five) for its high standards of service. The property is in a quiet neighborhood that gives you easy access to West End theaters and shops. Each of the nine tastefully decorated guest rooms has an array of amenities (such as hairdryers, minibars, tea- and coffee-making facilities, and color televisions) that you don't usually find in this price range. An English breakfast is served in a cheerful breakfast room, and a bar and limited room service are available. The staff can arrange baby-sitting if necessary.

See map p. 132. 66 Avonmore Rd. (northwest of Earl's Court), London W14 8RS. ☎ *020/7603-4296. Fax: 020/7603-4035.* www.avonmorehotel.co.uk. *Tube: West Kensington (then a five-minute walk north on North End Road and Mattheson Road to Avonmore Road). Rack rates: £60–£90 ($111–$167) double without bathroom, £80–£110 ($148–$204) double with bathroom. Rates include English breakfast. AE, MC, V.*

Bryanston Court Hotel
$$ **Marylebone**

In a neighborhood with many attractive squares, three houses were joined to form the 200-year-old Bryanston Court, one of Central London's finest moderately priced hotels. Family owned and operated, the freshly refurbished 54-room hotel has small guest rooms (and equally small bathrooms) that are comfortably furnished and well maintained. You find a comfy bar with a fireplace in the back of the lounge.

See map p. 132. 56–60 Great Cumberland Place (near Marble Arch), London W1H 7FD. ☎ *020/7262-3141. Fax: 020/7262-7248.* www.bryanstonhotel.com. *Tube: Marble Arch (then a five-minute walk north on Great Cumberland Place to Bryanston Place). Rack rates: £120 ($222) double. Rates include continental breakfast. AE, DC, MC, V.*

Cadogan Hotel
$$$$–$$$$$ **Chelsea**

Memories of the Victorian era fill this beautiful 65-room hotel, which is close to the exclusive Knightsbridge shops. The main floor includes a small, wood-paneled lobby and sumptuous drawing room (good for afternoon tea). The Cadogan (pronounced Ca-*dug*-en) is the hotel where Oscar Wilde was staying when he was arrested. (Room 118 is the Oscar Wilde Suite.) The large guest rooms, many overlooking Cadogan Place gardens, are quietly tasteful and splendidly comfortable, with large bathrooms. The sedate Edwardian restaurant is known for its excellent cuisine.

See map p. 132. 75 Sloane St. (near Sloane Square), London SW1X 9SG. ☎ *800/260-8338 in the U.S. or 020/7235-7141. Fax: 020/7245-0994.* www.cadogan.com. *Tube: Sloane Square (then a five-minute walk north on Sloane Street). Rack rates: £245–£350 ($453–$648) double. Rates don't include 17.5% VAT. AE, MC, V.*

Claverley Hotel
$$$–$$$$ Knightsbridge

On a country-quiet cul-de-sac a few blocks from Harrods and the best of Knightsbridge shopping, this cozy place is one of London's best B&Bs. Georgian-era accessories, 19th-century oil portraits, elegant antiques, and leather-covered sofas accent the public rooms. The 29 guest rooms are smart and cozy, with marble bathrooms with tubs and power showers. The hotel offers an excellent English breakfast and great value for this tony area.

See map p. 132. 13–14 Beaufort Gardens (off Brompton Road), London SW3 1PS. ☎ *800/747-0398 in the U.S. or 020/7589-8541. Fax: 020/7584-3410.* www.claverley hotel.co.uk. *Tube: Knightsbridge (then a two-minute walk south past Harrods on Brompton Road to Beaufort Gardens). Rack rates: £149–£219 ($276–$405) double. Rates include English breakfast. AE, DC, MC, V.*

Comfort Inn Notting Hill
$–$$ Notting Hill

Comfort Inn is a franchise, but you can get a lower rate if you book directly with the hotel rather than through central reservations. On a quiet, pretty street off Notting Hill Gate, the Comfort Inn stretches across five terrace houses and has 64 fair-size rooms on the three upper floors (there's an elevator). Rooms have been redecorated with a nice traditional look and equipped with firm new beds; a few newly redone rooms face a charming interior courtyard. Standard amenities include dataports, coffeemakers, and hairdryers. The bathrooms are also newly renovated. Breakfast is a self-service buffet.

See map p. 132. 6–14 Pembridge Gardens (near Pembridge Square), London W2 4DU. ☎ *020/7229-6666. Fax: 020/7229-3333.* www.lth-hotels.com. *Tube: Notting Hill Gate (then a two-minute walk north on Pembridge Gardens). Rack rates: £100 ($185) double. Rates include continental breakfast. AE, DC, MC, V.*

The Cranley
$$–$$$$ South Kensington

On a quiet street near South Kensington's museums, the Cranley occupies a quartet of restored 1875 townhouses. Luxuriously appointed public rooms and 39 high-ceilinged, air-conditioned guest rooms — with original plasterwork, a blend of Victorian and contemporary furnishings, and up-to-the-minute in-room technology — make this property a standout. The bathrooms are large and nicely finished, with tubs and showers. Rates include tea with scones in the afternoon, and champagne and canapés in the evening.

See map p. 132. 10–12 Bina Gardens (off Brompton Road), London SW5 0LA. ☎ *800/448-8355 in the U.S. or 020/7373-0123. Fax: 020/7373-9497.* www.thecranley.com. *Tube: Gloucester Road (then a five-minute walk south on Gloucester Road, west on Brompton Road, and north on Bina Gardens). Rack rates: £190–£220 ($352–$407) double. AE, DC, MC, V.*

Dorset Square Hotel
$$$–$$$$ **Marylebone**

This sophisticated 38-room luxury hotel occupies a beautifully restored Regency townhouse overlooking Dorset Square, a private garden surrounded by graceful buildings. Aggressively gorgeous inside and out, the hotel is the epitome of traditional English style. Each guest room is unique, but all are filled with a superlative mix of antiques, original oil paintings, fine furniture, fresh flowers, and richly textured fabrics. The bathrooms contain marble and mahogany.

See map p. 132. 39–40 Dorset Sq. (just west of Regent's Park), London NW1 6QN. ☎ *800/553-6674 in the U.S. or 020/7723-7874. Fax: 020/7724-3328.* www.dorset square.co.uk. *Tube: Marylebone (then a two-minute walk east on Melcombe to Dorset Square). Rack rates: £164–£240 ($303–$444) double. Rates don't include 17.5% VAT. AE, MC, V.*

Durrants Hotel
$$$ **Marylebone**

Opened in 1789 off Manchester Square, this 92-room hotel makes for an atmospheric London retreat. Durrants is quintessentially English, with pine- and mahogany-paneled public areas, a wonderful Georgian room that serves as a restaurant, and even an 18th-century letter-writing room. Most of the wood-paneled guest rooms are generously proportioned and nicely furnished, with decent-size bathrooms. Some rooms are large enough for families with children.

See map p. 132. George Street (across from the Wallace Collection), London W1H 6BJ. ☎ *020/7935-8131. Fax: 020/7487-3510.* www.durrantshotel.co.uk. *Tube: Bond Street (then a five-minute walk west on Oxford Street and north on Duke Street and Manchester Street). Rack rates: £165 ($305) double. AE, MC, V.*

Fielding Hotel
$$ **Covent Garden**

The Fielding sits on a beautiful old street (now pedestrian only) lit by 19th-century gaslights, just steps from the Royal Opera House. The hotel doesn't have an elevator, and the stairways are steep and narrow. The 24 rather cramped guest rooms have showers and toilets but aren't particularly memorable. However, this quirky hotel is an excellent value for such a central location. A small bar is on the premises, and the area is loaded with cafes, restaurants, and fab shopping.

See map p. 132. 4 Broad Court, Bow Street, London WC2B 5QZ. ☎ *020/7836-8305. Fax: 020/7497-0064.* www.the-fielding-hotel.co.uk. *Tube: Covent Garden (then a five-minute walk north on Long Acre and south on Bow Street). Rack rates: £100–£130 ($185–$241) double. AE, DC, MC, V.*

Five Sumner Place
$$ South Kensington

Winner of the English Tourist Board's "Bed & Breakfast of the Year" award for 2000, this 14-room charmer occupies a landmark Victorian terrace house that has been completely restored in elegant English style. The guest rooms are comfortably and traditionally furnished, and all have bathrooms (a few have refrigerators as well). The B&B offers a full range of services, including breakfast served in a Victorian-style conservatory, and welcomes families.

See map p. 132. 5 Sumner Place (just east of Onslow Square), London SW7 3EE. ☎ *020/7584-7586. Fax: 020/7823-9962.* www.sumnerplace.com. *Tube: South Kensington (then a three-minute walk west on Brompton Road and south on Sumner Place). Rack rates: £130 ($241) double. Rates include English breakfast. AE, MC, V.*

41
$$$$$ Victoria

Overlooking Buckingham Palace Mews, this unique 18-room boutique hotel is the epitome of luxury and offers superior personal service. The hotel lobby and breakfast room is an elegant conservatory that was once the waiting room for debutantes who were going to Buckingham Palace to be presented. Every detail in the beautifully furnished rooms, from the Frette sheets to the Penhaligon toiletries, is pure *luxe*. The staff here is wonderfully friendly.

See map p. 132. 41 Buckingham Palace Rd. (just north of Victoria Station), London SW1W 0PS. ☎ *877/955-1515 in U.S. or 020/7300-0041. Fax: 020/7300-0141.* www.41hotel.com. *Tube: Victoria (then a five-minute walk northeast along Buckingham Palace Road). Rack rates: £295–£315 ($546–$583) double. Rates include continental breakfast. Rates don't include the 17.5% VAT. AE, MC, V.*

The Gore
$$$–$$$$ South Kensington

Lovers of true Victoriana love the Gore, which sits on a busy road near Kensington Gardens and South Kensington museums. More or less in continuous operation since 1892, this hotel has loads of historic charm. Each of the 54 guest rooms is unique, filled with high-quality antiques and elegant furnishings. Even old commodes conceal the toilets. Bistro 190, the hotel restaurant, is hip and popular.

See map p. 132. 189 Queen's Gate (south of Kensington Gardens), London SW7 5EX. ☎ ***800/637-7200*** *in the U.S. or 020/7584-6601. Fax: 020/7589-8127.* www.gorehotel. com. *Tube: Gloucester Road (then a five-minute walk east on Cromwell Road and north on Queen's Gate). Rack rates: £190–£210 ($352–$389) double. Rates don't include 17.5% VAT. AE, DC, MC, V.*

Hazlitt's 1718
$$$–$$$$ Soho

Staying in this intimate, 23-room gem (built in 1718) is a delight, thanks in part to its old-fashioned atmosphere and location in the heart of hip Soho. The Georgian-era guest rooms are charming, with mahogany and pine furnishings and antiques, as well as lovely bathrooms, many with claw-foot tubs. Every room comes equipped with dataports for laptop computers; the hotel doesn't have an elevator, however. Rooms in the back are quieter; the front rooms receive more light, but restrictions on historic properties don't allow for double-glazed windows.

See map p. 132. 6 Frith St., Soho Square (just west of Charing Cross Road), London W1V 5TZ. ☎ ***020/7434-1771.*** *Fax: 020/7439-1524.* www.hazlittshotel.com. *Tube: Tottenham Court Road (then a five-minute walk west on Oxford Street and south on Soho Street to Frith Street at the south end of Soho Square). Rack rates: £205–£255 ($379–$472) double. Rates don't include 17.5% VAT. AE, DC, MC, V.*

Hotel 167
$–$$ South Kensington

Hotel 167, one of the more fashionable guest houses in South Ken, attracts both young visitors who like the price and businesspeople who like the central location. Every guest room has a decent-size bathroom (some with showers, others with tubs), and the overall ambience is bright and attractive. The 16 rooms are furnished with a mix of fabrics and styles. Have fun exploring this busy neighborhood!

See map p. 132. 167 Old Brompton Rd., London SW5 0AN. ☎ ***020/7373-0672.*** *Fax: 020/ 7373-3360.* www.hotel167.com. *Tube: South Kensington (then a ten-minute walk west on Old Brompton Road). Rack rates: £99–£110 ($183–$204) double. Rates include continental breakfast. AE, DC, MC, V.*

James House and Cartref House
$ Westminster and Victoria

One of the top ten B&Bs in London, James House and Cartref House (across the street from each other, with a total of 20 rooms) deserve their accolades. Each guest room is individually designed; some of the larger ones contain bunk beds, which makes them suitable for families. Fewer than half of the rooms have private bathrooms. You get an extremely generous English breakfast, and everything is in tip-top order. Neither house has an elevator, but guests don't seem to mind. Both houses are completely smoke free. It doesn't matter which house you're assigned; both are winners.

See map p. 132. 108 and 129 Ebury St. (near Victoria Station), London SW1W 9QD. James House ☎ *020/7730-7338; Cartref House* ☎ *020/7730-6176. Fax: 020/7730-7338.* www.jamesandcartref.co.uk. *Tube: Victoria Station (then a ten-minute walk south on Buckingham Palace Road, west on Eccleston Street). Rack rates: £70 ($130) double without bathroom, £85 ($157) double with bathroom. Rates include English breakfast. AE, MC, V.*

Luna Simone Hotel
$ Westminster and Victoria

The outside of this big, stucco-fronted, family-run hotel gleams bright white, and each freshly renovated guest room has a newly tiled private bathroom (with shower). The 36 rooms vary widely in size, but with their blue carpeting and cream-colored walls, they beat all the dowdy, badly designed hotels and B&Bs for miles around. The beechwood and marble-clad reception area is all new, too, as is the smart-looking breakfast room, now totally nonsmoking. The look throughout is refreshingly light, simple, and modern.

See map p. 132. 47–49 Belgrave Rd. (just west of Warwick Way), London SW1V 2BB. ☎ *020/7834-5897. Fax: 020/7828-2474.* www.lunasimonehotel.com. *Tube: Victoria (then a five-minute walk east on Belgrave Road). Rack rates: £60–£80 ($111–$148) double. Rates include English breakfast. MC, V.*

The Montague
$$$–$$$$ Bloomsbury

For service and sheer sumptuousness, you won't find a better hotel anywhere in the vicinity of the British Museum — which happens to be right across the street. Every room in this immaculately kept property has been individually decorated and features every amenity you can think of, from twice-daily maid service with evening turndown to luxuriously equipped bathrooms. You can have afternoon tea or a cocktail in the delightful, airy garden-side conservatory, and check out the Chef's Table restaurant for an enjoyable lunch or dinner.

See map p. 132. 15 Montague St. (east side of the British Museum), London WC1B 5BJ. ☎ *877/955-1515 in U.S. or 020/7637-1001. Fax: 020/7637-2516.* www.montague hotel.com. *Tube: Russell Square (then a five-minute walk south across Russell Square to Montague Street). Rack rates: £150–£240 ($278–$444) double. Rates don't include 17.5% VAT. AE, MC, V.*

St. Margaret's Hotel
$ Bloomsbury

The welcome at this hotel inspires devoted loyalty. Mrs. Marazzi is the second generation of her family to run this nonsmoking B&B, which

The big splurge

If you're looking for the crème de la crème of luxury, here are a few more five-star, $$$$$ suggestions (**Note:** Look for special rates on their Web sites):

- ✔ **Brown's Hotel,** 29–34 Albemarle St., London W1X 4BP. ☎ 020/7493-6020. Fax: 020/7493-9381. www.brownshotel.com.

- ✔ **Claridge's,** Brook Street, Mayfair, London W1A 2JQ. ☎ 800/223-6800 in the U.S. or 020/7629-8860. Fax: 020/7499-2210. www.savoy-group.co.uk.

- ✔ **The Dorchester,** 53 Park Lane, London W1A 2HJ. ☎ 800/727-9820 in the U.S. or 020/7629-8888. Fax: 020/7409-0114. www.dorchesterhotel.com.

- ✔ **Park Lane Sheraton Hotel,** Piccadilly, London W1Y 8BX. ☎ 800/325-3535 in the U.S. or 020/7499-6321. Fax: 020/7499-1965. www.sheraton.com/parklane.

- ✔ **The Savoy,** The Strand, London WC2R 0EU. ☎ 800/63-SAVOY in the U.S. or 020/7836-4343. Fax: 0171/240-6040. www.savoy-group.co.uk.

rambles over four houses. The 64 rooms are simple and immaculate, and no two are alike. Only about ten rooms have private bathrooms, but the Marazzis recently created some beautiful extra public bathrooms, so you can easily survive the sharing experience. Some rooms look out onto the quiet communal garden, which all guests may use. Just ask, and the staff can arrange baby-sitting for your little ones.

See map p. 132. 26 Bedford Place (south side of Russell Square), London WC1B 5JL. ☎ *020/7636-4277. Fax: 020/7323-3066.* www.stmargaretshotel.co.uk. *Tube: Russell Square (then a five-minute walk to Bedford Place). Rack rates: £64 ($118) double without bathroom, £92–£98 ($170–$181) double with bathroom. Rates include English breakfast. MC, V.*

Runner-up accommodations

Here are some further hotel suggestions if your top choices are booked.

Blooms Hotel

$$$$ **Bloomsbury** A luxurious country-house atmosphere prevails in this appealing hotel with a walled garden next to the British Museum. *See map p. 132. 7 Montague St., London WC1.* ☎ *020/7323-1717. Fax: 020/7636-6498.* www.grangehotels.com.

Dukes Hotel

$$$$ **St. James's** At Dukes, you get charm, style, and tradition in a 1908 townhouse hotel; the staff can arrange baby-sitting services for your children. *See map p. 132. 35 St. James's Place, London SW1A 1NY.* ☎ *800/381-4702 in the U.S. or 020/7491-4840. Fax: 020/7493-1264.* www.dukeshotel.co.uk.

Fairways Hotel

$ Paddington This large late-Georgian house from the 1820s exudes charming English ambience. *See map p. 132. 186 Sussex Gardens, London W2 1TU.* ☎ *020/7723-4871. Fax: 020/7723-4871.* www.fairways-hotel.co.uk.

Harlingford Hotel

$ Bloomsbury In the heart of Bloomsbury, this wonderfully personable, immaculately maintained hotel occupies three 1820s town houses. *See map p. 132. 61–63 Cartwright Gardens (north of Russell Square), London WC1H 9EL.* ☎ *020/7387-1551. Fax: 020/7387-4616.* www.harlingfordhotel.com.

Inperial Hotel

$$ Bloomsbury This large, full-service hotel isn't particularly glamorous, but you get a well-run hotel for a terrific value right on Russell Square. *See map p. 132. Russell Square, London WC1B 5BB.* ☎ *020/7278-7871. Fax: 020/7837-4653.* www.imperialhotels.co.uk.

Milestone Hotel & Apartments

$$$–$$$$ South Kensington You find superior service and a country-house feeling in this small, stylish hotel wonderfully situated across from Kensington Gardens. *See map p. 132. 1 Kensington Court, London W8 5DL.* ☎ *877/955-1515 in the U.S. or 020/7917-1000. Fax: 020/7917-1010.* www.milestonehotel.com.

Regent Palace Hotel

$–$$ Piccadilly Circus One of Europe's largest hotels, the 920-room Regent Palace provides affordable accommodations in the heart of the West End. *See map p. 132. 12 Sherwood St. (just north of Piccadilly Circus), London W1A 4BZ.* ☎ *020/7734-0716. Fax: 020/7734-6435.* www.regentpalacehotel.co.uk.

St. Martin's Lane

$$$$–$$$$$ Piccadilly Circus This hip hotel has an almost surreal lobby; three restaurants; and 204 beautifully minimalist, all-white guest rooms designed by Phillipe Starck. *See map p. 132. 45 St. Martin's Lane (next to the English National Opera), London WC2N 4HX.* ☎ *020/7300-5500. Fax: 020/7300-5501.* www.morganshotelgroup.com.

Twenty Nevern Square

$$$ Earl's Court This sumptuously refurnished boutique hotel is plush and glamorous, with individually designed rooms and decor that emphasizes natural materials. *See map p. 132. 20 Nevern Sq., London SW5 9PD.* ☎ *020/7565-9555. Fax: 020/7565-9444.* www.twentynevernsquare.co.uk.

Dining Out

For the past two decades or so, London has been in the grip of a gastronomic revolution. The Modern British cuisine many London restaurants now serve takes old standards and deliciously reinvents them with foreign influences and ingredients, mostly from France (sauces), the Mediterranean (olive oil, oregano, and garlic), and northern Italy (pasta, polenta, and risotto). Besides Modern British cuisine, London foodies continue to favor classic French and Italian cuisines. Indian cooking has been a favorite ethnic food for decades. London abounds with Indian restaurants (about 1,500 of them) serving curries and dishes cooked in clay tandoori pots.

At the same time, you find a renewed interest in and respect for traditional English fare. In the past, many people called English cooking dull and tasteless. But when done well, this country's cuisine is both hearty and delicious. The best traditional dishes are game, lamb, meat and fish pies, and the ever popular roast beef with Yorkshire pudding (a crispy concoction made with meat drippings and served with gravy). At the lower end, you find fish and chips, steak-and-kidney pie, and *bangers and mash* (sausages and mashed potatoes) with a side of peas and carrots. (For more information on English food, check out Chapter 2.)

Neighborhoods for ethnic eats

London has more than 5,000 restaurants, so you can probably find something to suit your tastes and your pocketbook. Unlike in some other large cities, ethnic restaurants aren't really confined to one particular area of London. You do find a few exceptions, however: Several Chinese restaurants cluster along Lisle, Wardour, and Gerrard streets in Soho's Chinatown; Notting Hill has long been a standby for low-price Indian and Caribbean restaurants; and a number of Middle Eastern (especially Lebanese) restaurants line Edgware Road. But otherwise, ethnic restaurants are scattered all over. In terms of sheer variety, Soho and neighboring Covent Garden offer the most choices in the West End, with British, African, Caribbean, Mongolian, American (North and South), French, Italian, Spanish, Thai, Korean, Japanese, Middle Eastern, Eastern European, Modern European, Turkish, and vegetarian all represented. South Kensington offers you another grab bag of culinary choices.

Strategies for budget dining

Eating out in London can be mind-bogglingly pricey. So where do you go for lower-cost meals? Try pubs, cafes, sandwich bars, pizza places, and ethnic restaurants — places where you're not paying for custom cooking and personal service. If you opt for a pricier establishment, always see if the restaurant of your choice has a set-price menu. More and more of London's top restaurants offer two- and three-course fixed-price meals that can slash an a la carte tab by one-third or more. Sometimes restaurants call these fixed-price meals pre- or post-theater menus, which

London's Top Restaurants

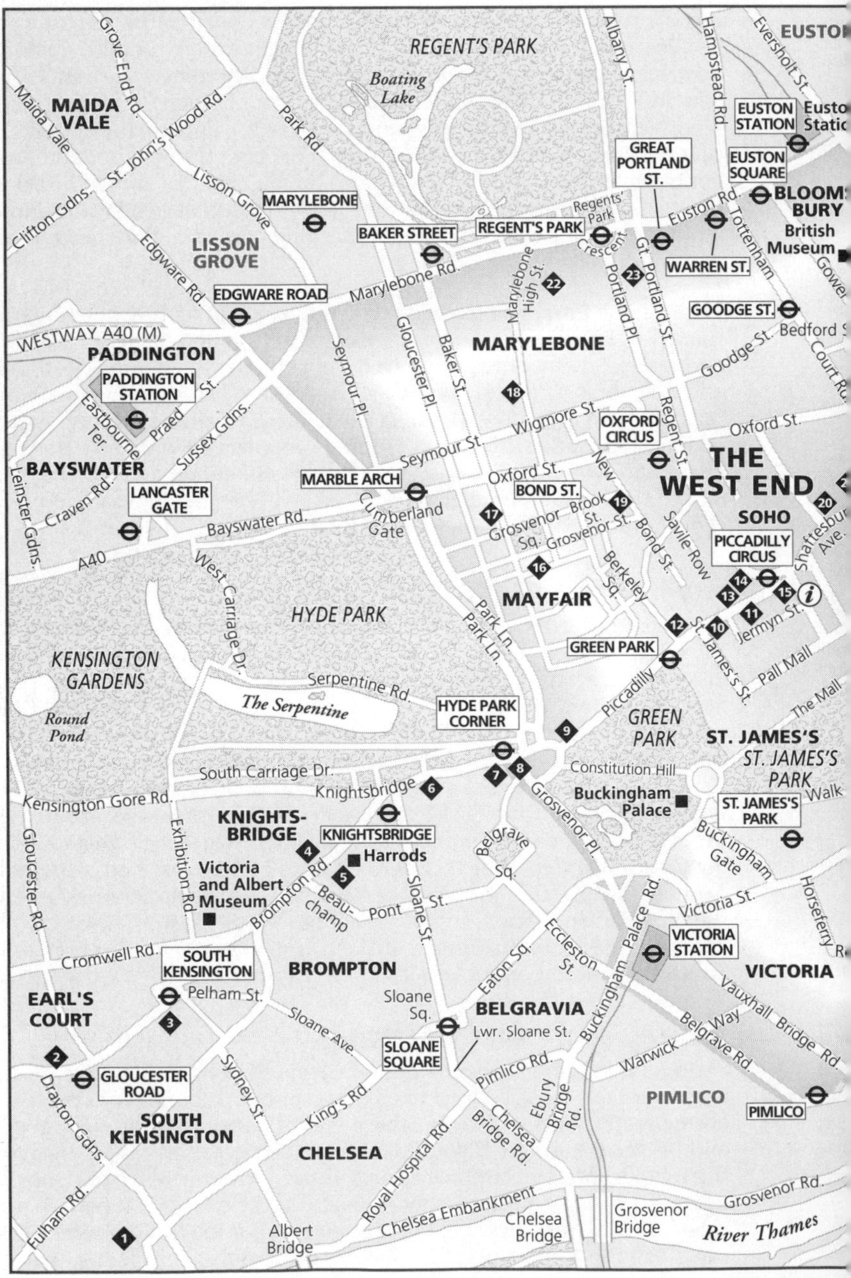

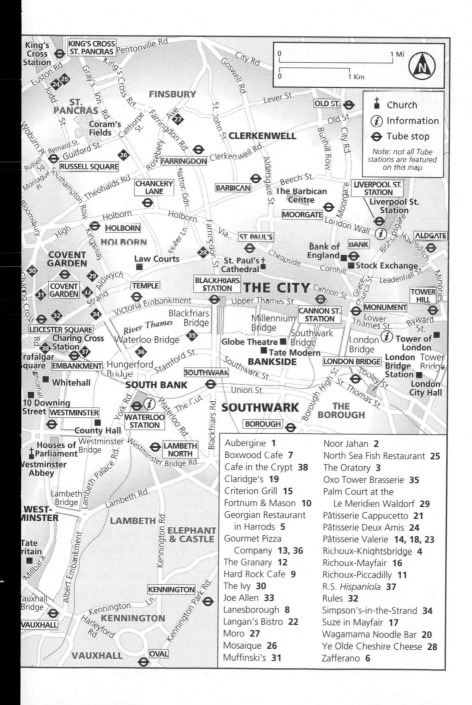

Aubergine **1**
Boxwood Cafe **7**
Cafe in the Crypt **38**
Claridge's **19**
Criterion Grill **15**
Fortnum & Mason **10**
Georgian Restaurant
  in Harrods **5**
Gourmet Pizza
  Company **13, 36**
The Granary **12**
Hard Rock Cafe **9**
The Ivy **30**
Joe Allen **33**
Lanesborough **8**
Langan's Bistro **22**
Moro **27**
Mosaique **26**
Muffinski's **31**

Noor Jahan **2**
North Sea Fish Restaurant **25**
The Oratory **3**
Oxo Tower Brasserie **35**
Palm Court at the
  Le Meridien Waldorf **29**
Pâtisserie Cappucetto **21**
Pâtisserie Deux Amis **24**
Pâtisserie Valerie **14, 18, 23**
Richoux-Knightsbridge **4**
Richoux-Mayfair **16**
Richoux-Piccadilly **11**
R.S. *Hispaniola* **37**
Rules **32**
Simpson's-in-the-Strand **34**
Suze in Mayfair **17**
Wagamama Noodle Bar **20**
Ye Olde Cheshire Cheese **28**
Zafferano **6**

means that the restaurant serves those menus only from about 5:30 p.m. to 7 p.m. and after 9:30 p.m. Wine can cost you a bundle, so forgo that glass of chardonnay if you need to watch your budget. And try your splurge dining at lunch, when prices often drop by one-third of the cost at dinner and you get the same food.

The top restaurants

For a key to the dollar-sign ratings that I use in the following listings, see the Introduction. For the locations of all the restaurants I discuss in this section, see the "London's Top Restaurants" map on p. 144.

Aubergine
$$$$ Chelsea FRENCH

Aubergine is one of London's top "name" restaurants, so you need to book weeks in advance. Chef William Drabble has earned a Michelin star for his delicate delivery of French haute cuisine. Every dish, from fish and lighter-Mediterranean-style choices *toassiette* of pork on creamed savoy cabbage and bacon, is a culinary achievement of the highest order. Cap off your meal with the celebrated cappuccino of white beans with grated truffle. Service is polished and efficient.

See map p. 144. 11 Park Walk, SW10. ☎ *020/7352-3449. Reservations essential. Tube: Sloane Square (then a ten-minute walk southwest on King's Road to Park Walk; or bus 11, 19, 22, or 211 southwest on King's Road from the Tube station). Fixed-price menus: lunch £32 ($59); dinner £55 ($102) for three courses, £72 ($133) for seven courses. AE, DC, MC, V. Open: Mon–Fri noon–2:15 p.m.; Mon–Sat 7–11 p.m.*

Boxwood Cafe
$$$ Knightsbridge MODERN BRITISH

This cafe may be the most stylish kid-friendly restaurant in London, but grownups can find plenty of comforting delights on the menu too. Created by Gordon Ramsay, Boxwood Cafe is chic without being fussy, and the same goes for the food, which emphasizes fresh and healthy dishes ranging from a baked macaroni of wild mushrooms and parmesan to fresh steamed fish, grilled calf's liver, roast chicken salad, veal, and steaks. The entire restaurant is nonsmoking.

See map p. 144. In the Berkeley Hotel, Wilton Place, SW1. ☎ *020/7235-1010. Tube: Knightsbridge (then a five-minute walk east on Brompton Road). Reservations recommended. Main courses: £14–£25 ($26–$46); fixed-price lunch £21 ($39); children's menu £7.50 ($14). AE, DISC, MC, V. Open: Mon–Fri noon–3 p.m.; Sat–Sun noon–4 p.m.; daily 6–11 p.m.*

Cafe in the Crypt
$ Trafalgar Square BRITISH

Eating in a crypt might not be everyone's idea of fun, but eating in this crypt — below St. Martin-in-the-Fields Church on Trafalgar Square — is an inexpensive London dining experience that you won't forget. The food is basic but good, served cafeteria style. Choose among a big salad bar and traditional main courses, such as shepherd's pie, filled rolls, and delicious soups. One fixture is that most traditional of British desserts, bread-and-butter pudding (bread soaked in eggs and milk with currants or sultanas and then oven-baked). The cavernous, candlelit room, with its great stone pillars, is wonderfully atmospheric.

See map p. 144. St. Martin-in-the-Fields, Duncannon Street, WC2. ☎ *020/7839-4342. Tube: Charing Cross (then a three-minute walk west to Trafalgar Square). Main courses: £5.95 £7.50 ($11–$14); fixed-price meal £5.25 ($9.70). No credit cards. Open: Mon–Wed 10 a.m.–7:30 p.m.; Thurs–Sat 10 a.m.–10:15 p.m.*

Criterion Grill
$$–$$$ Piccadilly   MODERN FRENCH/BRITISH

It's almost worth coming to the Criterion just to see its Byzantine palace interior with gold vaulted ceiling. The food — a mixture of modern French and British standards — doesn't quite match the grandeur of the décor, but it's generally quite good. You can order Brit faves like haddock or sausages, or French faves like slow-roast duck with apple sauce or steak au poivre. This place is smack-dab on Piccadilly Circus, making it wonderfully convenient. You can get a great deal with the fixed-price lunches and dinners.

See map p. 144. 224 Piccadilly, W1. ☎ *020/7930-0488. Reservations essential. Tube: Piccadilly Circus (the restaurant is on the southeast side of the Circus). Main courses: £11–£23 ($20–$43); fixed-price lunch and pre-theater dinner (5:30 7pm); £15–£18 ($28 $33). AE, DC, MC, V. Open: Daily noon–2:30 p.m., Mon–Sat 5:30–11:30 p.m.*

Fortnum & Mason
$$ St. James's   BRITISH

Fortnum & Mason, a posh London store famous for its food section, also has three restaurants: the lower-level Fountain (breakfast, lunch, tea, and dinner), the mezzanine-level Patio (lunch), and the fourth-floor St. James's (morning coffee, lunch, and afternoon tea). Although crowded with tourists, these restaurants remain pleasant places where you can get a good meal and a glimpse of the fading Empire. The Fountain serves sandwiches and daily specials. The Patio's lunch menu offers an assortment of pricey sandwiches and main courses, especially hot and cold pies (steak and kidney, curried fish and banana, chicken, and game) and Welsh *rarebit* (thick melted cheese poured over toast) prepared with Guinness stout. The well-heeled dine at the St. James's, where the menu is even more traditionally British: For starters, try the *kipper* (smoked herring) mousse or the potato and Stilton brûlée; main courses include pies and roast rib of Scottish beef. The more informal Fountain and Patio are good places to dine with a family, although St. James also welcomes children.

See map p. 144. 181 Piccadilly, W1. ☎ *020/7734-8040. Reservations accepted for St. James's only. Tube: Piccadilly Circus (then a five-minute walk west on Piccadilly).*

Main courses: £9–£24 ($17–$44); fixed-price menus: £20–£23 ($37–$43). AE, DC, MC, V. Open: St. James's and the Patio, Tues–Sat 10 a.m.–5:30 p.m.; the Fountain, Mon–Sat 8:30 a.m.–7:45 p.m.

Gourmet Pizza Company
$ St. James's   PIZZA/PASTA

If you're in the West End or across the river in Southwark and want an economical lunch or dinner in a family-friendly environment, stop at one of these bright, pleasant spots. You can choose among 20 pizzas (pizza as in pie, not slice). Everything from a B.L.T. version to one with Cajun chicken and prawns is available; about half the choices are vegetarian, and some are vegan. The crusts are light and crispy, and the toppings are fresh and flavorful. Rather than pizza, you may want to try ham and tomato tortellini with cream. The new branch at Upper Ground, Gabriel's Wharf (☎ 020/7928-3188; Tube: London Bridge), is right on the river.

See map p. 144. 7–9 Swallow Walk (off Piccadilly), W1. ☎ 020/7734-5182. Tube: Piccadilly Circus (then a five-minute walk west on Piccadilly and north on Swallow Street). Pizzas: £6–£9 (11–$17). Pastas: £7.75–£9.25 ($14–$17). AE, DC, MC, V. Open: Daily noon–10:30 p.m. (until midnight at Gabriel's Wharf location).

The Granary
$ Piccadilly Circus/Leicester Square   BRITISH

The newly refurbished Granary serves a simple but flavorful array of home-cooked dishes, listed daily on a chalkboard. Specials may include fresh pan-fried fish; lamb casserole with mint and lemon; steak and mushroom pie; or avocado stuffed with prawns, spinach, and cheese. Vegetarian meals include meatless versions of *paella* (a Spanish rice dish), lasagna, and *korma* (curried vegetables with Greek yogurt). The most tempting desserts are bread-and-butter pudding and brown Betty (both served hot). Large portions guarantee you won't go hungry. Kids enjoy the casual atmosphere and simple food.

See map p. 144. 39 Albemarle St., W1. ☎ 020/7493-2978. Tube: Green Park (then a five-minute walk east on Piccadilly to Albemarle) or Piccadilly Circus (then a five-minute walk west on Piccadilly). Main courses: £9–£11 ($17–$20). MC, V. Open: Mon–Fri 11:30 a.m.–7:30 p.m., Sat 11:30 a.m.–3:30 p.m.

Hard Rock Cafe
$$ Mayfair   NORTH AMERICAN

The original Hard Rock, now a worldwide chain of rock-and-roll/American-roadside-diner-themed restaurants, serves up comfort food amid a collection of rock memorabilia and loud music. The burgers aren't particularly good, so you may want to stick to the salads, all of them big enough for three. You can get some vegetarian dishes, too. Fajitas are another good choice, and they serve a pretty good homemade apple pie. Be prepared to stand in line on weekend evenings; teenagers love this place.

See map p. 144. 150 Old Park Lane, W1. ☎ *020/7629-0382. Tube: Hyde Park Corner (take the Park Lane exit; Old Park Lane is just east of Park Lane). Main courses: £7.50–£14 ($14–$26). AE, MC, V. Open: Sun–Thurs 11:30 a.m.–midnight, Fri–Sat 11:30 a.m.–1 a.m.*

The Ivy
$$ Soho BRITISH/FRENCH

The Ivy, with its 1930s look, tiny bar, glamour-scene crowd, and later-than-usual hours, is one of the hippest places to dine after the theater. The menu is simple, and the cooking is notable for skillful preparation of fresh ingredients. Popular menu items include white asparagus with sea kale and truffle butter, roast chicken and stuffing, roast beef and potatoes, and Mediterranean fish soup. Try one of the wonderful English desserts, such as sticky toffee pudding or caramelized bread-and-butter pudding. You need to book as far in advance as possible for this top dining spot.

See map p. 144. 1–5 West St., WC2. ☎ *020/7836-4751. Reservations required; book at least a month in advance. Tube: Leicester Square (then a five-minute walk north on Charing Cross Road; West Street is at the southeastern end of Cambridge Circus). Main courses: £9.50–£35 ($18–$65); fixed-price menu: Sat–Sun lunch £20–£22 ($37–$41). AE, DC, MC, V. Open: Daily noon–3 p.m. and 5:30 p.m.–midnight.*

Joe Allen
$$ Covent Garden NORTH AMERICAN

With its checkered tablecloths and crowded dining room, Joe Allen is the sort of gabby place where actors often come after a performance to wolf down chili con carne or gnaw on barbecued ribs. This spot keeps a low profile on a back street in Covent Garden. The food, American classics with some international twists, is sturdy and dependable, and the set menu is a real value: After a starter (maybe smoked haddock vichyssoise), you can choose main courses, such as pan-fried parmesan-crusted lemon sole, Cajun chicken breast, and grilled spicy Italian sausages. If you're an American feeling homesick, console yourself with a burger, a brownie, and a Coke. Come before the show for the best prices; come after for potential star-gazing.

See map p. 144. 13 Exeter St., WC2. ☎ *020/7836-0651. Reservations recommended. Tube: Covent Garden (then a five-minute walk south past the Market to Burleigh Street on the southeast corner of the Piazza and west on Exeter Street). Main courses: £9–£15 ($17–$28); fixed-price menus: lunch and pretheater dinner Mon–Fri £14–£16 ($26–$30).. AE, MC, V. Open: Mon–Fri noon–12:45 a.m., Sat 11:30 a.m.–12:45 a.m., Sun 11:30 a.m.–11:30 p.m.*

Langan's Bistro
$$ Marylebone BRITISH/FRENCH

Clusters of Japanese parasols, rococo mirrors, paintings, and old photographs cover this busy bistro's dining room, which sits behind a brightly colored storefront. The menu features English foods with an underplayed (some may say underdeveloped) French influence. Depending on the season, the fixed-price menu may start with smoked mackerel pate or a leek and Stilton tart and move on to grilled plaice with parsley butter or lamb kebab with polenta. Chocoholics have to try the dessert extravaganza known as "Mrs. Langan's chocolate pudding."

See map p. 144. 26 Devonshire St., W1. ☎ *020/7935-4531. Reservations recommended three days in advance. Tube: Regent's Park (then a five-minute walk south on Portland Place and west on Devonshire Street). Fixed-price menus: lunch or dinner £19 ($35) for two courses, £21 ($39) for three courses. AE, DC, MC, V. Open: Mon–Fri 12:30–2:30 p.m.; Mon–Sat 6:30–11 p.m.*

Moro
$$ Clerkenwell   SPANISH/NORTH AFRICAN

Clerkenwell, on the fringes of the City, has become a very hip neighborhood in recent years, and award-winning Moro has become this unpretentious area's best haute spot. The decor is modern and minimalist, and the North African cuisine is earthy and powerful. The kitchen uses only the best ingredients, organic whenever possible, in its daily-changing menu. I highly recommend the quail baked in flatbread with pistachio sauce and the tender wood-roasted pork, marinated in sherry. For dessert, try one the yummy house-specialty desserts: yogurt cake with pistachios or rosewater and cardamom ice cream.

See map p. 144. 34–36 Exmouth Market, EC1. ☎ *020/7833-8336. Reservations recommended. Tube: Farringdon (then a five-minute walk north on Farringdon to Exmouth Market). Main courses: £14–£18 ($26–$33); tapas: £3–£5 ($5.55–$9.25). AE, DC, MC, V. Open: Mon–Fri 12:30–2:30pm; Mon–Sat 7–10:30pm.*

Mosaique
$$ Holborn   MEDITERRANEAN

Tourists staying on the beaten track never find this wonderful restaurant, but the people who work in the area know it well. The interior is bright and cheerful, with yellow walls and white tablecloths glowing under skylights. The menu choices feature dishes from all across the Mediterranean region, prepared with an assured hand. You can dine here on the *mezes* (small plates), such as grilled *halloumi* or *tabbouleh,* or feast on a lamb or chicken "shish" (as in "kebab"), which comes with vegetables and rice. Vegetarian choices include risotto primavera and vegetable moussaka. At night, a jazz pianist adds to the ambience.

See map p. 144. 73 Gray's Inn Rd., WC1. ☎ *020/7404-7553. Reservations recommended. Tube: Chancery Lane (then a five-minute walk north on Gray's Inn Road). Main courses: £7.50–£15 ($14–$28); mezes: £2.95–£3.95 ($5.45–$7.30). AE, MC, V. Open: Mon–Fri noon–midnight; Sat 5pm–midnight.*

Noor Jahan
$$ **South Kensington**   **INDIAN**

Small, unpretentious, and always reliable, Noor Jahan is a neighborhood favorite. The marinated chicken and lamb dishes cooked tandoori style in a clay oven are moist and flavorful. Try the chicken *tikka* specialty, a staple of northern India, or sample one of the. *biriani* dishes — chicken, lamb, or prawns mixed with basmati rice, fried in ghee (thick, clarified butter), and served with a mixed vegetable curry. If you're unfamiliar with Indian food, the waiters will gladly explain the dishes.

See map p. 144. 2A Bina Gardens (off Old Brompton Road). ☎ *020/7373-6522. Reservations recommended. Tube: Gloucester Road (then a five-minute walk south on Gloucester Road, west on Brompton Road, north on Bina Gardens). Main courses: £6.50–£12 ($12–$22); fixed-price menu: £19 ($35). AE, DC, MC, V. Open: Daily noon– 2:45 p.m. and 6–11:45 p.m.*

North Sea Fish Restaurant
$$ **Bloomsbury**   **SEAFOOD**

If you get a craving for "real" fish and chips — not the generic frozen stuff that often passes for it — definitely try this unassuming "chippie" where the fish is *always* fresh. With its sepia prints and red velvet seats, the place is pleasant, comfortable, and popular with adults and kids. You may want to start with grilled fresh sardines or a fish cake before digging into a main course of cod or haddock. The fish is most often served battered and deep fried, but you can also order it grilled. The chips are almost as good as the fish.

See map p. 144. 7–8 Leigh St. (off Cartwright Gardens), WC1. ☎ *02073/875-892. Reservations recommended. Tube: Russell Square (then a ten-minute walk north on Marchmont Place and east on Leigh Street). Main courses: £8–£17 ($15–$31). AE, MC, V. Open: Mon–Sat noon–2:30 p.m. and 5:30–10:30 p.m.*

The Oratory
$$ **South Kensington**   **MODERN BRITISH**

Named for the nearby Brompton Oratory, a famous late-19th-century Catholic church, and close to the Victoria & Albert Museum and Knightsbridge shopping, this funky bistro serves up some of the best and least expensive food and wine in tony South Ken. The high-ceilinged room is decorated in what I call Modern Rococo, with enormous glass chandeliers, patterned walls and ceiling, and wooden tables with wrought-iron chairs. Take note of the daily specials on the chalkboard, especially any pasta dishes. Noteworthy dishes include homemade fish cakes, roasted field-mushroom risotto, and grilled calf's liver with bacon and deep-fried sage. For dessert, the sticky toffee pudding with ice cream melts in your mouth.

See map p. 144. 232 Brompton Rd., SW3. ☎ *020/7584-3493. Tube: South Kensington (then a five-minute walk north on Brompton Road). Main courses: £7–£15 ($13–$28);*

fixed-price menu: lunch specials £3.50–£6.95 ($6.45–$13). MC, V. Open: Daily noon–11 p.m.

Oxo Tower Brasserie
$$$$ South Bank   FRENCH/FUSION

Book well in advance, and insist on a window table at this sleek and stylish brasserie perched atop the landmark Oxo Tower on the South Bank. The Brasserie is less chi-chi than the adjacent Oxo Tower Restaurant, but you get marvelous food and pay about half the price of the place next door. Plus you can feast your eyes on the sublime river and city views. The food has taken on more fusion elements recently but remains as good as ever. Order such tasty dishes as roasted halibut with fried sweet potato or twice-cooked pork with coriander and chilies. The fixed-price lunch and pretheater menu makes this spot an affordable extravagance.

See map p. 144. Oxo Tower Wharf, Barge House Street, SE1. ☎ 020/7803-3888. Reservations essential; book at least one or two weeks in advance. Tube: Waterloo (then head north to the South Bank Centre and follow the Thames pathway east to the Oxo Tower, about a ten-minute walk). Main courses: £11–£17 ($19–$31); fixed-price lunch and pretheater menu (Mon–Fri) £17–£22 ($31–$41). AE, DC, MC, V. Open: Mon–Sat noon–3:15 p.m. and 5:30–11 p.m.; Sun 6–10 p.m.

R.S. Hispaniola
$$$ The Strand   BRITISH/FRENCH

Permanently moored in the Thames, this comfortably outfitted former passenger boat provides good food and spectacular views of the river traffic. The frequently changing menu offers a variety of sturdy and generally well-prepared dishes. On any given night, you may find calf's liver with olive mash, beef stroganoff with wild rice, rack of lamb marinated in honey, and several vegetarian dishes, such as linguini with leeks, red peppers, and basil oil. Most nights feature live music, and the place can be fun and romantic, if a bit touristy.

See map p. 144. River Thames, Victoria Embankment, Charing Cross, WC2. ☎ 020/7839-3011. Reservations recommended. Tube: Embankment (the restaurant is a few steps from the station). Main courses: £13–£18 ($24–$33); fixed-price lunch and dinner menu £25–£45 ($46–$83). AE, DC, MC, V. Open: Daily noon–3 p.m. and 6:30–11 p.m.; closed Dec 24–Jan 4.

Rules
$$$–$$$$ Covent Garden   BRITISH

If you want to eat classic British cuisine in a memorable (nay, venerable) setting, put on something dressy, and head for Maiden Lane. London's oldest restaurant, Rules was founded in 1798, and two centuries' worth of prints, cartoons, and paintings decorate the walls. The restaurant is completely nonsmoking, a rarity in London. If you're game for game, go for it, because that's what Rules is famous for. On the menu, you may find lobster and asparagus salad with mango dressing, or fallow deer with spiced red cabbage, blueberries, and bitter chocolate sauce. The food is delicious — traditional yet innovative, until you get to the puddings (desserts), which are a mix of nursery and dinner-dance classics. In recent years, the restaurant has added fish and a few vegetarian dishes.

See map p. 144. 35 Maiden Lane, WC2. ☎ 020/7836-5314. Reservations recommended. Tube: Covent Garden (then a five-minute walk south on James Street to Southampton Street behind Covent Garden Market and west on Maiden Lane). Main courses: £16–£21 ($30–$39); fixed-price menu: posttheater (Mon–Thurs 10 p.m.–11:30 p.m.) £18 ($33). AE, DC, MC, V. Open: Mon–Sat noon–11:30 p.m., Sun noon–10:30 p.m.

Simpson's-in-the-Strand
$$$ The Strand   BRITISH

Simpson's, open since 1828, boasts an army of formal waiters serving the best of staunchly traditional food. You find an array of the best roasts in London: sirloin of beef, saddle of mutton with red-currant jelly, and Aylesbury duckling. (Remember to tip the tail-coated carver.) For a pudding (dessert course), you may want to order treacle roll and custard or Stilton with vintage port. That's the downstairs restaurant. Simply Simpson, a brighter, lighter dining area on the second floor, is actually (gasp) nouvelle. This is also a great place to come for a real English breakfast. A jacket and tie are required for men downstairs; Simply Simpson has a smart-casual dress code (leave your tennis shoes and sweatpants or jeans in your hotel room).

See map p. 144. 100 The Strand (next to the Savoy Hotel), WC2. ☎ 020/7836-9112. Reservations required. Tube: Charing Cross (then a five-minute walk east along The Strand). Downstairs: main courses: £20–£24 ($37–$45); Simply Simpson: main courses: £10–£16 ($19–$30); fixed-price menus: £16–£19 ($30–$35); breakfast £16–£18 ($30–$33). AE, DC, MC, V. Open: Mon–Sat 7:15–10:30 a.m., 12:15–2:30 p.m., and 5–10:45 p.m.; Sun 6–8:30 p.m.

Suze in Mayfair
$–$$ Mayfair   PACIFIC RIM/INTERNATIONAL

For relaxed, charming, bistrolike ambience in Mayfair, check out Suze. The well-prepared food is Australasian with some international crossovers. Try the succulent New Zealand green-tipped mussels, a house specialty, or New Zealand scallops. You can also get New Zealand rack of lamb. You can choose among several sharing platters: cheese, Greek, Italian antipasti, seafood, and vegetarian. Save room for Pavlova, a light meringue covered with kiwi fruit, strawberries, passion fruit, and mangoes.

See map p. 144. 41 North Audley St., W1. ☎ 020/74913237. Reservations recommended. Tube: Marble Arch (then a five-minute walk east on Oxford Street and south on North Audley Street). Main courses: £6.25–£15 ($12–$28); platters to share: £4.95–£11 ($9.15–$20). AE, DC, MC, V. Open: Mon–Sat 11 a.m.–11 p.m.

Wagamama Noodle Bar
$ Soho JAPANESE

If you're exploring Soho and want a delicious, nutritious meal in a smoke-free room, try this trendsetting noodle bar modeled after the ramen shops of Japan. You pass along a stark, glowing corridor with a busy open kitchen and descend to a large open room with communal tables. The specialties are ramen, Chinese-style thread noodles served in soups with various toppings, and the fat white noodles called *udon*. You can also choose among rice dishes, vegetarian dishes, dumplings, vegetable and chicken skewers, and tempura. Your order is sent by radio signal to the kitchen and arrives the moment the food is ready. You may have to stand in line to get in, but it's worth the wait. Teens especially love the loud, hip, casual atmosphere. There are several other Wagamamas scattered all over London.

See map p. 144. 10A Lexington St., W1. ☎ *020/7292-0990. Reservations not accepted. Tube: Piccadilly Circus (then a five-minute walk north on Shaftesbury Avenue and Windmill Street, which becomes Lexington Street). Main courses: £5.50–9.25 ($10–$17); kids' menu: £3.50 ($6.50). MC, V. Open: Mon–Thurs noon–11 p.m.; Fri–Sat noon–midnight; Sun 12:30–10 p.m.*

Ye Olde Cheshire Cheese
$$ The City BRITISH

Opened in 1667 and a one-time haunt of Dr. Johnson, Charles Dickens, and Fleet Street newspaper scandalmongers, Ye Olde Cheshire Cheese is London's most famous chophouse. You find six bars and two dining rooms in this place, which is perennially popular with families and tourists looking for some Olde London atmosphere. The house specialties include "ye famous pudding" (steak, kidney, mushrooms, and game), Scottish roast beef with Yorkshire pudding and horseradish sauce, and Dover sole. If those choices put the kids off, they can choose sandwiches and salads.

See map p. 144. Wine Office Court, 145 Fleet St., EC4. ☎ *020/7353-6170. Tube: Blackfriars (then a ten-minute walk north on New Bridge Street and west on Fleet Street). Main courses: £7.25–£14 ($13–$26). AE, DC, MC, V. Open: pub Mon–Sat noon–11 p.m., Sun noon–10:30 p.m.; bar snacks and hot food daily noon–10 p.m.*

Zafferano
$$$$ Knightsbridge ITALIAN

If you want perhaps the best Italian food in London, served in a quietly elegant, attitude-free restaurant, head to Zafferano (but only after you've made reservations weeks in advance). The menu changes seasonally and retains classic favorites. The semolina pastas are perfectly cooked and come with various additions; you can sometimes get chestnut tagliatelle (wide noodle pasta) with wild mushrooms. The deliciously simple main courses may include roast rabbit with Parma ham and polenta, venison with polenta, tuna with rocket and tomato salad, and pan-fried prawns. For dessert, try ricotta and lemon cake with rum raisin ice cream.

See map p. 144. 15 Lowndes St., SW1. ☎ 020/7235-5800. Reservations essential. Tube: Knightsbridge (then a five-minute walk south on Lowndes Street, two streets east of Sloane Street). Fixed-price menus: lunch £24–£33 ($44–$61), dinner £30–£42 ($56–$78). AE, MC, V. Open: Daily noon–2:30 p.m. and 7–11 p.m. (Sun until 10:30 p.m.).

Treating Yourself to a Tea

The stereotype is true: Brits do drink tea. In fact, they drink 171 million cups per day (give or take a cup), though consumption is dropping, what with the new emphasis on coffee. Teatime is traditionally from about 3:30 to 5 p.m. Your afternoon tea can be a lavish affair served by a black-coated waiter in a hotel lobby, or you can have a quick "cuppa" with a slice of cake or a sandwich at a corner tea shop or *patisserie* (a bakery where you can sit down or get pastries to take away). Tea may be served fast-food style in paper cups, home-style in mugs, or more elegantly on bone china.

So what exactly, you ask, is the difference between afternoon tea and high tea?

- ✔ **Afternoon tea:** Tea with cakes, scones, or sandwiches (or all of them), served between 3 and 5 p.m.

- ✔ **High tea:** Served from about 5 to 6 p.m., this teatime is a more elaborate affair, including a light supper with a hot dish, followed by dessert and tea.

Casual tearooms and patisseries

In the following comfortable neighborhood tearooms and patisseries, you can get a good cup of tea along with a scone or other pastry or a plate of tea sandwiches for about £4 to £10 ($7.40–$19):

- ✔ **Muffinski's** (5 King St., WC2; ☎ 020/7379-1525; Tube: Leicester Square): Offers great homemade muffins, including low-fat and vegetarian ones. It's open Monday through Friday from 8 a.m. to 7 p.m., Saturday from 9 a.m. to 7 p.m., and Sunday from 10 a.m. to 6 p.m.

- ✔ **Pâtisserie Cappuccetto** (8 Moor St., W1; ☎ 020/7437-9472; Tube: Leicester Square): Serves breakfast, sandwiches, soups, and superb desserts Monday through Thursday from 8 a.m. to 11:30 p.m., and Friday and Saturday from 8 a.m. to 12:30 a.m.

- ✔ **Pâtisserie Deux Amis** (63 Judd St., WC1; ☎ 020/7383-7029; Tube: Russell Square): A good choice for a quick bite. It's open Monday through Saturday from 9 a.m. to 5:30 p.m. and Sunday from 9 a.m. to 1:30 p.m.

- ✔ **Pâtisserie Valerie** (44 Old Compton St., W1; ☎ 020/7437-3466; Tube: Leicester Square or Tottenham Court Road): Around since 1926, this place serves a mouthwatering array of pastries, but expect to stand in line, night or day. It's open Monday through Friday from 7:30 a.m. to 8 p.m., Saturday from 8 a.m. to 6:30 p.m., and Sunday from 9 a.m. to 6 p.m.

Pâtisserie Valerie also has two branches in Marylebone. One is at 105 Marylebone High St., W1 (☎ 020/7935-6240; Tube: Bond Street or Baker Street); the other is near Regent's Park at 66 Portland Place, W1 (☎ 020/7631-0467; Tube: Regent's Park). The Marylebone branch is open Monday through Saturday 7:30 a.m. to 6 p.m., and Sunday 9 a.m. to 6 p.m. The Regent's Park branch opens at 7:30 a.m. Monday through Saturday (8 a.m. on Sunday) and stays open until 7 p.m., and opens at 8 a.m. on Sunday.

✔ **Richoux:** This place has three old-fashioned tearooms in choice London locations. They serve food all day long, and they're kind to your budget:

> **Richoux-Knightsbridge** (215 Brompton Rd., SW3; ☎ 020/ 7823-9971; Tube: Knightsbridge)

> **Richoux-Mayfair** (41A South Audley St., W1; ☎ 020/7629-5228; Tube: Bond Street or Green Park)

> **Richoux-Piccadilly** (172 Piccadilly, W1; ☎ 020/7493-2204; Tube: Piccadilly Circus)

All locations keep the same hours: Monday through Friday 7 a.m. to 7 p.m., Saturday 7:30 a.m. to 7 p.m., and Sunday 8 a.m. to 6 p.m.

Elegant spots for high tea

A traditional afternoon English tea has cakes, sandwiches, and scones with clotted cream and jam, and is "taken" in a posh hotel or restaurant. These rather lavish affairs are expensive but memorable. At any one of the following places, you can get a proper traditional afternoon or high tea (respect the smart-casual dress code — don't wear tennis shoes and jeans):

✔ **Claridge's** (Brook Street, W1; ☎ 020/7629-8860; Tube: Bond Street): Serves a glamorous and expensive tea daily from 3 to 5:30 p.m. for £30 ($56). Reservations are a good idea.

✔ **Fortnum & Mason** (181 Piccadilly, W1; ☎ 020/7734-8040; Tube: Piccadilly Circus): Serves tea in the **St. James's Restaurant,** Monday through Saturday 3 to 5:30 p.m. for £20 ($37). Reservations aren't necessary.

✔ **Georgian Restaurant,** on the fourth floor of Harrods (87–135 Brompton Rd., SW1; ☎ 02/07225-6800; Tube: Knightsbridge): Serves high tea Monday through Saturday from 3:45 to 5:30 p.m. It costs £19 ($35) per person, and you don't need reservations.

✔ **Lanesborough** hotel (Hyde Park Corner, SW1; ☎ **02072/595-599;** Tube: Hyde Park Corner): You need reservations for high tea here, which is served daily 3:30 to 6 p.m. You pay £26 ($48); the price goes up to £34 ($63) if you add strawberries and champagne.

✔ **Palm Court** at the Le Meridien Waldorf Hotel (Aldwych, WC2; ☎ **02078/362-400;** Tube: Covent Garden): Serves afternoon tea Monday through Friday from 3 to 5:30 p.m. at a cost of £18 to £21 ($33–$39); reservations are required.

Chapter 12

Exploring London

● ●

In This Chapter

▶ Visiting London's many attractions

▶ Choosing a tour that's right for you

▶ Finding London's hot shopping spots

▶ Discovering London theater and nightlife

▶ Getting some fast facts about London

● ●

*T*wo millennia ago, London was *Londinium,* a walled colony of the Roman Empire. Today, this dazzling metropolis, home to more than 7 million people, is one of the most historic, cultured, and exciting cities on earth. London is a big city built (mostly) on a human scale, with charming old streets, bustling modern thoroughfares, plenty of greenery, plenty of traffic, and a vitality that spills over into the night. When the sun goes down and floodlights bathe London's historic buildings and monuments, all kinds of new possibilities spring up.

History-laden London can stir the imagination like few other cities. No matter how often you hear or read about places such as Westminster Abbey, Buckingham Palace, and the Tower of London, nothing can beat the thrill of actually visiting them. And although you'll no doubt keep yourself busy trying to see the important sights, save a little time for just wandering around London's streets. You can find a wealth of architectural styles, curious reminders of days gone by, and blue famous-person-lived-here plaques on houses all over the city. On some streets, you can almost hear the horses' hooves clopping on the cobblestones, as they did until about 1915. London grew from a series of villages, and that villagelike character survives in many London neighborhoods.

Discovering the Top Attractions

Where do you begin? If you're a dedicated museum maven, London's museums can keep you going for days, weeks, months, and even years. But the city is also loaded with famous monuments, fascinating historic buildings, and flower-filled parks. In this treasure trove of possibilities, you have to make some decisions. The sights in this section are my roster of the most important London attractions. For their locations, see the "London's Top Attractions" map on p. 160.

To beat the crowds, try to hit the top sights on your London list early in the day (preferably right when they open) or late in the afternoon. Westminster Abbey, to cite just one example, can receive upward of 15,000 visitors per day. Other top tourist draws, such as Buckingham Palace (when it's open to the public during August and September), the Tower of London, the British Museum, and Madame Tussauds can jam up as the day wears on.

British Museum
Bloomsbury

The **British Museum** ranks as the most-visited attraction in London, with a magnificent, wide-ranging collection of treasures from around the world. Wandering through its seemingly endless galleries, you can't help but be struck by humankind's enduring spirit and creativity. You can see permanent displays of antiquities from Egypt, Western Asia, Greece, and Rome, as well as prehistoric and Romano-British, medieval, Renaissance, modern, and Oriental collections. The most famous of the countless treasures are the superb **Parthenon Sculptures** that once adorned the Parthenon in Athens — sculptures that Greece wants returned. Other must-sees are the **Rosetta Stone** (which allowed archaeologists to decipher Egyptian hieroglyphics); the **Egyptian Mummies;** the **Sutton Hoo Treasure,** an Anglo-Saxon burial ship believed to be the tomb of a seventh-century East Anglian king; and **Lindow Man,** a well-preserved ancient corpse found in a bog. In December 2000, the museum's **Great Court** reopened with a glass-and-steel roof designed by Lord Norman Foster. Inaccessible to the general public for 150 years, the Great Court is now the museum's central axis. In the center, a circular building completed in 1857 served as the museum's famous **Reading Room.** Completely restored, this building now houses computer terminals where visitors can access images and information about the museum's vast collections. For a layout of the museum, see the "British Museum" map on p. 163.

If you get hungry along the way, you can find a cafe and a restaurant in the Great Court, and another cafe next to Room 12. Weekday mornings are the best times to go and avoid big crowds. You may want to pick up a *Visit Guide* (£2.50/$4.65) at the information desk in the Great Court to help you chart your way.

 If you have only limited time for the British Museum, consider taking one of the **90-minute highlight tours** offered daily at 10:30 a.m. and 1 and 3 p.m.; the tour costs £8 ($15). Audio tours covering some of the most important objects in the museum's collections cost £3.50 ($6.50). You can get tickets and information for both tours at the information desk in the Great Court.

See map p. 160. Great Russell Street (between Bloomsbury Street and Montgomery Street), WC1. ☎ *020/7636-1555.* www.thebritishmuseum.ac.uk. *Tube: Russell Square (then a five-minute walk south on Montgomery Street, along the west side of Russell Square, to the museum entrance on Great Russell Street). Admission: Free. Open: Sat–Wed 10 a.m.–5:30 p.m., Thurs–Fri 10 a.m.–8:30 p.m.; closed Jan 1, Good Friday, Dec 24–26. Most of the museum has wheelchair access by elevator; call for entrance information.*

London's Top Attractions

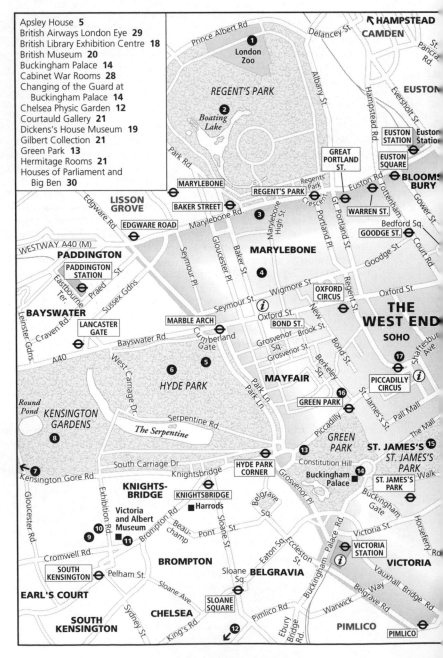

Apsley House **5**
British Airways London Eye **29**
British Library Exhibition Centre **18**
British Museum **20**
Buckingham Palace **14**
Cabinet War Rooms **28**
Changing of the Guard at
  Buckingham Palace **14**
Chelsea Physic Garden **12**
Courtauld Gallery **21**
Dickens's House Museum **19**
Gilbert Collection **21**
Green Park **13**
Hermitage Rooms **21**
Houses of Parliament and
  Big Ben **30**

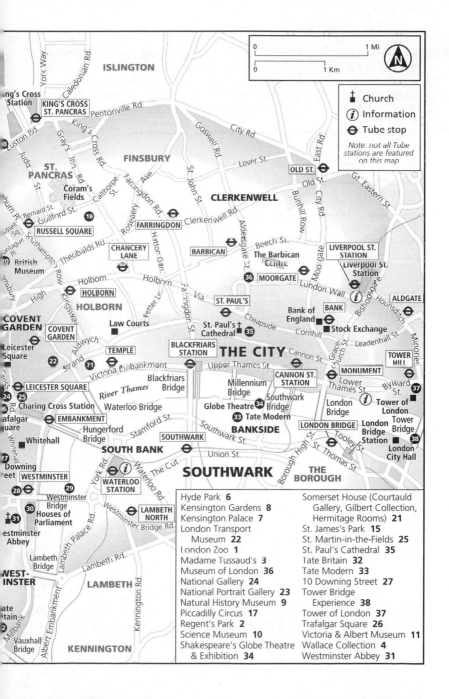

0 — 1 Mi
0 — 1 Km

N

† Church
(i) Information
⊖ Tube stop

Note: not all Tube stations are featured on this map

Hyde Park **6**
Kensington Gardens **8**
Kensington Palace **7**
London Transport Museum **22**
London Zoo **1**
Madame Tussaud's **3**
Museum of London **36**
National Gallery **24**
National Portrait Gallery **23**
Natural History Museum **9**
Piccadilly Circus **17**
Regent's Park **2**
Science Museum **10**
Shakespeare's Globe Theatre & Exhibition **34**

Somerset House (Courtauld Gallery, Gilbert Collection, Hermitage Rooms) **21**
St. James's Park **15**
St. Martin-in-the-Fields **25**
St. Paul's Cathedral **35**
Tate Britain **32**
Tate Modern **33**
10 Downing Street **27**
Tower Bridge Experience **38**
Tower of London **37**
Trafalgar Square **26**
Victoria & Albert Museum **11**
Wallace Collection **4**
Westminster Abbey **31**

The power of the written word

The incredible literary collection that was in the British Museum Reading Room (including its rare copy of the *Magna Carta,* the charter of liberties that was a forerunner to modern constitutions) has been moved to a remarkable new space in North London. For details, see the entry for the **British Library Exhibition Centre** in the section "Finding More Cool Things to See and Do," later in this chapter.

Buckingham Palace
St. James's Park and Green Park

All the pomp, majesty, scandal, intrigue, tragedy, power, wealth, and tradition associated with the British monarchy hide behind the monumental facade of **Buckingham Palace,** the London residence of the sovereign since Victoria ascended the throne in 1837.

An impressive early-18th-century structure, the palace was rebuilt in 1825 and further modified in 1913. From late July or early August (the dates change yearly) through September, when the royal family isn't in residence, you can buy a ticket to get a glimpse of the impressive staterooms used by Elizabeth II and the other royals. There isn't a guided palace tour; you just wander at your own speed through 18 rooms, most of them baroque, filled with some of the world's finest artworks. In these rooms, the queen receives guests on official occasions. You leave through the gardens where the queen holds her famous garden parties each summer. Budget about two hours for your visit.

On Monday through Thursday throughout the year, you can visit the **Royal Mews,** one of the finest working stables in existence, which house the magnificent Gold State Coach (used in every coronation since 1831) and other royal conveyances. The newly refurbished **Queen's Gallery,** which features changing exhibits of works from the Royal Collection, reopened early in 2002 in time for the queen's Golden Jubilee.

Buckingham Palace forms the centerpiece of **St. James's Park** and **Green Park,** two royal parks acquired by Henry VIII in the early 16th century. St. James's Park, the prettier of the two, was landscaped in 1827 by John Nash in a picturesque English style with an ornamental lake and promenades. Major ceremonial occasions are held in **The Mall,** a processional route between the palace and Whitehall and Horse Guards Parade. **St. James's Palace,** the former London abode of Prince Charles and his two sons, and adjacent **Clarence House,** residence of the Queen Mum until her death in 2002 and now the London home of Prince Charles, are between The Mall and **Pall Mall** (pronounced *Pell Mell*), a broad avenue running from Trafalgar Square to St. James's Palace. Neither residence is open to visitors.

British Museum

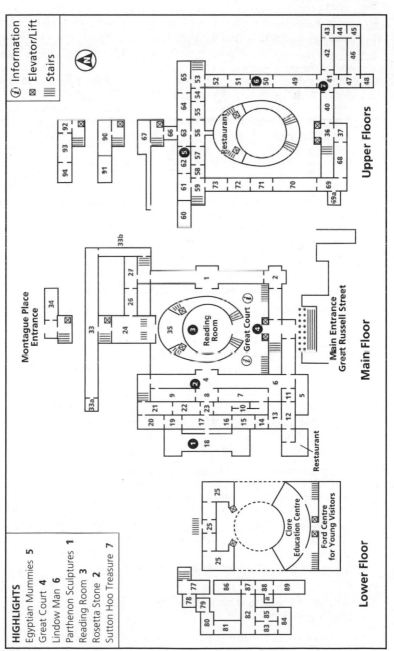

Information

⊠ Elevator/Lift

‖‖ Stairs

Upper Floors

Main Floor

Montague Place
Entrance

Main Entrance
Great Russell Street

Reading
Room

Great Court

Restaurant

Restaurant

Lower Floor

Clore
Education Centre

Ford Centre
for Young Visitors

HIGHLIGHTS

Egyptian Mummies **5**
Great Court **4**
Lindow Man **6**
Parthenon Sculptures **1**
Reading Room **3**
Rosetta Stone **2**
Sutton Hoo Treasure **7**

You can charge tickets for Buckingham Palace visits by calling ☎ **020/ 7766-7300.** A ticket office in Green Park is open daily July 29 to October 1 from 9 a.m. until 4 p.m. or until it sells the last ticket. Keep in mind that every visitor gets a specific time for entry into the palace, so you probably want to phone ahead for tickets. All phone-charged tickets cost an additional £1 ($1.85).

See map p. 160. Buckingham Palace Road, SW1. Palace Visitor Office and Royal Mews ☎ *020/7839-1377 (9:30 a.m.–5:30 p.m.) or 020/7799-2331 (24-hour recorded info).* www.royal.gov.uk. *Tube: St. James's Park (then a ten-minute walk north on Queen Anne's Gate and west on Birdcage Walk to Buckingham Gate); or Green Park (walk directly south through the park). Admission: Palace, £14 ($26) adults, £12 ($22) seniors over 60, £7 ($13) children under 17, £34 ($63) families (2 adults, 2 children under 17). Royal Mews, £6 ($11) adults, £5 ($9.25) seniors, £3.50 ($6.50) children, £14 ($26) families. Queen's Gallery, £7.50 ($14) adults, £6 ($11) seniors, £4 ($7.40) children. Open: Palace, Aug–Oct (dates may vary by a day or two) daily 9:30 a.m.–6:30 p.m. Royal Mews, Mar–July Sat–Thurs 11 a.m.–4 p.m. (last admission 3:15 p.m.); Aug–Sept daily 10 a.m.–5 p.m. (last admission 4:15 p.m.). Queen's Gallery, daily 10 a.m.–5:30 p.m (last admission 4:30 p.m.). Royal Mews and Queen's Gallery closed Dec 25–26. Visitors with disabilities must prebook; Royal Mews and Queen's Gallery are wheelchair accessible.*

Changing of the Guard at Buckingham Palace
St. James's Park

Free of charge, you can stand outside Buckingham Palace and watch the **Changing of the Guard.** The Foot Guards of the Household Division of the Army, the queen's personal guard, carry out the ritual. The Old Guard forms in the palace forecourt before going off duty and handing everything over to the New Guard, which leaves Wellington Barracks at 11:27 a.m. precisely and marches to the palace on Birdcage Walk, usually accompanied by a band. The Guard consists of 3 officers and 40 men but is reduced when the queen is away. The entire ceremony takes around 40 minutes. If you can't find a spot at the front of the railings of Buckingham Palace, you can see pretty well from the Victoria Memorial in front of the palace.

The pageantry of the Changing of the Guard is no longer a daily occurrence. The event takes place April to early June daily at 11:30 a.m., but only on alternate days at other times of the year. To avoid disappointment, call ahead or check the Web site listed in the following information.

See map p. 160. Buckingham Palace Road, SW1. ☎ *020/7321-2233 (24-hour recorded info).* www.army.mod.uk. *Tube: St. James's Park (then a ten-minute walk north on Queen Anne's Gate and west on Birdcage Walk to Buckingham Gate); or Green Park (walk directly south through the park). Admission: Free.*

Houses of Parliament and Big Ben
Westminster

The **Houses of Parliament,** situated along the Thames, house the landmark clock tower containing **Big Ben,** a huge bell whose booming chime

More changing of the guards

If you miss the Changing of the Guard, or if the event doesn't take place on the day of your visit, you can still get an eyeful of London pageantry by attending the **Mounted Guard Changing Ceremony** at the Horse Guards Building in Whitehall. The ceremony takes place Monday to Saturday at 11 a.m. and Sunday at 10 a.m. No ticket is required, but arrive early for a good view. To get there, take the Tube to Charing Cross, and walk south from Trafalgar Square along Whitehall (about a five-minute walk); the Horse Guards Building will be on your right.

is a familiar London sound. Designed in a neo-Gothic style by Sir Charles Barry and A.W.N. Pugin, the Parliament buildings were completed in 1857. Covering approximately 8 acres, they occupy the site of an 11th-century palace of Edward the Confessor. At one end (Old Palace Yard) is the **Jewel House,** built in 1366 and the former treasury house of Edward III, who reigned from 1327 to 1377.

For most visitors, a glimpse of the exterior of the Houses of Parliament is sufficient (you can get the best view from Westminster Bridge). If you want to sit in the **Stranger's Gallery** to hear the rancorous debates, you can line up (pardon me, *queue*) for tickets at the St. Stephen's entrance.

Previously, overseas visitors had to go through an elaborate procedure weeks in advance of their trip in order to tour the Houses of Parliament. Now, however, you can join **75 minute guided tours** in late summer and early fall (generally from the first week in July until early Oct). The tours cost £6 ($11), and you probably want to book in advance. The London ticket office in Westminster Hall (at the Houses of Parliament) opens in mid-July. You can reserve by phone at ☎ **0870/906-3773** or order tickets online at www.firstcalltickets.com. For the rest of the year, the procedure for getting a tour is much more difficult. If you're interested, you can find details on the Web at www.parliament.uk.

See map p. 160. Bridge Street and Parliament Square, SW1. ☎ *020/7219-4272. Tube: Westminster (you can see the clock tower with Big Ben directly across Bridge St. when you exit). Admission: Free. For free tickets, join the line at St. Stephen's entrance. Open: Stranger's Gallery House of Commons, Mon 7:30–10:30 p.m., Tues–Wed 11:30 a.m.–7:30 p.m., Thurs 11:30 a.m.–6:30 p.m., most Fridays 9:30 a.m.– 3 p.m.; House of Lords, Mon–Wed 2:30–10 p.m., Thurs 11 a.m.–7:30 p.m. Parliament isn't in session late July to mid-Oct or on weekends.*

Kensington Gardens
Kensington

One of London's loveliest and most family-friendly parks, **Kensington Gardens** adjoins Hyde Park west of the Serpentine lake. The park was laid out during the reign of William and Mary, after they moved into Kensington

Palace in 1689. Generations of children have gazed upon the famous bronze statue of **Peter Pan,** located north of the Serpentine Bridge. Commissioned in 1912 by Peter Pan's creator, J.M. Barrie, the statue marks the spot where Peter Pan (in the book *Peter Pan in Kensington Gardens*) entered the gardens to get to his home on Serpentine Island.

The park is also home to the **Albert Memorial,** an ornate neo-Gothic memorial honoring Queen Victoria's husband, Prince Albert; the lovely **Italian Gardens;** and the free **Serpentine Gallery** (☎ 020/7298-2100), which is gaining a reputation for showing cutting-edge art and is open daily (except Dec 24–27 and Jan 1) 10 a.m. to 6 p.m. The **Princess Diana Memorial Playground,** which opened in 2000, is in a fenced-in area at the park's northwest corner. If the weather is fine, give yourself enough time for a leisurely stroll — at least a couple of hours.

See map p. 160. Bounded by Kensington Palace Gardens and Palace Green on the west, Bayswater Road on the north, Kensington Road and Kensington Gore on the south. ☎ *020/7298-2100.* www.royalparks.gov.uk/parks/kensington_gardens.*Tube: High Street Kensington (then a ten-minute walk east on Kensington High Street) or Queensway (directly across from the northwest corner of the park). Admission: Free. Open: Daily dawn to midnight.*

Kensington Palace
Kensington

Acquired by William III in 1689 and remodeled by Sir Christopher Wren, the monarchy used **Kensington Palace** as a royal residence until 1760. Victoria was born in the palace and was informed here, in 1837, that she was the new queen of England (and could move to the grander Buckingham Palace). One wing of the palace was Princess Diana's London home after her divorce from Prince Charles. After her death, tens of thousands of mourners gathered in front of the palace and left a sea of floral tributes.

The palace was also the home of Princess Margaret (Queen Elizabeth's sister) until her death in 2002 and is still the home of the duke and duchess of Kent, so portions of the building are closed to visitors. But you can visit the **State Apartments.** A **free audio guide,** keyed to every room and exhibit, explains the history and background of what you're seeing. Before reaching the State Apartments, you pass through the **Royal Ceremonial Dress Collection**'s Dressing-for-Royalty exhibit, which takes you through the process of being presented at court, from the first visit to the tailor or dressmaker to the final bow or curtsy. Dresses worn by Queen Victoria, Queen Elizabeth II, and Princess Diana are on display. Give yourself about two hours to view the dress collection and the palace's rooms.

For a pleasant and not-too-expensive tea or snack after visiting Kensington Palace, stop in at **The Orangery** (☎ 020/7376-0239) in the gardens next to the palace. The cafe is open daily noon to 6 p.m. Lunches cost about £7 ($13); from 3 p.m., you can get a good tea for £7 to £14 ($13–$26).

See map p. 160. The Broad Walk, Kensington Gardens, W8. ☎ *0870/751-5170.* www. hrp.org.uk. *Tube: Queensway on the north side (then a ten-minute walk south through the park) or High Street Kensington on the southwest side (then a ten-minute walk through the park). Open: Mar–Oct daily 10 a.m.–5 p.m., Nov–Feb daily 10 a.m.– 4 p.m. Admission: £11 ($20) adults, £8.20 ($15) seniors and children 5 to 15. Despite some stairs, the palace is accessible for visitors with disabilities; call first.*

Madame Tussauds
Marylebone

Madame Tussauds wax museum is a world-famous tourist attraction, and people tend to either love it or hate it. The question is: Do you want to pay the exorbitant admission price and devote the time to see lifelike wax figures? (You need at least two hours to see everything.) The original moldings of members of the French court are undeniably fascinating. Madame Tussaud had direct access to the former royals — she made molds of their heads after they were guillotined during the French Revolution. And animatronic gadgetry makes the **Spirit of London** theme ride fun. But the **Chamber of Horrors** is definitely for the ghoulish (parents with little ones may want to think twice about wandering here). This is where you can see one of Jack the Ripper's victims lying in a pool of (wax?) blood and likenesses of mass murderers, such as Gary Gilmore and Charles Manson. You can find better stars next door at the **London Planetarium** (☎ 020/7935-6861).

Go early to beat the crowds; better still, reserve tickets by credit card (☎ 0870/400-3000) up to three days in advance and then go straight to the head of the line at your scheduled time.

See map p. 160. Marylebone Road, NW1. ☎ *02079/356-861.* www.madame-tussauds.com. *Tube: Baker Street (then a two-minute walk east on Marylebone Road). Admission: £20 ($37) adults, £17 ($31) seniors over 60, £16 ($30) children under 16; children under 4 not admitted. Combination tickets (including the London Planetarium): £22 ($41) adults, £19 ($35) seniors, £18 ($33) children. Open: Mon–Fri 9 a.m.–5:30 p.m.; Sat–Sun 9 a.m.–6 p.m. Tussauds is wheelchair accessible by elevator, but call first, because only three chair-users are allowed in at a time.*

National Gallery
Trafalgar Square

If great art is your passion, you may think that the **National Gallery** is paradise. The museum houses one of the world's most comprehensive collections of British and European paintings. All the major schools from the 13th to the 20th centuries are represented, but the Italians get the lion's share of wall space, with artists like Leonardo da Vinci, Botticelli, and Raphael on the roster. The French Impressionist and post-Impressionist works by Monet, Manet, Seurat, Cézanne, Degas, and van Gogh are shimmering and sublime. And because you're on English soil, check out at least a few of Turner's stunning seascapes, Constable's landscapes, and Reynolds' society portraits. And you don't want to miss the Rembrandts.

Budget at least two hours here. If you're hungry, stop by the second-floor restaurant for lunch, tea, or snacks.

Use the free **computer information center** to make the most of your time at the gallery. You can design a tour based on your artistic preferences and print out a customized tour map. You can also rent a portable **audio-tour guide** for ₤3 ($5.55). **Free guided tours** are offered daily at 11:30 a.m. and 2:30 p.m., with an additional tour on Wednesday at 6:30 p.m.

A ₤21 million ($39 million) revamp of the National Gallery began in 2003 and is scheduled to be completed by 2006. When work is finished, the gallery will have two new entrances in the east wing and a new shop and cafe, and a previously hidden inner courtyard will be transformed into a spacious atrium.

See map p. 160. Trafalgar Square, WC2. ☎ *020/7747-2885.* www.nationalgallery. org.uk. *Tube: Charing Cross (then a two-minute walk north across Trafalgar Square). Admission: Free, but admission charged for special exhibits, usually around £5 ($9.25) per person. Open: Daily 10 a.m.–6 p.m., Wed 10 a.m.–9 p.m.; closed Jan. 1, Good Friday, and Dec 24–26. The entire museum is wheelchair accessible.*

National Portrait Gallery
Trafalgar Square

What do the following people have in common: Sir Walter Raleigh, Shakespeare (wearing a gold earring), Queen Elizabeth I, the Brontë sisters, Winston Churchill, Oscar Wilde, Noël Coward, Mick Jagger, and Princess Di? Their portraits hang in the **National Portrait Gallery,** a visual *Who's Who* of famous Brits. The galleries are arranged in chronological order. The earliest portraits are in the **Tudor Gallery;** portraits from the 1960s to the 1980s are displayed in the **Balcony Gallery.** The rooftop cafe provides great West End views. Plan on spending at least two hours, but getting sidetracked here is easy, so you may want more time.

See map p. 160. St. Martin's Place (off Trafalgar Square behind the National Gallery), WC2. ☎ *020/7306-0055.* www.npg.org.uk. *Tube: Leicester Square (then a two-minute walk south on Charing Cross Road). Admission: Free; audio tour £3 ($5.55). Open: Sat–Wed 10 a.m.–6 p.m., Thurs–Fri 10 a.m.–9 p.m. All but the landing galleries are wheelchair accessible; call first for entry instructions.*

Picture-perfect Queen Mum

The royal-family portrait commissioned by the National Portrait Gallery to celebrate the Queen Mother's 100th birthday (in 2000) is the newest royal addition to go on display in the National Portrait Gallery. Artist John Wonnacott painted the canvas that portrays Queen Elizabeth, Prince Phillip, Prince Charles, and Princes William and Harry in conversation with the Queen Mother in the White Drawing Room in Buckingham Palace. Interestingly, Prince William — Charles' firstborn and thus the second in line to the throne — dominates the picture. The Queen Mother died in 2002.

Natural History Museum
South Kensington

Filled with magnificent specimens and exciting displays relating to natural history, this museum houses the national collections of living and fossil plants, animals, and minerals. The most popular attraction in this enormous Victorian-era museum is the huge **dinosaur exhibit,** with 14 complete skeletons; a pair of animatronic raptors; and a life-size, robotic T-Rex lunching on a freshly killed Tenontosaurus. Bug-filled **Creepy Crawlies** is another popular kid pleaser. The sparkling gems and crystals in the **Mineral Gallery** are literally dazzling, and in the **Meteorite Pavilion,** you can see fragments of rock that crashed into the earth from the farthest reaches of the galaxy. The museum offers enough to keep you occupied for at least two hours.

See map p. 160. Cromwell Road, SW7. ☎ *020/7942-5000.* www.nhm.ac.uk. *Tube: South Kensington (the Tube station is on the corner of Cromwell Road and Exhibition Road, at the corner of the museum). Admission: Free. Open: Mon–Sat 10 a.m.– 5:50 p.m., Sun 11 a.m.–5:50 p.m. Nearly all the galleries are flat or ramped for wheelchair users; call for instructions on entering the building.*

St. Paul's Cathedral
The City

After the Great Fire of 1666 destroyed the city's old cathedral, the great architect Christopher Wren was called upon to design **St. Paul's,** a huge and harmonious Renaissance-leaning-toward-baroque building. Nazi bombing raids wiped out the surrounding area, so Wren's masterpiece, capped by the most famous dome in London, rises majestically above a crowded sea of undistinguished office buildings. Grinling Gibbons carved the exceptionally beautiful choir stalls, which are the only impressive artworks inside.

Christopher Wren is buried in the crypt, and his epitaph, on the floor below the dome, reads "LECTOR, SI MONUMENTUM REQUIRIS, CIRCUMSPICE" ("Reader, if you seek his monument, look around you"). His companions in the crypt include Britain's famed national heroes: the Duke of Wellington, who defeated Napoleon at Waterloo; and Admiral Lord Nelson, who took down the French at Trafalgar during the same war. But many people want to see St. Paul's simply because Lady Diana Spencer wed Prince Charles here in what was billed as the fairy-tale wedding of the century.

You can climb up to the **Whispering Gallery** for a bit of acoustical fun or gasp your way up to the very top for a breathtaking view of London. You can see the entire cathedral in an hour or less. For an overview of the cathedral's layout, see the "St. Paul's Cathedral" map on p. 171.

The pedestrian-only **Millennium Bridge,** designed by Lord Norman Foster, links St. Paul's Cathedral to the Tate Modern art gallery on the other side of the Thames. The bridge was so shaky when it opened in 2000 that it was immediately closed for repairs. A steadier version reopened in 2001.

See map p. 160. St. Paul's Churchyard, Ludgate Hill, EC4. ☎ 020/7236-4128. www. stpauls.co.uk. *Tube: St. Paul's (then a five-minute walk west on Ludgate to cathedral entrance on St. Paul's Churchyard). Admission: £8 ($15) adults, £7 ($13) seniors and students, £3.50 ($6.50) children under 10. Guided tours: £2.50 ($4.65) adults, £2 ($3.70) seniors, £1 ($1.85) children. Audio tours (available 8:30 a.m.–3 p.m.) £3.50 ($6.50) adults, £3 ($5.55) seniors and students. Open: Mon–Sat 8:30 a.m.–4 p.m.; no sightseeing on Sun (services only). The cathedral is wheelchair accessible by the service entrance near the South Transept; ring the bell for assistance.*

Tate Britain
Pimlico

The Tate Gallery took this name to distinguish it from its new counterpart, Tate Modern, which opened in May 2000 on the South Bank. **Tate Britain** retains the older (pre-20th-century) collections of exclusively British art, plus works by major British stars like David Hockney and experimental works by Brits and foreigners living in Britain. Among the masterpieces on display in a host of newly refurbished galleries are dreamy works by the British pre-Raphaelites, the celestial visions of William Blake, bawdy satirical works by William Hogarth, genteel portraits by Sir Joshua Reynolds, bucolic landscapes by John Constable, and the shimmering seascapes of J.M.W. Turner. Plan on spending at least two hours here. A restaurant and cafe are on the lower level.

See map p. 160. Millbank, Pimlico SW1. ☎ 020/7887-8000. www.tate.org.uk. *Tube: Pimlico (then a ten-minute walk south on Vauxhall Bridge Road to the river and north on Millbank to the museum entrance). Bus: For a more scenic route, take bus 77A, which runs south along The Strand and Whitehall to the museum entrance on Millbank. Admission: Free; varying admission fees for special exhibits; audio tours £3 ($5.55). Open: Daily 10 a.m.–5:50 p.m. Most galleries are wheelchair accessible, but call first for details on entry.*

Tate Modern
Bankside

The former Bankside Power Station is the setting for the fabulous **Tate Modern,** which opened in May 2000. Considered one of the top modern art museums in the world, the Tate Modern houses a collection of international 20th-century art, displaying major works by some of the most influential artists of the last century: Picasso, Matisse, Dalí, Duchamp, Moore, and Bacon among them. A gallery for the 21st-century collection exhibits new art as artists create it. If you're a fan of contemporary art and architecture, don't miss this new star on the London art scene. Plan on spending at least two hours. The Tate Restaurant, open for lunch and tea, offers stunning views over the Thames; definitely call first to book a table.

See map p. 160. 25 Sumner St., SE1. ☎ 020/7887-8000. www.tate.org.uk. *Tube: Southwark (then a ten-minute walk north along Blackfriars Road and east along the riverside promenade) or Blackfriars (then a ten-minute walk south across Blackfriars Bridge). Admission: Free; special exhibits may have charges. Open: Mon–Thurs 10 a.m.–6 p.m., Fri–Sat 10 a.m.–10 p.m.*

St. Paul's Cathedral

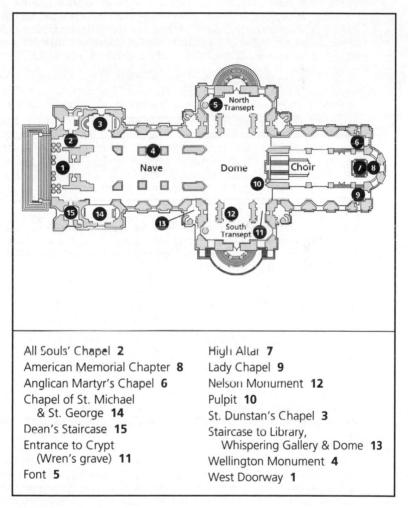

All Souls' Chapel **2**
American Memorial Chapter **8**
Anglican Martyr's Chapel **6**
Chapel of St. Michael
  & St. George **14**
Dean's Staircase **15**
Entrance to Crypt
  (Wren's grave) **11**
Font **5**

High Altar **7**
Lady Chapel **9**
Nelson Monument **12**
Pulpit **10**
St. Dunstan's Chapel **3**
Staircase to Library,
  Whispering Gallery & Dome **13**
Wellington Monument **4**
West Doorway **1**

Tower of London
The City

The **Tower of London** offers enough to keep you captivated for a good three to four hours, but *make sure* you save time for the **Crown Jewels,** which include the world's largest diamond (the 530-carat Star of Africa) and other breathtaking gems set into royal robes, swords, scepters, and crowns.

In 1066, William the Conqueror built the city's best-known historic site. The Tower served as his fortress and later as a prison, holding famous captives, such as Sir Walter Raleigh and Princess Elizabeth I. Anne Boleyn and

Catherine Howard (two of the eight wives of Henry VIII), the nine-day queen Lady Jane Grey, and Sir Thomas More were among those who lost their heads on **Tower Green.** According to Shakespeare, henchmen of Richard III murdered the two little princes (the sons of Edward IV) in the **Bloody Tower,** but many modern historians refute this story. For the layout of the tower, see the "Tower of London" map on p. 173.

Huge black ravens hop around the grounds of the Tower of London. A legend says that the tower and the British Commonwealth will fall if the ravens ever leave. Their wings have been clipped as a precaution.

See map p. 160. Tower Hill, EC3. ☎ *020/7709-0765.* www.hrp.org.uk. *Tube: Tower Hill (then a five-minute walk west and south on Tower Hill). Bus: Eastbound bus 25 from Marble Arch, Oxford Circus, or St. Paul's; it stops at Tower Hill, north of the entrance. Admission: £15 ($28) adults, £11 ($20) seniors and students, £9.50 ($18) children 5–15, £42 ($78) families (2 adults, 3 children). Tours: Yeoman Warders (also known as Beefeaters) give free one-hour tours of the entire compound every half-hour, starting at 9:30 a.m. (Sun at 10 a.m.) from the Middle Tower near the main entrance. The last guided walk starts about 3:30 p.m. in summer or 2:30 p.m. in winter (weather permitting). Open: Mar–Oct Mon–Sat 9 a.m.–5 p.m., Sun 10 a.m.–5 p.m.; Nov–Feb Tues–Sat 9 a.m.–4 p.m., Sun–Mon 10 a.m.–4 p.m.; closed Jan 1 and Dec 24–26. There's wheelchair access onto the grounds, but many of the historic buildings can't accommodate wheelchairs.*

Trafalgar Square
St. James's

Until very recently, **Trafalgar Square** was an island in the midst of a roaring traffic interchange surrounded by historic buildings, such as St. Martin-in-the-Fields church and the National Gallery. After a major urban redesign scheme, it reopened in 2003 with one side attached to the steps of the National Gallery, so visitors can easily get to the square without crossing any streets at all. Besides being a major tourist attraction, many large gatherings take place in Trafalgar Square, including political demonstrations, Christmas revels, and New Year's Eve festivities. The square honors military hero Admiral Lord Nelson (1758–1805), who lost his life at the Battle of Trafalgar. **Nelson's Column,** with fountains and four bronze lions at its base, rises some 145 feet above the square. At the top, a 14-foot-high statue of Nelson (who was 5 feet, 4 inches tall in real life) looks commandingly toward **Admiralty Arch,** which state and royal processions between Buckingham Palace and St. Paul's Cathedral pass through. You don't really need more than a few minutes to take in the square.

St. Martin-in-the-Fields (☎ 020/7930-0089), the famous neoclassical church at the northeast corner of Trafalgar Square, was designed by James Gibbs, a disciple of Christopher Wren, and completed in 1726; the 185-foot spire was added about 100 years later. The church was the precursor of dozens of similar-looking churches throughout colonial New England. (For a special place to dine inexpensively, try the **Cafe in the Crypt;** see Chapter 11 for details.) **The Academy of St. Martin-in-the-Fields,** a famous musical ensemble, frequently performs here. Lunchtime concerts are held

Tower of London

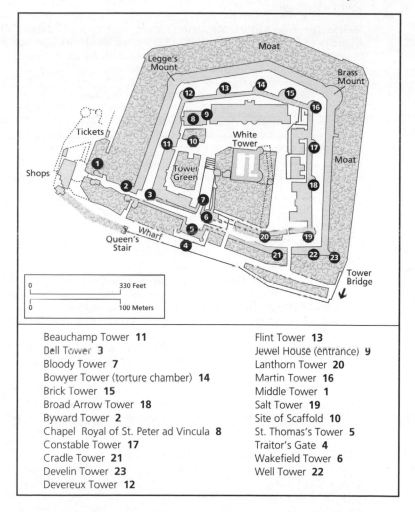

Beauchamp Tower **11**
Dell Tower **3**
Bloody Tower **7**
Bowyer Tower (torture chamber) **14**
Brick Tower **15**
Broad Arrow Tower **18**
Byward Tower **2**
Chapel Royal of St. Peter ad Vincula **8**
Constable Tower **17**
Cradle Tower **21**
Develin Tower **23**
Devereux Tower **12**

Flint Tower **13**
Jewel House (entrance) **9**
Lanthorn Tower **20**
Martin Tower **16**
Middle Tower **1**
Salt Tower **19**
Site of Scaffold **10**
St. Thomas's Tower **5**
Traitor's Gate **4**
Wakefield Tower **6**
Well Tower **22**

on Monday, Tuesday, and Friday at 1 p.m., and evening concerts are held Thursday to Saturday at 7:30. Concert tickets are £6 to £15 ($11–$28). For reservations by credit card, call ☎ **020/7839-8362.** The church is open Monday to Saturday from 10 a.m. to 6 p.m. and Sunday from noon to 6 p.m.; admission is free.

See map p. 160. Bounded on the north by Trafalgar, on the west by Cockspur Street, and on the east by Whitehall. Tube: Charing Cross (an exit from the Underground station leads to the square).

Victoria & Albert Museum
South Kensington

The **Victoria & Albert Museum** (known as the V&A) is the national museum of art and design. In the 145 galleries filled with fine and decorative arts from around the world, you can find superbly decorated period rooms, a fashion collection spanning 400 years of European designs, Raphael cartoons (designs for tapestries in the Sistine Chapel), the Silver Galleries, and the largest assemblages of Renaissance sculpture outside Italy and of Indian art outside India. The **Canon Photography Gallery** shows work by celebrated photographers. In November 2001, the museum opened its spectacular new British Galleries. Allow at least two hours just to cover the basics.

See map p. 160. Cromwell Road, SW7. ☎ 020/7942-2000. www.vam.ac.uk. *Tube: South Kensington (the museum is across from the Underground station). Admission: Free. Open: Thurs–Tues 10 a.m.–5:45 p.m., Wed 10 a.m.–10 p.m.; closed Dec 24–26. The museum is wheelchair accessible (about 95% of the exhibits are step free).*

Westminster Abbey
Westminster

The Gothic and grand **Westminster Abbey** is one of London's most important and venerable historic sites. The present abbey dates mostly from the 13th and 14th centuries, but a church has been on this site for more than a thousand years. Since 1066, when William the Conqueror became the first English monarch to be crowned here, every successive British sovereign save two (Edward V and Edward VIII) has sat on the **Coronation Chair** to receive the crown and scepter. In the **Royal Chapels,** you can see the **tomb of Henry VII,** with its delicate fan vaulting, and the **tomb of Queen Elizabeth I,** buried in the same vault as her Catholic half-sister, Mary I, and not far from her rival, Mary Queen of Scots. In **Poets' Corner,** some of England's greatest writers (including Chaucer, Dickens, and Thomas Hardy) are interred or memorialized. Other points of interest include the College Garden; Cloisters; Chapter House; and Undercroft Museum, which contains the Pyx Chamber, with its display of church plate (silver utensils once used in church services). In September 1997, the abbey was the site of Princess Diana's funeral, and in 2002, the funeral service for the Queen Mother took place here. The Abbey is within walking distance of the Houses of Parliament. For a floor plan of the Abbey, see the "Westminster Abbey" map on p. 175.

See map p. 160. Broad Sanctuary, SW1. ☎ 020/7222-7110. www.westminster-abbey.org. *Tube: Westminster (then a three-minute walk west following Parliament Square to Broad Sanctuary). Bus: The 77A going south along The Strand, Whitehall, and Millbank stops near the Houses of Parliament, near the Abbey. Admission: £8 ($15) adults; £6 ($11) seniors, students, and children 11–16; £18 ($33) families (2 adults, 2 children). Guided tours: Led by an Abbey Verger £4 ($7.40) per person (call for times); audio tours £3 ($5.55). Open: Cathedral, Mon–Fri 9 a.m.–3:45 p.m., Sat 9 a.m.–1:45 p.m.; no sightseeing on Sun (services only). College Garden, Apr–Sept 10 a.m.–6 p.m., Oct–Mar 10 a.m.–4 p.m. There's ramped wheelchair access through the Cloisters; ring the bell for assistance.*

Westminster Abbey

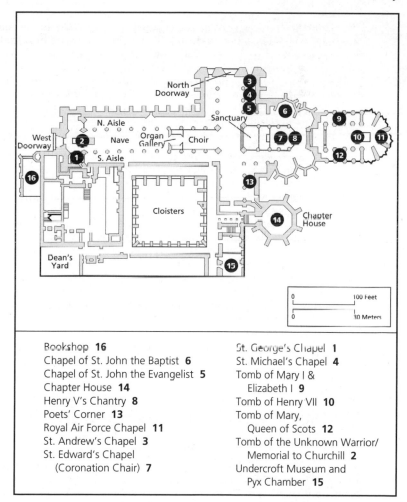

Bookshop **16**	St. George's Chapel **1**
Chapel of St. John the Baptist **6**	St. Michael's Chapel **4**
Chapel of St. John the Evangelist **5**	Tomb of Mary I &
Chapter House **14**	Elizabeth I **9**
Henry V's Chantry **8**	Tomb of Henry VII **10**
Poets' Corner **13**	Tomb of Mary,
Royal Air Force Chapel **11**	Queen of Scots **12**
St. Andrew's Chapel **3**	Tomb of the Unknown Warrior/
St. Edward's Chapel	Memorial to Churchill **2**
(Coronation Chair) **7**	Undercroft Museum and
	Pyx Chamber **15**

Finding More Cool Things to See and Do

London offers much more to see than the places I describe in the preceding section, which includes the essential A-list sights that almost everyone who visits London wants to see. If you have more time, you can pick and choose among the following attractions to round out your visit (and don't forget to check out the side trips I describe in Chapter 13). For the location of the following sights, see the map "London's Top Attractions" on p. 160.

✔ **Apsley House** (Hyde Park Corner, W1; ☎ **020/7499-5676;** Tube: Hyde Park Corner): An imposing neoclassical mansion designed by Robert Adam and completed in 1778, Apsley House was the London residence of Arthur Wellesley, the first duke of Wellington, who defeated Napoleon at Waterloo in 1815. With its sumptuous interiors and treasure trove of paintings, china, swords, and military honors, the house reflects the duke's position as the most powerful commander in Europe. A **free audio guide** explains all the details on a self-guided tour that lasts about an hour. Admission is £4.50 ($8.30) for adults, £3 ($5.55) for seniors, and free for children under 18. The house is open Tuesday to Sunday from 11 a.m. to 5 p.m. It's closed January 1, Good Friday, May 1, and December 24 to 26.

✔ **British Airways London Eye** (Bridge Road, SE1, beside Westminster Bridge on the South Bank; ☎ **0870/500-0600** for advance credit-card booking; Tube: Westminster): This 400-foot-high rotating wheel offers unparalleled views of London from its enclosed observation pods. Each glass-sided elliptical module holds about 25 passengers, with enough room to move freely about. Lasting about 30 minutes (equivalent to one rotation), the ride (or "flight") is remarkably smooth. The London Eye was scheduled to remain in operation through 2003 and has been such a hit that it will probably stay open several more years, though it may eventually be moved to a new location. You can save time by reserving a ticket in advance. Admission is £13 ($24) for adults, £10 ($19) for seniors, and £6.50 ($12) for children under 16. The London Eye is open daily from 9:30 a.m.; the last admission varies seasonally.

✔ **The British Library Exhibition Centre** (96 Euston Rd., Marylebone, NW1; ☎ 020/7412-7513; Tube: King's Cross/St. Pancras): This center houses the literary treasures of the British Museum. Here, you can see a copy of the *Magna Carta,* the illustrated *Lindisfarne Gospel* from Ireland, Shakespeare's first folio, and handwritten manuscripts by world-famous British authors such as Jane Austen and Thomas Hardy. Allow at least an hour, more if you love literature or literary history. Admission is free. The center is open Monday and Wednesday to Friday from 9:30 a.m. to 6 p.m., Tuesday from 9:30 a.m. to 8 p.m., Saturday from 9:30 a.m. to 5 p.m., and Sunday from 11 a.m. to 5 p.m.

✔ **The Cabinet War Rooms** (Clive Steps, King Charles Street, Westminster, SW1; ☎ 020/7930-6961; Tube: Westminster): The World War II bunker used by Winston Churchill and his chiefs of staff during "England's darkest hour" house the history-laden Cabinet War Rooms. A free audio tour guides you through this labyrinth of underground rooms where Churchill and his War Cabinet planned military campaigns. It has all been meticulously preserved, right down to the cigar waiting by Churchill's bed. You can almost hear the air-raid sirens. Admission is £10 ($19) for adults, £8 ($15) for seniors and students, free for children under 16. The rooms are open daily from 9:30 a.m. to 6 p.m. (last entry 5:15 p.m.). From the Tube, walk west (staying on the north side of the street) to Parliament Street; then turn right to reach King Charles Street.

✔ **Chelsea Physic Garden** (Swan Walk, 66 Royal Hospital Rd., Chelsea SW3; Tube: Sloane Square, then a 15-minute walk south on Lower Sloane Street and west to the end of Royal Hospital Road): This little-known gem of a garden sits on the grounds of the Royal Hospital. Set on 3½ acres, it dates to 1673 and is filled with plant species cultivated hundreds of years ago for their commercial and medicinal benefits. Admission is £5 ($9.25) adults, £3 ($5.55) students and children 5 to 15. The garden is open April through October Wednesday from 2 to 5 p.m. and Sunday from 2 to 6 p.m.; daily from 2 to 5 p.m. during the Chelsea Flower Show in May. Drop by the nice teahouse on the premises for a spot of tea.

✔ **The Charles Dickens Museum** (48 Doughty St., Bloomsbury, WC1; ☎ 020/7405-2127; Tube: Russell Square): The home of the great Victorian novelist and his family from 1837 to 1839. Here, the prolific Charles Dickens penned such famous works as *The Pickwick Papers, Oliver Twist,* and *Nicholas Nickleby.* The museum contains the world's most comprehensive Dickens library, portraits, illustrations, and rooms furnished as they were in Dickens' time. Admission costs £5 ($9.25) for adults, £4 ($7.40) for seniors, and £3 ($5.55) for children. Hours are Monday to Saturday from 10 a.m. to 5 p.m.

✔ **Hyde Park** (bounded by Knightsbridge to the south, Bayswater Road to the north, and Park Lane to the east; ☎ 020/7298-2100; Tube: Marble Arch or Lancaster Gate): This former private boar-and-deer-hunting domain of Henry VIII is now the largest and most popular of the Central London parks — and one of the largest urban green spaces in the world. With adjoining Kensington Gardens, Hyde Park is 630 acres of landscaped lawns; flowerbeds; avenues of trees; and a 41-acre lake known as the Serpentine, where you can row and sail model boats. Rotten Row, the park's 300-year-old riding track, was the country's first public road to be lit at night. At the northeastern tip, near Marble Arch, is Speakers' Corner, a famous Sunday-morning-venting spot for orators. **Free band concerts** are held in the park's bandshell on Sundays and Bank Holidays from May to August, and the **Dell Restaurant** (☎ 020/7706-0464) at the east end of the Serpentine offers cafeteria-style food and drinks. The restaurant is open in summer weekdays 10 a.m. to 6 p.m., weekends 10 a.m. to 7 p.m.; in winter weekdays 10 a.m. to 4 p.m., weekends 10 a.m. to 5 p.m. You can take a pleasant hour's stroll in the park, but you may be tempted to stay longer. The park is open daily from dawn to midnight.

✔ **The London Transport Museum** (The Piazza, Covent Garden, WC2; ☎ 020/7379-6344; Tube: Covent Garden): This museum chronicles the development of the city's famous Underground and double-decker bus system, and displays a wonderful collection of historic vehicles, including an 1829 omnibus, a horse-drawn bus, and

London's first trolley bus. Interactive exhibits allow younger visitors to operate the controls of a Tube train and get their tickets punched. After two hours, you may have to drag them away. Admission costs £5.95 ($11) for adults, £4.50 ($8.35) for seniors, free for children under 16 with adult. The museum is open Saturday to Thursday from 10 a.m. to 6 p.m. and Friday from 11 a.m. to 6 p.m. (last entry at 5:15 p.m.).

✔ **The London Zoo** (at the north end of Regent's Park, NW1; ☎ 020/7722-3333; Tube: Regent's Park, then bus C2 north to Delaney Street or Camden Town): Britain's largest zoo covers 36 acres, with about 8,000 animals in various species-specific houses. Check out the best houses: the **Insect House** (bird-eating spiders), the **Reptile House** (huge monitor lizards and a 15-foot python), the **Sobell Pavilion for Apes and Monkeys,** and the **Lion Terraces.** In the Moonlight World, special lighting effects simulate night for the nocturnal creatures so you can see them in action. The newest exhibit — Web of Life, in the Millennium Conservatory — brings together special animal displays with interactive activities to show the interconnectedness and diversity of different life forms. The Children's Zoo, with interactive exhibits placed at low height, is designed for 4- to 8-year-olds. Many families budget almost an entire day for the zoo; I recommend at least three hours. Admission is £14 ($26) adults; £12 ($22) seniors, students, and visitors with disabilities; £11 ($20) children 3 to 14; £45 ($83) families (2 adults, 2 children). The zoo is open daily from March 10 to October 26 from 10 a.m. to 5:30 p.m., October 27 to February 10 from 10 a.m. to 4 p.m., and February 11 to March 9 from 10 a.m. to 4:30 p.m. The zoo is closed December 25.

✔ **The Museum of London** (150 London Wall, EC2, in the Barbican district near St. Paul's Cathedral; ☎ 020/7600-3699; Tube: St. Paul's): One of the most comprehensive city museums in the world, the Museum of London sits in the original square-mile Londinium of the Romans, overlooking Roman and medieval city walls. Archaeological finds; paintings and prints; social, industrial, and historical artifacts; and costumes, maps, and models trace the city's history and development from prehistoric times to the 21st century. Of special interest is the gilt-and-scarlet **Lord Mayor's Coach,** built in 1757 and weighing 3 tons. Admission is free. The museum is open Monday to Saturday from 10 a.m. to 5:50 p.m. and Sunday from noon to 5:50 p.m. Closed January 1 and December 24 to 26.

✔ **Regent's Park** (just north of Marylebone Road, surrounded by Outer Circle Road; ☎ 020/7486-7905; Tube: Regent's Park or Baker Street): One of London's great green spaces and home of the **London Zoo.** People come to the park to play soccer, cricket, tennis, and softball; boat in the lake; visit Queen Mary's Rose Garden; and let their kids have fun in the many playgrounds. Summer lunch and evening bandstand concerts happen here, as well as puppet shows and other children's activities on weekdays throughout August. The park's northernmost section rises to the summit of Primrose Hill, which provides fine views of Westminster and the city. The park is open from dawn to dusk.

✔ **The Science Museum** (Exhibition Road, SW7; ☎ 020/7942-4454; Tube: South Kensington): This state-of-the-art museum covers the history and development of science, medicine, and technology. You can see rarities such as an 1813 steam locomotive, Arkwright's spinning machine, Fox Talbot's first camera, Edison's original phonograph, and the Apollo 10 space module on display. Kids 7 to 12 years old find the interactive displays challenging and fun. The **Garden Galleries** provide construction areas, sound-and-light shows, and games for younger kids. The Wellcome Wing, which opened in 2000, focuses on contemporary science and has an IMAX 3-D film theater. Allow at least two hours, more if you're going to see the film. A signposted exit in the Tube station goes directly to the museum. Admission to the museum is free; the IMAX theater (☎ 0870/870-4868 for advance booking) costs £7.50 ($14) for adults, £6 ($11) for seniors and children 5 to 15. The museum is open daily 10 a.m. to 6 p.m. It closes December 24 to 26.

✔ **Shakespeare's Globe Theatre & Exhibition** (New Globe Walk, South Bank, SE1, just west of Southwark Bridge; ☎ 020/7902-1500; Tube: London Bridge): Travel back to Elizabethan times as you tour this full-size replica of the roofless "wooden O" that served as the Bard's London theater. On **guided tours** through the oak-and-thatch theater and its workshops, you discover tons of info about Shakespeare and the London theater world of the Elizabethans. The exhibition (with theater tour) costs £8 ($15) for adults, £6.50 ($12) for seniors and students, £5.50 ($10) for children. From October to April the theater is open daily from 10 a.m. to 5 p.m.; during the May-to-September performance season, the Globe is open daily from 9 a.m. to noon.

✔ **The "new" Somerset House** (The Strand, WC2; ☎ 02078/454-600; www.somerset-house.org.uk; Tube: Temple, then a five-minute

Dinner and a show at the Globe Theatre

The Globe presents Shakespeare plays from May to September. Theatergoers sit on wooden benches or stand, as they did in Shakespeare's day, under the open sky. For tickets, call ☎ 020/7401-9919 in the U.K. or 020/7902-1475 from overseas; you can check out the current performance schedule at www.shakespeares-globe.org. Ticket prices range from £5 ($9.25) for standing room to £30 ($56). Even if you don't plan to see a play at the Globe, you can have a snack, tea, or a full meal in the theater. No reservations are required at **The Globe Cafe,** open daily from May to September 10 a.m. to 11 p.m. and from October to April 10 a.m. to 6 p.m. If you want lunch or dinner, reserve a table in advance at **The Globe Restaurant** (☎ 020/7928-9444), which is open daily from noon to 2:30 p.m. and 5:30 to 11 p.m.

From autos to art

The late Queen Mother once remarked how sad it was that the courtyard at **Somerset House** had become an Inland Revenue car park. It was just the spur needed to restore the 1,000-room civil-service palace, designed by Sir William Chambers (1724–1796), and open it to the public.

walk north on Arundel Street and west on The Strand): This house, with its three noteworthy art collections, offers a heady mix of high culture and street entertainment. It also has a new courtyard with dancing fountains and a riverside terrace with a great summer cafe. Admission to Somerset House is free; each gallery charges an admission fee of £5 ($9.25) for adults, £4 ($7.40) for seniors; children under 18 enter free. All three galleries are open daily from 10 a.m. to 6 p.m. (last admittance 45 to 60 minutes before closing), and close January 1 and December 24 to 26. The courtyard is open daily from 7:30 a.m. to 11 p.m. (7 p.m. in winter).

- **The Courtauld Gallery** (☎ 020/7848-2526): This gallery has been in Somerset House since 1989. Impressionist and Post-Impressionist paintings are the gallery's main strength. Major works include Manet's *Bar at the Folies Bergères;* Monet's *Banks of the Seine at Argenteuil; Lady with Parasol* by Degas; *La Loge* by Renoir; Van Gogh's *Self-Portrait with Bandaged Ear;* and several Cézannes, including *The Card Players.*

- The **Gilbert Collection** (☎ 020/7420-9400): In the South Building, this collection showcases glittering gold, silver, and mosaics valued at £75 million ($139 million) when Arthur Gilbert donated the 800-piece collection to the nation in 1996. You can see objects here from Princess Diana's old home, Althorp.

- The **Hermitage Rooms** (☎ 020/7845-4630): An offshoot of the State Hermitage Museum in St. Petersburg, this area exhibits pieces from the Russian Imperial collections in changing shows.

- **10 Downing Street** (10 Downing St., SW1; Tube: Westminster): The residence of the prime minister, many London visitors' must-see list, so I'm sorry to tell you that there's nothing to see here except a heavily guarded gate. By peering through the gate, you can get a glimpse (on the right side) of No. 10, the official residence of the British Prime Minister since 1732. The Chancellor of the Exchequer usually resides next door at No. 11 (the Blairs, with their large family, now reside there), and No. 12 serves as the office of the chief government whip, responsible for maintaining discipline and cooperation in the noisy House of Commons. These three small brick terrace houses, built on a cul-de-sac in 1680, stand in sharp contrast to the enormous 19th-century offices lining Whitehall, the government quarter around Downing Street.

✔ **Tower Bridge Experience** (North Pier, Tower Bridge, SE1; ☎ 020/7378-1928; Tube: Tower Hill): You get to go inside one of the world's most famous bridges to find out why, how, and when the bridge was built. Harry, a Victorian bridge worker brought to life by animatronics, tells you the story and explains how the mechanism for raising the bridge works. The experience takes about 90 minutes, and you definitely want to see the magnificent views up and down the Thames from the bridge's glass-enclosed walkways. Admission is £5.50 ($10) for adults; £4.25 ($7.85) for seniors, students, and children 5 to 15. The attraction is open daily from 10 a.m. to 6 p.m. (last admission 75 minutes before closing).

✔ **The Wallace Collection** (Hertford House, Manchester Square, Marylebone, W1; ☎ 020/7935-0687; Tube: Baker Street): In the palatial "town house" of the late Lady Wallace. The French works by such artists as Watteau and Fragonard are outstanding, but you also find masterworks from the Dutch (including Rembrandt), English, Spanish, and Italian schools. Vying for your attention are collections of decorative art, ornaments from 18th-century France, and European and Asian armaments. You need at least an hour just to give everything a cursory glance. Admission is free. The museum is open Monday to Saturday from 10 a.m. to 5 p.m. and Sunday from noon to 5 p.m.

Seeing London by Guided Tour

When it comes to London sightseeing tours, you're limited only by your imagination, stamina, and budget. You can tour London with an experienced guide by bus, by boat, or on foot.

Bus tours

Original London Sightseeing Tours (☎ 020/8877-1722; www.the originaltour.com) maintains a fleet of double-decker buses (many of them open on top) and offers hop-on/hop-off service at more than 90 boarding points around the city. You can choose among four tour routes. The **Original London Sightseeing Tour** lasts 90 minutes and passes every major sight in Central London and the South Bank; the tour starts from Piccadilly Circus (Tube: Piccadilly Circus) outside the Planet Hollywood restaurant on Coventry Street and departs every few minutes daily from 9 a.m. to 6 p.m. (to 9 p.m. in summer). You don't have to book any of the sightseeing tours in advance; you can pay on the bus. A ticket good for 24 hours on all routes costs £16 ($30) for adults and £10 ($19) for children under 16. For more information or to book online, check out the Web site.

The Big Bus Company (☎ 020/7233-9533; www.bigbus.co.uk) leaves from Green Park, Victoria, and Marble Arch daily every 15 to 30 minutes, from 8:30 a.m. to 7 p.m. (4:30 p.m. in winter) on three different routes that take anywhere from one-and-a-half to two-and-a-half hours. Tickets include a river cruise and walking tours, and cost £18 ($33) for adults and £8 ($15) for children ages 5 to 15. Valid for 24 hours, these tickets let you hop on and off at 54 locations. Big Bus often has special offers, too, throwing in cheap theater tickets, fast entry to popular attractions, and so on.

Another tour company with many guided excursions is **Golden Tours,** 4 Fountain Square, 123–151 Buckingham Palace Rd. (☎ 800/456-6303 in the U.S. or 020/7233-7030; www.goldentours.co.uk). It has comfy buses with restrooms, and the certified guides have a certifiable sense of humor. The daily **Historic & Modern London** tour is a full-day outing that includes the West End, Westminster Abbey, the Changing of the Guard (at Buckingham Palace or Horse Guards Parade), the City of London, St. Paul's Cathedral, the Tower of London, and a cruise from the Tower down to Charing Cross Pier; the price includes a pub lunch and all admissions. This tour costs you £64 ($118) for adults and £54 ($100) for kids under 16. Tours depart from the office at Buckingham Palace Road (Tube: Victoria) and other points in Central London. You can book your tickets directly or online, or you can ask your hotel concierge to do it at least two days in advance.

Boat tours

A cruise down the majestic Thames is a marvelous way to take in the city's sights. Sightseeing boats regularly ply the river between Westminster and the Tower of London; some continue downstream to Greenwich (site of the Prime Meridian, *Cutty Sark,* and the Old Royal Observatory) and upstream to Kew Gardens and Hampton Court (see Chapter 13 for descriptions of all three places). Along the way, you can see many of London's great monuments: the Houses of Parliament, Westminster Abbey, St. Paul's Cathedral, the Tower of London, and Tower Bridge. The main departure points along the Thames are at **Westminster Pier** (Tube: Westminster), **Waterloo Pier** (Tube: Waterloo), **Embankment Pier** (Tube: Embankment), **Tower Pier** (Tube: Tower Hill), and **Greenwich Pier** (Tube: Greenwich). Call the London Travel Information line at ☎ 020/7222-1234 line for recorded information on tours.

Evan Evans (☎ 020/7950-1777; www.evanevans.co.uk) offers three cruises. A **daily lunch cruise** departs at 12:15 p.m. from Embankment Pier aboard the *Silver Bonito;* this tour costs you £20 ($37) for adults, £12 ($22) for children. Another daily offering starts with a guided boat tour of the Thames, includes a tour of the Tower of London, and contin-ues by bus to The City and St. Paul's; this tour's price is £37 ($68) for adults and £32 ($59) for children 3 to 16. A **full-day tour** offered Monday to Saturday takes in Westminster Abbey, continues to Buckingham

Palace (or Horse Guards Parade) for the Changing of the Guard, St. Paul's Cathedral, and the Tower of London. This tour, which includes a pub lunch and a river cruise, costs £63 ($117) adults and £53 ($98) children.

Transport for London (☎ 020/7222-1234; www.tfl.gov.uk) runs a fleet of commuter and sightseeing boats on the Thames. A round-trip ticket from Westminster Pier to Greenwich costs £8.60 ($16) adults, £4.30 ($8) children, £22 ($41) for a family (2 adults, 2 children). Daily from March through November and on weekends the rest of the year, **Catamaran Cruisers** (☎ 020/7987-1185; www.catamarancruisers.co.uk) offers a one-hour circular cruise from Westminster Pier (Tube: Westminster) that passes most of London's major monuments and stops at Festival Pier, Bankside Pier, London Bridge City Pier, and St. Katharine's Pier (hop-on/hop-off service). All the boats provide live commentary and have a fully licensed bar. These tours cost £8 ($15) for adults, £6 ($11) for children, and £22 ($41) for families (2 adults, 3 children).

Bateaux London (☎ 020/7925-2215; www.catamarancruisers.co.uk) offers a **nightly dinner cruise** that leaves Embankment Pier (Tube: Embankment) at 7:15 p.m. and returns at 9:45 p.m. The cruise, which includes a two- or four-course dinner with live music and after-dinner dancing, costs £65 to £95 ($120–176), depending on the various add-ons that you choose. You can also take a one-hour **lunch cruise** with a multi-course set menu and live commentary Monday to Saturday for £20 to £30 ($37–$56) per person; the boat departs from Embankment Pier at 12:15 p.m. A two-hour **Sunday lunch cruise** departs from Embankment Pier at 12:15 p.m. and costs £38 to £45 ($70–$83) per person. You need to make advance reservations for all tours, and a smart-casual dress code applies (no sweatpants or running shoes).

An amphibious tour

London Duck Tours (☎ 020/7928-3132; www.londonducktours.co.uk) has adapted several World War II amphibious troop carriers, known as DUKWs, to civilian comfort levels and painted them bright yellow. It runs 80-minute road-and-river trips. Tours start behind County Hall (site of the British Airways London Eye giant observation wheel). It picks up passengers on Chicheley Street (Tube: Westminster, then walk across Westminster Bridge) and then rumbles through Westminster and up to Piccadilly, gathering bemused stares as it passes many of London's major tourist sites. Then the vehicle splashes into the Thames at Vauxhall for a 30-minute cruise as far as the Houses of Parliament. The tickets cost £18 ($33) for adults, £14 ($26) for seniors, £12 ($22) for children.

Walking tours

A walking tour is an affordable way to see London from street level in the company of a knowledgeable guide. This type of tour is great for history, literature, and architecture buffs, and older kids generally have a good time as well. The weekly events listings in *Time Out* magazine, which you can pick up at any news agent in London, include dozens of intriguing walks; a walk happens every day.

The Original London Walks, P.O. Box 1708, London NW6 4LW (☎ 020/
7624-3978; www.walks.com), offers a terrific array of tours, including
**Jack the Ripper's London, Christopher Wren's London, Oscar Wilde's
London,** and **The Beatles' Magical Mystery Tour.** Guides lead walks
every day of the week, rain or shine; tours last about two hours and end
near an Underground station. You don't need to make advance reservations. Call for schedules and departure points. A London Walk costs
£5.50 ($10) for adults and £4.50 ($8.35) for students with ID; kids walk
free with a parent. If you want to follow detailed strolls on your own,
check out the 11 tours in *Frommer's Memorable Walks in London,* by
Richard Jones (Wiley Publishing, Inc.).

Following an Itinerary

Every London visitor faces one problem: how to see as much as possible
in a limited amount of time. What do you do if you have only one, two, or
three days at your disposal? I provide one-, two-, and three-day itineraries
for top London sights in Chapter 4 (the first three days in the "Seeing
England's Highlights in One Week" section).

Shopping in London

When you think of shopping in London, what items come to mind? Silky
cashmere sweaters? Burberry raincoats? Hand-tailored suits and shirts?
Tartan plaids? Irish linens? Silver spoons? Old engravings? Bone china?
Books? Whatever you think of, you can find it somewhere in London, one
of the world's greatest shopping cities. In addition to the major department stores, you can find hundreds of small, enticing specialty shops
and boutiques that delight the eye and empty the wallet. For the location of all the shops listed in this section, see the "West End Shopping"
map on p. 186.

When to shop and how to find deals

Normal **shopping hours** are Monday to Saturday 10 a.m. to 5:30 p.m.,
with late closing (7 or 8 p.m.) on Wednesday or Thursday. Stores may
legally be open for six hours on Sunday, usually 11 a.m. to 5 p.m.

Stores in London have **two sale periods:** one in January and the other in
July. Discounts can range from 25 to 50 percent at leading department
stores. Harrods has the most famous January sale in London, but just
about every other store also has a big sale at this time.

The *VAT (value-added tax)* in London and throughout England is 17.5 percent. The VAT is added to the price on every price tag. Anyone who isn't
a resident of the European Union can get a VAT refund on retail goods,
but not on restaurant and hotel bills. For the details on how to recoup as
much as 15 percent of your shopping spree, see Chapter 5.

Where to shop and what to buy

Most of the department stores, designer shops, and *multiples* (chain stores) have their flagships in the **West End**. The key streets are **Oxford Street** for affordable shopping; **Regent Street** for fancier shops, more upscale department stores, and specialty dealers; **Piccadilly** for older, established department stores; **Jermyn Street** for traditional English luxury goods; and **Bond Street** for chic, upscale fashion boutiques. The **Covent Garden** area is great for all-purpose shopping. **Charing Cross Road** is known for its extraordinary number of bookstores, selling both new and old volumes.

Chelsea is known for **King's Road** (Tube: Sloane Square), a street that became world-famous during the Swinging Sixties. The young crowd still flocks to King's Road, but it's becoming more and more a lineup of chain stores, markets, and *multistores* (large or small conglomerations of indoor stands, stalls, and booths within one building). The area is also known for its design-trade showrooms and stores of household wares. King's Road begins on the west side of Sloane Square Tube station.

London has plenty of big department stores to choose among. **Harrods,** 87–135 Brompton Rd., SW1 (☎ **020/7730-1234**; Tube: Knightsbridge), may be the world's most famous department store. As firmly entrenched in London life as Buckingham Palace, this enormous emporium has some 300 departments, delectable Food Halls, and several cafes. **Fortnum & Mason,** 181 Piccadilly, W1 (☎ **020/7734-8040**; Tube: Piccadilly Circus), a department store, serves as the queen's London grocer. In a setting of deep-red carpets and crystal chandeliers, you find everything from pâté de foie gras and Campbell's soup to bone china, crystal, leather, antiques, and stationery. Dining choices include the **Patio, St. James's,** and **The Fountain** (for restaurant reviews, see Chapter 11). A Chelsea emporium founded in 1877, **Peter Jones,** Sloane Square, SW1 (☎ **020/7730-3434**; Tube: Sloane Square), is known for household goods, household fabrics and trims, china, glass, soft furnishings, and linens; the linen department is one of London's best.

Bargain hunters can zero in on goods manufactured in England. **The Filofax Centre,** 21 Conduit St., W1 (☎ **020/7499-0457**; Tube: Oxford Circus), carries the entire range of Filofax inserts and books at about half the price that you can get them in the States. Prices at the U.K.-based **Body Shop** stores are much lower than in the States. You can stock up on their politically and environmentally correct beauty, bath, and aromatherapy products at **The Body Shop,** 375 Oxford St., W1 (☎ **020/7409-7868**; Tube: Bond Street), which has branches in every shopping zone in London. **Dr. Marten's Department Store,** 1–4 King St., WC2 (☎ **020/7497-1460**; Tube: Covent Garden), is the flagship for internationally famous Doc Martens shoes. Prices are far better here than they are outside the United Kingdom.

The following sections describe where to go and what to look for in some of London's key shopping areas. For the locations of stores in the West End, see the "West End Shopping" map on p. 186.

West End Shopping

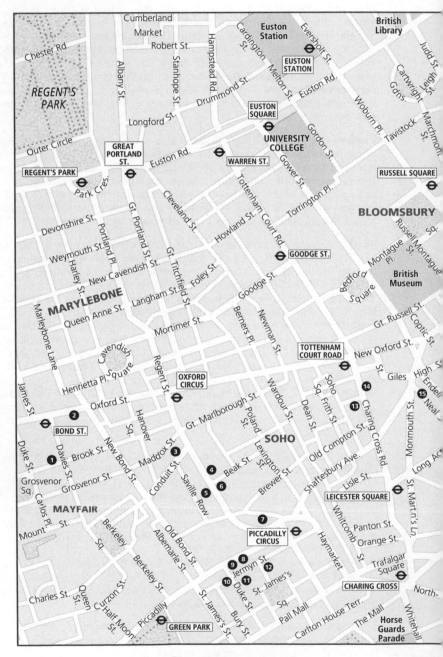

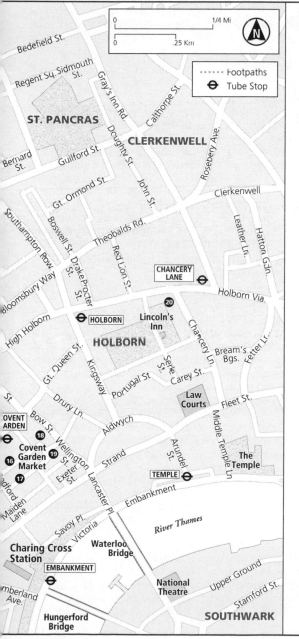

The Body Shop **2**
Burlington Arcade **5**
Church's **1**
Covent Garden
  Market **17**
Culpepper the
  Herbalist **18**
Dr. Marten's Department
  Store **16**
The Filofax Centre **3**
Floris **12**
Fortnum & Mason **9**
Hamleys **4**
Hatchards **8**
Hilditch & Key **10**
Irish Linen Company **5**
London Silver Vaults **20**
Murder One **14**
Neal's Yard
  Remedies **15**
Penhaligon's **19**
Royal Doulton Regent
  Street **6**
Scotch House **7**
Taylor of Old Bond
  Street **11**
W & G Foyle, Ltd. **13**

Bond Street

Divided into New (northern section) and Old (southern portion), Bond Street is the address for all the hot international designers. Here and on adjacent streets, you can find a large conglomeration of very expensive fashion boutiques. **Church's,** 133 New Bond St., W1 (☎ **020/7493-1474;** Tube: Bond Street), sells classy shoes said to be recognizable to all the snobby maîtres d'hôtel in London.

Charing Cross Road

For books, head to Charing Cross Road, where you find **W & G Foyle, Ltd.,** 113–119 Charing Cross Rd., WC2 (☎ **020/7440-3225;** Tube: Tottenham Court Road), which claims to be the world's largest bookstore and carries an impressive array of hardcovers and paperbacks, as well as travel maps, records, and sheet music. **Murder One,** 71–73 Charing Cross Rd., WC2 (☎ **020/7734-3485;** Tube: Leicester Square), specializes in crime, romance, science fiction, and horror books. Established in 1797, **Hatchards,** 187 Piccadilly, W1 (☎ **020/7439-9921;** Tube: Piccadilly Circus), is London's most historic and atmospheric bookstore. Some distance away, in Kensington, you can find the **Children's Book Centre,** 237 Kensington High St., W8 (☎ **020/7937-7497;** Tube: High Street Kensington), the best place in London to go for children's books; fiction is arranged according to age, up to 16.

Covent Garden

The **Covent Garden Market** (☎ **02078/369-136;** Tube: Covent Garden), which is actually several different markets, is open daily 9 a.m. to 5 p.m. The place can be a little confusing until you dive in and explore it all. The **Apple Market** is the fun, bustling market in the courtyard, where traders sell collectible nostalgia: glassware and ceramics, leather goods, toys, clothes, hats, and jewelry. On Monday, antiques dealers take over. On the backside, you can find the **Jubilee Market** (☎ **020/7836-2139**), with inexpensive crafts, clothes, and books. The **Covent Garden Market** itself (in the restored hall on The Piazza) is full of specialty shops selling fashions and herbs, gifts and toys, books and personalized dollhouses, hand-rolled cigars . . . you name it.

The Covent Garden area is a good place to find herbalists and shops sell-ing excellent English soaps, toiletries, and aromatherapy goods. **Culpeper the Herbalist,** 8 The Market, Covent Garden, WC2 (☎ **020/7379-6698;** Tube: Covent Garden), sells food, bath, and aromatherapy products, as well as dream pillows, candles, sachets, and many a shopper's fave: the battery-operated aromatherapy fan. **Penhaligon's,** 41 Wellington St., WC2 (☎ **020/7836-2150;** Tube: Covent Garden), is an exclusive-line Victorian perfumery dedicated to good grooming, with a large selection of per-fumes, aftershaves, soaps, candles, and bath oils for women and men. People the world over know **Neal's Yard Remedies,** 15 Neal's Yard (off Shorts Garden), WC2 (☎ **020/7379-7222;** Tube: Covent Garden), for its all-natural, herbal-based bath, beauty, and aromatherapy products in cobalt-blue bottles.

Jermyn Street

Two-block-long Jermyn Street, one of St. James's most exclusive nooks, is home to posh high-end men's haberdashers and toiletry shops, many of which have been doing business for centuries. **Taylor of Old Bond Street,** 74 Jermyn St., SW1 (☎ 020/7930-5544; Tube: Piccadilly Circus), carries the world's finest collection of men's shaving brushes, razors, and combs, plus soaps and hair lotions. **Floris,** 89 Jermyn St., SW1 (☎ 020/7930-2885; Tube: Piccadilly Circus), is a small mahogany-clad store that's been selling its own line of soaps and perfumes since 1851. For more than a century, **Hilditch & Key,** 73 Jermyn St., SW1 (☎ 020/7930-5336; Tube: Piccadilly Circus), has been selling what many people consider the finest men's shirts in the world: 100 percent cotton, cut by hand, with buttons fashioned from real shell.

 If you're shopping in Regent Street or Jermyn Street, visit the **Burlington Arcade,** running from Regent Street to Savile Row. This famous, glass-roofed Regency passage, lit by wrought-iron lamps and decorated with clusters of ferns and flowers, is lined with intriguing shops and boutiques. The **Irish Linen Company,** 35–36 Burlington Arcade, W1 (☎ 020/7493-8949; Tube: Piccadilly Circus), carries items crafted of Irish linen, including hand-embroidered handkerchiefs, and bed and table linens.

Regent Street

Curving Regent Street, just off Piccadilly Circus, is a major shopping street for all sorts of goods. If you're after English bone china, stop in at **Royal Doulton Regent Street,** 154 Regent St., W1 (☎ 020/7734-3184; Tube: Piccadilly Circus or Oxford Circus), which carries Royal Doulton, Minton, and Royal Crown Derby china. **Scotch House,** 84–86 Regent St., W1 (☎ 020/7734-0203; Tube: Piccadilly Circus), has a worldwide reputation for its comprehensive selection of cashmere and wool knitwear for men, women, and children; the shop also sells tartan garments and accessories, as well as Scottish tweed classics. If you're looking for toys or children's gifts, check out **Hamleys,** 188–196 Regent St., W1 (☎ 020/7494-2000; Tube: Piccadilly Circus), which stocks more than 35,000 toys and games on seven floors.

Shopping in the vaults

If you're searching for silver, go to the **London Silver Vaults,** Chancery House, 53–63 Chancery Lane, WC2 (☎ 020/7242-3844; Tube: Chancery Lane). Here, you go into real vaults — 40 in all — filled with a staggering collection of old and new silver and silver plate, plus a collection of jewelry.

Living It Up After Dark

London by day is lovely; London by night is lively. Whatever you're looking for — grand opera, a hip-hop dance club, or a historic pub — you
can find it here. As the cultural hub of the United Kingdom, London is
always brimming over with possibilities for after-dark adventures.

Finding out what's happening

You can find details for all London shows, concerts, and other performances in the daily newspapers: the *Daily Telegraph,* the *Evening Standard,*
the *Guardian,* the *Independent,* and the *Times.* For the most comprehensive listings of everything that's going on in London, plus thumbnail
descriptions and (usually scathing) critical opinion, buy a copy of the
weekly magazine *Time Out.* New editions hit London newsstands every
Wednesday. Online, www.londontheatre.co.uk provides a complete
listing of shows currently playing in London's West End, plus seating
plans for the theaters and theater news and reviews.

Getting tickets

The following ticket agencies accept credit card bookings 24 hours a
day, and all charge at least a 25 percent commission:

- ✔ **Albemarle Booking Agency** (☎ **020/7637-9041;** www.albemarle-
  london.com)

- ✔ **Keith Prowse** (☎ **800/669-7469** in the U.S. or 020/7836-9001; www.
  keithprowse.com)

- ✔ **Ticketmaster** (☎ **0870/606-9999;** www.ticketmaster.co.uk)

You can avoid the agencies' hefty fees if you go to the box office to buy
tickets or call the venue and order tickets by phone. With a credit card,
you can usually order tickets directly from the box office (or online in
some cases) before you leave home and pick them up after you arrive in
London.

Raising the curtain on performing arts and music

When you plan a night out in London, your biggest problem will be
choosing among all the possibilities.

Theater

When it comes to theater, London is the greatest. The **West End theater
district** — or **Theatreland,** as it's called — concentrates in the area
around Piccadilly Circus, Leicester Square, and Covent Garden. But the
theaters at the Barbican and South Bank Arts Centre are considered
West End theater venues as well. You can get tickets for even the biggest
hit shows more cheaply in London than in New York; you rarely pay
more than £40 ($74) for the best seats in the house. The city's many

"fringe" venues also play an important part in the theatrical vitality of London. Fringe is the London equivalent of Off or Off-Off Broadway in New York. If you want to see a show, look at the following theaters' schedules:

- ✔ **The Royal National Theatre,** South Bank Arts Centre, SE1 (☎ 020/ 7452-3000; www.nt-online.org; Tube: Waterloo): This company performs Shakespeare, classic revivals, musicals, and new plays in three theaters. For information on performances, call ☎ 020/7452-3400 (Mon–Sat 10 a.m.–11 p.m.); check the Web for information and an online booking form.

- ✔ **The Royal Shakespeare Company** (☎ 08706/091-110; www.rsc. org.uk): Based in Stratford-upon-Avon, this prestigious company performs in London at the **Gielgud Theatre,** Shaftesbury Avenue, W1 (☎ 020/7494-5085; Tube: Piccadilly Circus), and the **Theatre Royal Haymarket,** Haymarket SW1 (☎ 0870/901 3356; Tube: Piccadilly Circus).

- ✔ **Shakespeare's Globe Theatre,** New Globe Walk, Bankside, SE1 (☎ 020/7401-9919; www.shakespeares-globe.org; Tube: Cannon Street or London Bridge): This theater presents a June-to-September season of the Bard's plays in a reconstructed open-air Elizabethan theater. After a couple of hours, the benches can be a bit numbing, but you get to see Shakespeare performed not far from the original theater — and you're right beside the Thames.

The **Society of London Theatres** operates a **half-price ticket booth** in the clock tower building by the gardens in Leicester Square (Tube: Leicester Square). The booth doesn't have a phone info line, so you have to show up in person to see what's on sale that day. The booth is open Monday to Saturday from noon to 6:30 p.m.; on matinee days (Wed, Sat, and Sun), it sells only matinee tickets before 2 p.m. You can buy tickets only on the day of performance. The ticket booth accepts MasterCard and Visa. You pay exactly half the price, plus a nominal service fee (under £3/$5.55). The most popular shows usually aren't available, but you may luck out. Tickets for the English National Opera and other events are sometimes available as well. Ask for a free copy of *The Official London Theatre Guide,* which lists every show, with addresses and phone numbers, and includes a map of the West End theater district.

Opera, ballet, and classical music

The **Royal Opera** and **Royal Ballet** perform at the **Royal Opera House,** Covent Garden, WC2E (☎ 020/7304-4000 info line; www.royalopera. org; Tube: Covent Garden). Ticket prices for grand opera run £8 to £175 ($15–$324). The season runs September to August. For a summary of the opera and ballet season, check the Web site.

The **English National Opera** and **English National Ballet** perform at the **London Coliseum,** St. Martin's Lane, WC2N (☎ 020/7632-8300 for box office; www.eno.org; Tube: Leicester Square). The operas here are all sung in English. Seats run £5 to £75 ($9.25–$139); 100 balcony seats at £5 ($9.25) go on sale at 10 a.m. on the day of the performance (except for Sat evenings). The box office is open 24 hours Monday through Saturday for phone bookings and from 10 a.m. to 8 p.m. if you want to purchase tickets in person. The opera and ballet season runs September to July. To book online, go to the Web site.

The **London Symphony Orchestra** (www.lso.co.uk) makes the **Barbican Hall** at the Barbican Centre, Silk Street, EC2Y (☎ 020/7638-8891 for 24-hour recorded info; Tube: Barbican), its home base.

The three auditoriums of the **South Bank Centre,** South Bank, SE1 (☎ 020/7960-4242; www.sbc.org.uk; Tube: Waterloo), host classical music and dance concerts year-round. All manner of orchestras (some British, some international) perform symphonic works in the **Royal Festival Hall.** Chamber-music concerts and dance programs take place in the smaller **Queen Elizabeth Hall,** and recitals are held in the more intimate **Purcell Room.** You can get tickets and information on all three venues at the box office or online. For credit-card phone bookings, call ☎ 020/7960-4242. *Note:* The South Bank Centre is in the midst of a major renovation; Queen Elizabeth Hall will be closed for part of 2006.

You can see classical music performed at the **Royal Albert Hall,** Kensington Gore, SW7 (☎ 020/7589-2141 box office; Tube: High Street Kensington). This enormous, circular, domed concert hall has been a landmark in South Kensington since 1871. One of London's most eagerly awaited musical events is the mid-July to mid-September series of classical and pops concerts known as the **Proms.** Orchestras come from all over Europe to play.

Checking out the club and bar scenes

London is a big club town; the action doesn't really get hot until around midnight. For more options than the ones you can find in the following sections, check out the listings for music and clubs in *Time Out.* For the locations of places in the following sections, see the "London's Clubs, Pubs, and Bars" map on p. 194.

Jazz and other live music

London has plenty of small, smoky jazz clubs where you can groove 'til the wee hours. In Soho, **Ronnie Scott's,** 47 Frith St., W1 (☎ 020/7439-0747; Tube: Tottenham Court Road), has been London's preeminent jazz club for years, with dependably high-caliber performances. You have to order food (meals or snacks) on top of the £15 to £25 ($28–$46) cover. For something trendier, with fewer tourists, try Islington's **Blue Note,** 1 Hoxton Sq., N1 (☎ 020/7729-8440; Tube: Old Street), for its innovative and wide-ranging musical program. Cover ranges from £3 to £10 ($5.55–$19).

In Earl's Court, the **606 Club,** 90 Lots Rd., SW10 (☎ 020/7352-5953; Tube: Earl's Court or Fulham Broadway), is a basement club where young British jazz musicians play. You don't have to pay a cover to get in, but you have to order something to eat, and the club adds a charge of £5 ($9.25) to your bill to pay the musicians. You can find good food and diverse music (from Afro-Latin jazz to rap) at the **Jazz Cafe,** 5 Parkway, NW1 (☎ 020/7916-6060; Tube: Camden Town). Admission costs £12 to £18 ($22–$33).

How about a pizza with your jazz? In Soho, try the **Pizza Express Jazz Club,** 10 Dean St., W1 (☎ 020/7439-8722; Tube: Tottenham Court Road), where big names from the American jazz scene regularly perform; the cover is £10 to £20 ($19–$37). In Knightsbridge, you find **Pizza on the Park,** 11 Knightsbridge, SW1 (☎ 020/7235-5273; Tube: Hyde Park Corner), where the basement Jazz Room books mainstream jazz; admission costs £16 to £18 ($30–$33).

The **Ain't Nothing But Blues Bar,** 20 Kingly St., W1 (☎ 020/7287-0514; Tube: Oxford Circus), the only true-blue blues venue in town, features local acts and touring American bands. The cover charge is £3 to £5 ($5.55–$9.25) on Friday and Saturday; you get in free before 9:30 p.m.

Dance clubs

In Islington, **The Complex,** 1–5 Parkfield St., N1 (☎ 020/7288-1986; Tube: Angel), has four floors with different dance vibes on each. Open Friday and Saturday from 10 p.m. to 2 a.m.; admission is £10 to £12 ($19–$22).

The **Equinox,** Leicester Square, WC2 (☎ 020/7437-1446; Tube: Leicester Square), a lavishly illuminated club with London's largest dance floor, boasts one of the largest lighting rigs in Europe. A crowd as varied as London itself dances to virtually every kind of music, including dance hall, pop, rock, and Latin. The cover is £5 to £12 ($9.25–$22).

Lady Di's favorite scene in her club-hopping days, the **Hippodrome,** at the corner of Cranbourn Street and Charing Cross Road, WC2 (☎ 020/7437-4311; Tube: Leicester Square), is a cavernous place with a great sound system and lights to match. The club is tacky, touristy, and packed on weekends. The cover is £4 to £12 ($7.40–$22).

Venom Club/The Zoo Bar, 13–17 Bear St., WC2 (☎ 020/7839-4188; Tube: Leicester Square), features a trendy Euro-androgynous crowd and music so loud that you have to use sign language. This club boasts the slickest, flashiest, most psychedelic decor in London. The cover is £3 to £5 ($5.55–$9.25) after 10 p.m. (You can get in free before 10 p.m., but the place is empty.)

Bar Rumba, 36 Shaftesbury Ave., W1 (☎ 020/7287-2715; Tube: Piccadilly Circus), has a different musical theme every night: jazz fusion, phat funk, hip-hop, drum 'n' bass, soul, R&B, and swing. You have to be at least 21

London's Clubs, Pubs, and Bars

0 —— 1 Mi
0 —— 1 Km

↖ HAMPSTEAD
CAMDEN

❶ Delancey St.

Prince Albert Rd.

London Zoo

REGENT'S PARK

Boating Lake

Albany St.

St. Pancras Rd.

EUSTON

Eversholt St.

Hampstead Rd.

ST. JOHN'S WOOD

Wellington Rd.

Grove End Rd.

EUSTON STATION

EUSTON SQUARE

❿ Euston Station

MAIDA VALE

MAIDA VALE

Maida Vale

St. John's Wood Rd.

Park Rd.

Lisson Grove

GREAT PORTLAND ST.

Regents Park Crescent

Euston Rd.

BLOOMS- BURY

Clifton Gdns.

Edgware Rd.

LISSON GROVE

MARYLEBONE

BAKER STREET

REGENT'S PARK

Marylebone High St.

Gt. Portland St.

Portland Pl.

Tottenham Court Rd.

Gower St.

WARREN ST.

Bedford Sq.

GOODGE ST.

EDGWARE ROAD

Marylebone Rd.

MARYLEBONE

Goodge St.

THE WEST END

←❷ WESTWAY A40 (M)

NOTTING ←HILL

PADDINGTON

PADDINGTON STATION

Eastbourne Ter.

Praed St.

Seymour Pl.

Gloucester Pl.

Baker St.

Wigmore St.

OXFORD CIRCUS

Oxford St.

⑪ ⑫

Wardour St.

⑬

BAYSWATER

Sussex Gdns.

LANCASTER GATE

Bayswater Rd.

MARBLE ARCH

Seymour St.

Oxford St.

BOND ST.

New Bond St.

Regent St.

⑨

SOHO

⑭

⑮ Shaftesbury Ave. ⑯ ⑰

Leinster Gdns.

Craven Rd.

A40

Cumberland Gate

Grosvenor Sq.

Brook St.

Grosvenor St.

Savile Row

Berkeley Sq.

PICCADILLY CIRCUS

ⓘ

West Carriage Dr.

HYDE PARK

Park Ln.

Park Ln.

MAYFAIR

St. James's St.

PICCADILLY CIRCUS

KENSINGTON GARDENS

Round Pond

The Serpentine

Serpentine Rd.

HYDE PARK CORNER

GREEN PARK

Piccadilly

❽

Pall Mall

The Mall

←❸ Kensington Gore Rd.

South Carriage Dr.

Knightsbridge

❻ ❼

Constitution Hill

Buckingham Palace

GREEN PARK

ST. JAMES'S

ST. JAMES'S PARK

Gloucester Rd.

Exhibition Rd.

KNIGHTS- BRIDGE

KNIGHTSBRIDGE

Victoria and Albert Museum

Harrods

Brompton Rd.

Beauchamp Pl.

Pont St.

Sloane St.

❺

Belgrave Sq.

Grosvenor Pl.

Buckingham Palace Rd.

ST. JAMES'S PARK

Buckingham Gate

Birdcage Walk

Horseferry Rd.

Cromwell Rd.

Pelham St.

BROMPTON

Eaton Sq.

Sloane Sq.

BELGRAVIA

Eccleston St.

Victoria St.

VICTORIA STATION

ⓘ

VICTORIA

EARL'S COURT

SOUTH KENSINGTON

SOUTH KENSINGTON

Sydney St.

Sloane Ave.

SLOANE SQUARE

Lwr. Sloane St.

King's Rd.

Pimlico Rd.

CHELSEA

Ebury Bridge Rd.

Warwick Way

Belgrave Rd.

Vauxhall Bridge Rd.

PIMLICO

PIMLICO

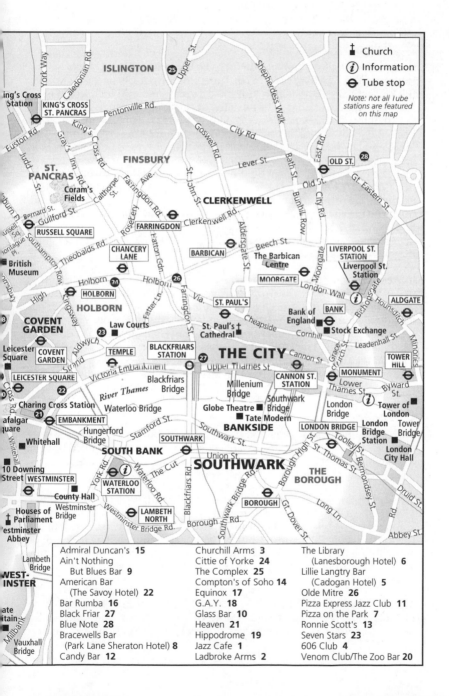

Admiral Duncan's **15**
Ain't Nothing
  But Blues Bar **9**
American Bar
  (The Savoy Hotel) **22**
Bar Rumba **16**
Black Friar **27**
Blue Note **28**
Bracewells Bar
  (Park Lane Sheraton Hotel) **8**
Candy Bar **12**

Churchill Arms **3**
Cittie of Yorke **24**
The Complex **25**
Compton's of Soho **14**
Equinox **17**
G.A.Y. **18**
Glass Bar **10**
Heaven **21**
Hippodrome **19**
Jazz Cafe **1**
Ladbroke Arms **2**

The Library
  (Lanesborough Hotel) **6**
Lillie Langtry Bar
  (Cadogan Hotel) **5**
Olde Mitre **26**
Pizza Express Jazz Club **11**
Pizza on the Park **7**
Ronnie Scott's **13**
Seven Stars **23**
606 Club **4**
Venom Club/The Zoo Bar **20**

years old to get in on Saturday and Sunday, and you have to be over 18
Monday to Friday. The cover is £3 to £12 ($5.55–$22).

English pubs

If you're looking for a pub in The City, the **Cittie of Yorke,** 22 High
Holborn, WC1 (☎ 020/7242-7670; Tube: Holborn or Chancery Lane), has
the longest bar in Britain and looks like a great medieval hall, which is
appropriate because a pub has existed at this location since 1430. The
Seven Stars, 53 Carey St., WC2 (☎ 020/7242-8521; Tube: Holborn), at the
back of the law courts, is tiny and modest except for its collection of Toby
mugs and law-related art. Many barristers drink here, so Seven Stars is a
great place to pick up some British legal jargon while you throw back a
few. The namesake of an inn built here in 1547, the **Olde Mitre,** Ely Place,
EC1 (☎ 020/7405-4751; Tube: Chancery Lane), is a small pub with an
eccentric assortment of customers. An Edwardian wonder of marble and
bronze art nouveau, the wedge-shaped **Black Friar,** 174 Queen Victoria St.,
EC4, (☎ 020/7236-5650; Tube: Blackfriars), features low-relief carvings of
mad monks, a low-vaulted mosaic ceiling, and seating carved out of gold
marble recesses.

In West London, the **Churchill Arms,** 119 Kensington Church St., W8
(☎ 020/7727-4242; Tube: Notting Hill Gate or High Street Kensington),
which is loaded with Churchill memorabilia, hosts an entire week of celebration leading up to Winston's birthday on November 30. Visitors are
often welcomed like regulars here, and the overall ambience is down to
earth and homey. The **Ladbroke Arms,** 54 Ladbroke Rd., W11 (☎ 020/
7727-6648; Tube: Holland Park), serves good pub food. With background
jazz and rotating art prints, the place strays a bit from a traditional pub
environment but makes for a pleasant stop and a good meal.

Classy bars

With surroundings far removed from the hurly-burly of London's streets,
the hotel bars in this section are elegant and dressy. Gents need to wear
a jacket and tie at the American Bar; a smart-casual dress code (no
jeans, sweatpants, or tennis shoes) applies for the others.

The **American Bar** in the Savoy hotel, The Strand, WC2 (☎ 020/7836-
4343; Tube: Charing Cross or Embankment), one of the most sophisticated gathering places in London, reputedly serves the best martini in
town. With a plush decor of Chinese lacquer, comfortable sofas, and
soft lighting, **Bracewells Bar** in the Park Lane Sheraton Hotel, Piccadilly,
W1 (☎ 020/7499-6321; Tube: Green Park or Hyde Park), is chic and
nostalgic.

The **Library** in the Lanesborough hotel, 1 Lanesborough Place, SW1
(☎ 020/7259-5599; Tube: Hyde Park Corner), is one of London's poshest drinking retreats and boasts an unparalleled collection of cognacs.

The **Lillie Langtry Bar** in the Cadogan Hotel, Sloane Street, SW1 (☎ 020/ 7235-7141; Tube: Sloane Square or Knightsbridge), takes you back to the charm and elegance of the Edwardian era, when Lillie Langtry, an actress and a society beauty (and a mistress of Edward VII), lived here.

Gay and lesbian bars and dance clubs

Check the gay listings in the weekly magazine *Time Out* to find out what's going on, because many clubs have special gay nights. The **Lesbian and Gay Switchboard** (☎ 020/7837-7324; www.llgs.org.uk) has 24-hour information on everything. For the location of venues described here, see the "London's Clubs, Pubs, and Bars" map on p. 194.

In terms of size, central location, and continued popularity, the best gay disco in London — which is the best disco here, period — is **Heaven,** Under the Arches, Craven Street, WC2 (☎ 020/7930-2020; www.heaven-london.com; Tube: Charing Cross or Embankment). Admission varies from £3 to £10 ($5.50–$18). Hours are 10:30 p.m. to 3 a.m. on Monday and Wednesday, 10:30 p.m. to 6 a.m. on Friday, and 10:30 p.m. to 5 a.m. on Saturday. **G.A.Y.**, London Astoria, 157 Charing Cross Rd., Soho, WC2 (☎ 0906/100-0160; www.g-a-y.co.uk; Tube: Tottenham Court Road), is the biggest gay dance venue in Europe. Admission costs £10 ($19). Hours are Saturday 10:30 p.m. to 5 a.m.

For general, where-it's-happening action, stroll along Old Compton Street (Tube: Leicester Square or Tottenham Court Road) in Soho. You may want to duck into **Admiral Duncan's,** 54 Old Compton St., W1 (☎ 020/ 7437-5300), or the two-floor **Compton's of Soho,** 53–55 Old Compton St., W1 (☎ 020/7479-7961). Both of these gay bar/pubs are Soho institutions, open Monday through Saturday noon to 11 p.m. and Sunday noon to 10:30 p.m. The city's largest women-only bar is **Glass Bar,** West Lodge, Euston Square Gardens, 190 Euston Rd., NW10 (☎ 020/7387-6184; Tube: Euston). This "non-scene" bar on two levels has a smart-casual dress code and is open Tuesday through Friday from 5 p.m. until late, on Saturday from 6 p.m. until late, and Sunday from 2 p.m. to 7 p.m.; you can't get in after 11:30 p.m. You can find a louder lesbi-scene at **Candy Bar,** 23–24 Bateman St., W1 (☎ 020/7437-1977; Tube: Tottenham Court Road), open seven nights a week (until 1 a.m. Mon–Thurs, 3 a.m. Fri–Sat, and 11 p.m. Sun).

Fast Facts: London

American Express

The main office is at 6 Haymarket, SW1 (☎ 020/79/30-4411; Tube: Piccadilly Circus). Full services are available Monday to Friday 9 a.m. to 5:30 p.m. and Saturday 9 a.m. to 4 p.m. At other times — Saturday 4 p.m. to 6 p.m. and Sunday 10 a.m. to 5 p.m. — only the foreign-exchange bureau is open. Other offices are at 78 Brompton Rd., Knightsbridge SW3 (☎ 020/7584-3431; Tube: Knightsbridge); 84 Kensington High St., Kensington W8 (☎ 020/7795-8703; Tube: High Street Kensington); 51 Great

Russell St., Bloomsbury WC1 (☎ 020/7404-8700; Tube: Russell Square); and 1 Savoy Court, The Strand WC2 (☎ 020/7240-1521; Tube: Charing Cross).

ATMs

You can find ATMs, also called *cashpoints,* at banks and in shopping areas throughout Central London.

Country Code and City Code

The country code for England is **44.** London's telephone area code is **020.** If you're calling a London number from outside the city, use **020,** followed by the eight-digit number. If you're calling within London, leave off the **020,** and dial only the eight-digit number.

Currency Exchange

In London, you can easily exchange cash or traveler's checks by using a currency-exchange service called a *bureau de change.* You find these services at the major London airports, at any branch of a major bank, at all major rail and Underground stations in Central London, at post offices, and at American Express and Thomas Cook offices.

Doctors and Dentists

Most hotels have physicians on call. Medical Express, 117A Harley St., W1 (☎ 020/7499-1991; Tube: Oxford Circus), is a private clinic with walk-in medical service (no appointment necessary) Monday to Friday 9 a.m. to 6 p.m. and Saturday 9:30 a.m. to 2:30 p.m. Dental Emergency Care Service, Guy's Hospital, St. Thomas St., SE8 (☎ 020/7955-2186; Tube: London Bridge) is open Monday to Friday from 8:45 a.m. to 3:30 p.m. for walk-in patients.

Embassies and High Commissions

London is the capital of the United Kingdom and, therefore, the home of all the embassies, consulates, and high commissions. United States: 24 Grosvenor Sq., W1 (☎ 020/7499-9000; www.usembassy.org.uk; Tube: Bond Street). Canada: MacDonald House, 38 Grosvenor Sq., W1 (☎ 020/7258-6600; www.canada.org.uk; Tube: Bond Street). Ireland: 17 Grosvenor Place, SW1 (☎ 020/7235-2171; www.ireland.embassyhomepage.com; Tube: Hyde Park Corner). Australia: Australia House, Strand, WC2 (☎ 020/7379-4334; www.australia.org.uk; Tube: Charing Cross or Aldwych). New Zealand: New Zealand House, 80 Haymarket (at Pall Mall), SW1 (☎ 020/7930-8422; www.nzembassy.com; Tube: Charing Cross or Piccadilly Circus).

Emergencies

For police, fire, or an ambulance, call ☎ **999.**

Hospitals

The following hospitals offer 24-hour emergency care: Royal Free Hospital, Pond Street, NW3 (☎ 020/7794-0500; Tube: Belsize Park); and University College Hospital, Grafton Way, WC1 (☎ 020/7387-9300; Tube: Warren Street or Euston Square). Many other London hospitals also have accident and emergency departments.

Information

The main Tourist Information Centre (Britain & London Visitor Centre, 1 Regent St., Piccadilly Circus, SW1; Tube: Piccadilly Circus) provides tourist information to walk-in visitors Monday 9:30 a.m. to 6:30 p.m., Tuesday to Friday 9 a.m. to 6:30 p.m., and Saturday and Sunday 10 a.m. to 4 p.m. You can find another Tourist Information Centre in the Arrivals Hall of the Waterloo International Terminal (open daily 8:30 a.m.–10:30 p.m.). For general London information, call ☎ 020/7234-5800.

Internet Access

easyEverything (www.easyeverything.co.uk) has cybercafes all over London. Most of them are open from 8:30 a.m. to 11 p.m. or midnight.

Maps

The best all-around street directory, *London A to Z,* is available at most news agents and bookstores. You can obtain a bus and Underground map at any Underground station.

Newspapers/Magazines

The *Times, Telegraph, Daily Mail,* and *Evening Standard* are all dailies carrying the latest news. The *International Herald Tribune,* published in Paris, and an international edition of *USA Today* are available daily. Most newsstands also sell *Time* and *Newsweek.* The weekly magazine *Time Out* contains an abundance of useful information about the latest happenings in London. *Gay Times,* a high-quality, news-oriented magazine covering the gay and lesbian community, is available at most news agents.

Pharmacies

They're called *chemists* in the United Kingdom. Boots has outlets all over London. Bliss the Chemist, 5 Marble Arch, W1 (☎ 020/7723-6116; Tube: Marble Arch), is open daily from 9 a.m. to midnight. Zafash Pharmacy, 233–235 Old Brompton Rd., SW5 (☎ 020/7373-2798; Tube: Earl's Court), is London's only 24-hour pharmacy.

Police

In an emergency, dial ☎ **999** (no coin required).

Post Offices

The Main Post Office, 24 William IV St., WC2 (☎ 020/7930-9580; Tube: Charing Cross), is open Monday to Saturday from 8:30 a.m. to 8 p.m. Other post offices and sub-post offices (windows in the back of news-agent stores) are open Monday to Friday from 9 a.m. to 5:30 p.m. and Saturday from 9 a.m. to 12:30 p.m. Look for red ROYAL MAIL signs outside.

Restrooms

The English often call toilets *loos.* They're marked by public-toilets signs on streets, in parks, and in a few Tube stations. You also find well-maintained public lavatories in all larger public buildings, such as museums and art galleries, large department stores, and rail stations. Public lavatories are usually free, but you may need a 20p coin to get in or to use a washroom. In some places (like Leicester Square), you find coin-operated "Super Loos" that are sterilized after each use. If all else fails, duck into the nearest pub.

Safety

London is generally a safe city, both on the street and in the Underground. As in any large metropolis, use common sense and normal caution when you're in a crowded public area or walking alone at night. The area around Euston Station has more purse-snatchings than anywhere else in London.

Smoking

Smoking is forbidden in the Underground (on the cars and the platforms) and on buses. Most restaurants have no-smoking tables, but they're sometimes separated from the smoking section by very little space. No-smoking rooms are available in more and more hotels, and some B&Bs are now entirely smoke free.

Taxes

The 17.5 percent value-added tax (VAT) is added to all hotel and restaurant bills and is included in the price of many items you buy. You can get this tax refunded if you shop at stores that participate in the Retail Export Scheme (signs are posted in the window). See Chapter 5 for more information.

Taxis

You can hail a cab from the street; if the "For Hire" light is lit, the cab is available. You can phone for cab at ☎ 020/7272-0272.

Transit Assistance

For 24-hour information on London's Underground, buses, and ferries, call Transport for London at ☎ 020/7222-1234; www.tfl.gov.uk.

Weather

For the daily London weather report, check out http://na.visitlondon.com/info/weather.

Web Sites

The official Web page for VisitLondon, www.visitlondon.com, is a good all-around resource for visitors to London and the United Kingdom in general. At www.londontown.com, you can browse sections on attractions, restaurants, nightlife, and hotels. For a useful list of gay and gay-friendly hotels, services, clubs, and restaurants, check out www.gaylondon.co.uk. Information on all London's airports is available at www.baa.co.uk. At www.royal.gov.uk, the official Royal Web site, you can find history, information, and trivia about the British monarchy.

Chapter 13

Day-tripping from London

● ●

In This Chapter

▶ Exploring the ancient university towns of Cambridge and Oxford
▶ Going upriver to Greenwich
▶ Discovering Hampton Court Palace
▶ Sniffing the roses at Kew Gardens
▶ Wandering through Blenheim Palace
▶ Visiting the royal residence at Windsor Castle

● ●

*W*ith so much to see and do in London, many visitors never leave the city. But several wonderful attractions are within easy commuting distance, and I share the best of them with you in this chapter. You can visit any one of the places described here in a day and be back in London in time for dinner and an 8 o'clock curtain. For locations of the destinations in this chapter, see the "Day Trips from London" map on p. 202.

Cambridge: Medieval Colleges on the River Cam

Students at Oxford refer to **Cambridge** as "the other place." Located 88km (55 miles) north of London in Cambridgeshire, Cambridge is most famous for its university. Every year, about 8,000 students apply to this prestigious school, which accepts only about 1,600. The beautiful colleges, many dating from the Middle Ages, are built around quiet inner quadrangles, or "quads." The River Cam runs past the colleges, and is particularly beautiful in April, when daffodils line its banks. Magnificent King's College Chapel is a definite must-see in Cambridge. For the locations of the attractions and restaurants I recommend in the following sections, see the "Cambridge" map on p. 203.

Getting to Cambridge

Direct trains depart hourly from London's King's Cross Station for the 45-minute journey to Cambridge. A round-trip "cheap day return" ticket costs £17 ($31); all travel must take place after 9:30 a.m. For schedules,

Day Trips from London

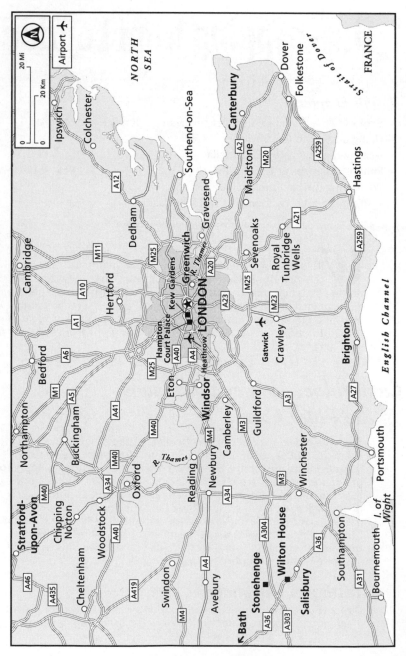

Cambridge

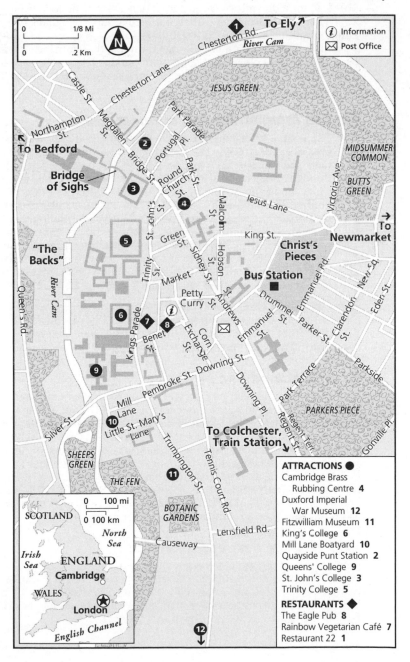

ATTRACTIONS ●
Cambridge Brass
  Rubbing Centre **4**
Duxford Imperial
  War Museum **12**
Fitzwilliam Museum **11**
King's College **6**
Mill Lane Boatyard **10**
Quayside Punt Station **2**
Queens' College **9**
St. John's College **3**
Trinity College **5**

RESTAURANTS ◆
The Eagle Pub **8**
Rainbow Vegetarian Café **7**
Restaurant 22 **1**

call ☎ 0845/7484950. You can go by **National Express** more cheaply —
£10 ($19) for a day-return (round-trip) ticket — but the trip from Victoria
Coach Station to Drummer Street Station in Cambridge takes two hours.
Contact National Express (☎ 0990/808080; www.nationalexpress.
com) for schedules. I don't recommend driving to Cambridge because
most of the city is closed to traffic (with parking lots on the outskirts).
If you drive from London, take the M11 north, and follow the signs to
Cambridge.

Finding information and taking a tour

✔ The **Tourist Information Centre,** Wheeler Street (☎ 0906/586-2526;
www.visitcambridge.org), has brochures on town and area attractions and can also book a room for you. The center is open Monday
through Friday from 10 a.m. to 5:30 p.m., Saturday from 10 a.m. to
5 p.m., and Sunday from 11 a.m. to 4 p.m. This office offers a **two-
hour city walking tour** (£8.50/$16) that includes colleges open to
the public. The walks leave from the Tourist Information Centre daily
at 1:30 p.m. throughout the year; from July to September, additional
walks depart at 10:30 a.m. and 2:30 p.m. Monday through Saturday;
and from October to March, another Saturday tour departs at
11:30 a.m.. For more information or to book a special guided tour,
stop in this office or call **Blue Badge Guides** at ☎ 01223/457-574.

✔ **City Sightseeing** (☎ 01708/864340; www.citysightseeing.co.
uk) offers a one-hour **open-top bus tour** (£8/$15). Buses depart
daily from the train station, starting at 9:45 a.m., and run every
15 to 20 minutes until 3 or 4 p.m., depending on the season.

Getting around Cambridge

Cambridge is a compact city, so you can walk everywhere. The distance
from the train station to the city center is about a mile (a 20-minute
walk), so hop on the No. 3 shuttle bus (£1/$1.85) that runs into town
every few minutes from in front of the station. Taxis are available right
outside the train and bus stations. Cambridge, with all its students, is a
big cycling city. If you want to rent a bike, during the summer months,
head to the rental stall right at the train station (no phone). You can also
rent bikes at **Geoff's Bike Hire,** 65 Devonshire Rd. (☎ 01223/365-629),
and **Mike's Bikes,** 28 Mill Rd. (☎ 01223/312-591). Expect to pay about
£8 ($15) a day, plus a refundable deposit for a standard bike.

Exploring the best of Cambridge

Cambridge has enough to keep you happily occupied for an entire day.
Wandering through the ancient courtyards of the colleges is fun, but so
many visitors (three and a half million a year) now descend on Cambridge
that several of the colleges have instituted visiting hours and admission
fees.

When visiting Cambridge, keep in mind that the colleges are completely closed to visitors during exam season, from mid-April until late June. Note, too, that open hours for the colleges can be restricted during term time from September to June. Summer is the best time to visit if you want to get into the college courtyards, but it's also the busiest tourist season.

Fitzwilliam Museum

The Fitzwilliam Museum is Cambridge's best museum and one of England's oldest museums. A palatial mid-19th-century building, the museum houses the original collections bequeathed to Cambridge University in 1816 by Viscount Fitzwilliam. Typical of an upper-class gentleman, Fitzwilliam collected antiquities from Egypt and Greece (mummies, sarcophagi, vases, and so on) and porcelain from all over Europe. You can see all these treasures, plus an amazing assortment of later bequests — pewterware, portrait miniatures, and illuminated manuscripts — on display in the **Lower Galleries.** You can find a rich and varied selection of European paintings and sculpture, including works by Picasso, Cezanne, and Renoir, in the **Upper Galleries.** Check out the rooms devoted to British painting to find important works by the poet/artist/mystic William Blake, English landscapes by Constable and Turner, satirical prints by Hogarth, and portraits by Gainsborough. The 20th-century gallery displays works by modern British artists, such as David Hockney, Lucian Freud, and Barbara Hepworth. **Guided tours** (£3/$4.80) are available on Sunday at 2:30 p.m. The museum houses a pleasant cafe for lunch or tea.

See map p. 203. Trumpington Street (near Peterhouse College). ☎ *01223/332-900. Admission: Free, but suggested donation £3 ($5.55). Open: Tues–Sat 10 a.m.–5 p.m., Sun noon–5 p.m.; closed Jan 1, Good Friday, May Day, and Dec 24–31.*

King's College

Founded by Henry VI in 1441, King's College encloses one of England's greatest architectural treasures: **King's College Chapel.** Located on the north side of the college's Great Court, the chapel was begun in 1446 and completed about 90 years later. The structure was built in a tall, slender, highly decorated Gothic style. The stunning interior conveys both strength and delicacy. Look up to the ceiling, and you see what many consider to be the finest fan vaulting in England. Nearly 500 years ago, Flemish glaziers made the enormous windows of richly colored stained glass that depict stories from the Old and New Testaments. A painting by Rubens, *Adoration of the Magi,* adorns the altar.

You may want to arrange your schedule so you can hear *Evensong* at King's College Chapel. In the late afternoons during term time, the chapel's famous boys' choir walks in procession across the college grounds in black and white robes to sing in the chapel (Tues–Sat, 5:30 p.m.; free). You can also hear the choir during Sunday services at 10:30 a.m. and 3:30 p.m. On Christmas Day, the famous Festival of Nine Lessons and Carols (a traditional Christmas service) sung by the choir is broadcast around the world from the chapel.

See map p. 203. On King's Parade. ☎ *01223/331-100. Admission (to college and chapel): £4.50 ($8.35) adults; £3 ($5.55) seniors, students, and children 12–17; free for kids under 12. Open: During the school year, Mon–Sat 9:30 a.m.–3:30 p.m., Sun 1:15–2:15 p.m.; the rest of the year, Mon–Sat 9:30 a.m.–4:30 p.m., Sun 10 a.m.–5 p.m. Closed Dec 26–Jan 1.*

Queens' College

Queens' College got its name because two queens — one the wife of Henry VI, the other the wife of Edward IV — endowed the college in 1448. For many, Queens' represents the quintessential and perhaps the most picturesque of all the Cambridge colleges. Step inside to the **Old Court,** and you can see a self-contained academic universe: library, chapel, hall, rooms, and kitchens, all clustered around a small green lawn. The unique sundial in Old Court dates from 1642 and is one of the country's finest. Not only can the sundial tell apparent solar time, but it also can calculate the sun's altitude, the date, the time of sunrise and sunset, and the zodiac sign. The last remaining half-timbered building in Cambridge, **President's Lodge,** is in the southeast corner of **Cloister Court.** (A *half-timbered building* is made of a wooden framework and has the spaces filled with plaster or brick.) Another unusual feature of Queens' is the **Mathematical Bridge** over the Cam. A copy of the original bridge built in 1749, the span was named because meticulous calculations made nails unnecessary.

See map p. 203. Queen's Lane. ☎ *01223/335-511. Admission: £1 ($1.85). Open: Nov 1–Mar 19 daily 1:45–4:30 p.m.; March 20–May 16 and June 20–Oct 31, Mon–Fri 1:45–4:30 p.m. and Sat–Sun 10 a.m.–4:45 p.m.; closed May 17–June 19.*

St. John's College

Before entering St. John's College, on St. John's Street next door to Trinity, take a moment to examine its magnificent **Tudor gateway.** All the fancy carving and statuary is the heraldic "signature" of Lady Margaret Beaufort (1443–1509), mother of Henry VII and grandmother of Henry VIII. A great patron of Cambridge, Lady Margaret founded Christ's College in 1505 and died before her second project, St. John's, was completed in 1511. Inside the First Court, you can see the original building of St. John's College. Two more courts lie beyond, and beyond those courts, you come to the famous **Bridge of Sighs,** built in 1831 over the River Cam. The covered wooden bridge is closed to the public; you can get a better view from a *punt,* or small boat. (For information about punt rentals, see "Finding more to see and do in Cambridge," later in this chapter.)

See map p. 203. St. John's Street. ☎ *01223/338-600. Admission: £1.75 ($3.25). Open: Daily 10 a.m.–5:30 p.m.*

Trinity College

Henry VIII founded Trinity College in 1546, and his coat of arms decorates the **Great Gate** on Trinity Street. Beyond the gate is the **Great Court,** a vast, asymmetrical expanse of lawn surrounded by fine Tudor buildings,

Trinity greats

The largest of the Cambridge colleges, Trinity also has the longest list of illustrious alums. Isaac Newton and Lord Byron; the poets John Dryden and Alfred Lord Tennyson; the novelists William Thackeray and Vladimir Nabokov; the composer Ralph Vaughan Williams; the philosopher Ludwig Wittgenstein; kings Edward VII and George VI; and the present heir to the throne, Prince Charles, all attended Trinity.

including a 15th-century clock tower. Rumor has it that Lord Byron (1788–1824), a Trinity student who became the most famous poet of his day, bathed naked with his pet bear in the fountain. Pass through "the screens" — a passageway between the dining hall and the kitchens — and you come to **Nevile's Court,** where Sir Isaac Newton tested his theory on the speed of sound. **Trinity College Library,** on the west side of Nevile's Court, is another famous Cambridge building. Designed by Sir Christopher Wren and begun in 1676, the library contains a treasure trove of rare books and manuscripts, many written by Trinity alums. The library's marble statue of Lord Byron, shown composing his poem *Childe Harold's Pilgrimage,* is a masterful work by the Danish sculptor Bertel Thorvaldsen. The four figures standing on the library's parapet are 17th-century representations of Divinity, Mathematics, Law, and Physics — the disciplines for which Trinity is best known.

See map p. 203. Trinity Street, ☎ *01223/338-400. Admission (college and library): £2.20 ($4.05). Open: College, daily 10 a.m.–6 p.m.; library, during the school year, Mon–Fri noon–2 p.m. and Sat 10:30 a.m.–2:30 p.m.; library, outside of term, Mon–Fri noon–2 p.m.*

Finding more to see and do in Cambridge

Visitors flock to Cambridge to see the historic colleges and breathe in the rarified academic atmosphere. Check out my additional suggestions for things to see and do:

✔ **Brass rubbing in the round church:** The Church of the Holy Sepulchre is one of England's few surviving Norman round churches. The building is no longer used for services but has taken on new life as the **Cambridge Brass Rubbing Centre** (☎ 01223/ 871-621). Instructions and materials are provided — all you supply is the elbow grease. The brasses are replicas, not originals. A rubbing costs £3 to £15 ($5.55–$28). Even if you don't want to rub, step inside for a look at this unique structure with its thousand-year-old rounded Norman arches and 600-year-old oak roof. The center is open daily in winter from 1 to 4 p.m. and in summer from 10 a.m. to 5 p.m.

✔ **Punting on the River Cam:** Cambridge takes its name from the lovely River Cam. The most famous section of the river is called "The Backs" because many of the colleges back onto its shores. Punting on the Cam is a time-honored tradition. Floating along in one of these flat-bottomed boats looks so romantic, so delightful, so easy! Rather than oars, the punter uses a long stick and propels the boat from the rear like a Venetian gondolier. But the stick frequently gets stuck in the muddy river bottom, and the boat often just doesn't obey orders. So unless you're adept at watersports, consider a **chauffeured punt tour** along the river. If you want to try navigating the river yourself, you can rent punts, rowboats, and canoes from **Scudamore's Punting Company** (☎ **01223/359-750;** www.scudamores.com). It has two locations: **Quayside Punt Station,** beside the Magdalene Street bridge, and **Mill Lane Boatyard,** beside the Silver Street bridge. The boatyards are open from Easter to October. The rental costs £14 to £16 ($26–$30) per hour, plus a refundable £60 ($111) deposit, for up to 6 people in a punt. You can arrange a chauffeured punt at these boatyards, too; the price usually comes out to about £10 ($19) per person.

✔ **Flying back in time:** Duxford, in the countryside about 8km (5 miles) south of Cambridge, was an important airfield during World War II. Today, with its preserved hangars, control tower, and Operations Room, the **Duxford Imperial War Museum** (☎ **01223/835-000**) is one of Europe's top aviation museums. You can check out a major exhibition on the 1940 Battle of Britain, in which Duxford played a major role, and more than 180 historic aircraft. You can also see a collection of tanks and military vehicles, including Field Marshal Montgomery's mobile tactical headquarters. The **American Air Museum** features American fighter planes and other artifacts. A free sightseeing train takes visitors around the 85-acre site. Pick up something to eat at the self-service restaurant on the grounds, or bring your own picnic. To get here, rail travelers can use the museum's free bus service, which runs hourly (9:40 a.m. to 3:40 p.m.) from the Cambridge train station. By car, drive south from Cambridge on the M11 to Junction 10. Admission costs £12 ($22) for adults, £9 ($17) for seniors and students, free for children under 16. The museum is open daily March 17 to October 27 from 10 a.m. to 6 p.m., and in winter daily from 10 a.m. to 4 p.m.; closed from December 24 to 26.

Dining in Cambridge

If you're looking for good vegetarian food, try the **Rainbow Vegetarian Cafe** (☎ **01223/321-551**). Located at 9A King's Parade, down a narrow passageway opposite King's College Gates, this subterranean haven is noted for its excellent daily specials, spinach lasagna, and a hearty Latvian potato bake with carrots, garlic, herbs, and cheese. Main courses cost £6.95 to £7.95 ($13–$15). The cafe takes MasterCard and Visa. It's open Tuesday through Saturday from 10 a.m. to 10 p.m.

You can get a good pub lunch at **The Eagle Pub,** 8 Benet St. (☎ **01223/505-020**). The pub, which dates to the 16th century, was a gathering place for both American and British pilots during World War II. You find a bit of everything on the menu, including fish and chips, bangers and mash, pasta, and beef stroganoff. Main courses cost £3.50 to £11 ($6.50–$20). The pub accepts American Express, Diners Club, MasterCard, and Visa. Food is served Monday through Saturday from noon to 3 p.m. (Sun until 4 p.m.) and from 5 to 9 p.m.; the pub is open until 11 p.m.

Restaurant 22, the restaurant in a converted Victorian house at 22 Chesterton Rd. (☎ **01223/351-880**), is the place to go if you're in the mood for fine dining. This dinner-only restaurant (open Tues–Sat 7–9:45 p.m.) is one of the best in Cambridge. The modern English cooking emphasizes local products of the highest quality. This place gets busy, so you probably want to make reservations. The set-price dinner costs £25 ($46). The restaurant takes MasterCard and Visa.

Greenwich: The Center of Time and Space

Time is of the essence in **Greenwich,** a town and borough of Greater London, about 6.5km (4 miles) east of The City. The world's clocks are set according to Greenwich Mean Time, and visitors from around the globe flock here to stand on the **Prime Meridian,** the line from which the world's longitude is measured. The main attractions in Greenwich, parts of which UNESCO has designated a World Heritage Site, are the Old Royal Observatory, the Queen's House, and the National Maritime Museum, all located in Greenwich Park, and the *Cutty Sark,* berthed on the Thames. The Royal Naval College, a grouping of historic buildings on the Thames, is one of the finest and most dramatically sited architectural and landscape ensembles in the British Isles. Greenwich offers enough to keep you fully occupied for a full day and is a great outing for kids.

Getting to Greenwich

The most interesting route to Greenwich is by **Docklands Light Rail,** which takes you past Canary Wharf and all the new Docklands development. The one-way fare costs £2 ($3.70). To get to Greenwich, ride the Tube to Tower Hill, where you connect to the DLR at its Tower Gateway station (near the Tower of London). Take the light rail to Island Gardens and then walk through the foot tunnel beneath the Thames to Greenwich. You come out next to the *Cutty Sark.* You can also take the Jubilee Underground line to North Greenwich and bus no. 188 from the station into town. **Transport for London** (☎ **020/7222-1234**) runs a fleet of boats from Westminster Pier to Greenwich Pier year-round. A round-trip ticket costs £8.60 ($16) for adults, £4.30 ($8) children, £22 ($41) for families (2 adults, 2 children).

Finding information and taking a tour

All the attractions in Greenwich are clearly signposted, and you can easily reach them on foot. The **Greenwich Tourist Information Centre,** Pepys House, Cutty Sark Gardens (☎ **0870/6082-000**), open daily from

10 a.m. to 5 p.m., offers one-and-a-half- to two-hour **walking tours** (at 12:15 and 2:15 p.m.) of the town's principal sights for £4 ($7.40). You don't need to make reservations, but you may want to call first to verify the schedule.

Exploring Greenwich

Cutty Sark

The majestic *Cutty Sark,* last of the tea-clipper sailing ships, was launched in 1869 and first used for the lucrative China Sea tea trade. Later, the ship carried wool from Australia, and after that (until the end of World War II), it served as a training ship. Today, the hold contains a collection of nautical instruments and paraphernalia. You can visit the ship on a self-guided tour and see everything in about 30 minutes.

King William Walk (along the Thames). ☎ *020/8858-3445. Admission: £4.50 ($8.35) adults, £3.20 ($5.90) children 5–15, £12 ($22) families. Open: Daily 10 a.m.–5 p.m.*

National Maritime Museum

The National Maritime Museum is dedicated to Britain's seafaring past. The paintings of ships tend to be boring, but you also find sailing crafts and models and an extensive exhibit on Admiral Lord Nelson, which includes hundreds of his personal artifacts (including the coat he was wearing when he was shot at the Battle of Trafalgar in 1805). New galleries with interactive technology explore modern maritime issues. You can see the entire collection in about 30 minutes.

In Greenwich Park. ☎ *020/8312-6608. Admission: Free. Open: Daily 10 a.m.–5 p.m.*

Old Royal Observatory

After leaving Queen's House (see the following listing), you can huff your way up the hill in the park to explore the "center of time and space." Situated on the **Prime Meridian** (longitude zero degrees), this observatory also houses a collection of original 18th-century chronometers (marked H1, H2, H3, and H4), beautiful instruments that were developed to help mariners chart longitude by time rather than by the stars.

In Greenwich Park. ☎ *020/8312-6608. Admission: Free. Open: Daily 10 a.m.–5 p.m.*

Queen's House

Adjacent to the National Maritime Museum is the splendidly restored Queen's House, designed by Inigo Jones in 1616 and later used as a model for the U.S. White House. Anne of Denmark, the wife of James I, commissioned Queen's House, the first classical building in England, and it was completed in 1635 (with later modifications). You can visit the royal apartments on a self-guided tour that takes about a half-hour; special exhibits are also held here.

In Greenwich Park. ☎ *020/8312-6608. Admission: Free. Open: Daily 10 a.m.–5 p.m.*

Royal Naval College

Near the *Cutty Sark,* the Royal Naval College occupies the site of Greenwich Palace, which stood here from 1422 to 1620 and was the birthplace of Henry VIII, Mary I, and Elizabeth I. Badly damaged by Oliver Cromwell's troops during the Civil War in the 17th century, the palace was later torn down. In 1696, a naval hospital for retired seamen was erected in its place. The riverside buildings, designed by Sir Christopher Wren, became the Naval College in 1873 and are today a UNESCO-designated World Heritage Site. The only rooms open to visitors are the **chapel** and the imposing **Great Hall,** with its dazzling painted ceiling; the body of Lord Nelson lay in state here in 1805.

King William Walk (along the Thames). ☎ *020/8858-2154. Admission: Free. Open: Daily 10 a.m.–5 p.m.*

Dining in Greenwich

If you're looking for a nice spot for lunch, try **Inside,** 19 Greenwich St. (☎ **020/8205-5060**). This contemporary restaurant serves Modern British cuisine and has vegetarian options. Main courses range from £11 to £17 ($20–$31) with daily fixed-price specials. It's open for lunch Wednesday to Friday from noon to 2:30 p.m., for dinner Tuesday to Saturday from 6:30 to 11 p.m., and for brunch on Saturday and Sunday (11 a.m.–1 p.m.).

Hampton Court Palace: Henry VIII's Riverside Estate

In 1514, Cardinal Thomas Wolsey, Henry VIII's Lord Chancellor, began building **Hampton Court** in East Moseley, Surrey, 21km (13 miles) west of London on the north side of the Thames. But Cardinal Wolsey got on the monarch's bad side when he opposed the king's request for a divorce from Catherine of Aragon. This opposition provided a convenient excuse for the greedy Tudor monarch to nab Hampton Court for himself and make the property a royal residence, a status it held from 1525 until 1760. Henry's fifth wife (of six), Catherine Howard, supposedly haunts the place to this day, though you'd think the hordes of tourists would have scared her away by now.

Getting to Hampton Court

Frequent trains from London's Waterloo Station make the half-hour trip to Hampton Court Station; a round-trip "cheap day return" fare costs £5.30 ($9.80). The palace entrance is a two-minute walk from the station. If you have plenty of time, you can take a boat from **Westminster Pier** to Hampton Court; the journey takes almost four hours. From April to September, boats usually run at 10 a.m. and 12:45 p.m.; call **Westminster Passenger Service** (☎ **020/7930-7770**; www.wpsa.co.uk) for more information. One-way fares (you can easily take the train back) are £11 ($20)

Ghost palace

So many people, from staff to visitors, have reported encounters with Catherine Howard's ghost in the "haunted gallery" at Hampton Court that psychologists from the University of Hertfordshire conducted an investigation to see if they could find a scientific explanation for the phenomenon. Catherine, the fifth wife of King Henry VIII, was locked up in Hampton Court prior to her beheading for adultery in 1542. One day, she supposedly escaped and in desperation ran along the 40-foot gallery to pound on the king's door and beg for mercy. Sightings in this gallery of a running, screaming apparition have been reported for centuries. After weeks of research, the ghost hunters came away empty-handed.

for adults, £7 ($13) for seniors, £5.25 ($9.70) for children 5 to 15, and £26 ($48) for families (2 adults, 2 children). By car, the palace is on A308 close to the A3, M3, and M25 motorways.

Exploring Hampton Court

Hampton Court Palace

The **Anne Boleyn Gate,** with its 16th-century astronomical clock, and the **Great Hall,** with its hammer-beam ceiling, are remnants from Hampton Court's Tudor days. In the late 17th century, Sir Christopher Wren significantly altered the place for William and Mary. Wren also designed the famous **Maze,** where you can wander in dizzy confusion. Inside the enormous palace, something of a maze itself, you can see various state apartments and private rooms, including the King's Dressing Room, the Tudor kitchens, wooden carvings by Grinling Gibbons, Italian paintings, and guides dressed in period costumes. If the weather is nice, take a few minutes to stroll through the lovely, manicured Thames-side gardens, or grab a bite to eat at the cafe and restaurant on the grounds.

East Moseley, Surrey. ☎ *020/8781-9500. Admission: £12 ($22) adults, £8.70 ($16) seniors and students, £7.70 ($14) children 5–15. Open: Apr–Oct daily 10 a.m.–6 p.m.; Nov–Mar Tues–Sun 9:30 a.m.–4:30 p.m., Mon 10:15 a.m.–4:30 p.m.; closed Jan 1 and Dec 24–26.*

Royal Botanic Gardens (Kew Gardens): Royal Pleasure Grounds

Located 14.5km (9 miles) southwest of Central London, the **Royal Botanic Gardens** at Kew — more familiarly known as **Kew Gardens** — are a feast for garden lovers' eyes (and noses).

Getting to Kew Gardens

The easiest way to get here is to take the **Underground** to Kew Gardens; from the station, the entrance on Kew Road is a ten-minute walk west on Lichfield Street. If you have more time, you can take a boat. From April to late September, the **Westminster Passenger Service Association** (☎ **02079/302-062;** www.wpsa.co.uk) operates vessels that leave from London's Westminster Pier daily from 10:15 a.m. to 2 p.m. Round-trip fares for the 90-minute journey cost £17 ($31) for adults, £11 ($20) for seniors, £8.25 ($15) for children 5 to 15, and £41 ($76) for families (2 adults, 2 children). The last boat from Kew back to London usually departs around 5:30 p.m. (depending on the tide).

Exploring Kew Gardens

Royal Botanic Gardens

A marvelous array of specimens, many first planted in the 17th and 18th centuries, thrive in the 300-acre gardens. Gardeners nurture orchids and palms in the Victorian conservatory. Also onsite, you can find a lake, aquatic gardens, a Chinese pagoda, and even a royal palace. **Kew Palace,** the smallest and most picturesque of the former royal compounds, is where King George III went insane. **Queen Charlotte's Cottage** was the mad king's summer retreat. Neither building is open to the public.

Kew. ☎ *020/8332-5622. Admission: £10 ($19) adults, free for children under 16. Tours: Free one-hour tours Mar–Nov daily 11 a.m. and 2 p.m. Open: daily 9:30 a.m–dusk; conservatory closes one hour before gardens.*

Oxford: Town and Gown

Oxford University, one of the world's oldest, greatest, and most revered universities, dominates the town of **Oxford,** about 87km (54 miles) northwest of London. With its skyline pierced by ancient tawny towers and spires, Oxford has been a center of learning for seven centuries (the Saxons founded the city in the tenth century). Roger Bacon, Sir Walter Raleigh, John Donne, Sir Christopher Wren, Dr. Samuel Johnson, Edward Gibbon, William Penn, John Wesley, Lewis Carroll, T. E. Lawrence, W. H. Auden, and Margaret Thatcher are just a few of the distinguished alumni who've taken degrees here. Even Bill Clinton studied at Oxford.

Although academically oriented, Oxford is far from dull. Its long sweep of a main street (High Street, known as "The High") buzzes with a cosmopolitan mix of locals, students, black-gowned dons, and foreign visitors. You can tour some of the beautiful historic colleges, each sequestered away within its own quadrangle (or quad) built around an interior courtyard; stroll along the lovely Cherwell River; and visit the Ashmoleon Museum. For the locations of the attractions and restaurants in the following sections, see the "Oxford" map on p. 215.

Getting to Oxford

Trains to Oxford leave from London's Paddington Station every hour; the trip takes about one hour and costs £16 ($30) for a round-trip "cheap day return" ticket. For train schedules, call ☎ 0845/748-4950. By car, take the M40 west from London, and follow the signs. Note, however, that parking in Oxford is a nightmare.

Finding information and taking a tour

The **Oxford Information Centre**, 15–16 Broad St. (☎ 01865/726-871), is open Monday to Saturday from 9:30 a.m. to 5 p.m. and on Sunday in summer from 10 a.m. to 3:30 p.m.. The center sells a good visitors' guide for £1 ($1.85) and conducts two-hour **walking tours** of the town and its major colleges (but not New College or Christ Church). Tours cost £6.50 ($12) for adults and £3 ($5.55) for children 5 to 15. They leave Sunday through Thursday at 11 a.m. and 2 p.m., Friday at 11 a.m. and 1 p.m., and Saturdays at 10:30 and 11 a.m. and 1 p.m. A special tour includes Christ Church on Friday and Saturday at 11 a.m. and 2 p.m.

City Sightseeing (☎ 01708/864-340; www.citysightseeing.co.uk) offers a one-hour **bus tour** (£9/$17) with hop-on/hop-off service. Buses depart daily from the train station starting at 9:30 a.m. and run every 15 to 20 minutes until 5 or 6 p.m., depending on the season.

The Oxford Story, 6 Broad St. (☎ 01865/790-055), packages Oxford's complexities into a concise and entertaining exhibit-cum-ride that takes you through 800 years of the city's history, reviewing some of the architectural and historical features that you may otherwise miss. It also fills you in on the backgrounds of the colleges and those people who've passed through their portals. Admission costs £6.95 ($13) for adults and £5.95 ($11) for children 5 to 15. The exhibit is open daily in July and August from 9:30 a.m. to 6 p.m. and from September through June from 10 a.m. to 4:30 p.m. (from 11 a.m. on Sun).

Exploring the best of Oxford

Many Americans arriving at Oxford ask, "Where's the campus?" Oxford doesn't have just one campus; it includes 45 widely dispersed colleges serving some 16,000 students. Instead of trying to see them all (impossible in a day), focus on seeing a handful of the better-known ones. Faced with an overabundance of tourists, the colleges have restricted visiting to certain hours and to groups of six or fewer; in some areas, you aren't allowed at all. Before heading off, check with the tourist office to find out when and what colleges you can visit.

You may want to start your tour with a bird's-eye view of the colleges from the top of **Carfax Tower** (☎ 01865/792-653) in the center of the city. The tower is all that remains from St. Martin's Church, where William Shakespeare stood as godfather for a fellow playwright. The tower is open daily November to March from 10:30 a.m. to 3:30 p.m.,

Oxford

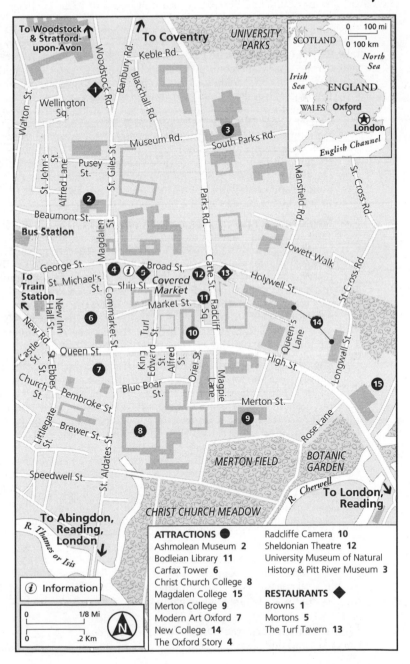

To Woodstock↑
& Stratford-
upon-Avon

↑To Coventry

UNIVERSITY
PARKS

Keble Rd.

Woodstock Rd.
Banbury Rd.
Blackhall Rd.
Walton St.

Wellington
Sq.

Museum Rd.

South Parks Rd.

St. John's St.
Alfred Lane
Pusey
St.
St. Giles St.

Parks Rd.

Mansfield Rd.
St. Cross Rd.

Beaumont St.

Bus Station

Magdalen St.

Jowett Walk

George St.
To
Train
Station
St. Michael's St.
New Inn Hall St.
New Rd.
Castle St.
St. Ebbes St.
Church St.
Pembroke St.
Littlegate St.
Brewer St.
St. Aldates St.

Broad St.
Ship St.
Covered Market
Market St.
Cornmarket St.
Turl St.

Catte St.
Radcliff Sq.
Holywell St.
Queen's Lane
Longwall St.

Queen St.

King Edward St.
Alfred St.
Oriel St.
Magpie Lane
Blue Boar St.

High St.

Merton St.

Rose Lane

Speedwell St.

MERTON FIELD

BOTANIC
GARDEN

R. Cherwell
To London,
Reading

CHRIST CHURCH MEADOW

**To Abingdon,
Reading,
London**
R. Thames or Isis

i Information

0   1/8 Mi
0   .2 Km
N

0   100 mi
0   100 km
SCOTLAND
North
Sea
Irish
Sea
ENGLAND
WALES Oxford
London
English Channel

ATTRACTIONS ●
Ashmolean Museum **2**
Bodleian Library **11**
Carfax Tower **6**
Christ Church College **8**
Magdalen College **15**
Merton College **9**
Modern Art Oxford **7**
New College **14**
The Oxford Story **4**

Radcliffe Camera **10**
Sheldonian Theatre **12**
University Museum of Natural
History & Pitt River Museum **3**

RESTAURANTS ◆
Browns **1**
Mortons **5**
The Turf Tavern **13**

and April to October from 10 a.m. to 5:30 p.m. Admission costs £1.60 ($2.95) for adults and 80p ($1.50) for children 5 to 15.

I recommend visits to the following four colleges:

✔ **Christ Church College** (☎ 01865/276-150): Facing St. Aldate's Street, Cardinal Wolsey (who built Hampton Court, described earlier in this chapter) began this college in 1525. Christ Church has the largest quadrangle of any college in Oxford and a chapel with 15th-century pillars and impressive fan vaulting. **Tom Tower** houses Great Tom, the 18,000-pound bell that rings nightly at 9:05, signaling the closing of the college gates. Several notable portraits, including works by Gainsborough and Reynolds, hang in the **Picture Gallery** and 16th-century **Great Hall.** Admission costs £4 ($7.40) for adults, £3 ($5.55) for seniors and children 5 to 15. The college and chapel are open Monday through Saturday from 9 a.m. to 5 p.m. and Sunday from 1 to 5:30 p.m.

✔ **Magdalen** (pronounced *Maud*-lin) **College** (☎ 01865/276-000): This college on High Street, founded in 1458, boasts the oldest botanical garden in England and the most extensive grounds of any Oxford college; you even find a deer park. The 15th-century bell tower, one of the town's most famous landmarks, is reflected in the waters of the Cherwell River. You can cross a small footbridge and stroll through the water meadows along the path known as Addison's Walk. Admission is £3 ($5.55) for adults and £2 ($3.70) for children 5 to 15. October to June, the college is open daily from 1 p.m. to dusk; off season, it's open daily from 2 to 6 p.m.

✔ **Merton College** (☎ 01865/276-310): Dating from 1264, this college stands near Merton Street, the only medieval cobbled street left in Oxford. The college is noted for its 14th-century library, said to be the oldest college library in England (admission to the library costs £1/$1.85). You can see an astrolabe (an astronomical instrument used for measuring the altitude of the sun and stars) thought to have belonged to Chaucer. The library and college are open Monday to Friday from 2 to 4 p.m., and Saturday and Sunday from 10 a.m. to 4 p.m.; both close for a week at Easter and at Christmas.

✔ **New College** (☎ 01865/279-555): On New College Lane, this college contains the first quadrangle to be built in Oxford (14th century), an architectural boilerplate for the quadrangles in many other colleges. The antechapel holds Sir Jacob Epstein's remarkable modern sculpture of Lazarus and a fine El Greco study of St. James. In the garden, you can see remnants of the old city wall that used to surround Oxford. Admission costs £2 ($3.70) from Easter to October, free off season. Easter to September, you can visit the college daily from 11 a.m. to 5 p.m.; off season, the hours are 2 to 4 p.m. daily.

Finding more to see and do in Oxford

Other attractions worth checking out in Oxford include the following:

✔ **Architectural highlights:** East of Carfax, at the north end of Radcliffe Square, is the **Bodleian Library,** Broad Street (☎ 01865/277-000), the world's oldest library, established in 1450. The **Radcliffe Camera,** the domed building just south of the Bodleian, is the library's reading room, dating from 1737. You can visit both on a one-hour guided tour ($4/$7.40) only; call or stop in at the bookstore for details. To one side of the Bodleian, you can see the **Sheldonian Theatre,** Broad Street (☎ 01865/277-299), which dates from 1669 and was the first major work by Sir Christopher Wren, designed when he was an astronomy professor at Oxford. Today, the college uses the building for lectures and concerts, and you get great city views from the cupola. Admission costs £1.50 ($2.80) for adults and £1 ($1.85) for children 5 to 15. It's open Monday through Saturday from 10 a.m. to 12:30 p.m. and 2 to 4:30 p.m.

✔ **Ashmolean Museum:** Located on Beaumont Street (☎ 01865/278-000), this is the oldest museum in England. A beautiful classical building from the 1840s houses the collections of the University of Oxford: European and Asian art; silver, ceramics; and antiquities from ancient Egypt, Greece, and Rome. You can get into the museum for free, and it's open Tuesday to Saturday from 10 a.m. to 5 p.m. and Sunday from noon to 5 p.m.

✔ **University Museum of Natural History:** Located on Parks Road (☎ 01865/270949), this free museum shows off a good collection of dinosaur skeletons and other curiosities in a marvelous glass-roofed Victorian hall. Entered from the Natural History Museum, the **Pitt Rivers Museum** (☎ 01865/270-949), is also free and worth poking your head into for its curiosity value. General Pitt Rivers gave his collection of ethnic artifacts to the university in 1884, and there are now more than half a million objects in old-fashioned cases crammed into a dimly lit room. Arranged by type rather than geography or date, the exhibits demonstrate how different peoples tackled the same tasks. Most redolent of adventure are the 150 pieces collected during Captain Cook's second voyage, from 1773 to 1774. The Pitt Rivers Museum is open Monday through Saturday from noon to 4:30 p.m. and on Sunday from 2 to 4:30 p.m.

✔ **Modern Art Oxford:** This leading center for contemporary visual arts, located on Pembroke Street (☎ 01865/722-733; www.modern artoxford.org.uk), holds ever-changing exhibitions of sculpture, architecture, photography, video, and other media. Admission is free. It's open Tuesday through Saturday from 10 a.m. to 5 p.m. and Sunday from noon to 5 p.m. You can make a tasty stop at Café Varvara for breakfast, lunch, or a tea-time snack. It opens Tuesday to Saturday at 9:30 a.m., and nothing costs much more than £5 ($9.25).

Dining in Oxford

Browns, 5–11 Woodstock Rd. (☎ 01865/319-655), a large, casual, upbeat brasserie, is one of the best places to eat in Oxford. It serves hearty food, including a good traditional cream tea, and has a large

convivial bar and a very pleasant outdoor terrace. Mummies and dad-
dies visiting their high-achieving offspring at the university bring them
here. Main courses run from £6 to £15 ($11–$28). Browns accepts
American Express, Mastercard, and Visa. The restaurant is open Monday
through Saturday from 11 a.m. to 11:30 p.m. and Sunday from noon to
11:30 p.m.

If you don't want to spend a lot for lunch, stop in at **Mortons,** 22 Broad St.
(☎ **01865/200860**). It makes delicious sandwiches on fresh baguettes
and serves a daily soup. You can eat upstairs, in the back garden, or take
your sandwich away and picnic elsewhere. Sandwiches cost about £2.50
($4.65). Mortons is open daily from 8:30 a.m. to 5 p.m.

For inexpensive pub grub (salads, soups, sandwiches, beef pie, chili con
carne, and so on) or a pint of beer, try **The Turf Tavern,** 4 Bath Place
(☎ **01865/243-235**). Dating to the 13th century, the tavern has served
the likes of Thomas Hardy; Richard Burton and Elizabeth Taylor; and Bill
Clinton, who was a frequent visitor during his student days at Oxford.
You reach the pub using St. Helen's Passage, which stretches between
Holywell Street and New College Lane. Main courses cost £4 to £8
($7.40–$15); the tavern accepts MasterCard and Visa. Food is served
Monday to Saturday from noon to 8 p.m.

Blenheim Palace: Ancestral Home of the Churchills

Located 13km (8 miles) north of Oxford in Woodstock, Oxfordshire,
Blenheim Palace is one of the most beautiful country estates in
England. Visiting the magnificent Baroque palace, birthplace of Sir
Winston Churchill, and strolling through the magnificently landscaped
grounds can take up the better part of a day, although you can sample
the highlights in three hours. The palace has several playgrounds and
activity areas for kids.

Getting to Blenheim Palace

From Oxford, the nearest train station, you can take a taxi (about
£10/$19) or bus no. 20 from the Oxford bus station (it stops at the palace
gate and costs £3.70/$6.85 for a day return). If you have a car, Blenheim
is a 10-minute drive from Oxford and a 45-minute drive from Stratford-
upon-Avon (see Chapter 19). Approaching Oxford from the M40, take the
Junction 9 turnoff, and follow the signs to Blenheim.

Exploring Blenheim Palace

Make the palace your first stop. To get there, you can walk or take a
narrow-gauge railway from the parking lot. I recommend that you join
up with a **palace tour** — tours start every five to ten minutes and last
about a half-hour — but you can also wander through at your own pace

Blenheim was built between 1705 and 1722 for John Churchill, first Duke of Marlborough, in recognition of his victory over the French at the Battle of Blenheim in 1704. The palace was a gift from Queen Anne, whose royal coat of arms is part of the decorations in the Great Hall. The principal architects were Sir John Vanbrugh, also responsible for Castle Howard in Yorkshire, and Nicholas Hawksmoor. Together, they devised the most beautiful baroque palace in England.

The remarkable **Great Hall** is 67 feet high, with stone carvings by Grinling Gibbons and a painted ceiling that shows Marlborough victorious at Blenheim. Sir Winston Churchill, England's prime minister during World War II, was born in a room west of the Great Hall in 1874. The **Churchill Exhibition** contains a variety of interesting exhibits, from letters to his baby curls. The **Green Drawing Room** and the two damask-covered rooms beyond it all have their original ceilings and family portraits painted by George Romney, Joshua Reynolds, John Singer Sargent, and Sir Anthony Van Dyck. A famous tapestry in the **Green Writing Room** shows Marlborough accepting Marshall Tallard's surrender at the Battle of Blenheim. In the **Saloon,** used as the state dining room, the silver-gilt dining table is laid with Minton china.

Three apartments known as the **State Rooms** display more hung tapestries showing Marlborough's victorious campaigns. The **Long Library,** famous for its extraordinary stucco decoration and two false domes, exhibits coronation robes, liveries, uniforms, and the coronets of the present duke and duchess. Sarah, the first duchess, designed much of the **chapel,** which not unexpectedly pays homage to the Duke of Marlborough.

Blenheim is set in acres of beautiful parkland with a variety of gardens designed by Capability Brown and the French landscape architect Achille Duchene. In spring, daffodils and bluebells cover the grassy banks. In summer, hoops of pink roses adorn the **Rose Garden.** Brown designed the **Grand Cascade,** a picturesque waterfall. A path leads to the lake, where you can rent a rowboat. Exotic butterflies inhabit **The Butterfly House.** The **Marlborough Maze,** the world's largest symbolic hedge maze, was designed to reflect the palace's history and architecture. You can have lunch, tea, or a snack during your rambles at one of the many cafes and restaurants scattered about.

Woodstock, Oxfordshire. ☎ *01993/811-325.* www.blenheimpalace.com. *Admission: £13 ($24) adults, £11 ($20) seniors and children 16–17, £7.50 ($14) children 5–15, £35 ($65) family (2 adults, 2 children). Open: Palace, mid-Feb–mid-Dec daily 10:30 a.m.–4:45 p.m (closed Mon–Tues Nov–Dec); grounds, daily summer 9 a.m.- 6 p.m., winter 9 a.m.–4 p.m.*

Windsor Castle: Official Royal Residence

Located in Windsor, Berkshire, 32km (20 miles) from the center of London, **Windsor Castle** is one of the queen's official residences. Some 900 years ago, William the Conqueror constructed the castle, an imposing skyline of towers and battlements rising from the center of the 4,800-acre

ANGLO FILES
ENGLAND

A royal pain

In June 2003, the royal family was royally freaked out when a man dressed in an Osama bin Laden costume managed to scale a wall at Windsor Castle, talk his way past security guards, and get into Prince William's 21st birthday party. The culprit, who climbed up onto the stage as William was making a speech thanking his grandmother, Queen Elizabeth II, for the costume party, turned out to be a comedian known for gatecrashing celebrity events. But the queen wasn't amused, and the security breach led to an apology from the police and a full-scale investigation.

Great Park, which has been used as a royal residence ever since. The town is also the site of Eton College, one of the most exclusive boys' schools in the world.

Getting to Windsor Castle

Trains leave every half-hour from Waterloo Station in London for the 50-minute trip (the stop is Windsor & Eton); the round-trip "cheap day return" fare is £7 ($13). If you're driving from London, take M4 west.

Exploring Windsor Castle

The **State Apartments,** open to visitors, range from the intimate chambers of Charles II to the enormous Waterloo Chamber, built to commemorate the victory over Napoléon in 1815. All are superbly furnished with important works of art from the Royal Collection. Sir Edwin Lutyens designed **Queen Mary's Dollhouse,** a marvelous palace in miniature, as a present for Queen Mary (wife of King George V) in 1921. From April through June, the **Changing of the Guard** takes place Monday through Saturday at 11 a.m. (on alternate days the rest of the year). From the ramparts of Windsor, you can look down on the playing fields of **Eton College,** where aristocrats and social climbers have been sending their boys for generations. You can explore the famous school and the charming town of Eton by strolling across the Thames Bridge.

Windsor, Berkshire. ☎ *01753/831-118.* www.windsor.gov.uk/attractions/ castle.htm. *Admission: £13 ($24) adults, £11 ($20) seniors and students, £6.50 ($12) children under 17, £32 ($59) families. Open: Mar–Oct daily 9:45 a.m.–5:30 p.m. (last entry 4 p.m.), Nov–Feb daily 9:45 a.m.–4:15 p.m. (last entry 3 p.m.); closed Jan 1, Mar 28, June 16, Dec 25–26.*

Part IV
The Southeast

The 5th Wave   By Rich Tennant

"He had it made after our trip to England. I give you, 'Clifford Fountain from Hever Castle'."

In this part . . .

*I*n this part, I introduce you to Kent and Sussex, the counties that form the wedge-shaped southeastern corner of England between London and the English Channel. The area is incredibly rich in history.

In Chapter 14, I take you to a trio of beautiful towns. Canterbury is famous for its magnificent cathedral, a place of pilgrimage for hundreds of years. Rye is a treasure trove of ancient streets lined with half-timbered inns and Georgian shops. Brighton, with its long beach, amusement pier, and fanciful Royal Pavilion, is a seaside resort that's a favorite weekend getaway spot for Londoners. In this chapter, I also tell you about visiting Battle, home to one of the most hallowed spots on English soil — the site where William the Conqueror fought King Harold for the English throne in 1066.

Moated castles, glorious gardens, and stately homes fill the Kentish countryside. In Chapter 15, I guide you through Dover Castle, with its 2,000-year history that stretches back to the time of the Romans. Hever Castle is noteworthy for its associations with Anne Boleyn and its magnificent gardens. Many castle connoisseurs, including several kings and queens who lived there, consider Leeds Castle the most beautiful in England. And speaking of beautiful, you won't find a more spectacular garden anywhere than the one at Sissinghurst. For a glimpse of how the other half lived, you can visit Knole, a country estate that just happens to have 365 rooms, or Chartwell, the country home of Sir Winston Churchill.

You can easily experience every place that I describe in this part in a day trip from London. Or you can stay overnight in any of the towns in Chapter 14 and be assured of a good hotel, fine restaurants, and atmosphere galore.

Chapter 14

Kent and Sussex

● ●

In This Chapter

▶ Visiting Canterbury and its cathedral

▶ Exploring the cobbled streets of Rye

▶ Reliving the Battle of Hastings

▶ Seeing the sights in Brighton

● ●

Kent and Sussex make up the southeast corner of England, an area that extends east and south from London to the English Channel. (See "The Southeast" map on p. 224.) At its narrowest point, near Dover, the channel separating England from France is only 32km (20 miles) wide. Because of its proximity to the European mainland, this part of England has always been of prime strategic importance. Two thousand years ago, the Romans landed on these shores and began their systematic conquest of what they called Britannia. In 1066, William the Conqueror sailed over from Normandy and fought King Harold for the crown of England at a place now called, appropriately enough, Battle. Kent and Sussex became the scene of ferocious air battles and daring sea escapes during World War II. (Dover Castle, which you can read about in Chapter 15, played a pivotal role in the country's coastal defenses.)

Despite all the historic dramas that have played out here, the country-side has an air of calm repose. The land is lush and green, with chalk *downs* (high, open, grassy land over a chalk–limestone subsoil) appearing near the coastline. Kent and Sussex (divided into West Sussex and East Sussex) are wealthy counties, favored spots for country living because of their mild climate and proximity to London.

In this chapter, I head first to Canterbury to explore the wonders of Canterbury Cathedral and the charming old town that grew up around it. From Canterbury, I travel to Rye and stroll the ancient lanes of a once-proud seaport that is today one of England's loveliest small towns. After exploring the battlefield and ruined abbey at Battle, I stop off in the lively resort town of Brighton for some fun beside the sea.

The Southeast

Canterbury: Tales from the Great Cathedral

Magnificent **Canterbury Cathedral** is one of England's glories. Spinning the yarns immortalized in *The Canterbury Tales,* Chaucer's pilgrims made their way here. For nearly 400 years, the devout, in search of miracles and salvation (and a bit of adventure), trekked to the cathedral's shrine of St. Thomas à Becket, archbishop of Canterbury. In 1170, Henry II's henchmen murdered him in the cathedral. The pilgrims didn't stop coming until Henry VIII had the shrine destroyed in 1538.

Modern pilgrims, called *day-trippers,* continue to pour into the Kentish city of Canterbury, on the River Stour. I recommend that you spend most of your time visiting the cathedral, which remains the town's greatest attraction, and exploring the picturesque semimedieval streets that surround it. You may also want to visit some of the small but noteworthy museums and attractions that can help you piece together an image of Canterbury through the centuries. For the locations of museums, hotels, restaurants, and attractions described in the following sections, see the "Canterbury" map on p. 227.

Getting to Canterbury

Canterbury, which is 99km (62 miles) east of London, has two train stations, Canterbury East and Canterbury West, both within easy walking distance from the city center. From London's Victoria Station, trains run about every half-hour to Canterbury East. Hourly trains from London's Charing Cross stop at Canterbury West. The journey takes one and a half hours and costs £18 ($33) for a "cheap day return" (round-trip) ticket from London. For train schedules and information, call ☎ **08457/484-950.**

National Express (☎ **0990/808-080;** www.nationalexpress.com) offers frequent, direct bus service from London's Victoria Coach Station to Canterbury's bus station on St. George's Lane, a few minutes' walk from the cathedral. The trip takes one hour and 50 minutes; day-return fare is £11 ($20).

To drive from London, take A2, then the M2; Canterbury is signposted all the way. The city center is closed to cars, but several parking areas are close to the cathedral.

Finding information and taking a tour

At the **Tourist Information Centre,** 12–13 Sun St. (☎ **01227/378-100;** www.canterbury.co.uk), opposite Christchurch Gate at the entrance to the cathedral precincts, you can buy tickets for **guided-tour walks** of the city and cathedral. The walks leave from here daily at 2 p.m. (in July and Aug, additional walks Mon–Sat at 11:30 a.m.). The cost is £4 ($7.40) for adults, £3.50 ($6.50) for seniors and students, £2.80 ($5.20) for children under 12, and £12 ($22) for families. From Easter through October, the center is open Monday through Saturday from 9:30 a.m. to 5:30 p.m. and Sunday from 10 a.m. to 4 p.m.; the rest of the year, it's open Monday through Saturday from 9:30 a.m. to 5 p.m.

Canterbury Historic River Tours, Weaver's House, 1 St. Peter's St. (☎ **07790/534-744**), offers half-hour **boat trips** on the Stour River with a commentary on the history of the buildings you pass. From April through September, river conditions permitting, boats depart daily every half-hour from 10 a.m. to 5 p.m. Tickets cost £4.80 ($8.90) for adults and £3.80 ($7.05) for children 5 to 15. Umbrellas are available in case of rain. The boats leave from behind the 15th-century Weaver's House (which you can get to through the Weaver's restaurant garden).

Staying in or near Canterbury

Canterbury itself has surprisingly few hotels, but you can find some other acceptable options in the vicinity.

Abbot's Fireside Hotel
$ Elham

This pretty 15th-century hotel sits in the middle of Elham, a village 16km (10 miles) south of Canterbury, midway between Canterbury and Dover. The hotel is small and cozy, with only six medium-size rooms (all with private bathrooms). You find welcoming log fires, exposed beams, and a good restaurant. The staff welcomes children.

See map p. 227. High Street, Elham (near Canterbury), Kent CT4 6TD. (By car from Canterbury: Take A2 southeast toward Dover; exit at Barham, and drive through town to next village, which is Elham.) ☎ **01303/840-265.** *Fax: 01303/840-852.* www.abbots fireside.com. *Rack rates: £45–£105 ($83–$194) double. Rates include English breakfast. AE, MC, V.*

Cathedral Gate Hotel
$ Canterbury

If you want to stay near the cathedral like the pilgrims of yore, you can't get any closer than this 27-room hotel adjoining Christchurch Gate (one of the gates into the cathedral precincts). Dating from 1438, the hotel has comfortable and modestly furnished rooms, and an overall ambience of sloping floors, massive oak beams, and winding corridors.

See map p. 227. 36 Burgate, Canterbury, Kent CT1 2HA. ☎ **01227/464-381.** *Fax: 01227/ 462-800.* www.cathgate.co.uk. *Rack rates: £26–£90 ($48–$167) double. Rate includes continental breakfast. AE, DC, MC, V.*

The Swallow Chaucer Hotel
$–$$ Canterbury

Originally a Georgian residence, the Chaucer stands opposite Canterbury's ancient city walls, about a 10-minute walk from the city center. This is a small, pleasant, recently refurbished hotel with 42 comfortable rooms, all of them different in size and layout, some with views over the city's rooftops to the cathedral. The bathrooms are a decent size. The locals really like the hotel's restaurant.

See map p. 227. 63 Ivy Lane (off Lower Bridge Street), Canterbury, Kent CT1 1TU. ☎ **01227/464427.** *Fax: 01227/450397.* www.swallow-hotels.com. *Rack rates: £55–£130 ($102–$241) double. AE, DC, MC, V.*

Dining in or near Canterbury

Restaurant options in and near Canterbury run the gamut from traditional to contemporary.

Augustine's
$–$$ Canterbury MODERN BRITISH

You find this fun, informal restaurant in a Georgian house just outside of the center of town, on the way to St. Augustine's Abbey. This spot is a

Canterbury

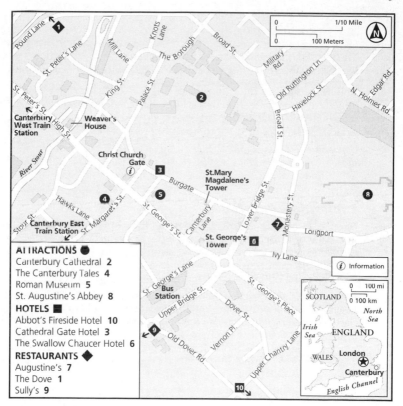

ATTRACTIONS ●
Canterbury Cathedral **2**
The Canterbury Tales **4**
Roman Museum **5**
St. Augustine's Abbey **8**
HOTELS ■
Abbot's Fireside Hotel **10**
Cathedral Gate Hotel **3**
The Swallow Chaucer Hotel **6**
RESTAURANTS ◆
Augustine's **7**
The Dove **1**
Sully's **9**

dependable neighborhood favorite that serves good cooking, including vegetarian dishes, using fresh, local ingredients. The relaxed atmosphere makes Augustine's a good spot for dining with children.

See map p. 227. 1–2 Longport. ☎ *01227/453-063. Reservations recommended. Main courses: £12–£25 ($22–$46); fixed-price lunch: £8.95 ($17). MC, V. Open: Tues–Sat noon–1:30 p.m. and 6:30–9 p.m., Sun noon–2 p.m. Closed Jan.*

The Dove
$$ Dargate   FRENCH/MEDITERRANEAN

Not many pubs serve food as good as this one, located a few miles southwest of town in the village of Dargate. The chef–owner offers a constantly changing menu that represents the best of French and Mediterranean-style cooking. A blackboard displays the daily specials. Whatever's fresh and in season appears on the menu, which may include cooked crab risotto, roast venison, grilled mackerel, braised beef, or duck.

See map p. 227. Plumpudding Lane. ☎ *01227/751-360. Reservations recommended. By car, from Canterbury: Take A290 north to A299, turn west and exit at Dargate. Main courses: £15–£25 ($28–$46). MC, V. Open: Tues–Sun noon–2 p.m.; Tues–Sat 7–9 p.m.*

Sully's
$$–$$$ Canterbury   TRADITIONAL BRITISH

This restaurant in the County Hotel is one of Canterbury's best. You can choose among a selection of traditional English dishes; try one of the more imaginatively conceived platters; or sample seasonal specialties, such as grilled lemon sole or roasted breast of pheasant.

See map p. 227. County Hotel, High Street. ☎ *01227/766-266. Reservations recommended. Fixed-price lunch: £17 ($31); fixed-price dinner: £23–£28 ($43–$52). AE, DC, MC, V. Open: Daily 12:30–2:30 p.m. and 7–10 p.m.*

Exploring Canterbury

Much of central Canterbury is a pedestrian-only zone, making it a pleasant place to stroll.

Canterbury Cathedral

Imagine how overwhelmed medieval pilgrims must have been when they first saw this massive and magnificent structure. The cathedral's origins date to A.D. 597, when St. Augustine arrived on a mission from Rome. Fire and Viking marauders destroyed the earlier church. What stands on the site today is the first cathedral in England to be built in the Gothic style. The crypt dates from about 1100 and the cathedral from the 13th century, with a central bell tower — called Bell Harry — added in the 15th century. After Archbishop Thomas à Becket was murdered in the cathedral in 1170, pilgrims from all over Europe began to flock to his shrine. Although Henry VIII destroyed Becket's shrine, its site is still marked in the **Trinity Chapel,** near the high altar. Noteworthy features of the cathedral include panels of rare **stained glass** and the medieval **royal tombs** of Henry IV and Edward the Black Prince. Give yourself at least an hour to visit the cathedral.

As you stroll the cathedral grounds, you may encounter flocks of well-behaved boys and girls wearing blazers and ties. They attend **King's School,** the oldest public school in England, housed in several fine medieval buildings (not open to the public) around the cathedral.

See map p. 227. 11 The Precincts. ☎ *01227/762-862. Admission: £5 ($9.25) adults; £4 ($7.40) seniors, students, and children 5–15. Open: Mon–Sat 9 a.m.–6 p.m. (Nov–Mar until 4:30 p.m.), Sun 9 a.m.–2 p.m. and 4:30–5:30 p.m.; closed to sightseeing during services.*

The Canterbury Tales

This museum and exhibition are informative and entertaining even if you don't know a thing about Geoffrey Chaucer (1342–1400) or *The Canterbury Tales,* his spirited and sometimes-bawdy stories about a group of medieval pilgrims on their way to visit Becket's shrine at Canterbury Cathedral. The pilgrimages that were so popular in Chaucer's time are re-created here in tableaux. You can hear five of Chaucer's tales and the story of St. Thomas à Becket's murder on **audio headsets.** Give yourself 45 minutes to an hour to see and hear the entire show.

See map p. 227. 23 St. Margaret's St., off High Street, in St. Margaret's Church. ☎ *01227/454-888. Admission: £6.95 ($13) adults; £5.95 ($11) seniors and students, £5.25 ($9.70) children 5–15. Open: Daily 10 a.m.–4:30 p.m. (Mar–Oct until 5 p.m., July–Aug from 9:30 a.m.).*

Roman Museum

Two millennia ago, following their conquest of England, Romans lived in Canterbury, which they called Durovernum Cantiacorum. This small but fascinating museum, in the excavated Roman levels of the city between the cathedral and High Street, chronicles their daily lives. Allow 30 minutes.

See map p. 227. Butchery Lane. ☎ *01227/785-575. Admission: £2.90 ($5.35) adults; £1.80 ($3.35) seniors, students, and children 5–15. Open: Year-round Mon–Sat 10 a.m.–5 p.m.; June–Oct Sun 1:30–5 p.m.*

St. Augustine's Abbey

Although the cathedral gets the lion's share of attention in Canterbury, another Christian site predates the cathedral by about 600 years. Set in a spacious park, about a 15-minute walk east from the town center, are the atmospheric ruins of St. Augustine's Abbey, founded in A.D. 598 and one of the oldest Anglo-Saxon monastic sites in the country. You tour this World Heritage site with an **interactive audio tour.** Allow 30 minutes.

Trek another five minutes east from St. Augustine's Abbey, and you encounter England's oldest parish church. No one knows for sure who founded **St. Martin's Church,** North Holmes Road (☎ **01227/459-482**), but it was already in existence when Augustine arrived from Rome to convert the Anglo-Saxon natives in A.D. 597. The tiny church was given to Queen Bertha, the French (Christian) wife of Saxon (pagan) King Ethelbert of Kent, as part of her marriage contract. The church is open daily from 9 a.m. to 5 p.m., and admission is free. Allow ten minutes at most; the church is tiny.

See map p. 227. Longport. ☎ *01227/767-345. Admission: £3.70 ($6.85) adults, £2.80 ($5.20) seniors and students, £1.90 ($3.50) children under 16. Open: Daily Apr–Sept 10 a.m.–6 p.m., Oct–Mar Wed–Sun 10 a.m.–4 p.m.; closed Jan 1 and Dec 24–26.*

Rye: Smugglers, Mermaids, and Writers

"**Rye** is like an old beautifully jewelled brooch worn at South-England's throat." So wrote Patric Dickinson, one of the many writers who have fallen under the spell of this remarkably beautiful coastal town in East Sussex. (See the "Rye" map on p. 231.) Henry James spent the last years of his life here, and E. F. Benson, author of *Mapp and Lucia,* was mayor. (Benson called the town "Tilling" in his novels.)

The town earned its official title, "The Ancient Town of Rye," nearly a millennium ago when Rye joined the federation of coastal defense towns known as the Cinque Ports. After a pleasurable stay in 1573, Queen Elizabeth I decreed that the town could use the additional title "Rye Royale." Located today about 3km (2 miles) inland from the English Channel, Rye was a powerful seaport that protected the coast from foreign marauders while carrying on a lively business in smuggling and piracy. That maritime history still clings to the cobblestone lanes threading through Rye.

Rye is small enough that you can see it all in about three hours but so charming that you may want to spend the night. The town claims to have more historic buildings than any other town in England, and preservationists carefully protect their appearance. As a result, you see buildings dating from the 13th century to the Victorian era, with no modern intrusions. Rye is also known for several excellent restaurants, many of which serve fresh, locally caught seafood. For the locations of hotels, restaurants, and attractions that follow, see the "Rye" map on p. 231.

Getting to Rye

Rye is 100km (62 miles) southeast of London. By train, you can visit Rye in an easy day trip. Trains depart hourly from London's Charing Cross Station, and you have to make a change at Ashford International; the total trip takes about one-and-a-half hours. The day return (round-trip) fare from London costs £21 ($39). For train schedules, call ☎ **08457/ 484-950.** The easy walk from Rye train station on Cinque Ports Street to Strand Quay, a good place to start your explorations, takes about ten minutes.

By car, Rye is 16km (10 miles) northeast of Hastings on A259. From London, take the M25, M26, and M20 east to Maidstone, turning southeast along A20 to Ashford; at Ashford, take A2070 south to Rye. Cars aren't allowed into the historic center, so you need to park in one of the nearby lots and walk from there. Currently, no bus service is available from London to Rye.

If you drive, you can easily combine a trip to Rye with a trip to Battle, scene of the momentous Battle of Hastings in 1066 (see the section "Battle: 1066 and All That," later in this chapter).

Finding information

One of Rye's old sail lofts (where sails were repaired) on Strand Quay now holds the Rye Heritage Center, home of the **Tourist Information Centre** (☎ 01797/226-696; www.rye-tourism.co.uk). You can obtain a free town map here, buy books and postcards, and rent an excellent **audio walking tour** (£2.50/$4.65) that guides you around the town. The

Rye

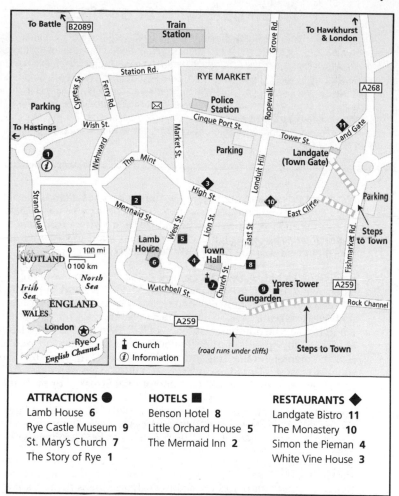

ATTRACTIONS ●
Lamb House **6**
Rye Castle Museum **9**
St. Mary's Church **7**
The Story of Rye **1**

HOTELS ■
Benson Hotel **8**
Little Orchard House **5**
The Mermaid Inn **2**

RESTAURANTS ◆
Landgate Bistro **11**
The Monastery **10**
Simon the Pieman **4**
White Vine House **3**

office can also help you find a hotel room. Office hours from April through October are Monday through Saturday from 9:30 a.m. to 5 p.m., Sunday 10 a.m. to 4 p.m., and from November through March, daily from 10 a.m. to 4 p.m.

Taking a tour of Rye

Renting the **audio walking tour** from the information office on Strand Quay (see the previous section, "Finding information") is the best available way to get to know Rye. Easy to use, and packed with interesting

Rye's calendar of events

During August, Rye holds its **Medieval Weekend,** with a parade of costumed locals, a two-day fair, and a street market on High Street. In September, the town stages the **Rye Festival of Music and the Arts,** which features concerts and exhibitions. The town celebrates Guy Fawkes Night (Nov 5) with the **Rye Bonfire Weekend:** Bonfire societies from all over Sussex participate in a parade and torchlight procession through the darkened streets before the ceremonial bonfire and fireworks. For information about the holiday, see the sidebar "Famous failure: Guy Fawkes," later in this chapter. For more information about the celebration, contact the Tourist Information Centre at ☎ 01797/226-696.

historical tidbits and ghost stories, the tour makes a circuit around the town, stopping to point out sights you may otherwise miss. Depending on how frequently you stop, the tour takes anywhere from one to three hours. If you stay overnight in Rye, you may want to consider an overnight rental of the **"Ghost Walks" audio tour.**

If you're a fan of E. F. Benson's novels set in Rye, you may want to consider taking the **"Mapp and Lucia's Rye" walking tour.** Conducted by the secretary of the E. F. Benson Society, the walk takes you past the characters' houses to the Benson memorials in St. Mary's Church and ends at Lamb House, the onetime residence of E. F. Benson. From the last week in May through September, the 90-minute walks take place on Wednesday and, in summer, on the first and third Saturday of the month at 2 p.m. The tour costs £4.95 ($9.15) per person. You don't need to reserve in advance; just show up at Hilder's Cliff (the end of High Street). For more information, call ☎ **01797/223-114** or 01797/226-696. (Before coming to Rye, you may also want to watch the film versions of the books: The Mapp and Lucia stories, written in the 1920s and 1930s, were filmed in ten one-hour segments for television in the 1980s and are available on video.)

Staying in Rye

Rye offers any number of charming, historic places to stay, some with gardens, some with views out over Romney Marsh.

Benson Hotel
$

A former vicarage, this comfortable, three-story brick B&B sits just off High Street. The four guest rooms have four-poster beds and private bathrooms. From your room, you can see out over Rye's rooftops or toward distant Romney Marsh.

See map p. 231. 15 East St., Rye, East Sussex TN31 7JY. ☎ *01797/225-131. Fax: 01797/ 225-512.* www.bensonhotel.co.uk. *Rack rates: £80–£104 ($148–$192) double. Rates include English or continental breakfast. MC, V.*

Little Orchard House
$–$$

This charming Georgian-era B&B is named for the romantic little orchard garden tucked behind the house. Period antiques and paintings decorate the two guest rooms; both have private bathrooms. The rate includes a generous country breakfast with many local and organic products.

See map p. 231. West Street, Rye, East Sussex TN31 7ES. ☎ and fax: 01797/223-831. www.littleorchardhouse.com. Rack rates: £78–£100 ($144–$185) double. Rates include English breakfast. V.

The Mermaid Inn
$$$–$$$$

When you enter this famous half-timbered inn, one of the oldest and loveliest in England, you're instantly wafted back to the "Olde England" of your dreams. The inn is hundreds of years old, full of ancient oak timbers, creaking floors, and huge fireplaces with log fires (plus a resident ghost or two). The 31 rooms, every one different, are spread over several levels and have modern bathrooms. This is the best hotel in Rye, and it has one of the best restaurants.

See map p. 231. Mermaid Street, Rye, East Sussex TN31 7EU. ☎ 01797/223-065. Fax: 01797/225-069. www.mermaidinn.com. Rack rate: £160–£220 ($296–$407) double. Rates include English breakfast. Special rates with dinner available. AE, DC, MC, V.

Dining in Rye

Rye is known for its restaurants, many of which serve fresh seafood. In addition to the eateries listed here, the Mermaid Inn (see the preceding section) uses fresh ingredients to create some of the best cuisine in town.

Landgate Bistro
$–$$ MODERN BRITISH

This highly regarded bistro close to the old town gate is known for the quality of its local produce, fish, and lamb. The cooking is sophisticated but not fussy. For starters, you may have chard and Roquefort tart or butternut squash risotto. Main courses may include free-range chicken; wild rabbit; or "very fishy stew," which uses fresh, locally caught fish.

See map p. 231. Landgate. ☎ 01797/222-829. Reservations recommended. Main courses: £6–£13 ($11–$24). AE, MC, V. Open: Tues–Sat 7–9:30 p.m.

The Monastery
$$ MODERN BRITISH/FRENCH

Many foodies consider the Monastery, on busy High Street, one of Rye's top restaurants. A sample menu may include garlic mushrooms with smoked bacon, poached salmon in white wine and dill, and lamb with red-currant jam and rosemary. In the summer, you probably want to reserve a table in advance.

See map p. 231. High Street. ☎ *01797/223-272. Reservations recommended. Main courses: £12–£15 ($22–28); fixed-price dinner: £19 ($35). MC, V. Open: Tues–Sun noon–2 p.m.; Tues–Sat 7–9:45 p.m.*

Simon the Pieman
$ LIGHT FARE/AFTERNOON TEA

At this charming tearoom in the shadow of St. Mary's Church, you can get a light lunch, cake and coffee, or an afternoon cream tea. Daily specials include homemade soups and sandwiches, and an enticing selection of cakes, pies, and fudge.

See map p. 231. Lion Street. ☎ *01797/22207. Lunch: £4–£8 ($7.40–$15); cream tea: £4.50 ($8.35). No credit cards. Open: Mon–Fri 9:30 a.m.–5 p.m., Sat 9:30 a.m.–5:30 p.m., Sun 1:30–5:30 p.m.*

Exploring Rye

Formerly a fortified island surrounded by the sea, Rye occupies a hill that now rises above the flat green expanse of Romney Marsh. From atop the former ramparts, you can see the River Rother, home to the local fishing fleet, winding its way toward the sea. Rye is a town to explore on foot (cars aren't allowed) and at your leisure. You can savor it in its entirety rather than in a specific church or museum. Rye is jam-packed with half-timbered Tudor and Elizabethan houses, handsome Georgian townhouses, secret passageways, quaint corners, cobbled lanes, windy viewpoints, enticing shops, and wonderful restaurants. (For more about the architectural styles mentioned here, see Chapter 2.)

Lamb House

This dignified red-brick Georgian house is full of literary associations. The house was the last residence of the American writer Henry James, who became a British citizen at the end of his life and lived here from 1898 to 1916. In this house, James entertained many other writers, including H. G. Wells, Rudyard Kipling, and Joseph Conrad. One guest, E. F. Benson, acquired the house after James's death. Benson, who became mayor of Rye, went on to write a series of satirical novels set in the town. Visitors to Lamb House, now a National Trust property, can see some of the rooms and personal possessions used by James and Benson. The house also has a charming walled garden. You can see the house and garden in under a half-hour.

See map p. 231. West Street. ☎ *01892/890-651 (regional office of National Trust). Admission: £2.90 ($5.35) adults, £1.40 ($2.60) children 5–15. Open: Apr–Oct Wed and Sat 2–5:30 p.m.*

Rye Castle Museum

Rye's local history museum has two sites. The 12th-century **Ypres Tower** displays medieval pottery, ironwork, and items having to do with smuggling (for which Rye was notorious). Originally built as part of the town's defenses, the tower is one of Rye's oldest buildings. The structure survived the burning of the town by the French in the late 14th century and was later used as a prison and a mortuary. From the terrace, you can view what was once Rye's busy harbor. The **Gungarden** below the tower received its name from the small cannons mounted there for the symbolic protection of Queen Elizabeth, the Queen Mother, who made an official visit in the 1980s. (The Queen Mum was Warden of the Cinque Ports, an honorary title formerly held by Winston Churchill.) On East Street, a former bottling factory has been converted into the **East Street Gallery,** the second half of the museum. In the Gallery, you can see a splendid 18th-century fire engine, paintings and engravings of Rye, an exhibition of the famous local pottery, and maritime memorabilia. You can breeze through both of these sites in less than a half hour.

See map p. 231. Pump Street (Ypres Tower) and East Street (Gallery). ☎ *01797/226-728. Admission: Joint ticket to both, £3 ($5.55) adults, £1.75 ($3.25) children 7–16, £5 ($9.25) families (2 adults, 2 children). Open: Apr–Oct Thurs–Mon 10:30 a.m.–1 p.m. and 2–5 p.m.; Nov–Mar Tower only Sat–Sun 10:30 a.m.–3:30 p.m.St. Mary's Church.*

St. Mary's Church

For almost 900 years, the parish church of St. Mary's has dominated the hill on which the old town stands. In 1377, French invaders looted the town, set it on fire, and carried the church bells off to France. The following year, men from Rye sailed to Normandy and brought the bells back. The church's turret clock, the oldest in the country, dates from 1561 and has an 18-foot-long pendulum. The church's "Quarter Boys" (bells that strike the quarters but not the hours) were added in 1760. The church has several interesting stained-glass windows, although none is very old. You can see the most beautiful window, by Sir Edward Burne-Jones and dating from 1891, in the north aisle. You can climb the church tower for a magnificent view out over the rooftops of Rye.

See map p. 231. Church Square. ☎ *01797/222-430. Admission: church, free; Tower, £1.50 ($2.80). Open: Church and tower, daily 9 a.m.–6 p.m. (4 p.m. in winter). The tower isn't accessible to wheelchairs.*

The Story of Rye

Located in the same building as the tourist-information center, this attraction uses an elaborate scale model of the town for a miniature sound-and-light show detailing highlights in Rye's long and sometimes-bloody history. Kids usually enjoy the spectacle. The show lasts approximately 20 minutes and provides a good overall introduction to Rye.

See map p. 231. Rye Heritage Center, Strand Quay. ☎ *01797/226-696. Admission: £2.50 ($4.65) adults, £1.50 ($2.80) seniors, £1 ($1.85) children 5–15. Open: Daily 10 a.m.–3 p.m.*

Battle: 1066 and All That

If you ever studied English history, the year 1066 probably rings a bell. That year, Duke William of Normandy defeated Harold, king of England, at the Battle of Hastings. After the battle, William became known as William the Conqueror. He had himself crowned king at Westminster Abbey and Winchester, and began construction of the Tower of London and other fortifications that you can still see today. William's conquest of England ended the post-Roman Anglo-Saxon era. For taxation purposes, the new monarch compiled a list of every property and building in his newly conquered land. The list became the famous *Domesday Book,* a unique record of England in the 11th century. (The original *Domesday Book,* housed in the Public Records Office in London, isn't accessible to the public. You can, however, look over its contents on the Web at www.domesdaybook.co.uk.)

But all this history started with a battle, and Battle marks the spot. In the town, preserved behind high brick walls, you can see the actual battlefield where the Saxon and Norman soldiers clashed on that fateful day in 1066. (Many people think that the Battle of Hastings took place in Hastings, but the conflict happened here, 9.5km (6 miles) inland.) If you have an interest in history, Battle is a memorable visit. Basing yourself in nearby Rye or Brighton, you can come to Battle as part of a larger tour of southeast England, or you can come to Battle for a day trip from London. Local tourist associations refer to the Sussex countryside around Battle as "1066 Country."

Getting to Battle

Battle is 92km (57 miles) south of London. Direct train service is available from London's Charing Cross Station (Battle is a stop on the London–Hastings line). The trip takes about 90 minutes; a standard day return (round trip) costs £18 ($33). You also can get train connections from Rye, about 29km (18 miles) southeast, via Hastings. The easy walk from the Battle train station to the battlefield entrance on High Street takes about ten minutes. (To get to the battlefield, turn left outside the station and right at Lower Lake, the first main street.) For train schedules and information, call ☎ 08457/484-950.

By car, Battle is about 9.5km (6 miles) north of Hastings on A2100. Parking lots are near the entrance to the battlefield.

Finding information

The **Battle Tourist Information Centre,** Battle Abbey Gatehouse, 88 High St. (☎ 01424/773-721; www.1066country.com/tics.htm), has a free town pamphlet that includes a map. The center is open daily from 10 a.m. to 6 p.m. in summer, 10 a.m. to 4 p.m. in winter.

Dining in Battle

A plethora of restaurants and tearooms beckons travelers along High Street. For hearty and traditional home-cooked English food, try the **Gateway Restaurant,** 78 High St. (☎ 01424/772-056), open daily from 9 a.m. to 5:30 p.m. Lunch specials usually include several old-fashioned pies: steak, ale, and mushroom; steak and kidney; and chicken, leek, and bacon. You can also get toasted sandwiches, baguettes with different fillings, an all-day brunch, or an afternoon cream tea (£4.50/$8.35). Lunch costs about £5 to £6 ($9.25–$11); the restaurant doesn't accept credit cards.

For another atmospheric place to get a simple hot lunch, snack, or afternoon tea with homemade cakes, check out the **Copper Kettle,** also on High Street (☎ 01424/772-727). It's in the Almonery, a lovely, beamed medieval hall (where the Town Council meets) with a pretty, walled garden. Lunch costs under £6 ($11), but you can't pay with a credit card. The shop is open Monday through Saturday from 9:30 a.m. to 4:30 p.m.

Famous failure: Guy Fawkes

In the front hallway of the Almonery, the building on High Street that houses the Copper Kettle (see the preceding section, "Dining in Battle"), you can see one of the oldest Guy Fawkes sculptures in the country, bearded and dressed in black and red with a pointed hat. Residents parade the figure around town before they light a bonfire on Guy Fawkes Night, November 5.

Who, you may ask, was Guy Fawkes (1570–1606)? Guy was the most famous guy behind the Gunpowder Plot, a conspiracy of Catholic extremists to blow up Protestant King James and the Houses of Parliament. On November 4, 1605, poor Guy was caught red-handed in the Palace of Westminster. The treasonous plot, and Guy Fawkes's subsequent execution, gave rise to a popular rhyme:

Please to remember / The 5th November:

Gunpowder, Treason and Plot.

We know of no reason / Why Gunpowder Treason

Should ever be forgot.

Every year since 1605, on November 5, residents of towns, villages, and cities throughout England light bonfires, toss firecrackers, and parade or burn an effigy of Guy Fawkes to celebrate his failure to blow up the king and the Parliament. Guy Fawkes Night is perhaps the longest-running tradition in England, even though the religious and royalist sentiments that inspired it have long vanished.

Exploring the Battle of Hastings Abbey and Battlefield

Make sure that you visit this site in Battle, and give yourself at least two unhurried hours to take it all in. This attraction offers a fascinating journey back in time. The preservationist organization English Heritage, which owns the site, has done a clever job of making the experience both interesting and informative. You receive an **audio guide** when you pay for your ticket.

The tour starts with an outdoor video presentation, *1066 — The Battle of Hastings,* that fills you in on the major events leading up to the battle. Next comes an exhibition, "Prelude to Battle," which uses text panels to draw you deeper into the story of the intrigues and the royal power struggle between King Harold and Duke William of Normandy. Finally, you walk onto the battlefield itself. The long (complete) tour takes about an hour; a shorter version takes about 45 minutes. Take the longer tour if you have time (and the weather is good).

Linked to your audio guide, descriptive panels line the pathway around the battlefield. The battle's unfolding events are presented as seen through the eyes of three different narrators: Aelfric, a Saxon thane; Henri, a French knight; and Edith, the wife of King Harold. As you tour the battlefield, you can follow the story and tactics used by both sides from these three perspectives. The vivid, firsthand accounts of the battle are fictional, but they bring history alive for kids of all ages.

King Henry VIII dissolved the great abbey that William had constructed to mark the spot where King Harold was slain. Today, the abbey is an atmospheric ruin, but you can explore several rooms.

Entrance at south end of High Street. ☎ *01424/773-792. Admission: £5.30 ($9.80) adult, £4 ($7.40) seniors, £2.70 ($5) children 5–15, £13 ($24) families (2 adults, 2 children). Open: Daily Apr–Sept 10 a.m.–6 p.m., Oct–Mar 10 a.m.–4 p.m. (last audio tour issued one hour before closing); closed Jan 1 and Dec 24–26. Uneven terrain makes much of the battle site inaccessible to wheelchair users; however, a short gravel path does wind through part of the site.*

Brighton: Fun Beside the Seaside

On the Sussex coast, a mere 81km (50 mlles) south of London, **Brighton** is England's most famous, and probably most popular, seaside town. (See the "Brighton" map on p. 239.) Brighton was a small fishing village until the Prince Regent, a fun-loving dandy who reigned as George IV from 1820 to 1830, became enamored of the place and had the incredible Royal Pavilion built. Where royalty moves, fashion follows, and Brighton, on the English Channel, eventually became one of Europe's most fashionable towns. (The long terraces of Georgian town homes that you see everywhere in Brighton date from that period.) Later in the 19th century,

Brighton

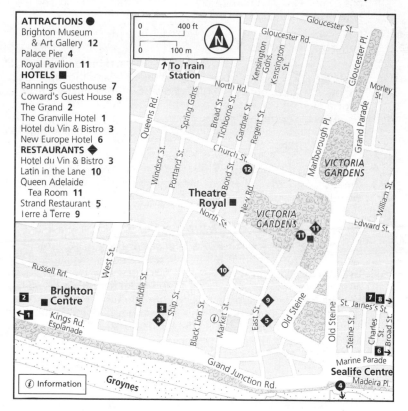

ATTRACTIONS ●
Brighton Museum
& Art Gallery **12**
Palace Pier **4**
Royal Pavilion **11**
HOTELS ■
Bannings Guesthouse **7**
Coward's Guest House **8**
The Grand **2**
The Granville Hotel **1**
Hotel du Vin & Bistro **3**
New Europe Hotel **6**
RESTAURANTS ◆
Hotel du Vin & Bistro **3**
Latin in the Lane **10**
Queen Adelaide
Tea Room **11**
Strand Restaurant **5**
Terre à Terre **9**

when doctors prescribed breathing sea air as a cure for everything from
depression to tuberculosis, the Victorians descended in hordes. (The
famous Brighton pier is from that era.) Today, Brighton is a popular
place for weekend getaways and conventions. People come to hang out
on the long stretch of beach, shop, stroll, and party the night away at
clubs and discos. Gays and lesbians are very much part of the local and
visitor scene.

Getting to Brighton

More than 40 trains a day run from London's Victoria Station to
Brighton. The trip takes about an hour; an off-peak (after 9:30 a.m.)
"cheap day return" round-trip ticket costs £17 ($31). For train schedules,
call ☎ **08457/484-950.**

National Express (☎ **0990/808-080;** www.nationalexpress.co.uk)
runs hourly buses from London's Victoria Coach Station. A same-day
round-trip ticket for the two-hour journey costs £9.80 ($18). If you drive,

the M23 from Central London leads to Brighton. The drive takes about one to one-and-a-half hours, but if the roads are clogged, the trip may take twice as long.

Finding information

Brighton's **Visitor Information Centre,** 10 Bartholomew Sq. (☎ 0906/ 11-2255; www.visitbrighton.com), sits opposite the town hall, about a ten-minute walk south from the train station. You can pick up a map and information on current events at the center. You can also reserve a hotel room here. The center is open Monday through Friday from 9 a.m. to 5 p.m., Saturday from 10 a.m. to 5 p.m., and Sundays in summer from 10 a.m. to 4 p.m.

At the Tourist Information Centre, gay and lesbian visitors can ask for the Visitors Guide to Lesbian and Gay Brighton, which lists gay-friendly guesthouses, pubs, and clubs.

Getting around Brighton

Brighton is a compact town, and the easiest way to get around is on foot. While here, forget about that frantic need for sightseeing, and relax. Brighton is all about relaxation. This is a place for leisurely strolling, either in the town or along the seaside promenades. Brighton is small enough you can't get lost and large enough to offer some good cultural diversions. **Brighton and Hove Bus Company** (☎ 01273/886-200) offers frequent and efficient service; the local fare is £1.30 ($2.40). You can usually find a taxi at the train station, or you can call **Streamline** (☎ 01273/ 747474) for a cab.

Staying in or near Brighton

Brighton is a favorite weekend getaway spot, and you can find many hotels and B&Bs. The Tourist Information Centre, 10 Bartholomew Sq. (☎ 0906/711-2255; www.tourism.brighton.co.uk), can also help you find a room.

The Grand
$$$–$$$$ **Brighton**

The grandest place to stay in Brighton is the Grand, a huge, dazzling white resort hotel built on the seafront in 1864. The Grand, the only five-star luxury hotel in Brighton, has 200 spacious and predictably gorgeous guest rooms, done mostly in blues and yellows, with big tile baths. The most expensive rooms have sea-facing balconies and floor-to-ceiling, double-glazed windows. The welcoming staff, attentive to the needs of families with children, can help arrange baby-sitting.

See map p. 239. King's Road, Brighton, East Sussex BN1 2FW. ☎ *01273/224-300. Fax: 01273/224-321.* www.grandbrighton.co.uk. *Rack rates: £170–£250 ($315–$463) double. Rates include English breakfast. Lower weekend and "leisure" rates available. AE, DC, MC, V.*

Brighton's gay and lesbian hotels and B&Bs

Several hotels and B&Bs in Brighton cater to gay and lesbian visitors. **Bannings Guesthouse,** 14 Upper Rock Gardens, Brighton, Sussex BN2 1QE (☎ **01273/681-403;** www.bannings.co.uk), is a snug Georgian townhouse for women only; the guest-house has six rooms, all with private bathrooms, which cost £50 to £56 ($93–$104) for a double, English breakfast included. **Coward's Guest House,** 12 Upper Rock Gardens, Brighton, Sussex BN2 1QE (☎ **01273/692-677**), is a dapper Regency-era townhouse that caters to men only; it has six rooms with private bathrooms, which rent for £50 to £65 ($93–$120) double, breakfast included. The **New Europe Hotel,** 31–32 Marine Parade, Brighton, Sussex BN2 1TR (☎ **01273/624-462;** Fax: 01273/624-575; www.legendsbar.co.uk), is the largest (30 rooms) gay-owned and -operated hotel in Brighton. A double room with private bathroom costs £60 to £65 ($111–$120), conti-nental breakfast included. The New Europe also houses Legends, one of the most pop-ular gay clubs in town. The hotel is closed until summer 2006 for refurbishment. For locations, see map p. 239.

The Granville Hotel
$–$$ Brighton

Located opposite the West Pier, Granville is a good choice if you're look-ing for a smaller, stylish, boutique hotel on the sea front. A former town-house, this place has 25 individually designed rooms, all with private bathrooms and some with four-poster beds. The hotel is completely non-smoking and welcomes families with children.

See map p. 239. 124 Kings Rd., Brighton, East Sussex BNT 2FA. ☎ *01273/326-302. Fax: 01273/728-294.* www.granvillehotel.co.uk. *Rack rates: £85–£145 ($157–$268) double. Rates include English or continental breakfast. MC, V.*

Hotel du Vin
$$–$$$$ Brighton

A sophisticated new addition to Brighton's hotel scene, the ultrastylish Hotel du Vin occupies a set of Mock Tudor and Gothic Revival buildings a stone's throw from the seafront. This is Brighton's most unique contem-porary hotel, with an impressive three-story lobby; a signature French bistro (reviewed in the following section); and 37 cool, uncluttered, and very comfortable bedrooms featuring marvelous beds with fine Egyptian linens, deep soaker tubs, and power showers.

See map p. 239. Ship Street, Brighton BN1 1AD. ☎ *01273/718-588. Fax: 01273/718-599.* www.hotelduvin.com. *Rack rates: £130–£230 ($241–$426) double. Rates include continental breakfast. AE, DC, MC, V.*

Dining in Brighton

Brighton is known for its restaurants. It boasts dozens of places to dine, at all levels of the culinary ladder.

Hotel du Vin Bistro
$$–$$$ MODERN FRENCH

The signature bistro of Brighton's most stylish new hotel is a sophisticated but comfortable spot with a menu that sticks to the basics and does them well. The two-course fixed-price menu is a good value and offers starters such as a salad of marinated goat's cheese and artichokes with pancetta, and main courses such as seared calf's liver or salt-cod pork belly with wilted spinach and baby carrots; a glass of wine comes with the fixed-price meal.

See map p. 239. In Hotel du Vin, Ship Street. ☎ **01273/718-588.** *Reservations recommended. Main courses: £15 ($27); fixed-price meal: £15 ($27). AE, DC, MC, V. Open: Daily noon–2:30 p.m. and 6–10 p.m.*

Latin in the Lane
$–$$ ITALIAN/SEAFOOD

At this restaurant, you can sample Italian antipasti, such as melon with Parma ham or mixed salami with fresh figs, and then go on to pastas or fish, which comes fresh from the market every day. You can't go wrong with the seafood risotto with wild mushrooms, cream, and white wine, or you may want to try the casserole of fresh, seasonal seafood and mussels in white wine, parsley, and garlic.

See map p. 239. 10–11 King's Rd. ☎ **01273/328-672.** *Reservations recommended for dinner on weekends. Main courses £7.50–£16 ($14–$30). AE, DC, MC, V. Open: Daily noon–2:15 p.m. and 6:30–11 p.m.*

Strand Restaurant
$$ MODERN BRITISH/SEAFOOD

One of the hippest (and friendliest) places for dining is the bow-fronted Strand. The ever-changing menu may include starters such as herby home-made vegetable soup, followed by chicken breast with creamy mush-rooms, smoked haddock lasagna, lamb *en croute,* or pan-fried filet steak with potatoes.

See map p. 239. 6 Little East St. ☎ **01273/747-096.** *Reservations recommended. Main courses: £13–£18 ($24–$33). AE, DC, MC, V. Open: Daily noon–10 p.m.*

Terre à Terre
$–$$ VEGETARIAN

Considered the best vegetarian restaurant in England, perhaps in Europe, Terre à Terre elevates meatless cuisine to the art it should be but rarely is. The food is impeccably fresh and beautifully presented. You can eat your

A pier of the realm collapses

Brighton has two famous piers, but only the Palace Pier is open to visitors today. The other, West Pier, was built in 1866 and reached its heyday in the 1920s, when it had a concert hall and charged admission to keep the riffraff at bay; it closed in 1975 for safety reasons. Plans to renovate West Pier, the only pier in Britain that has received the top heritage grade designation, gained urgency just before New Year's 2003, when a chunk of the ornate structure collapsed into the sea. At last report, there was still no consensus on what to do with what was once the greatest piece of marine architecture in England.

way through the menu with the Terre à Tapas, a superb selection of the best dishes, big enough for two. On the menu, you find imaginative dishes such as heirloom tomato consommé, and wild garlic and goat's cheese risotto.

See map p. 239. 71 East St. ☎ 01273/729-051. Reservations essential on weekends. Main courses: £12–£13 ($22–$24). DC, MC, V. Open: Tues–Sat noon–10:30 p.m., Sun 10 a.m.–10 p.m. (brunch 10 a.m.–1 p.m.).

Exploring Brighton

Brighton is a fun city to explore. It's compact enough that you can walk everywhere but large enough that you can discover quiet streets off the beaten tourist track. A stroll along the seaside promenade is an essential part of any trip to Brighton.

Brighton Museum & Art Gallery

Close to the Royal Pavilion on Church Street, you can find the city's small museum and art gallery, which has interesting collections of Art Nouveau and Art Deco furniture, glass, and ceramics, plus a fashion gallery. You can easily while away a spare hour here.

See map p. 239. Church Street. ☎ 01273/290-900. Admission: Free. Open: Mon–Tues and Thurs–Sat 10 a.m.–5 p.m., Sun 2–5 p.m.

Palace Pier

The town's famous amusement area (also called Brighton Pier) juts out into the sea just south of the Royal Pavilion. The pier was built in the late 19th century, when Brighton became a major holiday resort. Today, Palace Pier looks a bit tacky, but it's kept in good shape and still worth visiting. If the arcade games and rides don't interest you, you can just walk and enjoy the sea air. At night, all lit up with twinkling lights, the pier is almost cheerily irresistible.

See map p. 239. Seafront. Admission: Free. Open: 24 hours.

TIP

Tea at the pavilion

Before you leave the Royal Pavilion, consider having lunch or a cream tea in the nicely restored **Queen Adelaide Tea Room** (☎ 01723/292-736; see map p. 239), open daily 10:30 a.m. to 4:30 p.m. (to 5 p.m. in summer). Queen Adelaide, who used this suite in 1830, didn't appreciate the epicurean tastes of her husband, George IV. Dismissing his renowned French chefs, she reverted to English cuisine so dreary that Lord Dudley complained, "You now get cold pâté and hot champagne." The lunch selections range from £4 to £7 ($7.40–$13) and cream teas from £4 to £6 ($7.40–$11).

Royal Pavilion

Set in a small landscaped park, Brighton's must-see attraction is one of the most extraordinary palaces in Europe. John Nash redesigned the original farmhouse and villa on this site for George IV (when the king was still Prince Regent). The fun- and food-loving George lived here with his mistress, Lady Conyngham, until 1827. The king's brother, William IV, and their niece, Queen Victoria, also used the pavilion. Finding the accommodations too cramped and lacking a sea view, Victoria closed the Royal Pavilion, put the furnishings into storage, and moved to Osborne House on the Isle of Wight. The city of Brighton eventually got the furnishings back and opened the pavilion to the public. Give yourself about an hour for a leisurely walk-through tour.

The crazily wonderful exterior is an Indian fantasy of turrets and minarets. The interior, decorated in the Chinese style, is sumptuous and fantastically extravagant. The **Long Gallery** has a color scheme of bright blues and pinks; **Music Room** has a domed ceiling of gilded, scallop-shaped shells; and the **King's private apartments** on the upper floors epitomize the Regency lifestyle of the rich and royal.

See map p. 239. Bounded by North Street, Church Street, Olde Steine, and New Road. ☎ *01273/290-900. Admission: £6.10 ($11) adults, £4.30 ($7.95) students and seniors, £3.60 ($6.65) children under 16, £16 ($30) families (2 adults, up to 4 children). Open: Daily Oct–Mar 10 a.m.–5:15 p.m., Apr–Sept 9:30 a.m.–5:45 p.m. Closed Dec 25–26. Wheelchair users should call first to make arrangements.*

Seafront

Brighton and neighboring Hove stretch out along the English Channel. The entire seafront is a pebbly public beach used for swimming and sunning. If you're into sunbathing *au naturel,* Brighton has the only nude beach in England, about a mile west of Palace Pier. All along the seafront, you can find promenades for strolling.

Shopping in Brighton

The Lanes, Brighton's original fishing village, is now a warren of narrow streets filled with small shops selling upscale goods and many tourist trinkets. **North Laines** has more interesting shops, including some trendy outfitters. **Duke's Lane** is a good place to look for men's clothing, and **Duke Street** and **Upper North Street** are good for antiques.

Shops in Brighton are generally open Monday through Saturday from 10 a.m. to 6 p.m., with a later closing on Thursday or Friday. During the summer tourist season, some shops are open on Sunday and closed on Monday.

Stepping out in Brighton, night or day

Brighton is preeminently a resort town, a place where people go to relax and have fun. The nighttime scene is a lively one, especially from April through September.

The performing arts

The **Brighton International Festival** (☎ 01273/292-950; www.brighton-festival.org.uk), one of England's best-known arts festivals, happens in May and features a wide array of drama, literature, visual art, dance, and concert programs ranging from classical to hard rock. England's best actors regularly appear at the **Theatre Royal,** New Road (☎ 01273/328-488), which presents a full season of dramatic works.

The highly regarded **Brighton Philharmonic Orchestra** (☎ 01273/622-900) performs a season of classical concerts at **The Dome,** 29 New Rd. (adjacent to the Royal Pavilion). Built in 1803 as the stables for George IV's horses and remodeled into a concert hall in 1935, The Dome hosts concerts of all kinds. When internationally known performers come to town, they play at the 5,000-seat **Brighton Centre,** Russell Road (☎ 01273/202-881).

The pub and club scene

Brighton fills up on the weekends, especially in summer, with folks looking for a good time. You can find many choices for nighttime entertainment. Pick up a copy of the local entertainment weekly, *The Punter,* or look for *What's On,* a weekly events sheet posted around town, to find out what's happening. Pub hours are Monday through Saturday from 11 a.m. to 11 p.m. and Sunday from noon to 10:30 p.m. Dance clubs open later and sometimes remain open for 24-hour stretches on weekends. Clubs generally have a cover charge of £5 to £7 ($9.25–$13).

Clubbers usually start their evening at a bar or pub. One good place to begin is the 100-year-old **Colonnade Bar,** New Road (☎ 01273/328-728). An even older establishment — parts of it date to the 16th century — is **The Cricketers,** Black Lion Street (☎ 01273/329-472). Cuba, 160 King's Rd. (☎ 01273/770-505), is a popular beachside drinking spot. **Steamers,**

King's Road (☎ 01273/775-432), is also popular (and loud) on Friday and Saturday nights.

When you're ready to dance, you may want to try **Event II,** Kingswest on West Street (☎ 01273/732-627), which boasts state-of-the-art lighting and visual effects. At **Gloucester,** Gloucester Plaza (☎ 01273/699-068), you can find different music all through the week: from '70s and '80s retro hits to alternative and groove.

Gay and lesbian spots

Brighton's "Gay Village" centers on St. James's Street, east of the Royal Pavilion, and along the seafront. Ask at the tourist information center for a list of current gay and lesbian nightlife choices. All the gay pubs and bars are fairly close to one another. Pub hours are Monday through Saturday from 11 a.m. to 11 p.m. and Sunday from noon to 10:30 p.m. **Legends,** the smartly redecorated bar in the New Europe Hotel, 31–32 Marine Parade (☎ 01273/624-462), has a cabaret area for weekly entertainment. Summer weekends are a nonstop buzz at the big new **Amsterdam** hotel bar, 11–12 Marine Parade (☎ 01723/688-825). **The Harlequin,** 43 Providence Place (☎ 01273/620-630), a cabaret bar with weekly drag shows and karaoke, has been voted the best gay bar outside London. **Marlborough,** 4 Princes St. (☎ 01273/570-028), a traditional pub in the heart of town, is popular with lesbians. **Club Revenge,** 32 Old Steine St., opposite the Palace Pier (☎ 01273/606-064), spreads over two floors and holds about 700 people; the club has lasers, smoke machines, and views of the seafront. A sociable crowd packs the place.

Chapter 15

Kent's Best Castles, Stately Homes, and Gardens

In This Chapter

▶ Exploring Knole, one of England's largest homes
▶ Visiting Anne Boleyn's Hever Castle
▶ Charting your way to Chartwell, home of Winston Churchill
▶ Lollygagging in Leeds Castle
▶ Strolling through the great garden at Sissinghurst
▶ Viewing the White Cliffs from Dover Castle

The county of Kent is rich in castles, stately homes, and magnificent gardens. All are within about 81km (50 miles) of London, so you can visit them on day trips. Alternatively, you can incorporate Kent's most famous sights into a car tour of the Southeast. (For ideas on towns to visit, see Chapter 14.)

Kent is known as the Garden of England (see the "Kent's Castles, Stately Homes, and Gardens" map on p. 248). A mild year-round climate favors Kent, where fruit grows and hops ripen in the summer sun. Old walled orchards and conical *oast* (hops-drying) houses dot the landscape. Kent has more gardens open to the public than any other county in England. With the one exception of Dover Castle, the castles and stately homes that I describe in this chapter all have superbly landscaped grounds.

Don't worry about finding a meal. In every castle, home, and garden, you can find at least one restaurant or tea shop where you can get lunch, a snack, or tea.

The places in this chapter are all in the country. They're near small towns with rail stations but not always within easy walking distance of the station. You can, however, visit them all by train or bus, continuing by taxi when necessary. Taxis are generally available outside the train stations. If you drive yourself, make sure that you have a good map with you. I do provide directions to each sight, but as soon as you're off the motorway and main roads, Kent is full of winding lanes. The attractions all have parking onsite or in parking lots.

Kent's Castles, Stately Homes, and Gardens

Chartwell House **1**
Dover Castle **6**
Hever Castle **2**
Knole **3**
Leeds Castle **5**
Sissinghurst Castle
    Garden **4**

 The Web site www.traintaxi.co.uk provides information about taxi service from every train station in England. The site gives you the phone numbers of local taxi companies so that you can make reservations and have a cab waiting when you arrive.

Knole: A Room for Every Day of the Year

Set in a picturesque deer park, this great country homestead houses important collections of portraits, silver, tapestries, and 17th-century furniture. What make **Knole** so wonderfully unique are its size and the fact that the house has remained basically unaltered since 1603. A visit here is an ideal day trip from London; be sure to give yourself at least three hours to take it all in.

Getting to Knole

Frequent train service connects Sevenoaks Station, 2.5km (1½ miles) from the Knole, to London's Charing Cross Station. The journey takes 30 minutes and costs £7.20 ($13) for a "cheap day return" round-trip ticket. Call ☎ 08457/484-950 for train schedules. From the rail station, you can walk to the park entrance in the center of Sevenoaks or take the connecting hourly bus service. You can also find cabs at the station or call **Bluebird** (☎ 01732/45531) to reserve one in advance; one-way taxi fare to the entrance is about £4 ($7.40). By car, Knole is 8km (5 miles) north of Tonbridge, off A225.

Exploring Knole

With its skyline of gables, chimneys, battlements, and pinnacles, this enormous house resembles an entire village. Like a well-protected medieval community, Knole has a central gatehouse with an inner gate house (Bourchier's Tower). The gatehouses may conjure up visions of a traditional castle, but they are, in fact, entirely decorative.

Thomas Bourchier, Archbishop of Canterbury, purchased the land and original house at Knole in 1456. He set about transforming the fortresslike building into a home suitable for princes of the church (the Archbishop of Canterbury, as the spiritual head of the Church of England, wielded enormous wealth and power). Four more archbishops resided at Knole before Henry VIII took possession of the house (just as he took possession of Hampton Court Palace, home of Cardinal Wolsey). Henry VIII enlarged Knole until it was suitable as a royal palace, but he never spent much time there. His daughter Elizabeth I presented the house and estate to her cousin Thomas Sackville, the first Earl of Dorset, in 1566. His descendants have lived at Knole ever since. Knole was the childhood home of Vita Sackville-West, who created the gardens at Sissinghurst Castle. (See the section "Sissinghurst Castle Garden: Romance amongst the Roses," later in this chapter.)

In 1603, the first earl enlarged and embellished what would become one of England's greatest houses. Occupying some 4 acres, Knole was built with seven courtyards, representing the days of the week, 52 staircases, one for each week of the year, and 365 rooms, one for every day of the year. The 13 state rooms open to the public are magnificent representatives of the Elizabethan and Stuart eras. Rooms that you can tour include three long galleries, each with an adjoining state bedroom, and the King's Bedroom, which has a 17th-century bed decorated with gold and silver thread and topped with ostrich feathers.

In addition to its outstanding tapestries and textiles, important portraits by Van Dyck, Gainsborough, and Reynolds fill the house. Among the house's original features are the fine plasterwork ceilings, the carved wooden screen in the Hall, and the painted walls of the staircases. The elaborate marble-and-alabaster chimneypiece and mantle in the Ballroom (the former living quarters of Archbishop Bouchier) stretch from floor to ceiling and are considered one of the finest works of Renaissance sculpture in England.

Large herds of fallow and Japanese deer roam the parkland surrounding the house. The private garden is open only once a month and requires separate admission. Look for the tearoom, where you can get lunch or tea, on the premises.

See map p. 248. Tonbridge Road, Sevenoaks. ☎ 01732/462-100 or 01732/450-608 (recorded information). Admission: House £6.40 ($12) adults, £3.20 ($5.90) children 4–15, £16 ($30) families (2 adults, 2 children); garden £2 ($3.70) adults, £1 ($1.85) children 4–15; deer park free to pedestrians. Open: House mid-Mar–Oct Wed–Sun noon–4 p.m.; garden mid-Mar–Oct Wed 11 a.m.–4 p.m.; park daily; tearoom mid-Mar–Oct 2 Wed–Sun 10:30–5 p.m.

Hever Castle: Anne Boleyn Slept Here

A lovely, moated castle set amid immaculately landscaped gardens 48km (30 miles) south of London, **Hever Castle** was the childhood home of Anne Boleyn (1507–1536), the second wife of Henry VIII. Anne of Cleves, Henry's fourth wife, also lived here. In 1903, the American millionaire William Waldorf Astor bought the castle and created the beautiful gardens. Hever is a fairly easy day trip from London. Give yourself at least an hour for the house and another two hours to enjoy the gardens.

Getting to Hever Castle

From London's Victoria Station, trains depart throughout the day for two stations near Hever Castle. The trip takes an hour and costs £7.90 ($15) for a "cheap day return" round-trip ticket. You have to change trains at East Croyden. From **Hever Station,** you can take a pretty 1.6km (1-mile), 15-minute walk to the castle. Taxis aren't available at Hever station, but they are available from **Edenbridge Town Station,** located 5km (3 miles) from the castle. You probably want to book a cab in advance; without doing so, you may have to wait for an hour or more. Call **Rely On Cars** (☎ 01732/863-800) or **Edenbridge Cars** (☎ 01732/864-009); the one-way taxi fare from the train station to the castle costs about £5 ($9.25).

If you're traveling to Hever Castle on a Sunday, always check to find out whether the train stops at Edenbridge Town Station or Edenbridge Station. Due to train-scheduling changes on Sunday, you may have to get off at the **Edenbridge Station** and take a taxi to the castle; one-way fares are about £5 ($9.25). For taxi companies, see the preceding information for Edenbridge Town Station.

By car, Hever Castle is 5km (3 miles) southeast of Edenbridge, midway between Sevenoaks and East Grinstead off B2026. From London, take the M25, and exit at Junction 5 or 6.

Exploring Hever Castle

Hever Castle's long and varied history stretches back over seven centuries. To experience this rich history, you can wander through the rooms in the castle at your own pace; guides can answer your questions.

The castle's stone gatehouse and outer walls were constructed in the 13th century. In about 1500, the Boleyn (or Bullen, as it was then written) family added a more comfortable Tudor manor house within the walls. In the middle of divorcing his first wife, Catherine of Aragon, Henry VIII wooed Anne Boleyn at Hever Castle.

Henry VIII's desire for Anne Boleyn helped change the course of English history. When Catherine of Aragon didn't produce a male heir, the king turned his eye to Anne. Hoping that the 25-year-old Anne would give him the successor he wanted, Henry sought to divorce Catherine. When the pope refused Henry's request, Henry broke with the Catholic Church and established the Church of England with himself as head. He then married Anne, but she also failed to deliver a male child. (Her first child was Elizabeth I, who became one of England's greatest monarchs.) Eventually, Henry had Anne arrested on trumped-up charges of adultery and incest with her brother George. Both Boleyn siblings were executed, George first and then the unfortunate Anne, who was beheaded at the Tower of London. You may hear her called Anne of the Thousand Days because that's how long she was queen.

After Anne's demise and the death in childbirth of his third wife, Jane Seymour, the much-married monarch gave Hever Castle to his fourth wife, Anne of Cleves, who lived there after Henry divorced her. You can view costumed likenesses of Anne, Henry, and his other five wives in the **waxwork exhibition** "The Six Wives of Henry VIII," on the top floor of the castle.

William Waldorf Astor acquired Hever Castle in 1903 and spent a fortune restoring it. What you see today is a result of Astor's preservation efforts. Inside, splendid carving and paneling cover the castle walls. Antiques, some interesting works of art, including portraits of Anne Boleyn and her daughter, Elizabeth, and a Holbein painting of Henry VIII fill the rooms. You can also view two of Anne's prayer books. In 2003, two newly acquired portraits of Mary, Queen of Scots went on display.

The **gatehouse,** the last room you visit, contains a grisly collection of torture instruments, including beheading axes. Anne asked for a French axe to be used on her neck — she knew French axes did a quicker, cleaner job.

Between 1904 and 1908, Astor further enhanced the castle's parklike setting by creating the magnificent **gardens,** which include the **Italian Garden,** filled with statuary and sculpture collected in Italy and dating from Roman to Renaissance times; the **Maze;** a 35-acre lake; and the **rose garden.** The **Tudor herb garden,** close to the castle, opened in 1994.

You can find two self-service restaurants serving hot lunches, snacks, and teas on the premises.

See map p. 248. Edenbridge. ☎ 01732/865-224. Admission: Castle and garden £9.20 ($17) adults, £7.70 ($14) seniors, £5 ($9.25) children 5–15, £23 ($43) families (2 adults, 2 children). Open: Mar–Oct daily, gardens 11 a.m.–5 p.m., castle noon to 5 p.m.; Nov daily 11–4 p.m. Closed Dec–Feb.

Chartwell: The Private Life of a Famous Prime Minister

Chartwell House was the home of Sir Winston Churchill (1874–1965) from 1924 until he died. The home can't compare with the grandeur of Blenheim Palace (see Chapter 13), where Churchill was born, but if you're interested in the personal life of Britain's wartime prime minister and one of its great statesmen, **Chartwell** will fascinate you. Give yourself at least one-and-a-half hours to visit the house and gardens. If you're driving, you can easily combine a visit to Chartwell with a visit to Hever Castle or Knole (see previous sections in this chapter for information on both).

Getting to Chartwell

From London's Charing Cross Station, you can hop on frequent train service to **Sevenoaks,** 10.5km (6½ miles) east of Chartwell, and to **Oxted,** 6 miles west of Chartwell. The journey takes about 40 minutes and costs about £8.50 ($16) for a day-return (round-trip) ticket. Call ☎ 08457/484-950 for train schedules. From either station, you can take a cab to Chartwell. To reserve a taxi from Sevenoaks, call **Bluebird** (☎ 01732-45531); from Oxted, call **Terrys** (☎ 01883/712-623) or **D Line** (☎ 01883/715-576). The one-way taxi fare costs you approximately £8 ($15).

By car, Chartwell is 3km (2 miles) south of Westerham; fork left off B2026 after 2.5km (1½ miles).

Exploring Chartwell House

The National Trust administers Chartwell, a family home where the rooms and gardens remain much as Churchill left them. You can see Churchill's watercolors, pictures, maps, and personal mementos on display throughout, as are first editions of his books (Churchill won the Nobel Prize for Literature). He had endless energy and a wide range of interests: You can trace his career from his school days at Harrow to his years as a war correspondent, Chancellor of the Exchequer, parliamentarian, and prime minister. You can see some of his famous uniforms and hats on display, and you can hear tapes of his speeches. In addition to the house, you can visit the beautiful terraced gardens containing the lakes he dug; the brick wall he built with his own hands; the water garden where he fed his fish; and his garden studio, which holds many of his paintings.

See map p. 248. Westerham. ☎ 01732/866-368. Admission: House, garden, and studio £8 ($15) adults, £4 ($7.40) children 5–15, £20 ($37) families (2 adults, 2 children). Open: Mid-Mar–Oct Wed–Sun 11 a.m.–5 p.m.; also Tues July–Aug.

Leeds Castle: Castle of Queens, Queen of Castles

 Leeds Castle, tucked away in the Kent countryside (64km) 40 miles southeast of London, is one of the world's most beautiful castles. Built on two small islands, its stone facade mirrored in a lake, this treasure trove of history has enough in its rooms and gardens to beguile you for half your day. Coming here is an easy day trip by train or bus from London, or you may want to combine a visit with an overnight trip to Canterbury or Rye (both described in Chapter 14).

Getting to Leeds Castle

Trains run frequently from London's Victoria Station to **Maidstone** and **Bearsted** stations; Bearsted is closer to the castle. **Southeastern** (☎ 0845/000-2222; www.southeasterntrains.co.uk) offers an all-in-one ticket to Bearsted Station with connecting bus service to and from the castle; the trip costs £24 ($44) for adults, £13 ($24) for children. **National Express** (☎ 08705/808-080; www.nationalexpress.co.uk) runs a special bus-and-admission package from London's Victoria Coach Station every day that the castle is open. Buses leave at 9 a.m., arrive at Leeds Castle at 10:30 a.m., depart at 3 p.m , and arrive back in London by 4:50 p.m. The package costs £18 ($33) for adults, £13 ($24) for children. By car, from London's ring road, continue east along the M26 and M20; the castle is 6.5km (4 miles) east of Maidstone at the junction of A20 and the M20.

Exploring Leeds Castle

Part of Leeds' fascination lies in the stories of its various owners. The castle reflects the changing tastes and fortunes of several families and dozens of generations. The original buildings were wood, constructed in A.D. 857 during the Saxon era. After the Norman Conquest of 1066, the buildings were given to the French Crevecoeur family, who rebuilt them in stone. The castle's vineyard (still producing) is listed in the *Domesday Book,* tax records compiled in 1086. Under Edward I, in 1278, Leeds became a royal palace. During the medieval era, six queens of England lived there. Faces from many eras greet you as you walk through the castle. Look for the portrait of Catherine of Valois (it hangs near her apartments). Catherine, the widow of Henry V, eloped with Owen Tudor. Henry VIII, their great-grandson, stayed at the castle often and added the Tudor windows.

By the mid-16th century, Leeds was no longer a royal palace. A house was built on the larger island in the early 1600s. An owner in the 18th century, the 6th Lord Fairfax, owned 5 million acres of land in Virginia and was a mentor and friend to George Washington. After several more owners, Olive Lady Baillie purchased the house in 1926 and completely transformed the inside. Her collections of medieval and Renaissance tapestries, Chinese porcelain, paintings, and furniture give Leeds Castle a sumptuous quality.

The tour of Leeds Castle begins in the **Norman Cellar,** passes through the medieval **Queen's Rooms,** and into Henry VIII's richly decorated **Banqueting Hall.** The circuit then takes you into a suite of rooms decorated in the 1920s. The Gatehouse, where you enter, houses the **Dog Collar Museum,** with a collection that dates back to the 16th century.

You get your first glimpse of Leeds Castle from the **Wood Garden and Duckery,** which you pass through on the way to the entrance. In the spring, wood anemones carpet the banks of the stream; swans and wildfowl live here year-round. The **Culpeper Garden,** named for the castle's 17th-century owners, is a large cottage garden planted with lavenders, roses, lupines, and poppies that start blooming in early summer. The **Lady Baillie Garden** takes its inspiration from the Mediterranean. If you reach the center of the **Maze,** you're rewarded with entry into a mysterious underground grotto.

Visitors often overlook the **Aviary,** which opened in 1988 and houses more than 100 species of rare and endangered birds, including parrots, toucans, cockatoos, kookaburras, and cranes.

Two restaurants serve hot meals. You can also find a tearoom and snack stands throughout the grounds.

See map p. 248. Maidstone. ☎ *01622/765-400. Admission: £13 ($24) adults, £11 ($20) seniors and students, £9 ($17) children 4–15, £39 ($72) families (2 adults, 3 children). Open: Daily Apr–Oct 10 a.m.–5 p.m., Nov–Mar 10 a.m.–3 p.m.; closed Dec 25 and on two days in June and July for classical concerts.*

Sissinghurst Castle Garden: Romance amongst the Roses

The writer Vita Sackville-West and her diplomat husband, Sir Harold Nicolson, created **Sissinghurst,** one of the world's most famous gardens. Sissinghurst Castle, an Elizabethan manor house with a central red-brick tower, was in ruins when the Nicolsons bought it in 1930. Vita, who had grown up in the huge manor house at Knole (see "Knole: A Room for Every Day of the Year," earlier in this chapter), developed a garden scheme that is like a series of small, enclosed compartments, intimate in scale, romantic in atmosphere, and filled with color year-round. Her goal was to create a garden of "profusion, extravagance, and exuberance within the confines of the utmost linear severity."

Getting to Sissinghurst Castle Garden

The nearest train station, **Staplehurst,** is 9km (5½ miles) away. Direct trains run from London's Charing Cross Station; the trip takes just under an hour and costs £12 ($22) for a combined rail–bus ticket. From Staplehurst Station, take a Cranbrook bus to the village of Sissinghurst; from there, the castle gardens are an easy 2km walk (1¼-mile) on pavement and through countryside. From Staplehurst Station, you can also get a cab; a trip one-way to the gardens costs about £8 ($15); to reserve a taxi, call **MTC** (☎ **01580/890-003**) or **Weald** (☎ **01850/893-650**). For train information, call ☎ **0845/484-950.** By car, the garden is 3km (2 miles) northeast of Cranbrook and 1.6km (1 mile) east of Sissinghurst village on A262.

Exploring Sissinghurst Castle Garden

Sissinghurst features a beautiful garden with lush plantings that soften a strict formal design. The **White Garden,** with foliage and blossoms that are entirely white or silver, is probably the most celebrated of the several "rooms" that make up Sissinghurst. Every season has its highlights. In April and May, primroses carpet the **Nuttery,** and the **Spring Garden** explodes with blossoming daffodils and other bulb plants. The orchard holds an enticing **Wild Garden.** Many people come specifically to see the summer roses. Vita Sackville-West planted hundreds in every form and helped return some lost roses to cultivation. Lovely old varieties climb through trees and over walls. In June and July, a wave of fragrance ascends all over the garden from the thousands of roses blooming everywhere.

The **library** and the **tower study** where Vita worked are also open to visitors. You can have lunch or tea at the Granary Restaurant on the premises.

Note: Sissinghurst limits the number of guests in its garden at any given time. Upon your arrival, you receive a ticket that indicates your admittance time. Waiting times depend on the season and time of day. If you arrive during peak times (summer 11 a.m.–4 p.m.), you may have to wait an hour or more for admittance; the garden is least crowded in April, September, and October, and after 4 p.m. on Tuesday to Friday year-round. If you arrive after 4 p.m. on Tuesday to Friday, you can get in immediately. Wheelchairs can access only parts of the garden; baby strollers are not admitted (the paths are narrow and uneven), but free baby carriers are available.

See map p. 248. Sissinghurst, near Cranbrook. ☎ *01580/710-700 or 01580/710-701 (recorded information). Admission: £7.50 ($14) adults, £3.50 ($6.50) children, £19 ($35) families (2 adults, 2 children). Open: Mid-Mar–Oct Fri–Tues 11 a.m.–6.30 p.m.; last admission one hour before closing.*

Dover Castle: Towers and Tunnels

Dover is one of the busiest Channel ports, with thousands of visitors arriving daily on ferries and hovercraft from the Continent. Unfortunately, your first impulse upon seeing Dover may be to leave town as quickly as possible. The town is low on charm and has the transient, unfocused air of a place where people pass through but never stay. Many people want to visit Dover to see the famed white cliffs. A better reason to visit — the only reason, in my opinion — is to explore **Dover Castle.** Sitting high on a clifftop overlooking the Channel, the castle is awash with 2,000 years of history, right through World War II. Dover Castle puts on a good show, one that everyone can enjoy. You can go there as a day trip from London, or if you're arriving in Dover by ferry, you can visit the castle before heading on to other parts of the country. I don't recommend that you stay overnight in Dover.

Getting to Dover Castle

Dover is 124km (77 miles) southeast of London, on the English Channel. Frequent train service connects London's Victoria Station to **Dover Priory Station.** The trip takes about one hour and 50 minutes; a round-trip ticket costs about £30 ($56). Call ☎ **0845/484-950** for train schedules. From the train station, you can walk through the town to the castle — about a 2.5km trek (1½-mile), part of it uphill — or get a cab right outside the station (the one-way fare costs about £5/$9.25). From mid-May through mid-September, the daily **City Sightseeing** (www.citysightseeing.co.uk) bus service travels from the station to the castle entrance, stopping at other attractions, including the famed white cliffs, along the way. The sightseeing bus, which operates hourly between 10 a.m. and 4 p.m., costs £6.50 ($12) for adults, £5 ($9.25) for seniors and students, and £3 ($5.55) for children. I don't recommend traveling to Dover from London by bus as a day trip, because the trip takes anywhere from two hours and 40 minutes to three hours. By car, the castle is on the east side of Dover, signposted from the M20 and A2.

The castle covers some 70 acres and offers plenty to see. If you don't want to walk from place to place within the compound, take the free Land Train that makes a circuit of the grounds. You can get a free map when you enter.

Exploring Dover Castle

Start with the **Secret Wartime Tunnels.** The entrance to the tunnels is near the castle's general visitor entrance. You can visit these tunnels only with a **guided tour** (allow 40 minutes), and you may have to wait on busy days, but it's well worth it. The tour takes you into the labyrinth of underground tunnels that were used during World War II as a hospital and general war office. Wartime sound and light effects accompany your visit. The rooms have been preserved as they were during the war; you see the Underground Command Center, the hospital with its operating room, and the living quarters.

The other sites within the castle compound are set up as separate attractions (all included in your ticket price). In the **Keep Yard,** you find an introductory film that you can use to help plan what you want to see. You can view a 2,000-year-old **lighthouse tower** (called "the Roman pharos") dating from the Roman occupation of Britain and a much-restored Saxon church beside it. The **1216 Siege Experience,** an audio tour of an exhibit that includes sound and light effects, tells the story of the unsuccessful French siege of the castle. You can look out over the channel on the **Battlement Walk** and explore the **Medieval Tunnels.** Kids particularly enjoy the Secret Wartime Tunnels and the 1216 Siege Experience because of the special effects.

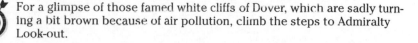

For a glimpse of those famed white cliffs of Dover, which are sadly turning a bit brown because of air pollution, climb the steps to Admiralty Look-out.

If all this clambering around makes you hungry, head to the restaurant in the Keep Yard, where you can get hot food and snacks.

See map p. 248. Dover. ☎ *01304/201-628. Admission: £8.95 ($17) adults, £6.70 ($12) seniors, £4.50 ($8.35) children 5–15, £22 ($41) families (2 adults, 2 children). Open: Daily Apr–Sept 10 a.m.–6 p.m., Oct 10 a.m.–5 p.m., Nov Mar 10 a.m.–4 p.m.; closed Jan 1 and Dec 24–26.*

Part V
The West Country

"I think I'll have the Cocoa Puffs shepherd's pie."

In this part . . .

The West Country is a bold, mysterious place. Rugged moors stretch like a spine down the center of a narrowing peninsula that begins in Hampshire and ends in Cornwall at the rocky headland called Land's End. Giant prehistoric landmarks — Stonehenge being the most famous — dot the landscape. Centuries of wind and rain have worn down the ancient Celtic crosses that stand like lonely sentinels in village churchyards. The sea beats incessantly along the peninsula's north and south coasts. The West Country also happens to have England's mildest climate, with spring coming earlier and autumn lingering later than in the rest of the country. All this helps to explain why the West Country is one of the most appealing regions in England to visit.

In Chapter 16, I introduce you to the best places in Hampshire and Wiltshire. Bucolic Hampshire was part of the ancient Saxon kingdom of Wessex. Winchester, the kingdom's most beautiful city, is a two-hour train ride from London. The landscape starts to change in Wiltshire, where Stonehenge, that great silent challenge to modern sensibilities, stands on the flat expanse of Salisbury Plain.

I devote Chapter 17 to Devon, home to the cathedral city of Exeter and enormous Dartmoor National Park, one of the most unspoiled natural landscapes in England.

In Chapter 18, I take you to Cornwall. Penzance on the south coast and St. Ives on the north make good bases for exploring Land's End and other special places in this westernmost county in the West Country.

Chapter 16

Hampshire and Wiltshire: Old Wessex and New Sarum

. . . .

In This Chapter

▶ Wending your way through Winchester
▶ Sauntering through Salisbury
▶ Visiting Stonehenge

. . . .

*T*he Hampshire countryside has a bit of everything: marshland and heath, traditional farms and quiet villages with thatched-roof cottages, ancient woodlands, rolling hills, narrow lanes, and *chalk downs* (high, open, grassy land over a chalk–limestone underlayment). Hampshire is basically an agricultural county known for special crops, such as watercress, strawberries, and hops, with large-scale farming appearing on the scene more recently. Along its south coast is the naval town of Portsmouth, with the Isle of Wight lying across the channel known as The Solent.

Wiltshire, adjoining Hampshire to the west, is a fertile county character-ized by undulating chalk downs and stretches of woodland. Over the centuries, farmers and herders have used much of the county for sheep grazing. The flat and mostly treeless expanse of Salisbury Plain, an area well known to prehistoric inhabitants of England, dominates the cen-tral part of Wiltshire. The Ridgeway, the oldest known path in England, crosses the plain, and ancient peoples erected mysterious stone-circle monuments like Stonehenge here. Salisbury is a good place to headquar-ter if you want to explore the Wiltshire countryside. Wilton House, one of England's finest stately homes, is close by, as are the magnificent gar-dens at Stourhead, one of the oldest and most famous landscape gar-dens in England.

For an overview, see the "Hampshire and Wiltshire" map on p. 262.

Hampshire and Wiltshire

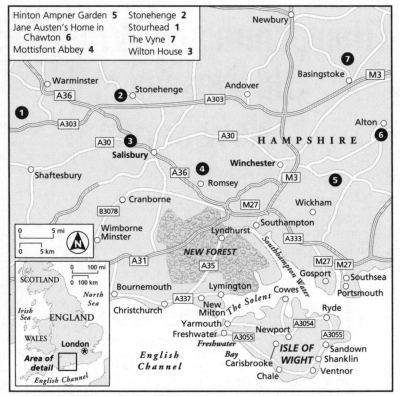

Hinton Ampner Garden **5**	Stonehenge **2**
Jane Austen's Home in	Stourhead **1**
Chawton **6**	The Vyne **7**
Mottisfont Abbey **4**	Wilton House **3**

Welcome to Wessex

Hampshire, along with Wiltshire and several other counties in southern England, was part of the ancient kingdom of Wessex formed by Saxons in the fifth century, following the withdrawal of Roman troops from England. Winchester, the Hampshire town of most interest to visitors, was the capital of this ancient kingdom. The countryside around Winchester is home to some famous manor houses and gardens.

Winchester: King Alfred Meets Jane Austen

King Alfred and Jane Austen didn't really meet, of course, because they lived almost a thousand years apart. But Alfred (849–899), the great Saxon king of Wessex, and Jane Austen (1775–1817), the brilliant novelist, are the most prominent personalities associated with Winchester, the capital of the ancient kingdom of Wessex. Elusive, legendary King Arthur has a spot of honor, too — King Arthur's Round Table has been on display here for more than 600 years. Another famous visitor was William the Conqueror, who came to Winchester to claim his crown after the Battle of Hastings (see Chapter 14). William founded the present cathedral, and in Winchester, he ordered the compiling of his inventory of England, the *Domesday Book*. But long before Arthur, Alfred, William, or Jane, the Romans lived here — Winchester's High Street was their east–west route through the city.

I recommend that you visit **Winchester** as a day trip from London (see the "Winchester" map on p. 264). Reaching Winchester and exploring the city are easy. One of the best-kept and prettiest small cities in England, it evokes its ancient heritage with pride. The cathedral alone is worth a trip. With a walk, lunch, and afternoon tea, you can spend a very pleasant day indeed in the old capital of Wessex.

Getting to Winchester

Frequent, direct train service (☎ 08457/484-950) goes from London's Waterloo Station to Winchester. The trip takes about one hour; a "cheap day return" round-trip ticket costs £21 ($39). The center of town is about a ½-mile from the station. To get there, you can easily walk (ten minutes), hop on a white park-and-ride bus (15p/30¢), or take a taxi (about $3.50/ $6.50) from the rank outside the station. **National Express** (☎ 0990/ 808-080;** www.nationalexpress.com) runs several buses a day from London's Victoria Coach Station; the fastest trip takes two hours (the longest, more than four hours); a round-trip ticket costs £13 ($24). The bus lets you off on Broadway, in the center of town. If you're driving from London, take the M3 to Junction 9. You can't drive in the town center; you can find parking lots on the roads coming into the city.

Finding information and taking a tour of Winchester

The ultrahelpful **Tourist Information Centre,** in the Guildhall on Broadway (☎ 01962/840-500; www.visitwinchester.co.uk), has loads of local info and a free, **self-guided walking tour** booklet. You can also buy tickets for guided walking tours that make a one-and-a-half-hour circuit around this fascinating city. Tours leave almost every day at 11 a.m. or 2:30 p.m., with additional walks during the summer. The tour costs £3 ($5.55) for adults, free for kids. The center is open April through September Monday through Saturday from 9:30 a.m. to 5:30 p.m. and Sunday from 11 a.m. to 4 p.m.; and October through March Monday through Saturday from 10 a.m. to 5 p.m.

Winchester

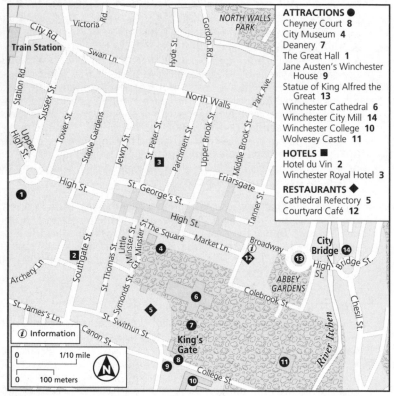

ATTRACTIONS ●
Cheyney Court **8**
City Museum **4**
Deanery **7**
The Great Hall **1**
Jane Austen's Winchester House **9**
Statue of King Alfred the Great **13**
Winchester Cathedral **6**
Winchester City Mill **14**
Winchester College **10**
Wolvesey Castle **11**

HOTELS ■
Hotel du Vin **2**
Winchester Royal Hotel **3**

RESTAURANTS ◆
Cathedral Refectory **5**
Courtyard Café **12**

Staying in Winchester

The Tourist Information Centre has a hotel-booking service. If you want to spend the night, I recommend the following hotels:

✔ **Hotel du Vin,** Southgate Street, Winchester, Hants SO23 9EF (☎ **01962/841-414;** Fax: 01962/842-458; www.hotelduvin.com): A stylish townhouse hotel with a good bistro. A double with breakfast costs £115 to £185 ($213–$342).

✔ **Winchester Royal Hotel,** St. Peter Street, Winchester, Hants SO23 8BS (☎ **01962/840-840;** www.winchester-hotels.co.uk): Comfortable, full of character, and close to the cathedral. Doubles with breakfast cost £116 ($215).

Finding lunch or a spot of tea

The **Courtyard Cafe** (☎ **01962/622-177**), in the Winchester Guildhall right behind the Tourist Information Centre, is a great, informal spot for a morning cappuccino; homemade soups, salads, and sandwiches at lunchtime; or an afternoon tea. Lunch costs about £6 to £8 ($11–$15). The cafe is also a gallery; prints and photographs line its walls. The cafe is open daily from 9:30 a.m. to 5 p.m.

The **Cathedral Refectory,** Inner Close (☎ **01962/853-224**), is behind a medieval wall next to the cathedral. This spot specializes in desserts and meals made from fresh local ingredients. Lunch costs about £6 to £10 ($11–$19). Hours are Monday through Saturday from 9:30 a.m. to 5 p.m. and Sunday from 10 a.m. to 5 p.m.

Exploring Winchester and the surrounding area

The main attraction in Winchester is the ancient cathedral. After viewing the cathedral, stroll through the town, using the walking tour I describe in the section "Strolling through Winchester: A walking tour," later in this chapter. Jane Austen fans can visit her former homes in Winchester and in the nearby village of Chawton, but you need at least two additional hours to visit Chawton if you rely on public transportation.

Visiting the top attraction: Winchester Cathedral

Nine-hundred-year-old Winchester Cathedral occupies the heart of the city and is the repository of many historic treasures. In all, 12 English kings lie here, indicative of Winchester's long reign as capital of Wessex and England after the Norman Conquest. The cathedral you see today was begun in 1079, after the Conquest, and has the longest *nave* (the long central hall of a church) in Europe. **Jane Austen's grave** is a simple stone floor marker in the north aisle. A few feet farther along is a **12th-century font** made of Tournai marble carved with stories of St. Nicholas (patron saint of pawnbrokers long before he became known as Old Saint Nick). Above and on either side of the **Great Screen,** an elaborate carving completed in 1476, you see **mortuary chests** containing the remains of Saxon kings and bishops. The beautiful **choir stalls** were carved in about 1308. Check out the **Winchester Bible,** an extraordinary illuminated manuscript, in the library. For a leisurely stroll through the cathedral, give yourself about 30 minutes.

The world-famous **Winchester Cathedral Choir** sings at all main services, including Evensong (a service in which part of the liturgy is sung), held Monday though Saturday at 5:30 p.m. and Sunday at 3:30 p.m. Visitors are welcome to attend.

See map p. 264. Winchester (in the town center). ☎ *01962/857-200. Admission: Free; £4 ($7.40) suggested donation. Open: Daily 8:30 a.m.–6 p.m. Tours: Free one-hour tours Mon–Sat hourly 11 a.m.–3 p.m.*

Strolling through Winchester: A walking tour

Winchester is a walking city par excellence, with all sorts of fascinating corners in which you can poke around. The walking tour in this section takes about two hours, longer if you linger. For all the sights this tour describes, see the "Winchester" map on p. 264.

1. **Winchester Cathedral and Precincts:** Begin your tour at Winchester Cathedral, described in the preceding section. Outside, adjacent to the cathedral, is the **Deanery,** formed from 13th-century buildings that had belonged to the Priory of St. Swithin (which stood here before Henry VIII dissolved all the monasteries in 1539). **Cheyney Court,** the picturesque half-timbered porter's lodge beside the ancient priory gate (King's Gate) was formerly the Bishop of Winchester's courthouse. The Deanery and Cheyney Court buildings aren't open to the public.

2. **Jane Austen's Winchester house:** Walk through King's Gate, and turn left onto College Street. Almost immediately, you come to a private house with a plaque on it. This is where Austen died on July 18, 1817, aged 42. Austen scholars believe she died of Addison's disease, a malfunctioning of the adrenal glands. The ailing writer came to Winchester from the nearby village of Chawton so she could be close to her doctor. She is buried in Winchester Cathedral. Farther down Queen Street, you see the buildings of **Winchester College,** the oldest public school in England, founded in 1382. Neither the Austen house nor the college allows public access.

3. **Winchester City Mill and Statue of King Alfred the Great:** Follow College Street to the end, and turn left. Then take the short, lovely walk along the narrow River Itchen, which served as part of the Roman defense system. To your left, you can see the remains of **Wolvesey Castle,** a 12th-century bishop's palace destroyed during the Civil War of 1642 to 1649. At the end of Bridge Street, you come to the City Bridge, an 1813 reconstruction of a Saxon span built 1,000 years earlier. The **Winchester City Mill** (☎ **01962/870-057**) is located on the opposite side of the bridge. You can stop in to have a look at the mill's restored machinery; an exhibition on the history and surroundings; and a pretty island garden that's home to kingfishers, otters, and water voles. The mill is open July through Christmas daily from 11 a.m. to 5 p.m.; in March, on Saturday and Sunday only; and from April to the end of June, Wednesday through Sunday. Admission costs £3 ($5.55).

   Turn left on Bridge Street, and you see the famous bronze **statue of King Alfred the Great** holding aloft his sword. What, you ask, made Alfred so great? Probably that he was an enlightened man in the Dark Ages and drove off the marauding Danes. A soldier, statesman, and scholar, he made Winchester the capital of his southern England kingdom, called Wessex. Winchester remained as powerful and prosperous as London even after the Norman Conquest of 1066.

4. **City Museum:** Walk down Broadway to The Square, and you find the small, attractive **City Museum** (☎ **01962/863-064**), with a room devoted to Roman Winchester and a fine Roman mosaic centerpiece. You can see everything in about 15 minutes. Admission is

free. Hours are April to October Monday through Saturday from 10 a.m. to 5 p.m., Sunday from noon to 5 p.m.; and November to March Tuesday to Sunday from noon to 4 p.m.

5. **King Arthur's Round Table** and **The Great Hall:** Continue down High Street, and turn left (south) through the Westgate, a fortified medieval gateway. All that remains of once-mighty Winchester Castle is the **Great Hall** (☎ **01962/846-476**) on Castle Avenue. The stone hall is famous for displaying something that isn't what legend claims it is: the Round Table of King Arthur and his knights. Looking like a giant Wheel of Fortune, the painted wooden table has hung here for some 600 years. King Arthur, if he ever existed, was probably a Romano-British chieftain of the fifth century. (Do the math.) Admission is free. The hall is open daily from 10 a.m. to 5 p.m. (until 4 p.m. on winter weekends).

Taking a side trip to Chawton

Jane Austen's house in Chawton is about 27km (17 miles) northeast of Winchester. **Stagecoach Hampshire Bus** (☎ **01256/464-501**) no. X64 runs from Winchester Bus Station to Chawton at ten minutes past each hour Monday through Saturday; on Sunday and holidays, bus no. 64 leaves at 20 minutes past the hour starting at 10:20 a.m. and every two hours thereafter. The trip takes about 30 minutes. Ask the driver to drop you at the Alton Butts stop, the one closest to the Austen house. From the bus stop, walk toward the railway bridge, cross the busy road, and continue, passing a brown tourist sign and following the road beneath an underpass. The walk from the bus stop to the house takes about 15 minutes. For more information, inquire at the Tourist Information Centre in Winchester. If you drive from Winchester, take A31 northeast; you can see a signposted turnoff to the house from the roundabout junction with A32.

Jane Austen's House in Chawton

Jane Austen's novels have been in print since they were first published nearly 200 years ago. Television and movie adaptations in the last few decades have made her work even more popular. The witty, eagle-eyed novelist did more than sleep in this sturdy red-brick Georgian house, where she lived with her mother and sister Cassandra from 1809 until 1817. Here, on a small round table in the parlor, she dipped her quill and revised her earlier novels, *Pride and Prejudice* and *Sense and Sensibility,* and wrote *Mansfield Park* and *Emma.* Creatively, this was where she spent the most productive years of her life. When she wasn't writing, she made patchwork quilts (you can see one on display in her bedroom) and jaunted around in her donkey carriage (on view in the old bakehouse). Austen family memorabilia spreads throughout the house, which has a charm and modesty evidently not unlike the great author herself. Allow a half-hour.

Chawton (northeast of Winchester). ☎ *01420/83262. Admission: £4.50 ($8.35) adults, £3.50 ($6.50) seniors and students. Open: Mar–Nov daily 11 a.m.–4 p.m.; Dec–Feb Sat–Sun 11 a.m.–4 p.m. Wheelchair access is very limited in the house.*

Touring more of the region's historic sights

The National Trust maintains several interesting properties in Hampshire. Among the best are

- ✔ **Hinton Ampner Garden,** Bramdean, Alresford (☎ **01962/771-305**): Features a 20th-century shrub garden with scented plants, over-flowing borders, and spring-flowering bulbs and fruit trees. To get there from Winchester, drive east on A272.

- ✔ **Mottisfont Abbey,** Mottisfont, Romsey (☎ **01794/340-757**): A delightful estate on the River Test with ruins of a 12th-century monastery and walled gardens containing the National Collection of Old-Fashioned Roses. The abbey is a few miles west of Winchester.

- ✔ **The Vyne,** Sherborne St. John, Basingstoke (☎ **01256/883-858**): A 16th-century manor with a Tudor chapel and lovely gardens. The manor is north of the village of Basingstoke, northeast of Winchester, off A339.

Salisbury: High-Spire Act

The tall, slender spire of Salisbury Cathedral rises from the plains of Wiltshire like a finger pointing toward heaven. **Salisbury,** or New Sarum as it was once called, lies in the valley of the River Avon, 145km (90 miles) southwest of London and about 48km (30 miles) west of Winchester (see the "Salisbury" map on p. 269). Filled with Tudor inns and tearooms, and dominated by its beautiful cathedral, this old market town is often over-looked by visitors eager to see Stonehenge, about 14.5km (9 miles) away.

Getting to Salisbury

Hourly trains travel from London's Waterloo Station to Salisbury (pro-nounced *Sauls*-bury); the journey takes one hour and 20 minutes and costs £24 ($44) for a "cheap day return" round-trip ticket. For informa-tion and schedules, call ☎ **08457/484-950. National Express (☎ 0990/ 808-080;** www.nationalexpress.com) has direct bus service from London's Victoria Coach Station; the bus terminal in Salisbury is about a ten-minute walk east of the train station. If you drive from London, head west on the M3 to the end of the run, continuing the rest of the way on A30.

Finding information on Salisbury

Salisbury's **Tourist Information Centre,** Fish Row (☎ **01722/334-956;** www.visitsalisbury.com), is open Monday through Saturday from 9:30 a.m. to 5:30 p.m. (also May–Sept Sun 10:30 a.m.–4:30 p.m.) To reach the center, take Fisherton Street on your far left as you leave the train station, cross the River Avon, and continue to follow the street; the street changes names several times and eventually becomes Fish Row.

Salisbury

ATTRACTIONS ●
Salisbury Cathedral **6**

HOTELS ■
Pembroke Arms Hotel **1**
Macdonald White
    Hart Hotel **5**
Red Lion Hotel **4**

RESTAURANTS ◆
Harper's Restaurant **3**
One Minster Street **2**

Staying in or near Salisbury

Salisbury's accommodations represent an appealing mix of historic architecture and modern comforts.

Macdonald White Hart Hotel
$–$$ Salisbury

A Salisbury landmark since Georgian times, the White Hart offers accommodations in the older section of the building or in a new motel-like section in the rear. The 68-room hotel was completely refurbished in 1995 and has a good restaurant. The rooms are nicely furnished, although some of the bathrooms are small. Some rooms are large enough for families, and the staff can help arrange baby-sitting.

See map p. 269. 1 St. John St., Salisbury, Wiltshire SP1 2SD. ☎ *01724/327-476.* www.macdonaldhotels.co.uk. *Rack rates: £84–£120 ($155–$222) double. Rates include English breakfast. AE, MC, V.*

Pembroke Arms Hotel
$$ Wilton

This elegant little eight-room hotel in Wilton, northwest of Salisbury off the A36, sits in a large garden opposite Wilton House, one of Wiltshire's most famous stately homes, and not far from Stonehenge. The en-suite double rooms are fairly spacious and traditionally furnished. The hotel is known for its restaurant. You can book a room only online, however; the Pembroke Arms doesn't maintain a reservations number.

See map p. 269. Minster Street, Wilton, Salisbury, Wiltshire SP2 0BH. www.pembrokearmshotel.activehotels.com. *Rack rates: £100–£120 ($185–$222) double. Rates include English breakfast. MC, V.*

Red Lion Hotel
$ Salisbury

Atmosphere fills every nook and cranny of this 750-year-old inn, from which the Salisbury–London stagecoach used to depart every night at 10. The cozy lounge is a popular spot for tea, and in good weather the vine-covered courtyard is a pleasant place for drinks. Although now part of the Best Western chain, the hotel has maintained its own venerable identity. Each guest room is uniquely furnished, some with fireplaces and four-poster beds.

See map p. 269. Milford Street., Salisbury, Wiltshire SP1 2AN. ☎ 01722/323-334. Fax: 01722/325756. www.the-redlion.co.uk. *£88–£109 ($163–$202) double. Rate includes English breakfast. AE, DC, MC, V.*

Dining in Salisbury

Salisbury has many good restaurants serving a range of cuisines.

Harper's Restaurant
$ MODERN BRITISH

For homemade, uncomplicated, wholesome food in the center of Salisbury (overlooking the marketplace), go to Harper's. You can order from two menus, one featuring cost-conscious bistro-style platters and the other a longer slate of all-vegetarian pasta dishes.

See map p. 269. 6–7 Ox Row, Market Place. ☎ 01722/333-118. Reservations recommended. Main courses: £8.50–£13 ($16–$24); fixed-price lunch £7.50 ($14), fixed-price dinner £8.90 ($16). AE, MC, V. Open: Mon–Sat noon–2 p.m. and 6:30–9:30 p.m., Sun June–Sept 6–9 p.m.

One Minster Street
$$$ TRADITIONAL ENGLISH

This creaky-timbered, wonderfully atmospheric 1320 chophouse and pub used to be called the Haunch of Venison and served old-fashioned English roasts and grills until 2003. The trendy new menu at the third-floor restaurant isn't always successful but does feature some good dishes, such as cassoulet with wild mushrooms and shank of pork with foie gras. Do check out the ancient pub rooms (still called the Haunch of Venison), even if you don't dine here.

See map p. 269. 1 Minster St. ☎ 01722/322-024. Main courses: £7.50–£15 ($14–$28); fixed-price menu £9.90 ($18) (served noon–1 p.m. and 6–7 p.m.). AE, MC, V. Open: Food served daily noon–2:30 p.m. and 6–9:30 p.m.; pub open Mon–Sat 11 a.m.–11 p.m., Sun noon–10:30 p.m.

Exploring Salisbury and the surrounding area

In many ways, Salisbury is a quintessential English country town, bustling during the day and quiet at night. Make a stroll around the quiet confines of the *cathedral close* (the enclosed precinct surrounding a cathedral) part of your exploration. Within the old cathedral gates, you can find several streets with 18th- and 19th century houses; it's the largest cathedral close in England. If you follow the Town Path through the water meadows west of the cathedral, you can see views of Salisbury Cathedral that have changed little since the days of John Constable (1776–1837), who painted the scene many times.

Salisbury Cathedral
Salisbury

Despite an ill-conceived renovation in the 18th century, this 13th-century structure remains the best example in England of Perpendicular Gothic, an architectural style in which vertical lines predominate (see Chapter 2 for more on English architectural styles). At 404 feet, the cathedral's spire is the tallest in the country. The cathedral's beautiful 13th-century octagonal **chapter house** possesses one of the four surviving original texts of the *Magna Carta.* The **cloisters** and an exceptionally large **close,** comprising about 75 historic buildings, add to the serene beauty of the cathedral. Allow about an hour.

See map p. 269. The Close, Salisbury. ☎ 01722/555-120. Admission: Free; suggested donation £4 ($7.40) adults, £3.50 ($6.50) children, £8.50 ($16) families. Open: Daily June–Aug Mon–Sat 7:15 a.m.–7:15 p.m., Sept–May 7:15 a.m.–6:15 p.m.

Stourhead
Stourton

Stourhead is a world-famous 18th-century landscape garden. The Palladian-style villa (see Chapter 2 for a discussion of English architectural styles), with its early Chippendale furniture and art treasures, was built in 1722 for a merchant banker, Henry Hoare. The gardens, laid out in 1741, represent a dramatic change in English garden design. Until the early 18th century, English gardens generally followed the formal, geometrical French style. At Stourhead, the landscape was fashioned to look more natural and more picturesque, with small temples, monuments, rare trees, flowering shrubs, and plants set around a beautiful lake. With its tranquil walks and long vistas, Stourhead is pleasant to visit any time of year, but the grounds explode into blossom in May and June.

See map p. 262. Stourton (from Salisbury, take A36 northwest to A303 west to Mere [about 40km/25 miles total]; Stourton is 5km/3 miles northwest of Mere off B3092). ☎ 01747/841-152. Admission: House and garden £9.90 ($18) adults, £4.80 ($8.90) children 5–15, £24 ($44) families (2 adults, 2 children). Open: Garden daily 9 a.m.–7 p.m.; house Apr–Nov Fri–Tues 11 a.m.–5 p.m.

Wilton House
Wilton

Wilton is one of England's great country estates. The home of the earls of Pembroke, the house is noted for its 17th-century state rooms designed by the celebrated architect Inigo Jones and for the historic events that took place here. Shakespeare's troupe may have entertained in Wilton House. Several centuries later, General Dwight Eisenhower and his advisers made preparations here for the D-Day landings at Normandy. Beautifully maintained furnishings and paintings by Van Dyck, Rubens, Brueghel, and Reynolds fill the house. You can visit the reconstructed **Tudor kitchen** and **Victorian laundry,** and see the **Wareham Bears,** a collection of some 200 miniature dressed teddy bears. The 21-acre grounds include **rose and water gardens, riverside and woodland walks,** and a huge adventure **playground** for children.

If you're without wheels, take the bus that stops on New Canal, a ten-minute walk north of Salisbury train station, to Wilton House; check with the tourist office for schedules (see "Finding information on Salisbury," earlier in this chapter).

See map p. 262. Wilton (5km/3 miles west of Salisbury on A30; follow signs). ☎ 01722/ 746-729. Admission: £9.25 ($17) adults, £8 ($15) seniors and students, £5.50 ($10) children 5–15, £24 ($44) families (2 adults, 2 children). Open: Apr 11–Oct 26 daily 10:30 a.m.–5:30 p.m.

Stonehenge: Visiting the Standing Stones

About 14.5km (9 miles) north of Salisbury, you can see one of the world's most renowned prehistoric sites and one of England's most popular attractions, the giant stone circle of Stonehenge. Recognizing its importance, UNESCO designated Stonehenge a World Heritage Site.

The crowds can reach epidemic proportions as the day wears on, so I recommend that you come here as early as possible.

Getting to Stonehenge

Wilts and Dorset buses (☎ 01722/336-855; www.wdbus.co.uk) depart from Salisbury bus station for Stonehenge about every two hours beginning at 10:25 a.m. and depart from Stonehenge for Salisbury about every two hours, with the last return to Salisbury at 3:45 p.m. Monday to Saturday and 6:55 p.m. on Sunday, when there is hourly service. The trip takes 40 minutes, and the fare is about £6.50 ($12) return. From mid-May through September, the bus company also offers a City Sightseeing Stonehenge Tour, an excellent and easy way to explore the region's fascinating history. The tour departs from the Salisbury train station daily at 9:55 and 11:55 a.m. and 1:55 p.m. Visitors ride a double-decker bus to Old Sarum and on to Stonehenge, where a guide explains the site. The cost is £15 ($28) for adults, £12 ($22) for seniors, and £8 ($15) for children ages 5 to 15; admission to Stonehenge is included in the price.

If you drive from London, head west on the M3 to the end of the run, continuing the rest of the way on A30 to Salisbury. From there, take A338 north to A303 and then head east to the turnoff on A360.

Exploring Stonehenge

Believed to be 3,500 to 5,000 years old, Stonehenge is a stone circle of megalithic pillars and lintels built on the flat Salisbury Plain. Many folks are disappointed when they actually see the site, which isn't as huge as modern-day megasensibilities expect. (A path surrounds the site and keeps visitors 50 feet from the stones.) Keep in mind, however, what a remarkable achievement, in terms of design and engineering skills, Stonehenge represents. Many of the stones, which weigh several tons, were mined and moved from distant sites in a time before forklifts, trucks, and dynamite. Such a feat indicates a high level of skill, dedication, and manpower.

Who built it, and what does it all mean? Researchers have discredited the old belief that the Druids built Stonehenge (the site is probably older than the Celtic Druids). Because Stonehenge is aligned to the summer equinox and can predict eclipses, a popular theory maintains that the site was an astronomical observatory. Whatever its purpose, Stonehenge was an important shrine or ceremonial gathering place of some kind. But in an age that thinks it knows everything, Stonehenge still keeps its tantalizing mysteries to itself.

See map p. 262. 14.5km (9 miles) north of Salisbury. ☎ 01980/624-715. Admission: £5.50 ($10) adults, £4.10 ($7.60) students and seniors, £2.80 ($5.20) children 5–15; admission includes audio guide. Open: Daily Mar 16–May and Sept–Oct 15 9:30 a.m.–6 p.m., June–Aug 9 a.m.–7 p.m., and Oct 16–Mar 15 9:30 a.m.–4 p.m.

Chapter 17

Devon: Moors, Tors, and Sandy Shores

. . . .

In This Chapter

▶ Examining Exeter
▶ Exploring Dartmoor National Park
▶ Touring Torquay and the English Riviera
▶ Seeing Plymouth, the Pilgrims' port

. . . .

*T*raveling westward from London through Wiltshire, you enter Devon, a scenically diverse county with a windy, unspoiled north coast, a popular south coast, and a giant national park in between. (See the "Devon" map on p. 275.) If you're looking for outdoor adventures in England, Devon is a good place to visit. You can go walking or pony trekking across Dartmoor National Park, with its high, open moorland and giant granite rock formations known as *tors*. You can go swimming along the south coast, with its clean, sandy beaches. Or you can relax in laid-back Torquay, taking leisurely boat rides or drives in an area known as the English Riviera. Devon's cities and villages are loaded with history. Exeter's magnificent cathedral dates from the 12th century, and Plymouth was where the Pilgrims set sail for the New World in 1620.

You can easily get to Exeter, Torquay, and Plymouth by train from London. Devon's good public transportation system lets you explore without a car by using local buses, small rail lines, and boats. If you want to see more of the countryside, consider renting a car in Exeter.

Devon, like neighboring Cornwall (see Chapter 18), has long been associated with the cream tea, which is available in the afternoon at just about every restaurant and teashop throughout the county. Devonshire clotted cream, a version of what the French call crème fraîche, appears "silvery," as opposed to Cornish cream's "golden" hue. A cream tea should be served with a scone (made without baking soda) and strawberry preserves.

Devon

Exeter: Sea Captains and Silversmiths

Exeter, one of England's oldest cities, began as the most westerly outpost of the Roman Empire (see the "Exeter" map on p. 276). Saxon King Alfred the Great refounded Exeter in the ninth century. By the 11th century, the time of the Norman Conquest, Exeter was one of England's largest towns. The English wool trade, which made villages in the Cotswolds (see Chapter 20) so prosperous during the Tudor era, also sustained Exeter until the 18th century. During World War II, the Germans bombed the center of the city. Much of Exeter's medieval core was gutted, but luckily, the city's greatest treasure, its magnificent Norman cathedral, wasn't destroyed. As

Exeter

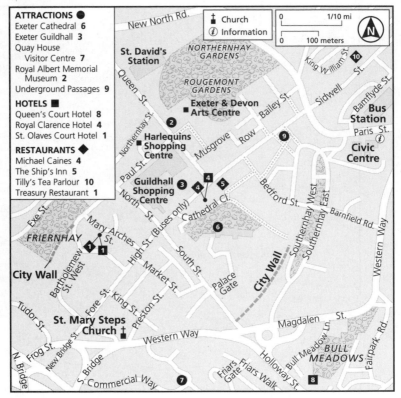

ATTRACTIONS ●
Exeter Cathedral **6**
Exeter Guildhall **3**
Quay House
  Visitor Centre **7**
Royal Albert Memorial
  Museum **2**
Underground Passages **9**

HOTELS ■
Queen's Court Hotel **8**
Royal Clarence Hotel **4**
St. Olaves Court Hotel **1**

RESTAURANTS ◆
Michael Caines **4**
The Ship's Inn **5**
Tilly's Tea Parlour **10**
Treasury Restaurant **1**

a result of the bombing and subsequent rebuilding, Exeter (like Plymouth) has a somewhat piecemeal look. The most picturesque part of town is the area around the cathedral; you also find a newly redeveloped area along the River Exe that's good for strolling and shopping. You may want to stay overnight in Exeter or just stay long enough to see the cathedral and other sights. From the cathedral, you can easily hop in a car and explore Dartmoor National Park, just a few miles to the west.

Getting to Exeter

Trains from London's Paddington Station depart hourly for the two-and-a-half-hour journey to Exeter's **St. David's** Station (a "supersaver return," advance-purchase round-trip fare costs £47/$87); local trains connect St. David's to **Exeter Central,** closer to the town center. For train schedules, call ☎ **08457/484-950. National Express** (☎ **0990/808-080;** www.nationalexpress.com) buses depart from London's Victoria Coach Station every two hours during the day; the trip takes four hours. Frequent bus service is also available for the one-hour trip between

Exeter's arts festival

The two-week Exeter Festival, held from late June to mid-July, features candlelit classical music concerts in the cathedral, plus jazz, rock, theater, and opera performances throughout the city. For information, call the **Exeter Festival Office** (☎ **01392/265-198**).

Exeter and Plymouth. (See the section "Plymouth: Where the Pilgrims Set Sail," later in this chapter.) By car from London, take the M4 west, cutting south to Exeter on the M5 (junction near Bristol).

Finding information and taking a tour

The **Tourist Information Centre**, in the Civic Centre, Paris Street (☎ **01392/265-700**; www.exeter.gov.uk), is open Monday to Saturday from 9 a.m. to 5 p.m. and June through October also on Sunday from 10 a.m. to 4 p.m. You can book a hotel room at this center.

Free 90-minute guided tours leave daily throughout the year from opposite the Royal Clarence Hotel in the Cathedral Close, the area immediately adjacent to Exeter Cathedral. From April through October, tours depart at 10:30 and 11 a.m. and at 2, 2:30, and 7 p.m. From November to March, tours leave at 10:30 a.m. and 2 p.m.

Staying in Exeter

Exeter has a full range of hotels and B&Bs.

Queen's Court Hotel
$

You'd be hard pressed to find a better hotel in this price range. Queen's Court sits on a quiet, leafy square just a few minutes' stroll from High Street and the cathedral. The hotel has 18 freshly redecorated rooms, all with bath and shower. The staff is attentive, and the restaurant serves tasty The Olive Tree food. For an English breakfast, add £8 ($15) to your room price.

See map p. 276. 6–8 Bystock Terrace, Exeter, Devon EX4 4HY. ☎ *01392/272-709. Fax: 01392/491-390.* www.queenscourt-hotel.co.uk. *Rack rates: £85–£95 ($157–$176) double. AE, MC, V.*

Royal Clarence Hotel
$$

This Georgian-era hotel opposite the cathedral has just been given a complete makeover and is now one of the most stylish and innovative boutique hotels in the region. The 56 rooms have been redecorated in a strikingly modern style; the rooms in front look out onto the cathedral.

Some units are big enough for families, and the hotel can help arrange baby-sitting. Michael Caines, the hotel restaurant, is one of Exeter's top dining spots (see "Dining in Exeter," later in this chapter).

See map p. 276. Cathedral Yard, Exeter, Devon EX1 1HD. ☎ *01392/319-955. Fax: 01392/ 439-423.* www.abodehotels.co.uk/exeter. *Rack rates: £110–£140 ($204–$259) double. AE, DC, MC, V.*

St. Olaves Court Hotel
$$

Set in its own walled garden close to the cathedral, this intimate hotel was created from a townhouse built in 1827. An original spiral staircase runs to many of its 15 guest rooms. Furnished with antiques, the rooms have period charm and decent-size bathrooms with new showers. The standards are high throughout. You can dine on excellent gourmet cuisine in the hotel's Treasury Restaurant.

See map p. 276. Mary Arches Street (off High Street), Exeter, Devon EX4 3AZ. ☎ *800/ 544-9993 in the U.S. or 01392/217-736. Fax: 01392/413-054.* www.olaves.co.uk. *Rack rates: £115–125 ($213–$231) double. Rates include continental breakfast. AE, DC, MC, V.*

Dining in Exeter

From Modern British cuisine to simple pub fare, Exeter has a restaurant to suit every taste. Here are some that I like.

Michael Caines
$$–$$$ MODERN BRITISH

This classy, smoke-free hotel restaurant is one of Exeter's dining hot spots. Many of the dishes are made with local, organically grown products. The menu changes all the time, but you may find lentil and foie gras soup or seafood risotto as a starter, with main courses featuring fresh fish, lamb, venison, or chicken with interesting accompaniments. The restaurant has a special children's menu, and kids under 5 eat free. **Michael Caines Cafe,** adjacent to the restaurant, is less fancy in cuisine and decor, but also a great place to dine. Michael Caines also presides over the famous kitchen at Gidleigh Park (see "Staying in Dartmoor National Park," later in this chapter).

See map p. 276. In the Royal Clarence Hotel, Cathedral Yard. ☎ *01392/310-031. Reservations recommended. Main courses: Restaurant £17–£25 ($31–$46), fixed-price lunch £18–£22 ($33–$41); cafe £8–£17 ($15–$31). AE, DC, MC, V. Open: Daily noon–2:30 p.m. and 7–10 p.m.*

The Ship's Inn
$ TRADITIONAL ENGLISH/PUB

For an atmospheric, inexpensive pub lunch, try this restaurant. The Ship's Inn is the oldest pub in Exeter; Francis Drake and Sir Walter Raleigh frequented the place more than 400 years ago. The menu has plenty of simple offerings, like soups and sandwiches, but you can also get home-made steak, kidney or chicken and mushroom pie, and good fish and chips.

See map p. 276. St. Martin's Lane. ☎ 01392/272-040. Main courses: £6.25–£7.95 ($12–$15). MC, V. Open: Meals served Sun–Mon noon–3 p.m., Tues–Thurs noon–9 p.m., Fri noon–6 p.m., Sat 11 a.m.–6 p.m.; pub open Mon–Sat 11 a.m.–11 p.m., Sun noon–10:30 p.m.

Tilly's Tea Parlour
$ TEAS/LIGHT FARE

Pop into Tilly's if you want an old-fashioned cream tea with rich Devonshire cream and home-baked scones. You can also get breakfast and lunch; daily specials are posted. Kids enjoy the relaxed atmosphere and the dessert selection.

See map p. 276. 40 Sidwell St. ☎ 01392/213-633. Main courses: £2.50–£5.50 ($4.65–$10). No credit cards. Open: Daily 9 a.m.–5:30 p.m.

Treasury Restaurant
$$–$$$ CONTINENTAL

Locals and visitors alike love the restaurant in this Georgian town-house hotel because of its reliably high standards of cooking. For starters, you may find pan-fried scallops, with rack of lamb, filet steak, fresh fish, or roasted duck breast to follow. The desserts are wonderful.

See map p. 276. In the St. Olaves Court Hotel, Mary Arches Street. ☎ 01392/217-736. Reservations recommended. Main courses: £15–£25 ($28–$46); fixed-price menus £26–£29 ($48–$54). AE, DC, MC, V. Open: Daily 8 a.m.–9:30 p.m.

Exploring Exeter
You can see the noteworthy sights in Exeter in a couple of hours and on foot.

Exeter Cathedral

The cathedral's twin towers are of Norman origin, built in the 12th century. The west front has remarkable rows of sculptured saints and kings, the largest surviving array of 14th-century sculpture in England. The original Norman interior was remodeled in the 13th century, in a soaring Decorated Gothic style. The remarkable fan-vaulted roof is the longest of its kind in the world. The cathedral's astronomical clock is reputedly the source of the "Hickory Dickory Dock" nursery rhyme. Allow 30 minutes.

See map p. 276. 1 The Cloisters. ☎ 01392/255-573. Admission: Free; suggested dona-tion £3.50 ($6.50). Open: Daily 9:30 a.m.–5 p.m. Guided Tours: Mar–Oct Mon–Sat 11 a.m. and 2:30 p.m., Sun 4 p.m.

Exeter Guildhall

One of England's oldest municipal buildings, the Guildhall was referred to in surviving documents as far back as 1160. Its colonnaded front was a Tudor addition of 1593. Inside, you can find a display of silver; the city has long been known for its silverwork.

See map p. 276. High Street. ☎ *01392/265-500. Admission: Free. Open: Mon–Fri 10:30 a.m.–1 p.m. and 2–4pm.*

Quay House Visitor Centre

Start your walk along Exeter's revamped Quayside area. Just south of the town center, you come across a small port to which seagoing ships have access by means of an 9km-long (5½-mile) canal dug in the 16th century. The Visitor Centre provides an **audiovisual program** that fills you in on key events in Exeter's 2,000-year history.

See map p. 276. Quayside. ☎ *01392/265-213. Admission: Free. Open: Daily Easter–Oct 10 a.m.–5 p.m., Oct 11–Easter Sat–Sun 11 a.m.–4 p.m.*

Royal Albert Memorial Museum

The city's large Victorian-era museum has collections of paintings, local glassware, clocks and watches, silver, and Roman artifacts. The Royal Albert also administers St. Nicholas Priory (off Fore Street), the guest wing of a 700-year-old Benedictine Priory that later became an Elizabethan merchant's home.

See map p. 276. Paul Street. ☎ *01392/665-858. Admission: Free. Open: Mon–Sat 10 a.m.–5 p.m.*

Underground Passages

This labyrinth of vaulted underground tunnels was dug beneath High Street during the medieval era to bring fresh water to the city. An **introductory video and a tour** tell you the tunnels' history. Kids love the tour, which explores the ancient tunnels. Note: The Underground Passages have closed for redevelopment and won't reopen until 2007.

See map p. 276. Boots Corner, off High Street. ☎ *01392/265-887. Admission: £3.75 ($6.95) adults, £2.75 ($5.10) children 5–15. Open: Easter–Sept Mon–Sat 10 a.m.–5 p.m.; Oct–Easter Tues–Fri 2–5 p.m., Sat 10 a.m.–5 p.m. Wheelchair users have very limited access.*

Shopping for Exeter silver

Exeter is known for its silver, identifiable by the three-castle mark stamped onto the article. At **Burford,** 1 Bedford St. (☎ **01392/254-901**), you can find spoons that date from the 18th century and earlier. Ten dealers share space in **The Quay Gallery Antiques Emporium,** on the Quay off Western Way (☎ **01392/213-283**), selling furniture, porcelain, metalware, and collectibles.

Dartmoor National Park: Back to Nature

A protected national park since 1951, **Dartmoor** is one of England's unique natural landscapes (see the "Dartmoor National Park" map on p. 282). Dartmoor National Park's eastern boundary is only 21km (13 miles) west of Exeter. Dartmoor encompasses some 953 sq. km (368 square miles) of high, open moorland covered with yellow-flowering *gorse* (a spiny, yellow-flowered shrub), purple heather, and windswept granite outcroppings called *tors*. Moorland rivers and their many small waterfalls rush down green, wooded valleys. The last unspoiled landscape in England, Dartmoor is home to wild ponies and many other kinds of wildlife. More than 800km (500 miles) of public footpaths and bridle paths crisscross this remarkably atmospheric landscape. Although a national park, the land in Dartmoor is privately owned, and about 33,000 people live and work in the area.

Scattered throughout Dartmoor are grand country hotels, cozy village inns, and countryside B&Bs. The ancient village of **Chagford,** about 32km (20 miles) west of Exeter, makes a good base for touring. Open moors with high granite tors surround the town, which overlooks the River Teign in its deep valley. In addition to enjoying the splendid countryside, you can visit Dartmoor's two historic houses: **Buckland Abbey,** near Plymouth, was the home of Sir Francis Drake; and **Castle Drogo,** just a mile from Chagford, was the last castle built in England.

Getting to the park

You can take the train to Exeter (see the section "Getting to Exeter," earlier in this chapter) and then use local buses to connect you with villages in Dartmoor. **Transmoor Link** (☎ 01392/382-800) operates buses throughout the summer. If you're driving, Exeter is the nearest large city to the park. From Exeter, continue west on B3212 to Chagford or other Dartmoor villages.

You may want to take the train to Exeter and then rent a car. The following car-rental companies have offices in Exeter:

- ✔ **Avis,** 29 Marsh Green Rd. (☎ 01392/259-713)
- ✔ **Budget,** Unit 2 Grace Rd. Central (☎ 01392/496-555)
- ✔ **Hertz,** 12 Marsh Barton Rd. (☎ 01392/207-207)

The car-rental agencies cluster in the Marsh Barton industrial area, a couple of miles south of Exeter's town center. To get there, you can call a local taxi at ☎ 01392/433-433.

Finding information

Dartmoor National Park's main information hub is **High Moorland Visitor Centre,** Tavistock Road, Princetown, Yelverton, Devon PL20 6QF (☎ 01822/890-414). The center is open daily from 10 a.m. to 5 p.m. in

Dartmoor National Park

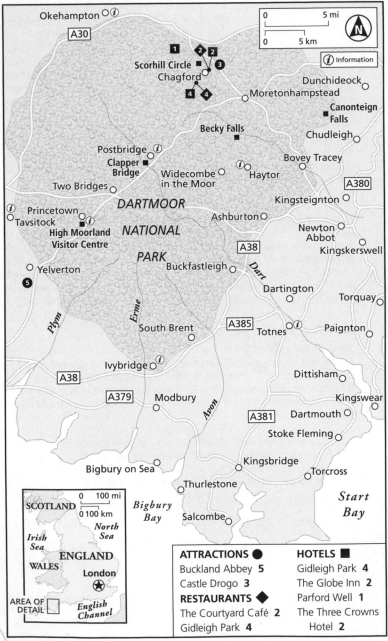

Okehampton

A30

Scorhill Circle

Chagford

Dunchideock

Moretonhampstead

Canonteign Falls

Chudleigh

Becky Falls

Postbridge

Clapper Bridge

Bovey Tracey

Widecombe in the Moor

Haytor

Two Bridges

A380

DARTMOOR

Kingsteignton

Princetown

Tavsitock

Ashburton

Newton Abbot

High Moorland Visitor Centre

NATIONAL

Kingskerswell

PARK

A38

Buckfastleigh

Yelverton

Dartington

Torquay

Dart

South Brent

A385

Totnes

Paignton

Ivybridge

Dittisham

A38

A379

Modbury

Kingswear

A381

Dartmouth

Stoke Fleming

Bigbury on Sea

Kingsbridge

Torcross

Thurlestone

Start Bay

Bigbury Bay

Salcombe

0   5 mi
0   5 km

ⓘ Information

Plym

Erme

Avon

SCOTLAND

North Sea

Irish Sea

ENGLAND

WALES

London

AREA OF DETAIL

English Channel

0   100 mi
0 100 km

ATTRACTIONS ●
Buckland Abbey **5**
Castle Drogo **3**
RESTAURANTS ◆
The Courtyard Café **2**
Gidleigh Park **4**

HOTELS ■
Gidleigh Park **4**
The Globe Inn **2**
Parford Well **1**
The Three Crowns
Hotel **2**

summer and from 10 a.m. to 4 p.m. in winter. Smaller park information centers with limited opening times are in **Haytor** (☎ 01364/661-520), **Newbridge** (☎ 01364/631-303), and **Postbridge** (☎ 01822/880-272). Tourist Information Centres for Dartmoor are in **Ivybridge** ☎ 01752/897-035), **Okehampton** (☎ 01837/53020), **Tavistock** (☎ 01822-612-938), and **Totnes** (☎ 01803/863-168). You can also find information on the Web site of the Dartmoor National Park Authority: www.dartmoor-npa.gov.uk.

Taking a tour of the park

Year-round, the Dartmoor National Park Authority offers **guided walks** — a great way to introduce yourself to Dartmoor's special landscape. Walks range from easy one-and-a-half-hour village strolls to six-hour treks covering 14.5 to 19km (9–12 miles) of moorland. For details, contact the High Moorland Visitor Centre (see the preceding section). The walks cost £2 to £4 ($3.70–$7.40), depending on their length. You don't need to make a reservation; just show up at the departure point. Going to the park's Web site at www.dartmoor-npa.gov.uk is the fastest way to get information about the walks.

Staying in Dartmoor National Park

Dartmoor is a special world, with unspoiled countryside that's still wild in parts. Several old villages lie within the area Dartmoor National Park covers. Chagford has one of the most convenient locations and offers more amenities than other villages.

Gidleigh Park
$$$$$ Near Chagford

Staying at this marvelous country-house hotel is an unforgettable experience. Located 3km (2 miles) outside of Chagford, Gidleigh Park was built in 1929 on 45 acres of beautifully landscaped gardens with a river running through the property. The hotel has impeccably high standards, but it isn't fussy or formal. The 15 enormous guest rooms have fine marble baths and a wonderfully old-fashioned English ambience. The hotel is famous throughout the West Country for its cuisine (see "Dining in Dartmoor National Park," later in this chapter), and the room rate includes a sumptuous four-course dinner. If you're looking for a dream splurge, this hotel is it.

See map p. 282. Gidleigh Road, Chagford, Devon TQ13 8HH. ☎ *01647/432-367. Fax: 01647/432-574.* www.gidleigh.com. *Rack rates: £440–£600 ($814–$1,110) double. Rates include English breakfast, morning tea, and dinner. MC, V.*

The Globe Inn
$ Chagford

A 16th-century stone-built inn that served stagecoaches, The Globe Inn sits in the center of charming Chagford. Downstairs, you find two bars and a restaurant serving traditional English dishes and daily specials. Upstairs are nicely furnished guest rooms with private bathrooms. The inn can pack a picnic lunch for you on request.

See map p. 282. High Street, Chagford, Devon TQ13 8AJ. ☎ *01647/433-485. Rack rates: £50–£60 ($93–$111) double. Rates include English breakfast. V.*

Parford Well
$ Near Chagford

This professionally run B&B is wonderfully attuned to guests' needs (including privacy). Tim Daniel, the owner, worked as a hotelier in London before starting this country retreat. The modern house, set within a walled garden, holds three guest rooms decorated with an understated English elegance. The rooms are quiet, comfortable, and very cozy.

See map p. 282. Sandy Park, Devon TQ13 8JW. ☎ *01647/433-353.* www.parford well.co.uk. *Rack rates: £56–£75 ($104–$139) double. Rates include English breakfast. No credit cards.*

The Three Crowns Hotel
$ Chagford

The Three Crowns Hotel is in a 13th-century granite building that was formerly the home of the Wyddons, an important local family. Over the years, the home was renovated into a comfortable hotel with rooms that have modern amenities and private bathrooms. With its mullioned windows, massive oak beams, and open fireplace, the downstairs lounge is a good spot for a drink. The hotel restaurant serves traditional English cuisine; main courses cost £10 to £13 ($19–$24). Kids usually enjoy the hotel's atmosphere and village setting.

See map p. 282. High Street, Chagford, Devon TQ13 8AJ. ☎ *01647/433-444. Fax: 01647/433-117.* www.chagford-accom.co.uk. *Rack rates: £75 ($139) double. Rates include English breakfast. MC, V.*

Dining in Dartmoor National Park

The restaurant at Gidleigh Park is one of the culinary highlights of England, but you also can find simple pubs and country cafes in the Dartmoor villages.

The Courtyard Cafe
$ Chagford   VEGETARIAN

Part of a local store dedicated to all things organic and sustainable, this cafe makes a good spot for a vegetarian lunch. Consider the menu's home-made soup, vegetarian pizzas and quiches, and fresh salads. Don't pass up local Devonshire ice cream, one of the specialties.

See map p. 282. 76 The Square. ☎ *01647/432-571. Main courses: £4–£7 ($7.40–$13). No credit cards. Open: Mon–Sat lunch noon–3 p.m.; tea or snacks 9 a.m.–5:30 p.m.*

Gidleigh Park

$$$$ Near Chagford   ENGLISH/INTERNATIONAL

Even if you're not staying at Gidleigh Park, you may want to consider eating there. The restaurant has been acknowledged with a raft of awards and honors, including two Michelin stars. The seven-course tasting menu changes weekly, but it may include such delicacies as crab ravioli with ginger and lemongrass, roast wild local salmon, roast duckling with honey and spices, roast saddle of venison, or fresh fish. You can choose from various fixed-price menus at lunch and dinner; nothing will disappoint you. Chef Michael Caines opened another restaurant in the Royal Clarence Hotel in Exeter (see "Staying in Exeter," earlier in this chapter).

See map p. 282. Gidleigh Road. ☎ **01647/432-367.** *Fax: 01647/432-574.* www. gidleigh.com. *Reservations essential. Fixed-price dinner £75–£80 ($139–$148); fixed-price lunch £27–£41 ($50–$76). Open: Daily 12:30–2 p.m. and 7–9 p.m.*

Exploring in and around Dartmoor National Park

Dartmoor is home to some of England's wildest and windiest expanses, where wild ponies still graze, giant tors rise among fields of bracken, and streams rush through forested valleys. People have lived in Dartmoor for centuries, and small villages make up a part of its timeless landscape.

Buckland Abbey
Yelverton

Tucked away in its own secluded valley above the River Tavy, 5km (3 miles) west of Yelverton, Buckland was originally a small but influential Cistercian monastery. Parts of the abbey date from around 1278, but the main parts of the house were built in the 16th century when Sir Richard Grenville remodeled the dissolved abbey into a noble residence. The tower over the church's crossing and many other original features of Buckland Abbey are still visible.

The great Elizabethan navigator Sir Francis Drake bought Buckland in 1581, shortly after circumnavigating the world. The house, today a National Trust property, displays memorabilia of Drake and Grenville. Behind the house lies a monastic tithe barn, where the monks stored the food that the farmers were required to give them. On the estate grounds, you can find an herb garden and take some delightful walks. Give yourself at least an hour to see everything.

See map p. 282. 5km (3 miles) west of Yelverton off A386. ☎ **01822/853-607.** *Admission: £6 (11) adults, £3 ($5.55) children 5–15, £15 ($28) families (2 adults, 2 children). Open: Mid-Mar–Oct Fri–Wed 10:30 a.m.–5:30 p.m., Nov–mid-Mar Sat–Sun 2–5 p.m. Wheelchair users can access most of the house and grounds; call in advance to make arrangements.*

Castle Drogo
Drewsteignton

The architect Sir Edwin Lutyens designed this granite castle, which was built for a self-made millionaire, Julius Drewe, between 1910 and 1930. Perched on a rocky cliff above the Teign River, the castle commands panoramic views of Fingle Gorge and Dartmoor. Drewe wanted his dream house — the last castle built in England — to combine the grandeur of a medieval castle with the comforts of the 20th century. Designed for easy, elegant living, the interior includes a kitchen, a scullery, and elaborately appointed bathrooms. Go outside to see the terraced formal garden with roses and herbaceous borders, as well as woodlands with flowers in spring. You can see the house and gardens in about an hour.

See map p. 282. 6.5km (4 miles) northeast of Chagford, or 9.5km (6 miles) south of Exeter-Okehampton Rd. (A30). ☎ *01647/433-306. Admission: Castle and grounds, £6.50 ($12) adults, £3.20 ($5.90) children, £16 ($30) families (2 adults, 2 children). Open: Castle, mid-Mar–Oct Wed–Mon 11 a.m.–5.30 p.m.; garden daily 10.30 a.m.–5:30 p.m. Visitors in wheelchairs can access most of the castle and grounds; call in advance to make arrangements.*

Dartmoor National Park

You can find more remains of prehistoric huts, enclosures, burial monuments, stone rows, and stone circles in Dartmoor National Park than anywhere else in Europe. You need a detailed ordnance survey map to find these ancient sites (you can buy maps at the visitor centers; see the section, "Finding Information," earlier in this chapter). **Scorhill Circle,** 6.5km (4 miles) west of Chagford, is a prehistoric stone circle. Near **Postbridge,** a village about 23km (14 miles) south of Chagford, you can see a legacy of Dartmoor's medieval past in the form of a *clapper bridge,* a giant slab of flat rock spanning the East Dart River.

Dartmoor is popular walking country, but don't attempt any long-distance hikes without taking sensible precautions. Always have an ordnance survey map of the area with you, and be prepared for sudden changes in the weather.

If you're not a walker, you can explore Dartmoor by car. Two main roads cross the open moorland. B3212 enters and crosses the eastern side of the high moor through the best area of heather moorland, which you can see at its peak bloom in late August. B3357 cuts through the center, sometimes running alongside the West Dart River and passing the tors. From the villages, smaller lanes lead off into the moorland.

Torquay: Relaxing on the English Riviera

Torquay (pronounced Tor-*key*), 37km (23 miles) southeast of Exeter, lies on sheltered Tor Bay, an inlet of the English Channel, in an area known as the English Riviera. The area isn't like the French Riviera except that it has mild temperatures, many sunny days, and easy access to the sea.

Victorian health-seekers made the town a popular spot. The pre–jet set crowd that brought Torquay a touch of British glamour from the 1950s to the 1970s has long since departed on cheap flights to more exotic locales.

Torquay is now essentially a resort town for honeymooners, retirees, and families. Visitors come to Torquay to hang out and take it easy. Torquay and the neighboring towns of **Brixham** and **Paignton** form **Torbay,** a cluster of resorts around **Tor Bay.** You can find several safe, sandy beaches, parks, seaside promenades, and gardens along Torbay, which is a center for yachting and watersports. At night, concerts, productions from London's West End, vaudeville shows, and ballroom dancing keep the vacationers entertained. I don't suggest that you go out of your way to visit Torquay, but it does make for a good overnight if you're touring the West Country (see the "Devon" map on p. 275).

Getting to Torquay

Trains run throughout the day from London's Paddington and Waterloo stations to Torquay, whose station is in the town center on the seafront. The trip takes three to four hours and costs £42 ($78) for a round-trip ticket. You can also take direct service from Exeter's St. David's Station; the trip takes only 40 to 50 minutes. For train schedules and fares, call ☎ 08457/484-950. **National Express** (☎ 0990/808-080; www.national express.com) buses leave from London's Victoria Coach Station every couple of hours during the day. The trip takes five to six hours and costs £34 ($63) round-trip. From Exeter, the bus journey takes less than an hour and costs £6.60 ($12) round-trip. If you're driving from Exeter, take A38 south, and continue on A380.

Getting around and touring Torquay

If you don't have a car, you can make local excursions by boat. From May through October, the **Brixham Ferry** provides daily service between Torquay and Brixham for £4.50 ($8.35) round-trip. **Neptune Cruises** (☎ 01803/295-280) runs a daily 11 a.m. excursion cruise from Torquay up the Dart River to Dartmouth, returning at 4:45 p.m.; the trip costs £9 ($17). You can buy tickets at the kiosk on the quay or at the Stagecoach Travel office, Vaughn Parade. For more information, contact the Tourist Information Centre (see the following section).

Finding information

The **Tourist Information Centre,** Vaughan Parade (☎ 01803/297-428), is open Monday through Saturday from 9 a.m. to 5 p.m. It has plenty of information on local attractions and a hotel-finding service.

Staying and dining in Torquay

If you're going to stay in Torquay, I recommend that you find a seafront hotel with a good restaurant and rooms with views over Tor Bay. Try the following, which all have good restaurants, evening entertainment, and recreational facilities, and offer special short-break rates for two or more nights:

✔ **The Imperial Hotel,** 1 Park Hill Road, Torquay, Devon TQ1 2DG (☎ **01803/294-301;** Fax 01803/298-293; imperialtorquay@ paramount-hotels.co.uk); This hotel overlooks Tor Bay and is the dowager empress of Torquay luxury resort hotels. Doubles start at £170 ($315), with English breakfast.

✔ **Livermead Cliff Hotel,** Sea Front, Torquay, Devon TQ2 6RQ (☎ **01803/299-666;** Fax: 01803/294-496; www.livermeadcliff. co.uk): This hotel sits right on the water's edge with steps down to a beach. Doubles with sea views go for £116 to £140 ($215–$259), with English breakfast.

✔ **The Livermead House,** Sea Front, Torquay, Devon TQ2 8QJ (☎ **01803/294-361;** Fax: 01803/200-758; www.livermeadhouse. co.uk): With its heated swimming pool and sun patio, Livermead House is another good choice on the seafront. Doubles with sea views go for £130 to £156 ($241–$289), with English breakfast.

✔ **Osborne Hotel,** Hesketh Crescent, Meadfoot, Torquay, Devon TQ1 2LL (☎ **01803/213-311;** Fax: 01803/296-788; www.osborne-torquay. co.uk): Part of a beautiful Regency building, this hotel has sea-facing doubles, with English breakfast, from £114 to £164 ($211–$303).

Exploring Torquay

Torquay's only nonaquatic tourist attraction of note is **Torre Abbey,** The Kings Drive (☎ **01803/293-593**), about a ¼-mile east of the town center. A prosperous abbey founded in 1196, Torre was later converted to a luxurious private residence and now serves as Torquay's municipal museum. It has painting galleries, furnished period rooms, ancient cellars, and gardens. The **Agatha Christie Memorial Room** displays the personal possessions, paintings, books, and original manuscripts of the famous mystery writer, who was born in Torquay. Admission costs £3 ($5.55) for adults, £2.50 ($4.65) for students and seniors, and £1.50 ($2.80) for children 8 to 15. The abbey is open from Easter to November daily 9:30 a.m. to 6 p.m.

The English Riviera coastline stretches some 35km (22 miles), from Torquay to the family resort town of Paignton and the harbor and fishing town of Brixham. In 1874, Isaac Singer, founder of the sewing-machine empire, built the **Oldway Mansion** (☎ **01803/201-201**), which is on Torquay Road in Paignton, a short drive south of Torquay. His son Paris enhanced the mansion's decor and had a rehearsal space and performance hall built for his mistress, the dancer Isadora Duncan. The house is open Monday to Saturday from 9 a.m. to 5 p.m., and Sunday from 2 to 5 p.m. from June through September. Admission costs £1 ($1.85).

Plymouth: Where the Pilgrims Set Sail

Many Americans want to visit **Plymouth** because the Pilgrims set sail from this port on the Mayflower in 1620. They landed 66 days later in Massachusetts. Don't go to Plymouth expecting to find a quaint Elizabethan city. During World War II, German bombs gutted the ancient town, and the way the town has been rebuilt isn't what you would call picturesque. I don't recommend staying in Plymouth, but you may want to stop off here as part of your exploration of the West Country (see the "Devon" map on p. 275). I suggest that you give yourself a couple of hours here; have a cream tea; and head out to someplace more scenic, perhaps Dartmoor or neighboring Cornwall.

Getting to Plymouth

Frequent direct trains leave from London's Paddington Station for the three-and-a-half- to four-hour journey to Plymouth. You also can get direct service from Exeter's St. David's Station (one hour) and from Torquay (one hour) to Plymouth. For train fares and schedules, call ☎ 08457/484-950. The Plymouth Train Station is on North Road, north of the town center. Western National Bus no. 83/84 runs from the station into the heart of town. **National Express** (☎ 0990/808-080; www.nationalexpress.com) runs buses from London's Victoria Coach Station; the trip takes five to nine hours. Buses also run directly to Plymouth from Exeter and from Torquay. Driving from Exeter, head southwest (skirting around Dartmoor National Park) on A38. From Torquay, head west on A385, and continue southwest on A38.

The **Plymouth Discoverer** (☎ 01752/222-221) bus runs year-round in Plymouth, making a circuit from the railway station to the Barbican, the seafront, and back.

Taking a cruise in Plymouth

If you're feeling seaworthy, you may want to take a **boat tour** of Plymouth Sound. **Plymouth Boat Cruises** (☎ 01752/822-797) offers a one-hour **Grand Circular cruise** that passes the Mayflower Steps, commercial docks, and nuclear-submarine base, and continues to the Tamar River. Boats depart from April through September daily every 30 minutes from 10:45 a.m. through the afternoon; the fare costs £5 ($9.25) for adults, £4.50 ($8.35) for seniors, £2.50 ($4.65) for children 5 to 15, and £11 ($20) for families (2 adults, 3 children). It also has **four-hour cruises** up the Tamar River and **two-hour sea cruises.** Cruise boats depart from Phoenix Wharf, a short walk south from the Barbican. You can purchase tickets from the Tourist Information Centre, the National Marine Aquarium, or the kiosk at Phoenix Wharf.

Finding information

You can find the **Tourist Information Centre** at Island House, the Barbican (☎ 0870/225-4950; www.visitplymouth.co.uk). A second information center, **Plymouth Discovery Centre,** is at Crabtree Marsh Mills. Both are open from Easter through September, Monday through Saturday 9 a.m. to 5 p.m. and Sunday 10 a.m. to 4 p.m.; winter hours are Monday through Friday 9 a.m. to 5 p.m. and Saturday from 10 a.m. to 4 p.m.

Locating a spot for lunch or tea

You may want to stop in at the **Tudor Rose Tea Rooms,** 36 New St. (☎ 01752/255-502), a convenient and inexpensive little tearoom and lunch spot dating from 1640 that has an outdoor garden; it's close to the Mayflower Steps but away from the crowds on the quay. Tudor Rose serves traditional home-cooked English food and afternoon cream teas. A sandwich or a cream tea costs about £4 ($7.40). Hours are Tuesday through Saturday from 10 a.m. to 5:30 p.m. The Tudor Rose doesn't accept credit cards.

Exploring Plymouth

Plymouth was badly bombed in World War II, and the area around Plymouth Harbor is the only part of town where you'll probably want to spend any time.

The Barbican

This small segment of the Elizabethan town of Plymouth, reconstructed around the harbor, is Plymouth's primary tourist area. Today's mall-like atmosphere makes it difficult to imagine Plymouth as it was in Elizabethan days, when it was one of England's greatest ports. Sir Francis Drake, whose house, Buckland Abbey, you can see near Dartmoor (see "Exploring in and around Dartmoor National Park," earlier in this chapter), became Plymouth's mayor after he made his famous round-the-world voyage on the *Golden Hinde.* Drake left Plymouth in 1577 from a quay in the Barbican area and was gone for three years.

On Plymouth Harbor.

Black Friars Distillery

The former Black Friars priory was turned into a gin distillery in 1793 and has been in continuous operation ever since. In 2005, a new Visitor Centre opened with a cafe, but you have to pay a pretty steep price to tour this facility, and you don't really get what you pay for. The distillery makes the only English gin with an *appelation contrôlée,* which means the Plymouth Gin brand can be made only here. The distillery still makes the gin with water from Dartmoor, in the original copper stills.

60 Southside St. ☎ *01752/665-292.* www.plymouthgin.com. *Admission (including 1½-hr. tour): £6 ($11) adults. Distillery tours offered daily 10:30 a.m.–4:45 p.m.*

Plymouth: Departure point for the U.S.

The Pilgrims may have been the earliest and most famous emigrants to leave Plymouth, England, for Plymouth, Massachusetts, but they were hardly the last. During the 19th century, estimates show that more emigrant ships bound for the United States left from Plymouth than from anywhere else in Europe. More than 100 towns in New England are named after places in Devon.

The Hoe

If you walk south from the Barbican, you come to the Hoe, a promontory overlooking Plymouth Sound, an inlet of the English Channel. The River Tamar, the age-old boundary between Devon and Cornwall and a Royal Navy anchorage for more than 400 years, flows into the sound from the west. To the east, you can see the River Plym, from which Plymouth takes its name. On the Hoe, you can see 17th-century ramparts surrounding a citadel and an 18th-century lighthouse, Smeatons Tower.

South of the Barbican.

Mayflower Steps

To commemorate the spot from which the *Mayflower* sailed for the New World, a neoclassical stone archway was erected in 1934 at the base of West Pier in the Barbican. The flags of the United States and the United Kingdom fly above the spot, but otherwise, little distinguishes it. You can read a full list of the names of all who sailed on the side of Island House, now the Barbican's Tourist Information Centre. Some of the Pilgrims reputedly lodged at the house before setting sail.

On Plymouth Harbor in the Barbican.

National Marine Aquarium

This popular and well-designed aquarium gives you insight into the lives of the aquatic creatures that inhabit the rivers of Devon and the waters of Plymouth Sound. The exhibits start with the watery environment of a moorland stream on Dartmoor; continue to a river; and then move down an estuary and beyond, from the shoreline to the continental shelf. You see fish, anemones, corals, seahorses, jellyfish, and sharks. The large tanks and variety of fish inevitably fascinate children.

Rope Walk, Coxside (follow signs from the Barbican). ☎ *01752/600-301.* www.national-aquarium.co.uk. *Admission: £8.75 ($16) adults, £7.25 ($13) seniors, £5.25 ($9.70) children 5–15, £25 ($46) families (2 adults, 2 children). Open: Daily 10 a.m.– 6 p.m. (until 5 p.m. Nov–Mar).*

Chapter 18

Cornwall: Saints, Salts, Sea, and Sun

- -

In This Chapter

▶ Pausing in Penzance

▶ Traveling to Land's End

▶ Strolling the quaint streets of St. Ives

▶ Frolicking in Fowey

▶ Stopping in at Cornwall's best houses and gardens

- -

The Tamar River west of Plymouth is the age-old boundary between Devon and Cornwall. (See the "Cornwall" map on p. 293.) At one time, the river was also a kind of dividing line between Cornwall and the rest of "civilized" England. The Cornish, who spoke their own language until the 18th century, were always considered a race apart. Their land, Cornwall, jutting like a toe out into the Atlantic, was a place of myth and mystery, associated with legendary figures such as Tristan and Isolde and King Arthur.

Cornwall has a special mystique that comes from its rocky landscape; its warm, buttery light; and the windy blue seascapes that you encounter at every turn. A history that stretches back more than 3,000 years to a time when Phoenician traders sailed up the Cornish coast to trade for the tin that was mined here haunts Cornwall. In Cornish churchyards, you can see ancient Celtic crosses from the fifth and sixth centuries, the time when men and women known as "saints" (missionaries from Ireland and Wales) first brought Christianity to this pagan land. Many Cornish places are named for these early saints. Along the Cornish coast, you find picturesque stone-built fishing villages huddled alongside small, sheltered harbors. The former haunts of fishermen and sea salts, and more than a few pirates and smugglers, they're a reminder of Cornwall's strong seafaring traditions.

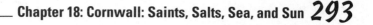

Cornwall

Castle on St. Michael's Mount	1
Cotehele	4
Eden Project	2
Lanhydrock	3

Today, tourism keeps Cornwall afloat. In summer, the warm, often-sunny climate draws hordes of vacationers. In this chapter, I take you first to the lively market town of Penzance, the end of the line as far as train travel goes. The major attraction in Penzance is St. Michael's Mount, a castle that began life as a monastery. From Penzance, you can easily reach Land's End, the westernmost point in England, exploring the south-coast fishing villages of Newlyn and Mousehole on the way. The picturesque village of St. Ives on the north coast (a few miles from Penzance) became an artists' colony in the early 20th century. Today, with a branch of the Tate Museum and plenty of good hotels and restaurants, St. Ives is one of the nicest spots to stay in Cornwall. I also point you in the direction of other worthwhile sights — from major tourist attractions, such as the Eden Project, to historic houses and special gardens — scattered throughout Cornwall.

ANGLO FILES
ENGLAND

Princely perks: The Duchy of Cornwall

In his redistribution of English lands, William the Conqueror gave Cornwall to one of his relatives. In the 14th century, Edward III created the Duchy of Cornwall as an estate for the eldest sons of the monarch. Cornwall, through 24 dukes, has remained a duchy ever since. Prince Charles, the oldest son of Queen Elizabeth II, is the present Duke of Cornwall. Income from the Duchy of Cornwall, in leased lands and estates, amounts to tens of millions of pounds every year and is a "nice little earner" for Charlie.

Penzance: As in "The Pirates of . . ."

Penzance, 124km (77 miles) southwest of Plymouth (see the "Cornwall" map on p. 293), is the most westerly town in England and a good base for exploring Land's End and western Cornwall. Penzance is the end of the line for mainline trains from London, 451km (280 miles) to the northeast. Built on hills overlooking Mount's Bay, Penzance is temperate enough to grow palm trees and plants that can't survive elsewhere in England.

Gilbert and Sullivan made Penzance famous in their operetta *The Pirates of Penzance,* but the town doesn't trade on that musical connection. In reality, Penzance has survived several major calamities: Barbary pirates raided the town, and Spaniards sacked and burned it in the 16th century, Cromwell partially destroyed it during the 17th-century Civil War, and the Germans bombed it in the 1940s. Despite all that, Penzance is an unusually friendly town. This town is the only part of England where you may hear yourself addressed as "my love."

Getting to Penzance

Express InterCity trains depart throughout the day from London's Paddington Station for the five-hour journey to Penzance. The round-trip advance-purchase supersaver fare costs £62 ($115). For train schedules, call ☎ 08457/484-950. **National Express** (☎ 0990/808-080; www.nationalexpress.com) operates daily bus service from London's Victoria Coach Station, but the trip takes seven-and-a-half to nine hours. If you're driving, the fastest route is A30, which cuts across Devon and Cornwall from Exeter.

Good train service connects London to Penzance and St. Ives, the two places I recommend as touring headquarters in Cornwall. If you don't have a car, excellent local bus service serves towns throughout the county; for more information, contact **Western National** (☎ 01208/79898; www.firstwesternnational.co.uk). If you want to rent a car, the following car-rental agencies have offices in Penzance:

✔ **Economy Hire,** Heliport Garage (☎ 01736/366-636)

✔ **Enterprise,** The Forecourt, Longrock (☎ 01736/332-000)

✔ **Europcar,** Station Yard (☎ 01736/360-078)

Finding information and taking a tour of Penzance

The **Tourist Information Centre,** Station Road (☎ 01736/362-207; www.penzance.co.uk), is open Monday through Friday from 9 a.m. to 5 p.m., Saturday 9 a.m. to 4 p.m. (until 1 p.m. Oct–May), and Sunday 10 a.m. to 1 p.m. (June–Sept only).

Belerion Walks, Avon House, 13 Penare Rd. (☎ 01736/362-452), offers year-round **guided walks** of the town; tours last about 90 minutes and cost £4 ($7.40). Call to reserve a spot. **Harry Safari** (☎ 01736/711-427; www.harrysafari.com) runs a four-hour **guided tour,** which offers one of the best ways to see this part of Cornwall. Guides drive you through the area in a minivan to all sorts of hidden corners and scenic spots. The tour costs £20 ($37); you can have them pick you up in Penzance or St. Ives.

A cruise around Mounts Bay, passing St. Michael's Mount and local coastal beauty spots where you may see seals or dolphins, makes for a fun excursion. **MVS Mermaid & Viking** (☎ 01736/368-565) operates two-hour coastal cruises at 3 p.m. (most days); these cruises cost £8 ($15) adults, £6.50 ($12) children 5 to 15. Boats leave from the marina area.

Staying in Penzance

Penzance is a holiday town with many hotels and B&Bs. I've listed a few of my faves in this section. See also The Summerhouse Restaurant with Rooms in the section "Dining in Penzance," later in this chapter

The Abbey
$$–$$$

The Abbey, in a 17th-century building overlooking Penzance harbor, is the most stylish guesthouse in Penzance. The hotel uses bold colors and

Special events in Penzance

Daphne du Maurier, whose famous novel *Rebecca* is set in Cornwall, lived in Bodinnick in nearby Fowey (see "Fowey and the Saint's Way: River Town and Holy Track," later in this chapter). Every year in May, Penzance sponsors the **Daphne du Maurier Festival of Arts and Literature,** featuring all kinds of performers and events. For information, call the box office at ☎ 01726/223-535 or check out the town's Web site at www.penzance.co.uk.

antiques to convey an atmosphere of overstuffed English elegance. It's like staying in a small, luxuriously appointed house. The nine guest rooms are lovely, and so are the bathrooms. You can arrange to have dinner in the hotel, or you may prefer the equally stylish Abbey Restaurant next door (see the section "Dining in Penzance," later in this chapter).

Abbey St., Penzance, Cornwall TR18 4AR. ☎ *01736/366-906. Fax: 01736/351-163.* www. theabbeyonline.com. *Rack rates: £120–£190 ($222–$352) double. Rates include English breakfast. AE, DC, MC, V.*

The Georgian House Hotel
$

This 18th-century Georgian building, formerly the house of a mayor of Penzance, reputedly has a resident ghost. But the real spirit of the 11-room B&B is modern art: The dining room, where you're served breakfast, is painted with murals inspired by Picasso and Matisse. Guest rooms are comfortable and well equipped, and a nice lounge and bar are on the premises. The hotel is right on Chapel Street, the most interesting street in town.

20 Chapel St., Penzance, Cornwall TR18 4AW. ☎ *01736/365-664. Fax: 01736/365-664. Rack rates: £52–£56 ($96–$104) double. Rates include English breakfast. AE, MC, V.*

Mount Prospect Hotel
$$

This 21-room hotel, overlooking Mounts Bay and the town, is one of the best places to stay in Penzance. Impeccably maintained, the hotel features comfortable, well-furnished rooms, many with sea views and good-size bathrooms (most with bath and shower). Kids enjoy the on-site pool. A special rate, which includes dinner at the hotel's fine restaurant, is a noteworthy bargain. Nonguests can also dine here on Modern British cuisine; the restaurant serves dinner nightly from 7 to 8:30.

Britons Hill, Penzance, Cornwall TR18 3AE. ☎ *01736/363-117. Fax: 01736/350-970.* www.hotelpenzance.com. *Rack rates: £115 ($213) double with English breakfast; £155 ($287) double with English breakfast and dinner. AE, MC, V.*

Dining in Penzance

You won't lack for dining options in Penzance. Many of the restaurants feature fresh seafood.

Abbey Restaurant
$$–$$$ MODERN EUROPEAN

At this stylish restaurant next to the Abbey Hotel, you enter a luscious red womb of a bar–lounge and walk up to an airy dining room with views out over Penzance harbor. Chef–owner Ben Tunnicliffe cooks in a modern European style that makes use of fresh local fish, meat, and produce. For starters, try pan-fried foie gras or crab cakes with cucumber chutney. Main courses change often but may include wild sea bass with fettuccine, pancetta, and artichokes or end of lamb. The Abbey has an excellent wine list.

Abbey Street. ☎ *01736/330-680. Reservations recommended. Main courses: £16–£25 ($30–$46). MC, V. Open: Fri–Sat noon–2 p.m.; Tues–Sat 7–10 p.m.*

Harris's Restaurant
$$–$$$ MODERN BRITISH/FRENCH

For a restaurant to stay in business for more than 30 years, it must be doing something right. This well-established restaurant, located down a narrow cobbled lane off Market Jew Street, is one of Penzance's best and most highly regarded. The cooking emphasizes fresh, local produce and seafood, with dishes such as crab Florentine and grilled scallops.

46 New St. ☎ *01736/364-408. Reservations recommended. Main courses: £16–£19 ($30–$35). AE, MC, V. Open: Tues–Sat noon–2 p.m. and 7–10 p.m.; closed three weeks in winter.*

The Summer House Restaurant with Rooms
$$$ ITALIAN

Head to this restaurant-inn in a Regency-era house just off the promenade if you're in the mood for innovative Mediterranean-style food. The set-price menus change daily, depending on what's fresh in the market, and you can choose from an interesting Italian wine list. In the summer, you can dine by candlelight in the beautiful walled garden. If you want to stay here, there are five large, stylishly furnished rooms with private bathrooms; a double with choice of English or continental breakfast goes for £80 to £95 ($140–$176), plus £26 ($48) for a three-course dinner.

Cornwall Terrace, Penzance, Cornwall TR18 4HL. ☎ *01736/363-744. Fax: 01736/360-959.* www.summerhouse-cornwall.com. *Reservations required. Fixed-price dinner £25 ($46). MC, V. Open: Restaurant Mar–Nov Tues–Sun 7–10 p.m.; hotel closed Dec–Feb.*

Sylvester's Restaurant
$–$$ CONTINENTAL

In a historic wharf building next to the Wharfside Shopping Centre, Sylvester's is an informal restaurant that catches plenty of tourist trade. The place serves good, inexpensive, home-cooked meals, including local seafood dishes, with minimum fuss.

Wharf Road. ☎ *01736/366-888. Main courses: Lunch £5–£8 ($9.25–$15); fixed-price dinner £15 ($28). AE, MC, V. Open: Easter–Oct daily 10:30 a.m.–9:30 p.m.; Nov–Easter Mon–Thurs 10:30 a.m.–5:30 p.m., Fri–Sat 10:30 a.m.–9:30 p.m.*

The Turks Head
$ INTERNATIONAL/PUB

The atmospheric, low-ceilinged Turks Head claims to be the oldest tavern in town because an inn on this spot has been welcoming travelers since the 13th century. You get good, hearty food, everything from fisherman's pie and seafood platters to ratatouille and chicken *tikka masala,* a spicy Indian dish.

49 Chapel St. ☎ *01736/363-093. Main courses: £6–£10 ($11–$19). MC, V. Open: Food served daily 11 a.m.–2:30 p.m. and 6–10 p.m.; pub open Mon–Sat 11 a.m.–11 p.m., Sun 11 a.m.–10:30 p.m.*

Exploring in and around Penzance

St. Michael's Mount is the must-see attraction in Penzance. The town itself doesn't offer a lot in the way of special interest or tourist attractions, though Chapel Street has some interesting buildings. Garden lovers may enjoy visiting Trengwainton Garden outside of town.

Castle on St. Michael's Mount
Mount's Bay

For nearly 350 years, this amazing island–castle in Mount's Bay has been the home of the St. Aubyn family. Connected to the mainland by a 500-foot-long causeway, the castle incorporates parts of an earlier 12th-century Benedictine priory that was founded as the daughter house of Mont St. Michel in Normandy. Later, in the 16th and 17th centuries, St. Michael's Mount was an important fortress to protect the coastline from foreign attack. (The beacon on top of the church tower was lit to warn of the approach of the Spanish Armada in 1588.) A royalist stronghold during the Civil War, the fort was forced to surrender after a long siege. The St. Aubyn family still inhabits part of the castle and has lived there since 1659.

Visitors enter through the **West Door,** above which hangs the St. Aubyn family crest. The **Entrance Hall,** altered in the 19th century, was the living area for the Captain of the Mount in the 16th and 17th centuries. The little adjacent chamber, known as **Sir John's Room,** is the owner's private sitting room. Sporting weapons and war memorabilia hang in the **Armoury.** The snug **Library** is in the oldest (12th-century) part of the castle, as is the dining room, which served as the monks' refectory. The **Priory Church** on the island's summit has beautiful rose windows. In a newer section of the castle, you can see the elegant rococo-style **Blue Drawing Rooms.**

St. Michael's Mount is one of the most-visited National Trust properties in Britain. Give yourself at least three hours for a visit, and be aware that you have to climb many stairs to reach the castle. If the tide is in, boatmen known as *hobblers* can ferry you over or back. If you need some nourishment after all those stairs, you can refuel at one of two restaurants on the island, open April to October only, where you can have lunch or tea. Lunch costs about £4 to £8 ($7.40–$15); a cream tea, about £4 ($7.40).

To get here by bus, take bus no. 20 or 22 from Penzance to Marazion, the town opposite St. Michael's Mount.

See map p. 293. On St. Michael's Mount, Mount's Bay (take A30 from Penzance). ☎ *01736/710-507.* www.stmichaelsmount.co.uk. *Admission: £5.50 ($10) adults,*

£2.75 ($5.10) children under 17, £14 ($26) families (2 adults, 2 children). Open: Mid-Mar to Oct Sun–Fri 10:30 a.m.–5:30 (last admission 4:45 p.m.); Nov to mid-Mar usually Mon, Wed, and Fri by conducted tour only at 11 a.m., noon and 2 and 3 p.m.; call to verify.

Chapel Street
Penzance

Chapel Street, running north–south from St. Mary's Church near the water-front up to Parade Street, is the most architecturally significant street in Penzance. Strolling the length takes only a few minutes, and doing so gives you a glimpse of the Penzance of yore. Chapel Street has always been a mixture of residential and commercial buildings. Facades that look Georgian (from the late 18th and early 19th centuries) often hide much older buildings. Two hundred years ago, the **Union Hotel,** with its Assembly Rooms, was the center of the town's social activities. Across the road from the Union Hotel is the **Egyptian House,** built in 1835 with Egyptian motifs and ornamentation. Other houses on the street belonged to mayors, mariners, and traders. Just below the Regent Hotel is the **Old Custom House,** a fine building whose interior retains many original 18th-century features (it's now a shop selling antiques, crystal, and German Christmas ornaments). Farther down is the **Turks Head,** which claims to be the oldest inn in Penzance (see the section "Dining in Penzance," earlier in this chapter). The austere **Wesleyan Chapel** of 1814 is situated across from the inn. Nearby, marked by a blue plaque, you can see the home of Maria Branwell, the beloved "Aunt Branwell" who moved to Yorkshire to raise Charlotte, Emily, Anne, and Branwell Brontë after their mother died. Chapel Street's most impressive building is **St. Mary's Church,** rebuilt in the 1830s on the site of an earlier medieval chapel.

Penlee House Gallery & Museum
Penzance

Built as a private residence in 1865, Penlee House now serves as Penzance's art gallery and museum. The painting collection focuses on the Newlyn School of artists, mostly landscape painters active in the area between 1880 and 1930. The museum has exhibits ranging from Stone Age to the present day. You can tour the entire museum in about 30 minutes. The Orangery Cafe is a nice spot for tea or a light lunch.

Morrab Road. ☎ 01736/363-625. Admission: £2 ($3.70) adults, free for children 5–15. Open: Mon–Sat 10 a.m.–5 p.m., (10:30 a.m.–4:30 p.m. Oct–Apr).

Trengwainton Garden
West of Penzance

Nowhere else on mainland Britain can you find a garden with plants as exotic as the ones grown here. Trengwainton (pronounced as it's spelled, Treng-*wain*-ton), which means the "House of the Spring" in Cornish, is set in the granite hills behind Penzance, and commands panoramic views of

Mount's Bay and the Lizard Peninsula. The first walled gardens were constructed in the 18th century, but the plantings didn't really flourish until the late 1920s, under Sir Edward Bolitho. Several species of rhododendrons, which Bolitho planted from seeds collected in Asia, flowered for the first time outside their native habitat in this garden. You see color throughout the year, from camellias and magnolias in early spring to acres of blue hydrangea in late summer. You can have lunch or a Cornish cream tea in the teahouse. The garden is a National Trust property. Give yourself at least an hour to enjoy it.

To get here by bus, take the First National bus no. 10/A from Penzance to St. Just; ask the driver to let you off along the way at the stop nearest Trengwainton. (For bus schedules, check with the Tourist Information Centre; see "Finding information and taking a tour of Penzance," earlier in this chapter.)

3km (2 miles) west of Penzance, .5km (½ mile) west of Heamoor off Penzance-Morvah Road (B3312). ☎ *01736/362-297 or 01637/875-404. Admission: £4.50 ($8.35) adults, £2.20 ($4.05) children under 17, £11 ($20) families (2 adults, 2 children). Open: Mid-Feb to Oct Sun–Thurs 10 a.m.–5 p.m. (until 5:30 p.m. Apr–Sept).*

The Penwith Peninsula: A Driving Tour from Penzance to Land's End

On a map, the **Penwith Peninsula** west of Penzance looks like a giant toe dipping into the Atlantic. You can take a great driving tour of this area, which I outline in this section. B3315 follows the peninsula's southern coastline past the fishing villages of Newlyn and Mousehole — good places to stop and explore for an hour or so — to famous Land's End, where you can pick up the fast A30 back to Penzance. The distances here aren't that great; driving this loop without stopping takes about an hour, but the trip makes a pleasant half- or full-day excursion from Penzance or St. Ives. If you don't have a car, bus service runs from Penzance to Newlyn, Mousehole, and Land's End. For times and schedules, check with the tourist office or the local bus service, **First Western National** (☎ 01209/719-988; www.firstwesternnational.co.uk).

Stop #1: Newlyn

Just a couple of miles south of Penzance lies the port of Newlyn, home of England's second largest fishing fleet. Chances are that any fresh fish or lobster that you eat in Penzance or even St. Ives was landed in the waters near Newlyn. *Pilchards* (mature sardines) have traditionally been the biggest catch off these shores. In general, though, the pilchard fishing industry that was the mainstay of Cornwall's coastal villages from the medieval era until the early part of the 20th century is now a tiny fragment of what it once was. **The Pilchard Works Museum and Factory**, The Coombe (☎ 01736/332-112), is the last remaining salt pilchard factory in England; the factory has a small adjunct museum that explains the process of curing pilchards; for almost a hundred years, this factory has supplied salt (cured) pilchards to the same Italian company. The museum is open Easter through October weekdays from 10 a.m. to 6 p.m.

The seascapes and the quality of light along this part of the Cornish coast lured several artists to the area in the late Victorian era. You can see the paintings of the Newlyn School in Penzance at Penlee House. (See the section "Exploring in and around Penzance," earlier in this chapter.) The **Newlyn Art Gallery,** Newlyn Green (☎ 01736/363-715), has a small collection of the distinctive Arts and Crafts copper work that was produced in Newlyn from 1890 to 1950. The gallery is open Monday to Saturday from 10 a.m. to 5 p.m.

If the sea air has you feeling *peckish* (hungry), you can find the best fish and chips in town at the **Tolcarne Inn,** Tolcarne Place (☎ 01736/365-074). Or you may want to try fresh crab or Newlyn fish pie (white and smoked fish and prawns in white wine sauce, topped with cheese and breadcrumbs). Meals (lunch and dinner daily) are served in a publike room with a beamed ceiling. Main courses go for £5 to £10 ($9.25–$19); the inn accepts MasterCard and Visa.

Stop #2: Mousehole

A few miles south of Newlyn lies the former fishing village of Mousehole (pronounced *Muz*-zle). With its curving quay, its small protected harbor, and its quaint stone cottages, Mousehole is a pretty place. The town attracts many tourists who come for lunch or tea and a look around. The town itself is the attraction here.

One very good restaurant to try is **Cornish Range,** 6 Chapel St. (☎ 01736/731-488), open daily in the summer and Wednesday to Saturday in the winter for lunch and dinner. On the menu, you find fish soup, crab Florentine, roast cod and mullet, and many other fresh fish dishes. Main courses go for £13 to £18 ($24–$33). MasterCard and Visa are accepted. Cornish Range also rents out three guest rooms, each with private bath, for £80 to £90 ($148–$167) per night, including breakfast. If you're looking for a good, unfussy Cornish cream tea, pop into **Pam's Pantry,** 3 Mill Lane (☎ 01736/731-532), open February to November daily 9:30 a.m. to 6:30 p.m. This cash-only hole-in-the-wall also serves Newlyn crab in soups, sandwiches, and salads. A cream tea costs about £4 ($7.40), and main courses go for £5 to £8 ($9.25–$15).

Stop #3: The Minack Theatre

The oceanside **Minack Theatre** (☎ 01736/810-694; www.minack.com) was carved out of a rocky hillside in Porthcurno, a village 14.5km (9 miles) southwest of Penzance (from Mousehole, continue south on B3315, and follow the signs). The theater is legendary because of its outdoor setting, overlooking the ocean. If you stay in Penzance or St. Ives, an evening here makes for a memorable experience. From May to

September, theater companies from all over England stage performances of everything from Shakespeare to musical comedies, a tradition dating to 1932. Bring a cushion, a sweater, and a raincoat, just in case. You can check out the Visitor Centre even if you're not seeing a play. Theater tickets cost £6 to £7.50 ($11–$14). The Exhibition Hall, which has information on the theater's history, is open daily from 9:30 a.m. to 5:30 p.m. (Oct–Mar 10 a.m.–4 p.m.). The theater presents evening performances Monday through Friday at 8. and matinees on Wednesday and Friday at 2 from the end of May to mid-September.

Stop #4: Land's End

Atlantic-facing Land's End, where high granite cliffs plunge down to the roaring sea, is one of the country's most famous and dramatic landmarks. But a theme-park development that you have to pass through to reach the headland mars the grandeur of this windy point, the westernmost on mainland Britain. A well-marked path leads out to an observation point, and you can follow other coastal paths if the day is fine. The British-owned Scilly Isles are 45km (28 miles) out to sea; otherwise, nothing lies between England and the eastern coast of North America.

St. Ives: Artists' Haven by the Sea

It's easy to understand why this former fishing village on the north coast of Cornwall attracts artists. The sea at **St. Ives** changes color like a jewel shimmering in the sunlight. The town's whitewashed stone cottages and painted stucco villas stretch along rocky coves and a long, curving sand beach. A relaxing place to stay, St. Ives is much smaller than Penzance. A branch of London's Tate museum commemorates a group of local artists, including Barbara Hepworth and Ben Nicholson, who lived and worked in the town. The town is still a favorite hangout for artists and craftspeople. You can find dozens of small galleries for browsing, in addition to plenty of good restaurants specializing in locally caught seafood.

Getting to St. Ives

Trains run throughout the day from London's Paddington Station to the area. For St. Ives, you change trains at St. Erth on the main line to Penzance, or you can take a train direct from Penzance. The total trip takes about five-and-a-half to six hours. For train information, call ☎ 08457/484-950. Long-distance buses from London's Victoria Coach Station take up to nine hours; call **National Express (☎ 0990/808-080)** for more information. Driving from Penzance, you can take A30 northeast to its junction with A3074, and follow A3074 north.

For information about renting a car in Penzance, see the section "Getting to Penzance," earlier in this chapter.

Finding information about St. Ives

The **Tourist Information Centre** in the Guildhall, Street-an-Pol (☎ 01736/ 796-297), is open Monday through Friday from 9:30 a.m. to 5:30 p.m.; Saturday from 10 a.m. to 1 p.m. (mid-May to Aug 9:30 a.m.–5:30 p.m.); and from mid-May through September Sunday 10 a.m. to 1 p.m. The center dispenses information on the area, stocks brochures on local attractions, and operates a room-finding service.

Staying in St. Ives

St. Ives draws visitors year-round, but it's particularly busy in the warm summer months. Dozens of hotels and B&Bs occupy this small Cornish town. Here are my recommended choices.

Garrack Hotel & Restaurant

$$–$$$

This hotel is renowned for its restaurant and has special rates that include dinner. The Garrack is in a traffic-free area of St. Ives, with views looking out over the gardens to the sea. Some of the 18 guest rooms are in a former private house; the others, in a modern wing and separate cottage. All have private bathrooms. Kids love the indoor pool. The romantic sea-view restaurant serves fresh fish and lobster from Newlyn; organic beef, lamb, and venison; and produce from its own garden. A four-course fixed-price meal costs £26 ($48). Even if you stay elsewhere, you may want to eat here (reservations required).

Burthallan Lane, St. Ives, Cornwall TR26 3AA. ☎ **01736/796-199.** *Fax: 01736/798-955.* www.garrack.com. *Rack rates: £126–£180 ($233–$333) double with English breakfast; £168–£228 ($311–$422) double with English breakfast and dinner. AE, DC, MC, V.*

Pedn-Olva Hotel

$$–$$$

Located right on the edge of a commanding cliff, this hotel was stylishly refurbished in 2001 and has 30 rooms with the best sea views in St. Ives. Most of the rooms (and bathrooms) are smallish, but the panoramic views are mesmerizing. The hotel has a fine restaurant, sunny terraces, and a pool, and you have only a two-minute walk to the center of town or the beach. It's a light, bright, airy hotel with a lot of nice features.

Porthminster Beach, St. Ives, Cornwall TR26 2EA. ☎ **01736/796-222.** *Fax: 01736-797-710.* www.pednolvahotel.co.uk. *Rack rates: £110–£145 ($204–$268) double. Rates include English breakfast. AE, DC, MC, V.*

Tregony

$

This well-maintained, nonsmoking B&B in a pretty, bay-fronted Victorian house sits just above the Tate St. Ives and Porthmeor Beach. The B&B has five guest rooms, two of them with sea views and all with private bathrooms with showers. This B&B's staff welcomes families with children.

Clodgy View, St. Ives, Cornwall TR26 1JG. ☎ *01736/795-884.* Fax: 01736/798-942. www. tregony.com. *Rack rates: £56–£60 ($104–$111) double. Rate includes English breakfast. MC, V.*

Dining in St. Ives

As you may expect, many St. Ives restaurants feature fresh seafood. Here are my dining choices.

Josephs
$–$$ SEAFOOD/INTERNATIONAL

This small, smart cafe–restaurant overlooking the harbor specializes in seafood, with four or five choices daily. You can also get duck, chicken, and steak. Pastas are served at lunchtime. Try the seafood spaghetti, made with scallops and prawns.

39A Fore St. ☎ *01736/796-514. Reservations recommended for dinner. Main courses: £9.50–£15 ($18–$28). MC, V. Open: Daily 10 a.m.–4:30 p.m. and 6:30–9:45 p.m.*

Porthminster Beach Cafe
$$–$$$ MODERN BRITISH/INTERNATIONAL

This pleasant cafe on Porthminster Beach overlooking St. Ives Bay serves some interesting dishes. The offerings emphasize fresh fish, but tasty vegetarian options are always on the menu. A meal may consist of seared scallops, prawn risotto, or baked Newlyn cod.

Porthminster Beach. ☎ *01736/795-352. Reservations recommended for dinner. Main courses: £14–19 ($26–$35). MC, V. Open: Apr–Oct daily 11 a.m.–4 p.m. and 7–10 p.m.*

Russets Restaurant
$$ SEAFOOD/INTERNATIONAL

This intimate restaurant, a favorite with both locals and visitors, wisely specializes in fresh seafood. Don't pass up crab soup if it's available. Or you may want to try fish stew with *aioli* (a cold sauce made with crushed garlic, egg yolks, olive oil, and lemon). If you're not into fish, you can choose breast of duck, chicken, or lamb.

18A Fore St. ☎ *01736/794-700. Reservations recommended for dinner. Main courses: Lunch £7–£15 ($13–$28), dinner £10–£30 ($19–$56). AE, DC, MC, V. Open: Daily noon–2 p.m., 7–10 p.m. (closed Mon Nov–Mar).*

Exploring St. Ives

Over a century ago, artists started coming to St. Ives for the wonderful light and atmosphere. The sculptor Barbara Hepworth decided to stay, and her house is one of the town's most magical places to visit. Tate St. Ives is the biggest tourist draw. The sandy beaches and high headlands with views of the sea make for great walks.

Barbara Hepworth Museum and Sculpture Garden

This wonderful adjunct of the Tate St. Ives (just a couple of minutes' walk from that museum) gives remarkable insight into the work of Dame Barbara Hepworth, one of the great sculptors of the 20th century. You get to see Hepworth's actual studio and sculpture garden. She lived here from 1949 until her death in 1975 at age 72. On the lower level, you can find an informative exhibit on her life and career. Then you go upstairs to a marvelous living area and from there out into the **sculpture garden.** On display throughout are about 47 sculptures and drawings from 1928 to 1974, photos, working tools, and Hepworth memorabilia.

Barnoon Hill. ☎ 01736/796-226. Admission: £4.50 ($8.35) adults, £2.25 ($4.15) seniors and students; combined ticket with Tate St. Ives £8.50 ($16) adults, £4.25 ($7.85) seniors and students. Open: Mar–Oct daily 10 a.m.–5:30 p.m.; Nov–Feb Tues–Sun 10 a.m.–4:30 p.m.

Tate St. Ives

A branch of the Tate museum in London, Tate St. Ives opened in 1993 and quickly became the town's biggest attraction. The museum is devoted exclusively to modern art and particularly to the works of artists who lived in Cornwall. St. Ives itself has been an artists' colony since 1928. Personally, I think the building, which sits on the site of the old town gasworks, is ungainly and confusing, although the spaces are filled with light and have some fine seaward views. The museum has no permanent collection but presents changing exhibitions four times a year; the paintings, sculptures, and ceramics on display are chosen from works in the Tate's vast collection (the British National Collection of Modern Art). You can also find works by contemporary artists. You can have lunch or a snack at the pleasant cafe on the premises. The Gallery also manages the nearby Barbara Hepworth Museum and Sculpture Garden (see the preceding listing).

Porthmeor Beach. ☎ 01736/796-226. Admission: £5.50 ($10) adults, free for seniors and children under 18; combined ticket with Barbara Hepworth Museum £8.50 ($16) adults, £4.25 ($7.85) students. Open: Mar–Oct daily 10 a.m.–5:30 p.m.; Nov–Feb Tues–Sun 10 a.m.–4:30 p.m.

Finding more to see near St. Ives

Cornwall, like Wiltshire and Devon, is full of prehistoric sites, although nothing as grand as Stonehenge. The following list describes three ancient sites near St. Ives that you may want to check out; before you set out, stop at the Tourist Information Centre (see the section "Finding information about St. Ives," earlier in this chapter) for more exact directions:

✔ **Chysauster** (*Kie*-sis-ter): The remains of a remarkable Iron Age village with four pairs of houses, each fronting a village street. Each house is oval in plan, with roughly circular rooms that open to a central courtyard. Now roofless, the rooms were apparently covered with stone or thatch, although the courtyards were open. During the excavation, archaeologists discovered hearths, pottery, and other domestic debris lying on the paved floors. Each house also had a stone-fenced back garden. From St. Ives, drive south on B3311, turning west toward New Mill and the marked site.

✔ **Lanyon Quoit:** This huge granite slab, 17 feet by 9 feet and 18 inches thick, rests on three upright stones. This formation is all that remains of a Neolithic tomb. From St. Ives, drive west on B3306 to a signposted turnoff just before Morvah. Drive a couple of miles farther south to see Trengwainton Garden (see the section "Exploring in and around Penzance," earlier in this chapter).

✔ **Zennor Quoit** (also called Mulfra Quoit): An unusual type of Early Bronze Age megalithic tomb, which originated in Brittany and is found throughout the Penwith area of Cornwall. Divided into chamber and antechamber, a large round *cairn* (a heap of stones used as a marker) originally covered the tomb, but all trace of this marker has disappeared, leaving the internal structure standing free. From St. Ives, drive west on B3306 to the signposted turnoff. Be prepared for a 15-minute walk on a path that's often wet and overgrown.

Fowey and the Saint's Way: River Town and Holy Track

Located on the south coast, about midway between Plymouth and Penzance, **Fowey** (pronounced *Foy*) is a small, scenic harbor town with several historic buildings and an interesting past. The town stretches along the green, wooded banks of the River Fowey, a shipping channel that empties into St. Austell Bay. The river is a favorite spot for pleasure boats of all kinds. A car-ferry service runs between Fowey to Bodinnick, on the east side of the river. Daphne du Maurier, who used Cornwall as a setting for her most famous novel, *Rebecca,* grew up in Bodinnick, part of Fowey.

You can pick up a free map and guide to the town and surrounding villages at Fowey's **Tourist Information Centre,** The Ticket Shop, 4 Custom House Hill (☎ 01726/833-616). The center is open daily from Easter through September (Mon–Fri 9 a.m.–5:30 p.m., Sat 9 a.m.–5 p.m., Sun 10 a.m.–5 p.m.); the center closes on Sunday in the off season.

If you want lunch or tea in Fowey, **The Toll Bar,** Lostwithiel Street (☎ 01726/833-001), has a nice outdoor terrace overlooking the river and sea. The **Marina Hotel & Waterside Restaurant,** Esplanade, Fowey, Cornwall PL23 1HY (☎ 01726/833-315; www.themarinahotel.co.uk), has 12 lovely rooms, most of them overlooking the river, and a fine-dining restaurant. A double room with breakfast goes for £100 to £144 ($185–$266).

This region has been great walking country for thousands of years. The 42km-long (26-mile) **Saint's Way** begins at Padstow on the north coast, crosses the moors of central Cornwall, and ends at Fowey. During the Bronze Age and Iron Age, Saint's Way was a coast-to-coast trading route that avoided the treacherous waters off Land's End. Later, Saint's Way became the route for missionaries and pilgrims crossing from Ireland to take ships from Fowey to France and on to Rome or Santiago de Compostela in Spain. You can see hill forts, granite Celtic crosses, holy wells, and ancient churches all along the route.

Cotehele, Eden Project, and Lanhydrock: Three Great Cornish Gardens

Cornwall, blessed with the mildest climate in England, is equally blessed with magnificent gardens. Check out these three places where plant lovers can revel in nature. Two of them are former estates with fascinating houses; the third is new.

Cotehele

Set on the steep, wooded slopes of the River Tamar, west of Plymouth, **Cotehele** (pronounced *Co-teel*; ☎ 01579/351-346) is a marvelous manor house with magnificent gardens — one of the least altered medieval houses in England. Built of granite and slate, Cotehele blends in naturally with the landscape. The rooms inside, unlit by electricity, display a wonderful collection of ancient furniture, textiles, and tapestries. The chapel contains the oldest working domestic clock in England, still in its original place. Formal gardens, terraces, and a daffodil meadow surround the house, situated near the top of the valley. The steep valley gardens below contain many species of exotic plants that thrive in Cornwall's mild climate. The house is a National Trust property. A good restaurant is in the nearby medieval barn. You need at least two hours to see everything. Admission costs £7.40 ($14), £3.70 ($6.85) for children, £18 ($33) for families (2 adults, 2 children). From mid-March through October, the house is open Saturday through Thursday from 11 a.m. to 5 p.m. (in Oct until 4:30 p.m.); the gardens are open year-round from 10:30 a.m. to dusk. To get to Cotehele from Plymouth, take A38 northwest and then A388, turning east on A390 and south at Harrowbarrow (see the "Cornwall" map on p. 293).

Eden Project

A few miles west of Fowey, overlooking St. Austell Bay, you come to a major tourist attraction called **Eden Project** (☎ **01726/811-911**; www. edenproject.com), which opened in March 2001. The Eden Project is both an educational resource and an environmental showcase. The site comprises two gigantic geodesic conservatories, one devoted to the rainforest, and the other to the fruits and flowers of the Mediterranean, South Africa, and California. Sunflowers, lavender, and hemp are among the plants that grow outside, on the acres of landscaped grounds. The project grows plants from all sorts of different terrains in microhabitats. Eden Project is intriguing and definitely worth a couple of hours. A trip here is a fun way to introduce kids to plants and environmental issues. Admission is £13 ($24) for adults, £9.50 ($18) for seniors, £5 ($9.25) for children 5 to 15, and £30 ($56) for families (2 adults, 3 children). The attraction is open daily from 9:30 a.m. to 6 p.m. (Nov–Mar until 4:30 p.m.). St. Austell is the nearest town. The Eden Project is signposted from A390, A30, and A391 (see the "Cornwall" map on p. 293).

Lanhydrock

Set in a beautiful landscape overlooking the valley of the Fowey River, Lanhydrock (Lan-*hi*-druck) is one of the grandest homes in Cornwall. The magnificent Long Gallery, with its 17th-century plaster ceiling depicting scenes from the Old Testament, is one of the few rooms that survived a disastrous fire in 1881. You can view approximately 50 rooms that reflect the organization and lifestyles in a rich Victorian household that depended on servants to keep it running efficiently. Lanhydrock reveals the other side of grand living: the kitchens, sculleries, and larders where the staff toiled.

Different kinds of gardens — from Victorian *parterres* (ornamental gardens with paths between the beds) to woodland gardens with camellias, magnolias, and rhododendrons — surround the house. An avenue of ancient beech and sycamore trees runs from the 17th-century gatehouse down to a medieval bridge across the Fowey. The National Trust manages the property. You need at least two hours to take it all in. Admission costs £7.90 ($15), £3.95 ($7.30) children, £10 ($19) for families (2 adults, 2 children). The house is open April through October Tuesday to Sunday from 11 a.m. to 5:30 p.m. (in Oct until 5 p.m.). The garden is open daily year-round from 10 a.m. to 6 p.m. Lanhydrock is about 16km (10 miles) north of Fowey and 4km (2½ miles) east of Bodmin; the home is signposted from A30, A38, and B3268.

Part VI
England's Heartland

The 5th Wave   By Rich Tennant

"I appreciate that our room looks out onto several Regency fountains, but I had to get up 6 times last night to go to the bathroom."

In this part...

Central England encompasses many more counties than the two I describe in this part. But the bordering counties of Warwickshire and Gloucestershire are, to my mind, the heart of England's heartland. William Shakespeare, whose words have become a permanent part of the English language, was born and died in Warwickshire. And Gloucestershire can boast some of the most beautiful countryside and villages in England.

In Chapter 19, I take you through Shakespeare's hometown, Stratford-upon-Avon, where you can visit the houses that the great poet and playwright called home. From Stratford, you can make an easy day trip to mighty Warwick Castle, the most impressive castle in this piece of central England.

Chapter 20 begins with the Regency spa town of Bath, a place that epitomizes the graceful, glamorous world of Jane Austen and Georgian England. From Bath, you can head to Cheltenham, a smaller spa town in Gloucestershire, or tour the Cotswolds, where picturesque medieval market towns of honey-colored stone stand as proud reminders of the days when the wool trade brought prosperity to the region.

Chapter 19

Stratford-upon-Avon and Warwick Castle

* *

In This Chapter

▶ Visiting Shakespeare's hometown

▶ Spending time in mighty Warwick Castle

* *

*W*illiam Shakespeare is the one name that people around the world associate with England. Shakespeare (1564–1616) was a universal genius: His plays and poems transcend geographical boundaries and strike a chord common in all humanity. It's no wonder, then, that **Stratford-upon-Avon,** the town where he was born and died, is one of the most visited places in England. **Warwick Castle** is only a few miles away, and you can easily get there by train from Stratford, so you may want to visit both when you're in the area. Bath and the Cotswolds are also nearby (see Chapter 20). For an overview of the area, see the "England's Heartland" map on p. 312.

Stratford-upon-Avon: In the Bard's Footsteps

Do I need to tell you whose spirit pervades this market town on the River Avon, 147km (91 miles) northwest of London? Stratford-upon-Avon is a shrine to the world's greatest playwright, William Shakespeare, who was born, lived much of his life, and is buried here. In summer, crowds of international tourists overrun the town, which hustles its Shakespeare connection in every conceivable way.

Stratford boasts many fine Elizabethan and Jacobean buildings, but it's not really a quaint village anymore. (See the "Stratford-upon-Avon" map on p. 314.) If you arrive by train, you get your first glimpse of Stratford: a vast parking lot across from the station. Don't let this less-than-Shakespearean view put you off. Stratford hasn't completely lost the charms of its formerly bucolic setting — you can find plenty of charming corners as you explore. Besides the literary pilgrimage sights, the top draw in Stratford is the **Royal Shakespeare Theatre,** where Britain's foremost actors perform.

England's Heartland

SCOTLAND
0   100 mi
0   100 km
North Sea
Irish Sea ENGLAND
WALES Area of Detail
London
English Channel

Dudley

Birmingham

Coventry

Kidderminster

Rugby

Redditch

Warwickshire

M5

Warwick

Worcestershire

A46

Worcester

Stratford-upon-Avon

M40

Kiftsgate Court Gardens   Hidcote Manor

Herefordshire   Evesham   Banbury

Hereford   Broadway   Chipping Campden

A44   THE   A44   Moreton-in-Marsh

COTSWOLDS   Stow-on-the-Wold   Chipping Norton

Cheltenham   A429

Upper and Lower Slaughter

Gloucester   A40   Woodstock

Chedworth Roman Villa   Bourton-on-the-Water

A417   A40   Oxford

M5   Gloucestershire

Cirencester   Oxfordshire

Abingdon

A419

Swindon

M4

Bristol   0   15 Mi

To Bath   0   15 Km

Wiltshire

Stratford has much to see and enjoy. I recommend that you spend at least a day here. Consider an overnight stay if you're a theater lover, but make sure that you book your theater seat in advance. (See the section "Seeing a play in Stratford-upon-Avon," later in this chapter.)

Getting to Stratford-upon-Avon

Direct trains leave frequently from London's Paddington and Marylebone Station; the fastest direct trains take about two hours. The "supersaver return" advance-purchase round-trip ticket costs £39 ($72), but you can actually save money by buying two single (one-way) fares for £15 ($28) each way. Call ☎ **08457/484-950** for information, fares, and schedules.

National Express (☎ 0990/808-080; www.nationalexpress.com) offers daily bus service from London's Victoria Coach Station; a direct trip lasts a little more than three hours and costs £16 ($30) for a same-day round-trip ticket. By car from London, take the M40 toward Oxford, and continue to Stratford-upon-Avon on A34.

Finding information about Stratford-upon-Avon

Stratford's **Tourist Information Centre**, Bridgefoot (☎ 01789/293-127; www.shakespeare-country.co.uk), provides information and maps of the town and its principal sites. The center has a currency exchange and also offers a **room-booking service** at ☎ 01789/415-061. The center is open Easter through October, Monday through Saturday from 9 a.m. to 6 p.m. and Sunday from 11 a.m. to 5 p.m.; November to Easter, Monday through Saturday from 9 a.m. to 5 p.m. and Sunday from 10:30 a.m. to 4:30 p.m.

Getting around and touring Stratford-upon-Avon

Stratford is compact, and you can walk everywhere. The train and bus stations are less than a 15-minute walk from the town center.

City Sightseeing, 14 Rother St. (☎ 01708/866-000; www.citysight seeing.co.uk), offers guided tours of Stratford that leave from outside the tourist office. Open-top, double-decker buses depart every 15 to 30 minutes daily between 9:30 a.m. and 5:30 p.m. You can take the one-hour ride without stops, or get off and on at any or all the town's five Shakespeare properties, including Mary Arden's House in Wilmcote (see the section "Exploring the best of Stratford-upon-Avon," later in this chapter). The tour ticket is valid all day but doesn't include admission to any of the houses. The bus tour cost is £8 ($15) for adults, £6 ($11) for seniors and students, and £3 ($5.55) for children under 12. You can buy your ticket on the bus.

Staying in Stratford-upon-Avon

Make reservations if you plan to sleep, perchance to dream, in Stratford — particularly on weekends during the theater season and during the summer. For those popular periods, make reservations at least a couple of weeks in advance. The Tourist Information Centre (see "Finding information about Stratford-upon-Avon," earlier in this chapter) can also help you find accommodations.

Hamlet House
$

This unpretentious, well-maintained B&B in a Victorian townhouse is a convenient three-minute walk from the train station and close to everything else in Stratford. Two of its five guest rooms have private bathrooms; the others share a toilet and shower. Yvonne and Paul, the owners, are helpful and hospitable, and they welcome children. The breakfast is hearty.

Stratford-upon-Avon

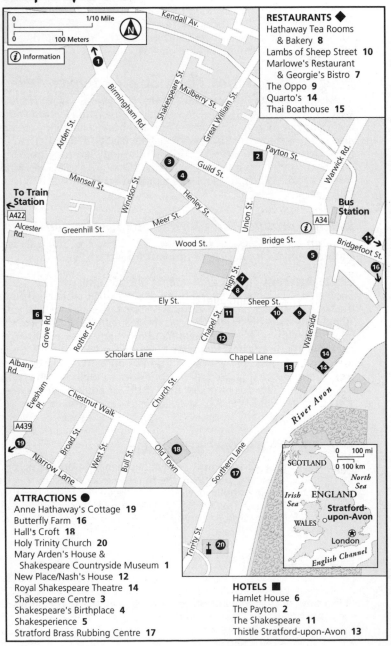

0   1/10 Mile
0   100 Meters

(i) Information

Kendall Av.

Birmingham Rd.

Arden St.

Mansell St.

Shakespeare St.

Mulberry St.

Great William St.

Windsor St.

Guild St.

Payton St.

Warwick Rd.

To Train Station
A422

Alcester Rd.

Greenhill St.

Henley St.

Meer St.

Union St.

Wood St.

Bridge St.

Bus Station
A34

Bridgefoot St.

High St.

Ely St.

Sheep St.

Chapel St.

Scholars Lane

Chapel Lane

Grove Rd.

Rother St.

Albany Rd.

Evesham Pl.

Chestnut Walk

Church St.

Waterside

River Avon

A439

Broad St.

West St.

Bull St.

Old Town

Narrow Lane

Southern Lane

Trinity St.

RESTAURANTS ◆
Hathaway Tea Rooms
  & Bakery **8**
Lambs of Sheep Street **10**
Marlowe's Restaurant
  & Georgie's Bistro **7**
The Oppo **9**
Quarto's **14**
Thai Boathouse **15**

0   100 mi
0   100 km

SCOTLAND

North Sea

Irish Sea

ENGLAND

Stratford-upon-Avon

WALES

London

English Channel

ATTRACTIONS ●
Anne Hathaway's Cottage **19**
Butterfly Farm **16**
Hall's Croft **18**
Holy Trinity Church **20**
Mary Arden's House &
  Shakespeare Countryside Museum **1**
New Place/Nash's House **12**
Royal Shakespeare Theatre **14**
Shakespeare Centre **3**
Shakespeare's Birthplace **4**
Shakesperience **5**
Stratford Brass Rubbing Centre **17**

HOTELS ■
Hamlet House **6**
The Payton **2**
The Shakespeare **11**
Thistle Stratford-upon-Avon **13**

See map p. 314. 52 Grove Rd., Stratford-upon-Avon, Warwickshire CV37 6PB. ☎ *01789/204-386.* www.hamlethouse.com. *Rack rates: £42–£54 ($78–$100) double. Rates include English breakfast. No credit cards.*

The Payton
$

The five en-suite guest rooms in this Georgian-era townhouse are larger and more stylish than the rooms at Hamlet House. The B&B is charming and quiet, located on a side street that's just a three-minute walk from the town center.

See map p. 314. 6 St. John St., Stratford-upon-Avon, Warwickshire CV37 6UB. ☎ */fax 01789/266-442.* www.payton.co.uk. *Rack rates: £68 ($126) double. Rates include English breakfast. MC, V.*

The Shakespeare
$$–$$$

The Shakespeare successfully blends old and new. Parts of this centrally located hotel date from 1635 and preserve the original Tudor-era beams and stone floor, but all 76 rooms were completely refurbished in 2005 in a comfortably elegant and traditional style. The rooms come with a host of modern amenities, and all the bathrooms have bathtubs with showers.

See map p. 314. Chapel Street, Stratford-upon-Avon, Warwickshire CV37 6ER. ☎ *0870/400-8182. Fax: 01789/415-411.* www.macdonaldhotels.co.uk. *Rack rates: £138–£158 ($255–$292) double. Rates include English breakfast. AE, DC, MC, V.*

Thistle Stratford-upon-Avon
$$–$$$

If this hotel were any closer to the Royal Shakespeare Festival theaters, the guests would be on stage. Thistle is a British chain of full-service hotels, offering comfortable if somewhat dowdy rooms (63 of them in this hotel) with an abundance of amenities. The building dates to 1791 and has been decorated to look like a traditional Georgian townhouse. Bards Restaurant serves good English and continental cuisine.

See map p. 314. Waterside, Stratford-upon-Avon, Warwickshire CV37 6BA. ☎ *800/ 847-4358 in U.S. and Canada or 01789/294-949. Fax: 01789/415-874.* www.thistle hotels.com. *Rack rates: £125–£170 ($231–$315) double. AE, DC, MC, V.*

Dining in Stratford-upon-Avon

As you may expect in a town that attracts visitors from around the globe, Stratford-upon-Avon isn't lacking in restaurants. I've listed my dining choices in this section, but don't hesitate to explore others on your own.

Hathaway Tea Rooms & Bakery
$ TEAS/LIGHT FARE

Come here to enjoy afternoon tea in atmospheric surroundings. The tea-rooms are on the second floor of a building that dates from 1610. Cream tea comes with homemade fruit scones, clotted cream, and jam, and high tea includes a variety of sandwiches. You can also get an English breakfast and light meals through the day.

See map p. 314. 19 High St. ☎ *01789/292-404. Main courses: £5.50–£7.50 ($10–$14); cream teas: £4.50 ($8.35); high teas: £6.20 ($11). No credit cards. Open: Daily 9 a.m.–5:30 p.m.*

Lambs of Sheep Street
$$ MODERN BRITISH

Although it's in one of Stratford's oldest buildings, with low ceilings and timber framing, Lamb's serves Modern British cooking with flair. Typical menu offerings include roasted saddle of lamb, duck breast with cabbage and potatoes, and nonmeat choices such as open ravioli with sautéed wild mushrooms or tomato risotto with grilled vegetables and pesto.

See map p. 314. 12 Sheep St. ☎ *01789/292-554. Reservations recommended. Main courses: £10–£17 ($19–$31); fixed-price lunch and dinner: £15–£20 ($28–$37). AE, MC, V. Open: Daily noon–2 p.m.; Mon–Sat 5–10 p.m., Sun 6–9:30 p.m.*

Marlowe's Restaurant & Georgie's Bistro
$–$$$$ BRITISH/MODERN BRITISH

These adjoining eateries share an Elizabethan townhouse. Marlowe's is the classier "silver service" restaurant. The bar, where a fire blazes in winter, leads to an oak-paneled dining room where you can sample specialties such as Drunken Duck (duck marinated in gin, red wine, cracked pepper, and juniper berries). In summer, you can dine on the patio. For a relaxed, informal meal, ask to be seated at Georgie's, the bistro area. Try fish and chips or pork and leek sausages.

See map p. 314. 18 High St. ☎ *01789/204-999. Reservations required for Marlowe's. Main courses: Marlowe's £13–£21 ($24–$39), Georgie's £7–£13 ($13–24); fixed-price lunch and dinner at Marlowe's: £20–£23 ($37–$43). AE, MC, V. Open: Daily noon–2 p.m. and 5:45–11 p.m.*

The Oppo
$$ BRITISH/INTERNATIONAL

This cozy, oak-beamed restaurant in a 16th-century building in the heart of Stratford serves good bistro fare. Lunch and dinner choices include a mix of traditional and Modern British cuisine, with some pasta dishes and Cajun breast of chicken. For dessert, you can't go wrong with the sticky toffee pudding, a traditional favorite.

See map p. 314. 13 Sheep St. ☎ *01789/269-980. Reservations recommended. Main courses: £9–£17 ($17–$31). MC, V. Open: Daily noon–2 p.m. and 5–11 p.m.*

Quarto's
$$–$$$ **BRITISH/CONTINENTAL**

This lovely restaurant in the Royal Shakespeare Theatre looks out on the River Avon, with its gliding white swans. The menu offers a bit of everything — on the daily-changing menu, you may find pot roast guinea fowl, roast cod, loin of pork, rib of beef, and stuffed baby peppers. The restaurant serves a special fixed-price lunch special on matinee days.

See map p. 314. In the Royal Shakespeare Theatre. ☎ 01789/293-226. Reservations required. Main courses: £15–£19 ($28–$35); fixed-price matinee lunch: £16 ($30). AE, MC, V. Open: Noon–2:30 p.m. on matinee days, Mon–Sat 5:45 p.m.–midnight.

Thai Boathouse
$–$$ **THAI**

This Thai restaurant above a boathouse with views of the River Avon is a fun and flavorful place to dine. Traditional Thai starters include chicken and beef satays, deep-fried spring rolls, or hot and sour soup. Pork, chicken, seafood, and vegetarian main courses are prepared with curries, herbs, and spices. The fixed-price meals are a good value.

See map p. 314. Swan's Nest Lane (on the river between Clopton Bridge and foot-bridge). ☎ 01789/297-733. Main courses: £8–£11 ($15–$20), fixed-price meals: £11–£20 ($20–$37). AE, MC, V. Open: Daily noon–2:30 p.m., 5:30–10:30 p.m.

Exploring the best of Stratford-upon-Avon

You can easily spend the better part of a day visiting the Shakespeare sights in Stratford.

One ticket gets you into the five sites administered by the **Shakespeare Birthplace Trust** (☎ **01789/201-807;** www.shakespeare.org.uk): Anne Hathaway's Cottage, Hall's Croft, Mary Arden's House, New Place/Nash's House, and Shakespeare's Birthplace. You can pick up the ticket at your first stop. This five-in-one ticket costs £13 ($24) for adults, £12 ($22) for seniors and students, £6.50 ($12) for children 5 to 15, and £29 ($54) for families (2 adults, 3 children). All the Shakespeare sites have access limitations, so visitors in wheelchairs may want to call ahead for more information.

To follow Shakespeare's life from birth to death, you can visit the sights in the order in which they appear in this section.

Shakespeare's Birthplace
Stratford-upon-Avon

The Bard, son of a glover and wool merchant, first saw the light of day on April 23, 1564, in this house, the logical place to begin your tour. You enter through the modern **Shakespeare Centre,** where you can spend a few minutes browsing the exhibits that illustrate his life and times. The house, filled with Shakespeare memorabilia, is actually two 16th-century half-timbered houses joined together: His father's shop was on one side and the family residence on the other. After visiting the bedroom where wee Willie was (probably) born, the Elizabethan kitchen, and other rooms, you can walk through the garden. You need at least 30 to 60 minutes for a thorough visit; be prepared for crowds.

See map p. 314. Henley Street. ☎ *01789/204-016. Admission: £6.70 ($12) adults, £5.50 ($10) seniors and students, £2.60 ($4.80) children 5–15, £15 ($28) families (2 adults, 3 children). Open: Daily Apr–May and Sept–Oct 10 a.m.–5 p.m.; June–Aug 9 a.m.–5 p.m. (Sun from 9:30 a.m.); Nov–Mar 10 a.m.–4 p.m. (Sun from 10:30 a.m.); closed Dec 24–26.*

Anne Hathaway's Cottage
Shottery

Anne Hathaway, who came from a family of *yeoman* farmers (farmers who owned and worked their own land), lived in this lovely thatched cottage until 1582, the year she married 18-year-old Shakespeare. (Anne was seven years older than Will.) Many original 16th-century furnishings, including the courting *settle* (a type of bench that courting couples sat on), are preserved inside the house, which Anne's descendents occupied until 1892. Before leaving, stroll through the beautiful garden and orchard. Allow about 30 minutes.

To visit the cottage, located about a mile south of Stratford, take a bus from Bridge Street, or better still, walk there along the well-marked country path from Evesham Place.

See map p. 314. Cottage Lane, Shottery. ☎ *01789/204-016. Admission: £5.20 ($9.60) adults, £4 ($7.40) seniors and students, £2 ($3.70) children 5–15, £12 ($22) families (2 adults, 3 children). Open: Daily Apr–May and Sept–Oct 9:30 a.m.–5 p.m. (Sun from 10 a.m.); June–Aug 9 a.m.–5 p.m. (Sun from 9:30 a.m.); Nov–Mar 10 a.m.–4 p.m.; closed Jan 1, Good Friday, and Dec 24–26.*

New Place/Nash's House
Stratford-upon-Avon

In 1610, Shakespeare was a relatively prosperous man whose plays had been seen by Queen Elizabeth. He retired to New Place, a Stratford house he had purchased a few years earlier and where he died in 1616. The house was later torn down. Of New Place, only the garden remains. You enter the garden through Nash's House, which belonged to Thomas Nash, husband of Shakespeare's granddaughter. The house contains 16th-century period rooms and an exhibit illustrating Stratford's history. A knot garden landscaped in an Elizabethan style with clipped boxwood borders adjoins the house. You can see the house and garden in 15 to 30 minutes.

To reach the site from Anne Hathaway's Cottage, retrace your steps to Shakespeare's Birthplace and then walk east on Henley Street and south on High Street, which becomes Chapel Street.

See map p. 314. Chapel Street. ☎ *01789/204-016. Admission: £3.50 ($6.50) adults, £3 ($5.55) seniors and students, £1.70 ($3.15) children 5–15, £9 ($17) families (2 adults, 3 children). Open: Daily Apr–May and Sept–Oct 11 a.m.–5 p.m.; June–Aug 9:30 a.m.– 5 p.m. (Sun from 10 a.m.); Nov–Mar 11 a.m.–4 p.m.; closed Dec 24–26.*

Hall's Croft
Stratford-upon-Avon

Shakespeare's daughter, Susanna, probably lived with her husband, Dr. John Hall, in this magnificent Tudor house with a walled garden. The house is furnished in the style of a middle-class 17th-century home. You can view exhibits illustrating the theory and practice of medicine in Dr. Hall's time. The word *croft,* by the way, means a small farm. You can see Hall's Croft in less than a half-hour. To get here from New Place, travel south on Chapel and Church streets, and turn east on Old Town.

You can take a convenient break from your Shakespeare pilgrimage at **Drucker's Cafe,** Old Town (☎ **01789/292-107**), a cozy, informal eatery attached to Hall's Croft. Sandwiches and homemade soup cost about £3 ($5.55), and a pot of tea runs £1.50 ($2.80). The cafe is open daily from 10 a.m. to 5 p.m. in summer, until 4 p.m. in winter.

See map p. 314. Old Town. ☎ 01789/292-107. Admission. £3.50 ($6.50) adults, £3 ($5.55) seniors and students, £1.70 ($3.15) children 5–15, £9 ($17) families (2 adults, 3 children). Open: Daily Apr–May and Sept–Oct 11 a.m.–5 p.m.; June–Aug 9:30 a.m.–5 p.m. (Sun from 10 a.m.); Nov–Mar 11 a.m.–4 p.m.; closed Dec 24–26.

Holy Trinity Church
Stratford-upon-Avon

Shakespeare died on his birthday (April 23), aged 52, and is buried in this beautiful parish church near the River Avon. His wife, Anne; his daughter, Susanna; and Susanna's husband, John Hall, lie beside him in front of the altar. A bust of the immortal Bard looks down on the gravesite. For a man who wrote some of the world's most enduring lines, his tomb's inscription is little more than trivial verse, ending with "and curst be he who moves my bones." Obviously, Shakespeare didn't want to leave Stratford — ever. You can visit the entire church in about 15 minutes. To reach the church from Hall's Croft, walk south to Southern Lane, which runs beside the River Avon, and follow it south to Trinity Street, where you can find a path to the church.

See map p. 314. Old Town. ☎ 01789/266-316. Admission: Church free, Shakespeare's tomb £1 ($1.85). Open: Mar–Oct Mon–Sat 8:30 a.m.–6 p.m., Nov–Feb Mon–Sat 8:30 a.m.– 4 p.m.; year-round Sun 2–5 p.m.

Mary Arden's House & Shakespeare Countryside Museum
Wilmcote

For more than 200 years, Palmers Farm, a Tudor farmstead with an old stone dovecote and outbuildings, was identified as the girlhood home of Mary Arden, Shakespeare's mother. Recent evidence revealed, however, that Mary Arden actually lived in the house next door, at Glebe Farm. In 2000, the house at Glebe Farm was officially designated the Mary Arden House. Dating from 1514, this house contains country furniture and domestic utensils; in the barns, stable, cowshed, and farmyard, you can see an extensive collection of farm implements illustrating life and work in the local countryside from Shakespeare's time to the present.

For a leisurely look at everything, give yourself about 45 minutes.

To reach this last Shakespeare shrine, drive north to Wilmcote on A34. The house is also a stop on the City Sightseeing bus tour (see "Getting around and touring Stratford-upon-Avon," earlier in this chapter).

See map p. 314. Wilmcote (about 5.5km/3½ miles north of Stratford on A34). ☎ *01789/ 204-016. Admission: £5.70 ($11) adults, £5 ($9.25) seniors and students, £2.50 ($4.65) children 5–15, £14 ($26) families (2 adults, 3 children). Open: Daily Apr–May and Sept–Oct 10 a.m.–5 p.m.; June–Aug 9:30 a.m.–5 p.m.; Nov–Mar 10 a.m.–4 p.m.; closed Dec 24–26.*

Finding more to see and do in Stratford-upon-Avon

Most people come to Stratford to see the Shakespeare sites. If you have the kids with you, and old houses bore them silly, here are a handful of alternative attractions that they can enjoy:

- ✔ **Avon Boating,** Swan's Nest Boatyard, Swan's Nest Lane (☎ **01789/ 267-073**): Offers half-hour boat trips on the Avon River from April to October. Boats depart daily, approximately every 20 minutes, from 10 a.m. to 5 p.m. The trip costs £3.50 ($6.50) for adults and £2 ($3.70) for children.

- ✔ **Butterfly Farm,** Tramway Walk, Swan's Nest Lane (☎ **01789/299- 288**): An enclosed greenhouse filled with hundreds of colorful, free-flying butterflies. You can discover various insect displays amid the tropical plants and flowers of a re-created rainforest. Besides the butterflies, kids enjoy seeing forest insects and spiders. Admission costs £4.75 ($8.80) for adults, £4.25 ($7.85) for seniors and students, £3.75 ($6.95) for children 5 to 15, and £14 ($26) for families (2 adults, 2 children). The farm is open daily from 10 a.m. to 6 p.m. in the summer and from 10 a.m. to dusk in the winter.

- ✔ **Shakespearience,** Waterside Theatre, Waterside (☎ **01789/290- 111**): Stratford's newest attraction presents the life and works of Shakespeare in a unique way by using show technology and special effects. The one-hour show includes information about the Bard of Stratford and dramatic highlights from nine of his best-loved plays. Tickets cost £7.25 ($13) for adults; £6.25 ($12) for seniors, students, and children under 12; and £23 ($43) for families (2 adults and 2 children). Shakespearience is open daily (except Christmas) from 10 a.m. to 5 p.m. (11 a.m.–4 p.m. in winter).

- ✔ **Stratford Brass Rubbing Centre,** Avon Bank Gardens, Southern Lane (☎ **01789/297-671**): This center has dozens of interesting replica brasses from English churches and provides all the materials that you need to make an on-the-spot rubbing for £1 to £20 ($1.85–$37). You can easily create a brass rubbing (and have fun doing it), even if you're not exactly an artist. To make a brass rubbing, you rub a hard wax crayon over paper covering the memorial brass; the impression that you make is the *rubbing*. The center is open daily from 10 a.m. to 6 p.m. in the summer and Saturday and Sunday from 11 a.m. to 4 p.m. in the winter.

Seeing a play in Stratford-upon-Avon

The **Royal Shakespeare Theatre,** Waterside, Stratford-upon-Avon CV37 6BB (☎ **01789/403-403;** www.rsc.org.uk), is the home of the prestigious **Royal Shakespeare Company,** which typically stages five Shakespeare plays during a season running from November to September. The company performs the plays in the Festival Theatre, which has a *proscenium stage* (a traditional stage), or in The Swan, a *thrust stage* (a stage that extends into the audience) with side galleries. Although demand depends on the play, you should order your tickets at least two to three weeks in advance. The theater always holds a few tickets for sale on the day of a performance, but you may not get a good seat if you wait till the last minute. The box office is open Monday through Saturday from 9 a.m. to 8 p.m. but closes at 6 p.m. on days when no performances are scheduled. Ticket prices are £5 to £45 ($9.25–$83). You can book tickets online through the Royal Shakespeare Company Web site.

Shopping in Stratford-upon-Avon

Stratford's weekly **Market,** held on Friday, dates back over 800 years. The **Shakespeare Bookshop,** in the Shakespeare Centre, Henley Street (☎ **01789/201-819**), is the region's best bookshop for Shakespeare-related material. The nearby **Pickwick Gallery,** 32 Henley St. (☎ **01789/294-861**), carries a wide variety of old and new engravings. **Elaine Rippon Craft Gallery,** Shakespeare Craft Yard off Henley Street (☎ **01789/415-481**), designs, creates, and sells sumptuous silk and velvet accessories, and carries fine British contemporary crafts.

Warwick Castle: Warlords and Ladies

The ancient county town of Warwick (pronounced *War*-ick) sits on a rocky hill on the north side of the River Avon, about 13km (8 miles) northeast of Stratford. Although you can explore some intriguing old streets in the town, most visitors come here with one goal in mind: to visit mighty Warwick Castle, one of England's most popular tourist attractions. Dramatically sited above the river on the town's south side, the castle is a splendid example of a medieval fortress that's been adapted over the centuries to reflect its inhabitants' tastes and ambitions.

Give yourself at least three hours to visit the castle and the lovely gardens and parkland around it; if you want to wander through the town, add an hour or two.

Warwick Castle was built as a medieval fortress and, as such, has a large number of steps and narrow doorways, which present limitations for mobility-restricted visitors. Travelers with disabilities are encouraged to call first or check the Web site, www.warwick-castle.co.uk, for more information.

Getting to Warwick

The castle sits right in the center of Warwick, a 15-minute walk from the train or bus station. **Stagecoach** (☎ **0870/608-2608**) provides direct bus service from Stratford for £3.70 ($6.85) round-trip; the trip takes about 15 minutes. **Chiltern Railways** (☎ **08705/165-165**) runs direct trains to Stratford and Warwick from London's Marylebone station; the trip takes one hour and 45 minutes and costs about £30 ($56) for a round trip. **National Express** (☎ **0990/808-080**) offers daily bus service between Victoria Coach Station in London and Warwick; the two-hour-and-45-minute trip costs £40 ($74) round trip. National Express also runs buses to Warwick from Riverside bus station in Stratford-upon-Avon. By car from Stratford, take Junction 15 off the M40, and continue for 3km (2 miles).

Dining at Warwick Castle

Being robbed by a highwayman wasn't an uncommon experience for travelers 200 years ago. At Warwick Castle's **Highwayman's Supper,** guests hear the highwayman's side of the story. The themed event's setting is the castle in the 18th century on a night when the Earl of Warwick is away, and the castle housekeeper gives the guests a private viewing of the staterooms. Afterward, in the coach house, a five-course meal is served (with unlimited wine, ale, or soft drinks), accompanied by 18th-century music, dancing, and bawdy tall tales. The castle holds a Highwayman's Supper most Fridays and Saturdays throughout the year and nightly (except Sun) in December until Christmas. The supper costs £45 ($83) per person (slightly higher during Dec). For reservations and further information, call ☎ **01926/406-602**. *Note:* This event is unsuitable for guests under 18 years of age.

Exploring Warwick Castle

You can explore the entire castle complex, but save most of your time — at least one hour — to wander through the **Private Apartments.** In these rooms, you encounter lifelike figures that are part of an exhibition called the Royal Weekend Party. In 1898, the Countess of Warwick hosted a weekend party for Edward, Prince of Wales, later Edward VII. A century later, the wax artists at Madame Tussauds created likenesses of the guests, including a twentysomething Winston Churchill (seen leafing through a book in the **Library**) and the Duke of York, later George V (seen lighting a cigarette in the **Card Room**). Upstairs, their hostess (known to her friends as Daisy) is dressing for dinner, and so are some of her guests, including Consuelo, Duchess of Marlborough (a member of the Vanderbilt family); Lord Curzon (Viceroy of India); and the Countess' special guest, the future King Edward VII. All the room settings are meticulous re-creations that use original furniture from the time of the party. The **Chapel** and **State Rooms**

are next to the Private Apartments. The 16th-century **Great Hall** is the longest (99m/330 ft.) and largest of the rooms on view. The hall overlooks the river and has a collection of arms and armor. The other rooms were mostly decorated from 1770 to 1790. The **Cedar Room** has Van Dyke portraits, and paintings by Velasquez and Rubens hang in the Red Drawing Room.

Several exhibitions use sound and light effects and wax figures to tell stories about the castle. **Death or Glory** regales you with the story of former resident Richard Neville, "the Kingmaker," preparing for battle. Another, in the **Ghost Tower,** tells of the murder of Fulke Greville, one of the castle's owners. After visiting the very depressing **dungeon,** you may want to walk along the castle **ramparts** for a breath of fresh air. The castle overlooks beautiful parkland and **gardens** laid out by Capability Brown, one of the greatest landscape gardeners of 18th-century England. Peacocks roam freely through the grounds, and the River Avon runs through them.

Warwick. ☎ *0870/442-2000. Admission (price is slightly less in low season): £15 ($28) adults, £11 ($20) seniors and students, £9 ($17) children 5–15, £42 ($78) families (2 adults, 2 children). Open: Daily Apr–Sept 10 a.m.–6 p.m.; Oct–Mar 10 a.m.–5 p.m.*

History and architecture of Warwick Castle

Warwick Castle reflects more than a thousand years of turbulent English history. The castle was the ancestral home of the Earls of Warwick, key players in medieval England's brutal political conflicts — not the sort of guys you want messing with you. One of them, Richard Neville (known as "the Kingmaker"), was so powerful that he helped depose both Henry VI and Edward IV. Another Earl of Warwick executed Joan of Arc.

For their family stronghold, the earliest earls chose a strategic site first fortified by the Saxons and later, in 1068, by the Normans. About three centuries later, the 11th Earl of Warwick expanded the Norman stronghold into the enormous walled and turreted fortress that visitors see today. When James I granted the castle to Sir Fulke Greville in 1604, the new owner spent a fortune converting the inner buildings into a luxurious mansion. Extensive restorations were made after a disastrous fire in 1871. Lord Brooke, the most recent owner, sold the ancestral mansion to the owners of Madame Tussauds wax museum, who have added some entertainment features.

Architecturally, the castle marks the transitional period between the formidable but dreary strongholds of medieval England and the more domestic fortified houses that replaced them. The massive outer walls and defense towers date to the 14th century. From the Porter's Lodge (1800), a winding path cut in the solid rock leads to a double gateway between two massive towers. In the grassy inner court, you can see the Bear and Clarence Towers on the right, a castle–mound (all that's left from Norman times) rising in front, and the domestic buildings on the left.

Finding more to see and do in Warwick

I don't recommend staying overnight in Warwick, but you may want to stroll through town to check out the buildings in this list:

✔ **Lord Leycester Hospital** (☎ **01926/491-422**): Established in 1571 by Robert Dudley, Earl of Leicester (a favorite of Queen Elizabeth I), this marvelous grouping of half-timbered almshouses leans against the old West Gate. The hospital buildings, some dating from around 1400, give you a good picture of what buildings in the town looked like before a fire destroyed most of them in 1694. If you spot someone wearing a black cape with a silver pendant in the shape of a boar, he's one of the Brethren (retired servicemen) who live at the hospital and welcome visitors. Inside, you can visit the beautiful galleried **courtyard,** the **Great Hall** and magnificent **Guildhall,** and the **Chaplains' Dining Hall.** In the wonderfully atmospheric Brethren's Kitchen, with stone floors and exposed oak beams, you can get a good afternoon tea for about £5 ($9.25). Admission costs £3.50 ($6.50) adults, £3 ($5.55) seniors, and £2.50 ($4.65) children. The hospital is open Tuesday through Sunday from 10 a.m. to 4 p.m. (5 p.m. in winter).To get to the hospital from Warwick Castle, follow Castle Street up the hill to High Street, and turn left.

✔ **St. Mary's Church** (☎ **01926/403-940**): This church (on Church Street) had to rebuild its tower and nave after the great fire of 1694. Spared by the fire was the Beauchamp Chantry, the location of a famous gilded bronze tomb effigy of Richard Beauchamp, a powerful Earl of Warwick who died in 1439. (A *chantry,* by the way, is a chapel endowed by a family for the chanting of Masses, usually for the chapel's principal founder.) The tomb of Robert Dudley is against the north wall. The church, less than a five-minute walk from Warwick Castle, is open daily from 10 a.m. to 6 p.m. (Nov–Mar until 4 p.m.).

Chapter 20

Bath and the Best of the Cotswolds

In This Chapter

▶ Basking in Bath

▶ Checking out Cheltenham

▶ Exploring charming Cotswolds villages

▶ Strolling through Cirencester

The Cotswold Hills occupy a region in central England that's been inhabited for some 6,000 years. Tucked into this gentle landscape, you can find prehistoric mounds, the remains of Roman villas, magnificent gardens, old manor houses, and amazingly preserved towns that grew rich on Cotswold wool during the Middle Ages. For hundreds of years, merchants came from London and as far away as Florence to buy Cotswold fleeces for shipment around the world.

This area of grassy limestone hills, woodlands, cool green ravines, and high open plateaus (known as *wolds*) is roughly bordered by Bath to the south, Oxford to the east, Stratford-upon-Avon to the north, and Cheltenham to the west. This area isn't large: From north to south, the Cotswolds stretch some 126km (78 miles). More than 80 percent of the land is still farmland; a network of distinctive dry stone walls marks the fields.

Many people enjoy touring the Cotswolds. They visit the medieval villages just to stroll around, shop (the Cotswolds have more antiques stores than anywhere else in England), and have an afternoon cream tea. Although the region has many lovely villages, in this chapter, I include only the ones that hold the most interest for casual village-hoppers: **Bourton-on-the-Water, Upper and Lower Slaughter, Broadway,** and **Chipping Campden. Bath,** which starts this chapter, is a must-see city even if you don't plan to tour the Cotswolds. Other worthwhile stops include the smaller cities of **Cheltenham** and **Cirencester.**

(Fairford)

Visitors on a tight schedule won't find the public transportation options in the Cotswolds very useful. You can best explore this area by car. Otherwise, getting from one village to the next is difficult.

Bath: Hot Mineral Springs and Cool Georgian Splendor

Bath, 185km (115 miles) west of London, sits on the doorstep of the Cotswolds but not quite in them (see the "Bath" map on p. 327). Plan to devote at least a day to this beautiful spa town on the River Avon. Bath makes a good base for exploring the region, though you can also visit on a day trip from London.

In ancient times, the area was known far and wide for its hot mineral springs, which drew the Celts and later the Romans, who settled here in A.D. 75 and built a huge bath complex to soak their weary bones. Centuries later, in 1702, Queen Anne dipped her royal bod into the soothing sulfurous waters and sparked a trend that transformed Bath into an ultrafashionable spa. Aristocrats, socialites, social climbers, and flamboyant dandies like Beau Nash held sway. Jane Austen, a demure visitor, used Bath as an upwardly genteel setting for her class-conscious novels.

Filled with remarkable curving *crescents* (row houses built in a long, curving line) and classically inspired buildings built of toffee-colored stone, the town you see today is a fabulous legacy from the Georgian era. Its architectural legacy is so important that UNESCO named Bath a World Heritage Site. For more on the city's architecture, see the sidebar "Building blocks of history: Bath," later in this chapter.

Getting to Bath

Trains for Bath leave from London's Paddington Station every 30 minutes, and the trip lasts about 90 minutes. Standard round-trip fare costs £35 ($65). **National Express** (☎ 08705/808-080; www.nationalexpress.com) runs frequent buses from London's Victoria Coach Station. Depending on departure time, the trip takes three to four hours; round-trip ("day return") fare costs £16 ($30). By car, take the M4 to Junction 18 and then drive a few miles south on A46.

Bath is one of the most convenient places for renting a car to tour the Cotswolds. Car-rental agencies in town include the following:

- ✔ **Arrows Self-Drive Hire,** Claverton Buildings, Widecombe, ☎ 01225/422-262

- ✔ **Avis,** Riverside Business Park, ☎ 01225/446-680

- ✔ **Enterprise,** Riverside Business Park, ☎ 01225/443-311

Bath

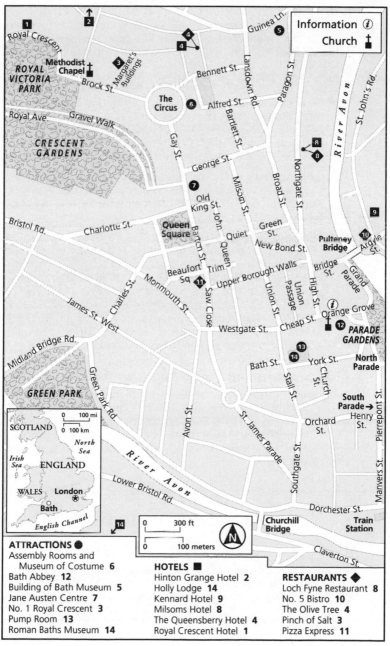

Information ⓘ
Church ✝

ATTRACTIONS ●
Assembly Rooms and
 Museum of Costume **6**
Bath Abbey **12**
Building of Bath Museum **5**
Jane Austen Centre **7**
No. 1 Royal Crescent **3**
Pump Room **13**
Roman Baths Museum **14**

HOTELS ■
Hinton Grange Hotel **2**
Holly Lodge **14**
Kennard Hotel **9**
Milsoms Hotel **8**
The Queensberry Hotel **4**
Royal Crescent Hotel **1**

RESTAURANTS ◆
Loch Fyne Restaurant **8**
No. 5 Bistro **10**
The Olive Tree **4**
Pinch of Salt **3**
Pizza Express **11**

Finding information and taking a tour of Bath

Bath's **Tourist Information Centre** (☎ **01225/477-101;** www.visitbath. co.uk), on the town square in front of Bath Abbey, has a currency exchange and room-finding service. The center is open Monday through Saturday from 9:30 a.m. to 5 p.m. and Sunday from 10:30 a.m. to 4 p.m.

If you want to take a tour of Bath, you have the following options:

✔ **Free guided walks:** The Tourist Information Centre offers these tours around Bath. The walks leave from outside the Pump Room, adjacent to the center, daily at 10:30 a.m., plus Sunday through Friday at 2 p.m. From May through September, the center offers an additional evening walk at 7 on Tuesday, Friday, and Saturday.

✔ **Jane Austen's Bath:** The Tourist Information Centre also gives this walk, which departs from the center daily at 1:30 p.m. in July and August and on Saturday and Sunday only the rest of the year. The tour costs £3.50 ($6.50).

✔ **The Bath Tour: City Tour** (☎ **07721/559-686**) presents one-hour open-top bus tours with live guides and plenty of commentary. This tour costs £6.50 ($12) for adults and £4.50 ($8.35) for seniors and students. **City Sightseeing** (☎ **01871/666-0000**) offers basically the same tour but with audio commentary at a cost of £9 ($17) for adults, £6.50 ($12) for seniors and students, and £4.50 ($8.35) for children. Tours for both companies depart from the bus station every 15 minutes in summer, hourly the rest of the year. Tickets are valid all day, and you can get off and on to explore places along the route.

Exchanging money and locating ATMs

You can change money at the **Tourist Information Centre** in the center of town (☎ **01225/477-101**); at **American Express,** 5 Bridge St. (☎ **01225/444-767**); and at **Marks & Spencer,** 16–19 Stall St. (☎ **01225/462-591**). The following banks have 24-hour cash machines: **Barclays** on Manvers Street, **HSBC** on Milson Street, **Lloyds** on Milson Street, and **NatWest** on High Street.

Special events in Bath

Bath's Regency (1714–1830) buildings provide wonderful settings for performances during the **International Music Festival** in mid-May and the **Mozartfest** in November. In March, the city hosts a well-known **Literature Festival.** For information on these events, contact the **Bath Festival's Box Office,** 2 Church St., Abbey Green, Bath BA1 1NL (☎ **01225/463-362**), or check out the city's Web site at www.visitbath.co.uk.

Staying in and around Bath

Beautiful Bath has plenty of hotels and B&Bs.

Hinton Grange Hotel
$$–$$$ Hinton

This hotel appeals to romantics looking for a special hideaway in the southern Cotswolds countryside. A 15th-century farmhouse, barns, and stables were converted to make this classy hotel, situated on 6 acres of parkland. With low beams, stone walls, blazing fires, and candlelight in the lounges and dining rooms, the atmosphere is Olde English all the way. Most of the 19 guest rooms are large, with open coal fireplaces, beamed ceilings, Victorian bathing alcoves, antique decor, and terraces opening into the grounds.

See map p. 327. Hinton, near Dyrham (from Bath, take A46 north to Dyrham exit), Somerset SN14 8HG. ☎ *0117/937-2916. Fax: 0117/937-3285.* www.hinton grange.co.uk. *Rack rates: £120–£170 ($222–$315) double. Rates include English breakfast. AE, DC, MC, V. No children under 14.*

Holly Lodge
$ Bath

This skillfully converted townhouse B&B has plenty of charm. All seven cozy, nonsmoking bedrooms have private bathrooms. Each one is individually furnished, and two have four-poster beds. Breakfast is served in a pretty conservatory.

See map p. 327. 8 Upper Oldfield Park, Bath, Somerset BA2 3JZ. ☎ *01225/424-042. Fax: 01225/481-138.* www.hollylodge.co.uk. *Rack rates: £48–£97 ($89–$179) double. Rates include English breakfast. AE, DC, MC, V.*

Kennard Hotel
$$ Bath

On the east side of Pulteney Bridge, within walking distance of everything in Bath, this elegant hotel with 14 guest rooms occupies a beautifully restored Georgian townhouse from 1794. All the rooms are individually furnished to a high standard, have their own bathrooms, and offer an abundance of amenities

See map p. 327. 11 Henrietta St., Bath, Somerset BA2 6LL. ☎ *01225/310-472. Fax: 01225/460-054.* www.kennard.co.uk. *Rack rates: £98–£118 ($181–$218) double. Rates include English breakfast. AE, MC, V.*

Milsoms Hotel
$–$$ Bath

Located above the Loch Fyne restaurant (see the review in the section "Dining in Bath," later in this chapter), Milsoms offers a great location, good value, and a kind of unique charm. Each of the nine rooms has been individually decorated with a fresh, contemporary look. Note: You have to climb a fairly steep flight of stairs to get to the reception area; the hotel doesn't have an elevator.

See map p. 327. 24 Milsom St., Bath, Somerset BA1 1DG. ☎ **01225/750-128.** *Fax: 01225/750-129.* www.milsomshotel.co.uk. *Rack rates: £85–£115 ($157–$213) double. Rates include English breakfast. AE, DC, MC, V.*

The Queensberry Hotel
$$–$$$$$ Bath

A large Georgian townhouse built in 1772, the Queensberry occupies a prime position near the Assembly Rooms and the Royal Crescent, two major attractions. The 29 rooms in this stylish boutique hotel are decorated with flair and comfort. For information on the hotel's award-winning restaurant, The Olive Tree, see the section "Dining in Bath," later in this chapter.

See map p. 327. Russel Street, Bath, Somerset BA1 2QF. ☎ **01225/447-928.** *Fax: 01225/446-065.* www.thequeensberry.co.uk. *Rack rates: £145–£295 ($268–$546) double. AE, DC, MC, V.*

Royal Crescent Hotel
$$$$$ Bath

"Sumptuous" is the only word to describe this hotel, which occupies part of Bath's most famous crescent. Every room is different, and all have been furnished in an elegant style that's in keeping with the building's historical character. You can visit an on-site spa with a heated pool, and an award-winning restaurant, Pimpernel's, for fine dining. If you want to splurge in Bath, this hotel is your best choice.

See map p. 327. 16 Royal Crescent, Bath, Somerset BA1 2LS. ☎ **01225/823-333.** *Fax: 01225/339-401.* www.royalcrescent.co.uk. *Rack rates: £290 ($537) double. AE, DC, MC, V.*

Dining in Bath

Bath's sophisticated dining scene features many cuisines. Here are my favorite places to eat.

Loch Fyne Restaurant
$–$$$ SEAFOOD

Loch Fyne is a seafood restaurant chain, and quite a good one. You can find a selection of seasonal oysters and mussels; smoked salmon; and seafood main courses such as Cornish monkfish Caesar salad, roast fillet of cod, poached smoked haddock, and traditional fish pie. The menu also features vegetarian dishes. With its high ceilings, marble pillars, and natural wooden floors and furniture, this restaurant gives you an attractive place to dine.

See map p. 327. 24 Milsom St. ☎ **01225/750-120.** *Reservations recommended. Main courses: £8–£25 ($15–$46). AE, MC, V. Open: Sun–Thurs noon–10 p.m. Fri–Sat noon–11 p.m.*

No. 5 Bistro
$$ FRENCH

This pleasant, smoke-free bistro in the city center is decorated with bright prints, plants, and candles. The varied daily menu may include baked ricotta with olive, spinach, and sun-dried tomato soufflé; Provençal fish soup; chargrilled loin of lamb; or vegetarian dishes, such as roast stuffed peppers and vegetable gratin.

See map p. 327. 5 Argyle St. ☎ **01225/444-499.** *Reservations recommended. Main courses: £14–£16 ($26–$30); fixed-price lunch: £6.95 ($13); fixed-price dinner: £8.95 ($17). AE, MC, V. Open: Daily noon to 2:30 p.m. and 6:30–10 p.m.*

The Olive Tree
$$ INTERNATIONAL

This popular hotel restaurant has a Mediterranean ambience and a menu drawn from all over the globe. You can find dishes such as crispy pig's cheek salad, roast breast of rabbit with potato cakes, and pan-fried sea bass with baked butternut squash and *pancella* dressing. For dessert, try almond and cherry steamed sponge cake.

See map p. 327. Queensberry Hotel, Russel St. (just north of Assembly Rooms). ☎ **01225/447-928.** *Reservations recommended. Main courses: £16–£23 ($30–$43); fixed-price lunch: £16 ($30). AE, DC, MC, V. Open: Tues–Sun noon to 2 p.m.; daily 7–10 p.m.*

Pinch of Salt
$–$$$ MODERN FRENCH

A delightful bistro with stone floors and orange walls covered with art, Pinch of Salt is a casual place where you can dine really well on delicious French cuisine. Traditional ingredients and masterful preparation go into the creation of daily-changing dishes, such as lasagna of creamed oyster mushrooms, spinach and asparagus with black truffle salad, or wild sea bass with orange-scented couscous. The wine list is reasonably priced.

See map p. 327. 11 Margarets Buildings (off Brock Street). ☎ **01225/421-251.** *Reservations recommended. Main courses: £13–£17 ($24–$31); fixed-price lunch: £10 ($19). MC, V. Open: Mon–Sat noon–2:30 p.m. and 7–10:30 p.m.*

Pizza Express
$ PIZZA/PASTA

If you're looking for a kid-friendly restaurant in Bath, head to Pizza Express. The service is relaxed and friendly; kids get crayons and paper; and the pizzas are great. The menu doesn't feature anything particularly spectacular or showy, but the food is consistently good.

See map p. 327. 1–3 Barton St. ☎ **01225/420-119.** *Main courses: £7–£13 ($13–$24). AE, MC, V. Open: Daily 11:30 a.m.–midnight.*

Exploring Bath

Bath's legacy of architecture from the Regency era (1811–1830) is so important that the city is a UNESCO World Heritage Site. To view the historic buildings and visit the sights, you can easily walk everywhere in this compact town. If you're interested in guided walks or a bus tour, see the section "Finding information and taking a tour of Bath," earlier in this chapter.

Assembly Rooms and Museum of Costume

A classic building worth visiting is the Assembly Rooms, the site of all the grand balls and social climbing in 18th-century Bath. The complex houses the excellent Museum of Costume, where you can see just what those dandies and their ladies wore. You can walk through the Assembly Rooms in just a few minutes; allow a half-hour if you're also visiting the Museum of Costume.

See map p. 327. Bennett Street. ☎ **01225/477-785.** *Admission: Assembly Rooms free; museum £6.25 ($12) adults, £5.25 ($9.70) seniors and students, £4.25 ($7.85) children 6–18, £17 ($31) families (2 adults, 2 children). Open: Museum daily 10 a.m.–5 p.m.; closed Dec 25 and 26; Assembly Rooms sometimes closed for private functions.*

Bath Abbey

The 18th-century abbey dominates the adjacent town square. Step inside for a look at the graceful fan vaulting; the great east window; and the unexpectedly simple memorial to Beau Nash, the most flamboyant of the dandies who frequented Bath in its heyday.

See map p. 327. Abbey Church Yard. ☎ **01225/422-462.** *Admission: £2.50 ($4.65). Open: Mon–Sat 9 a.m.–6 p.m. (Nov–Mar until 4:30 p.m.); Sun 1–2:30 p.m. and 4:30–5:30pm.*

Bridges, Crescents, Circuses, and Parades

Bath was built for promenading. Filled with beautiful squares and sweeping residential crescents, it remains a wonderful town for walking. Stroll along the **North Parade** and the **South Parade, Queen Square** (where Jane Austen lived), and **The Circus.** Built in 1770 and inspired by Florence's Ponte Vecchio, **Pulteney Bridge** spans the River Avon a few blocks south of the Assembly Rooms. The bridge is one of the few in Europe lined with shops and restaurants.

Building blocks of history: Bath

Queen Anne sparked the royal enthusiasm for Bath's healing waters, but it wasn't until a few years later, during the Georgian and Regency eras (1714–1830), that Bath became one of the social hot spots of England. In about 100 years, what had been a small provincial spa town was transformed into one of Europe's most elegant cities. The extraordinary building boom created Bath's famous curving crescents of sumptuous townhouses, garden squares, and dozens of beautifully proportioned detached homes and public buildings. This period's architecture was unusually restrained (unlike many of the personalities); it's based on classical models and motifs that present harmonious and well-proportioned facades.

If you're interested in the architecture, stop in and spend an hour or so at the **Building of Bath Museum,** The Countess of Huntingdon's Chapel, The Vineyard (off Paragon Street; ☎ **01225/333-895**; see map p. 327). The museum examines the city's Georgian and Regency architecture and interiors. Exhibits detail the crafts used in the course of construction and introduce the architects who contributed to Bath's remarkable development. The museum is open mid-February through November Tuesday through Sunday from 10:30 a.m. to 5 p.m. Admission is £4 ($7.40) for adults, £3 ($5.55) for seniors and students, and £1.50 ($2.80) for children 5 to 15. To reach the museum from the Assembly Rooms, head east on Alfred Street and north on Paragon Street; you can see the museum on your left.

Jane Austen Centre

Truth be told, Jane Austen didn't really like Bath very much, but she was a keen observer and drew on it for her witty portraits of 18th-century society. In a Georgian townhouse on a street where she once lived, text-heavy exhibits and a video tell you more about the life and times of this brilliant daughter of a country pastor and convey a sense of what life was like in Bath during the Regency period. If you're an Austen fan, allow about 30 minutes for your visit. If you're not a fan, this rather dull place won't convert you.

See map p. 327. 40 Gay St. ☎ **01225/443-000.** *Admission: £5.95 ($11) adults, £4.50 ($8.35) seniors and students, £2.95 ($5.45) children, £16 ($30) families (2 adults, 2 children). Open: Daily 10 a.m.–5:30 p.m. (Nov–Feb until 4:30 p.m.).*

No. 1 Royal Crescent

The Royal Crescent is a magnificent, curving row of 30 townhouses regarded as the epitome of England's Palladian style (a classical style incorporating elements from ancient Greek and Roman buildings). John Wood the Younger designed the crescent in 1767. No. 1 Royal Crescent is a gorgeously restored 18th-century house with period furnishings. A tour of the interior gives you a vivid picture of how the elite lived during the Regency era. Allow about 30 minutes.

See map p. 327. Royal Crescent. ☎ *01225/428-126. Admission: £4 ($7.40) adults; £3.50 ($6.50) seniors, students, and children 6–16; £12 ($22) families (2 adults, 2 children). Open: Mid-Feb–Oct Tues–Sun 10:30 a.m.–5 p.m., Nov Tues–Sun 10:30 a.m.–4 p.m.; last admission a half-hour before closing. Closed Dec–mid-Feb.*

Pump Room

The Pump Room overlooks the Roman baths, and it was here in the late 18th century that the fashionable congregated to sip the waters. You can enter and taste the supposedly healthful liquid for yourself (but it's not Perrier). You can use the amusingly old-fashioned Pump Room for *elevenses* (morning coffee or tea), lunch, or afternoon tea, usually with live musical accompaniment. Main courses go for £9 to £10 ($17–$19); afternoon tea costs £6 to £8 ($11–$15).

See map p. 327. Stall Street. ☎ *01225/477-785. Admission: Free. Open: Daily Mar–June and Sept–Oct 9:30 a.m.–5 p.m., July–Aug 9:30 a.m.–10 p.m., Nov–Feb 10 a.m.–4:30 p.m.*

Roman Baths Museum

Ancient British tribes considered the hot, healing waters of Bath's mineral springs sacred, but the Romans built the enormous complex that forms the nucleus of this subterranean museum, one of Bath's most important attractions. Upon entering, you take a portable, self-guided audio tour keyed to everything on display, including the original Roman baths and heating system; the tour is informative, well done, and fun for children and adults. Give yourself about one hour to see the museum.

In July and August, you can visit the atmospheric Roman Baths Museum at night with a *torch* (Britspeak for flashlight).

See map p. 327. Pump Room, Stall Street (beside Bath Abbey). ☎ *01225/477-785. Admission: £9.50 ($18) adults, £8.50 ($16) seniors and students, £5.30 ($9.80) children 6–18, £25 ($46) families (2 adults, 2 children). Open: Daily Jan–Feb and Nov–Dec 9:30 a.m.–4:30 p.m., Mar–June and Sept–Oct 9:30 a.m.–5 p.m., July–Aug 9 a.m.–9 p.m.*

Cheltenham: A Little Bath

Like Bath, its more glamorous neighbor 64km (40 miles) to the south, Cheltenham was a spa town. Mineral springs were discovered in 1716, and people came to sip the healthy (but not very tasty) water. The first pump room was installed in 1742, but Cheltenham didn't become fashionable until 1788, when George III came to take a five-week "course" of the waters. The town still has its wide, leafy promenades; public gardens; and pretty Regency-era architecture. Although technically falling just outside the boundaries of the Cotswolds, Cheltenham is a good town in which to base yourself for exploring the region. Here, you find plenty of hotels, cafes, and some fine restaurants, plus good shopping and far fewer tourists than in Bath. Considered the cultural center of the Cotswolds, Cheltenham hosts two major international events: the **Cheltenham Festival of Literature** in May and the **International Festival of Music** in early July (☎ **01242/227-979;** www.cheltenhamfestivals.co.uk).

Getting to Cheltenham

Trains run frequently from London's Paddington Station to Cheltenham Spa, Cheltenham's small train station. Some trains run direct; others require a change at Swindon or Bristol Parkway. The trip on a direct train takes two hours and costs £29 ($54) for an advance-purchase round trip. For train information, call ☎ **08457/484-950. National Express** (☎ **08705/808-080**) runs several buses a day from Victoria Coach Station in London to the Royal Well bus station in the center of Cheltenham. The trip takes three to five hours; round-trip fare costs £24 ($44). National Express also runs buses to Cheltenham from Oxford (a 90-minute trip) and Stratford-upon-Avon (a one-hour trip). If you come by car, Cheltenham is close to Junction 11 of the M5; the town is 66km (41 miles) west of Oxford on A40.

Traveling among the local villages

You can get from Cheltenham to several of the Cotswolds villages on buses; ask for the pamphlet "Getting There by Public Transportation" in the Cheltenham tourist office (see the following section). **Pulhams Coaches** (☎ **01451/820-369**) is the area's most useful bus service, running daily between Cheltenham and Bourton-on-the-Water (see the section "Bourton-on-the-Water: Bridges on the Windrush," later in this chapter).

Finding information and taking a tour of Cheltenham

The **Tourist Information Centre,** 77 Promenade (☎ **01242/522-878;** www.visitcheltenham.gov.uk), has many useful brochures on the town and Cotswolds region. You can book accommodations in the office or by calling ☎ **01242/517-110.** The center is open Monday to Saturday from 9:30 a.m. to 5:15 p.m.

From about June 12 through September 12, the Tourist Information Centre offers guided walking tours of Regency-era Cheltenham, pointing out the best of the town's fine architecture and floral decorations. The tours depart at 11 a.m. Monday to Friday, last about one-and-a-quarter hours, and cost £3 ($5.55).

The train station is about 1.6km (1 mile) from the town center. You can walk everywhere or call a taxi (☎ **01242/580-580**).

Staying in Cheltenham

Here are my recommended choices for staying in Cheltenham.

Hotel on the Park
$$ Pittville Park

I highly recommend this immaculate hotel overlooking Pittville Park just north of the town center. The hotel is in a beautifully restored 1830s villa, and each of the 12 guest rooms has been carefully designed and furnished. The feeling throughout is intimate and opulent but not at all stuffy.

38 Evesham Rd., Cheltenham, Glos GL52 2AH. ☎ **01242/518-898.** www.hotelon thepark.co.uk. *Rack rates: £114–£144 ($211–$266) double. AE, DC, MC, V.*

Lawn Hotel
$ Pittville Park

Located just inside the iron gates leading to Pittville Park, this nonsmoking B&B caters to vegetarians and vegans. The B&B has nine high-ceilinged rooms, four with private bathrooms and one with a four-poster bed. The house dates from the 1840s and has many nice touches.

5 Pittville Lawn, Cheltenham, Glos GL52 2BE. ☎ *and fax* **01242/526-638.** *Rack rates: £45–£50 ($83–$93) double. No credit cards.*

Parkview
$ Town center

This friendly B&B is in a row of Regency townhouses off Albert Road. The B&B has three large guest rooms, but only one has a private bathroom (with shower). The other two rooms share a bathroom with an enormous tub and shower. Families with children are welcome.

4 Pittville Crescent, Cheltenham, Glos GL52 2QZ. ☎ **01242/575-567.** *Rack rates: £45–£55 ($83–$102) double. Rates include English breakfast. No credit cards.*

Dining in Cheltenham
Cheltenham has several good restaurants. Here are three of the best.

The Daffodil
$$ MODERN BRITISH

This very hip restaurant was created from an Art Deco movie palace and looks like the gleaming set of a Busby Berkeley musical. The food is good but not surprising, and sometimes the ambience trumps the meal. For main courses, you can find steak, kidney, and Guinness (stout) pie topped with an oyster; roasted rack of lamb; and Mediterranean vegetable tart.

18–20 Suffolk Parade. ☎ **01242/700-055.** *Reservations recommended for dinner. Main courses: £11–£17 ($20–$31); fixed-price meals: £10–£30 ($19–$56). AE, DC, MC, V. Open: Mon–Sat noon to 2:30 p.m. and 6:30–10 p.m.*

Le Petit Blanc
$$ FRENCH

A stylish brasserie that welcomes kids (and has a kids' menu), Le Petit Blanc has steel tables offset by vibrant fabrics. The nice bar menu includes items such as pea and ham soup with baguette, or you can order scones and jam. For a main course, try fish soup; tomato risotto; herb pancakes; roast rabbit; or confit of guinea fowl, wild mushrooms, and Madeira.

In Macdonald Queen's Hotel, The Promenade. ☎ **01242/266-800.** *Reservations required weekends. Main courses: £9.50–£18 ($18–$33), fixed-price lunch or dinner: £12–£15 ($22–$28). AE, DC, MC, V. Open: Daily noon–3 p.m. and 6–10:30 p.m.*

The Retreat
$ INTERNATIONAL

The Retreat's been around since 1981 and is one of the most popular spots in town for lunch (the restaurant becomes a bar at night). You can order a simple sandwich or something much more substantial from a menu that changes every day. You can always order fish, pasta, and steak; the restaurant doesn't fat-fry anything. The place also has a nice courtyard garden.

10–11 Suffolk Parade. ☎ **01242/235-436.** *Main courses: £6–£13 ($11–$24). AE, DC, MC, V. Open: Mon–Sat noon–2:15 p.m.*

Exploring Cheltenham

The main sights in Cheltenham serve as pleasant reminders of a genteel, bygone era. You won't find anything truly extraordinary here, however, so you may want to save your valuable time for exploring the nearby Cotswolds villages, such as Bourton-on-the-Water, Upper and Lower Slaughter, Broadway, or Chipping Campden. (I detail all these villages later in this chapter.) In less than two hours, you can see Cheltenham's main sights, all free, including:

- ✔ **Cheltenham Art Gallery and Museum,** Clarence Street (☎ **01242/ 237-431**): Notable for its collection of 19th-century Arts and Crafts furniture, silver, jewelry, ceramics, carvings, and textiles. (Cheltenham was a center of the Arts and Crafts movement started by William Morris.) You also find exhibits on local history and a small 20th-century gallery with a Stanley Spencer painting. The gallery and museum are open Monday through Saturday from 10 a.m. to 5:20 p.m. and Sunday from 2 to 4 p.m.

- ✔ **Imperial Gardens:** Cheltenham's gardens often win first place in the national "Britain in Bloom" contest. The gardens are in an open square and seasonally planted. To reach them, walk south from the Tourist Information Centre on Promenade until the street becomes Montpellier Walk.

✔ **The Pittville Pump Room,** Pittville Park (☎ **01242/523-852**): The
Pump Room opened in 1830, a remnant of spa days, when health-
conscious people came to Cheltenham to sip the alkaline water (for
the digestion), take carriage rides (for the air), and promenade (for
the exercise). Inside the Pump Room is a ballroom and an area
where you can taste the water (the only natural, consumable alkaline waters in Great Britain). On Sunday from the end of May until
the end of September, the Pump Room is open for lunch and afternoon cream teas, accompanied by classical music.

Shopping in Cheltenham

Cheltenham is a regional hub, so you find many appealing shops.
Antique stores cluster in the **Suffolk quarter** along Suffolk Road, Great
Norwood Street, and Suffolk Parade. You can find boutiques, art gal-
leries, and crafts and specialty shops in the **Montpellier quarter** along
Montpellier Walk and the Promenade.

Bourton-on-the-Water: Bridges on the Windrush

Like other villages in the Cotswolds, Bourton-on-the-Water grew rich
from the wool trade during the medieval era. But its history actually
dates to Roman times, when the town served as an outpost along the
Fosse Way, a strategic Roman road that cut across England from the
North Sea to St. George's Channel. (Today, the road is A429.) The "water"
in the village's name is the River Windrush, which flows gently through
the village's heart, its narrow channel lined with low, graceful stone
bridges. Virtually all the village buildings are made of a local honey-
colored stone that gives off a soft, mellow glow. When the wool trade
ended, Bourton became a forgotten backwater, which helped preserve
its wealth of medieval buildings. Today, this town, with an almost endless succession of shops, tearooms, and tourist attractions, is perhaps
the most commercialized of the Cotswolds villages. You probably want
to visit during spring or fall, avoiding the summer influx of tourists. The
Tourist Information Centre is on Victoria Street (☎ **01451/820-211**).

Getting to Bourton-on-the-Water

By car from Cheltenham, 24km (15 miles) to the southeast, take A40. The
village doesn't have parking; you find *car parks* (Britspeak for parking
lots) on Station Road and Rissington Road. Trains run from London's
Paddington Station to Moreton-in-Marsh; from Moreton-in-Marsh, you
can take a **Pulhams Coaches** (☎ **01451/820-369**) coach 9.5km (6 miles)
to Bourton. The same company runs about four buses a day from
Cheltenham.

Stopping for a spot of tea in Bourton-on-the-Water

The **Mad Hatter Tearoom,** Victoria Street (☎ 01451/821-508), serves hot meals all day, including fish and chips, for about £6 ($11); cream teas cost £3.50 ($6.50).

Exploring Bourton-on-the-Water

Many people come here just to stroll leisurely through the village, shop, and have an afternoon cream tea. If you're looking for additional activities, check out these attractions:

- **Birdland,** Rissington Road (☎ 01451/820-480): This series of aviaries has more than 350 species of some 1,200 birds, including penguins, cranes, storks, and waterfowl. You find a picnic area, cafe, and children's playground. Admission costs £4.60 ($8.50) for adults, £3.60 ($6.65) for seniors, and £2.60 ($4.80) for children 4 to 14. Birdland is open daily April through October from 10 a.m. to 6 p.m. and November through March from 10 a.m. to 4 p.m.

- **Cotswold Motoring Museum and Toy Collection,** The Old Mill (☎ 01451/821-255): Housed in an 18th-century water mill, this museum displays a collection of vintage cars, toys, motorbikes, and advertising signs. Admission costs £2.95 ($5.50) for adults and £1.95 ($3.50) for children. It's open daily mid-February to November from 10 a.m. to 6 p.m.

- **The Cotswold Perfumery,** Victoria Street (☎ 01451/820-698): This perfume factory has an on-site shop. Half-hour tours of the facility, including the compounding room, perfume laboratory, and perfume garden, cost £5 ($9.25) for adults and £3 ($5.55) for seniors and children. Call or stop in to reserve a spot on the tour. The perfumery is open daily from 9:30 a.m. to 5:30 p.m. (Sun from 10:30 a.m.).

- **The Cotswold Pottery,** Clapton Row (☎ 01451/820-173): This small country pottery exhibits and sells hand-thrown pots of exceptional quality. Hours are Monday through Saturday from 10 a.m. to 5 p.m. and Sunday from 10:30 a.m. to 4 p.m.

- **The Model Village at the Old New Inn,** High Street (☎ 01451/820-467): Opened in 1937, this miniature re-creation of the village remains the town's most popular attraction. Local stone was used to re-create a pint-size version of the entire village of Bourton-on-the-Water; you can walk through and see everything at one-ninth its actual height. Kids get a kick out of feeling like a giant. Admission costs £2.75 ($5.10) for adults and £2 ($3.70) for children. Summer hours are daily from 9 a.m. to 5:45 p.m.; in winter, it's open daily from 10 a.m. to 4 p.m.

- **St. Lawrence's Church;** In the center of the village, this church was constructed in the 12th century. The tower dates from 1784.

Upper Slaughter and Lower Slaughter: Quiet and Atmospheric

Just 2.5km (1½ miles) northwest of Bourton-on-the-Water sits **Lower Slaughter,** the prettiest village in the Cotswolds. With the River Eye running through it, Lower Slaughter is a picture of quiet, commercial-free elegance. There's really nothing to "do" here except stroll through the peaceful country lanes with their stone houses. You can stop in at **The Old Mill,** a working mill on Mill Lane (☎ 01451/820-052), and have tea in its riverside tearoom. The mill is open daily from 10 a.m. to 6 p.m. in the summer and until 4 p.m. in the winter.

If you fall under the spell of Lower Slaughter, you can stay here — in a pretty place that costs a pretty penny. A double room with breakfast at **The Washbourne Court Hotel,** Lower Slaughter, Gloucestershire GL54 2HS (☎ 01451/822-143; www.washbournecourt.co.uk), goes for £120 to £150 ($222–$278).

A 1.6km (1-mile) country footpath known as Warden's Way connects Lower Slaughter with **Upper Slaughter,** the next village. A leisurely walk between the two takes about an hour each way. The well-marked footpath skirts the edge of the River Eye, passing meadows with grazing sheep and old cottages surrounded by gardens. (The trail actually begins in Bourton-on-the-Water, along the ancient Roman footpath known as the Fosse Way.) Upper Slaughter is a small, peaceful, commercial-free village where you can stroll and savor the Olde English atmosphere.

Broadway: Village Shopping

Located 29km (18 miles) northeast of Cheltenham, Broadway is a picture-perfect Cotswold village. Saxons first settled the village in the sixth century. In the 16th century, Broadway became an important stagecoach stop. During the Victorian age, Broadway's charm and tranquility drew painters and writers. Today, visitors come to bask in the ambience of the golden-yellow stone buildings, which mostly date from the 16th century through Georgian times. Broadway doesn't have the kind of tourist attractions that Bourton-on-the-Water has, but day-trippers still pack the village during the summer tourist season. Visitors come here to stroll, shop, and have lunch or afternoon tea. High Street has so many upscale shops that you sometimes hear it called "the Bond Street of the Cotswolds" (a reference to London's chic shopping street).

Getting to Broadway

Broadway is 93km (58 miles) north of Bath and 24km (15 miles) southwest of Stratford-upon-Avon. Trains run daily from London's Paddington Station to Moreton-in-Marsh, 13km (8 miles) away; call ☎ 08457/484950 for train information. A taxi can take you from Moreton-in the-Marsh to Broadway; call **Bourton** (☎ 01481/820-972) or **Shipston** (☎ 01608/ 661-592).

Finding information about Broadway

The small **Tourist Information Centre,** 1 Cotswold Court (☎ 01386/ 852-937), is open February through December, Monday through Saturday from 10 a.m. to 1 p.m. and 2 to 5 p.m.

Staying in Broadway

You can find one lodging option in the village at the 16th-century **Lygon Arms,** High Street, Broadway, Worcestershire WR12 7DU (☎ 01386/ 852-255; www.thelygonarms.co.uk). Doubles in this full-service luxury hotel go for £119 to £319 ($220–$590). The 69-room hotel has acres of grounds, a health spa, and every amenity you can think of.

If you want to stay in an exceptionally beautiful house in the Cotswold countryside, try **Mill Hay,** Snowshill Road, Broadway, Worcestershire WR12 7JS (☎ 01386/852-498; www.millhay.co.uk). The house, with only three guest rooms, is a spacious, golden stoned Queen Anne with 3 acres of extraordinary gardens. Doubles with English breakfast go for £120 to £160 ($222–$296).

Stopping for a spot of tea in Broadway

For an informal lunch or old-fashioned cream tea in Broadway, try **Small Talk,** 32 High St. (☎ 01386/853-676; www.broadway-cotswolds.co.uk/ smtalk.html), next to the Lygon Arms hotel. The cafe is open daily from 9 a.m. to 5 p.m. Lunch costs a reasonable £5 to £8 ($9.25–$15); a cream tea with homemade scones goes for £4.50 ($8.35). Buy sandwiches here if you want to have a picnic. Small Talk rents out six charming guest rooms, all with private bathrooms; prices start at £50 ($93).

Exploring Broadway and vicinity

Soak up the atmosphere of this Cotswold village by taking a leisurely stroll along **High Street.** Along the way, you pass little antiques shops, boutiques, galleries, and pubs. You may want to spend a few minutes looking at the antique toys and 100-year-old teddy bears on display in the **Broadway Teddy Bear Museum,** 76 High St. (☎ 01386/858-323). In an 18th-century shop called Broadway Bears and Dolls, the museum is open Tuesday through Sunday and costs £2.50 ($4.65) for adults and £1.75 ($3.25) for seniors and children under 14.

If you want to savor a bit of Elizabethan ambience, stop in for a meal, a drink, or afternoon tea at the half-timbered **Lygon Arms** (☎ 01386/ 852-255; see the section "Staying in Broadway," earlier in this chapter). This wonderfully atmospheric hotel, in business since 1532, has crackling fires, exposed beams, and paneled lounges.

On Snowshill Road, 1.6km (1 mile) south of town, sits **St. Eadburgha's,** a lovely medieval church built of the characteristic local stone. Another .5km (½-mile) brings you to a local landmark and one of England's outstanding viewpoints: **Broadway Tower** (☎ **01386/852-390**) was built in the early 19th century as a *folly* (a picturesque building evoking an earlier age) high atop Broadway Hill. From the hilltop, you can see 12 surrounding counties. The tower and surrounding land are now a country park. In the tower, you can find exhibits connected with its past as a retreat for William Morris, founder of the Arts and Crafts movement; red deer and Cotswold sheep roam the grounds, and children can visit an animal park and playground. Stop in at the restaurant on the premises, or bring a picnic. Admission to the park is free. The Tower and park are open daily April through October from 10:30 a.m. to 5 p.m.; winter hours are daily 11 a.m. to 3 p.m.

The countryside to the northwest of Broadway, near the town of Evesham, is known as the **Vale of Evesham.** The area has some of England's most productive fruit-growing land. For a few weeks between mid-March and mid-May, the roadsides blaze with the soft pinks of cherry, apple, and pear blossoms, and the white of flowering plums.

Chipping Campden: Picture Perfect

Have your camera ready as you enter this village, because you can see a picture everywhere you turn. Chipping Campden was a wool town in the Middle Ages. Here, you find thatched-roof cottages with walls of mellow yellow Cotswold stone and beautiful High Street with Tudor and Elizabethan buildings.

The **Tourist Information Centre,** 2 Rosary Ct., High Street (☎ **01386/ 841-206**), is open daily from 10 a.m. to 5 p.m.

Getting to Chipping Campden

By car from Broadway, take B463 east 6.5km (4 miles); from Cheltenham, 32km (20 miles) to the west, head north on A435 and A46 and then turn southeast on A44. The closest train service is from London's Paddington Station to Moreton-in-Marsh, 11km (7 miles) away; from Moreton-on-Marsh, you can take a taxi to Chipping Campden. Call **Bourton** (☎ **01481/820-972**) to reserve a cab.

Staying and dining in Chipping Campden

Head to the **Noel Arms Hotel,** High Street, Chipping Campden, Gloucestershire GL55 6AT (☎ **01386/840-317;** www.noelarmshotel.com), for a fine meal and a comfortable bed. This 14th-century coaching inn has a modern wing, but the original section retains many original features, such as stone fireplaces and beamed ceilings. A double room with full

English breakfast costs £125 to £185 ($231–$342). You probably want to make reservations for the restaurant, which offers a classy international menu with meat, fish, and vegetarian choices. Fixed-price lunches cost £16 to £18 ($30–$33); fixed-price dinners go for £23 to £26 ($43–$48); and a sumptuous afternoon cream tea served in one of the lounges costs £19 ($35).

For good, unfancy lunches and teas, try **The Bantam Tea Rooms,** also on High Street (☎ **01386/840-386;** www.thebantam.co.uk). A traditional lunch of cottage pie or steak and kidney pie costs about £6 ($11), and a cream tea costs under £5 ($9.25). The place is open daily from 10 a.m. to 5 p.m. (Sun from 11 a.m.). The Bantam also rents out charming, inexpensive rooms nestled up under the eaves, all with private bathrooms; doubles cost £70 to £75 ($130–$139), full English breakfast included.

Kiftsgate Court and Hidcote Manor Gardens

The Cotswolds are blessed with many beautiful gardens, two of which, near Chipping Campden and Broadway, you'll want to see if you're at all interested in English gardens. The two gardens, Kiftsgate Court and Hidcote Manor, are only about a mile apart.

Just east of the village of Mickleton off the B4632 from Broadway, **Kiftsgate Court Gardens** (☎ **01386/438-777**) is the creation of three generations of women gardeners. Heather Muir started Kiftsgate in the 1920s. Her daughter, Diany Binny, added to the gardens in the 1950s. Diany's daughter, Anne, now looks after them. Kiftsgate was designed as a series of connecting gardens, each with its own distinct character. The newest addition is a contemporary water garden. You can get a light lunch or homemade tea from June to August. Admission costs £5 ($9.25) for adults and £1.50 ($2.80) for children under 16. In April, May, August, and September, the garden is open Wednesday, Thursday, and Sunday from 2 to 6 p.m. In June and July, it's open Monday, Wednesday, Thursday, Saturday, and Sunday from noon to 6 p.m. Allow at least an hour.

One of the great gardens of England, **Hidcote Manor** (☎ **01386/438-333**), lies 6.5km (4 miles) northeast of Chipping Campden and 14.5km (9 miles) south of Stratford-upon-Avon. Set on 10 acres, Hidcote Manor is comparable in beauty, skill, and ingenuity to Sissinghurst in Kent (see Chapter 15). In 1907, Major Lawrence Johnstone began to create a series of hedged outdoor rooms linked by the corridors of its main vista. The rooms are furnished with all sorts of topiary and an amazing variety of plantings that add color, texture, and contrast. Give yourself at least an hour to see this garden, a National Trust property. A restaurant serves lunch from noon to 2:30 p.m. and teas from 3 to 5:30 p.m. Admission is £6.60 ($12) for adults, £3.30 ($6.10) for children 5–15, and £16 ($30) for families (2 adults, 2 children). The gardens are open mid-March through October Saturday through Wednesday from 10:30 a.m. to 6 p.m. (until 5 p.m. in Oct). Access for visitors with disabilities is limited in parts.

Exploring Chipping Campden

You can walk through the village and see everything in about 30 minutes. First, at the north end of town, visit **St. James's Church,** which prosperous wool merchants built in the 15th century. The church is a fine example of the Perpendicular Gothic style, a medieval building style in which vertical lines dominate. Nearby is a grouping of medieval **almshouses,** built to house six poor men and six poor women. High Street contains many beautiful Cotswold stone buildings dating from the 14th to the 17th centuries. The imposing **Market Hall** was built in 1627 for the town's local produce market.

Cirencester: Market Town with a Roman Past

Regarded as the unofficial capital of the Cotswolds, Cirencester (pronounced *Sih*-ren-*ses*-ter) is a bustling market town 26km (16 miles) south of Cheltenham. During the Middle Ages, Cirencester was a center of the great Cotswold wool industry. But long before that, in Roman times, Cirencester was the second-largest town in Britain. Known then as Corinium Dobunnorum, the town stood at the crossroads of five major roads. Like Bath and Cheltenham, Cirencester makes for a good touring base in the Cotswolds. Londoners in search of weekend and summer homes in the Cotswolds have recently "discovered" the town, and many good restaurants and quality shops have opened.

Getting to Cirencester

The nearest train station is at Kemble, 6.5km (4 miles) to the southwest. Trains run from London's Paddington Station; it's an 80-minute trip, which may involve a transfer at Swindon, depending on the train that you take. For train information, call ☎ **08457/484-950.** A bus (no. 51) runs to Cirencester from Cheltenham via Stroud Valley Monday through Saturday. **National Express** (☎ **0990/808-080;** www.nationalexpress. com) offers direct service from London's Victoria Coach Station; the trip takes two hours and 15 minutes.

Finding information about Cirencester

The **Tourist Information Centre,** Corn Hall, Market Place (☎ **01285/ 654-180**), sells an inexpensive town map with a walking tour. The center also has a room-booking service. From April through September, the center is open Monday from 9:45 a.m. to 5 p.m. and Tuesday through Saturday from 9:30 a.m. to 5 p.m.

You can exchange money at Lloyds Bank on Castle Street.

Staying in Cirencester

Cirencester doesn't offer many hotel or B&B choices. Here are two options.

Corinium Hotel
$ Cirencester

This pleasant, family-owned hotel with a walled garden was a wool merchant's house in Elizabethan days. The hotel was later refaced with mellow Cotswold stone, and the stables and coach house were converted into a restaurant and bar. The guest rooms, all with private bathrooms, are fresh and comfortable

12 Gloucester St., Cirencester, Gloucestershire GL7 2DG. ☎ **01285/695-711.** *Fax: 01285/885-807.* www.coriniumhotel.co.uk. *Rack rates: £75–£95 ($139–$176) double. Rates include English breakfast. AE, MC, V.*

Stratton House Hotel
$$ Cirencester

Stratton House was built as a private residence in the 17th century and converted into a 40-room hotel in 1947. Surrounded by lawns and a lovely walled garden, it has the look and feel of a gracious Cotswolds country house. The rooms come in all shapes and sizes, and they're furnished in traditional English style. Bathrooms are on the small side. There's a good restaurant on the premises, as well as a very pleasant drawing room and bar.

Gloucester Road, Cirencester, Gloucestershire GL7 2LE. ☎ **01285/651-761.** *Fax: 01285/640024.* www.strattonhousehotel.co.uk. *Rack rates: £125–£140 ($231–$259) double. Rates include English breakfast. AE, DC, MC, V.*

Dining in Cirencester

Now that Londoners, many of whom have country homes in the Cotswolds, have "discovered" Cirencester, the number and variety of restaurants has increased. Here are my recommendations.

Ann's Pantry
$ TRADITIONAL

This old-fashioned lunch and tearoom is upstairs at the rear of an intriguing antiques shop. You can get a sandwich or a daily lunch special, which may be mussels with leeks, duck, or chicken curry. The cream tea with Cornish clotted cream is very good.

Cirencester Arcade, 25 Market Place. ☎ **01285/644-214.** *Main courses: £4–£7 ($7.40–$13); cream tea: £3.50 ($6.50). AE, MC, V. Open: Mon–Sat 9:30 a.m.–5 p.m., Sun noon to 5 p.m.*

Harry Hare's Restaurant & Brasserie
$ INTERNATIONAL

Harry Hare's serves English, French, Italian, and vegetarian dishes in a cheerful, informal setting, and it has a kids' menu, too. The place has a country Gothic look with plank floors, an old fireplace, and wicker chairs. The food is good, and you can choose from an ample wine list.

3 Gosditch St. ☎ **01285/652-375.** *Main courses: £6–£10 ($11–$19). AE, MC, V. Open: Daily 10:30 a.m.–10:30 p.m.*

Slug and Lettuce
$ PUB/TRADITIONAL

This friendly pub restaurant is part of a national chain. You can get a good ribeye steak, beef and Guinness stout sausages, smoked haddock fish-cakes, and other traditional dishes.

17 West Market Place. ☎ **01285/653-206.** *Main courses: £6–£11 ($11–$20). MC, V. Open: Mon–Sat 11 a.m.–11 p.m., Sun noon to 10:30 p.m.; food served Sun–Thurs until 9 p.m., Fri–Sat until 8 p.m.*

Swan Yard Cafe
$ TRADITIONAL

At this great, informal, all-purpose cafe, you can order a sandwich, quiche, or homemade soup. If it's available, try Homity pie, a traditional dish made with mashed potatoes, onions, and garlic — like shepherd's pie without the meat. The cafe is in Swan's Yard, which you can find to your left as you face the parish church.

West Market Place. ☎ **01285/641-300.** *Main courses: £3.50–£6 ($6.50–$11). MC, V. Open: Mon–Sat 9:30 a.m.–5p.m., Sun 11 a.m.–4 p.m.*

Tatyan's
$–$$ CHINESE

This well-known Chinese restaurant serves Peking, Hunan, and spicy Szechuan dishes. On the menu, you find dishes such as sizzling prawns, chicken with ginger, and sweet and sour pork.

27 Castle St. ☎ **01285/641-126.** *Main courses £5.50–£16 ($10–$30); fixed-price lunch for two: £12–£20 ($22–$37). AE, MC, V. Open: Mon–Sat noon–2 p.m. and 6–10:30 p.m., Sun 6–10:30 p.m.*

Exploring Cirencester

Two millennia ago, only London was larger and more powerful than Cirencester, then called Corinium Dobunnorum. The town was a Roman administrative center for the area around the southern Cotswold hills, one of the most prosperous regions in Roman Britain. You can still see the remains of the **Roman amphitheatre,** constructed in the second century A.D. to accommodate some 8,000 spectators. The entrance is on Cotswold Avenue, on the south side of town (free admission).

Newly reopened in 2004 after a two-year, multimillion-pound refurbishment, the **Corinium Museum,** Park Street (☎ 01285/655-611), is one of England's best small museums. The museum focuses entirely on the history of Cirencester from the Iron Age through the medieval wool era. In the antiquities on display, the Roman era predominates. You can see an outstanding collection of mosaic floors and re-created Roman-era interiors. In the dramatic new Anglo-Saxon Gallery, the museum has recreated the grave of a wealthy sixth-century Anglo-Saxon princess. You can easily while away an hour here. The museum is open Monday through Saturday from 10 a.m. to 5 p.m. and Sunday from 2 to 5 p.m. Admission is £3.70 ($6.85) for adults and £2 ($3.70) for students and children.

If you look south across Park Street from the museum, you see an enormous **yew hedge,** reputedly the highest in Europe. Planted in 1720, the hedge is now 40 feet high. The yew hedge is part of **Cirencester Park,** the Earl of Bathurst's 3,000-acre estate designed by the poet Alexander Pope. The park is open to the public; use the entrance gates on Cecily Hill.

Cirencester's importance as a wool town during the Middle Ages reflected in the size of its **Parish Church of St. John the Baptist (☎ 01285/653-142),** which dominates the Market Place. The church isn't quite as large as a cathedral, but it comes close. Special details include the fan-vaulted porch and a rare 15th-century pre-Reformation pulpit. The church displays a silver-gilt cup made for Anne Boleyn in 1535.

Shopping in Cirencester

Cirencester is a local market town, which means that people come from miles around to do their shopping. A **street market,** one of the oldest in the country, is held on Monday and Friday in the central Market Place in front of the parish church. On Friday, you can shop in an **antiques market** in Corn Hall next to the Tourist Information Centre; on Saturday, you can find a **crafts market** in the same space.

If you're looking for antiques or local crafts, you can also try these shops:

- ✔ **Brewery Arts Centre,** Brewery Court, (☎ 01285/657-181): Resident craft workers sell everything from baskets to handmade porcelain, glass, jewelry, and leather goods. You can find a good cafe on the premises.

- ✔ **Rankine Taylor Antiques,** 34 Dollar St., (☎ 01285/652-529): This shop sells silver, 17th- to 19th-century glass, and furniture.

- ✔ **William H. Stokes,** The Cloister, 6/8 Dollar St. (☎ 01285/653-907): This place specializes in furniture, tapestries, and items from the 16th and 17th centuries.

Chedworth Roman Villa

You can see the remains of one of the largest and finest Roman villas in Britain about a half-hour's drive from Cirencester. The villa sits at the end of a green, wooded valley. The National Trust administers the site, which includes the excavated remains of a water shrine, two bathhouses, and even a lavatory. Shedlike roofs protect fine fourth-century mosaics. Start your tour with the short introductory video and then wander at will. No one knows if this complex of buildings was a religious center or a giant Roman farm. Maybe it was both. You can see the entire site in under an hour.

Admission is £5 ($9.25) for adults, £2.50 ($4.65) for children 5 to 15, and £13 ($24) for families (2 adults, 2 children). The site is open April to October Tuesday through Sunday from 10 a.m. to 5 p.m.; November to March, it's open Tuesday through Sunday from 11 a.m. to 4 p.m. Call ☎ **01242/890-250** for more information. To get there from Cirencester, head north on A429, turn west at Fossebridge, and follow the signs for 5km (3 miles) to Chedworth.

If you need to pick up some swanky groceries, head to the Cirencester Waitrose, an upscale supermarket on Sheep Street. Gloucestershire Royals, such as Princess Anne (who lives in the countryside nearby) and Princess Michael of Kent, have been seen stocking up in this store.

The 5th Wave · By Rich Tennant

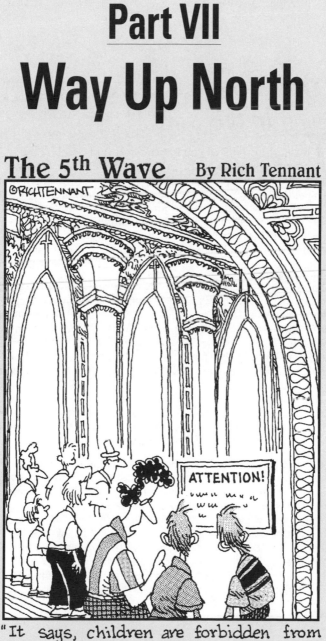

"It says, children are forbidden from running, touching objects, or appearing bored during the tour."

In this part . . .

This part introduces you to Yorkshire and Cumbria, large counties "way up north," close to Scotland. Scenically, the region has a quite different appeal from central and southern England, which are softer and greener. Gray-stone villages and mile upon mile of open moorland, rocky shoreline, small lakes, and treeless mountains fill the flinty northern landscape. Yorkshire and Cumbria are places of rugged character and independence. Local accents are sometimes closer to Scots than to the "Oxbridge" accents heard in the south.

Chapter 21 covers Yorkshire in the northeast. York, with its vast cathedral and medieval walls, is one of England's great cities. Magnificent Castle Howard and Scarborough, a fun-loving resort town on the North Sea, are close by. In this chapter, I also tell you about Yorkshire's two national parks: North York Moors, extending over a vast tract of heather-covered moorland and North Sea coastline, and Yorkshire Dales, a peaceful world of rolling farmland and traditional villages. Many people forever associate the Yorkshire moors with the novels *Wuthering Heights* and *Jane Eyre*. Haworth, where you can visit the home of the authors Emily and Charlotte Brontë, is a literary shrine second only to Stratford-upon-Avon.

Chapter 22 visits Cumbria, also known as the Lake District, in the northwest corner of England. Lake District National Park, which encompasses the entire county, protects a hauntingly beautiful world of lakes, bracken-covered mountains, and lovely stone villages. Tourists from around the world come to this remote part of England to hike, boat on Lake Windermere, bask in the glorious scenery, and visit the homes of William Wordsworth in Grasmere and Beatrix Potter near Lake Windermere. Keswick, on a pretty lake called Derwentwater, is another Lake District town that's well worth visiting.

Chapter 21

Yorkshire

In This Chapter

▶ Visiting York and its great cathedral
▶ Having some fun in Scarborough
▶ Seeing North York Moors and Yorkshire Dales National Parks
▶ Stopping at the Brontës' Haworth

A land of great and varied contrasts, Yorkshire is blessed with some of the most dramatic landscapes in England, and some of the most tranquil. (See the "Yorkshire" map on p. 352.) This northern region's windswept moors, sheltered dales, rocky coastline, and rushing streams — or *becks*, as people call them up north — draw walkers from around the world to the countryside. But Yorkshire was an industrial powerhouse during the 19th century, and many of its cities and towns are pretty grim reminders of those Industrial Revolution days. (Don't worry; I'm not taking you to any industrial heritage towns.) In Yorkshire, you can attune your ears to the broad, Scotslike accents of the North.

I begin this chapter with **York,** Yorkshire's most visited city. Ringed by medieval walls, with a stupendous cathedral and winding medieval streets, York is one of the most beautiful and fascinating cities in England. From York, you can make an easy trip by train and taxi to the splendor of **Castle Howard** and the haunting **Eden Camp,** a World War II prisoner-of-war camp. **Scarborough,** on the 160km (100-mile) stretch of Yorkshire coast, is a resort town on the North Sea, also easily accessible by train from York. If you want to explore Yorkshire's two national parks and the Brontë country in and around Haworth, you may want to rent a car in York rather than depend on public transportation. **North York Moors National Park** is known for its unspoiled coastline and vast stretches of heather-crowned moorland. Farther inland to the west lies **Yorkshire Dales National Park,** with its old stone villages, rolling farmland, and dramatic limestone formations. This chapter ends in **Haworth,** where the Brontës created their evocative masterpieces of moorland passion, *Wuthering Heights* and *Jane Eyre.*

Yorkshire

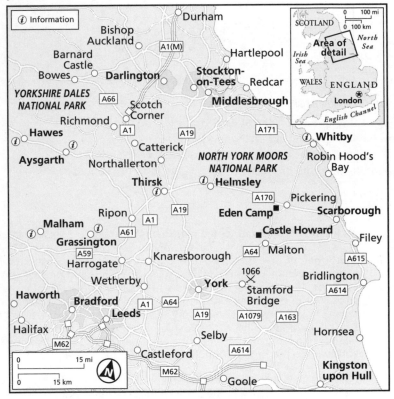

York: Ancient Walls and Snickelways

York is only 314km (195 miles) north of London, close enough for a day trip but worlds apart in character. York is the capital of the North and one of England's most historic cities. Under the Romans, who built a major fort here, the city was known as Eboracum. For hundreds of years after that, York was a thriving Viking settlement called Jorvik. And finally, after the Norman Conquest, it became York, queen of the North.

Interesting museums, historic buildings of all kinds, good hotels, excellent shops, and fine restaurants make York a popular tourist city, and rightly so. Enormous York Minster, the largest Gothic structure north of the Alps, dominates the city. And, amazingly, the old town's 800-year-old walls and fortified gateways still girdle the old town center.

York is considered the best-preserved medieval walled city in England. (A bloody history reputedly makes York the most haunted city in England, too.) You can soak up the city's history while exploring its

York

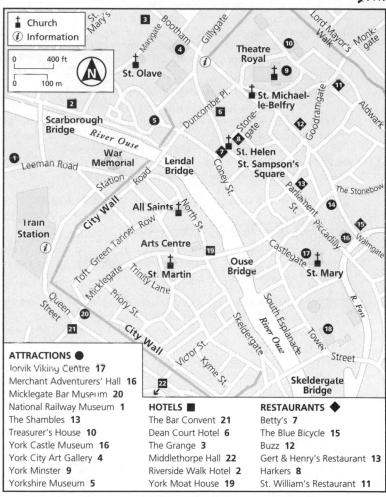

| ‡ Church |
| ⓘ Information |

0 400 ft
0 100 m

N

ATTRACTIONS ●
Jorvik Viking Centre **17**
Merchant Adventurers' Hall **16**
Micklegate Bar Museum **20**
National Railway Museum **1**
The Shambles **13**
Treasurer's House **10**
York Castle Museum **16**
York City Art Gallery **4**
York Minster **9**
Yorkshire Museum **5**

HOTELS ■
The Bar Convent **21**
Dean Court Hotel **6**
The Grange **3**
Middlethorpe Hall **22**
Riverside Walk Hotel **2**
York Moat House **19**

RESTAURANTS ◆
Betty's **7**
The Blue Bicycle **15**
Buzz **12**
Gert & Henry's Restaurant **13**
Harkers **8**
St. William's Restaurant **11**

maze of ancient streets and *snickelways* (hidden alleyways). You can get everywhere on foot and see many attractions in just a day. York makes a good base for exploring the rest of Yorkshire, with Castle Howard just a few miles to the east.

Getting to York

Direct trains leave frequently throughout the day from London's King's Cross Station for the two-hour trip to York's Rougier Street Station. The cheapest advance purchase round-trip fare costs £52 ($96). For train schedules and information, call National Rail Enquiries at ☎ 08457/484-950. The train station is a five-minute walk from York's historic center. Buses cost you considerably less than trains (£29/$54 round-trip) but take a minimum of five hours. **National Express (☎ 0990/808-080)** has service throughout the day from Victoria Coach Station in London. If you're driving from London, take the M1 expressway north to Junction 45, east of Leeds, and from there, continue northeast on A64 to York.

Renting a car or calling a taxi

You don't need a car if you're traveling to York by train and staying in the city. But if you want to explore more of the fascinating Yorkshire countryside, you can rent a car in York. **Practical Car & Van Rental (☎ 01904/624-828;** www.practical.co.uk) has good rates, a city-center location, and weekend specials. **Hertz** has an office on Station Road, near the railway station (**☎ 01904/612-586;** www.hertz.com).

If you need a taxi, contact **Station Taxis (☎ 01904/623-332**).

Finding information about York

You can visit two places for information in York. At both of the following places, you can get an inexpensive guidebook with a map, book a room, and obtain information on guided tours:

- ✔ A convenient branch of the **Tourist Information Centre** (no phone) is right in the train station. The office is open Monday through Saturday from 9 a.m. to 5 p.m. (until 6 p.m. in summer) and Sunday from 10 a.m. to 4 p.m. (until 5 p.m. in summer).

- ✔ The main **Tourist Information Centre,** De Grey Rooms, Exhibition Square (**☎ 01904/621-756;** www.visityork.org), near York Minster, has the same open hours as the train-station branch (see preceding bullet).

Exchanging money and locating ATMs

Both Tourist Information Centres (see the preceding section) have a currency exchange. You can also try **American Express,** 6 Stonegate (**☎ 01904/670-030**); **HSBC,** 13 Parliament St. (**☎ 01904/884-001**); and **Royal Bank of Scotland,** 6 Nessgate (**☎ 01904/642-961**).

Special events in York

York celebrates its Viking heritage with feasts, music, and pageantry during the **Jorvik Viking Festival (☎ 01904/636-668**), held in mid-February. The acclaimed **York Early Music Festival (☎ 01904/632-220;** www.ncem.co.uk) has special programs at Easter and in July. York has one of Europe's most prestigious horse-racing courses; **York Racecourse (☎ 01904/620-911;** www.yorkracecourse.co.uk) holds meets from May to October and is the site of the Royal Ascot racing meet in 2006.

Taking a tour in York

More guided tours are offered in York than in just about any other city in England, excluding London. You can explore the city by foot, bus, or boat. The city is small enough that you can easily get around and see everything by yourself, but you may find a guided tour useful because you can see parts of the town that you may otherwise miss.

During the summer, you can hire a horse-drawn carriage in front of the Dean Court Hotel near York Minster. A 15-minute ride around the cathedral *close* (the walled precinct surrounding the cathedral) costs £3.50 ($6.50) for adults and £2.50 ($4.65) for children.

Boat tours

What could be more fun than cruising down the River Ouse through the middle of England's most historic walled city? Departing from the pier below Lendal Bridge, **York Boat** (☎ 01904/647-204; www.yorkboat. co.uk) provides a 45-minute tour with live commentary that nicely complements a walking tour. From mid-February through November, at least four boats depart each day; you can buy your ticket on board. The tour costs £6.50 ($12) for adults, £5.50 ($10) for seniors, £3.50 ($6.50) for children 5 to 15, and £19 ($35) for families (2 adults, 3 children).

Bus tours

City Sightseeing (☎ 01904/625-618) runs open-top, double-decker tour buses on a circuit of all the main sights in York (one hour total). The ticket, valid all day so you can hop on and off as you want, costs £8 ($15) for adults, £6 ($11) for seniors and students, £4 ($7.40) for children 5 to 15, and £18 ($33) for families (2 adults, 2 children). The buses run year-round from about 9:30 a.m. to 5 p.m.; you can get on at the train station and buy your ticket from the driver.

Walking tours

Thumbs up to the **York Association of Voluntary Guides** (☎ 01904/ 640-780) for its free two-hour guided tours of the city. The tours depart daily at 10:15 a.m. year-round from Exhibition Square in the city center. Additional tours start at 2:15 and 6:45 p.m. in summer. You don't need to make a reservation; just show up.

Yorkwalk (☎ 01904/622-303; www.yorkwalk.co.uk) offers a series of two-hour walks on intriguing subjects on different days of the week. All walks start at the Museum Gardens Gates on Museum Street just north of Lendal Bridge; the cost is £5 ($9.25) for adults and £2 ($3.70) for children. Essential York, Roman York, Romantic York, and the Jewish Heritage Walk are some of the offerings; I'm sorry that I didn't have time for the Historic Toilet Tour. Call or visit the Web site to find out times and topics or pick up the leaflet at the Tourist Information Centre.

Staying in York

The largest city in northern England, York has a fine array of hotels and B&Bs. My recommended choices are listed here.

The Bar Convent

$

This convent building is an inexpensive, unusual, and convenient place to stay. The accommodations are in a Georgian building on the corner of Nunnery Lane and Blossom Street, a five-minute walk from the train station. The seven rooms, refurbished in 2005, are comfortable but nothing fancy; only one has a private bathroom. The convent, which houses a neoclassical chapel and a museum, was founded in 1686 and was active as a school until 1985. The on-site cafe serves inexpensive meals.

See map p. 353. 17 Blossom St., York YO24 1AQ. ☎ *01904/264-902. Fax: 01904/631-792.* www.bar-convent.org.uk. *Rack rates: £55 ($102) double with shared bathroom, £66 ($122) double with bathroom. Rates include continental breakfast. MC, V.*

Dean Court Hotel

$$–$$$

You can't get any closer to York Minster than this full-service hotel almost directly beneath the towers. The building, originally used to house clergy, dates from 1850 and was converted into a 39-room hotel after World War I; it's now part of the Best Western chain. The rooms are comfortable, although some are quite small, and they're decorated with traditional patterned fabrics and wallpapers. The restaurant serves traditional English and international fare at lunch and dinner.

See map p. 353. Duncombe Place, York YO1 2EF. ☎ *01904/625-082. Fax: 01904/620-305.* www.deancourt-york.co.uk. *Rack rates: £125–£205 ($231–$379) double. Rates include English breakfast. AE, DC, MC, V.*

The Grange

$$$–$$$$

Created from a classical Regency brick town house, The Grange is a small, elegant hotel close to the city walls and a few minutes' walk from York Minster. The 30 individually designed rooms use antique furniture and convey a comfortable English charm. Bathrooms are nicely done. The hotel offers room service and two good restaurants: The Ivy, serving classic French and Modern British cuisine, is considered one of the best restaurants in York; the Brasserie offers informal dining in the old brick vaulted cellars.

See map p. 353. 1 Clifton, York YO30 6AA. ☎ *01904/644-744. Fax: 01904/612-453.* www.grangehotel.co.uk. *Rack rates: £145–£210 ($268–$389) double. Rates include English breakfast. AE, MC, V.*

Middlethorpe Hall
$$$–$$$$ South of York

You can find one of the country's finest hotels in a 26-acre park 2.5km (1½ miles) south of York. Middlethorpe Hall is an elegant country house that was built in 1699. It was the residence of Lady Mary Wortley Montagu, a famous diarist of the early 18th century. The hotel offers a high standard of personal service and comfort, and features beautifully restored rooms, lovely gardens (with a 350-year-old cedar tree), a health spa, and a fine restaurant. Some of the 30 guest rooms are in the main house; others are in the remodeled stable house. The furnishings are traditional, and each roomy bathroom has a tub and shower. At dinner, served in the hall's original paneled dining room, men are requested to wear a jacket and tie.

See map p. 353. Bishopthorpe Road, York YO23 2GB. ☎ *800/260-8338 in U.S. or 01904/641-241. Fax: 01904/620-176.* www.middlethorpe.com. *Rack rates: £175–£235 ($324–$435) double. AE, MC, V.*

Riverside Walk Hotel
$

If you're looking for a nice B&B, check out this guesthouse in a Victorian terrace house overlooking the river. Riverside Walk is close to everything in town (a ten-minute walk to York Minster or National Railway Museum) and has 12 nicely furnished bedrooms, all with private bathrooms. The B&B is completely nonsmoking. Children are welcome.

See map p. 353. 9 Earlsborough Terrace, York YO30 7BQ. ☎ *01904/620-709. Fax: 01904/671-743. Rack rates: £50–£60 ($93–$111) double. Rates include English breakfast. MC, V.*

York Moat House
$–$$$

This modern 200-room hotel within the city walls overlooking the River Ouse is part of a British chain that caters mostly to business travelers and has good weekend deals for tourists. The rooms are nicely decorated and have small but adequate bathrooms; ask for a river-facing room with a view of York Minster. A fitness center is on the premises.

See map p. 353. North Street, York YO1 6JF. ☎ *01904/459-988. Fax 01904/641-793.* www.moathousehotels.com. *Rack rates: £75–£200 ($139–$370) double. Rates include English breakfast. Parking £6 ($11). AE, DC, MC, V.*

Dining in York
York suffers no shortage of good restaurants. Here are my recommendations.

Betty's
$ TRADITIONAL ENGLISH/SWISS/TEAS

Founded in 1919, Betty's is a wonderfully old-fashioned Art Nouveau tea-room–patisserie–restaurant. Sandwiches, salads, and a dozen or so hot dishes, both fish and meat, are available. Specialties include smoked salmon muffins, Yorkshire rarebit, locally made sausages, and haddock and prawns in white-wine cream sauce. The pastries, all made according to secret recipes, are superb. At the shop in front, you can buy specialties, such as Yorkshire fat rascals: warm scones with citrus peels, almonds, and cherries.

See map p. 353. 6–8 St. Helen's Sq. ☎ *01904/659-142. Main courses: £6–£9 ($11–$17); cream tea: £6–£11 ($11–$20). AE, MC, V. Open: Daily 9 a.m.–9 p.m.*

The Blue Bicycle
$$ MODERN BRITISH/INTERNATIONAL

If you're looking for atmosphere and good food, try this appealing restaurant overlooking the canal-like Ouse River. It has a brasserie-style menu with a few standard menu items, daily specials, and a char-grill for meat and fish dishes. The dinner menu usually features several varieties of fish cooked various ways, plus chicken, beef, and a vegetarian offering. The Blue Bicycle also rents out two self-contained luxury rooms in the center of York for £150 ($278) per room per night.

See map p. 353. 34 Fossgate. ☎ *01904/673-990. Reservations recommended. Main courses: £15–£20 ($28–$37). AE, MC, V. Open: Daily noon–2:30 p.m. and 6–9 p.m.*

Buzz
$$–$$$ JAPANESE

The cool minimalist interior of this friendly bar–restaurant perfectly complements the Japanese menu. Come to this great spot for sushi or sashimi. Or you can also get tempura; ramen soup noodles; and bento boxes with sushi, beef, chicken, and vegetarian options. During the day, the restaurant also serves as an Internet cafe.

See map p. 353. 20–24 Swinegate. ☎ *01904/640-222. Main courses: £12–£17 ($22–$31); fixed-price lunch and early dinner: £17 ($31). MC, V. Open: Daily noon to 2:30 p.m. and 5–10:30 p.m.*

Gert & Henry's Restaurant
$–$$ ENGLISH

This cozy, comfortable, unpretentious restaurant in a half-timbered building makes a good choice for a casual dinner. The menu sticks pretty much to traditional English dishes and seafood (including fish and chips) but also offers good salads and a few pastas.

See map p. 353. Jubbergate, The Market. ☎ *01904/621-445. Main courses: £5.95–£15 ($11–$28). MC, V. Open: Daily 10 a.m.–2:30 p.m. and 4–10 p.m.*

Harkers
$ ENGLISH/PUB FOOD

Stop in at Harkers, in the former Yorkshire Insurance Company building dating from 1824, for a simple pub lunch. The menu features traditional dishes, such as chicken and onion pie, fish and chips, ploughman's lunch (bread, cheese, and salad), and Cumberland sausages. The place can become something of a mob scene after work.

See map p. 353. St. Helen's Square. ☎ *01904/672-795. Main courses: £5.50–£9.95 ($10–$18). MC, V. Open: Pub Mon–Sat 11 a.m.–11 p.m., Sun noon–10:30 p.m.; food served daily noon–7 p.m.*

St. William's Restaurant
$–$$$ TRADITIONAL/MODERN BRITISH

For an affordable lunch, dinner, or tea, check out this small, attractive restaurant in front of St. William's College at the east end of York Minster. The menu changes daily but always has some delicious choices, such as seared sea bass with sautéed peppers and saffron risotto, pork loin wrapped in Cumbrian ham, or traditional roast beef and Yorkshire pudding. This spot is good for a simple cappuccino or an afternoon cream tea with scones and cakes. It's set up like a cafeteria during the lunch hour and becomes a bistro in the evening.

See map p. 353. 3 College St. ☎ *01904/634-830. Main courses: Lunch £6.95 ($13), dinner £14–£16 ($26–$30). AE, DC, MC, V. Open: Daily 10 a.m.–5 p.m. and 6 p.m.–9:30 p.m.*

Exploring York

York is a delightful city to explore, full of old streets, lanes, *snickelways* (alleyways), and many tourist attractions. Keep a map with you, because you can easily get lost on the city's medieval streets.

The City Walls and Micklegate Bar Museum

Almost 5km (3 miles) of medieval walls enclose the center of York. Fortified gateways (or *bars*) still serve as entrances to the old part of town. A path (open daily 8 a.m. to dusk) runs along the top of the walls, with plenty of great views along the way. You find stairways up to the top of the walls at the four gates.

Micklegate, the southern entry used by royalty, is a good place to start your wall walk. Housed in the 800-year-old fortified tower, the tiny **Micklegate Bar Museum** (☎ **01904/634-436**), looks at the social history of the gate in a quirky, humorous light. From February through October, the museum is open daily from 9 a.m. to 5 p.m.; in November and December, it's open weekends from 9 a.m. to dusk (closed in Jan). Admission costs £2.50 ($4.65) for adults, £1.25 ($2.30) for seniors and students, and 50p (95¢) for children 5 to 15. You can see it all in about 15 minutes.

Jorvik Viking Centre

If you want to revisit the Viking Age, hop into one of the time cars here to be transported back to A.D. 948, when Eric Bloodaxe was king and York was Jorvik, a thriving Viking port and trading town. The scenes you see — of village life, market stalls, crowded houses, and the wharf — are meticulous recreations based on archaeological finds in this area; even the heads and faces of the animatronic characters you see were modeled on Viking skulls. You can see artifacts unearthed on this site on display. Give yourself about an hour.

See map p. 353. Coppergate. ☎ *01904/643-211. Admission: £7.50 ($14) adults, £6.30 ($12) seniors and students, £5.50 ($10) children 5–15. Open: Apr–Oct daily 9 a.m.–5:30 p.m.; Nov–Mar daily 9 a.m.–4:30 p.m.*

Merchant Adventurers' Hall

In the medieval era, guilds ran English towns. This 14th-century stone and half-timbered guildhall belonged to York's most powerful guild, the Merchant Adventurers (it controlled trade into and out of the city). This building, one of the largest and best-preserved guildhalls in the country, has a great hall for business, a hospital for charitable work, and a chapel for worship. Allow half an hour for a tour with an audio guide.

See map p. 353. Fossgate. ☎ *01904/654-818. Admission: £2.50 ($4.65) adults, £2 ($3.70) seniors and students, £1 ($1.85) children 5–15. Open: Apr–Sept Mon–Thurs 9 a.m.–5 p.m., Fri–Sat 9 a.m.–3:30 p.m., Sun noon to 4 p.m.; Oct–Mar Mon–Sat 9 a.m.–3:30 p.m.*

National Railway Museum

As you probably guessed, this museum is devoted to England's railroad system. The great exhibits appeal to both adults and children. The earliest train cars on display date from the 1840s and look like stagecoaches on tracks. You can peek into the windows of private royal coaches, from Queen Victoria's of 1869, with its bulky furniture (the engineer had to stop when the queen wanted to move from one car to the next), to Queen Elizabeth's streamlined, functional carriage, used until 1977. You see a replica of the first steam locomotive (1830) and a display of the new Eurostar high-speed train. You need at least an hour for a thorough visit of this fascinating museum. On some trains, kids can climb up into the engineer's area.

See map p. 353. Leeman Road. ☎ *01904/621-261. Admission: Free. Open: Daily 10 a.m.–6 p.m.; closed Dec 24–26.*

The Shambles

Until 150 years ago, The Shambles was a street where butchers displayed their finest cuts in open windows on wide shelves called *shammels*. Today, this narrow, winding lane, with buildings so close that they shut out the light, is England's most famous medieval street. Gift shops have replaced the butcher shops, so you can get in a bit of retail therapy as you stroll.

No. 35 The Shambles is a shrine to St. Margaret Clitheroe, a butcher's wife executed during the Reformation for hiding Catholic priests in her attic; she was canonized in 1970.

Treasurer's House

This elegant town house in Minster Yard was originally the home of the Treasurer of York Minster. Built in 1620, the house was extensively remodeled during the Victorian era by an eccentric Yorkshireman who cared so passionately about interior décor that he threatened to return to haunt the place if anyone ever moved any of his furniture. The furniture hasn't been moved, and the house features beautiful period rooms with collections of 17th- and 18th-century furniture, glass, clocks, and china. You can see the entire collection in about 30 minutes. Stroll through the pretty walled garden, even if you don't visit the house. The tearoom belowstairs is a good place for lunch or tea.

See map p. 353. Minster Yard. ☎ *01904/624-247. Admission: £4.80 ($8.90) adults, £2.40 ($4.45) children 5–15. Open: Mid-Mar to Oct Sat–Thurs 11 a.m.–4:30 p.m.; closed Nov to mid-Mar.*

York Castle Museum

You can see 400 years of social history at York's top museum, which happens to be England's most popular folk museum. Using a treasure trove of now-vanished everyday objects, the exhibitions re-create slices of life from past historical eras. The museum took over York's 200-year-old prison buildings, with graffiti still on the walls of the dingy cells. You can walk down a reconstruction of Kirkgate, a cobbled Victorian shopping street; see a Jacobean dining room; visit a moorland cottage and a gypsy caravan; and call in at a Victorian police station and an Edwardian pub. You can check out the Jane Austen Costume Collection's fashion and fabrics. Kids love the giant dollhouses. Allow at least an hour.

See map p. 353. Eye of York (near Clifford's Tower). ☎ *01904/653-611. Admission: £6.50 ($12) adults, £3.50 ($6.50) children 5–15, £15 ($28) families (2 adults, 1 child). Open: Daily 9:30 a.m.–5 p.m.*

Ghostly legions

In 1953, apprentice heating engineer Harry Martindale was working in the basement of the Treasurer's House when he heard what sounded like marching feet. As he watched in amazement, a battalion of ghostly Roman soldiers marched right through the cellar. As it turns out, the Treasurer's House was built over the main Roman road. You can check out the haunted cellar of Treasurer's House yourself on one of the daily cellar tours, which cost £2 ($3.70).

York City Art Gallery

The city's art museum, with freshly refurbished galleries and a new cafe, is in an Italian Renaissance-style building completed in 1879. The collections on view span seven centuries of Western European painting and include pictures by Parmigianino, Bellotto, Lely, and Reynolds, and a small collection of 20th-century studio pottery. You can see the entire collection in less than an hour.

See map p. 353. Exhibition Square (city center). ☎ 01904/687-687. Admission: Free. Open: Daily 10 a.m.–5 p.m.; closed Jan 1 and Dec 25–26.

York Minster

Awesome York Minster, the largest Gothic cathedral in northern Europe, was built between 1220 and 1472. Architecturally, it spans the entire range of Gothic style: Early English (1220–1260), Decorated (1280–1350), and Perpendicular (1361–1472). The chief cathedral in the north of England, York Minster contains half of all the medieval stained glass in the country. The **Five Sisters' Window** from 1260 is the oldest complete window in the Minster. (*Minster,* by the way, means a church, usually with cathedral status, attached to a monastery.) The **Great West Window,** painted in 1338 and set in heart-shaped tracery, is known as the "Heart of Yorkshire."

Above the south door, a magnificent **Rose Window** (1500) commemorates the union of the royal houses of Lancaster and York. Painted in 1310, the **Jesse Window** in the south nave depicts Jesus's family tree. The Minster's Decorated Gothic **nave** (the main central space in the interior), begun in 1291 and finished in the 1350s, is one of Europe's widest. A 15th-century **Choir Screen** decorated with statues of 15 kings of England, from William I (the Conqueror) to Henry VI, separates the nave from the choir. In the south transept, you can descend into the **Undercroft** (the rooms under the church), where excavations have revealed the Roman basilica (an assembly hall, not a Christian church) that stood here nearly 2,000 years ago. You can take a well-designed "time walk" to see Roman, Anglo-Saxon, and Norman remains. The walk leads to the 12th-century **Crypt** and the **Treasury,** where silver plate and other church treasures are on display. From the nave, a separate entrance leads to the 13th-century **Chapter House,** filled with fine stone carvings and medieval glass. You can also ascend the minster's soaring tower for a bird's-eye view of York and the surrounding region. Give yourself at least one hour to see everything in the cathedral.

See map p. 353. Minster Yard. ☎ 01904/557-216. Admission: £7 ($13) adults, £5 ($9.25) seniors and students, £2 ($3.70) children. Open: Mon–Sat 9 a.m.–4:45 p.m., Sun noon to 3:45 p.m.

York Minster

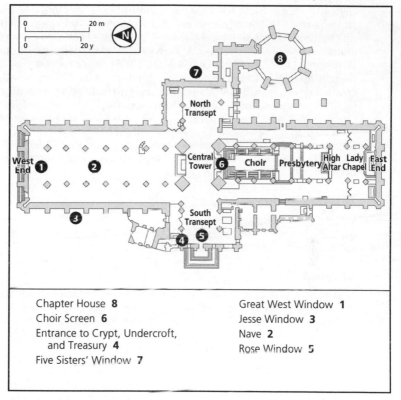

Chapter House **8**

Choir Screen **6**

Entrance to Crypt, Undercroft,
and Treasury **4**

Five Sisters' Window **7**

Great West Window **1**

Jesse Window **3**

Nave **2**

Rose Window **5**

Yorkshire Museum

The Yorkshire Museum is somewhat old-fashioned and heavy on the text panels, but if you start in the Roman section and walk through to the end, you get a sound presentation of Yorkshire's history from two millennia ago through the 16th century. You can view elegant Roman jewelry, mosaics, and Anglo-Saxon silver. Viking treasures include swords and battleaxes. The Middleham Jewel, a 15th-century pendant decorated with a large sapphire, was found in 1985 in North Yorkshire. The museum lies in 10 acres of landscaped gardens amid the ruins of St Mary's Abbey, once the wealthiest abbey in the north. On the grounds, you can see a 15th-century timberframed building known as The Hospitium. Give this museum about an hour.

See map p. 353. Museum Gardens (in the center of York). ☎ *01904/551-800. Admission: £4 ($7.40) adult, £2.50 ($4.65) children 5–15, £9 ($17) families (2 adults, 1 child). Open: Daily 10 a.m.–5 p.m. Closed Jan 1 and Dec 25–26.*

Shopping in York

High-end shops, including designer clothes boutiques and fine jewelry stores, are on **Swinegate,** a street that was once — you guessed it — a hog market. The **Quarter** area around Swinegate is known for its independent, one-of-a-kind shops. At **Newgate Market,** between Parliament Street and The Shambles (☎ 01904/551-355), you can find York's biggest open-air market, open daily with more than 100 stalls selling crafts, clothes, candles — you name it. If you're looking for antiques, head over to **The Red House Antiques Centre,** 1 Duncombe Place (the street runs south from York Minster; ☎ 01904/637-000), where more than 60 dealers sell quality, time-touched merchandise in a beautiful Georgian building. **The Miniature Scene,** 42 Fossgate (☎ 01904/638-265) is one of the U.K.'s biggest and best-stocked specialist dollhouse accessories stores.

Stepping out at night in York

York has an active nightlife scene, especially during the summer, when the air is warmer and the light lingers longer. You may want to take a special nighttime tour or head out to a pub.

Ghost walks

Apparently, plenty of supernatural activity takes place in York, which some claim is England's most haunted city. Evening ghost walks, with entertaining commentary and sometimes a bit of spookery thrown in, are a regular year-round industry. You have several tours from which to choose. You can buy your tickets on the spot. Tours cost £3.50 to £4 ($6.50–$7.40) for adults, £2 to £3 ($3.70–$5.55) for seniors, students, and children 5 to 15.

- ✔ **The Ghost Hunt of York** (☎ 01904/608-700): "Andy Dextrous," ghost hunter, leads this fun, one-hour walk and performance. Walks leave nightly at 7:30 from The Shambles, York's medieval street.

- ✔ **The Ghost Trail** (☎ 01904/633-276): You get more traditional ghost-storytelling on this walk, which leaves nightly at 7:30 from the front entrance of York Minster.

- ✔ **Original Ghost Walk of York** (☎ 01759/373-090): This walk began in 1973 and features really good storytelling, exploring the area's folklore, legend, and dreams. Walks leave nightly at 8 from The King's Arms Pub, Ouse Bridge.

The best pubs and bars

The Cross Keys, Goodramgate (☎ 01904/686-941), close to York Minster, is a popular pub with a beer garden and live music. Also on Goodramgate, you can find **Old White Swan** (☎ 01904/540-911), with a warm-weather courtyard, three bars, and home-cooked food. **The Punchbowl,** 7 Stonegate (☎ 01904/615-491), is a 300-year-old pub serving traditional Yorkshire ales and filling pub food. The half-timbered

Black Swan, Peasholme Green (☎ 01904/686-911), dates from the 15th century and is known for its folk-music performances. The modern **Bar 38,** Coney Street (☎ 01904/674-428), is a hip hangout with a riverside terrace, cocktail happy hour, and a good bar menu.

Performing arts

Theatre Royal, St. Leonard's Place (☎ 01904/623-568; www.theatre-royal-york.co.uk), and the **Grand Opera House,** Cumberland Street (☎ 01904/671-818; www.york-operahouse.co.uk), offer a year-round schedule of plays and concerts.

Day-tripping from York: Castle Howard and Eden Camp

If you're staying in York or the vicinity, you may want to visit Castle Howard and Eden Camp, both easily accessible from York by car, train, or taxi. The two places are close to each other but worlds apart. Castle Howard gives you a glimpse of the wealth and power of the English aristocracy, and Eden Camp tells the story of ordinary men and women living under extraordinary circumstances.

Getting to Castle Howard

Castle Howard is 24km (15 miles) north of York off A64 (20 minutes by car). From York, you can get a train to Malton (local Scarborough line, and then take a taxi (about £10/$19) 14.5km (9 miles) to the castle; to reserve a taxi, call **Station** (☎ 01653/696-969). In the summer, **Coastliner Coaches** (☎ 01653/692-556) operates buses from York and Scarborough.

Exploring Castle Howard

Set against a backdrop of North Yorkshire's Howardian Hills, anyone who's seen the television series *Brideshead Revisited* will instantly recognize Castle Howard. The castle is a truly magnificent sight — not really a castle, but certainly one of England's grandest stately homes. The largest house in Yorkshire, Castle Howard has been the home of the Howard family since the 17th century.

Sir John Vanbrugh designed Castle Howard (assisted by Nicholas Hawksmoor) and built it for the third Earl of Carlisle. The castle was Vanbrugh's first project; his second was Blenheim Palace (see Chapter 13). The facade showcases elegant architectural details, including statues, long arched windows, and a beautiful cupola crowning the center of the house.

The castle doesn't offer any guided tours; you're free to walk through at your own pace. Guides staff every room and can fill you in on the history. The marble entrance hall, lit by the dome, is particularly impressive, as is the Long Gallery, but the house has many superb rooms, all filled with fine furniture, statues, and china. The collection of paintings includes works by Rubens, Tintoretto, Van Dyke, Canaletto, and Reynolds, as well as a famous portrait of Henry VIII by Hans Holbein. *Brideshead* memorabilia fills one room.

The 1,000-acre park is landscaped with lakes, fountains, rose gardens, and shady woodland gardens. On the grounds, at the end of a short walk, you can find Vanbrugh's classically inspired Temple of the Four Winds and a circular mausoleum by Hawksmoor. You can choose among three restaurants: **The Hayloft Cafe** in the Stable Courtyard and **The Fitzroy Room** in the main house, both open daily from 10 a.m. to 5 p.m.; and **The Lakeside Cafe,** open weekends and holidays only, near the Great Lake. To see the house and gardens, you need a minimum of two hours, preferably three.

Malton. ☎ *01653/648-333. Admission: £9.50 ($18) adults, £8.50 ($16) seniors, £6.50 ($12) children 5–15. Open: Mar–Oct daily 11 a.m.–4 p.m. (grounds open at 10 a.m.).*

Getting to Eden Camp

Eden Camp is just north of the Malton train station, 8km (5 miles) east of Castle Howard off A64 York-Scarborough Road at the junction of A169 to Pickering. From York, take a train to Malton (local Scarborough line) and then take a taxi (about £10/$19) to Eden Camp; to reserve a taxi at the Malton train station, call **Station** (☎ **01653/696-969**).

Exploring Eden Camp

In 1942, Malton became the site of the Camp Eden prisoner-of-war camp. The first inmates, 250 Italians captured in North Africa, worked constructing the 35 wooden huts that you see today. The Italians left in 1944 and were followed by Germans, who remained until 1948. While at the camp, the prisoners worked on local farms under the control of the War Agriculture Officer.

Eden Camp's huts have now been re-equipped to tell about life in Britain during World War II (1939–1945). Realistic scenes, sounds, and smells have been created to help you imagine life at a time when food was strictly rationed, blackouts were a nightly occurrence, and 80,000 civilians were killed in bombing raids over England. Each hut covers a different aspect of the story, starting with the rise of the National Socialist Party, Hitler, and the outbreak of war. The sound of Vera Lynne singing "We'll Meet Again" is a haunting reminder of a time when people didn't know what the next day would bring. Eden Camp has much to see, so give yourself at least two hours.

Old Malton. ☎ *01653/697-777. Admission: £4.50 ($8.35) adults, £3.50 ($6.50) seniors and children 5–15. Open: Daily 10 a.m.–5 p.m. Closed Dec 24–mid-Jan.*

Scarborough: Cliffs and Arcades

The first and largest resort town on the Yorkshire coast, Scarborough is famous for its giant curving swath of sandy beach on the North Sea. The town clusters around two splendid bays (North Bay and South Bay), with a headland in between. South Cliff, the neighborhood around South Bay and the harbor with its Esplanade, is the main part of town. Scarborough is a fun place to visit for a day or to stay overnight if you're exploring North York Moors National Park (see the section "Yorkshire's Two National Parks: Moors and Dales," later in this chapter).

The seafront in Scarborough is a gaudy hodgepodge of noisy arcades, fish and chips shops, and tourist traps; its cheesiness is part of what makes the area fun. The town that covers the cliffs and hills above is more Victorian in character. Victorian-era cliff lifts still convey people up and down from the cliffs to the beach, just as they did when Scarborough was a preeminent Victorian spa town (people came to drink the mineral waters and to swim in the sea). In the end, Scarborough isn't a town where you go for heavy doses of culture. Popular with families, Scarborough is a good place to hang out on the beach, breathe the fresh sea air, and have a good time.

Getting to Scarborough

Scarborough is 56km (35 miles) northeast of York and 407km (253 miles) north of London. Local trains run all day between York and Scarborough. Trains leave London's Victoria Station almost every hour for York, where you change trains for the one-hour trip to Scarborough. For train information, call ☎ **08457/484950. Yorkshire Coastliner (☎ 01653/692-556;** www.yorkshirecoastliner.co.uk) operates two to four buses a day from York to Scarborough. By car from York, take A64 northeast.

Getting around Scarborough

The town is small enough that you can walk everywhere, but the hills from beach to town can make for a steep climb. For taxi service, call **Streamline Taxis (☎ 01904/638-833)** or **Station Taxis (☎ 01904/366-366)**.

Finding information and taking a tour of Scarborough

The main **Tourist Information Centre,** Unit 15A, Brunswick Shopping Centre, Westborough (☎ **01723/383-637;** www.discoveryorkshire coast.com), has maps, a room-booking service, and information on local attractions. The center is open Monday to Saturday from 9:30 a.m. to 5:30 p.m. and Sunday from 11 a.m. to 5 p.m. A smaller **Tourist Information Centre (☎ 01723/383-637)** is along the beach at Harborside; this center is open from Easter through October daily from 9:30 a.m. to 5:30 p.m. and from November to Easter on Sunday only.

Step Back in Time (☎ 01723/859-466; www.ScarboroughGuidedTours. ic24.net) is a local guide service that conducts guided walks on request.

Staying in Scarborough

Scarborough has plenty of hotels and B&Bs to choose from. I recommend the following choices.

Biederbecke's Hotel
$–$$ Town center

Biederbecke's, in an 1835 building at the end of a Victorian *crescent* (row houses built in a long, curving line), is Scarborough's most stylish hotel. The 27 guest rooms are comfortable and well furnished, with good-size tiled bathrooms (most with tub-shower combinations and bidets). Even if you don't stay here, stop in for a drink at the **Red Square Cocktail Bar,** with its blue and orange walls, contemporary furniture, and giant poster of Lenin. The bar is the hippest hangout in town. I describe the hotel restaurant, **Marmalade's,** in the section "Dining in Scarborough," later in this chapter.

1–3 The Crescent, Scarborough YO11 2PW. ☎ *01723/365-766. Fax: 01723/367-433.* www.beiderbeckes.com. *Rack rates: £90–£130 ($167–$241) double. Rates include English breakfast. AE, MC, V.*

Bradley Court Hotel
$ South Cliff

Bradley Court Hotel is a good, moderately priced hotel without sea views but within walking distance of town and beach. The 40-room hotel is Victorian with somewhat dowdy English modern furnishings. You find some nice connected rooms that families can put to good use up in the former attics and a few larger "premier" rooms. All rooms have private bathrooms with tubs and showers. You get a good breakfast with your room. Request a room in back if traffic noise bothers you.

Filey Road, Scarborough, YO11 2SE. ☎ *01723/360-476. Fax: 01723/376-661.* www.bradleycourthotel.co.uk. *Rack rates: £57–£85 ($105–$157) double. Rates include English breakfast. MC, V.*

The Esplanade Hotel
$–$$$ South Cliff

If you want a spacious room that has a big bathroom with tub and shower and panoramic sea views, you can't beat The Esplanade. The hotel is a large and rather old-fashioned place, created a century ago from three mid-19th-century houses on the top of the South Cliff above The Esplanade. A wonderful roof terrace overlooks South Bay and the town.

Belmont Road, Scarborough YO11 2AA. ☎ *01723/360-382. Fax: 01723/376-137.* www.theesplanade.co.uk. *Rack rates: £47–£192 ($87–$355) double. Rates include English breakfast. AE, V.*

Granville Lodge
$ Town center

This pretty, well-maintained hotel is in a Victorian building close to the town center. All 40 rooms have private bathrooms, and some have four-poster beds. The lodge has a good restaurant; ask about special rates that include dinner.

Belmont Road. ☎ **01723/367-668.** *Fax: 01723/363-089.* www.granville. scarborough.co.uk. *Rack rates: £52–£58 ($96–$107) double. Rates include English breakfast. MC, V.*

Dining in Scarborough

The restaurant scene in Scarborough has improved in recent years. Here are my recommended choices for dining.

Cafe Italia
$ COFFEE/LIGHT FARE

This small, atmospheric Italian coffee bar sits on a street over to one side of the Grand Hotel. Come here for good coffee, focaccia sandwiches, and ice cream.

36 St. Nicholas Cliff (near the Grand Hotel). ☎ **01723/501-975.** *Lunch: £4–£7 ($7.40–$13). No credit cards. Open: Mon–Sat 10 a.m.–4 p.m.*

Marmalade's
$–$$ INTERNATIONAL

This is Scarborough's liveliest and most sophisticated restaurant. The large, varied menu includes vegetarian offerings, such as Thai vegetable curry. Carnivores can choose from steak, chicken, rack of lamb, seared venison, and veal dishes, all served with intriguing sauces and side dishes. You can also find fresh fish on the menu. For simpler, cheaper fare, like fish and chips or meat and potato pie, eat in the bar.

1–3 The Crescent (in Biederbecke's Hotel). ☎ **01723/365-766.** *Reservations recommended for weekend dinner. Main courses: Restaurant £10–£16 ($19–$30); bar £6 ($11). AE, MC, V. Open: Daily 11 a.m.–3 p.m.; Mon–Sat 6–10 p.m., Sun 6–9 p.m.*

Mother Hubbard's
$ FISH AND CHIPS

This family-style fish restaurant serves the best fish and chips in town. You're not paying for decor or frills here, although the dining room is pleasant and cheery. Go for the haddock and chips; the batter is light and crispy. You can also get fresh cod or lemon sole.

43 Westborough. ☎ **01723/376-109.** *Main courses £5.50–£9 ($10–$17). No credit cards. Open: Mon–Sat 11:30 a.m.–6:45 p.m.*

Exploring Scarborough

Scarborough consists of an upper town and a lower area beside the beach. The town has always been more about enjoying the pleasures of the seaside than anything else.

Art Gallery

Scarborough's small art gallery sits next to Wood End Museum (see listing later in this section). The most interesting works on display relate to the Scarborough area during the Victorian age. You can see everything in about 15 minutes.

The Crescent. ☎ *01723/374-753. Admission (includes Rotunda Museum and Wood End Museum): £2.50 ($4.65) adults, £1.50 ($2.80) seniors and children 5–15, £6 ($11) families (2 adults, 2 children). Open: June–Sept Tues–Sun 10 a.m.–5 p.m., Oct–May Thurs–Sat 11 a.m.–4 p.m.*

Rotunda Museum

The history and architecture of this small, circular museum are more interesting than its collections. Built in 1829 to contain the rock collections of William Smith (known as the father of English geology), it was one of England's first purpose-built museums. You don't need more than a few minutes to wander through; the second floor, with its original painted frieze and curving wall cabinets, is worth checking out Your ticket allows admission to Wood End and the Art Gallery (I describe both in this section).

Vernon Road. ☎ *01723/374-839. Admission (includes Art Gallery and Wood End Museum): £2.50 ($4.65) adults, £1.50 ($2.80) seniors and children 5–15, £6 ($11) families (2 adults, 2 children). Open: June–Sept Tues–Sun 10 a.m.–5 p.m.; Oct–May Tues, Sat–Sun 11 a.m.–4 p.m.*

Scarborough Castle

The headland between Scarborough's North and South bays was originally the site of a fourth-century Roman signal station. The castle here, built in the 12th century, is partially in ruins, but you get panoramic views of the coastline from its battlemented walls. An audio tour (included in the admission price) fills you in on the castle's turbulent history. Give yourself an hour, but add more time if you want to enjoy the headland walks.

Castle Road. ☎ *01723/372-451. Admission: £3.30 ($6.10) adults, £2.50 ($4.65) seniors, £1.70 ($3.15) children 5–15. Open: Mid-Mar–Sept daily 10 a.m.–6 p.m.; Oct–Mar Thurs–Mon 10 a.m.–4 p.m.*

Scarborough Sea Life & Marine Sanctuary

Northeast England's leading marine animal rescue center, this place also operates as an aquarium, with fish, seals, sea otters, sea turtles, and other denizens of the deep. More than 30 multilevel viewing areas allow you to get close to various sea creatures, from sharks to shrimps. Kids enjoy the touch pools, where they can pick up velvet crabs, starfish, and anemones. You can watch feeding demonstrations and many marine-themed presentations.

Scalby Mills, North Bay. ☎ *01723/376-125. Admission: £6.50 ($12) adults, £4.75 ($8.80) children 5–15, £21 ($39) families (2 adults, 2 children). Open: Daily Oct–June 10 a.m.–5 p.m., July–Sept 10 a.m.–8 p.m.*

Wood End Museum

Wood End was the childhood vacation home of the miserable Sitwell siblings, Edith, Osbert, and Sacheverell, who went on to become literary figures. The Victorian house now contains a library of their works and a pretty boring collection of stuffed animals (the real kind) from the Museum of Natural History. This museum is of interest only to fans of the Sitwells and requires about 10 minutes to see.

The Crescent. ☎ *01723/367-326. Admission (includes Art Gallery and Rotunda Museum): £2.50 ($4.65) adults, £1.50 ($2.80) seniors and children 5–15, £6 ($11) families (2 adults, 2 children). Open: June–Sept Tues–Sun 10 a.m.–5 p.m.; Oct–May Wed, Sat, and Sun 11 a.m.–4 p.m.*

The fishing village of Whitby

The old fishing, whaling, and smuggling village of Whitby, with its quaint cobbled streets and picturesque houses, is 32km (20 miles) up the Yorkshire coast from Scarborough, in North York Moors National Park. Smaller and less touristy than Scarborough, Whitby makes a pleasant day trip from York or Scarborough. The port at Whitby has been in use for more than 1,000 years. Nowadays, people come to stroll the town's winding maze of streets and enjoy the coastal scenery, with its cliffs, coves, and bays. (The beaches are clean, but the North Sea is pretty cold for swimming, or "bathing," as the Brits call it.)

The River Esk divides the town into east and west sections. From Tate Hill Pier on the east side, Church Lane climbs up to the 199 steps leading to the **Church of St. Mary,** whose churchyard was one of the inspirations for Bram Stoker's *Dracula.* The imposing ruins of **Whitby Abbey,** founded in the seventh century, dominate the clifftop above. On the beachfront on the west side of town, you can find a **monument to Captain Cook,** who left Whitby in locally made ships for his circumnavigation of the globe. (Cook claimed Australia and New Zealand for Great Britain.)

You can see all the sights in Whitby on **The Whitby Tour** (☎ **0191/521-0202**), a 50-minute, open-top-bus tour that operates daily from April to October. The tour costs £4 ($7.40) for adults and £3 ($5.55) for seniors and students. Tours begin at about 10 a.m. (from Langborne Road, near the Tourist Information Centre) and depart hourly until 4 p.m.

For a map and more information, stop in at the **Tourist Information Centre,** Langborne Road (☎ **01947/602-674**), open daily from 9:30 a.m. to 4:30 p.m. (until 6 p.m. in summer). Daily bus service goes from Scarborough to Whitby, but you can't find any easy train connections. The Tourist Information Centre in Scarborough can give you up-to-the-minute bus schedules. If you're driving from Scarborough, take A171 north.

Seeing the performing arts in Scarborough

The **Stephen Joseph Theatre** (☎ 01723/370-541; www.sjt.uk.com), opposite the train station on the corner of Westborough and Valley Bridge Road, was created from an Art Deco movie theater. The space is known as "Alan Ayckborne's theatre" because the British playwright–director opens his plays here before doing so in London. Troupes from around the country present a full season of offerings. The **theater restaurant** (☎ 01723/368-463), a good place for a preshow meal, serves traditional and Modern British main courses, salads, and desserts.

Yorkshire's Two National Parks: Moors and Dales

Two national parks have helped preserve Yorkshire's famous moors, dales, and coastline. Using York or Scarborough as a base, you may want to explore the vast heather-covered moors and Yorkshire coastline that make up North York Moors National Park. York also makes a good base for touring Yorkshire Dales National Park, as does Windermere in Cumbria (see Chapter 22), at the park's northwestern corner. Both parks attract hordes of summer ramblers and long-distance hikers. Visitors on a limited schedule can rent a car in York (see the section "Renting a car or calling a taxi," earlier in this chapter) for touring one or both of the parks.

North York Moors National Park

Vast stretches of heather moorland — the largest expanses in England and Wales — make the North York Moors unique. In late summer, the countryside turns into a great flowing sea of purple. Wonderful views cut across *dales* (rich farmland, where people have worked for centuries) and sweep out to the North Sea. Old crosses and standing stones remind you of the moorland's ancient human heart. The 1,434 sq. km park (554-sq.-mile) is also an important protected area for birds and wildlife.

From Scalby Mills near Scarborough to Saltburn in the north, picturesque, cliff-clinging villages such as Whitby (see "The fishing village of Whitby" sidebar, earlier in this chapter), where fishing boats tie up at the harbors below, dot the coastal section. Commercial development along the coast and throughout the moors has been limited, so the area retains much of its rugged, down-to-earth character.

Getting to North York Moors National Park

Motorways encircle the park: A170 skirts the southern boundary; A19 and A172 traverse the western edge; and A171 follows the eastern coastline and then cuts across the park's northern boundary. The only major road through the park is A169. Within the park, you find small roads, so having a good map is essential (you can pick one up at a visitor center). If you're traveling by car from York, head northeast on A64; you can cut north on A169 at Malton to the Visitor Centre at Pickering or continue on A64 to Scarborough and there pick up A171, the coastal road. See the sections "Getting to York" and "Getting to Scarborough," earlier in this chapter, for train and bus information from London.

Getting around North York Moors National Park

The popular **North Yorkshire Moors Steam Railway** (☎ 01751/472-508; www.northyorkshiremoorsrailway.com) chugs along a wonderfully scenic 29km (18-mile) route through the heart of the park between the village of Grosmont (near Whitby) and the market town of Pickering. All-day Return Rover tickets let you hop off at any of the train's five restored stations for a walk through a village or the surrounding moors. The ticket costs £12 ($22) for adults, £11 ($20) for seniors, and £6 ($11) for children 5 to 15. Trains run daily from April through October.

Walking is the best way to discover this area's beauty. More than 3,220km (2,000 miles) of public paths allow you to explore even the remotest parts of the countryside. If you do go walking (or even if you drive), make sure you get Ordnance Survey Outdoor Leisure maps 26 and 27, which show every path and road. The National Park publishes "Walks Around . . ." booklets for various sections of the park, including Robin Hood's Bay, The Moors Centre, Goathland, Rosedale, and Sutton Bank. You can pick up the maps and booklets at the park information centers listed in the following section.

Finding information about the North York Moors

You can get information about the park from the **North York Moors National Park Authority,** Head Office, The Old Vicarage, Bondgate, Helmsley, York YO62 5BP (☎ 01439/770-657; www.visitthemoors.com); **The Moors Centre,** Danby, Whitby (☎ 01287/660-654); or **Sutton Bank National Park Centre,** Sutton Bank, Thirsk (☎ 01845/597-426). All these centers are open daily in March, November, and December from 11 a.m. to 4 p.m., April through October daily from 10 a.m. to 5 p.m., and in January and February on Saturday and Sunday from 11 a.m. to 4 p.m.

Exploring North York Moors National Park

North York Moors National Park was home to three great medieval religious houses. At **Mount Grace Priory,** near Osmotherley off A19, you can see how the Carthusian monks lived, each with his own cell and garden. Farther south, between Thirsk and Helmsley off A170, is **Byland Abbey,** which was the home of a Cistercian order. The majestic ruins of **Rievaulx Abbey,** oldest and most famous of the three, housed more than 600 monks. This National Trust property is located in the southwest section of the park, 3km (2 miles) west of Helmsley off B1257. You can reach all these sites in easy day trips from York if you have a car.

The patchwork of fields and open moorland in the **Esk Valley** exudes an aura of timelessness. Near **Lealholm** and **Glaisdale,** old stone tracks mark the routes walked by generations of farmers and travelers. The watermill in the farming hamlet of **Danby** was the village's most important building; the mill is more than 350 years old and still working. Nearby, you can see the ruins of **Danby Castle,** built in the 14th century as a fortified home. A short stroll down to the river takes you to **Duck Bridge,** first used 600 years ago. For the locations of all these sights, consult Ordnance Survey Outdoor Leisure maps 26 and 27 or the booklet "Walks Around . . . ," both available at the park information centers (see the preceding section).

Yorkshire Dales National Park

Covering some 1,813 sq. km (700 sq. miles), Yorkshire Dales National Park is home to a collection of varied landscapes: heather-capped moors, swift moorland rivers, colorful hay meadows, and rugged limestone crags. Bustling market towns and traditional sandstone villages nestle among fields and rolling farmland dotted with stone barns and stacked dry-stone walls. Yorkshire Dales has different moods, wild and windswept in one place, quietly pastoral and rustic in another.

Getting to Yorkshire Dales National Park

The A1 to the east, A66 to the north, and the M6 to the west flank Yorkshire Dales National Park. Although driving is the easiest way to explore the park, you can also take public transportation. For information on local bus service, call ☎ 0113/245-676. The nearest railway stations are Darlington and Northallerton; for train information, call ☎ 08457/484950. **National Express** (☎ 0990/808-080; www.nationalexpress.com) runs buses to Darlington.

Finding information for the Yorkshire Dales

You can obtain information at the park's Web site, www.yorkshire dales.org. You can get maps, general information, and help with accommodations at **National Park Centres** in the following towns: **Aysgarth** (☎ 01969/663-424), open daily April to October; **Grassington** (☎ 01756/752-774), open daily from Easter through October; **Hawes** (☎ 01969/667-165), open year-round; and **Malham** (☎ 01729/830-363), open daily from April through October and on Saturday and Sunday the rest of the year.

Exploring Yorkshire Dales National Park

The Yorkshire Dales are ideal for walking — paths crisscross the entire park. For the best walking areas and towns to explore, check out the following (for maps and information, visit any of the National Park Centres, listed in the preceding section):

- ✔ **Aysgarth:** Where the river cascades down a series of waterfalls, this place is one of the park's scenic highlights.

- ✔ **Dales Way:** This popular footpath passes through the village of **Grassington,** in the scenic Upper Wharfedale section.

✔ **Hawes:** In Upper Wharfedale, is said to be the highest market town in England. In this lively place, you can find shops selling local crafts and famous Wensleydale cheese. Hawes's old train station, next to the National Park Centre, is now the **Dales Countryside Museum** (☎ 01969/667-494), where you can find out more about the 10,000-year human history of the Yorkshire Dales.

✔ **Malham:** This town closest to the park's remarkable limestone formations has more good hiking. During the summer, up to half a million visitors swamp this 200-person village.

Haworth: On the Trail of the Brontës

Emily Brontë's *Wuthering Heights* or Charlotte Brontë's *Jane Eyre* may have sparked your interest in Yorkshire and the moors. Emily and Charlotte lived with a third sister, Anne, also a novelist *(The Tenant of Wildfell Hall)*, and their brother Branwell in the West Yorkshire town of Haworth, 72km (45 miles) southwest of York. Grim industrial cities (such as Leeds, Bradford, Halifax, and Keighley) surround Haworth, which wouldn't be on anyone's radar if not for the Brontë clan. For more than a century now, people from around the world have trekked up the cobbled Main Street of Haworth to see the house where these three women, daughters of a local parson, wrote their compellingly passionate novels. Although Branwell's failed career as a portrait painter led him to drink and drugs, he did paint the famous portrait of Charlotte, Emily, and Anne that now hangs in London's National Portrait Gallery.

Getting to Haworth

The nearest train station with service from a major city is Leeds. From Leeds, you can take the West Yorkshire Metrotrain to Keighley, 5km (3 miles) south of Haworth. The Keighley and Worth Valley Railway runs steam trains between Keighley and Haworth (year-round on the weekends and from late June to early Sept daily). There's regular bus service to Haworth from Keighley and Bradford (13km/8 miles away). For local train and bus information, call ☎ 01535/645-214; for national train information, call National Rail Enquiries ☎ 08457/484-950. If you're driving from York, take A64 west to Leeds and A6120 to Shipley; from there, take A650 to Keighley and B6142 to Haworth.

Finding information and taking a tour of Haworth

For information on the town, stop at the **Tourist Information Centre,** 2–4 West Lane (☎ 01535/642-329; www.haworth-village.org.uk), open daily from 9:30 a.m. to 5:30 p.m. (until 5 p.m. Nov–Mar; closed Dec 24–26). Well-marked walks lead from the town into the heather-covered moors so memorably evoked in the Brontë sisters' works. At the center, you can pick up a leaflet describing the most popular walks.

Dining in Haworth

If you want a well-prepared dinner, try **Weaver's Restaurant,** 15 West Lane (☎ **01535/643-822**). You absolutely have to make reservations, because this restaurant is the best (and busiest) in town. The menu features both traditional and Modern British cooking. Main courses go for £9 to £16 ($17–$30), and a set-price lunch or dinner costs £16 ($30). The restaurant is open Tuesday through Sunday from 11:30 a.m. to 2:30 p.m. and Tuesday through Saturday from 7 to 9:30 p.m. If you want a casual lunch, check out the offerings — pubs, tearooms, and cafes — lining Main Street and West Lane. A pub lunch averages around £8 to £10 ($15–$19).

Exploring Haworth

Haworth really should rename itself Brontëville, because the Brontë name is on everything from tea shops to trinket outlets. The one must-see literary shrine is the **Brontë Parsonage Museum** (☎ **01535/642-323**; www.bronte.org.uk), the house where the literary-minded siblings spent most of their lives. Built in 1778 at the top of the village behind the parish church, the house is furnished much as it would have been when the Brontës lived there. The museum displays a collection of personal memorabilia, manuscripts, and even some of Charlotte's clothes (she was tiny). The museum is open daily April through September from 10 a.m. to 5:30 p.m. and October through March daily from 11 a.m. to 5 p.m.; it's closed December 24 to 27 and all of January. Admission costs £4.90 ($9.05) for adults, £3.60 ($6.65) for seniors and students, £1.60 ($2.95) for children age 5 to 15, and £11 ($20) for families (2 adults, 3 children). Depending on your interest, allow 30 to 60 minutes to visit the museum.

After visiting the house, you can stop in at the parish church, which looks much different than it did in the Brontë sisters' days. Charlotte, the only one to wed, was married here in 1854 and buried here a year later, aged 39. Emily, who died in 1848 at age 30, also rests in the family vault. Anne died in Scarborough at age 29 and is buried there.

Chapter 22

The Lake District

In This Chapter

▶ Touring the Lake District
▶ Visiting Hill Top, home of Beatrix Potter
▶ Visiting Dove Cottage, Wordsworth's home in Grasmere
▶ Savoring the spectacular countryside around Keswick

*1*n 1974, the counties of Cumberland and Westmorland joined with a bit of Lancashire to officially create **Cumbria** in the northwest corner of England. But actually, Cumbria existed about 1,000 years before that as an ancient Celtic kingdom. And before that, about 5,000 years ago, the region was the home of Neolithic tribes that manufactured stone axes and erected stone circles. Today, this area, roughly 435km (270 miles) northwest of London and covering some 2,300 sq. km (885 sq. miles), is protected as the **Lake District National Park.** The largest national park in the United Kingdom, it's also one of the most popular.

If you can, give yourself at least a couple of days in the Lake District. I cover three towns and lakes in this chapter: **Bowness** and **Grasmere** on Lake Windermere, and **Keswick** on Derwentwater. You find good hotels and restaurants in all three, and all are convenient for exploring this fascinating region, which stretches from Lancashire north to the Scottish border, east to the counties of Yorkshire, Durham, and Northumberland, and west to the Irish Sea. (See "The Lake District" map on p. 378.)

ANGLO FILES
ENGLAND

Odes and bunny rabbits

The Lake District's two most famous residents were the poet William Wordsworth and Beatrix Potter, who wrote and illustrated children's books. The landscape inspired both writers, and they used it in their work. Wordsworth composed his poetry outdoors, often in the area around Grasmere. Potter used Lakeland settings for her tales about Peter Rabbit and Jemima Puddle-Duck.

The Lake District

Lake District lingo

The Lake District and northern England in general have a unique topography. Nowhere else in the country can you find the mixture of mountains, lakes, and streams that characterizes this area. These natural features even have special names. Here are a few words that you may encounter:

- ✔ *Tarn:* A steep-banked mountain lake or pool
- ✔ *Beck:* A mountain stream
- ✔ *Mere:* A small, still lake
- ✔ *Fells:* Mountains

The Lake District: Natural Beauty and Literary Treasures

The Lake District, or Lakeland as it's also called, is a hauntingly beautiful place with a distinct personality. Treeless peaks covered with *bracken* (large, coarse ferns) surround a series of tranquil, jewel-like lakes radiating like spokes around 3,210-foot-high Scafell Pike, England's highest mountain. Having a sense of wide-open spaces is rare in England, and that's why the Lake District is so popular with hikers. Wonderful hiking trails lace the entire region, passing fern-fringed streams, stands of purple foxglove, hedgerows bursting with dog roses, ancient stone circles, and cottages made of gray-green Lakeland slate.

The weather in the Lake District is unpredictable — squalls can suddenly appear. Be prepared for fine, thin rains; vapory mists; and blustery winds. If you're thinking about hiking, bring waterproof boots and rain gear. To check on the rapidly changing weather conditions, call the **Weatherline** at ☎ **01787/75757.**

Getting to the Lake District

Bowness-on-Windermere, Grasmere, and Keswick all make good bases for exploring the region. Several trains a day operate between London's Euston station and Oxenholme, the nearest main-line station to Lake Windermere. The trip takes about five hours and costs £65 ($120) for an advance-purchase round-trip ticket. From Oxenholme, local train service runs to Windermere. **National Express** (☎ **08705/808-080;** www.national express.com) runs buses from London's Victoria Coach Station to Windermere, but the trip by bus takes more than six-and-a-half hours. The closest airports are Manchester, Leeds, and Newcastle. Driving from London, the fastest route is the M1 to Birmingham, where you pick up the M6 heading north. From the M6, take A590 and then A591 northwest to Windermere.

Getting around the Lake District

Having a car opens up the entire region, but you may run into heavy (and sometimes aggravating) traffic in the summer. You may want to rent a car in York (see Chapter 21) and drive west through Yorkshire Dales National Park to the Lake District. (Otherwise, you can rent a car in Leeds or Manchester.) But boats and local buses (this area has no train service) can get you to all the towns and tourist sites that I describe in this chapter without too much difficulty. The distances aren't great; in some cases, you can even walk. For all public transport questions — to, from, and within Cumbria — call the **Cumbria Traveline** at ☎ **0870/ 608-2608** (daily 7 a.m.–8 p.m.; www.traveline-cumbria.co.uk). You can also check the district's Web site at www.golakes.co.uk.

Stagecoach Cumbria (☎ **0870/606-2608;** www.stagecoachbus.co.uk) operates buses between all the towns I describe in the following sections. A one-day **Explorer pass,** good for unlimited travel, is £8.50 ($16) for adults and £5.50 ($10) for children 5 to 15. You can buy the Explorer and longer-term tickets on the bus or at any tourist information center (see the sections about finding information for each region, later in this chapter, for locations).

Taking a tour of the Lake District

If you don't have a car, why not consider taking a guided tour of the Lake District? You have many options, including the following:

- ✔ **Countrywide Holidays,** Miry Lane, Wigan, Lancashire WN3 4AG (☎ **01942/823-456;** www.countrywidewalking.com): Offers safe and sociable walks led by experienced guides from different Lakeland locales; prices vary according to the walk you choose.

- ✔ **Cumbrian Discoveries,** Mickle Bower, Temple, Sowerby, Penrith CA10 1RA (☎ **01768/362-201;** www.toursofdiscovery.co.uk): Arranges tailor-made tours on foot, by car, and by minibus. Prices depend on your itinerary.

- ✔ **Lakeland Safari Tours,** 23 Fisherbeck Park, Ambleside LA22 0A (☎ **01539/433-904;** www.lakesafari.co.uk): Offers full- and half-day tours in a luxury six-seater for £22 ($41) for a half-day tour or £33 ($61) for a full day.

- ✔ **Lakes Supertours,** 1 High St., Windermere LA23 1AF (☎ **01539/ 442-751;** www.lakes-supertours.co.uk): Picks you up at your hotel for minibus trips to Beatrix Potter's house, Wordsworth's Dove Cottage, and Lakeland beauty spots. Prices depend on the type and length of your tour.

Lake Windermere: The Largest Lake in England

Glinting like a long, thin blade within its surrounding fells, 16km-long (10-mile) Windermere is England's longest lake. Windermere is also the region's most popular lake, a center for sailing, rowing, and yachting. (You can swim here, too, but the water's pretty brisk.) The town of **Windermere** (right around the train station) blends into **Bowness-on-Windermere** (also called Bowness) on the lake's eastern shore. Both towns are busy tourist-resort centers and good central spots to base yourself. You can walk from Windermere to Bowness in about 15 minutes; a local bus runs frequently from the train station at Windermere to Bowness Pier, a departure point for lake cruises. People come to Lake Windermere to hike, take boat trips, and visit the sites associated with Beatrix Potter.

Finding information and exchanging money near Lake Windermere

A few steps from the train station, Windermere's **Tourist Information Centre,** Victoria Street (☎ **015394/46490;** www.golakes.co.uk), sells maps and local guides and has a hotel-booking service. The center is open daily from 9 a.m. to 5 p.m. (until 6 p.m. Apr–Sept and until 7:30 p.m. July–Aug). A **National Park Information Centre** (with a bureau de change) is at Bowness Bay (☎ **015394/42895**), next to the boat landing. See also the listing for the Lake District Visitor Centre in the section "Exploring around Lake Windermere," later in this chapter.

Barclays, Crescent Road, Windermere (☎ **015394/46111**), changes money weekdays from 9:30 a.m. to 4:30 p.m. and has an ATM.

Touring by boat or foot

You can explore the lake and the dramatically beautiful countryside around it relatively easily — and you don't need a car to do it.

Lake cruises

Various boat trips are available year-round on Lake Windermere. From the piers at Bowness, ferries make regular trips to Waterhead (near Ambleside) on the north shore and Lakeside on the southern end; others make a circular tour, stopping at points all around the lake. The boats are fitted out for sightseeing, with big windows and open decks. From mid-May to mid-August, you can also take an evening wine cruise. A round trip from Bowness to Ambleside is £6.95 ($13) for adults, £3.60

($6.65) for children 5 to 15, and £19 ($35) for families (2 adults, 2 children). For more information, contact **Windermere Lake Cruises** (☎ **01539/531-188;** www.windermere-lakecruises.co.uk).

Windermere Ferry (☎ **0860/813-427**), which shuttles passengers, cyclists, and cars between Bowness and Far Sawrey, on the western shore, is the cheapest way to get across the lake. Ferries depart about every 30 minutes throughout the day from Ferry Nab, south of the excursion-boat piers. The one-way passenger fare costs 40p (75¢); a car costs £2.50 ($4.65).

A **Freedom of the Lake pass** is valid on all scheduled boats — including Windermere Lake Cruises and Windermere Ferry — on Lake Windermere for 24 hours. The pass costs £13 ($24) for adults, £6.25 ($12) for children 5 to 15, and £32 ($59) for families (2 adults, 2 children).

Walks and rides

You won't find much solitude around Lake Windermere during the summer months, but some good, nonstrenuous walks can give you some memorable views. One of the easiest, and a good choice if you have older kids in tow, is the 4km-round-trip (2½-mile) trail from the Windermere Tourist Information Centre on Victoria Street to Orrest Head (234m/784 ft.). The trail gives you plenty of photo-op panoramas of the lake and the villages along the shore.

The Lake District is wonderful biking country, but be aware that cars can jam the local roads during the summer. You can rent bikes at **Country Lanes Cycle Centre** (☎ **015394/44544**), in the Windermere railroad station. It's open daily from 9 a.m. to 5 p.m. Easter through October. Bike rental is £17 ($31), plus deposit.

Staying near Lake Windermere

Lake Windermere is one of England's premier tourist attractions, so you'll have no problem finding a hotel or B&B. My favorites are listed here.

Linthwaite House
$$$–$$$$$ **Bowness**

This large Victorian house overlooking Lake Windermere offers high-quality accommodations and wonderful service. The 26 rooms, all with private bathrooms, are appealingly decorated in a variety of styles that combine elegance and upscale comfort. The hotel has a notable restaurant and its own small tarn. Check the Web site for special offers.

Crook Road, Bowness-on-Windermere, Cumbria LA23 3JA. ☎ *015394/88600. Fax: 015394/88601.* www.linthwaite.com. *Rack rates: £160–£280 ($296–$518) double. Rates include English breakfast. AE, MC, V.*

Miller Howe Hotel
$$$–$$$$$ Windermere

Miller Howe is one of those great country-house hotels that can turn a holiday into heaven. The hotel sits on a hill amid acres of landscaped gardens and enjoys a spectacular view of Lake Windermere. The restaurant is one of the most famous in the country (see the review in the section "Dining near Lake Windermere," later in this chapter), and guests come specifically to dine here. (The rates look high, but if you figure in the cost of the masterful six-course dinner that comes with the room, it's actually pretty reasonable.) The house is warm and sumptuous, with fires, cozy lounges, and pampering service. The spacious and beautifully furnished rooms (12 in all) have big bathrooms with tubs and showers. If you don't stay, consider dining here.

Rayrigg Road, Windermere, Cumbria LA23 1EY. ☎ *015394/42536. Fax: 015394/45664.* www.millerhowe.com. *Rack rates: £190–£280 ($352–$518) double. Rates include English breakfast and dinner. AE, DC, MC, V.*

The Old England
$$–$$$ Bowness-on-Windermere

If you want to stay right on the water's edge, book a room at this well-appointed hotel. The hotel is just steps from Bowness Pier, and gardens lead down to the hotel's own jetties. Originally built as a lakeside mansion in the Victorian era, the hotel has grand-size public rooms and 76 comfy guest rooms with private bathrooms. In the summer, the hotel has a heated outdoor pool, a favorite with kids. You can have a nice lunch or dinner at the restaurant, overlooking the water.

Bowness-on-Windermere, Cumbria LA23 3DF. ☎ *0870/400-8130. Fax 01539/443-432.* www.macdonald-hotels.co.uk. *Rack rates: £140–£200 ($259–$370) double. Rates include English breakfast. AE, MC, V.*

Dining near Lake Windermere

As a busy tourist center, Windermere has plenty of restaurants. In this section, I list my favorites.

Aunty Val's Tea Rooms
$ Bowness-on-Windermere   TEAS/TRADITIONAL ENGLISH

Here's a good, quiet spot for an inexpensive lunch or tea. You can get homemade soup; toasted sandwiches; and a couple of hot main courses, such as steak and kidney pie, meat and potato pie, or a Cornish pasty (usually meat and onions baked in a crust). If you've never had hot sticky toffee pudding with cream, try it here. You can also choose from an assortment of homemade pastries.

Church Street, Bowness-on-Windermere. ☎ *015394/88211. Main courses: £3.50–£6 ($6.50–$11). No credit cards. Open: Daily 11 a.m.–5 p.m.; closed Fri Nov and May.*

The Hole in't Wall
$ Bowness-on-Windermere   PUB/INTERNATIONAL

Back in 1612, one side of this building was an alehouse (it still is), and the other was a blacksmith's shop. A hole in the wall connected the two. Now the place has a dark, wood-paneled interior with a fireplace. The food runs the gamut from whole roast pheasant to fisherman's pie, a daily curry, and daily specials listed on the blackboard. The menu always includes something that kids can enjoy. Set off a bit from the main tourist track in Bowness, it's an atmospheric spot to sample Cumbrian ales.

Lowside, Bowness-on-Windermere. ☎ *015394/43488. Main courses: £5.50–£10 ($10–$19). MC, V. Open: Mon–Sat 11 a.m.–11 p.m., Sun noon–10:30 p.m.*

Miller Howe Cafe
$ Windermere   MODERN BRITISH

Lakeland Ltd., right behind the Windermere train station, is one of England's largest retailers of creative kitchenware and food-related paraphernalia. The store contains this good cafe, where you can get a well-prepared lunch or tea. Options include homemade soups, sandwiches, salads, and quiches. Many families with children come here for lunch. You may want to stop in for some shopping, even if you don't eat here — you can find plenty of gift possibilities. (The cafe isn't related to the gourmet restaurant in the Miller Howe Hotel.)

Lakeland Ltd., Station Precincts, Windermere. ☎ *015394/88100. Main courses: £5–£9.50 ($9.25–$18). MC, V. Open: Mon–Fri 9 a.m.–6 p.m., Sat 9 a.m.–5 p.m., Sun 11 a.m.–4 p.m.*

Miller Howe Hotel Restaurant
$$$$ Windermere   MODERN BRITISH

Dinner at this fine hotel restaurant is a somewhat ritualistic affair. It has only one seating, at 8 p.m., and the six-course menu is the same for everyone (with a la carte options). A typical meal may start with a trio of canapés (with *áballontine* of foie gras) and advance to a first course of seared scallops wrapped in cabbage followed by champagne sorbet. The main course may be local lamb in red-wine–rosemary sauce, with vegetables, followed by dessert. The elegant, two-tiered, candlelit dining room overlooks Lake Windermere, and you definitely find it a culinary high point of the Lake District. If you're staying at the hotel, your room rate includes dinner.

In the Miller Howe Hotel, Rayrigg Road, Windermere. ☎ *015394/42536. Reservations required. Six-course fixed-price dinner: £43 ($80); 3-course fixed-price lunch: £22 ($41). AE, DC, MC, V. Open: Daily lunch and dinner.*

Exploring around Lake Windermere

You probably don't want to spend too much time in the town of Windermere itself. The lake and surrounding countryside are what make this part of England so special.

Beatrix Potter Gallery
Hawkshead

You can see ample evidence of Beatrix Potter's skills as an illustrator of her own children's stories in this National Trust collection of her original drawings and watercolors. You also can find an exhibition about Potter's life. The gallery is in what was the office of Potter's husband, a local attorney. After visiting the gallery, spend a little time wandering around Hawkshead, one of the region's prettiest villages. If you're a Potter fan, allow at least 30 minutes; add another 30 minutes if you want to wander around Hawkshead.

The poet William Wordsworth was a student at **Hawkshead Grammar School**, founded in 1585 (no phone). It's open Easter through October Monday through Saturday from 10 a.m. to 1 p.m. and 2 to 5 p.m.; admission costs £2 ($3.70) for adults and 50p (95¢) for children.

Main Street, Hawkshead. ☎ *015394/36355. Admission: £3.50 ($6.50) adults, £1.70 ($3.15) children 5–15, £8.70 ($16) family (2 adults, 2 children). Open: Mid-Mar–Oct Sun–Wed 10:30 a.m.–4:30 p.m. (also Thurs in Aug).*

Hill Top
Near Sawrey

Beatrix Potter wrote and illustrated many of her famous children's tales in this 17th-century stone cottage. She was born in London but spent summer holidays in the Lake District with her family. The international success of *The Tale of Peter Rabbit* allowed her to buy this small, pretty house and move permanently to the Lakeland village of Near Sawrey. Potter deeded her house to the National Trust before she died in 1943, and the interior — one of the darkest you'll ever see — remains as she left it, complete with her furniture, bone china, and garden. Because the house is so small, only a certain number of visitors are allowed in at any one time. Hill Top uses a timed-entry admission policy, which may keep you waiting in the summer. After you go inside, allow about 15 minutes to visit the house. You can get a pub lunch at the **Tower Bank Arms** (☎ 015394/ 36336) in front of the house.

Between April and October, you can take bus no. 505 or 506 from the train station in Windermere to Hill Top.

Near Sawrey, Ambleside (west side of Lake Windermere, 3.2km (2 miles) south of Hawkshead). ☎ *015394/36269. Admission: £5 ($9.25) adults, £2 ($3.70) children 5–15, £12 ($22) families (2 adults, 2 children). Open: Mid-Mar–Oct Sun–Wed 10:30 a.m.–4:30 p.m. (also Thurs in Aug).*

From Peter Rabbit to preservation

You can thank the creator of Peter Rabbit for some of the beautiful landscapes you see in the Lake District today. Beatrix Potter treasured the beautiful scenery and invested the earnings from her best-selling children's books in buying parcels of land and ensuring its preservation when she bequeathed it to the National Trust. In case you're interested, *The Tale of Peter Rabbit* has never been out of print since it was first published in 1902; to date, it has been reprinted more than 300 times, translated into 35 languages, and sold some 40 million copies worldwide.

The Lake District Visitor Centre
Brockhole

Housed in a lakeside mansion with terraced gardens, this visitor center presents an extensive overview of the national park and its special features. It offers all sorts of activities: Kids can go wild on an adventure playground; visitors can enjoy interactive exhibits and daily guided walks, too. The gardens and grounds, with views down to Lake Windermere and beyond, are home to a wide variety of unusual shrubs and plants. **The Cafe,** which specializes in traditional Cumbrian recipes, serves meals daily from noon to 2 p.m. From the visitor center's jetty, you can hop on one of Windermere Lake Cruises' circular cruises (see the section "Touring by boat or foot," earlier in this chapter). From April to October, a boat from Bowness can take you to the Lake District Visitor Centre.

Brockhole, Windermere (between Windermere and Ambleside on A591). ☎ *015394/ 46601.* www.lake-district.gov.uk. *Admission: Free. Parking: £4 ($7.40) per car. Open: Building mid-Mar to Oct daily 10 a.m.–5 p.m.; grounds daily year-round.*

Windermere Steamboat Museum
Windermere

This small lakeside museum displays a unique collection of boats used on Lake Windermere during the last 150 years. The oldest boat is a steam launch from 1850. You also can find exhibits on the history of boating and racing on the lake. You can see the boats and displays in under 30 minutes. The center offers a fun, 50-minute cruise around Belle Isle (an island in Lake Windermere) in an Edwardian steam launch; call ahead to reserve a seat. The cruise costs £5.50 ($10) for adults and £2.50 ($4.50) for children 5 to 15.

Rayrigg Road, Windermere. ☎ *015394/45565. Admission: £4.75 ($8.75) adult, £2.50 ($4.65) child 5–15, £9.50 ($18) family (2 adults, 3 children). Open: Mid-Mar–Oct daily 10 a.m.–5 p.m.*

The World of Beatrix Potter
Bowness-on-Windermere

If you grew up on Beatrix Potter stories and think that her illustrations are cute, you may enjoy this miniature theme park — having a child along helps, too. The attraction is a series of small, skillfully re=created scenes related to those famous Potter characters Peter Rabbit and Jemima Puddle-Duck. You can have tea in the Tailor of Gloucester ('another Potter story) tearoom, and of course, you can shop for Potter-inspired merchandise. You can see everything in under an hour.

The Old Laundry, Bowness-on-Windermere. ☎ ***015394/88444.*** *Admission: £5 ($9.25) adults, £4 ($7.40) children. Open: Daily 10 a.m.–4:30 p.m. (summer until 5:30 p.m.)*

Grasmere: Wordsworth Territory

Grasmere Village draws fans of William Wordsworth in the way that Near Sawrey draws Beatrix Potter-holics. High fells surround this lovely Lakeland village with the River Rothay running through it. The village is 13km (8 miles) north of Windermere on its own jewel of a lake, Lake Grasmere. Wordsworth called the area "the loveliest spot that man hath ever found." By bus, the trip from Windermere to Grasmere Village takes less than 30 minutes. You can also take the ferry to Ambleside, at the north end of Lake Windermere (the stop is called Waterside), and continue by bus. Keep in mind that this is an extremely popular tourist route, and summer traffic includes tour buses. Grasmere Village is about a quarter-mile from Dove Cottage and Lake Grasmere.

Rydal, the village where Wordsworth lived out his final years in relative affluence as England's poet laureate, is about midway between Ambleside and Grasmere.

Finding information about Grasmere

The Lake District National Park Authority's **Waterhead Information Centre** (☎ **015394/32729**), next to the ferry landing at Waterhead, has books and maps, and can advise you on good walks in the area. The center is open April through September daily from 9:30 a.m. to 5:30 p.m. **Grasmere Information Centre** (☎ **015394/35245**), across from the parish church and behind the Grasmere Garden Centre, is another good resource for local information. Both have a *bureau de change.*

Touring on foot

Several pleasant short walks begin in Grasmere. Check with the Grasmere Information Centre (see the preceding section) for maps and suggestions. More experienced hikers may want to tackle the 5.5km (3½-mile) round-trip trail to the rocky summit of Helm Crag; the walk takes about two hours. You can also walk east on Easedale Road to the nearby peaks known as "The Lion and the Lamb" and "The Lady at the Organ."

Staying in and around Grasmere

Grasmere is a small village with a good selection of accommodations. My recommended choices follow.

Harwood Hotel

$ Grasmere

Located right in the center of Grasmere, this small hotel built of traditional Lakeland stone dates to the 1850s and was operated as a temperance guest house. The house is now a comfortable B&B with eight nicely decorated rooms, two of them with four-poster beds. Four of the rooms have en-suite bathrooms, and the others have private bathrooms outside the room. A nice coffee lounge and Newby's Bakery & Deli, which serves local specialties (and can pack you a picnic lunch), are part of the hotel. *Note:* On weekends, the hotel requires a two-night minimum stay.

Red Lion Square, Grasmere, Ambleside, Cumbria LA22 9SP. ☎ *015394/35248. Fax: 015394/35545.* www.harwoodhotel.co.uk. *Rack rates: £39–£59 ($72–$109) double. Rates include English breakfast. AE, MC, V.*

White Moss House

$$$ Rydal Water

This Lakeland villa, built in 1730 overlooking Rydal Water and the surrounding fells, was the home of William Wordsworth's son, and the Wordsworth family inhabited it until the 1930s. The villa is now a small, wonderfully atmospheric country-house hotel with just seven guest rooms and a separate cottage suite on the hillside. All the rooms are individually decorated in a traditional country-house style. The room rate includes a memorable five-course dinner prepared by Peter Dixon, a Master Chef of Great Britain. His Modern British cooking makes use of local free-range and organic products; the restaurant has an exemplary wine cellar. You can take several lovely walks right from the hotel. Check the Web site for special offers.

Rydal Water (off A591, 2.5km/1½ miles south of Grasmere), Grasmere, Cumbria LA22 9SE. ☎ *015394/35295.* www.whitemoss.com. *Rack rates: £158–£190 ($292–$352) double; additional £3 ($5.55) per person for one-night stays. Rates include English breakfast and five-course dinner. AE, MC, V.*

Wordsworth Hotel

$$$ Grasmere

If you want to stay at the poshest place in town, head to this hotel in the heart of the village. Set on two acres of landscaped grounds, with a heated indoor pool and sauna and an upscale country ambience throughout, the Wordsworth Hotel features 35 individually decorated rooms that have large, modern bathrooms (with tubs and showers) and luxury-hotel amenities, such as room service and nightly shoeshines. You can book a room rate that includes a multicourse dinner served in The Prelude restaurant (see "Dining in Grasmere," later in this chapter), but if you're going that route, I'd recommend White Moss House over the Wordsworth.

Grasmere, Ambleside, Cumbria LA22 9SW. ☎ *015394/35592. Fax: 013594/35765.* www.grasmere-hotels.co.uk/wordsworth. *Rack rates: £110–£180 ($204–$333) double. Rates include English breakfast. AE, DC, MC, V.*

Dining In Grasmere

Remember that hotels such as White Moss House include a marvelous multicourse dinner in the price of the room. You can also find good take-away food at Newby's Bakery & Deli in the Harwood Hotel. Here are some other good restaurant choices for Grasmere.

Lamb Inn
$ TRADITIONAL ENGLISH/PUB

If you want a pub meal in nice, nonfancy surroundings, this is a good choice. You can get a bowl of homemade soup, sandwiches, roast lamb, or spicy Cumberland sausages. Other offerings include fish and chips, Yorkshire puddings, and vegetarian dishes. Kids enjoy the casual atmosphere and can usually find something on the menu they like.

In the Red Lion Hotel, Red Lion Square, Grasmere. ☎ *015394/35456. Main courses: £5.95–£8.95 ($11–$17). AE, MC, V. Open: Pub Mon–Sat 11 a.m.–11 p.m., Sun noon to 10:30 p.m.; food served daily noon to 2:30 p.m. and 5:30–9 p.m.*

The Prelude
$$$$ MODERN BRITISH

The restaurant in the Wordsworth Hotel is a dress-up kind of place with good food and attentive service. You choose from a three-course fixed-price menu that changes daily. Starters may include pan-fried scallops or a terrine of rabbit, pistachio, and foie gras. Main courses always include fresh fish and offerings such as roast duck breast or fillet of beef.

Wordsworth Hotel. ☎ *015394/355-592. Reservations required. Fixed-price dinner: £38 ($70). AE, DC, MC, V. Open: Daily for lunch and dinner.*

Villa Columbina
$ MODERN BRITISH/MEDITERRANEAN

This roadside restaurant is close to Dove Cottage, the main tourist attraction in Grasmere. It's not the most atmospheric spot, but it serves good home-cooked food and afternoon teas. You can get soup, sandwiches, pastas, and daily specials. Kids enjoy the casual atmosphere.

Town End, Grasmere. ☎ *015394/35268. Main courses: £4.50–£8.50 ($8.35–$16). MC, V. Open: Mon–Sat 10 a.m.–4:30 p.m., Wed–Sat 6:45–9 p.m.*

Exploring in and around Grasmere

William Wordsworth made the small village of Grasmere famous, and his two homes draw the lion's share of tourists. The village itself is so small that you can see everything in it in less than an hour.

Dove Cottage and The Wordsworth Museum
South of Grasmere

Picturesque 400-year-old Dove Cottage was the home of William Wordsworth (1770–1850), one of England's most famous Romantic poets and the one most identified with the Lake District. Wordsworth composed most of his greatest poems in Dove Cottage, where he lived between 1799 and 1808 with his wife; his children; and his sister Dorothy, whose journals chronicle their daily lives. A guide takes you through the entire house, which has been altered little over the years. You can view some of the family's personal possessions. Tours are limited to about 20 people at a time, so you may have to wait. A few steps away is the Wordsworth Museum, which documents the poet's life and works with manuscripts, books, and paintings. You need about 20 minutes for the tour and another 30 minutes for the museum — twice that if you're a Wordsworth fan.

On A591 (.5km/¼ mile south of Grasmere Village). ☎ *015394/35544. Admission: £6 ($11) adults, £5.50 ($10) seniors, £3.75 ($6.95) children 5–15, £15 ($28) families (2 adults, 2 children). Open: Daily 9:30 a.m.–5:30 p.m.; closed last three weeks in Jan and Dec 24–26.*

Wordsworth: The silent nightingale

William Wordsworth is considered one of England's great poets. The sights and scenes of the Lake Country, where he was born, spent most of his mature years, and died, influenced much of his poetry. Traveling in France after his graduation from Cambridge, Wordsworth fell in love with Annette Vallon, who gave birth to his daughter Caroline. He never married Annette, apparently because the French Revolution prevented his return to France.

In 1798, Wordsworth co-authored *Lyrical Ballads,* a volume that included "Tintern Abbey," the work that introduced Romanticism, with its love of nature, to England. In this poem, Wordsworth extolled not the great but the ordinary man: "That best portion of a good man's life, / His little, nameless, unremembered acts / Of kindness and of love."

In 1802, the poet married Mary Hutchinson, an old school friend. With Mary, he had five children. *The Prelude,* completed in 1805, is a long autobiographical poem. Some of his other famous poems include "Daffodils" and "Intimations of Immortality" ("Though nothing can buy back the hour / Of splendour in the grass, of glory in the flower"). From 1847 until his death in 1850, Wordsworth was England's poet laureate, appointed by Queen Victoria. He was called "the silent nightingale" because during those years he never composed a poem.

The Grasmere Gingerbread Shop
Grasmere

You smell this place before you see it, and I recommend that you stop in. This famous shop, in a tiny cottage next to the parish church, sells a marvelous gingerbread made from a 150-year-old secret recipe developed by Sarah Nelson and kept in a local bank vault. You can buy the gingerbread fresh or in sealed packs (a great gift idea). The shop also sells Kendal Mint Cakes, a supersweet mint bar that Sir Edmund Hilary used to raise his blood sugar while climbing Mount Everest.

Church Cottage (next to the parish church), Grasmere. ☎ *015394/35428.* www.gingerbread.co.uk. *Open: Apr–Oct Mon–Sat 9:15 a.m.–5:30 p.m., Sun 12:30–5:30 p.m.; Nov–Mar Mon–Sat 9:30 a.m.–4:30 p.m., Sun 12:30–5:30 p.m.*

Grasmere Parish Church
Grasmere

Grasmere's parish church is dedicated to St. Oswald, the seventh-century king of Northumbria. The oldest part of the gray stone church dates from the 13th century. The building has an attractive interior, much altered in later centuries. The Wordsworths worshiped here and are buried in the churchyard beside the river, close to eight yew trees planted by the poet. You can visit the church and churchyard in 15 minutes.

Grasmere. ☎ *015394/35428. Open: Daily 9 a.m.–5 p.m.*

Rydal Mount
South of Grasmere

In 1813, Wordsworth moved his family to Rydal Mount, a much grander house between Ambleside and Grasmere. From here, the man who immortalized the Lake District countryside had commanding views of Lake Windermere, Rydal Water, and the surrounding fells. The house still belongs to the poet's descendants, but they have opened much of it to the public, and you can wander through the dining room, drawing room, family bedrooms, and study. Take time to stroll through the gardens Wordsworth designed; Dora's Garden, ablaze with daffodils in the spring, was planted in memory of his daughter Dora. You can easily spend 30 minutes here, longer if you wander in the garden.

On A591 (4km/2½ miles south of Grasmere and 2.5km/1½ miles north of Ambleside). ☎ *015394/33002. Admission: £4.50 ($8.35) adults, £3.75 ($6.95) seniors, £1.50 ($2.80) children. Open: Mar–Oct daily 9:30 a.m.–5 p.m.; Nov–Feb Wed–Mon 10 a.m.–4p.m.; closed Jan 10–31.*

Steam Yacht Gondola
Coniston Water

An opulent Victorian-style yacht with velvet and leather seats makes a 45-minute circuit of Coniston Water, one of the loveliest of Lakeland's lakes. All you need to do is sit back and enjoy the scenery. Cruises leave hourly beginning at 11 a.m. until 4 p.m.

Coniston Pier, Coniston Water (take Lake Road south from Ambleside past Coniston Village; turn left at gas station to reach pier). ☎ *015394/35599. Admission: £4.50 ($8.35) adults, £2.80 ($5.20) children, £14 ($26) family (2 adults, 4 children). Open: Apr–Oct 11 a.m.–4 p.m.*

Keswick: Lakeland Central

Compared with tiny Grasmere, Keswick (pronounced *Kes*-ick) is a large, bustling market town. Situated on a lovely lake (Derwentwater), Keswick is a lively regional hub that turns into a busy resort on weekends and during the summer (see the "Keswick" map on p. 393). The town, with its narrow streets and sturdy gray stone buildings, stands on the banks of the River Greta beneath the slopes of the Skiddaw Range. Some of the most beautiful walking country in England lies around Keswick.

Getting to Keswick

Keswick lies about 32km (20 miles) north of Lake Windermere and 18km (11 miles) north of Grasmere. Cumbria Stagecoach bus no. 555 departs from Grasmere several times a day; the trip takes about 30 minutes. The bus drops you off just a couple of blocks from Main Street, and you can walk everywhere from there. Taxis wait right at the bus stop, or you can call **Davies Taxis** at ☎ **017687/72676.**

Finding information and exchanging money at Keswick

The **National Park Information Centre,** Moot Hall, Market Square (☎ **017687/72645**), is open daily from 9:30 a.m. to 5:30 p.m. (until 4:30 p.m. in winter). The center has maps, guidebooks, local information, and a *bureau de change.* The staff sells detailed leaflets on the best local walks. You can also find visitor information on the Web at www.keswick.org.

National Westminster Bank, 28 Main St. (☎ **01768/72091**), is open weekdays from 9 a.m. to 5 p.m. and has a *bureau de change* and an ATM.

Staying in or near Keswick

Here are my recommended choices for staying in Keswick.

Keswick

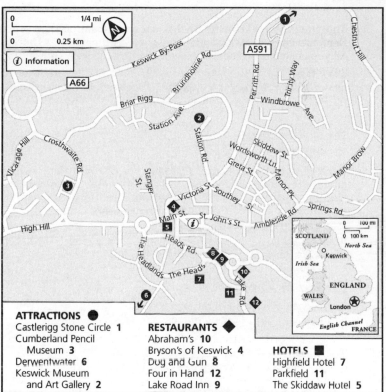

ATTRACTIONS ●

Castlerigg Stone Circle **1**
Cumberland Pencil
 Museum **3**
Derwentwater **6**
Keswick Museum
 and Art Gallery **2**

RESTAURANTS ◆

Abraham's **10**
Bryson's of Keswick **4**
Dog and Gun **8**
Four in Hand **12**
Lake Road Inn **9**

HOTELS ■

Highfield Hotel **7**
Parkfield **11**
The Skiddaw Hotel **5**

Highfield Hotel
$$ Keswick

Highfield was built as two Victorian-era houses and still has some interesting features, including two turrets that are now guest rooms with views across Hope Park toward Derwentwater. The nonsmoking hotel's 20 roomy units have traditional English decor. All rooms have private bathrooms (most with showers). The hotel is noted for its food, and the price of your room includes dinner.

See map above. The Heads, Keswick CA12 5ER. ☎ *017687/72508.* www.highfield keswick.co.uk. *Rack rates: £110–£150 ($204–$278) double. Rates include English breakfast and dinner. AE, MC, V.*

Parkfield
$ **Keswick**

This friendly, nonsmoking B&B has a great location right at the head of Derwentwater, steps away from Keswick's theater and shopping street. Here, you find eight nicely furnished rooms, all with shower and toilet.

See map p. 393. The Heads, Keswick CA12 5ES. ☎ *017687/72328.* www.parkfield keswick.co.uk. *Rack rates: £60 ($111) double. Rate includes English breakfast. AE, MC, V.*

The Skiddaw Hotel
$$ **Keswick**

Located right in the center of town, the 40-room Skiddaw is your best choice for a centrally located, full-service hotel. The rooms are comfortable and decorated in a kind of traditional, no-surprises way, and most of the bathrooms have tub-shower combinations.

See map p. 393. Main Street, Keswick, Cumbria CA12 5BN. ☎ *017687/72071. Fax: 017687/74850.* www.skiddawhotel.co.uk. *Rack rates: £110–£138 ($204–$255) double. Rate includes English breakfast. AE, MC, V.*

Dining in Keswick

Simple, hearty meals are the order of the day in Keswick. You can get a good meal at the following places.

Abraham's
$ **VEGETARIAN/TRADITIONAL ENGLISH**

This nonsmoking tearoom is a great place for a filling breakfast; a light, healthy lunch; or a rich dessert. The informal atmosphere makes it a popular spot for families. The salad menu usually includes dishes such as vegetarian flan; chicken, ham, and chestnut pie; or prawns. The homemade soup is always vegetarian. The blackboard lists daily specials.

See map p. 393. Third floor of George Fisher Ltd. Outdoor Equipment Store, 2 Borrowdale Rd. ☎ *017687/71333. Main courses: £5–£7 ($9.25–$13). No credit cards. Open: Daily 10:30 a.m.–5:30 p.m. (5 p.m. in winter).*

Bryson's of Keswick
$ **TRADITIONAL ENGLISH/TEAS**

The first floor is a wonderful bakery where you can buy apple and black-currant pies, tarts, cakes, muffins, and breads — great treats for kids of all ages. The second floor serves meals, concentrating on local specialties such as spicy Cumberland sausage, Cumbrian ham, and locally caught trout. You can get an excellent cream tea here, too.

See map p. 393. 42 Main St. ☎ *017687/72257. Main courses: £6–£7 ($11–$13). No credit cards. Open: Mon–Sat 9 a.m.–5:30 p.m., Sun 9 a.m.–5 p.m.*

Dog and Gun
$ TRADITIONAL ENGLISH/PUB

This pub serves some good traditional dishes. You may want to try home-made lamb curry, roast beef and Yorkshire pudding, goulash, or steak and kidney pie.

See map p. 393. Lake Road (just off the market square). ☎ *017687/73463. Main courses: £5–£6 ($9.25–$11). MC, V. Open: Pub Mon–Sat 11 a.m.–11 p.m., Sun noon–10:30 p.m.; food served daily noon–2:30 p.m. and 5:30–9 p.m.*

Four in Hand
$–$$ MODERN BRITISH

This old coaching inn has an attractive dining room (with fireplace) that serves top-end bar food. A house specialty is lamb steak cooked in rich red-wine and onion sauce. Fish dishes typically include poached salmon with cream and dill sauce. Also available are hearty local favorites such as Cumberland sausage and vegetarian offerings such as mushroom stroganoff.

See map p. 393. Lake Road. ☎ *017687/72665. Main courses: £7.50–£13 ($14–$24). MC, V. Open: Winter Mon–Sat noon to 3 p.m. and 5–11 p.m., Sun 5–10:30 p.m.; summer Mon–Sat 11 a.m.–11 p.m., Sun noon to 10:30 p.m.*

Lake Road Inn
$ TRADITIONAL ENGLISH/PUB

This cozy, old-fashioned pub, near the Dog and Gun, serves such staples as homemade soup, roast chicken, lasagna, braised shoulder of lamb, and locally caught trout with white-wine-and-parsley sauce. You may want to stop in to sample a Cumbrian ale.

See map p. 393. Lake Road (head south from the tourist office on Borrowdale Road and turn right on Lake Road, about a 2-minute walk). ☎ *017687/72404. Main courses: £4.75–£8.50 ($8.80–$16). MC, V. Open: Easter–Oct pub Mon–Sat 11 a.m.–11 p.m., Sun noon to 10:30 p.m.; food served daily noon to 2:30 p.m. and 5:30–9 p.m. Closed Nov–Easter.*

Exploring in and around Keswick

You may find the indoor tourist attractions in and around Keswick inter-esting, but they're not all that important. The landscape itself makes the place special, and invites walks and boat rides.

Castlerigg Stone Circle
Near Keswick

If you have time for only one walk in the Lake District, make it this one, which appeals to older kids as much as to adults. The walk leads to the best preserved of the 40 or so prehistoric stone circles found throughout Cumbria. The circle's unrivaled setting, on the flat top of a low hill above

Keswick, surrounded by high fells, adds greatly to its appeal. Castlerigg consists of 33 standing stones forming a circle, with another 10 stones arranged as a rectangular enclosure. The circle was probably constructed about 3000 B.C. No one can say definitively what its purpose was, but it may have served as the focal point for a scattered tribe of Neolithic people involved in making stone axes. Although much smaller than Stonehenge (and lacking the lintels that cap the stones there), Castlerigg conveys the same sense of timeless mystery.

See map p. 393 From the National Park Information Centre in Keswick, follow the signposted trail that leads 2.5km (1½ miles) east along A591 to Castlerigg Stone Circle; walking to the circle and back takes about 2½ hours. You can drive here following A591; a parking lot is across from the stones.

Cumberland Pencil Museum
Keswick

This museum devoted to the humble pencil is worth 30 minutes of your time. The exhibits inevitably pique the interest of children and their parents. The Elizabethans used pure graphite, discovered near Keswick in the early 1500s, to make cannonball molds, and local farmers used it to mark their sheep. In 1832, the precious carbon became the source of lead for a thriving local pencil industry. After watching an introductory video, you can wander past the displays (oldest pencils in the world and so on) and discover the answer to that burning question: How do they get the lead into the pencil? If you're looking for high-quality colored pencils, the shop is an excellent source.

See map p. 393. Southey Lane (take Main Street north to Southey Lane). ☎ 017687/73626. Admission: £3 ($5.55) adults, £1.50 ($2.80) seniors and children 5–15, £7.50 ($14) families (2 adults, 2 children). Open: Daily 9:30 a.m.–4 p.m.

Derwentwater
Southwest of Keswick

Many folks consider Derwentwater, studded with islands and enfolded in a landscape of low, bare hills with craggy peaks, the prettiest of all the lakes. The lake is about 5km (3 miles) long and 22m (72 ft.) deep. At its northern end, closest to Keswick, is a popular park. **Keswick Launch** (☎ 017687/72263; www.keswick-launch.co.uk), located at the lake's north end, operates 50-minute cruises from Easter through November daily starting at 10 a.m. (Sat and Sun only Dec–mid-Mar). The small launches make a circuit of the lake and stop at several docks, where you can get out and walk. The cruise costs £6 ($11) for adults, £3 ($5.55) for children 5 to 15, and £14 ($26) for a family (2 adults, 3 children). During the summer, an evening wine cruise is available.

Keswick Museum and Art Gallery
Keswick

This small Victorian museum has nothing of major importance, but a look at the paintings, manuscripts, crystals, and bric-a-brac collected over the years is fun. The most famous exhibit is a 500-year-old mummified cat found in the roof of Clifton Church, Penrith, in 1842; kids find this desiccated feline absolutely fascinating.

See map p. 393. Fitz Park, Station Road. ☎ *017687/73263. Admission: £1 ($1.85) adults, 50p (95¢) children 5–15. Open: Easter–Oct Tues–Wed 10 a.m.–4 p.m., Thurs 10 a.m.–7 p.m.*

Shopping in Keswick

My favorite shop in Keswick is **Ye Olde Friars,** 6–8 Market Square (☎ **017687/72234**), an old-fashioned candy store that sells black treacle, butter toffee, and other locally made sweets. **George Fisher Ltd.,** 2 Borrowdale Rd. (☎ **017687/72178**), is one of the largest specialist outdoor-clothing and -equipment stores in the country. **The Tea Pottery,** Central Car Park (☎ **017687/73983**), sells goofy and expensive handmade teapots.

Discovering Keswick's performing arts

Theatre by the Lake, Lakeside (☎ 017687/74411; www.theatrebythe lake.com), is a new 400-seat theater with a year-round repertory of plays, films, dance, concerts, and theatrical events.

Part VIII
The Part of Tens

The 5th Wave   By Rich Tennant

"Douglas, I'd like to talk to you about the souvenirs you brought back from our trip to England."

In this part . . .

*E*verything in this part is extra. You can have a great time in England without even looking at these chapters. But if you do read this part, I can turn you on to some extra-special places that you may otherwise miss. I describe everything in this part elsewhere in the guide. These top ten lists just give you an easy way to find out about some special-interest areas that you may want to explore further. Literature is one of the great links between England and other parts of the world. So, in Chapter 23, I give you the lowdown on ten famous English writers, from William Shakespeare to Beatrix Potter, and tell you how you can visit places where they lived and worked.

Then, because more and more people are interested in gardens and gardening every day, in Chapter 24, I introduce you to ten great English gardens that you can visit.

In Chapter 25, I point out some magnificent English cathedrals and churches that you may want to include on your itinerary.

And no book about England would be complete without at least a few pages devoted to the monarchy. After all, the kings and queens of England take on almost mythic status in British history, whether they accomplished heroic feats or suffered humiliating losses. In Chapter 26, I introduce you to a few notable royals, past and present, to give you a glimpse of how the rulers of England — and the rule of England — has changed over the past 2,000 years.

Chapter 23

Ten Writers and the Places They Lived

In This Chapter

▶ Seeing the England of Austen, the Brontës, and Henry James

▶ Visiting the London museum of Dickens

▶ Discovering the Lake District of Wordsworth and Beatrix Potter

▶ Venturing into the gardens of Vita Sackville-West

▶ Making a literary pilgrimage to Shakespeare's Stratford-upon-Avon

I don't know about you, but some of my earliest memories of England came from literature. Long before I ever visited the Lake District, I had seen the distinctive landscape in Beatrix Potter's illustrated children's tales. Peter Pan, who lived in Kensington Gardens, made me curious about London. As I grew older, I read English novels and went to plays written by Shakespeare. If you're literary minded, you can track down several places in England associated with your favorite authors. Even if you stay in London for your entire trip, you can do some literary sleuthing. Blue plaques on London buildings identify the abodes of famous writers and artists. Some of England's most famous poets, novelists, and playwrights are buried or commemorated in Poets' Corner, Westminster Abbey (see Chapter 12).

Jane Austen

One of England's most enduringly popular writers is Jane Austen (1775–1817). Her highly polished novels depict social and domestic life in Regency England — that is, the period just before Dickens and the Victorians. Austen's fictional world is full of wit and romance. She never married. When she was 21, her father, a minister, retired and moved his family to **Bath,** where you can see the house she lived in and visit the **Jane Austen Centre,** a museum dedicated to her life and times.

After her father's death, Austen lived in the quiet village of **Chawton** with her mother and sister Cassandra. The **Jane Austen House,** which you can visit, is a small red-brick dwelling that her wealthy brother

Edward gave her. In this house, she began revising her earlier drafts of *Sense and Sensibility* (published in 1811) and *Pride and Prejudice* (published in 1813). Austen continued writing and publishing novels until 1817, when illness forced her to move to **Winchester** for medical help. You can pay your respects at Austen's grave in **Winchester Cathedral.** You can find information on all the Jane Austen sites in Chapter 16.

Charlotte, Emily, and Anne Brontë

A trip to **Haworth** in Yorkshire (see Chapter 21) brings you to the **Brontë Parsonage Museum,** home of that trio of sibling scribes, Charlotte (1816–1855), Emily (1818–1848), and Anne (1820–1849) Brontë. The windswept moors that figure so prominently in Emily's *Wuthering Heights* and Charlotte's *Jane Eyre* surround the town, which markets the Brontë name in every conceivable way. Like Jane Austen, the Brontës were the children of a minister. They were educated (in grim schools, like the one called Lowood in *Jane Eyre*) but had no independent means of support, so all three had to work as governesses. Anne's *The Tenant of Wildfell Hall* and Charlotte's *Jane Eyre* both have governess heroines.

Charlotte and Emily spent a brief time at a school in Brussels (where Charlotte fell in love with her married teacher), but otherwise, the Brontës stayed close to the parsonage, writing the novels that would make them famous. Tragedy struck when Anne, 29, and Emily, 30, died in quick succession of tuberculosis. Charlotte eventually married one of her father's curates but died at age 39.

Charles Dickens

Charles Dickens (1812–1870) was one of the most prolific and best-loved novelists of the Victorian era. When Dickens was a boy, his father was thrown into debtor's prison, and young Charles was forced to work in a factory. His subsequent rise to fame as a reporter, editor, and novelist is as remarkable as anything in his fiction. *David Copperfield* is Dickens's most autobiographical novel.

Dickens didn't flinch at exposing the horrors of the day and tackling social issues, such as child labor and London's teeming slums. Some of his characters (Ebenezer Scrooge in *A Christmas Carol*, to cite just one example) have become as famous as Shakespeare's. Dickens moved around constantly, but in London, you can visit the **Charles Dickens Museum,** located in the house where he penned *Oliver Twist, The Pickwick Papers,* and *Nicholas Nickleby.* The museum contains the world's most comprehensive Dickens library, plus portraits, illustrations, and rooms furnished as they were in his lifetime. See Chapter 12 for more details on the museum.

Henry James (and E. F. Benson)

Novelist Henry James (1843–1916) was an American, but he loved England so much that he became a British citizen. In his long career, James wrote 20 novels, 112 stories, 12 plays, and literary criticism. The son of one of the best-known intellectuals in mid-19th-century America, he grew up in Manhattan. (William James, his brother, was one of the earliest psychologists.)

An Irish grandfather provided the wealth that endowed the family with the privileges of culture, travel, education, and social affluence — attributes found in Henry James's fictional characters, many of whom are Americans living in England or Italy. After living in Paris, James moved to England, living first in London and then in Sussex. **Lamb House,** his last home, is just one of many reasons to visit the beautiful Sussex town of **Rye.** (E. F. Benson, who wrote the *Mapp and Lucia* novels, later owned Lamb House.) For more on Rye, see Chapter 14.

Beatrix Potter

The life of famed children's-book writer and illustrator Beatrix Potter (1866–1943) is singularly lacking in drama and tragedy. Born in South Kensington, London, she was an only and lonely child but had many pets that she carefully observed and sketched. When Beatrix was 16, her parents rented a summer house in the Lake District. They returned every year afterward, and Beatrix fell in love with the beautiful countryside.

Many years later, when *The Tale of Peter Rabbit,* her first published book, sold 50,000 copies, she bought **Hill Top,** her house in **Near Sawrey,** close to Lake Windermere. The house is now open to the public. Potter's illustrations and watercolors are on display at the **Beatrix Potter Gallery** in nearby **Hawkshead.** The gallery is in a building that held the law offices of William Heelis, whom she married when she was 47. Over the years, Beatrix Potter used her earnings to buy thousands of acres in the Lake District (and became a prize-winning sheep farmer). She wanted the countryside that had so inspired her to be preserved for future generations, and she left it all to the National Trust. Here's one little-known fact about Potter: She discovered the process by which fungi reproduce, but the scientific world didn't acknowledge her research until the 1990s. You can read more about the Lake District and its Potter sites in Chapter 22.

Vita Sackville-West

Not many people read the novels and poems of Vita Sackville-West (1892–1962) anymore, but many people know about her life. She was born at **Knole,** an enormous house in Kent, and she later wrote an entertaining book called *Knole and the Sackvilles.* Virginia Woolf (1882–1941) used Vita as the inspiration for the gender-bending hero/heroine in her brilliant novel *Orlando,* which also has Knole as a setting. Vita, famous for her lesbian affairs, married the diplomat Harold Nicholson and had two children. Nigel Nicholson, one of their sons, wrote about his parents in *Portrait of a Marriage,* later filmed for television. Vita and Harold worked together to create the magnificent gardens at **Sissinghurst Castle,** now one of the world's most famous gardens. Check out Chapter 15 for more on Knole and Sissinghurst. Vita's garden books still sell; her best novel is *The Edwardians.*

William Shakespeare

England's most famous literary pilgrimage site is **Stratford-upon-Avon,** where you can visit the homes occupied by William Shakespeare (1564–1616) and his family. Before visiting **Shakespeare's Birthplace,** on Henley Street, spend a few minutes in the adjacent **Shakespeare Centre,** where exhibits illustrate the life and times of this Elizabethan genius. **Anne Hathaway's Cottage,** about a mile south of Stratford, was the home of the woman Shakespeare married when he was 18 and she was 25.

A relatively prosperous Shakespeare retired to **New Place** on Chapel Street; the only part that remains is the garden. **Nash's House,** next door, belonged to Thomas Nash, husband of Shakespeare's granddaughter. Nearby **Hall's Croft** is a magnificent Tudor house where Shakespeare's daughter Susanna probably lived with her husband, Dr. John Hall. Shakespeare and his family are buried in **Holy Trinity Church.** About 5.5km (3½ miles) north of Stratford is **Mary Arden's House.** For decades, this Tudor farmstead was assumed to be the girlhood home of Shakespeare's mother, but scholars have recently suggested that Shakespeare's mum probably lived in the house next door. I cover Stratford-upon-Avon in Chapter 19.

William Wordsworth

When William Wordsworth died in 1850 at the age of 80, he was poet laureate of England and perhaps the world's most famous poet. His fame rests on the poems in *Lyrical Ballads* and *The Prelude.* A champion of the Romantic Movement, which emphasized imagination and emotion and extolled nature, Wordsworth is closely associated with the **Lake District,** where he lived most of his life.

Born in Cumberland (today's Cumbria) in 1770, Wordsworth was the son of a lawyer. He attended **Hawkshead Grammar School** in the village of **Hawkshead** (also the location of the Beatrix Potter Gallery) and studied at Cambridge. Wordsworth composed most of his greatest poems in **Dove Cottage,** Grasmere, where he lived between 1799 and 1808. In 1813, Wordsworth moved his family to **Rydal Mount,** a much grander house between Ambleside and Grasmere. He and other family members are buried in the churchyard of Grasmere Parish Church. For more details on all these sites, see Chapter 22.

Chapter 24

Ten Great English Gardens

In This Chapter
▶ Wandering through castle and estate gardens
▶ Appreciating glorious English-style gardens
▶ Discovering botanical and experimental gardens

*E*ngland is famous for its spectacular gardens. You don't need to be a specialized or even knowledgeable gardener to appreciate and enjoy these wonderful creations. Gardens are living art forms meant to beguile your senses and refresh your spirit. Most, but not all, of the gardens I describe in this chapter are planted around grand stately homes and castles, which may be part of your visit. Four of the gardens are in or near London, and the rest are scattered throughout the country.

If you plan to visit gardens on your trip, May and June are probably the prime months, but the flowering season continues into September. Britain's Gardens, a map with brief descriptions of 100 gardens in England, Scotland, Wales, and Ireland, is available free from VisitBritain. (See the Appendix for an address.)

Castle Howard

Gardens are never static. Plants grow and die; styles change; and new owners make their own marks on the landscape. The 1,000-acre park at Castle Howard in Yorkshire is an example of how a garden can change over time.

The castle is famous for its 18th-century landscape, dotted with ornamental temples and *follies* (ornamental buildings that serve as focal points in a landscape). John Vanbrugh's classically inspired Temple of the Four Winds and the circular mausoleum by Nicholas Hawksmoor are particularly notable. When the South Parterre was laid out between 1715 and 1725, the house's architectural drama was extended into the surrounding landscape with obelisks, urns, statues, and a 50-foot column.

Most of that visual drama was removed in the 1850s, when the Atlas Fountain and a *parterre* (an ornamental garden with paths between its beds) of boxwood, plants, and gravel were installed. In the late 19th century, grass and yew hedges replaced the parterre. The walled Rose Garden and Ray Wood, full of rare rhododendrons and plants that survive in their own protected microclimate, were planted only in the last half-century. And the work goes on today, allowing visitors to stroll through fields and woodland, over bridges, and beside lakes. You can get to Castle Howard in an easy day trip from York; see Chapter 21 for more information.

Chelsea Physic Garden

This 3½-acre gem, hidden behind the high brick walls surrounding Chelsea Royal Hospital, is the second-oldest botanical garden in England. When the Worshipful Society of Apothecaries founded the garden in 1673, *physic* referred to medicine and medicinal agents. The goal of the apothecaries was to develop medicinal and commercial plant species. Seeds from this garden, for example, were used to start the cotton industry in the British colony of Georgia, first settled in 1733. Planted in the garden are some 7,000 exotic herbs, shrubs, trees, and flowers. This garden also boasts England's earliest rock garden. See Chapter 12 for more details.

Eden Project

Located on the south coast of Cornwall, the Eden Project is a garden of the 21st century. It's not an old-fashioned pleasure ground like the other gardens I mention in this chapter, but an intriguing educational showcase meant to stimulate an awareness of the Earth and humanity's dependence on plants and all living things. Already a major tourist attraction, the Eden Project consists of two giant geodesic conservatories sunk in deep craters. One dome covers the rainforest; and the other dome features the fruits and flowers of the Mediterranean, South Africa, and California. Outside, on the acres of landscaped grounds, plants from all sorts of terrains grow in specially created microhabitats. You can find more information in Chapter 18.

Hever Castle

In the early 16th century, when Anne Boleyn was growing up at Hever Castle, the grounds looked nothing like they do today. The superb landscaping was created about a century ago, after the American millionaire William Astor bought Hever in 1903. Astor, who'd been American ambassador to Italy, created the castle's magnificent Italian Garden between 1904 and 1908. This garden combines the formal structure and design elements of Italian Renaissance gardens with English plantings. A remarkable collection of Roman to Renaissance statuary and sculpture collected in Italy fills Astor's creation.

In other parts of the grounds, you find a maze, a 35-acre lake, and the obligatory English rose garden. The Tudor herb garden, built close to the castle in 1994, gives you an idea of what gardens were like in Anne Boleyn's day. You can visit this garden as a day trip from London; see Chapter 15.

Hidcote Manor

When you see a garden such as Hidcote Manor's, you have to marvel at the patience and love that went into creating it. An American officer, Lawrence Johnstone, bought the Cotswold estate in 1907. What this amazing gardener did with a high, windswept limestone scarp is nothing short of amazing. Johnston created a series of terraces and planted unusual hedges (as windbreaks) to form compartments off a long central axis. Rare and exotic plants — including rhododendrons, camellias, and magnolias that are lime intolerant — are planted in beds of sawdust. Hidcote is in some ways the forerunner of Sissinghurst because it comprises a variety of garden "rooms." Anyone touring the Cotswolds must stop here. For more information on Hidcote, see Chapter 20.

Kew Gardens

The Royal Botanic Gardens at Kew — more commonly known as Kew Gardens — are perfect for a half-day trip from London. (Getting there takes about a half-hour on the Underground.) The 300-acre gardens date to 1730, when Frederick, Prince of Wales, leased the property and helped lay out the grounds. His widow, Augusta, and his son, George III, really developed Kew. They enlisted botanists who began to bring plants from all over the world. Capability Brown later redesigned the gardens and destroyed many of the earlier buildings, but the 163-foot-high Chinese pagoda remains. The Palm House, a great glass-house conservatory, was completed in 1848. On the grounds, you can find picturesque Kew Palace, used by King George III (who went temporarily insane), and Queen Charlotte's Cottage, a royal summer retreat. From April through September, you can reach Kew by boat from London's Westminster Pier. See Chapter 13 for more details on Kew Gardens.

Lanhydrock

Gardens are usually meant to beautify and set off a house, and this garden is no exception. The beautiful gardens of Lanhydrock surround one of the largest stately homes in Cornwall. Here, different kinds of gardens — from Victorian parterres to woodland gardens where camellias, magnolias, and rhododendrons grow in dappled shade — embellish the great house and overlook the Fowey River valley below. An avenue of ancient beech and sycamore trees runs from the 17th-century gatehouse down to a medieval bridge across the Fowey. You can find details about Lanhydrock in Chapter 18.

Sissinghurst Castle Garden

This world-famous garden in Kent represents what many people consider the most beautiful example of an English garden. The sheer profusion and abundance of plants gives Sissinghurst a romance uniquely its own. The writer Vita Sackville-West and her diplomat husband, Sir Harold Nicolson, bought the ruined castle in 1930 and jointly created the gardens. Harold designed the various "compartments" or "rooms" of the garden, and Vita "furnished" them with plants, trees, and shrubs that provide color all year round. See Chapter 23 for more on Vita Sackville-West.

The White Garden, with foliage and blossoms that are entirely white or silver, is the most famous garden area at Sissinghurst. This area uses typical English plants, such as primroses and daffodils, extensively. Roses, many of them fragrant old varieties that were nearly lost, were planted by the hundreds and now climb through trees and over walls. You can visit Sissinghurst as a day trip from London, but be aware that you get in by timed ticket; see Chapter 15 for more information.

Stourhead

Stourhead in Wiltshire represents a new kind of gardening style that swept through England starting in the early 1700s. Before that, the wealthy based their show-off gardens on French models, with strictly geometric and low-to-the-ground designs. The new style favored a natural look, with flowing, irregular lines; plantings of trees and shrubs; and ornamental lakes rather than giant fountains.

The architect Henry Flitcroft laid out the gardens at Stourhead in 1741 for Henry Hoare, a wealthy merchant banker who'd already built a mansion on the site in the Palladian style (a classical style incorporating elements from ancient Greek and Roman buildings). Flitcroft transformed small ponds into lakes spanned by a bridge and used classically inspired buildings as architectural ornaments along the edges. Picturesque views and tranquil vistas are what Stourhead is all about. For more details on Stourhead, see Chapter 16.

Warwick Castle

Lancelot "Capability" Brown (1716–1783) was one of the most famous landscape gardeners in 18th-century England. In the 1750s, Brown introduced what has since become known as the English landscape garden, which is meant to look like an enhanced and perfected natural landscape. You can see his work in the park at Warwick Castle in Warwickshire. The grounds, sloping down to the River Avon, have winding paths and are planted with giant trees. One unusual feature at Warwick is the peacock-shaped topiary in front of the conservatory where a flock of peacocks freely roams. See Chapter 19 for details on visiting the castle.

Chapter 25

Ten (Or So) Great English Churches

● ●

In This Chapter
▶ Visiting England's most important churches and cathedrals
▶ Discovering the magnificent architecture of these sacred places

● ●

Churches and cathedrals are special places where you can come in direct contact with England's long history. Enter a church in just about any village, no matter how quiet and tiny, and you're in the place where countless generations have gathered to worship, celebrate, and grieve. Within the church, you may find a 900-year-old baptismal font, elaborate tombs with reclining figures, memorial stones, medieval brasses, ancient stained glass, and medieval carved figures and ornaments in wood and stone.

Over the centuries, even the smallest churches become fascinating almanacs of changing styles. The country is also blessed with an amazing assortment of magnificent cathedrals, huge places where monarchs have been crowned and famous people are buried. No matter how great or small, England's churches are architectural treasures, and I urge you to visit some of those I describe in this chapter.

Canterbury Cathedral: Pilgrim Central

Throughout the Middle Ages, pilgrims from throughout Europe flocked to this great cathedral in Kent. Their goal: to see the shrine of Saint Thomas à Becket, an archbishop killed in the cathedral in 1170 by henchmen of Henry II. (People believed if they prayed at the shrine, they would receive special indulgences after death.) The popularity of Becket's shrine, which added enormous wealth to the monastery at

Canterbury, rankled the absolutist monarch Henry VIII (who reigned from 1509–1547). Becket's shrine was destroyed when Henry abolished all monasteries. Declaring himself the head of the Church of England, Henry VIII outlawed loyalty to the pope as the head of the church, and monasteries were closed, destroyed, or converted.

In the cathedral, you can still see where the shrine stood, behind the high altar. In Canterbury, you can also visit **St. Martin's,** which may be the oldest church in England, and the ruins of St. Augustine's Abbey, established in A.D. 597. For more on Canterbury, see Chapter 14.

Exeter Cathedral: A Medieval Sculpture Gallery

The twin towers of Exeter Cathedral in Devon date from Norman times (12th century), but the entire church was remodeled in the 14th century. The ornamentation and architectural detailing both outside and in are representative of the aptly named Decorated Gothic style. Check out the cathedral's most remarkable exterior feature: the image screen on the west end. The screen contains row upon row of niches filled with wonderfully carved figures of saints and kings dating from the late 14th and early 15th centuries. This screen is the largest collection of medieval sculpture in the entire country. Inside, the cathedral's 300 feet of uninterrupted fan vaulting is the longest in England. You can find more information on Exeter Cathedral in Chapter 17.

King's College Chapel: Unparalleled Lightness

When entering this tall, thin church in Cambridge, you immediately notice how light and airy it feels. The building's style, called Perpendicular Gothic, emphasizes the vertical, carrying the eyes upward to a roof of beautiful fan vaulting. Enormous windows, glowing with stained glass, add to the sense of lightness. Hearing the famed King's College boys' choir sing in this chapel is an unforgettable experience. For more information, see Chapter 13.

St. Martin-in-the-Fields: West End Landmark

St. Martin-in-the-Fields is a London landmark. Prominently sited on Trafalgar Square, the 18th-century neoclassical church with its raised portico and graceful steeple served as the prototype for dozens of churches in New England. St. Martin's is a lively social center in the West End. The crypt holds a popular cafe and a brass-rubbing center, and the church itself hosts weekly concerts by the Academy of St. Martin-in-the-Fields. See Chapter 12 for more details.

St. Paul's Cathedral: Wren's Crowning Achievement

When the old St. Paul's burned down in London's Great Fire of 1666, the architect Christopher Wren designed a new cathedral on the same site. Wren was responsible for dozens of churches throughout the city, but none so grand as St. Paul's. Started in 1673 and completed in 1711, the cathedral is considered his masterpiece, and he's buried in the crypt along with national heroes like the Duke of Wellington and Admiral Lord Nelson. German bombers blitzed the entire area during World War II, but St. Paul's survived with only minor damage. In 1981, the cathedral was the site of the wedding of Prince Charles and Lady Diana Spencer. Today, the mighty dome of St. Paul's, a famous London landmark, rises high above a sea of bland office buildings. You can find details on visiting St. Paul's in Chapter 12.

Salisbury Cathedral: High in the Sky

Rising some 404 feet, the spire of Salisbury Cathedral in Wiltshire is the tallest in England. What is unique about this cathedral is that its structure was planned and built as a single unit. In other cathedrals, building usually went on for centuries, often incorporating portions of earlier structures and changing styles along the way. But at Salisbury, the work began in 1220 and was completed just 40 years later. (The one exception is the spire, which was added in 1334.) As a result, Salisbury Cathedral is probably the most beautiful and harmonious example of the Early English style. See Chapter 16 for details.

Westminster Abbey: England's Crowning Glory

London's Westminster Abbey holds a hallowed place in English history because nearly all the kings and queens of England since William the Conqueror have been crowned there. The Coronation Chair, made of English oak, has been used since 1307. The present cathedral, begun under Henry III in the 13th century, was built in French Gothic style. Be sure to check out the architectural highlight of the Henry VII Chapel, raised above the general level of the abbey and roofed with intricate fan vaulting; the Florentine sculptor Torrigiani created Henry VII's black-and-white touchstone tomb. The abbey is also the final resting place of Queen Elizabeth I; her Catholic half-sister Mary Tudor; and Mary, Queen of Scots, Elizabeth's one-time rival for the throne.

Approximately 3,300 people are buried in Westminster Abbey, including the poet Geoffrey Chaucer, the writer Dr. Samuel Johnson, the scientists Charles Darwin and Sir Isaac Newton, the composers George Frederic Handel and Henry Purcell, and the actor Sir Laurence Olivier. For more information on Westminster Abbey, refer to Chapter 12.

Winchester Cathedral: Saxon Power Base

Winchester was the capital of England before William of Normandy
arrived in 1066 and won the English throne. Before 1066, Saxon kings
were crowned not in London but in Winchester Cathedral, a tradition
that William continued — although he had himself crowned in London's
Westminster Abbey as well. To this day, the caskets of some of the pre-
Conquest Saxon rulers of England rest in Winchester Cathedral. You also
can find the grave of the early-19th-century novelist Jane Austen here.

Winchester Cathedral boasts the longest nave (the main central space
in the interior) in Europe, at 556 feet, but its massive foundations were
built on nothing more than a raft of logs laid on a bog. By 1900, the building was sinking. William Walker, an underwater diver, worked beneath
the foundations for five years (in water so black he couldn't see his
hands), removing the decayed wood handful by handful so that the
cathedral could be underpinned with concrete. For more on Winchester
Cathedral, see Chapter 16.

York Minster: England's Largest Gothic Church

When missionaries from Rome arrived in the late sixth century to convert England, York in the north, like Canterbury in the south, was established as an archbishopric. The importance of York as a city is reflected
in the overwhelming size of its church. The largest Gothic church in
England, York Minster has more rare medieval stained glass than any
other church in the country. Many English cathedrals are built on the
sites of earlier churches, but York Minster was built over a Roman military headquarters. If you visit, go down into the undercroft (the rooms
below the church), where excavations have revealed Roman walls and
streets. I describe York and its magnificent church in more detail in
Chapter 21.

Chapter 26

Ten Important Royals — Past and Present

In This Chapter

▶ Meeting a few notable royals

▶ Noting the changes over two millennia

I am not a royalist, but the kings and queens of England fascinate me. These are people who lived lives of penultimate power and humiliating defeat, people who killed to stay on the throne and were killed by others who wanted it, people who inspired their subjects and treated them like dirt, people who sometimes changed the course of history and sometimes disgraced the nation they ruled.

Choosing just ten is difficult, but in the thumbnail sketches that follow, you can get a glimpse of how the rulers of England — and the rule of England — has changed over the past 2,000 years.

Queen Boudicca (A.D. 30?–60): Braveheart of the Britons

I've always thought Boudicca's story would make a fantastic film, but who would play this fierce Celtic queen who painted her face blue and led 100,000 British troops again the invading Romans in A.D. 60? Angelina Jolie?

Boudicca's story goes back to the earliest period of Britain's recorded history. She was probably born about A.D. 30. In A.D. 48, she married Prasutagus, king of the Iceni, and bore him two daughters. The Iceni were a Celtic tribe that had been made a Roman client state in A.D. 43. When Prasutagus died, he left his kingdom — as required by Roman law — to the Roman emperor. But hoping to provide for his two daughters, he left a portion of his personal estate to them. For the Romans, that was a perfect excuse to confiscate all of Prasutagus's belongings and punish the Iceni for "disobeying" Roman law. Just days after her husband's death, Boudicca was publicly whipped, and her teenaged daughters were raped by Roman soldiers.

The outrages committed by the invading foreigners changed Boudicca's life forever. As more Roman troops arrived to begin the job of conquering all the native Britons, Boudicca managed to raise an army among formerly warring local tribes. The Celts were much feared by the Romans because Celtic women fought alongside the men, painting their faces blue to frighten the enemy and uttering terrifying shrieks as they attacked with swords, axes, and clubs. Boudicca and her army destroyed Roman forts and killed their inhabitants. Finally, at a site that was probably somewhere in the West Midlands, Boudicca faced the army of Suetonus Paulinus, the Roman governor of Britannia. She had more troops, but Suetonius and his legionnaires had the discipline that helped Rome conquer the Western world. The Romans slaughtered the Celts under Boudicca. It's not known what happened to Boudicca herself. Some accounts say she took poison. The alternative, had she lived, would have been worse. She would have been paraded in chains at a public triumph in Rome and then publicly tortured in the Coliseum.

The next time you cross Westminster Bridge in London, look up, and you can see a bronze statue of Boudicca on the north side. Thomas Hornicraft's mid-19th-century work shows a wild-haired superwoman in a horse-drawn chariot with her two daughters.

Alfred the Great (849–899): A Warrior and a Scholar

You can see a statue of Alfred the Great on Bridge Street in Winchester, the capital of the old Anglo-Saxon kingdom of Wessex. Alfred is the only English monarch to carry the title "the Great," and that alone makes him an intriguing character. His story goes back to the ninth century A.D. when England was being relentlessly attacked and terrorized by the Danes, more commonly known as the Vikings.

Youngest son of King Æthelwulf, Alfred became King of Wessex in 871. Wessex was an Anglo-Saxon kingdom patched together in southern and southwestern England after the departure of the Romans in A.D. 410. Alfred finally and decisively defeated attacking Danes led by Guthorm at the Battle of Eddington. As a condition of the peace treaty, Guthorm withdrew his forces from Wessex while Alfred recognized Danish control over East Anglia and parts of Mercia. This partition of England became known as the Danelaw, and though the Anglo-Saxon kings soon brought the Danelaw back under their rule, they did not attempt to interfere with the laws and customs of the area, many of which survived until after the Norman Conquest in 1066.

Alfred created a series of fortifications to surround his kingdom and provide security from invasion. *Burh,* the Anglo-Saxon word for these forts, is still recognizable in the modern English place-names ending in -*bury*. The reign of Alfred was known for more than military success, however. He promoted better education and helped make learning important in an age when education had gone into a decline because of Danish looting of monasteries and churches, the traditional centers of learning. Alfred was also a codifier of law and a patron of the arts. A warrior and a scholar, he translated Latin books into the Anglo-Saxon tongue. With the kind of leadership he provided, it's no wonder he was proclaimed "the Great."

William the Conqueror (1028–1087): Winner Takes All

The illegitimate son of the Duke of Normandy, William received the duchy of Normandy upon his father's death in 1035. He spent the next several years consolidating his strength on the continent through marriage, diplomacy, war, and savage intimidation. By 1066, the disputed succession in England offered William an opportunity for invasion.

When Edward the Confessor died childless, the English crown was offered to Harold Godwinson (an Anglo-Saxon), even though Edward had purportedly promised the throne to William of Normandy, his second cousin. Insisting that Harold had sworn allegiance to him in 1064, William prepared for battle. But as the new King Harold anxiously awaited William's arrival on England's south shores, Harold Hardrada, the King of Norway, invaded England from the north. Harold's forces marched north to defeat the Norse at Stamford Bridge on September 25, 1066. Two days after the battle, William landed unopposed at Pevensey, forcing Harold to move south to a new battle. The Battle of Hastings took place on October 14, 1066. Harold and his brothers died fighting, thus removing any further organized Anglo-Saxon resistance to the Normans. The Anglo-Saxon earls and bishops soon submitted and crowned him William I on Christmas Day 1066.

William's acquisitive nature never left him. Uprisings were ruthlessly crushed until, by 1072, the whole of England was conquered and united. Lands were confiscated and reallocated to the Normans. In 1085, William commissioned the *Domesday Book* to survey land ownership, assess property, and establish a tax base. Although he began his invasion with papal support, William refused to let the church dictate policy within English and Norman borders. Ruthless and cruel, the Conqueror exacted a high toll from his subjects, but he also laid the foundation for the economic and political success of England. Buildings from his reign include Windsor Castle and the Tower of London (see Chapter 12), but perhaps the most atmospheric reminder of William the Conqueror is at Battle (see Chapter 14), where you can visit the battlefield that was William's first conquest in England.

Henry II (1133–1189): Family Plots

Henry II, the first of the Plantagenets, was one of the most effective English kings. He refined Norman government and created a self-standing bureaucracy that could keep the country running even if it had a weak or incompetent ruler. But Henry's personal life was one unending soap opera, with more plots and counterplots than I can possibly detail here.

Henry was raised in the French province of Anjou. His vast continental possessions more than doubled with his marriage to Eleanor of Aquitane, the ex-wife of King Louis VII of France. Crowned King of England in October 1154, Henry was technically a vassal of the king of France, but in reality, he owned more territory and was more powerful than Louis.

Throughout his reign, Henry instituted reforms meant to weaken traditional feudal ties and strengthen his own position, but in the process, he became involved in the murder of his best friend, Thomas à Becket. The church courts instituted by William the Conqueror had become a safe haven for criminals, and Henry wanted to transfer sentencing to the royal courts. Becket, named Archbishop of Canterbury in 1162, vehemently opposed such a weakening of church courts. He also angered Henry by opposing the coronation of Henry's eldest son. When an exasperated Henry publicly voiced his desire to be rid of the contentious archbishop, four thuggish knights took the king at his word and murdered Becket in his own cathedral on December 29, 1170. (You can see the exact spot if you visit Canterbury Cathedral; see Chapter 14.)

Henry's sons, with the encouragement of their mother, repeatedly rebelled against their father and his plans for dividing his many lands and titles. Eleanor, equally ruthless and scheming, was kept a virtual prisoner for 16 years. Henry died in 1189, two days after his son Richard, with the assistance of Philip II Augustus of France, attacked and defeated him, forcing Henry to accept a humiliating peace.

Henry VIII (1491–1547): Take My Wife — Please!

The significance of Henry's reign is generally overshadowed by his six marriages. There is something pathological about Henry's many marriages, even if they were in pursuit of an elusive male heir.

Henry's first wife was Catherine of Aragon (widow of his brother, Arthur) whom he married in 1509 and divorced in 1533; the union produced one daughter, Mary. Henry married his pregnant mistress Anne Boleyn in 1533; she gave him another daughter, Elizabeth. But Anne was executed in 1536 on trumped-up charges of infidelity, a treasonous charge for the king's consort but never for the king. The same month Anne was beheaded, the lusty monarch married Jane Seymour, who died giving birth to Henry's lone male heir, Edward, in October 1536. After viewing Hans Holbein's beautiful portrait of the German princess Anne of Cleves, Henry arranged to marry her early in 1540. When she arrived, however, Henry found her so homely that the marriage was never consummated. In 1540, with Anne of Cleves scratched off the list, he married Catherine Howard, who was executed for infidelity two years later and reputedly haunts Hampton Court Palace to this day. Catherine Parr became Henry's sixth and last wife in 1543, and provided for the needs of both Henry and his children until his death in 1547.

So what did Henry do besides bed and wed? Most notably, he altered England as well as the whole of Western Christendom by separating the Church of England from Roman Catholicism. The separation was actually just another byproduct of Henry's obsession with producing a male heir. When Catherine of Aragon failed to produce a prince, Henry sought an annulment from the pope in order to marry Anne Boleyn. When Cardinal Wolsey failed to secure a legal annulment, Henry summoned the Reformation Parliament, which passed 137 statutes in 7 years, influencing political and ecclesiastical affairs in a way previously unknown. By 1536, all ecclesiastical and government officials were required to approve publicly of the break with Rome and take an oath of loyalty. Henry's dissolution of the Catholic monasteries filled royal coffers, as revenues from the sale of church lands went either to the crown or the nobility. The break with Rome, coupled with an increase in governmental bureaucracy, led to royal supremacy that lasted until the execution of Charles I and the establishment of the Commonwealth a century after Henry's death.

Elizabeth 1 (1533–1603): Heart and Stomach of a King

In contrast to her much-married father, Henry VIII, Elizabeth I never wed and was known as the Virgin Queen. When she ascended the throne in 1558, the conflicts between Catholics and Protestants tore at the very foundation of English society. Elizabeth's Catholic predecessor and half-sister, Mary, along with her advisors, had bled the royal treasury dry trying to restore the Catholic church's authority in England.

Instead of being a fanatic like Mary, Elizabeth was strong willed, tolerant, and intelligent. In religious matters, she devised a compromise that basically reinstated her father's Protestant reforms. Another volatile problem was her cousin, Mary, Queen of Scots, who gained the loyalty of Catholic factions and instituted several plots to overthrow Elizabeth. After irrefutable evidence of Mary's involvement in such plots came to light, Elizabeth sadly succumbed to pressure from her advisors and had the Scottish princess executed in 1587.

The persecution of continental Protestants forced Elizabeth into war, which she desperately tried to avoid. She sent an army to aid French Huguenots (Calvinists who had settled in France) after a 1572 massacre in which over 3,000 Huguenots lost their lives, and she assisted Belgium in its bid to gain independence from Spain. After Elizabeth rejected a marriage proposal from Philip II of Spain, the indignant Spanish monarch, incensed by English piracy and exploration in the New World, sent his much-feared Armada to attack England. "I know I have but the body of a weak and feeble woman," Elizabeth told her troops, "but I have the heart and stomach of a king." England won the sea battle and emerged as the world's strongest naval power.

In many ways, Elizabeth's reign has come to be regarded as a Golden Age. Literature bloomed in the works of Spenser, Marlowe, and Shakespeare. Francis Drake and Walter Raleigh expanded English influence in the New World. Elizabeth's religious compromise laid many fears to rest and sought to prevent murderous strife. Fashion and education came to the fore because of Elizabeth's thirst for knowledge, courtly behavior, and extravagant dress. Good Queen Bess, as she came to be called, maintained a regal air until the day she died, at 70 years of age and after a very successful 44-year reign. Few English monarchs have enjoyed such political power while maintaining the devotion of the whole of English society.

George III (1738–1820): "My Lords and Peacocks . . ."

George III was in no way an exemplary ruler, but I've long been fascinated by him because he was king at the time of the American Revolution and because he went mad. The only thing he really excelled at was procreation. He married Charlotte of Mecklenburg-Strelitz in 1761, and the prolific couple produced 15 children.

George was descended from the Hanoverian (German) line of succession that first came to the English throne in 1714. Determined to recover royal prerogatives lost to the Whig Party by George I and George II, George III methodically weakened the Whigs through bribery, coercion, and patronage, hand-picking yes-men of mediocre talent and servile minds to serve as Cabinet members.

George's commitment to taxing the American colonies to pay for military protection led to hostilities in 1775. The colonists proclaimed independence in 1776, but George obstinately continued the war until the final American victory at Yorktown in 1781. Bouts with madness (attributed to a disease called porphyria) and the way he handled the American Revolution eroded the king's support. The Peace of Versailles, signed in 1783, established British acknowledgment of the United States of America.

Other major events and people marked George III's reign. The British Army under the Duke of Wellington (whose London residence, Apsley House, you can visit; see Chapter 12) and the British Navy under Lord Horatio Nelson (honored by Nelson's Column in London's Trafalgar Square; see Chapter 12) defeated French forces under Napoleon. England also went to war again with the United States between 1812 and 1814, this time over the British practice of pressing American seamen into service in the British Navy.

It's safe to say that by the time he began an address with "My Lords and Peacocks," it was time for George to step down. Personal rule was given to his son George, the Prince Regent, in 1811. George III died blind, deaf, and mad at Windsor Castle (see Chapter 13) on January 29, 1820. You can see Kew Palace, his favorite residence, on a visit to the Royal Botanic Gardens (also known as Kew Gardens; see Chapter 13).

George IV (1762–1830): A Dandy King for the Regency

George IV, eldest son of George III and Charlotte, was the opposite of his father (are we starting to see a pattern here?): conservative in his infrequent political involvement and licentious in affairs of the heart. As Prince Regent, he had many mistresses until he secretly married the Catholic widow Maria Fitzherbert in 1785. When George III found out about it, he had the marriage declared illegal because his son would have been ineligible to reign with a Catholic wife. In 1795, George IV married again, this time to his cousin Caroline of Brunswick, who was something of a slob and whom he detested. Caroline took their only child and moved to Italy, returning to England to claim the rights of queen when George succeeded his father in 1820. George created one of the greatest scandals of his reign when he had Caroline barred from his coronation.

Bright, witty, and able on the one hand, indolent, spoiled, and lazy on the other, George was in some ways the psychological forerunner of many modern royals. Although he was scandalous with his mistresses and extravagant in his spending, he was also a patron of the arts and donated his father's immense book collection as the foundation of the British Museum Library. His support for building projects inspired the Regency style of architecture, at its most fanciful in the Royal Pavilion in Brighton (see Chapter 14). But his extravagances came at a time of social distress and general misery following the Napoleonic Wars and the tremendous changes brought forth by the Industrial Revolution. He was basically a party boy who couldn't overcome his sense of royal entitlement to provide true leadership.

Queen Victoria (1819–1901): Mother of Monarchs

Victoria, who gave her name to an era, was the daughter of Edward, Duke of Kent and Strathearn, and Victoria of Saxe-Coburg-Saalfeld. Her father died when she was an infant, and her mother enacted a strict regimen that turned its back on the scandal-ridden courts of Victoria's uncles, George IV and William IV. Popular respect for the Crown was at a low point at her coronation in 1837, but the modest and straightforward young queen, just 18 years old, eventually won the hearts of her subjects. She refused any further influence from her domineering mother, and though she had no direct input in policy decisions, she wanted to be informed of political matters. (After the Reform Act of 1832, legislative authority resided in the House of Lords, with executive authority resting within a cabinet formed by members of the House of Commons; the monarch was essentially powerless.)

Victoria married Prince Albert of Saxe-Coburg in 1840, a marriage that was apparently happy and certainly fertile: She bore nine children. The public, however, was not fond of Victoria's German prince, and Albert was excluded from holding any official political position, was never granted a title, and was named Prince Consort only after 17 years of marriage. Victoria did nothing without her husband's approval. His interests in art, science, and industry spurred him to organize the Crystal Palace Exhibition in 1851, a highly profitable industrial convention whose proceeds were used to purchase lands in Kensington for the establishment of several museums (one of which is the Victoria & Albert Museum; see Chapter 12). Following his death from typhoid in 1861, Victoria went into seclusion for more than 25 years, not emerging until the Golden Jubilee of 1887. An entire generation had never seen the face of their queen. In that period, she had the Albert Memorial erected in Kensington Gardens (see Chapter 12).

During her reign, the British Empire doubled in size, encompassing Canada, Australia, India, and various lands in Africa and the South Pacific. Victoria was named Empress of India in 1878. England's success in avoiding European conflicts for almost a century (1815 through 1914, the Crimean War of 1853 to 1856 being the major exception) was due, in large part, to the marriages Victoria arranged for her children. Either directly or by marriage, she was related to the royal houses of Germany, Russia, Greece, Romania, Sweden, Denmark, Norway, and Belgium. Nicholas II of Russia was married to Victoria's granddaughter Alexandra, and the dreaded Emperor of Germany, Kaiser Wilhelm II, was her grandson "Willy."

The era we now call Victorian England was one in which the queen's rigid ethics and uninspired personal tastes generally reflected those of the middle class. When she died of old age, an entire era died with her.

Queen Elizabeth II (1926–): Monarchy Amid Media

Elizabeth II, who became queen in 1952, is the best known of the seven remaining monarchs in Europe. The eldest daughter of George VI and Elizabeth Bowes-Lyon, she married a distant cousin, Philip Mountbatten, in 1947 and had four children: Charles, Prince of Wales; Anne; Andrew; and Edward. (For an account of some recent royal scandals involving Elizabeth's kids, see the "Recent royal events" sidebar in Chapter 2.)

In the modern world, where wealth and celebrity take the place of actual accomplishment, monarchs are basically privileged show dogs whose pedigrees allow them to amass enormous fortunes, live in a rarified world, and be newsworthy for no reason other than they are royal. Seen in the unflattering light of her children, Elizabeth shines like an old fashioned beacon of virtue and traditional values. She has never embarrassed her nation, and she is a hard and disciplined worker, the most widely traveled head of state in the world. She celebrated her Golden Jubilee in 2002 and appears determined to remain on the throne for quite some time — perhaps as long as Victoria.

Yet overall, the popularity of the English monarchy is in sharp decline. In large part, this is because the disliked and derided Windsor children have tarnished the royal name (Princess Diana was the only recent royal to reach the hearts of the public). But it also has to do with a growing sense that the monarchy is simply irrelevant. It provides an enormous boost to tourism and sells lots of books and newspapers, but in a world of democratic models and historical amnesia, how can an elitist monarchy achieve any meaningful relationship with the modern public?

But it's hard to imagine England without a king or a queen and the traditions associated with royalty. And perhaps the monarchy is worth preserving for that reason alone.

One of my favorite stories about Elizabeth II appeared in Paul Burrell's book *A Royal Duty.* One night, the queen asked if he would like to accompany her as she viewed the latest likeness sent from Madame Tussauds for her approval. The queen and her butler walked through the hallways and corridors of Buckingham Palace until they came to an enormous, dark drawing room. When the lights were switched on, a lifelike effigy of the queen was seen standing in the center of the room. Elizabeth slowly circled her wax twin, carefully scrutinizing her image. Then she pronounced herself satisfied, turned off the lights, and left herself in the dark.

Appendix

Quick Concierge

American Express

The main London office is at 6 Haymarket, SW1 (☎ 020/7930-4411; Tube: Piccadilly Circus). Branch offices are in Bath, 5 Bridge St. (☎ 01225/447-256); Brighton, 82 North St. (☎ 01273/712-905); Cambridge, 25 Sidney St. (☎ 01223/345-203); Oxford, 4 Queen St. (☎ 01865/207-105); Plymouth, 139 Armada Way (☎ 01752/502-705); Salisbury, 34 Catherine St. (☎ 01722/411-200); and York, 6 Stonegate (☎ 01904/676505).

Area/City Codes

Every U.K. telephone number in this book begins with a zero, followed by a city or area code, followed by a slash and the local number. You must dial the zero and area or city code only if you're calling from outside the area of the local number but within the United Kingdom. For information on calling the United Kingdom from outside the country, see "Telephone," later in this Appendix.

ATMs

ATMs, sometimes called *cashpoints,* are widely available in cities and towns throughout the country. Your bank or credit card may require a special PIN (personal identification number) to operate in overseas ATMs. You can obtain this PIN from your bank before you leave on your trip.

Business Hours

Banks are usually open Monday through Friday 9:30 a.m. to 3:30 p.m.

Business offices are open Monday through Friday 9 a.m. to 5 p.m.; the lunch break lasts

an hour, but most places stay open during that time. Pubs are allowed to stay open Monday through Saturday 11 a.m. to 11 p.m. and Sunday noon to 10:30 p.m. Some bars stay open past midnight. London stores generally open at 9 a.m. and close at 5:30 p.m. Monday through Saturday, staying open until 7 p.m. on Wednesday or Thursday. Elsewhere in the country, stores may be open for a half-day on Saturday. Larger stores in London and in heavily touristed areas may be open on Sunday as well.

Credit Cards

American Express, Diners Club, MasterCard, and Visa are widely accepted in London and throughout the United Kingdom. If your card gets lost or stolen in England, call the following U.K. numbers: Visa ☎ 01604/230-230 (800/645-6556 in the U.S. for Citicorp Visa); American Express ☎ 01273/696-933 (800/221-7282 in the U.S.); MasterCard ☎ 01702/362-988 (800/307-7309 in the U.S.); or Diners Club ☎ 0800/460-800 (800/525-7376 in the U.S.).

Currency Exchange

You find currency exchanges (called *bureaux de change*) in railway stations, at most post offices, and in many tourist information centers. See Chapter 5 for more on currency exchange.

Customs

If you're a U.S. citizen, you may bring home $800 worth of goods duty free, provided you've been out of the country at least 48 hours and haven't used the exemption in the past 30 days. This limit includes not more than 1 liter of an alcoholic beverage, 200 cigarettes, and 100 cigars. Antiques more than 100 years old and works of art are exempt from the $800 limit, as is anything you mail home from abroad. You may mail up to $200 worth of goods to yourself (marked "for personal use") and up to $100 worth to others (marked "unsolicited gift") once each day, as long as the package doesn't include alcohol or tobacco products. You have to pay an import duty on anything over these limits. You're charged a flat rate of 10 percent duty on the next $1,000 worth of purchases. For more specific guidance, download the free pamphlet *Know Before You Go* from the Customs Department Web site (www.customs.ustreas.gov), or contact the U.S. Customs Service, 1300 Pennsylvania Ave., NW, Washington, DC 20229 (☎ 877/287-8867), and request it.

Returning Canadian citizens are allowed a $750 exemption and can bring back duty free 200 cigarettes, 2.2 pounds of tobacco, 40 imperial ounces (1.2 qt.) of liquor, and 50 cigars. You need to declare all valuables that you're taking with you to the U.K., such as expensive cameras, on Form Y-38 before you depart Canada. For a clear summary of Canadian rules, ask for the booklet *Declare,* issued by the Canada Customs and Revenue Agency (☎ 800/461-9999 in Canada or 204/983-3500; www.ccra-adrc.gc.ca).

Australian citizens are allowed an exemption of $400 or, if under 18, $200. Personal property mailed back home should be marked "Australian Goods Returned" to avoid payment of duty. On returning to Australia, you can bring in 250 cigarettes or 250 grams of loose tobacco and 1.125 ml of alcohol. If you're returning with valuable goods you already own, such as foreign-made cameras, you should file Form B263. A helpful brochure, *Know Before You Go,*

is available from Australian consulates or Customs offices. For more information, contact the Australian Customs Service (☎ 1300/363-263; www.customs.gov.au).

New Zealand citizens have a duty-free allowance of $700. If you're older than 17, you can bring in 200 cigarettes, 50 cigars, or 250 grams of tobacco (or a mix of all three if the combined weight doesn't exceed 250 grams), plus 4.5 liters of wine and beer or 1.125 liters of liquor. New Zealand currency doesn't carry import or export restrictions. Fill out a certificate of export, listing the valuables you're taking out of the country. (That way, you can bring them back without paying duty.) You can find the answers to most of your questions in *New Zealand Customs Guide for Travelers Notice No. 4,* a free pamphlet available at New Zealand consulates and Customs offices. For more information, contact New Zealand Customs, The Customhouse, 17–21 Whitmore St., Box 2218, Wellington (☎ 04/473-6099 or 0800/428-786; www.customs.govt.nz)

Doctors

See "Hospitals," later in this Appendix. For a doctor in London, see "Doctors and Dentists" in the "Fast Facts" section of Chapter 12.

Electricity

British current is 240 volts, AC cycle—roughly twice the voltage of North American current, which is 115–120 volts, AC cycle. You won't be able to plug the flat pins of your appliance's plugs into the holes of British wall outlets without suitable converters or adapters (available from an electrical supply shop). Be warned that you'll destroy the inner workings of your appliance (and possibly start a fire) if you plug an American appliance directly into a European electrical outlet without a transformer.

Embassies and High Commissions

All embassies, consulates, and high commissions are in London, the capital of the U.K. In case you lose your passport or have some other emergency, here's a list of addresses and phone numbers:

Australia: The high commission is at Australia House, Strand, WC2 (☎ 02073/794-334; Tube: Charing Cross), open Monday through Friday 10 a.m. to 4 p.m.

Canada: The high commission is at MacDonald House, 1 Grosvenor Square, W1 (☎ 02072/586-600; Tube: Bond St.), open Monday through Friday 9 a.m. to 5 p.m.

Ireland: The embassy is at 17 Grosvenor Place, SW1 (☎ 02072/352-171; Tube: Hyde Park Corner), open Monday through Friday 9:30 a.m. to 1 p.m. and 2:15 to 5 p.m.

New Zealand: The high commission is at New Zealand House, 80 Haymarket at Pall Mall, SW1 (☎ 02079/308-422; Tube: Charing Cross or Piccadilly Circus), open Monday through Friday 9 a.m. to 5 p.m.

United States: The embassy is at 24 Grosvenor Square, W1 (☎ 02074/999-000; Tube: Bond Street), open Monday through Friday from 8:30 a.m. to noon and 2 to 4 p.m. (the embassy has no afternoon hours on Tuesday).

Emergencies

For police, fire, or an ambulance, dial ☎ 999 (you don't need to pay when calling from a public phone).

Holidays

Americans may be unfamiliar with some British holidays, particularly the spring and summer Bank Holidays (the last Monday in May and in August), when everyone takes off for a long weekend. Most banks and many shops, museums, historic houses, and other places of interest are closed on Bank Holidays, and public transport services are reduced. The same holds true for other major British holidays: New Year's Day, Good Friday, Easter Monday, May Day (the first Monday in May), Christmas Day, and Boxing Day (Dec 26). London crowds swell during school holidays: mid-July to early September, three weeks at Christmas and at Easter, and a week in mid-October and in mid-February.

Hospitals

Visitors to the U.K. can get free *emergency* care in Emergency Outpatient Centers of National Health hospitals, but you have to pay for any inpatient or followup care. Check with your insurance company or HMO to see if medical expenses are covered while you're out of the country. If you need a doctor, ask your hotel, consulate, or embassy to recommend one. If you find yourself in a life-threatening emergency situation, dial ☎ 999 for an ambulance. For a list of hospitals offering 24-hour emergency care in London, see "Hospitals" in the "Fast Facts" section of Chapter 12. See Chapter 10 for insurance and medical matters.

Information

See "Where to Get More Information," later in this Appendix, to find out where to get visitor information before you leave home.

Internet Access and Cybercafes

For Internet access in London, see the "Fast Facts" section of Chapter 12. For the rest of the country, check at local Tourist Information Centres to find out if you can get public Internet access. Usually, you find cybercafes only in larger cities; public libraries in smaller towns often have Internet access.

Liquor Laws

No alcohol is served to anyone under 18. Children under 16 aren't allowed in pubs except in certain rooms and then only when accompanied by a parent or guardian. Restaurants can serve liquor during the same hours as pubs (see "Business Hours," earlier in this Appendix, for these hours); however, only people who are eating a meal on the premises can get a drink. In hotels, liquor may be served 11 a.m. to 11 p.m. to both guests and nonguests; after 11 p.m., only guests may be served.

Mail

At press time, postcards and airmail letters to North America cost 47p (87¢) for 10 grams; letters generally take seven to ten days to arrive from the United States. Travel time for letters to the United States from the United Kingdom varies wildly but usually takes between seven and ten days as well. You can send mail within the United Kingdom first or second class. See "Post Offices," later in this Appendix.

Maps

London A to Z, which you can find in various formats from news agents and bookstores, is the best street directory to London. You can obtain a London bus and Underground map at any Underground station. If you drive through England, get one of the best road atlases : the large-format maps produced by the Automobile Association (AA), Collins, Ordnance Survey, and Royal Automobile Club (RAC). The best maps for walkers are the detailed Ordnance Survey maps; check out their selection, including digital maps, online at www.ordsvy.gov.uk. London's Stanfords, 12–14 Long Acre, WC2 (☎ 02078/361-321; Tube: Leicester Square), is the world's largest map shop.

Newspapers/Magazines

The *Times, Daily Telegraph, Daily Mail, Guardian,* and *Evening Standard* are all dailies carrying the latest news. The *International Herald Tribune,* published in Paris, and an international edition of *USA*

Today, beamed via satellite, are available daily. Copies of *Time* and *Newsweek* are also sold at most newsstands.

Pharmacies

Pharmacies are called *chemists* in the United Kingdom. Boots is a chain of chemists with outlets all over the country. Make sure that you bring generic prescriptions with you, not brand names. For a list of pharmacies in London, see "Pharmacies" in the "Fast Facts" section of Chapter 12.

Police

In an emergency, dial ☎ 999 (you don't need to pay when calling from a public phone).

Post Offices

In London, the Main Post Office, 24 William IV St., WC2 (☎ 02079/309-580; Tube: Charing Cross), is open Monday through Saturday 8:30 a.m. to 8 p.m. Other post offices and sub-post offices (windows in the back of news-agent stores) throughout the country are open Monday through Friday 9 a.m. to 5:30 p.m. and Saturday 9 a.m. to 12:30 p.m. Many sub-post offices and some main post offices close for an hour at lunchtime. A red sign identifies post offices.

Restrooms

The English often call toilets *loos.* In London, they're marked by PUBLIC TOILETS signs on streets, parks, and Tube stations. You also find well-maintained lavatories that anybody can use in all larger public buildings, such as museums and art galleries, large department stores, and rail stations. Toilets are always available at major tourist attractions. Public lavatories are usually free, but you may need a 20p coin to get in or to use a proper washroom. In some places (like Leicester Square in London), you find coin-operated toilets that are sterilized after each use.

Safety

In London, as in any large metropolis, use common sense and normal caution when you're in a crowded public area or walking alone at night.

Smoking

Most U.S. cigarette brands are available in England. Smoking is strictly forbidden in the London Underground (in the cars and on the platforms) and on buses, and it's increasingly frowned on in many other places. Most restaurants have nonsmoking tables, but they're usually in the same room with smokers. Nonsmoking rooms are available in more and more hotels, and some B&Bs are now entirely smoke free.

Taxes

The 17.5 percent value-added tax (VAT) is added to all hotel and restaurant bills and is included in the price of most items you purchase. You can get a refund if you shop at stores that participate in the Duty-Free Shopping scheme (signs are posted in the window). See Chapter 5 for details on getting your VAT refunded.

Taxis

In London, you can hail a cab from the street; if the "For Hire" light is lit, it means the cab is available. You can phone for a London radio cab at ☎ 02072/720-272. Elsewhere, you can often find taxis waiting outside train and bus stations, although it's a good idea to reserve a taxi in advance at smaller stations in the country.

Telephone

For directory assistance, dial ☎ 192. The country code for the United Kingdom is **44.** To call England from the United States, dial **011-44,** the area or city code, and then the 6-, 7-, or 8-digit phone number. If you're in England and dialing a number within the same area code, the local number is all you need.

Three types of public pay phones are available in England: those that take only coins; those that accept only phone cards; and those that take coins, phone cards, and credit cards. Phone cards are available in four values — £3 ($5.55), £5 ($9.25), £10 ($19), and £20 ($37) — and are reusable until the total value has expired. You can buy the cards from newsstands and post offices. At coin-operated phones, insert your coins before dialing. The minimum charge is 20p (35¢). The credit-call pay phone operates on credit cards: Access (which is interchangeable with MasterCard), American Express, Diners Club, and Visa. You find these type of pay phones most commonly at airports and large rail stations.

To make an international call from England, dial the international access code (00), then the country code, then the area code, and finally the local number. Or call through one of the following long-distance access codes: AT&T USA Direct (☎ 0800/890-011), Canada Direct (☎ 0800-/890-016), Australia (☎ 0800/890-061), and New Zealand (☎ 0800/890-064). Common country codes are United States and Canada, **1;** Australia, **61;** and New Zealand, **64.**

Time Zone

England follows Greenwich mean time (five hours ahead of eastern standard time). Clocks move forward one hour on the last Sunday in March and back one hour on the last Sunday in October. Most of the year, including summer, Britain is five hours ahead of the time observed on the East Coast of the United States. Because the United States and Britain observe daylight saving time at slightly different times of year, Britain is only four hours ahead of New York for a brief period (about a week) in autumn, and it's six hours ahead of New York for a brief period in spring.

Tipping

In restaurants, they often add service charges of 15 to 20 percent to the bill. Sometimes, this tip is clearly marked; other times, it isn't. When in doubt, ask. If service isn't included, adding 15 percent to the bill is customary. Sommeliers get about £1 ($1.85) per bottle of wine served. Tipping in pubs isn't done, but in cocktail bars the server usually gets about £1 ($1.85) per round of drinks. Tipping taxi drivers 10 to 15 percent of the fare is standard. Barbers and hairdressers expect 10 to 15 percent. Tour guides expect £2 ($3.70), although this tip isn't mandatory. Theater ushers aren't tipped.

Train Information

For information on train schedules and departure stations, call ☎ 0457/484-950, 24 hours a day. You can also find info online at www.trainline.co.uk.

Weather Updates

Weather information for the United Kingdom is available online at www.weather.co.uk.

Toll-Free Numbers and Web Sites

Major airlines serving England

Air Canada
☎ 888/247-2262 in the U.S.
www.aircanada.ca

Air New Zealand
☎ 800/262-1234 or 800/262-2468

in the U.S.
☎ 800/663-5494 in Canada
☎ 0800/737-767 in New Zealand
www.airnewzealand.com

American Airlines
☎ 800/433-7300
www.aa.com

British Airways
☎ 800/247-9297
☎ 0345/222-111 or 0845/77-333-77
in Britain
www.british-airways.com

British Midland
☎ 0800/788-0555 in Britain
www.britishmidland.com

Continental Airlines
☎ 800/525-0280
www.continental.com

Delta Air Lines
☎ 800/221-1212
www.delta.com

Icelandair
☎ 800/223-5500 in the U.S.
☎ 354/50-50-100 in Iceland
www.icelandair.is

Northwest Airlines
☎ 800/225-2525
www.nwa.com

Qantas
☎ 800/227-4500 in the U.S.
☎ 612/9691-3636 in Australia
www.qantas.com

United Airlines
☎ 800/241-6522
www.united.com

Virgin Atlantic Airways
☎ 800/862-8621 in the U.S.
☎ 0293/747-747 in Britain
www.virgin-atlantic.com

Major car-rental agencies operating in England

Alamo

☎ 800/327-9633 in the U.S.
☎ 0800/272-200 in Britain
www.goalamo.com

Avis

☎ 800/331-1212 in the U.S.
☎ 0990/900-500 in Britain
www.avis.com

Budget

☎ 800/527-0700 in the U.S.
☎ 0541/565-656 in Britain
www.budgetrentacar.com

Hertz

☎ 800/654-3131 in the U.S.
☎ 0990/6699 in Britain
www.hertz.com

National

☎ 800/CAR-RENT in the U.S.
☎ 0990/565-656 in Britain
www.nationalcar.com

Major hotel chains in England

Hilton Hotels

☎ 800/HILTONS in the U.S.
☎ 0800/88844 in Britain
www.hilton.co.uk

Hyatt Hotels & Resorts

☎ 800/228-9000 in the U.S.
☎ 0845/888-1234 in Britain
www.hyatt.com

Le Meridien Hotels & Resorts

☎ 800/225-5843 in the U.S.
☎ 0800/028-2840 in Britain
www.lemeridien.com

Macdonald Hotels & Resorts

☎ 888/892-0038 in the U.S.
☎ 0870/830-4812 in Britain
www.macdonaldhotels.com

Moat House Hotels

☎ 800/641-0300 in the U.S.
☎ 0870/225-0199 in Britain
www.moathousehotels.com

Red Carnation Hotels

☎ 877/955-1515 in the U.S.
☎ 0845/634-2665 in Britain
www.redcarnation.com

Relais & Chateaux

☎ 800/735-2478 in the U.S.
☎ 0800/2000-0002 in Britain
www.relaischateaux.com

Sheraton Hotels & Resorts

☎ 800/325-3535 in the U.S.
☎ 0800/3253-5303 in Britain
www.sheraton.com

Thistle Hotels Worldwide

☎ 800/847-4358 in the U.S.
☎ 0800/181716 in Britain
www.thistlehotels.com

Where to Get More Information

For more information on England, you can visit the tourist offices and Web sites listed in the following sections.

Locating tourist offices

For general information about London, contact an office of VisitBritain (formerly the British Tourist Authority) at one of the following addresses (or on the Web at www.visitbritain.com):

- **In the United States:** The main VisitBritain office for North America is at 551 Fifth Ave., Suite 701, New York, NY 10176-0799 (☎ 800/462-2748).

- **In Australia:** Level 2, 15 Blue St., North Sydney, NSW 2060 (☎ 02/9021-4400).

- **In Ireland:** 18–19 College Green, Dublin 2 (☎ 01/670-8000).

- **In New Zealand:** Level 17, NZI House, 151 Queen St., Auckland 1 (☎ 09/303-1446).

For more specific information on particular regions, contact the following regional tourist boards:

- **Cumbria Tourist Board** (the Lake District), Ashleigh, Holly Road, Windermere, Cumbria LA23 2AQ. (☎ 01539/44444; www.golakes.co.uk).

- **East of England Tourist Board,** Toppesfield Hall, Hadleigh, Suffolk IP7 5DN (☎ 01473/822-922; www.visiteastofengland.com).

- **Heart of England Tourist Board,** Woodside, Larkhill Road, Worcester WR5 2E2 (☎ 01905/763-436; www.visitheartof england.com).

- **North West England Tourist Board,** Swan House, Swan Meadow Road, Wigan Pier, Wigan WN3 5BB (☎ 01942/821-222; www.visitnorthwest.com).

- **South East England Tourist Board,** The Old Brew House, Warwick Park, Tunbridge Wells, Kent TN2 5TU (☎ 01892/ 540-766; www.visitsoutheastengland.com).

- **Southern England Tourist Board,** 40 Chamberlayne Rd., Eastleigh, Hampshire SO50 5JH (☎ 01703/620-006).

- **West Country Tourist Board,** 60 St. David's Hill, Exeter, Devon EX4 4SY (☎ 01392/425-426; www.westcountrynow.com).

- **Yorkshire Tourist Board,** 312 Tadcaster Rd., York YO24 1GS (☎ 01904/707-961; www.yorkshirevisitor.com).

Surfing the Net

You can find useful and quite specific Web sites scattered throughout this book. In the following sections, I point you toward some of the best of them.

Tourist info on England

For general information on all of England, try these sites for starters:

- ✔ www.visitbritain.com: The Web page for the official British travel agency is a good resource for visitors to London and to the United Kingdom in general.

- ✔ www.enjoyengland.com: The English Tourist Board's official site has information on cities and regions throughout the country.

- ✔ www.knowhere.co.uk: On this site, local residents provide a mish-mash of insider information for cities and towns throughout the United Kingdom.

- ✔ www.backpackers.co.uk: Travelers who want to backpack through England can find useful information, including hostels and inexpensive accommodations, at this site.

- ✔ www.nationaltrust.org.uk: The National Trust administers hundreds of properties, from castles to gardens to everything in between, throughout the U.K.

- ✔ www.english-heritage.org.uk: English Heritage maintains and administers important historic sites throughout the country.

General info on specific cities

The following Tourist Information Centre Web sites provide directories for hotels, restaurants, and attractions in cities throughout England:

- ✔ **Bath:** www.visitbath.co.uk or www.heritagecities.co.uk

- ✔ **Brighton:** www.visitbrighton.com or www.heritagecities.co.uk

- ✔ **Cambridge:** www.visitcambridge.org

- ✔ **Canterbury:** www.visitcanterbury.co.uk

- ✔ **Dover:** www.whitecliffscountry.org.uk

- ✔ **Greenwich:** www.greenwich.gov.uk

- ✔ **Oxford:** www.oxford.gov.uk/tourism or www.heritagecities.co.uk

- ✔ **Penzance:** www.penzance.co.uk/tourism

- ✔ **Plymouth:** www.plymouthcity.co.uk

✔ **Salisbury:** www.salisbury.gov.uk/leisure

✔ **Stratford-upon-Avon:** www.shakespeare-country.co.uk or www.heritagecities.co.uk

✔ **Winchester:** www.winchester.gov.uk

✔ **Windsor:** www.windsor.gov.uk

✔ **York:** www.york-tourism.co.uk or www.heritagecities.co.uk

Visitor info for counties, regions, and national parks

The following sites give you general information on specific counties, regions, and national parks in England:

✔ **Cornwall:** www.cornwall-calling.co.uk, www.cornwall-online.co.uk, or www.chycor.co.uk

✔ **Cotswolds, Gloucestershire:** www.visitcotswolds.co.uk or www.visit-glos.org.uk

✔ **Dartmoor National Park:** www.dartmoor-npa.gov.uk

✔ **Devon, English Riviera:** www.english-riviera.com

✔ **Lake District:** www.visitcumbria.com or www.cumbria-the-lake-district.co.uk

✔ **North York Moors National Park:** www.visitthemoors.com

✔ **South Kent:** www.whiteclittscountry.org.uk

✔ **Warwickshire around Stratford:** www.shakespeare-country.co.uk

✔ **Yorkshire:** www.yorkshirevisitor.com or www.discoveryorkshirecoast.com

✔ **Yorkshire Dales National Park:** www.yorkshiredales.org.uk

News on daily events, transportation, and the royals

If you're looking for news about daily events or royal happenings, log on to the following Web sites:

✔ **www.guardian.co.uk:** The *Daily Guardian*, a daily newspaper, provides up-to-the minute online news coverage.

✔ **www.timesonline.co.uk:** The *London Times*, the oldest and most traditional of London daily papers, is a good source for general news and culture.

✔ **www.trainline.co.uk:** This site provides information on train schedules.

✔ **www.pti.org.uk:** This very useful site (especially if you don't have a car) provides information on all forms of public transportation throughout the country.

✔ **www.royal.gov.uk:** If you want to read history, information, and trivia about the Windsors and the British monarchy in general, check out the official royal Web site.

Online sites for London

For tourism, cultural, entertainment, or transportation information on London, check out the following sites:

✔ **www.visitlondon.com:** VisitBritain maintains this "official" London Web site, which is loaded with information.

✔ **www.londontown.com:** This site features special offers on hotels, B&Bs, and theater tickets.

✔ **www.timeout.com/london:** The weekly listings magazine *Time Out* gives you the lowdown on London's cultural events, entertainment, restaurants, and nightlife.

✔ **www.gaylondon.co.uk:** This is a useful list of gay and gay-friendly hotels, services, clubs, and restaurants.

✔ **www.baa.co.uk:** You can get information on London's airports on this site.

✔ **www.tfl.gov.uk:** This is the Web site for Transport for London, which is in charge of all forms of public transportation in the city: Tube, buses, ferry service, and so on.

Index

• A •

AAA, 63, 83, 92
AARP, 63, 83, 92
The Abbey (Penzance), 295–296
Abbey Restaurant (Penzance), 296–297
Abbot's Fireside Hotel (Elham), 226
Abraham's restaurant (Keswick), 394
The Academy of St. Martin-in-the-Fields
     (London), 172–173
accommodations
  Bath, 329–330
  bed-and-breakfast inns (B&Bs), 88–89
  best room and rates, 92–94
  boutique and deluxe hotels, 91
  Brighton, 240–241
  Broadway, 341
  Canterbury, 225–226
  cash-only, 65
  Cheltenham, 335–336
  children and, 96
  Chipping Campden, 342–343
  Cirencester, 344–345
  cost of, 57–58, 88
  cost-cutting tips, 58, 62, 63, 134
  Dartmoor National Park, 283–284
  Exeter, 277–278
  gay and lesbian, 241
  Grasmere, 388–389
  hotel chains, 91, 428
  hotels, 89–92
  Internet access, 111
  Keswick, 392–394
  with kitchen, 63
  Lake Windermere, 382–383
  landmark and country-house hotels, 91
  London, 87, 88, 131–142
  with meals (full board), 59
  nonsmoking, 88, 94
  Penzance, 295–296
  price range, 2–3, 58, 90, 134
  rack rate, 2, 92, 134
  without reservations, 131
  reservations needed for London, 87
  reservations online, 93–94
  Rye, 232–233
  Scarborough, 367–369
  self-catering, 91–92, 96
  St. Ives, 303–304
  Stratford-upon-Avon, 313–315
  tipping, 68
  Torquay, 287–288
  VAT (value-added tax) on, 426
  Winchester, 264
  York, 356–357
  Yorkshire Dales National Park, 374
Agatha Christie Memorial Room
     (Torquay), 288
air travel
  airfare, 62, 70–71
  booking online, 71–72
  customs regulations, 116, 422–423
  deep vein thrombosis and, 107
  to London, 115–119
  security matters, 111–112
airlines, 69–70, 76, 427
airports
  Gatwick, 29, 70, 117–118
  Heathrow, 29, 69–70, 116–117
  Internet kiosks at, 109
  London City Airport, 70, 118–119
  Luton airport, 70, 119
  Manchester, 30, 70
  Stansted, 70, 118
  Web sites, 200
Albert Memorial (London), 166
Alfred the Great (King of Wessex),
     263, 266, 414–415
almshouses, 344
American Air Museum (Cambridge), 208
American Express, 65, 66, 422
Anne Boleyn Gate (Hampton Court
     Palace), 212
Anne Hathaway's Cottage (Shottery),
     318, 404
Anne (Princess), 84, 126, 348
Anne (Queen), 326, 333
Ann's Pantry restaurant
     (Cirencester), 345

antiques, shopping for
  BADA Antiques & Art Fair, 36
  Cheltenham, 338
  Cirencester, 347
  the Cotswolds, 28, 341
  Exeter, 280
  York, 364
Apsley House (London), 176
aquarium, Plymouth, 291
architecture, English, 18–19
Arden, Mary (Shakespeare's mother),
    319–320, 404
area/city codes, 198, 422
aromatherapy, London, 185, 188
Art Gallery (Scarborough), 370
Ascot racecourse (near Windsor), 37
Ashmolean Museum (Oxford), 217
Assembly Rooms (Bath), 332
Aster House (London), 134
Astons Apartments (London), 134–135
ATMs, 64, 65, 422
attractions. *See also* London, attractions
  avoiding crowds, 42, 159
  Bath, 332–334
  Battle, 238
  Brighton, 243–244
  Cambridge, 204–208
  Canterbury, 228–229
  Cheltenham, 337–338
  for children, 96–97
  Cornwall, 27–28
  cost of, 59–60
  cost-cutting tips, 60, 62, 63
  Dartmoor National Park, 285–286
  Exeter, 279–280
  Kent, 27, 247
  Keswick, 395–397
  Knole, 249–250
  Oxford, 214–217
  Penzance, 298–300
  Rye, 234–235
  Scarborough, 369–372
  St. Ives, 304–305
  Stratford-upon-Avon, 317–321
  Torquay, 288
  Winchester, 265
  York, 29, 359–363
Aubergine (London), 146
Augustine's (Canterbury), 226–227
Aunty Val's Tea Rooms (Bowness), 383

Austen, Jane (author)
  about, 27, 263, 401–402
  Bath and, 326, 328
  homes of, 266, 267, 401–402
  Jane Austen Centre, 333, 401
autumn season, 33–34
aviaries, 254, 339
Avon Boating (Stratford-upon-Avon), 320
Avonmore Hotel (London), 135
Aysgarth (Yorkshire), 374

• *B* •

babysitters, 97
BADA Antiques & Art Fair (London), 36
bakeries (patisseries), London, 155–156
ballet, London, 191–192
Bannings Guesthouse (Brighton), 241
The Bantam Tea Rooms (Chipping
    Campden), 344
The Bar Convent (York), 356
Barbara Hepworth Museum and
    Sculpture Gardens (St. Ives), 305
Barbican Hall (London), 192
The Barbican (Plymouth), 290
Barrie, J.M. (*Peter Pan in Kensington
    Gardens*), 97, 166
bars. *See* clubs, pubs, and bars
Bath
  accommodations, 329–330
  attractions, 332–334
  described, 10, 28, 326
  dining, 330–332
  festivals, 36, 328
  history of, 333
  map of, 327
  tourist information, 328
  tours, 328
  traveling to, 326
Bath Abbey (Bath), 332
Bath Festival's Box Office, 328
Battle, 12, 26, 236–238
Battle of Hastings, 236, 238
Battle of Hastings Abbey, 238
Bayswater (London), 125
BBC Henry Wood Promenade Concerts, 38
beaches
  best, 10
  Brighton, 239, 244, 271
  Scarborough, 29, 366, 367, 369

St. Ives, 302
Torquay, 287
Beatrix Potter Gallery (Hawkshead), 385, 403
Becket, Saint Thomas à (archbishop of Canterbury), 409–410
bed-and-breakfast inns (B&Bs), 88–89
beer, 21, 60, 61
Belgravia (London), 124
Benson, E. F. (*Mapp and Lucia*), 230, 403
Benson Hotel (Rye), 232
best of England
castles and estates, 11
cathedrals and churches, 11–12, 409–412
cities, towns, and villages, 10–11
gardens, 13, 405–408
historic landmarks, 12
London, 9–10, 24, 26
museums, 10
romantic landscapes, 13–14
shopping, 14
Betty's (York), 358
Biederbecke's Hotel (Scarborough), 368
Big Ben (London), 164–165
biking
Cambridge, 204
Lake Windermere, 382
Birdland (Bourton-on-the-Water), 339
Black Friars Distillery (Plymouth), 290
Blenheim Palace (Woodstock), 11, 218–219
Bloombury (London), 121
Blooms Hotel (London), 141
The Blue Bicycle (York), 358
boating and boat tours
Canterbury, 225
Derwentwater, 396
Henley Royal Regatta, 38
to Kew Gardens, 213
Lake Windermere, 381–382
London, 182–183
Oxford and Cambridge Boat Race, 36
Penzance, 295
Plymouth, 289
punting on the River Cam, 208
Stratford-upon-Avon, 320
York, 355
Bodleian Library (Oxford), 217
Boleyn, Anne (Queen), 212, 250, 251, 416
Bond Street (London), 185, 188
books, recommended, 22, 97–98

bookstores, London, 188
Boudicca (Celtic queen), 15, 413–414
Bourton-on-the-Water (the Cotswolds), 338–339
boutique and deluxe hotels, 91
Bowness, 29, 381
Boxwood Cafe (London), 146
Bradley Court Hotel (South Cliff), 368
brass rubbings, 207, 320–321
Brewery Arts Centre (Cirencester), 347
Bridge of Sighs (Cambridge), 206
Brighton
accommodations, 240–241
attractions, 243–244
beaches, 239, 244, 271
described, 26–27, 238–239
dining, 242–243
gay and lesbian travelers and, 102, 241, 246
map of, 239
nightlife, 245–246
shopping, 245
tourist information, 240
transportation, 239–240
Brighton International Festival, 36, 245
Brighton Museum & Art Gallery, 243
Brighton Philharmonic Orchestra, 245
British Airways London Eye (London), 176
The British Library Exhibition Centre (London), 176
British Museum (London), 159, 162, 163
BritRail passes, 58–59, 60, 73, 80–81
Brixham, 287
Broadway, 340–342
Broadway Teddy Bear Museum, 341
Broadway Tower (Broadway), 342
Brontë, Anne (novelist), 375, 376, 402
Brontë, Branwell (artist), 375
Brontë, Charlotte (novelist), 29, 375, 376, 402
Brontë, Emily (novelist), 29, 375, 376, 402
Brontë Parsonage Museum (Haworth), 375, 402
Brown's Hotel (London), 141
Browns (Oxford), 217–218
Bryanston Court Hotel (London), 135
Bryson's of Keswick, 394
bucket shops (consolidators), 71

Buckingham Palace (London), 11, 38, 162, 164
Buckland Abbey (Yelverton), 281, 285
budget for trip. *See also* cost-cutting tips; money
  accommodations, 57–58
  attractions, 59–60
  cost of things in London, 61–62
  dining, 59
  gasoline for rental car, 59, 62, 86
  shopping and nightlife, 60–61
  taxes, 68
  tipping, 68
  transportation, 58–59
Building of Bath Museum, 333
Burford (Exeter), 280
bus travel. *See also* tours; transportation
  children and, 129, 130
  from London, 81
  in London, 129–130
  overview, 77, 81
  passes, 130
  Travelcards for, 128–129
business hours, 422
Butterfly Farm (Stratford-upon-Avon), 320
Buzz (York), 358
Byland Abbey (Yorkshire), 373

• C •

Cabinet War Rooms (London), 176–177
Cadogan Hotel (London), 135–136
Cafe in the Crypt (London), 146–147
Cafe Italia (Scarborough), 369
calendar of events, 35–40, 232
Cambridge
  attractions, 204–208
  colleges, open hours, 205
  dining, 208–209
  map of, 203
  Oxford and Cambridge Boat Race, 36
  tourist information, 204
  transportation, 201, 204
Cambridge Brass Rubbing Centre, 207
Canon Photography Gallery (London), 174
Canterbury
  accommodations, 225–226
  attractions, 228–229
  described, 26, 224–225

  dining, 226–228
  map of, 227
  tourist information, 225
  traveling to, 225
Canterbury Cathedral, 12, 224, 228, 409–410
The Canterbury Tales (Chaucer), 12, 16, 26, 228–229
The Canterbury Tales museum, 228–229
Captain Cook monument (Whitby), 371
car rental. *See also* car travel
  booking online, 84
  cost-cutting tips, 83, 84
  driver's license/age requirements, 82
  gasoline costs and, 59, 62, 86
  going without, 58
  insurance for, 83–84
  rental agencies, 428
car travel. *See also* car rental; transportation
  driving on the left, 81–82
  emergencies, 85
  London congestion charge for, 82
  motorways, carriageways, and roundabouts, 84–85
  overview, 77
  parking, in London, 82
  rules of the road, 85, 131
Carfax Tower (Oxford), 214, 216
cash, carrying, 64
Castle Drogo (Drewsteignton), 11, 281, 286
Castle Howard, 11, 29, 351, 365–366, 405–406
Castle on St. Michael's Mount (Mount's Bay), 298
Castlerigg Stone Circle (near Keswick), 395–396
castles, best, 11
Cathedral Gate Hotel (Canterbury), 226
Cathedral Refectory (Winchester), 265
cathedrals and churches, best, 11–12, 409–412
cellphones, 107–108
Central London (London), 120
Chagford, 27, 281
chain hotels, 91
Changing of the Guard
  Buckingham Palace, 164
  Windsor Castle, 220
Chapel Street (Penzance), 299

Charing Cross (London), 121
Charing Cross Road (London), 185, 188
Charles Dickens Museum (London),
      177, 402
Charles (Prince), 17, 18, 294
Chartwell House (Kent), 11, 252–253
Chaucer, Geoffrey (*The Canterbury Tales*),
      12, 16, 26, 228–229
Chawton, 27, 267–268
Chedworth Roman Villa
      (Cirencester), 348
Chelsea Crafts Fair, 39
Chelsea Flower Show (London), 36–37
Chelsea (London), 125, 185
Chelsea Physic Garden (London), 177, 406
Cheltenham, 28, 334–338
Cheltenham Art Gallery and Museum, 337
Cheltenham Festival of Literature, 39, 335
children. *See* families with children
china (porcelain), London, 189
Chinese New Year (London), 35
Chipping Campden, 342–344
Christ Church College (Oxford), 216
Christie, Agatha (author), 288
Christmas lights (London), 40
The Chunnel, 72, 119
Church of St. Mary (Whitby), 371
churches and cathedrals, best, 11–12,
      409–412
Churchill, Sir Winston (prime minister)
   birthplace of, 218
   homes of, 11, 252–253
   World War II bunker of, 176
Chysauster (near St. Ives), 306
The Circus (Bath), 332
Cirencester, 344–348
Cirencester Park, 347
Cirencester Waitrose, 348
cities, towns and villages, best, 10–11
City Museum (Winchester), 266–267
City of London Festival, 37
The City of London (London), 120
Clarence House (London), 162
Claridge's (London), 141, 156
Claverley Hotel (London), 136
Cloister Court (Cambridge), 206
clubs, pubs, and bars
   Brighton, 245–246
   business hours, 20, 422
   gay and lesbian, 197, 246

London, 192–197
   tipping and, 20–21, 68, 427
   visiting, 20–21
   York, 364–365
Comfort Inn Notting Hill (London), 136
consolidators (bucket shops), 71
Copper Kettle (Battle), 237
Corinium Hotel (Cirencester), 345
Corinium Museum (Cirencester), 347
Cornish Range (Mousehole), 301
Cornwall, 13, 27–28, 292–293
cost-cutting tips
   accommodations, 58, 62, 63, 134
   airfare, 62, 70–71
   attractions, 60, 62, 63
   BritRail pass savings, 80–81
   car rental, 83, 84
   dining, 63, 143, 146
   overview, 62–63
   train travel, 63
   Travelcards, 128–129
Cotehele, 13, 307
Cotswold Motoring Museum and Toy
      Collection, 339
Cotswold Perfumery, 339
Cotswold Pottery, 339
the Cotswolds, 10, 13, 28, 325
country code and city code, 198
country-house hotels, 91
Courtauld Gallery (London), 180
The Courtyard Cafe (Chagford), 284
Courtyard Cafe (Winchester), 264–265
Covent Garden (London), 185, 188–189
Coward's Guest House (Brighton), 241
The Cranley (London), 136–137
credit cards
   abbreviations, 2
   credit-reporting bureaus, 67
   emergency numbers, 66, 422
   using, 64–65
Criterion Grill (London), 147
Crown Jewels (London), 60, 171
Culpeper the Herbalist (London), 188
Cumberland Pencil Museum
      (Keswick), 396
Cumbria, 29, 377
currency exchange, 63–64, 66, 422
customs regulations, 116, 422–423
Cutty Sark (Greenwich), 209, 210

• D •

The Daffodil (Cheltenham), 336
Dales Countryside Museum
    (Yorkshire), 375
Danby Castle (Yorkshire), 374
Danby (Yorkshire), 374
Daphne du Maurier Festival of Arts and
    Literature (Penzance), 295
Dartmoor National Park, 27, 281–286
day trips from London
    best way to travel, 77
    Blenheim Palace, 218–219
    Cambridge, 201, 203–209
    Greenwich, 209–211
    Hampton Court, 211–212
    map of, 202
    Oxford, 213–218
    Royal Botanic Gardens (Kew Gardens),
        212–213, 407
    Windsor Castle, 219–220
day trips from York, 365–366
Dean Court Hotel (York), 356
debit cards, 65
deep vein thrombosis (economy-class
    syndrome), 107
Dell Restaurant (London), 177
dentists, London, 198
The Derby (in Surrey), 37
Derwentwater (southwest of
    Keswick), 396
Devon, 27, 274, 275
Diana (Princess), 17, 47, 131, 166
Dickens, Charles (novelist), 17, 177, 402
dining. *See also specific restaurants*; tea
    Bath, 330–332
    Battle, 237
    Brighton, 242–243
    Cambridge, 208–209
    Canterbury, 226–228
    Cheltenham, 336–337
    with children, 96
    cost of, 2–3, 59
    cost-cutting tips, 63, 143, 146
    Dartmoor National Park, 284–285
    English cuisine, 20, 143
    ethnic cuisine, 20, 143
    Exeter, 278–279
    fast-foods, 96

    Grasmere, 389
    Haworth, 376
    Keswick, 394–395
    London, 143–155
    Oxford, 217–218
    Penzance, 296–298
    Plymouth, 290
    Rye, 233–234
    Scarborough, 369
    St. Ives, 304
    Stratford-upon-Avon, 315–317
    tipping, 68, 427
    Torquay, 287–288
    VAT (value-added tax), 68, 426
    Winchester, 264–265
    York, 357–359
disabilities, travelers with, 98–101
doctors
    hospitals and, 424
    London, 198
Dog and Gun (Keswick), 395
The Dorchester (London), 141
Dorset Square Hotel (London), 137
Dove Cottage (south of Grasmere), 390
The Dove (Dargate), 227–228
Dover Castle, 26, 256–257
Dover, white cliffs of, 26, 257
Dr. Marten's Department Store
    (London), 185
driving. *See* car travel
Drucker's Cafe (Stratford-upon-Avon), 319
du Maurier, Daphne (*Rebecca*), 295
Duck Bridge (Yorkshire), 374
Dukes Hotel (London), 141
Durrants Hotel (London), 137
duty-free shopping, 426
Duxford Imperial War Museum
    (Cambridge), 208

• E •

The Eagle Pub (Cambridge), 208–209
Earl's Court (London), 125
easyInternet café, 110
economy-class syndrome (deep vein
    thrombosis), 107
Eden Camp (Yorkshire), 351, 366
Eden Project (Cornwall), 13, 308, 406

Elaine Rippon Craft Gallery (Stratford-upon-Avon), 321
electricity, 423
Elizabeth I (Queen)
about, 16, 17, 417–418
books and movies about, 22, 23
tomb of, 51, 174
Elizabeth II (Queen), 17, 37, 39, 421
embassies and high commissions, 198, 424
emergencies
hospitals, 424
on the road, 85
English National Ballet (London), 191
English National Opera (London), 191
English Riviera, 286, 288
escorted tours, 73–75, 100
The Esplanade Hotel (South Cliff), 368
estates, best, 11
ethnic food, London, 143
Eton College (Windsor), 220
Eurostar high-speed trains, 72, 73, 119
events calendar, 35–40, 232
Exeter, 27, 275–280, 281
Exeter Cathedral, 12, 279, 410
Exeter Guildhall, 280

• F •

Fairways Hotel (London), 142
families with children
accommodations for, 96
attractions for, 96–97
babysitter for, 97
BritRail Family Pass, 81
bus travel and, 129, 130
dining, 96
Family Travelcard, 129
itinerary for, 47–49
traveling advice for, 95–96
fast-food dining, 96
Fawkes, Guy (conspirator), 39, 237
ferry
to England, 73
to Fowey, 306
Lake Windermere, 382
to Torquay, 287
Fielding Hotel (London), 137–138
The Fitzroy Room (Castle Howard), 366

Fitzwilliam Museum (Cambridge), 205
Five Sumner Palace (London), 138
Football Association FA Cup Final, 36
Fortnum & Mason (London), 147–148, 156, 185
41 (London), 138
Four in Hand (Keswick), 395
Fowey (Cornwall), 28, 306–307
freeways (motorways), 84–85
frequent-flier programs, 63, 83, 92
Frommer's Memorable Walks in London (Jones), 131, 184

• G •

gardens
best, 13, 405–408
itinerary for garden lovers, 49–50
Garrack Hotel & Restaurant (St. Ives), 303
gasoline (petrol), 59, 62, 86
Gateway Restaurant (Battle), 237
Gatwick airport, 29, 70, 117–118
gay and lesbian travelers
accommodations, 241
bars and dance clubs, 197, 246
Brighton and, 102, 241, 246
Pride in the Park, 38
Web sites, 200, 432
Gay's the Word (London), 102
George III (King), 213, 407, 418 419
George IV (King), 244, 419
The Georgian House Hotel (Penzance), 296
Georgian Restaurant (London), 156
Gert & Henry's Restaurant (York), 358
ghost walks/hauntings, 212, 361, 364
Gidleigh Park (near Chagford), 285
Gilbert Collection (London), 180
Glaisdale (Yorkshire), 373
The Globe Cafe (London), 179
The Globe Inn (Chagford), 283–284
The Globe Restaurant (London), 179
The Gore (London), 138–139
Gourmet Pizza Company (London), 148
The Granary (London), 148
The Grand (Brighton), 240
Grand Opera House (York), 365
The Grange (York), 356

The Granville Hotel (Brighton), 241
Granville Lodge (Scarborough), 368–369
Grasmere, 29, 387–392
The Grasmere Gingerbread Shop, 391
Grasmere Parish Church, 391
Grassington (Yorkshire), 374
Great British Heritage Pass, 60
Great Court (Cambridge), 206–207
Great Gate (Cambridge), 206
Green Park (London), 162
Greenwich, 209–211
Guy Fawkes Night, 39, 237

• *H* •

Hall's Croft (Stratford-upon-Avon), 319, 404
Hamlet House (Stratford-upon-Avon),
    313, 315
Hampshire, 27, 261, 262
Hampton Court Flower Show
    (East Moseley), 38
Hampton Court Palace (East Moseley),
    11, 211–212
Hard Rock Cafe (London), 148–149
Harkers (York), 359
Harlingford Hotel (London), 142
Harper's Restaurant (Salisbury), 270
Harris's Restaurant (Penzance), 297
Harrods (London), 185
Harry Hare's Restaurant & Brasserie
    (Cirencester), 345–346
Harry Potter series, 97
harvest festivals, 39
Harwood Hotel (Grasmere), 388
Hathaway Tea Rooms & Bakery
    (Stratford-upon-Avon), 316
Hawes (Yorkshire), 375
Hawkshead Grammar School, 385
Hawkshead (Lake District), 29
Haworth, 29, 351, 375–376
The Hayloft Cafe (Castle Howard), 366
Hazlitt's 1718 (London), 139
health issues, 106–107
heartland of England, 5, 28, 312
Heathrow airport, 29, 69–70, 116–117
Heathrow Express train, 117
Henley Royal Regatta, 38

Henry II (King), 416
Henry VII (King), 174
Henry VIII (King)
    about, 16, 251, 416–417
    Canterbury Cathedral and, 409–410
    Hampton Court Palace and, 211
    Trinity College founded by, 206
Hepworth, Barbara (sculptor), 304–305
Hermitage Rooms (London), 180
Hever Castle, 11, 27, 250–252, 406
Hidcote Manor Gardens (Chipping
    Campden), 28, 343, 407
high seasons, 30–31
Highfield Hotel (Keswick), 393
Highway Code booklet, 85
Highwayman's Supper (Warwick
    Castle), 322
Hill Top (Near Sawrey), 385
Hinton Ampner Garden (Bramdean), 268
Hinton Grange Hotel (Bath), 329
Hippodrome (London), 193
historic landmarks, best, 12
history
    architectural periods of, 18–19
    of England, 15–18
    history buffs itinerary, 51–53
The Hoe (Plymouth), 291
Holborn (London), 121
The Hole in't Wall (Bowness), 384
holidays, 424
Holly Lodge (Bath), 329
Holy Trinity Church (Stratford-upon-
    Avon), 319
horse racing, 37, 354
horse-drawn carriage tour (York), 355
hospitals, 198, 424
hotel chains, 91, 428
Hotel du Vin Bistro (Brighton), 242
Hotel du Vin (Brighton), 241
Hotel du Vin (Winchester), 264
Hotel on the Park (Pittville Park), 336
Hotel 167 (London), 139
hotels, 89–92. *See also* accommodations
Houses of Parliament (London),
    38, 164–165
hovercraft, 73
Hyde Park (London), 177

• I •

illness, avoiding, 106–107
Imperial Gardens (Cheltenham), 337
Imperial Hotel (London), 142
The Imperial Hotel (Torquay), 288
Inside (Greenwich), 211
insurance
 car rental, 83–84
 escorted tours and, 74
 travel and medical, 74, 105–106
International Festival of Music
  (Cheltenham), 38, 335
International Music Festival (Bath), 36, 328
Internet access, 109–111, 199, 424
Italian Gardens (London), 166
itineraries. *See also* day trips from London
 with children, 47–49
 day trips from York, 365–366
 driving tour from Penzance to Land's
  End, 300–302
 garden lovers, 49–50
 history buffs, 51–53
 one week, 42–45
 two weeks, 45–47
The Ivy (London), 149

• J •

James, Henry (novelist), 234, 403
James House and Cartref House
  (London), 139–140
Jane Austen Centre (Bath), 333, 401
Jane Austen's Bath, 328
Jane Austen's House in Chawton,
  267, 401–402
Jane Austen's Winchester house, 266
jazz in London, 192–193
Jermyn Street (London), 185, 189
Jewel House (London), 165
Joe Allen restaurant (London), 149
Jones, Richard (*Frommer's Memorable
  Walks in London*), 131, 184
Jorvik Viking Centre (York), 360
Jorvik Viking Festival (York), 35, 354
Josephs (St. Ives), 304

• K •

Kennard Hotel (Bath), 329
Kensington Gardens (London), 165–166
Kensington (London), 125
Kensington Palace (London), 11, 166–167
Kent, 27, 247–248
Kenwood Lakeside Concerts, 38
Keswick, 29, 392–397
Keswick Museum and Art Gallery, 397
Kew Gardens (Royal Botanic Gardens),
  212–213, 407
King Arthur's Round Table, 263, 267
King's College (Cambridge), 205–206
King's College Chapel (Cambridge),
  205, 410
King's Road (London), 185
Kitsgate Court (Chipping Campden), 343
Knightsbridge (London), 124
Knole, 11, 27, 248–250

• L •

Lake District, 11, 29, 377–380
Lake District National Park, 377
Lake Road Inn (Keswick), 395
Lake Windermere, 29, 381–387
The Lakeside Cafe (Castle Howard), 366
Lamb House (Rye), 234, 403
Lamb Inn (Grasmere), 389
Lambs of Sheep Street (Stratford-upon-
  Avon), 316
Landgate Bistro (Rye), 233
landmark hotels, 91
Land's End (Cornwall), 28, 293, 302
Lanesborough (London), 157
Langan's Bistro (London), 149–150
Lanhydrock (Cornwall), 308, 407
Lanyon Quoit (near St. Ives), 306
Latin in the Lane (Brighton), 242
Lawn Hotel (Pittville Park), 336
Le Petit Blanc (Cheltenham), 337
Lealholm (Yorkshire), 373
Leeds Castle, 27, 253–254
Leicester Square (London), 121
lighting ceremony (London), 40

Linthwaite House (Bowness), 382
liquor laws, 424–425
Literature Festival (Bath), 36, 328
Little Orchard House (Rye), 233
Livermead Cliff Hotel (Torquay), 288
The Livermead House (Torquay), 288
Loch Fyne Restaurant (Bath), 330
London. *See also* day trips from London;
    London, attractions
  accommodations, 87, 88, 131–142
  best of, 9–10, 24, 26
  clubs, pubs, and bars, 192–197
  congestion charge for driving in, 82
  cost of things in, 61–62
  dining, 143–155
  fast facts, 197–200
  neighborhoods, 120–126
  nightlife, 190–197
  overview, 115, 119–120, 158
  parking in, 82
  postal districts, 120
  safety of, 131
  shopping, 14, 184–189
  tearooms, 155–157
  tourist information, 35, 126–127
  tours, 181–184
  train stations in, 79–80
  travel times from, 29–30, 77
  traveling around, 82, 127–131, 200
  traveling to, 72–73, 115–119
  Web sites, 432
London, attractions
  Apsley House, 176
  Big Ben, 164–165
  British Airways London Eye, 176
  The British Library Exhibition
      Centre, 176
  British Museum, 159, 162, 163
  Buckingham Palace, 162, 164
  The Cabinet War Rooms, 176–177
  Changing of the Guard, 164
  Charles Dickens Museum, 177, 402
  Chelsea Physic Garden, 177, 406
  Houses of Parliament, 164–165
  Hyde Park, 177
  Kensington Gardens, 165–166
  Kensington Palace, 11, 166–167
  The London Transport Museum, 177–178

The London Zoo, 178
Madame Tussauds, 167
map of, 160–161
Mounted Guard Changing Ceremony, 165
The Museum of London, 178
National Gallery, 167–168
National Portrait Gallery, 168
Natural History Museum, 169
Regent's Park, 178–179
The Science Museum, 179
Shakespeare's Globe Theatre, 179, 191
The Somerset House, 179–180
St. Paul's Cathedral, 12, 169–170, 171
Tate Britain, 170
Tate Modern, 170
10 Downing Street, 180–181
Tower Bridge Experience, 181
Tower of London, 12, 60, 171–172, 173
Trafalgar Square, 172–173
Victoria & Albert Museum, 174
The Wallace Collection, 181
Westminster Abbey, 174–175
London City Airport, 70, 118–119
London Coliseum, 191–192
London Film Festival, 39
London Marathon, 36
London New Year's Day Parade, 35
London Planetarium, 167
London Silver Vaults, 189
London Symphony Orchestra, 192
The London Transport Museum, 177–178
London Underground (Tube)
  cost of, 58, 61
  from Heathrow airport, 116–117
  to Kew Gardens, 213
  security matters, 117
  Travelcards for, 128–129
  using, 127–128
The London Zoo, 178
Lord Leycester Hospital (Warwick), 324
Lord Mayor's Coach (London), 178
Lord Mayor's Procession (London), 39
lost items
  credit cards, 422
  luggage, 106
  passport, 105
  wallet, 66–67
low seasons, 30–31

Lower Slaughter, 340
luggage
  carry on, 112
  London Underground and, 116, 117
  lost, 106
Luna Simone Hotel (London), 140
Luton airport, 70, 119
Lygon Arms (Broadway), 341

• M •

Macdonald White Hart Hotel
  (Salisbury), 269
Mad Hatter Tearoom (Bourton-on-the-
  Water), 339
Madame Tussauds (London), 167
magazines/newspapers, 199, 425, 431
Magdalen College (Oxford), 216
mail, sending, 425
Malham (Yorkshire), 375
The Mall (London), 162
Manchester airport, 30, 70
Mapp and Lucia (Benson), 230, 232
maps
  Bath, 327
  Brighton, 239
  British Museum, 163
  Cambridge, 203
  Canterbury, 227
  Dartmoor National Park, 282
  day trips from London, 202
  Devon, 275
  England's Heartland, 312
  Exeter, 276
  Hampshire, 262
  Kent's castles, stately homes, and
    gardens, 248
  Keswick, 393
  Lake District, 378
  London attractions, 160–161
  London clubs, pubs, and bars, 194–195
  London hotels, 132–133
  London neighborhoods, 122–123
  London restaurants, 144–145
  London, West End Shopping, 186–187
  obtaining, 199, 425
  Oxford, 215
  regions of England, 25

Rye, 231
Salisbury, 269
Southeast England, 224
St. Paul's Cathedral, 171
Stratford-upon-Avon, 314
Tower of London, 173
Westminster Abbey, 175
Wiltshire, 262
Winchester, 264
York, 353
York Minster, 363
Marina Hotel & Waterside Restaurant
  (Fowey), 307
Market (Stratford-upon-Avon), 321
Marlborough Maze (Woodstock), 219
Marlowe's Restaurant & Georgie's Bistro
  (Stratford-upon-Avon), 316
Marmalade's (Scarborough), 369
Mary Arden's House & Shakespeare
  Countryside Museum (Wilmcote),
  319–320, 404
Marylebone (London), 124
Mathematical Bridge (Cambridge), 206
Mayfair (London), 121, 124
Mayflower Steps (Plymouth), 291
Medieval Weekend (Rye), 232
Merchant Adventurers' Hall (York), 360
The Mermaid Inn (Rye), 233
Merton College (Oxford), 216
Michael Caines Cafe (Exeter), 278
Michael Caines (Exeter), 278
Micklegate Bar Museum (York), 359
Middlethorpe Hall (York), 357
Milestone Hotel & Apartments
  (London), 142
Mill Hay (Broadway), 341
Millennium Bridge (London), 169
Miller Howe Cafe (Windermere), 384
Miller Howe Hotel Restaurant
  (Windermere), 384
Miller Howe Hotel (Windermere), 383
Milsoms Hotel (Bath), 329–330
The Minack Theatre (Porthcurno), 301–302
The Miniature Scene (York), 364
The Model Village at the Old New Inn
  (Bourton-on-the-Water), 339
Modern Art Oxford, 217
The Monastery (Rye), 233–234

money. *See also* budget for trip;
cost-cutting tips
  ATMs and carrying cash, 64, 65, 422
  credit cards, 64–65
  currency exchange, 63–64, 66, 422
  debit cards, 65
  lost or stolen wallet, 66–67
  tipping, 20–21, 68, 130, 427
  traveler's checks, 65–66
  typical costs in London, 61–62
  VAT (value-added tax), 67–68, 184,
    199–200, 426
The Montague (London), 140
Moro (London), 150
Mortons (Oxford), 218
Mosaique (London), 150
Mother Hubbard's (Scarborough), 369
motorways (freeways), 84–85
Mottisfont Abbey, 268
Mount Grace Priory (Yorkshire), 373
Mount Prospect Hotel (Penzance), 296
Mounted Guard Changing Ceremony
    (London), 165
Mousehole (Cornwall), 28, 301
movies, recommended, 23
Mozartfest (Bath), 328
Muffinski's (London), 155
Museum of Costume (Bath), 332
The Museum of London, 178
museums, best, 10

• *N* •

Nash, John (architect), 244
Nash's House (Stratford-upon-Avon),
    318, 404
National Express buses, 81, 117
National Gallery (London), 167–168
National Marine Aquarium (Plymouth), 291
National Maritime Museum
    (Greenwich), 210
National Portrait Gallery (London), 168
National Rail Enquiries, 78, 79
National Railway Museum (York), 360
Natural History Museum (London), 169
Near Sawrey (Lake District), 29
Nevile's Court (Cambridge), 207

New College (Oxford), 216
New Europe Hotel (Brighton), 241
New Place/Nash's House (Stratford-upon-
    Avon), 318, 404
Newgate Market (York), 364
Newlyn (south of Penzance), 300–301
newspapers/magazines, 199, 425, 431
Nicholson, Harold (Sissinghurst gardens
    developer), 24, 27
nightlife
  Brighton, 245–246
  cost of, 60–61
  gay and lesbian, 197, 246
  information and tickets, 190
  Keswick, 397
  London, 190–197
  Scarborough, 372
  York, 364–365
No. 5 Bistro (Bath), 331
No. 1 Royal Crescent (Bath), 333–334
Noel Arms Hotel (Chipping Campden),
    342–343
Noor Jahan (London), 151
North Parade (Bath), 332
North Sea Fish Restaurant (London), 151
North York Moors National Park, 29, 351,
    372–374
North Yorkshire Moors Steam
    Railway, 373
northern England, 5, 28–29
Notting Hill Carnival (London), 38–39
Notting Hill (London), 125

• *O* •

The Old England (Bowness), 383
The Old Mill (Lower Slaughter), 340
Old Royal Observatory (Greenwich), 210
Old White Swan (York), 364
Oldway Mansion (Torquay), 288
The Olive Tree (Bath), 331
One Minster Street (Salisbury), 270–271
one week itinerary, 42–45
opera, 191–192, 365
The Oppo (Stratford-upon-Avon), 316
The Orangery cafe (London), 166
The Oratory (London), 151–152

Osborne Hotel (Torquay), 288
Oxford
  attractions, 214–217
  college visiting hours, 214
  described, 213
  dining, 217–218
  map of, 215
  tourist information, 214
  traveling to, 214
Oxford and Cambridge Boat Race, 36
The Oxford Story, 214
Oxford Street (London), 185
Oxford University, 213
Oxo Tower Brasserie (London), 152

• P •

package tours, 62–63, 75–76, 83
Paddington (London), 125
Paignton, 287
Palace Pier (Brighton), 243–244
palaces, best, 11
Pall Mall (London), 162
Palm Court (London), 157
Pam's Pantry (Mousehole), 301
Parford Well (near Chagford), 284
Parish Church of St. John the Baptist
    (Cirencester), 347
Park Lane Sheraton Hotel (London), 141
Parkfield (Keswick), 394
Parkview (Cheltenham), 336
passport
  lost, 105
  obtaining, 103–105
  Passport Control and Customs, 116
patisseries (bakeries), London, 155–156
The Payton (Stratford-upon-Avon), 315
Pedn-Olva Hotel (St. Ives), 303
Pembroke Arms Hotel (Wilton), 270
Penlee House Gallery & Museum
    (Penzance), 299
Penwith Peninsula (Cornwall), 300
Penzance
  accommodations, 295–296
  attractions, 298–300
  boating and boat tours, 295

Daphne du Maurier Festival of Arts and
    Literature, 295
  described, 28, 293, 294
  dining, 296–298
  driving tour to Land's End, 300–302
  tourist information, 295
  traveling to, 294–295
performing arts. See nightlife
Peter Jones (London), 185
Peter Pan in Kensington Gardens (Barrie),
    97, 166
Peter Pan statue (London), 97, 166
petrol (gasoline), 59, 62, 86
pharmacies, 199, 425
Piccadilly Circus (London), 121
Piccadilly (London), 185
Pickwick Gallery (Stratford-upon-
    Avon), 321
The Pilchard Works Museum and Factory
    (Newlyn), 300–301
Pimlico (London), 124
Pinch of Salt (Bath), 331
Pitt Rivers Museum (Oxford), 217
The Pittville Pump Room, 338
Pizza Express (Bath), 331–332
planning trip. See also budget for trip;
    cost-cutting tips; itineraries
  airline security, 111–112
  BritRail pass purchase, 80–81
  car rental reservation, 84
  cellphone use, 107–108
  customs regulations, 116, 422–423
  health issues, 106–107
  hotel reservations, London, 87
  Internet access, 109–111
  passport, 103–105
  scheduling your time, 29–30
  travel and medical insurance, 74, 105–106
  Visitor Travelcards, 129
Plymouth, 27, 289–291
Plymouth Discovery Center, 290
Poets' Corner (London), 174
police, 198, 199, 425
porcelain (china), London, 189
Porthminster Beach Cafe (St. Ives), 304
Portsmouth, 261
post office, 199, 425

postal districts of London, 120
Potter, Beatrix (author/illustrator)
  about, 29, 403
  Beatrix Potter Gallery, 385, 403
  at Hill Top, 385
  Lake District and, 377, 386
  The Tale of Peter Rabbit, 386
  The World of Beatrix Potter, 387
pottery, 14
The Prelude (Grasmere), 389
President's Lodge (Cambridge), 206
Pride in the Park (London), 38
Prime Meridian (Greenwich), 209, 210
Princess Diana Memorial Playground
    (London), 166
Proms (London), 192
pubs. *See* clubs, pubs, and bars
Pulhams Coaches, 335
Pulteney Bridge (Bath), 332
Punchbowl (York), 364
Purcell Room (London), 192

• Q •

Quarter area (York), 364
Quarto's (Stratford-upon-Avon), 317
The Quay Gallery Antiques Emporium
    (Exeter), 280
Queen Adelaide Tea Room (Brighton), 244
Queen Charlotte's Cottage, 213
Queen Elizabeth Hall (London), 192
Queen Mary's Dollhouse (Windsor), 220
Queen Square (Bath), 332
Queens' College (Cambridge), 206
Queen's Court Hotel (Exeter), 277
Queen's House (Greenwich), 210
The Queensberry Hotel (Bath), 330

• R •

Radcliffe Camera (Oxford), 217
RailEurope, 80, 129
Rainbow Vegetarian Cafe (Cambridge), 208
rainfall, 31
Rankine Taylor Antiques (Cirencester), 347
Rebecca (du Maurier), 295
The Red House Antiques Centre
    (York), 364

Red Lion Hotel (Salisbury), 270
Regent Palace Hotel (London), 142
Regent Street (London), 185, 189
Regent's Park (London), 178–179
regions of England
  heartland, 5, 28, 312
  map of, 25
  northern, 5, 28–29
  southeast, 4, 26–27, 224
  west country, 4–5, 27–28
Restaurant 22 (Cambridge), 209
restrooms, 199, 425
The Retreat (Cheltenham), 337
Richoux tearooms (London), 156
Rievaulx Abbey (Yorkshire), 373
River Cam, 201, 208
Riverside Walk Hotel (York), 357
Roman amphitheatre (Cirencester), 346
Roman Baths Museum (Bath), 28
Roman Museum (Canterbury), 229
romantic landscapes, best, 13–14
Rotunda Museum (Scarborough), 370
roundabouts, 84
Royal Academy Summer Exhibition, 37
Royal Albert Hall (London), 192
Royal Albert Memorial Museum
    (Exeter), 280
Royal Ascot (near Windsor), 37
Royal Ballet (London), 191
Royal Bank of Scotland, 354
Royal Botanic Gardens (Kew Gardens),
    212–213, 407
Royal Ceremonial Dress Collection
    (London), 166
Royal Clarence Hotel (Exeter), 277–278
Royal Crescent Hotel (Bath), 330
Royal family
  cost to U.K. taxpayers, 18, 68
  portraits of, 168
  recent events involving, 18
  Web site, official, 200
  Windsor Castle as residence of, 219
Royal Festival Hall (London), 192
Royal Mews (London), 162
Royal National Theatre (London), 191
Royal Naval College (Greenwich), 209, 211
Royal Opera House (London), 191
Royal Opera (London), 191
Royal Pavilion (Brighton), 27, 244

Royal Shakespeare Company, 191, 321
Royal Shakespeare Theatre (Stratford-upon-Avon), 321
R.S. Hispaniola (London), 152
Rules restaurant (London), 152–153
Russets Restaurant (St. Ives), 304
Rydal, 29, 387
Rydal Mount (south of Grasmere), 391
Rye
  accommodations, 232–233
  attractions, 234–235
  calendar of events, 232
  described, 10, 26, 229–230
  dining, 233–234
  guided tours, 231–232
  map of, 231
  tourist information, 230–231
  traveling to, 230
Rye Bonfire Weekend, 232
Rye Castle Museum, 235
Rye Festival of Music and the Arts, 232

• S •

Sackville-West, Vita (Sissinghurst gardens creator), 27, 250, 254, 403–404
safety issues
  airline security, 111–112
  London and, 199
  London Underground, 117
  overview, 426
  terrorist bombings, 17–18
Saint's Way (Cornwall), 307
Salisbury, 27, 261, 268–273
Salisbury Cathedral, 271, 411
salt pilchard factory, 300–301
The Savoy (London), 141
Scarborough, 29, 351, 366–372
Scarborough Castle, 370
Scarborough Sea Life & Marine Sanctuary, 370
The Science Museum (London), 179
Scorhill Circle (Dartmoor National Park), 286
Scotch House (London), 189
Seafront (Brighton), 244
seasons, 30–35
senior travelers, 94, 97–98
Serpentine Gallery (London), 166

Serpentine (London), 177
Shakespeare Bookshop (Stratford-upon-Avon), 321
The Shakespeare (Stratford-upon-Avon), 315
Shakespeare, William (playwright), 28, 311, 317–319, 404
Shakespeare's Birthplace (Stratford-upon-Avon), 317–318
Shakespeare's Globe Theatre (London), 179, 191
Shakespearience (Stratford-upon-Avon), 320
The Shambles (York), 360–361
Sheldonian Theatre (Oxford), 217
The Ship's Inn (Exeter), 278–279
shoes, London, 185, 188
shopping
  best, 14
  Brighton, 245
  business hours, 184, 422
  Cheltenham, 338
  Cirencester, 347
  cost of, 60–61
  duty-free, 426
  Exeter, 280
  Keswick, 397
  London, 14, 184–189
  sale periods, 184
  Stratford-upon-Avon, 321
  VAT (value-added tax) and, 184
  York, 364, 365
silver, 189, 280
Simon the Pieman (Rye), 234
Simpson's-in-the-Strand (London), 153
Sissinghurst Castle Garden, 27, 254–255, 407–408
The Skiddaw Hotel (Keswick), 394
Slug and Lettuce (Cirencester), 346
Small Talk (Broadway), 341
smoking, 199, 426
soccer, 36
Society of London Theatres, 191
Soho neighborhood (London), 121
Somerset House (London), 179–180
South Bank Centre (London), 192
The South Bank (London), 126
South Kensington (London), 125
South Parade (Bath), 332

southeast England, 4, 26–27, 224
spring season, 31, 32
St. Augustine's Abbey (Canterbury), 229
St. Eadburgha's (Broadway), 342
St. Ives (Cornwall), 28, 293, 300–305
St. James's Church (Chipping
      Campden), 344
St. James's (London), 124
St. James's Palace (London), 162
St. James's Park (London), 162, 164
St. John's College (Cambridge), 206
St. Lawrence's Church (Bourton-on-the-
      Water), 339
St. Margaret's Hotel (London), 140–141
St. Martin-in-the-Fields (London),
      172–173, 410
St. Martin's Church (Canterbury), 229, 410
St. Martin's Lane (London), 142
St. Mary's Church (Rye), 235
St. Mary's Church (Warwick), 324
St. Michael's Mount (Penzance), 11, 28,
      293, 298–299
St. Olaves Court Hotel (Exeter), 278
St. Patrick's Day celebration (London), 36
St. Paul's Cathedral (London),
      12, 169–170, 171, 411
St. William's Restaurant (York), 359
Stansted airport, 70, 118
State Apartments (London), 166
State Opening of Parliament (London), 39
Steam Yacht Gondola (Coniston
      Water), 392
Stephen Joseph Theatre
      (Scarborough), 372
Stonehenge, 27, 62, 261, 272–273
The Story of Rye, 235
Stourhead (Wiltshire), 271–272, 408
The Strand and Covent Garden
      (London), 121
Strand Restaurant (Brighton), 242
Stranger's Gallery (London), 165
Stratford Brass Rubbing Centre, 320–321
Stratford-upon-Avon
   accommodations, 313–315
   attractions, 317–321
   described, 28, 311–312
   dining, 315–317
   map of, 314
   shopping, 321

tourist information, 313
tours, 313
traveling to, 28, 312–313
Stratton House Hotel (Cirencester), 345
subway. *See* London Underground (Tube)
Sully's (Canterbury), 228
The Summer House Restaurant with
      Rooms (Penzance), 297
summer season, 30–31, 32–33
Suze in Mayfair (London), 153
The Swallow Chaucer Hotel
      (Canterbury), 226
Swan Yard Cafe (Cirencester), 346
Swinegate (York), 364
Sylvester's Restaurant (Penzance), 297

• *T* •

The Tale of Peter Rabbit (Potter), 386
Tate Britain (London), 170
Tate Modern (London), 170
Tate St. Ives, 305
Tatyan's (Cirencester), 346
taxes, value-added (VAT), 67–68, 184,
      199–200, 426
taxis
   locating, 426
   tipping, 68, 130, 427
   from train stations, 117, 248
   Web sites, 248
tea
   afternoon tea, 20, 59
   Bourton-on-the-Water, 339
   Bowness, 383
   Broadway, 341
   Chipping Campden, 343
   cream tea, 20, 274
   high tea, 59, 156–157
   Keswick, 394
   London, 155–157
   Plymouth, 290
   Rye, 234
   Stratford-upon-Avon, 316
   Upper Slaughter, 340
   Winchester, 264–265
telephone
   cellphones, 107–108
   country code/city code, 198, 422
   using, 426

temperatures and rainfall, 31
10 Downing Street (London), 180–181
tennis, Wimbledon, 37
Terre à Terre (Brighton), 242–243
Thai Boathouse (Stratford-upon-Avon), 317
Thames Festival, 39
Thames river, 120, 182–183
theater
  Brighton, 245
  City of London Festival, 37
  Keswick, 397
  London, 179, 190–191
  Minack Theatre (near Porthcurno),
    301–302
  Oxford, 217
  Porthcurno, 301–302
  Scarborough, 372
  Stratford-upon-Avon, 321
  tickets, 60–61, 191
  Web sites, 190
  York, 365
Theatre by the Lake (Lakeside), 397
Theatre Royal (Brighton), 245
Theatre Royal Haymarket (London), 191
Theatre Royal (York), 365
Thistle Stratford-upon-Avon, 315
The Three Crowns Hotel (Chagford), 284
Tilly's Tea Parlour (Exeter), 279
time zone, 426
tipping, 20–21, 68, 130, 427
Tolcarne Inn (Newlyn), 301
The Toll Bar (Fowey), 306–307
Tor Bay, 287
Torquay, 27, 286–288
Torre Abbey (Torquay), 288
tourist information
  Bath, 328
  Battle, 236
  Bourton-on-the-Water, 338
  Brighton, 240
  Broadway, 341
  Cambridge, 204
  Canterbury, 225
  Cheltenham, 335
  Chipping Campden, 342
  Cirencester, 344
  Dartmoor National Park, 281, 283
  Exeter, 277
  Fowey, 306

Grasmere, 387
Greenwich, 209–210
Haworth, 375
Heathrow airport, 116
Keswick, 392
Lake Windermere, 381
London, 35, 126–127
Oxford, 214
Penzance, 295
Plymouth, 289–290
Rye, 230–231
Salisbury, 268–269
Scarborough, 367
St. Ives, 303
Stratford-upon-Avon, 313
Torquay, 287
tourist offices, locating, 429
Web sites, 35, 200, 430–432
Whitby, 371
Winchester, 263
York, 354
tours. See also boating and boat tours;
    itineraries
  Bath, 328
  Battle of Hastings, 238
  Cambridge, 204
  Canterbury, 225
  Cheltenham, 335
  Dartmoor National Park, 283
  escorted, 73–75
  Exeter, 277
  Grasmere, 387
  Greenwich, 210
  Hampshire, 268
  Lake District, 380
  Lake Windermere, 382
  London, 181–184
  Oxford, 214
  package, 75–76
  Penzance, 295
  Rye, 231–232
  Scarborough, 367
  Stratford-upon-Avon, 313
  Whitby, 371
  Winchester, 265–267
  York, 355, 364
Tower Bridge Experience (London), 181
Tower of London, 12, 60, 171–172, 173
Trafalgar Square (London), 172–173

train travel
BritRail pass, 58–59, 60, 73, 80–81
cost of, 62, 63
Eurostar, 72, 73, 119
to London from the Continent, 72–73, 119
London train stations, 79–80
schedules and fares, 78, 427
transportation from train stations, 248
using the rail system, 77–79
Web sites, 431
transportation. *See also specific types of travel*
to Bath, 326
to Battle, 236
to Blenheim Palace, 218
to Bourton-on-the-Water, 338
in Brighton, 240
to Brighton, 239–240
to Broadway, 340–341
in Cambridge, 204
to Cambridge, 201, 204
to Canterbury, 225
to Chartwell, 252
to Cheltenham, 335
to Chipping Campden, 342
choosing, 77
to Cirencester, 344
Cornwall and, 81
cost of, 58–59
the Cotswalds and, 81
to Dartmoor National Park, 281
to Dover Castle, 256
in Exeter, 281
to Exeter, 276, 277
from Gatwick airport, 118
to Grasmere, 387
to Greenwich, 209
to Hampton Court, 211–212
to Haworth, 375
from Heathrow airport, 117
to Hever Castle, 250
to Kent, 247–248
to Keswick, 392
to Knole, 249
in the Lake District, 81, 380
to the Lake District, 379
to Leeds Castle, 253
in London, 82, 127–131, 200
to London, 72–73, 115–119

to North York Moors National Park, 372–373
to Oxford, 214
to Penzance, 294–295
to Plymouth, 289
to Rye, 230
to Salisbury, 268
to Scarborough, 367
to Sissinghurst Castle, 255
to Stonehenge, 272–273
to Stratford-upon-Avon, 312, 313
to Torquay, 287
Travelcards for, 58, 128–129
Web sites, 431–432
to Winchester, 263
to Windsor Castle, 220
in York, 354
to York, 353–354
to Yorkshire Dales National Park, 374
travel and medical insurance, 74, 105–106
Travel Guard Alerts, 105–106
travel times
from London, 29–30, 77
scheduling, 29–30
Travelcards, 58, 128–129
traveler's checks, 65–66
Treasurer's House (York), 361
Treasury Restaurant (Exeter), 279
Tregony (St. Ives), 303–304
Trengwainton Garden (West of Penzance), 299–300
Trinity College (Cambridge), 206–207
trip-cancellation insurance, 105
Trooping the Colour (London), 37
Tudor gateway (Cambridge), 206
Tudor Rose Tea Rooms (Plymouth), 290
The Turf Tavern (Oxford), 218
The Turks Head (Penzance), 297–298
Twenty Nevern Square (London), 142
two week itinerary, 45–47

• *U* •

Underground. *See* London Underground (Tube)
Underground Passages (Exeter), 280
University Museum of Natural History (Oxford), 217
Upper Slaughter, 340

• V •

Vale of Evesham (the Cotswolds), 342
VAT (value-added tax), 67–68, 184,
    199–200, 426
Victoria & Albert Museum (London), 174
Victoria Coach Station (London), 81
Victoria (Queen), 17, 166, 244, 420
Villa Columbina (Grasmere), 389
VisitBritain (Web site), 35, 98, 430
VisitLondon (Web site), 200, 432
Visitor Travelcards, 58, 192
The Vyne (Basingstoke), 268

• W •

Wagamama Noodle Bar (London), 154
The Wallace Collection (London), 181
wallet, lost or stolen, 66–67
Warwick Castle, 11, 28, 311, 321–323, 408
The Washbourne Court Hotel
    (Lower Slaughter), 340
weather, 31–32, 200, 427
Weaver's Restaurant (Haworth), 376
Wembley Stadium (Web site), 36
Wessex, kingdom of, 262, 263
west country, 4–5, 27–28
West End (London), 121, 124, 185, 186–187
West End theater district (London), 190
West London, 124–125
West Pier (Brighton), 243
Westminster Abbey (London), 12, 159,
    174–175, 411
Westminster (London), 124
Whitby Abbey, 371
Whitby (Yorkshire), 29, 371, 372
White Moss House (Rydal Water), 388
William H. Stokes (Cirencester), 347
William (Prince), 168, 220
William the Conqueror (King)
    about, 415
    at Battle of Hastings, 16, 26
    Tower of London and, 171
    Winchester and, 263
Wilton House, 272
Wiltshire, 261–262
Wimbledon Lawn Tennis
    Championships, 37

Winchester, 27, 263–268
Winchester Cathedral, 265, 266, 412
Winchester City Mill, 266
Winchester Royal Hotel, 264
Windermere Steamboat Museum, 386
Windsor Castle, 11, 219–220
winter season, 30, 34–35
Wood End Museum (Scarborough), 371
Wordsworth Hotel (Grasmere), 388–389
Wordsworth Museum (south of
    Grasmere), 390
Wordsworth, William (poet)
    about, 390, 404
    burial site, 391
    Grasmere and, 387
    at Hawkshead Grammar School, 385, 404
    homes of, 390, 391, 404
    Lake District and, 377
The World of Beatrix Potter (Bowness-on-
    Windermere), 387
Wren, Christopher (architect)
    Hampton Court Palace and, 212
    rebuilding London, 12
    Royal Naval College and, 211
    Sheldonian Theatre and, 217
    St. Paul's Cathedral and, 169, 411

• Y •

Ye Olde Cheshire Cheese (London), 154
York
    accommodations, 356–357
    attractions, 29, 359–363
    day trips from, 365–366
    described, 10, 351–353
    dining, 357–359
    guided tours, 355
    Jorvik Viking Festival, 35, 354
    map of, 353
    nightlife, 364–365
    shopping, 364, 365
    tourist information, 354
    traveling to, 353–354
York Castle Museum, 361
York City Art Gallery, 362
York Early Music Festival, 354
York Minster, 12, 362–363, 412
York Moat House (York), 357

York Racecourse, 354
Yorkshire, 351
Yorkshire Dales National Park, 29, 351,
  374–375
Yorkshire Museum (York), 363

• Z •

Zafferano (London), 154–155
Zennor Quoit (near St. Ives), 306
zoo, London, 178

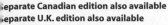

SPORTS, FITNESS, PARENTING, RELIGION & SPIRITUALITY

0-7645-5146-9   0-7645-5418-2

Also available:
- Adoption For Dummies
  0-7645-5488-3
- Basketball For Dummies
  0-7645-5248-1
- The Bible For Dummies
  0-7645-5296-1
- Buddhism For Dummies
  0-7645-5359-3
- Catholicism For Dummies
  0-7645-5391-7
- Hockey For Dummies
  0-7645-5228-7

- Judaism For Dummies
  0-7645-5299-6
- Martial Arts For Dummies
  0-7645-5358-5
- Pilates For Dummies
  0-7645-5397-6
- Religion For Dummies
  0-7645-5264-3
- Teaching Kids to Read
  For Dummies
  0-7645-4043-2
- Weight Training For Dummies
  0-7645-5168-X
- Yoga For Dummies
  0-7645-5117-5

TRAVEL

0-7645-5438-7   0-7645-5453-0

Also available:
- Alaska For Dummies
  0-7645-1761-9
- Arizona For Dummies
  0-7645-6938-4
- Cancún and the Yucatán
  For Dummies
  0-7645-2437-2
- Cruise Vacations For Dummies
  0-7645-6941-4
- Europe For Dummies
  0-7645-5456-5
- Ireland For Dummies
  0-7645-5455-7

- Las Vegas For Dummies
  0-7645-5448-4
- London For Dummies
  0-7645-4277-X
- New York City For Dummies
  0-7645-6945-7
- Paris For Dummies
  0-7645-5494-8
- RV Vacations For Dummies
  0-7645-5443-3
- Walt Disney World & Orlando
  For Dummies
  0-7645-6943-0

GRAPHICS, DESIGN & WEB DEVELOPMENT

0-7645-4345-8   0-7645-5589-8

Also available:
- Adobe Acrobat 6 PDF
  For Dummies
  0-7645-3760-1
- Building a Web Site For Dummies
  0-7645-7144-3
- Dreamweaver MX 2004
  For Dummies
  0-7645-4342-3
- FrontPage 2003 For Dummies
  0-7645-3882-9
- HTML 4 For Dummies
  0-7645-1995-6
- Illustrator cs For Dummies
  0-7645-4084-X

- Macromedia Flash MX 2004
  For Dummies
  0-7645-4358-X
- Photoshop 7 All-in-One Desk
  Reference For Dummies
  0-7645-1667-1
- Photoshop cs Timesaving
  Techniques For Dummies
  0-7645-6782-9
- PHP 5 For Dummies
  0-7645-4166-8
- PowerPoint 2003 For Dummies
  0-7645-3908-6
- QuarkXPress 6 For Dummies
  0-7645-2593-X

NETWORKING, SECURITY, PROGRAMMING & DATABASES

0-7645-6852-3   0-7645-5784-X

Also available:
- A+ Certification For Dummies
  0-7645-4187-0
- Access 2003 All-in-One Desk
  Reference For Dummies
  0-7645-3988-4
- Beginning Programming
  For Dummies
  0-7645-4997-9
- C For Dummies
  0-7645-7068-4
- Firewalls For Dummies
  0-7645-4048-3
- Home Networking For Dummies
  0-7645-42796

- Network Security For Dummies
  0-7645-1679-5
- Networking For Dummies
  0-7645-1677-9
- TCP/IP For Dummies
  0-7645-1760-0
- VBA For Dummies
  0-7645-3989-2
- Wireless All In-One Desk Reference
  For Dummies
  0-7645-7496-5
- Wireless Home Networking
  For Dummies
  0-7645-3910-8